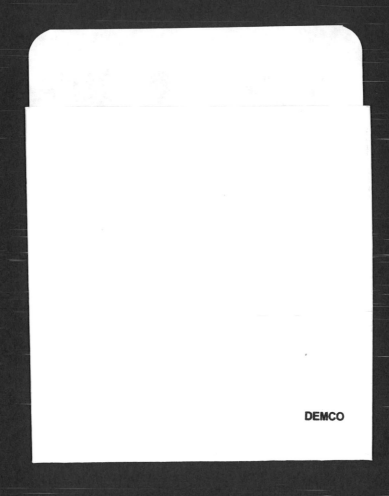

DEMCO

Teaching Children to Read

Putting the Pieces Together

Fourth Edition

D. Ray Reutzel
Utah State University

Robert B. Cooter, Jr.
The University of Texas at Arlington

PEARSON

Merrill
Prentice Hall

Upper Saddle River, New Jersey
Columbus, Ohio

Library of Congress Cataloging in Publication Data

Reutzel, D. Ray (Douglas Ray), 1953–
    Teaching children to read : putting the pieces together / D. Ray Reutzel, Robert B. Cooter.—4th ed.
        p. cm.
    Includes bibliographical references and index.
    ISBN 0-13-112189-8
        1. Reading (Elementary) 2. Reading (Elementary)—Language experience approach. 3. Language arts (Elementary) I. Cooter, Robert B. II. Title

    LB1573.R48 2004
    372.41—dc21

                                                      2003056143

Vice President and Executive Publisher: Jeffery W. Johnston
Senior Editor: Linda Ashe Montgomery
Development Editor: Hope Madden
Editorial Assistant: Laura Weaver
Production Editor: Mary M. Irvin
Production Coordination: Lea Baranowski, Carlisle Publishers Services
Design Coordinator: Diane C. Lorenzo
Cover Designer: Jason Moore
Cover Image: Susan Sturgill
Production Manager: Pamela D. Bennett
Director of Marketing: Ann Castel Davis
Marketing Manager: Darcy Betts Prybella
Marketing Coordinator: Tyra Poole

Photo credits: Text: Robert B. Cooter, Jr., pp. 459, 461, 513; Scott Cunningham/Merrill, pp. 20, 28, 75, 90, 114, 137, 148, 269, 272, 489; KS Studios/Merrill, p. 84; Anthony Magnacca/Merrill, pp. 24, 107; provided by D. Ray Reutzel, pp. 173, 330, 331, 333, 336, 338, 339, 344, 353, 366, 367, 393, 403; Anne Vega/Merrill, pp. 42, 51; Todd Yarrington/Merrill, p. 71. **Insert:** Scott Cunningham/Merrill, pp. 1, 5 (bottom), 6, 7, 8; Mary Kate Denny/PhotoEdit, p. 4; Anthony Magnacca/Merrill, p. 2 (top); Jeff Maloney/Getty Images, Inc., p. 5 (top); Joseph Nettis/Photo Researchers, Inc., p. 3; courtesy of the Wiggand family, p. 2 (bottom).

This book was set in Souvenir by Carlisle Communications, Ltd. It was printed and bound by Courier Kendallville, Inc. The cover was printed by Phoenix Color Corp.

Pearson Education Ltd.   Pearson Education Australia Pty. Limited
Pearson Education Singapore Pte. Ltd.   Pearson Education North Asia Ltd.
Pearson Education Canada, Ltd.   Pearson Educación de Mexico, S.A. de C.V.
Pearson Education—Japan   Pearson Education Malaysia Pte. Ltd.

10 9 8 7 6 5 4 3 2 1
ISBN: 0-13-112189-8

To my sweetheart, Pam, and my wonderful children and grandchildren as well as the teachers and colleagues with whom I work, thank you for the support all of you continuously offer me in the work of literacy.
—D. Ray Reutzel

For my brother, John C. T. Cooter, a gentle soul and a favorite friend of countless children.
—Robert B. Cooter, Jr.

EDUCATOR LEARNING CENTER: AN INVALUABLE ONLINE RESOURCE

Merrill Education and the Association for Supervision and Curriculum Development (ASCD) invite you to take advantage of a new online resource, one that provides access to the top research and proven strategies associated with ASCD and Merrill—the Educator Learning Center. At **www.EducatorLearningCenter.com** you will find resources that will enhance your students' understanding of course topics and of current educational issues, in addition to being invaluable for further research.

How the Educator Learning Center will help your students become better teachers

With the combined resources of Merrill Education and ASCD, you and your students will find a wealth of tools and materials to better prepare them for the classroom.

Research

- More than 600 articles from the ASCD journal *Educational Leadership* discuss everyday issues faced by practicing teachers.
- A direct link on the site to Research Navigator™ gives students access to many of the leading education journals, as well as extensive content detailing the research process.
- Excerpts from Merrill Education texts give your students insights on important topics of instructional methods, diverse populations, assessment, classroom management, technology, and refining classroom practice.

Classroom Practice

- Hundreds of lesson plans and teaching strategies are categorized by content area and age range.
- Case studies and classroom video footage provide virtual field experience for student reflection.
- Computer simulations and other electronic tools keep your students abreast of today's classrooms and current technologies.

Look into the value of Educator Learning Center yourself

Preview the value of this educational environment by visiting **www.EducatorLearningCenter.com** and clicking on "Demo." For a free 4-month subscription to the Educator Learning Center in conjunction with this text, simply contact your Merrill/Prentice Hall sales representative.

Preface

In working toward completing the fourth edition of *Teaching Children to Read: Putting the Pieces Together,* we drew upon a number of important elements. First, we considered the outcome of a wonderful professional experience we had several years ago when we decided to leave our university positions and return to teaching children. We tried out the various ideas and strategies about reading and writing that we had been collecting and verified how to practically apply them in the classroom.

We built upon this foundation with the findings of research on reading instruction. A strong research base for decision making is important for sound teaching. For this new edition, we completely updated our text to include the most recent information drawn from scientifically based research on balanced reading and writing instruction.

Finally, we decided to sculpt these ideas in such a way as to present the principles and theories you need to understand the teaching of reading, offer to you the best methods and assessments you'll need to create a classroom reading program, and provide a clear picture of the classroom itself. This revision is designed to illustrate precisely, from environment to procedures, what reading instruction in the elementary classroom should look like.

ORGANIZATION

The first thing you will notice about this text is that we have focused the chapters into three distinct parts. By pulling the text apart into these discrete sections, we will give you a better sense of how the elements of literacy fit together to create the whole literacy picture. We intend the practical nature of this text to give you the pieces of the literacy puzzle you need to become a creative problem solver and effective reading teacher.

Part I: Principles and Foundations: Understanding Literacy Development   The first chapter describes the characteristics of effective reading teachers and the principles that support literacy development. The second chapter presents the role language development plays in reading preparedness. A thoroughly updated Chapter 3 relates how reading theories form the basis of models for reading instruction.

Part II: Methods and Assessment: Strategies That Support Literacy Development   Chapters 4 through 9 consider strategy instruction and assessment, which is linked to the seven core elements of reading instruction, presented in Part I. In Part II you'll find an entirely new chapter, which focuses on understanding and developing reading fluency (Chapter 7), as well as an updated chapter on examining the components of basal reading programs (Chapter 8).

Part III: Classroom Practice: Organizing and Planning for Literacy Instruction   The final four chapters comprise a meticulous walk through the processes of planning and implementing effective reading instruction in primary and intermediate classrooms, integrating the disparate theory, research, instruction, and assessment chapters into seamless classroom descriptions. From one chapter to another, the reading and writing process is set up as a continuum beginning with emergent readers and writers, continuing on to developing readers and writers who benefit from reading and writing workshops, and ending with the honing of skills with independent readers and writers by supporting their needs for using content area and reference materials. These chapters will help you gain a sense of how teaching practices are sequenced to be developmentally appropriate.

New to This Edition

- **Comprehensive reading instruction.** This strong new focus calls for a balance in skills and strategies, reading and writing, and research-based instruction and assessment to implement the best literacy instruction.
- **Characteristics of Teachers.** Chapter 1 delineates the seven characteristics of highly effective reading teachers. This is what you must know and be able to do to become a master reading teacher.
- **Organizing Classrooms.** Part III of the text builds upon the information presented in Parts I and II by delineating ways to organize classrooms to promote literacy development and help ensure children's success in reading. This finely tuned information includes strategies on how to prepare and set up learning centers and how to plan for literacy instruction even before school begins and throughout the school year.
- **Connecting to Standards.** These features connect chapter concepts with the IRA/NCTE standards in classroom teaching. Link directly to these and all major standards from our Companion Website at www.prenhall.com/reutzel to continue making these connections, and to keep abreast of these continually updated principles.
- **Online Lessons and Strategies.** Margin notes within chapters will connect chapter concepts with online strategies and lesson plans specifically for struggling readers and writers. You'll find these valuable tools on our Companion Website at www.prenhall.com/reutzel.
- **Companion Website.** In addition to the Online Lessons and Strategies and important Standards materials, our Companion Website contains self-assessments to help you gauge your understanding of each chapter's concepts, a threaded message board for nationwide discussions, chapter objectives, and important literacy related Internet links.

ACKNOWLEDGMENTS

First, we owe a great deal of credit to the many teachers, parents, and children of the classrooms where we have visited over several editions and continually experiment to try out new ideas and strategies. The insights we gain from teachers and learners, both in Utah and Texas, profoundly influence our understanding of how children solve the language learning puzzle. We are especially thankful for the support of our colleagues at Utah State and the University of Texas at Arlington. You who have been reactors to our evolving ideas have offered many hints for improvement. We appreciate your wisdom and advice.

We also wish to express our gratitude to our reviewers for this and previous editions—Helen R. Abadiano, Central Connecticut State University; Kathy Barclay, Western Illinois University; Carole L. Bond, University of Memphis; Alexander Casereno, University of Portland; Martha Combs, University of Nevada, Reno; Susan J. Daniels, University of Akron; Laurie Elish-Piper, Northern Illinois University; M. Jean Greenlaw, University of North Texas; Judith Mitchells, Weber

State University; Kouider Mokhtari, Oklahoma State University; William J. Oehlkers, Rhode Island College; Peter Quinn, St. John's University; Timothy Rasinski, Kent State University; Rudy Rodriquez, University of North Texas; Mahmoud Suleiman, California State University, Bakersfield; Dan Tutolo, Bowling Green State University; James E. Walker, Clarion University of Pennsylvania; and Brad Wilcox, Brigham Young University—for your words of encouragement, timely insights, and help in shaping the organization and content for this fourth edition.

A particular debt of gratitude is extended to Scott Greenwood of West Chester University for his work with us on the Standards Connections and to Helen Hoffner of Holy Family University for her excellent contributions to the Companion Website and Instructor's Manual. Your work brings greater meaning to ours.

D. R. Reutzel and R. B. Cooter, Jr.

DISCOVER THE COMPANION WEBSITE ACCOMPANYING THIS BOOK

The Prentice Hall Companion Website: A Virtual Learning Environment

Technology is a constantly growing and changing aspect of our field that is creating a need for content and resources. To address this emerging need, Prentice Hall has developed an online learning environment for students and professors alike—Companion Websites—to support our textbooks.

In creating a Companion Website, our goal is to build on and enhance what the textbook already offers. For this reason, the content for each user-friendly website is organized by chapter and provides the professor and student with a variety of meaningful resources.

For the Professor

Every Companion Website integrates **Syllabus Manager™**, an online syllabus creation and management utility.

- **Syllabus Manager™** provides you, the instructor, with an easy, step-by-step process to create and revise syllabi, with direct links into Companion Website and other online content without having to learn HTML.
- Students may log on to your syllabus during any study session. All they need to know is the web address for the Companion Website and the password you've assigned to your syllabus.
- After you have created a syllabus using **Syllabus Manager™**, students may enter the syllabus for their course section from any point in the Companion Website.
- Clicking on a date, the student is shown the list of activities for the assignment. The activities for each assignment are linked directly to actual content, saving time for students.
- Adding assignments consists of clicking on the desired due date, then filling in the details of the assignment—name of the assignment, instructions, and whether or not it is a one-time or repeating assignment.
- In addition, links to other activities can be created easily. If the activity is online, a URL can be entered in the space provided, and it will be linked automatically in the final syllabus.

- Your completed syllabus is hosted on our servers, allowing convenient updates from any computer on the Internet. Changes you make to your syllabus are immediately available to your students at their next log on.

Common Companion Website features for students include:

For the Student

- **Chapter Objectives**—Outline key concepts from the text.
- **Interactive Self-quizzes**—Complete with hints and automatic grading that provide immediate feedback for students.

    After students submit their answers for the interactive self-quizzes, the Companion Website **Results Reporter** computes a percentage grade, provides a graphic representation of how many questions were answered correctly and incorrectly, and gives a question-by-question analysis of the quiz. Students are given the option to send their quiz to up to four email addresses (professor, teaching assistant, study partner, etc.).
- **Web Destinations**—Links to www sites that relate to chapter content.
- **Message Board**—Virtual bulletin board to post or respond to questions or comments from a national audience.

To take advantage of the many available resources, please visit the *Teaching Children to Read,* Fourth Edition, Companion Website at

www.prenhall.com/reutzel

Contents

Chapter 3   Theoretical Roots of Reading Instruction   68

PART II: METHODS AND ASSESSMENT: STRATEGIES THAT SUPPORT LITERACY DEVELOPMENT   95

Chapter 4   Phonemic Awareness and Phonics Instruction   96

Chapter 5   Increasing Vocabulary and Word Knowledge   120

Chapter 6   Improving Reading Comprehension   154

Chapter 7   Developing Reading Fluency   196

Chapter 8   Materials and Programs for Literacy Instruction: Basals and Beyond   220

Chapter 9 Assessing Literacy Learning 262

PART III: CLASSROOM PRACTICE: ORGANIZING AND PLANNING FOR LITERACY INSTRUCTION 323

Chapter 10 Organizing for Reading Instruction: Starting Out Right in Grades K–3 324

Chapter 11   Providing Effective K–3 Literacy Instruction: Every Child a Reader   378

Chapter 12   The Transition Years: Grades 4–6   420

Chapter 13   Reading in the Middle School   490

Contents

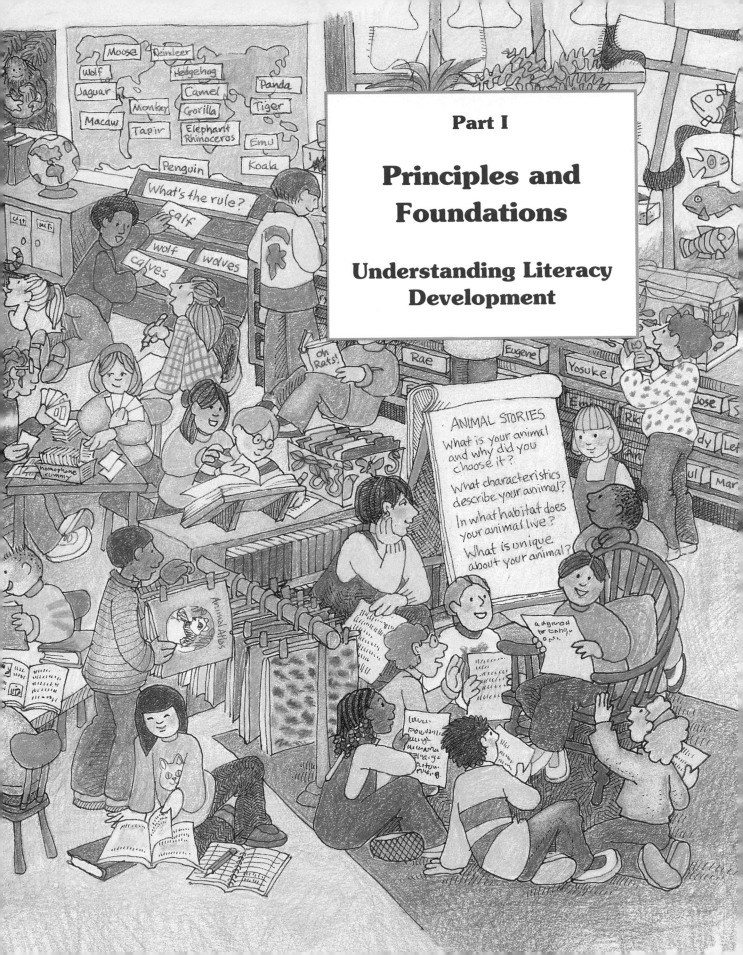

Part I

Principles and Foundations

Understanding Literacy Development

chapter 1

Introducing Comprehensive Reading Instruction for All Learners

Focus Questions

When you are finished studying this chapter, you should be able to answer these questions:

1. What is the nature of the current debate in reading education?

2. What are the seven characteristics of highly successful reading teachers?

3. What is meant by "comprehensive reading instruction"?

4. How does a *transitions approach* differ from an *eclectic approach*?

5. Why is it said that making transitions toward comprehensive reading instruction is "evolutionary . . . not revolutionary"?

6. At what point in the transition is it appropriate to develop your own system of beliefs? Explain.

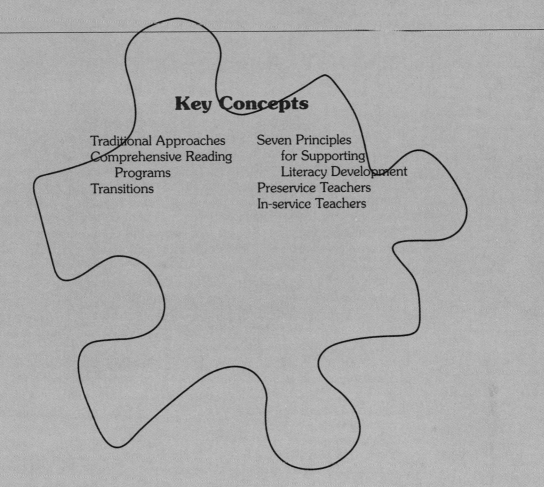

Key Concepts

Traditional Approaches
Comprehensive Reading
Programs
Transitions

Seven Principles
for Supporting
Literacy Development
Preservice Teachers
In-service Teachers

For many centuries those entrusted with the responsibility of teaching others to read have searched for effective ways to pass this invaluable skill on to others. American educators in the 19th century weighed in on the best-practices debate, an argument that continues to this day. As we travel the country, friends and strangers have asked us such questions as *Do you believe in teaching phonics? Why do some children struggle so much in learning to read? Is learning to read all that hard?* One thing is certain: there are many opinions as to how we should teach children to read.

READING IN TODAY'S SOCIETY

Visit Chapter 1 of our Companion Website at www.prenhall.com/ reutzel to look into the chapter objectives, standards and principles, and pertinent web links associated with Introducing Comprehensive Reading Instruction for All Learners.

Concern over the widening achievement gap for America's school children has resulted in an unprecedented national focus on ways to improve reading instruction (NAEP, 2000; Neuman, 2001; Rayner, Foorman, Perfetti, Pesetsky, & Seidenberg, 2001, 2002). At no time since the 1950s, when the issue was *Why Johnny Can't Read* (Flesch, 1955), has so much national political attention and funding been focused on reading research, teacher development, and reading instructional practices.

Literacy demands on our society increased exponentially as we progressed from the Industrial Age to the Information Age (Bronfenbrenner, McClelland, Wethington, Moen, & Ceci, 1996). The U.S. Bureau of Labor, in a report issued to the nation's governors, indicated that 85% of employment in the twenty-first century would require skilled or professional levels of training—all of which require the ability to read and read well (U.S. Bureau of Labor, 1995).

In spite of the increasing needs for a literate workforce, American students have not increased significantly in reading achievement. In fact, the National Assessment of Educational Progress (NAEP)(U.S. Department of Education: Office of Educational Research and Improvement, 2001) has registered no appreciable gains in fourth-grade reading achievement in decades. In the eight-year period from 1992 to 2000, the score did not vary by more than three points on a scale of 0 to 500. To make matters worse, reading achievement has continued to decline exponentially for children of poverty and urban minorities (Cooter, 2003; NAEP, 2000). In his presidential initiative called "America's Reading Challenge," former President Clinton declared,

> Forty percent of all children are now reading below basic levels on national reading assessments. Children who cannot read early and well are hampered at the very start of their lives. This will be truer as we move into the twenty-first century. To participate in America's high-skill workplaces, to cruise—much less use—the Internet, all children need to read better than ever before (U.S. Department of Education, 1997)

The High Price of Reading Failure

Research has linked poverty, incarceration, crime, and violence to illiteracy.

The cost of reading failure to both our society and individuals is very high. For many years researchers have found a high correlation between poor early reading and later failure in school (Juel, 1988; Torgesen, Wagner, Rashotte, Alexander, & Conroy, 1997). Evidence is also mounting that low reading achievement is strongly linked to adolescent/young adult substance abuse as well as criminal behavior (National Institute of Child Health and Human Development, 2000b). Further, there is a clear link between poor reading performance in early elementary years and later incarceration (Downing, 1990; Newman, 1996; Pray, 1983). Fielding, Kerr, and Rosier (1998) concluded,

> Poverty, incarceration, crime, and violence all have a common denominator in our society. That commonality is exclusion. Most of these children grew into adulthood unable to read in an information society. . . . The most expensive burden we place on our society is those students we have failed to teach to read well. The silent army of low readers who move through our schools, siphoning off the lion's share of administrative resources, emerge into society as adults still lacking the single prerequisite for managing their lives and acquiring additional training. They are chronically unemployed, underemployed, or unemployable. They form the single largest identifiable group of those whom we incarcerate, and to whom we provide assistance, housing, medical care, and other social services. They perpetuate and enlarge the problem by creating another generation of poor readers. (pp. 5–7)

Today's children are growing up in an information age in which reading and writing play a central and critical role both economically and socially (Armbruster, Lehr, & Osborn, 2001; Burns, Griffin, & Snow, 1999; Snow, Burns, & Griffin, 1998). Literacy cannot be oversold in today's economic marketplace. Now as never before teachers need to understand how children can be taught to read and write successfully.

WHAT IS ESSENTIAL TO READING INSTRUCTION: HELPING EVERY CHILD SUCCEED

How Did *YOU* Learn to Read?

Because the stakes are so high, there has been a kind of cold war over the last several decades as to how we can help children, *all* children, become good readers. Some have argued for a back-to-basics approach with lots of workbook and drill activities. Others have favored a "softer" approach using a lot of incidental learning and easy-to-read storybooks. Before we explore reading and instructional approaches to reading we would like to ask you a few questions. *Do you remember how you were taught to read in school?* Or, put another way, *How do think children learn to read?* These questions are likely to provoke a flood of very different and sometimes emotional responses. We have asked our students in university courses over the years to respond to these questions. Here is a sprinkling of their responses.

Reflect on how you first learned to read.

"Little children start learning to read by being read aloud to."

"Kids learn to read from their parents and brothers and sisters."

"I remember learning the sounds of the alphabet letters and discovering how they made words."

"I remember memorizing a favorite book and reading it again and again until the letters and words made sense to me."

"Writing, that's how I learned to read. I asked my Mom how to write my name. That led to more questions about how to write other words and the names of other people."

What *Is* This Thing Called Reading?

We often follow up this discussion by asking our students to define what they mean by *reading*. This question, too, provides some interesting insights. Here is a sampling of their responses.

"I think reading is when you make the sounds of the letters and put them together to make words."

"Reading is understanding what is on the page."

"Phonics is the first part of reading and comprehension is the last."

In response to these discussions with our college students/future teachers, we were naturally led to pose several additional questions to our students: What is involved in the reading process? Are there different beliefs, hypotheses, explanations, or theories about how children *learn* to read? Are there different beliefs as to how children should be *taught* to read? How do these differ? What do teachers need to know about children's language acquisition, or reading and writing development? How is our language structured, and how does language structure play a role in a child's learning to read?

At this juncture you may be wondering what you have gotten yourself into. We admit that the responsibilities of teaching children to read are challenging. However, you don't need to know all of the answers to these questions now. In fact, you probably won't have all of the answers when you finish reading this book. It is our intention that you will, however, have a better idea of what it takes to be successful at teaching reading and can work toward those goals. When you read the next section, you will get a picture of what we consider to be characteristics of highly successful reading teachers.

THE SEVEN CHARACTERISTICS OF HIGHLY SUCCESSFUL READING TEACHERS

We have learned over the years that successful reading teachers enjoy some common characteristics (see Figure 1.1). Here is what you must know and be able to do in order to become a master teacher of reading:

1. Understand the role of language as a critical part of children's reading development
2. Assess learner needs to plan appropriate instruction
3. Construct well-organized and print-rich learning environments
4. Use research-based instruction

Figure 1.1   The seven characteristics of highly successful reading teachers

5. Explicitly teach and model how to apply literacy skills and strategies in every area of study
6. Adapt instruction for learners with special needs
7. Involve the school, family, and community

In the following section we briefly define each of these seven characteristics. Then, throughout the remainder of the book, we go much deeper to help you set your goals and expectations toward becoming a master reading teacher.

1. *Understanding the role of language as a critical part of children's reading development.* Reading is one of four primary language forms: listening, speaking, reading, and writing. As one of the four "language arts," it is necessarily dependent on students having robust listening and speaking vocabularies. Studies indicate, for instance, that children from poverty typically start school with only half the vocabulary of children from higher-income backgrounds (Graves & Slater, 1987; Healy, 1990; Snow, Burns, & Griffin, 1998; Payne, 1998). But they also show that *all* students can be helped to read 1 million words per year in their classrooms and, as a powerful by-product, acquire some 1,000 words yearly in the process (Nagy, Anderson, & Herman, 1987; Krashen, 1993). Highly effective reading teachers continually find creative and permanent ways of building up vocabulary and concept knowledge in their students.

Reading is dependent on students having robust listening and speaking vocabularies.

2. *Assessing learner needs to plan appropriate instruction.* Reading assessment informs our teaching. Highly effective reading teachers realize that they must learn which reading skills each child already knows, and does not know, in order to plan appropriate instruction. Master teachers are able to quickly test each student's knowledge, create a kind of reading road map of what is known, and then teach children according to their specific needs (Cooter, 2004). Best assessments are conducted over time and compare the child's past and present abilities. This view of reading assessment provides a comprehensive portrait of the learner's progress (Farr & Tone, 1994; B. Hill & Ruptic, 1994).

Reading assessment allows teachers to teach children according to their specific reading needs.

3. *Constructing well-organized and print-rich learning environments.* The highly effective reading teacher is an extremely good classroom manager (Wong & Wong, 1998). Procedures and routines are taught from the first day of school so students have the security of knowing what is expected. These teachers also infuse the classroom with print in every form, using word walls, message centers, student writing samples, lots of books from every genre, learning centers, and real world objects that inspire study and reflection. Rome was not built in a day, nor are well-organized print-rich classrooms. Thus, there is the need for new teachers to set goals each year as they make positive transitions toward creating these kinds of learning environs.

Print-rich, well-organized classrooms promote the study of and reflection on words and reading.

4. *Using research-based instruction.* Great teachers must have a plethora of tools in their educational toolboxes if every child is to reach his full potential. For example, there is a veritable mountain of research on the best ways of teaching the skills of reading to different student populations. Perkins (2001) has identified research-proven methods for helping urban African American children become excellent readers. Escamilla and her colleagues (Galindo & Escamilla, 1994; Medina & Escamilla, 1995) have also provided us with compelling ideas for teaching reading to children who speak Spanish as their first language.

Figure 1.2   Comprehensive reading instruction

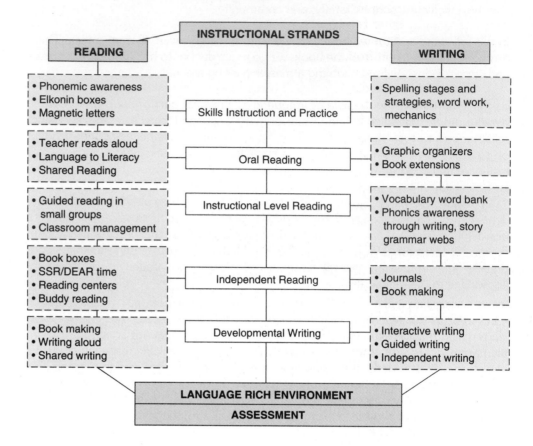

Comprehensive Reading Instruction

Evidence-based instruction includes the fundamental teaching and learning strands important in scaffolding reading instruction.

Effective reading teachers use an *evidence-based* (Snow et al., 1998) instructional "backbone" in planning instruction for all students. This backbone includes the fundamental teaching and learning strands important in scaffolding reading instruction. Figure 1.2 is one example of a comprehensive reading instruction backbone depicting key instructional strands (Cooter, 1998) used in a major school district.

5. *Explicitly teaching and modeling how to apply literacy skills and strategies in every area of study.*   Effective teaching uses a great deal of teacher *modeling* and the *gradual release of responsibility* (Pearson & Gallagher, 1983). Modeling means showing students how a new skill to be learned looks when a competent reader (the teacher) uses it. As students begin to understand, effective teachers gradually release the "doing" of the skill to students, but with a good deal of support, of course. When the student has become proficient using the new reading skill, then she is helped to apply it in myriad situations. We call this *generalizing usage of the skill.* For example, a new phonics skill used to "decode" unknown words in print, once mastered, can be applied to decoding unfamiliar "weather words" when reading a nonfiction science passage called *Storms of the Century.* Thus, highly effective teachers help children understand how each new skill is a valuable tool in their reading toolbox.

Modeling is showing students how a new skill to be learned looks when a competent reader (i.e. the teacher) uses it.

6. *Adapting instruction for learners with special needs.* It is essential that we work to meet reading needs of *all* children: *no one is to be left behind.* Master reading teachers know that we have some students with special learning needs that may require some program modifications. Whether due to physical, language, cognitive, cultural, or other factors, all children should be provided with flexible, high-quality instruction in the regular classroom whenever possible. Homeroom teachers receive in-class support from reading specialists, special education teachers, and educational psychologists so that children can enjoy learning with their peers. In this way, highly effective reading teachers deliver comprehensive reading instruction in an inclusive environment. They recognize that children benefit from classroom diversity in ways that carry into adulthood.

The importance of learning with their peers necessitates reading specialists, special education teachers, and educational psychologists to aid special needs readers.

7. *Involving the school, family, and community.* Parents and other family members have a profound influence on the development of a child's reading ability. Highly effective teachers encourage them to become active participants by encouraging them to create homes that stimulate reading growth (Rasinski & Fredericks, 1988). They help parents find ways to support learning begun at school in enjoyable ways. In other words, master teachers support parents in their roles as "first teachers."

Parental involvement is paramount in developing a child's reading ability.

Research has also shown that community groups can be mobilized to help children succeed in reading (Cooter, 2003). These efforts sometimes include citywide *DEAR Days* (Drop Everything and Read) to raise community awareness, volunteer grandparent groups like "Off Our Rockers" reading with children, and summer reading programs held at community churches at lunchtime ("read and feed" programs). Many corporate sponsors are interested in fundraisers that help schools create Literacy Materials Centers crammed full of high-quality books, pocket charts, and other instructional aids. Clearly, the highly effective reading teacher is a community activist when it comes to promoting reading.

One first step to becoming a successful reading teacher is to understand the theoretical underpinnings of reading instruction and learn what a classroom reading program might look like. Thus, to help you envision how to teach reading, it might be wise to identify for you what has influenced reading instruction over the last few years.

Standards Note
Standard 2.14: The reading professional will understand that goals, instruction, and assessment should be aligned. As you read about the practices that entail a comprehensive approach, list the parallel assessments that will lead to curricular coherence. Be prepared to share these with your classmates.

READING INSTRUCTION: LOOKING BACK AND LOOKING FORWARD

For many years, there has been a storm of controversy over reading instruction—some educators favoring traditional direct instruction reading programs with a heavy emphasis on phonics and others advocating "whole language" approaches. Recently, however, there have been those who advocate instead a position in the "radical middle"—reading programs that are more balanced or comprehensive. But, let's not get too far ahead of ourselves. Let's begin by looking at where the field has been over the last several decades and where it is likely to go in the next.

Traditional Approaches to Reading Instruction

For the purpose of our discussion, we define **traditional approaches** for reading instruction as those relying heavily on worksheets, volumes of seat work, either whole-class instruction or ability grouping exclusively, round robin reading, and exclusive use

Traditional approaches for reading rely heavily on parts-to-whole skill instruction, worksheets, and "round robin" reading.

of basal reader textbooks. It is also common to find that skill instruction is unconnected to the reading of texts in traditional basal reader programs, which is termed *teaching skills in isolation* or *parts-to-whole* instruction.

Teachers drawn toward using traditional basal programs *exclusively* argue that the basal reader is successful, especially as measured by standardized tests, state-mandated competency tests, and other measures of reading achievement commonly used in most school systems. In addition, many teachers like the structured aspects of basal reader manuals, which save them a great deal of planning time. Thus, many teachers understandably feel that basal readers are efficient classroom tools, help children learn to read, and provide documentation of reading success. While basal readers can be quite useful and certainly have an important role in many school districts, they are not by themselves sufficient in meeting the needs of all children.

A Whole Language Approach

Whole language is a form of teaching loosely adapted from New Zealand, but lacking regular skill instruction.

Whole language, a curious and mostly American phenomenon, was a loosely adapted version of some much heralded approaches to teaching reading developed by New Zealand educators. Taking an almost polar opposite stance from the traditionalists, whole language proponents decried the use of worksheets, seat work, or grouping children (other than heterogeneous or "mixed" grouping). They used shared reading and literature response groups rather than ability groups as primary strategies.

Teacher-directed, explicit skill instruction was also left out—even ridiculed—by many whole language supporters. Indeed, they shunned direct skill instruction in any form and believed that children learned skills best by reading or by having books read to them, leaving critics to conclude that whole language advocates believed that literacy skills are learned by some sort of osmosis!

The incomplete teaching that is whole language instruction contributed to the collapse of programs in California and other states in the late 1980s and early 1990s.

"Whole languagers" used only trade-book literature, and all instruction was *whole*—words were almost never broken down or removed from context for analysis. Unfortunately for many students, this sort of incomplete teaching contributed to the virtual collapse of reading programs in California and other states during the late 1980s and early 1990s. As a result of an unprecedented fall in reading test scores in California, a state-level reading task force composed of talented reading teachers, researchers, and other stakeholders was assembled. Their report, *Every Child a Reader* (California Reading Task Force, 1995), concluded that a more balanced approach to the teaching of reading was needed, an approach that is "research-based and combines skills development with literature and language-rich activities." (p. iii)

Balanced Reading Instruction: An Attempted Compromise

Balanced reading instruction was a much hoped for compromise between traditionalists and whole language advocates.

The balanced reading movement was the much-hoped-for compromise for ending the *Reading Wars* (Reutzel & Cooter, 2003). The crusade for *balanced reading instruction* began in 1990 with a small group of educators who issued *Balance: A Manifesto for Balance in the Teaching of Literacy and Language Skills* (Thompson, 1997). Some U.S. schools and districts caught on to the balanced reading movement early. But, it was not until the results of the 1994 National Assessment of Educational Progress (NAEP) became public in California that the balanced reading movement really acquired national momentum.

Bill Honig (1995), then Superintendent of Public Instruction in California, was instrumental in focusing national attention on the deficits of whole language instruction. He contended that whole language instruction was not meeting the needs of diverse students and that what was needed was a more "balanced" reading instructional approach. Honig's (1995) call for "Balanced Reading" was forcefully captured in the document *Every Child a Reader: Report of the California Reading Task Force* (1998). Other voices of reason and moderation emerged from what became known as *the radical middle* in support of a "balanced reading approach" to reading instruction.

As the national discussion progressed, questions came into focus—"balancing *what* and by *whom?*" Some national voices defined balance as an approach to reading instruction that brought equilibrium to two opposing views on teaching reading—whole language and phonics. What emerged from trying to define balanced reading instruction was the familiar notion of the "scales of justice." The concept of "balance" was to even up the sides of the scale with equal portions of phonics and whole language on either side, as portrayed by Reutzel and Cooter (2003) in Figure 1.3. Soon, it became apparent that to define "balanced reading instruction" as an act to even up the sides of the scale invited one more round of "this versus that" thinking.

Others challenged, from an historical viewpoint, the idea that balanced reading instruction was "new" and needed redefining at all (Reutzel, 1999a). This opinion held that balanced reading dated back to the popular "balanced reading" practices of the 1960s in New Zealand, also known as "READING TO, WITH, and BY" children (Mooney, 1990; Department of Education, 1985). As far as these reading educators were concerned, "balanced reading" had already been defined and proven effective for many years.

Still others felt that the concept of "balance" represented a *philosophy* rather than a defined set of practices. Balance was seen as a disciplined form of eclecticism grounded in the judgment and skill of informed teachers (Fitzgerald, 1999; Pearson, 2000; Speigel, 1999; Strickland et al., 1997). In some ways, this group attempted to describe balance by stating what it was and was not. Terms applied to define balanced reading instruction as a philosophy included flexible, realistic, decision-making approach, consistency, and comprehensive (Speigel, 1999; Fitzgerald, 1999).

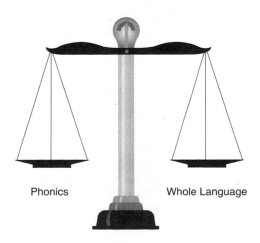

Figure 1.3 Balance as achieving instructional equilibrium

Phonics   Whole Language

By what type of reading instruction do you recall being taught?

Standards Note
Standard 16.2: The reading professional will be able to reflect on his or her practice to improve instruction and other resources to students. As you read about comprehensive reading instruction, list the essential features that set it apart from traditional and whole language approaches. Then analyze and reflect upon your own practices as a literacy professional.

Comprehensive Reading Instruction: A Research-Based Solution

Comprehensive reading programs have emerged as the leading research-based alternative to traditional and holistic approaches. Comprehensive reading programs teach students skills in reading and writing based on their individual needs, and within the context of appropriately leveled reading materials of interest to the learner.

Comprehensive reading instruction programs are an evidence-based alternative to traditional and holistic approaches.

Comprehensive reading programs often use basal readers, "decodable text," and other more traditional programmed reading materials; but they also include daily encounters with fiction and nonfiction trade books. In comprehensive reading classrooms, one typically sees oral reading by teachers and children alike, direct skill instruction and practice in guided oral reading groups (Fountas & Pinnell, 1996, NRP, 2000), reading by students in books they can manage independently, and "process" writing and spelling instruction.

The Politics of Comprehensive Reading Instruction

Comprehensive reading instruction has become a popular issue supported by major political leaders.

Comprehensive reading instruction has taken root in many states and has gained prominence as a political issue. During the 1998 Texas gubernatorial campaign, for instance, comprehensive reading instruction was a major plank in the election platform of then-Governor George W. Bush. The same was true in recent elections in many other states, including California. On the national proscenium, U.S. Secretary of Education Rod Paige pushed to the forefront initiatives that support comprehensive reading programs involving "scripted" materials (i.e, those that literally tell teachers word-for-word what should be said during instruction). *We advocate comprehensive reading programs that go well beyond the scripting of instruction, and call for the unfettered influence of highly educated and skilled teachers in the reading classroom.* These political and other trends indicate that reading issues will remain center stage for some time to come.

Comprehensive reading programs promote student empowerment.

Empowering Young Teachers and Readers

Many teachers feel that a comprehensive reading instruction perspective does a better job of empowering students and teachers. This is accomplished, at least in part, by teacher-directed skill instruction coupled with massive amounts of reading in appropriately challenging books, the teaching of composition skills through the writing process, and developing stronger vocabularies through speaking and read aloud experiences. These activities are carefully selected to engage and activate students' own experiences and are inherently more stimulating. Preliminary research suggests that teachers and students in comprehensive reading programs tend to perform very well in comparison to those using traditional approaches (Wharton-McDonald et al., 1997). So, how do you set up a comprehensive reading program? Understanding how to create comprehensive reading programs and become a highly skilled and successful reading teacher happens gradually over time through a process we call transitions—a process that takes years, not months. In the final section of this chapter we share our observations about the transitions process and the challenges it sometimes presents to the committed professional.

MAKING TRANSITIONS TOWARD COMPREHENSIVE READING INSTRUCTION

Transitions is a philosophical position that encourages teachers to initiate changes in literacy beliefs and practices by building bridges, not walls, to develop *comprehensive reading programs* in their classrooms. The bridges to be built connect, in part, the seemingly opposing worlds of traditionalists and whole language advocates. The bridges connect what research says is best practice from all instructional approaches.

First, we advocate *patience* when it comes to making the transition to comprehensive reading instruction, especially concerning (a) how quickly the transition is to occur, and (b) whether or not teachers can use some ideas from traditional and/or balanced perspectives. Our perspective, like the ideas we present in this book for creating a comprehensive reading curriculum, was first formed several years ago when we returned to full-time classroom teaching. We explored the usefulness of many of the comprehensive reading program strategies suggested by leaders in the field. So as not to fall into the "throwing out the baby with the bath water" syndrome, we also considered traditional and whole language strategies for teaching reading that might have value in a comprehensive reading program.

A major point of interest in our classroom experiences dealt with the challenges facing teachers moving from traditional and balanced forms of teaching to comprehensive reading programs. Our perspective was further refined during the late 1990s when we both participated in a massive teacher education initiative known as the Dallas Reading Plan and the Utah Balanced Literacy Project involving some 7,000 teachers from urban, suburban, and rural classrooms (see Cooter, 2003; Reutzel & Fawson, 2003). As a result of these experiences, we feel that we have come to a better understanding of the debate between whole language, traditionalist, and comprehensive reading instruction positions.

A transitional attitude encourages teachers to make changes by beginning from where they are and gradually adopting and embracing scientifically based comprehensive reading instructional practices. Thus, teachers springboard from current instructional methods or beliefs to comprehensive reading practices—such as strategic assessment of benchmark or "milestone" reading skills, teaching interactive writing, direct skill instruction in a variety of formats, the use of a variety of children's fiction and nonfiction books, leveled books, decodable books, predictable books, and guided oral reading groups. As teachers experience success with comprehensive reading approaches, a new spirit of adventure in teaching and learning enters the reading classroom. Several key elements of transitions are described in the paragraphs that follow.

Transitions Means Philosophical Movement

One aspect of transitions is the notion of *movement*. Over time, most teachers will gradually move toward more comprehensive reading strategies and further away from dependence on the practices and beliefs of the past. Comprehensive reading programs, as described in this book and others (e.g., Fountas & Pinnell, 1996; May & Rizzardi, 2002; Mooney, 1990; Pressley, 2002; *Reading in Junior Classes,* 1985; Roller, 2002; Snow et al., 1998), have a long track record of success in English-speaking countries. As has been said so well, "Once you see it in action, you can't go back." (Esch, 1991, p. D1)

Transitions encourage teachers to initiate changes in literacy beliefs and practices by building bridges between traditional and whole language reading approaches in their classrooms.

Eclectic approaches are "blended" programs that lack a consistent theoretical base.

One reason the notion of *movement* is important is that it distinguishes a transitions approach from those commonly referred to as "eclectic" approaches. In an **eclectic approach,** teachers simply borrow elements from two or more approaches to create their own approach. Eclectic approaches frequently grow out of what is considered new or trendy, rather than being organized according to an articulated belief system and evidence-based practices—*random acts of teaching,* you might say. Once designed, an eclectic approach is always changing; it is relatively fluid because it is at the mercy of fashion. Transitions approaches, on the other hand, change continuously, too, but they inspire one forward in an informed direction—improved comprehensive reading instruction and student success based on scientific reading research.

Transitions Takes Time

Transitions is also about *time*—time to learn, update your knowledge, explore, and grow professionally as a teacher of reading. A transitions position acknowledges that teachers make changes toward comprehensive reading instruction in their own way and at their own rate. With this multiyear perspective in mind, one must reasonably expect that teachers will make transitions quietly, little by little, step-by-step, over a substantial period of time (Routman, 2003).

Transitions Involves Curriculum Integration

Comprehensive reading teachers often integrate the language arts and content subject areas so as to deepen students' learning. Integration requires much planning, time, and skill to achieve. One well-known teacher, Regie Routman (1988), wrote about her own gradual transitions toward integrating her curriculum:

> At this point in time I am comfortable integrating the four language modes—listening, speaking, reading, and writing. . . . I don't always use thematic units; I occasionally teach from part to whole [i.e., instead of whole to parts to whole—*authors' note*]; I am still struggling hard to integrate more areas of curriculum with the language arts—an ideal that is very difficult to attain. I anticipate that this struggle will go on for years. (p. 26)

Transitions Involves Risk Taking

Closely related to the notion of allowing teachers time to make changes at their own pace and in their own way is the recognition that *risks* are associated with making these changes. There is sometimes the feeling that one is "walking the tightrope without a net" when trying somewhat different ideas in the classroom, especially in this age of high stakes testing in most states. Silvia Ashton-Warner (1963) long ago acknowledged the risks and frustration sometimes associated with making changes in reading instruction when she wrote:

> If only I had the confidence of being a good teacher. But I'm not even an appalling teacher. I don't claim to be a teacher at all. I'm just a nitwit somehow let loose among children. (p. 198)

Transitions teachers build "safety nets" for students as they make gradual curriculum changes.

Transitions teachers are supportive of each other and themselves. They build "safety nets" for themselves and others by understanding that transitions toward comprehensive reading instruction take time and will not happen all at once. These safety nets are to be not only tolerated, but also appreciated as a normal evolutionary step. The movement toward comprehensive reading instruction is evolutionary—not revolutionary

(Pearson, 1989), meaning it won't happen overnight. One teacher gradually transitioning into her own comprehensive reading program remarked,

> The basal program acts like a safety net for me. I've used it successfully for years and I know that the curriculum objectives required by the school system will be met and documented when I use basal materials. But I do want *more* for my students. My transitions program allows me to keep my basal safety net while learning more about balanced literacy. This year I reduced my classroom time in the basal to only three days per week. That allowed me to begin to do more with the writing workshop, whole to parts to whole skill instruction, and children's literature. Next year, I plan to use the basal *even* less to allow for other comprehensive reading practices. *(Darlene DeCrane, Bowling Green, OH)*

The Transitions Model: A Modest Proposal for Change

Regardless of how, when, where, what, or why teachers begin making transitions toward comprehensive reading instruction, there are at least eight interrelated dimensions of this multifaceted process.

Figure 1.4 is a model that shows how transitions involve gradual change along the following dimensions: instructional beliefs, reading materials, curriculum design, instructional grouping, cultural diversity, assessment, classroom environments, and family and community involvement.

The transitions model contains eight interrelated dimensions to move through toward comprehensive reading instruction.

Figure 1.4 Dimensions of transitions: A model of change in reading instruction

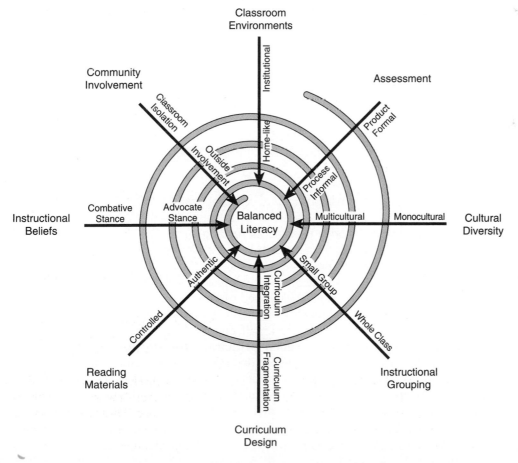

1. Transitions in *instructional beliefs* may range from an initial "combative" stance regarding comprehensive reading beliefs to the opposite end of the continuum—an "advocate's" stance.
2. Using traditional *reading materials and basal programs* while acquiring a variety of appropriately challenging reading materials better fitted to comprehensive teaching of reading makes up another dimension of transitions.
3. Teachers' *design of the reading curriculum* may change during transitions from emphasizing the use of isolated skill building worksheets exclusively toward reading skills instruction embedded in varied texts with carefully orchestrated, guided feedback and instruction (such as "decodable texts," poetry, song, raps, and chants).
4. Teachers in transition often find themselves moving from whole-class teaching to effective use of *small group and one-to-one* instructional modes, such as guided reading groups (Fountas & Pinnell, 1996; Morrow, 1988b), research "clubs," and needs-based, interest, and cooperative learning groups.
5. Transitions in *family and community involvement* means moving from classroom isolation to greater family involvement and, where sensible, the inclusion of other community stakeholders as important parts of reading instruction (Cooter, Mills-House, Marrin, Mathews, & Campbell, 1999).
6. Transitions in *classroom learning environments* means movement from rigid institutional environments (children seated in rows) with impoverished access to books that limit student interactions to more homelike, "language friendly" environments for learning (children seated at tables) with access to many and varied print materials.
7. Transitions in *cultural diversity* involve a shift from what may be termed monocultural and monolingual views of society to a multicultural and multilingual outlook in the literacy-learning classroom.
8. Transitions in *assessment* range from *product only assessments*—formal assessments best represented by standardized achievement tests—to including *process assessments*—criterion assessments providing on-the-spot analyses of children's reading and writing development in specific skill areas.

To begin your own transitions toward comprehensive reading instruction, it is important to know the essential elements of scientifically based reading research so you can use these findings to judge ideas about reading instruction. For master teachers, a knowledge of scientifically based research helps them screen new teaching strategies and also decide which practices currently in place can be eliminated from the busy school schedule (so as to allow for the infusion of the best practices). For new teachers, a knowledge of scientifically based research can help them select comprehensive reading instructional practices that can move them beyond the exclusive use of basal readers and overreliance upon ineffective practices.

The seven principles for supporting literacy development provide a springboard for teachers developing a belief system.

We have assembled a list of **seven principles for supporting literacy development** for this purpose, along with a description of each. Although not intended to be exhaustive, it should serve as a starting place for teachers as they make transitions toward comprehensive reading instruction. We begin with our goal statement, then continue with a list of principles that help us select components for a comprehensive reading program.

Seven
Principles
For Supporting Literacy Development

The primary goal of comprehensive reading programs is to help all students become independent, fluent readers in the early education years, then help them expand their literacy abilities throughout their schooling. This goal has now been adopted by school districts throughout the United States and implies that we have a vision of "every classroom as good as our best." It is accomplished by adhering to the seven principles outlined on these pages.

Principle
one

Begin with the teacher's knowledge of student reading processes. A great deal of research has been amassed over the years that collectively describes stages and milestone skills associated with reading and writing development. Comprehensive reading teachers use *evidence-based* (Snow, Burns, & Griffin, 1998; Strickland, Snow, Griffin, Burns, & NcNamara, 2002) instruction in teaching all students.

Rely on process and product student assessments that link directly to the knowledge base of reading. Assessment informs our teaching and makes it possible to group children efficiently and effectively according to their learning needs. Highly effective reading teachers realize that they must learn which reading skills each child already has and does not have in order to plan appropriate instruction (Barrentine, 1999; Calkins, Montgomery, & Santman, 1998; Embretson, 2003). Classroom assessment should examine students' literacy processes as well as products. Assessment should be used to encourage the learner about his or her progress, not merely to document scores for accountability purposes. Best assessments are conducted over time and compare students' past and present abilities. This is accomplished partly through the accumulation of numerous learning artifacts using multiple methods of collection. This system of assessment provides a comprehensive view of the learner's progress (Farr & Tone, 1994; B. Hill & Ruptic, 1994).

Principle
three

Involve families in support of the reading development process.
Parents and other primary care-givers have a profound influence on the development of their child's reading ability. Highly effective teachers encourage them to become active participants by creating homes that stimulate reading growth (DeBruin-Parecki & Krol-Sinclair, 2003). They help parents find ways to support learning begun at school in numerous enjoyable ways. In other words, master teachers support parents in their roles as "first teachers."

Support Reading To, With, and By students. *Reading To, With, and By* (Mooney, 1990) is a flexible and practical model for instruction that can be useful in creating comprehensive literacy programs (Reutzel & Cooter, 2003). This model has embedded within it key strands of teaching, including skill instruction and practice, instructional-level reading routines, oral reading by students and teachers alike, massive but pleasurable amounts of reading practice, and a great deal of writing instruction and composition. The key practices that occur daily are as follows:

Reading TO Children—Every student is read to each day by a masterful reader. This can take the form of teacher read alouds, reading one to one by a peer or adult, or what is sometimes called "lap reading," most often with a family member.

Reading WITH Children—The teacher reads with students daily. This commonly occurs in small groups during a guided reading session (Fountas & Pinnell, 2001), in "House Calls" wherein the teacher visits one to one with students, in large group choral reading sessions, or during shared reading experiences.

Reading BY Children—Children should have daily independent reading opportunities. It may simply be a time set aside during the day for twenty or so minutes of pleasure reading (i.e., Drop Everything and Read, or "DEAR" time; Sustained Silent Reading, or "SSR"), or it may be in the form of performance reading,  as with a Readers' Theater group. Sometimes students read to each other in a buddy or assisted reading period—for instance, a second grader reading to a fifth grade partner once a week.

Principle five

Integrate the development of reading with writing instruction and composition. In our own classroom experiences, as well as in our work with large urban school districts, we have seen firsthand the power of teaching writing as an essential element of reading instruction. Students who become writers rapidly improve as readers. When learning spelling strategies (part of the *editing* stage), for instance, students learn phonetic elements in words much more easily and become better decoders of words in print when reading. Similarly, as students learn story grammar elements (e.g., setting, characterization, challenges, resolution, etc.), their reading comprehension soars. Teachers establishing comprehensive literacy programs see writing instruction as indispensable and embed it within daily teaching routines.

Develop reading and writing skills via "whole-to-parts-to-whole" instruction. Children learning to become better readers must be helped to learn certain aspects of print (Richgels, 2001). However, that does not mean that instruction in such areas as phonics or comprehension should focus on these elements isolated from meaningful text (e.g., traditional skill and drill instruction). To teach in this way often confuses children as to what real reading is all about and fails to connect the new skills with the reading act (Strickland, 1998). For example, if reading instruction begins with the reading of meaningful text, the skill to be learned could be taught within the context of the story.

In the final stages of learning, the reading skill or strategy should be taken back into reading and reapplied in other contexts (U.S. Department of Education, 1985). This *whole-to-parts-to-whole* way of teaching skills helps students understand the relevance and usefulness of what they have learned.

Address the needs of *all* children. It is essential that we all work to meet reading needs of *all* children: *so that no one is to be left behind.* Master reading teachers know that we have some students with special learning needs who may require some instructional and environmental modifications. Whether due to physical, language, cognitive, cultural, or other factors, all children should be provided with flexible, high-quality instruction in the regular classroom whenever possible (Allington, 2001; Walker, 2000). A successful comprehensive literacy program includes all children, recognizing that all students benefit from classroom diversity in ways that carry into adulthood.

CHALLENGES FACING PRESERVICE TEACHERS IN MAKING TRANSITIONS

Preservice teachers, those studying to become elementary school teachers, face special challenges in delivering comprehensive reading instruction. Challenges facing preservice teachers are quite different from those of **in-service teachers** (those currently serving as classroom teachers). Preservice hurdles that can be addressed through the transitions approach include the following:

- Disharmony with past belief systems and practices
- Conflicting views among educators
- Overcoming tradition in the schools

Preservice teachers are people studying to become elementary school teachers.

In-service teachers are educators currently practicing the profession.

Disharmony with Past Belief Systems and Practices

Everyone who has ever attended elementary school has some preconceived notions about what reading instruction is *supposed* to be. To maintain an open mind and overcome biases based on past experiences, preservice teachers can do at least two things: They should find out what beliefs they currently hold, and then carefully review alternative philosophies and methods for teaching reading. This book is organized to facilitate this process. Once preservice teachers know what they know (and don't know), it becomes easier to begin making mental transitions toward new research findings and best practices for teaching reading. It is important to remember that (a) everyone holds biases about teaching and learning, either consciously or unconsciously, and (b) we should keep an open mind about teaching children until all possibilities have been explored.

Conflicting Views Among Educators

Another challenge for preservice teachers is the reality that not all teachers (or researchers) agree as to the best ways of teaching reading. For example, it is quite possible for students to take college courses from professors whose classroom experiences were very traditional and who feel movement toward comprehensive reading programs is not desirable. An important thing to remember is that colleges are organized, ideally, to present many different viewpoints. The purpose of collegiate work is *education,* not *indoctrination*. Maintaining an open mind is important if preservice teachers are to become as well informed and effective as they need to be.

Educators often hold differing views of learning and teaching.

Overcoming Tradition in the Schools

Another obstacle is inertia, or tradition, in schools. Many preservice teachers who are practice teaching in schools are intimidated and feel that they are know-nothings. Although it is true that preservice teachers, by definition, lack experience, it is not true that they are uneducated or cannot have useful insights. Preservice teachers are necessarily part of the change process occurring in schools today. Many classroom teachers and administrators are still learning about comprehensive reading programs; preservice teachers play an important role in helping other educators stay current and begin their own transitions. Preservice teachers should be seen as change agents who contribute to the improvement of schools while gaining much needed experience from seasoned educators. When viewed in this way, preservice

Preservice teachers contribute much to the cause of improving reading instruction.

and in-service teachers become true professional colleagues who can assist each other in making transitions toward comprehensive reading instruction.

CHALLENGES FACING IN-SERVICE TEACHERS

Unlike preservice teachers, in-service teachers have had time to get used to the responsibilities associated with daily classroom teaching. The initial feelings of uncertainty have been replaced with a strong desire to find more effective ways of helping children become literate. As in-service teachers begin the process of moving into transitions, they almost immediately become aware of obstacles that can zap one's creative energies unless they are recognized and addressed. Most common hurdles for practicing teachers are related to the following:

- Time commitment
- Comfort zones
- Administrative risk taking

Time Commitment

Many reading teachers complain that transitions toward comprehensive reading programs require a great time commitment in the early stages. True! For example, in addition to reading current books on comprehensive reading programs (a short list is recommended at the end of this chapter), many teachers need to become better acquainted with popular children's literature, pull together instructional resources (e.g., literacy materials centers), assemble teacher-made books and bulletin boards, order decodable books and big books (for primary levels), review computer software and other technology, and perhaps design thematic units. (Note: These and many other teaching ideas are discussed fully in later chapters.)

Teachers also need to find ways of aligning performance objectives required by the school district and state with their own research-based notions of what the curriculum should include. Without a doubt, comprehensive reading instruction requires significant planning time, especially during the first few years. But once teachers are off and running, comprehensive reading programs become relatively easy to maintain and modify. More importantly, the enjoyment both teachers and children experience as a result of this hard work makes the effort worthwhile.

Comfort Zones

Another problem is that of comfort zones. That is, it is often difficult to get teachers who have been practicing their profession for even a few years to begin something as different and challenging as making transitions toward comprehensive reading instruction. Ultimately, teachers who continue to experiment and update their teaching strategies throughout their careers tend to have greater success with student development and performance, usually experience fewer discipline problems in these energized classrooms, and enjoy the teaching profession rather than burn out.

Administrative Risk Taking

Finally, a certain amount of administrative risk taking is involved whenever new program changes are considered, especially for principals. Many wonderful, innovative elementary principals are very supportive of classroom change. Some principals (like

---

In-service teachers make significant time commitments when moving into transitions.

Standards Note
Standard 2.9: The reading professional will understand how contextual factors in the school can influence student learning and reading (e.g., grouping procedures, school programs, and assessment). Reading "programs," implicitly, mean materials. Assuming that you intend to be a practitioner of comprehensive reading instruction, you'll need lots of materials in order to do it well. Reread the process sections and draw up a good wish list for your classroom, prioritizing your needs.

Principals in schools moving into comprehensive reading instruction join their teachers and students in becoming risk takers.

Comprehensive reading programs require significant planning time, but once off and running, they become relatively easy to maintain and modify.

some teachers), however, are somewhat resistant to change. It is critical that teachers making transitions toward comprehensive reading instruction view, as *part of the process,* the necessity of educating principals—"bringing them along" as to how they are modifying their classrooms and why. They must find ways to make the principal part of their classroom family by inviting her into the classroom frequently and getting the principal meaningfully involved with children in comprehensive reading activities. It is important to remember that most people become teachers because they like to be around children; principals are simply teachers who have taken on administrative assignments. (Note: the term *principal* comes from the ancient title *principal teacher.*) Offering your principal "hands-on" opportunities will help inform her about your new literacy goals and build positive and supportive relationships.

Check your understanding of chapter concepts by using the self assessment for Chapter 1 on our Companion Website at www.prenhall.com/reutzel.

Concept Applications

In the Classroom

1. Outline your reading and language arts block schedule or that of a teacher whom you have interviewed. Would you characterize this schedule as favoring a more traditional, basal-oriented approach, or does it include a number of comprehensive reading program elements? Hint: Use the *seven principles for supporting literacy development* to validate your judgment if you feel the schedule favors comprehensive reading practices.
2. Consider your teaching environment (resources, principal's attitude, school board and central office policies, etc.) or that of an in-service colleague. What are some of the potential "comfort zones"? Will some administrative risk taking be required to facilitate transitions toward comprehensive reading teaching? Explain.

3. Draw up a comprehensive list of activities you are currently using in your classroom or those that you plan to use. Next, construct an evaluation checklist using the *seven principles for supporting literacy development* as a guide. Evaluate each of your classroom activities using the seven principles as the standard. Which of your activities qualify under one or more categories? Do any activities fail to meet any of the principles? If so, what should you do? (Possibly you will need to create some new principles!)

Recommended Readings

Armbruster, B. B., Lehr, F., & Osborn, J. (2001). *Put reading first: The research building blocks for teaching children to read.* Washington, DC: The Partnership for Reading— NIL, NICHHD, and U.S. Department of Education.

Au, K. H. (1997). *Literacy instruction in multicultural settings.* Belmont, CA: Wadsworth.

Burns, M. S., Griffin, P., & Snow, C. E. (1999). *Starting out right: A guide to promoting children's reading success.* Washington, DC: National Academy Press.

Cooter, R. B. (Ed.). (2003). *Perspectives on rescuing urban literacy education: Spies, saboteurs & saints.* Mahwah, NJ: Erlbaum.

Reutzel, D. R., & Cooter, R. B. (2003). *Strategies for reading assessment and instruction: Helping every child succeed* (2nd ed.). Upper Saddle River, NJ: Merrill/Prentice Hall.

Wong, H., & Wong, R. (1998). *The first days of school: How to be an effective teacher.* Mountain View, CA: Harry K. Wong.

2

Language Learning and the Stages of Literacy Development

Focus Questions

When you are finished studying this chapter, you should be able to answer these questions:

1. What are Piaget's four stages of cognitive development?

2. How does Vygotsky relate children's language growth to cognitive development?

3. What are four affective factors that influence children's motivation to learn language in all its modes?

4. What are the stages of children's oral language development?

5. What are the stages of children's reading development?

6. What are the stages of children's writing and spelling development?

Key Concepts

Emergent Literacy
Sensorimotor
Preoperational
Concrete Operations
Formal Operations
Zone of Proximal
    Development
Internalization
Affect
Behaviorist Theory
Innatist Theory
Cognitive Theory
Social Interaction Theory

Analogical
    Substitution
Preindependent Reading
Independent Reading
Picture-Governed
Print-Governed
Prephonemic Stage
Early Phonemic Stage
Letter-Naming Stage
Transitional Stage
Story Grammar
Environmental Print
Print Concepts

Young children are constantly noticing the presence of printed language in the world around them. Denver, age three, runs through the local supermarket and stops abruptly, pointing to a box of cereal, "Look Mom, here's the Fruit Loops!"

Sorcha, age 2, sits on her porch with her doll and a copy of her favorite book held upside down. "Now listen while I read you this story," she whispers to her silent playmate.

In a day-care center, Dylan, age four, is busily scribbling with crayons on a neatly folded piece of paper. The teacher looks at his work. She notices what appears to be a picture of a cake and candles with some scribbles underneath the picture. At the bottom is the carefully scrawled signature of Dylan. She asks, "Dylan, what are you writing?"

Dylan excitedly points to each set of scribble marks and replies, "I'm writing a birthday card to my Daddy."

Visit Chapter 2 of our Companion Website at www.prenhall.com/ reutzel to look into the chapter objectives, standards and principles, and pertinent web links associated with Language Learning and the Stages of Literacy Development.

ON BECOMING LITERATE

Emergent Literacy

Emergent literacy is a term that implies children are becoming literate beginning at birth and continue to develop as literate beings throughout life. We can observe in the behavior of even the very youngest children evidence of the process of becoming literate. Although their reading and writing behaviors may not be conventional in the sense of those behaviors accepted by adults, young children, regardless of age, maturity, or intelligence, are nonetheless learning the uses of printed language in a variety of situations and contexts. N. Hall (1987) described the assumptions about how children learn to read and write.

Emergent literacy represents a profound change in how people believe early literacy is acquired.

1. Acting like a reader is part of becoming a reader.
2. Reading and writing are closely related processes and should not be artificially isolated for instruction.
3. Learning to read and write is essentially a social process and is influenced by a search for meaning.
4. Most preschool children already know a great deal about printed language without exposure to formal instruction.
5. Becoming literate is a continuous, developmental process.
6. Children need to *act* like readers and writers to *become* readers and writers.
7. Children need to read authentic and natural texts.
8. Children need to write for personal reasons.

From the earliest studies into language learning begun in about 1956, researchers in language acquisition carefully studied and observed young children to de-

Standards Note
Standard 2.7: The reading professional will understand emergent literacy and the experiences that support it. Make note of eight assumptions about how young children learn to read and write related to emergent literacy theory.

Acting like a reader is part of becoming a reader.

termine how they solved the puzzle of printed language. Many researchers in the mid-twentieth century debated whether young children should be exposed to real books right away in beginning reading instruction or put into "reading readiness," or pre-reading activities (e.g., circling pictures that have matching sounds, identifying letters in isolation), before being allowed to attempt primary level books.

Durkin (1966) found that some young children could already read and write before exposure to formal schooling and instructional methodologies. Clay concluded in her early work with 5-year-old children in New Zealand that "there is nothing in this research that suggests that contact with printed language forms should be withheld from any five-year-old child on the grounds that he is immature." (1967, p. 24) More recently, scientific and practical evidence confirm Clay's findings (see Neuman, 2001) rejecting the notion of reading readiness stages and delaying exposure to books and other printed material. Y. M. Goodman (1986) studied the knowledge of at-risk beginning readers and found that these children possessed a great deal of understanding about the functions and uses of printed language. Since the early studies about how young children learn to read and write, many researchers have extended these findings, particularly concerning family involvement. We know that children need extensive opportunities to experience books and stories at home before they can profit from school reading instructional practices. D. Taylor (1983) found homes rich with social and cultural examples of print and print use in the families she studied. She stated that "perhaps, it is only after children have shared stories and experienced reading and writing as complex cultural activities that they will be able to learn on an individual level through the traditional pedagogical practices of the first-grade classroom" (p. 98). These and other studies have helped us understand how young children become literate. In the next section, we discuss how children develop the ability to think and reason, after which we discuss language and how it works. Finally, we describe how children acquire oral language as well as how they develop emergent reading and writing behaviors.

Children may need extensive opportunities to experience books and stories before they can profit from school reading instructional practices.

COGNITIVE, SOCIAL, AND AFFECTIVE ASPECTS OF LANGUAGE DEVELOPMENT

Contributions of Piaget: Cognitive Development

Knowledge of the relationship between a child's language development and cognitive growth is essential for understanding the development of reading and writing. The work of Jean Piaget, a renowned Swiss psychologist, is central to this understanding.

Piaget believed that the development of oral language, the foundation for other language skills like reading and writing, resulted from cognitive growth (Tomasello, 1996). Cognitive development occurred as a result of maturation (nature) rather than as a result of environmental forces and conditions (nurture). And, cognitive growth and maturation were thought to occur in a predetermined sequence or order through four ascending stages (see Figure 2.1). Though children were thought to progress through these four cognitive developmental stages sequentially, the ages at which children entered or exited each of the stages could vary dramatically. Piagetians called this difference in timing or lag among children in moving from one stage of cognitive development to another *décalage*.

Piaget demonstrated that young children in the **sensorimotor** stage (birth to 2 years of age) use oral language *egocentrically*—largely to meet their own needs.

Piaget viewed language development as a product of cognitive growth.

Figure 2.1 Piaget's Stages of Cognitive Development

Developmental Stages	Characteristics of Language Development
Stage 1 Sensorimotor (ages 0–2)	• Once children begin to speak, they use *egocentric speech.* Speech is audible to others but directed at self because children, from a cognitive perspective, do not see themselves as separate from others. • Children may overgeneralize (cars refer to all vehicles) or under-generalize (cat refers to only his cat) word use.
Stage 2 Preoperational (ages 2–7)	• Children use *socialized speech,* language that allows them to interact with others. • Children understand the symbolic use of words, that language can be used to represent actual objects. • Maturation must take place for students to understand *conservation* of objects and *reversibility.* Conservation refers to a cognitive understanding that if the shape of an object is changed, its mass or substance may not. Reversibility can refer to an understanding of language where a child recognizes that if he has a sister, then he is his sister's brother. • By age 3, sentence use becomes more strategic as learned nouns and verbs can be reversed to form questions. • Children begin to develop the ability to keep from centering attention on only one quality or attribute of an object or concept. Referred to as *decentration,* it allows students to relate parts to a whole, important if early reading instruction asks students to identify the parts of words first. • As children mature, sentences become more complex as children begin to cognitively recognize cause-and-effect relationships.
State 3 Concrete Operational (ages 7–11)	• Children develop the ability to solve problems and think deductively. • The use of language increases as children confidently describe and think about their environment, discovering complex relationships of sequence, order, cause and effect, and classification. • The more experiences children have, the more opportunity for the development of language.
Stage 4 Formal Operational (ages 11–Adult)	• Children become increasingly sophisticated and able to think abstractly and logically using language to discuss distant concepts, events, and experiences. • Children and adults are able to abstract meaning from text without actually having a direct experience.

*Children in the **sensorimotor** stage use language egocentrically to meet their own needs.*

Children's oral language at this stage is called *egocentric speech.* Children at this stage of cognitive development do not see others as separate from themselves. In other words, the world of spoken or oral language for the youngest child exists for meeting their needs, not for communicating socially with others. The ability to take into account the views of others, called *socialized speech,* does not occur until much later, somewhere between the ages of 7 and 8.

During the **preoperational** stage (2 to 7 years of age), children use language to interact with others beyond the desire to meet their own needs. This level of cognitive development, according to Piaget, occurs as a result of physical and biological maturation. As maturation changes children's view of the world, these cognitive insights are reflected in their use of oral language. During the preoperational stage, children begin to recognize the symbolic nature of language—language can be used to represent an actual object, a concept, or an event. For example, the spoken word *baby* represents a real baby, separate and distinct from a picture of a baby. Acquiring this understanding is a critical prerequisite for furthering reading and writing development. Children must realize that a spoken word *represents* the meaning or identity of an object—separate from the object itself or from a picture—to come to understand that words are also *symbolic* representations of objects and concepts. Children's preoperational experiences help to develop their sense of how language works as a "labeling system" for ideas and objects in the real and social world.

In the preoperational stage, children also learn the concept of *conservation,* that mass or substance does not change when the shape or form of an object is transformed. For example, when a ball of clay is flattened, the mass or substance is not altered by the change in shape. Another concept developed during this stage is *reversibility.* Children in this stage do not understand that relationships between events and objects can be reversed. For example, a young boy at this age may recognize that he has a sister, but not realize that he is a brother to his sister. Attaining the ability to conserve concepts and reverse relationships helps young readers move their recognition of words and concepts read in the context of a familiar book or setting, such as words on a cereal box, to another, less familiar setting, such as the same words found on word cards or wall charts.

During the preoperational stage of cognitive development, children develop the ability to relate the parts of an object to the whole. This development are an example of the Piagetian concept of *decentration*—the ability to keep from centering attention on only one quality or attribute of an object or concept. This development is of particular importance because children are often introduced to reading in a manner that requires them to identify the parts of words first. Many children can, for example, recognize the first letter in their name and often think all words that begin with that letter are their name! But as they develop decentration, they learn how all letters fit together to make a word.

In the third stage, **concrete operations** (7 to 11 years of age), children develop the ability to solve problems and think deductively. Language can now be used as a tool for discovering relationships such as sequence or order, cause and effect, and categorization. Piaget maintained that much is learned from interacting with others and manipulating objects in the environment. Actual experience with manipulating objects in the environment has a direct impact on language development. Consequently, experience with using oral language precedes the study of oral or written language parts. When children develop their oral language knowledge and begin to relate this knowledge to written language, they seek to understand more about the functions and parts of written language. Vasily Sukhomlinksy, an acclaimed Russian educator, in his book entitled *To Children I Give My Heart* (1981), believed that young children's life experiences and their oral language development are the wellspring of cognitive development.

> I begin [sic] to take the children on journeys to the source of words: I opened the children's eyes to the beauty of the world and at the same time tried to show their hearts the music of words. I tried to make it so that words were not just names of people, places, things, or phenomena, but carried with them emotional coloration—their

During the **preoperational** *stage, conservation, reversibility, and decentration are cognitive concepts that are beginning to be learned.*

Only when language is initially experienced whole will the parts make sense to the learner.

Children's preoperational experiences help to develop their sense of how language works.

own aroma, subtle nuances. Until the child feels the aroma of words, sees their subtle nuances, it [*sic*] is not prepared to begin to study reading and writing. And if the teacher begins this too early, he or she dooms the children to a difficult task. . . . The process of learning to read and write will be easy if it is a clear, exciting bit of life for the children, a filling out of living images, sounds, and melodies. (p. 125–126)

In Piaget's **formal operations** stage (11 years of age to adult), children are able to think abstractly and logically. Now they can use oral and written language to discuss, read, and write about abstract concepts, events, and experiences. Language becomes an important vehicle for transcending the boundaries of space and time. Before this stage, children needed to be in the presence of an object or event to manipulate or experience it; now thought can proceed without the immediate presence of objects or events. This cognitive ability is crucial for reading development. Learning from text requires that the reader be able to abstract concepts, events, and experiences from text rather than from direct experience or manipulation of objects. In fact, it is hard to imagine a child learning from reading who cannot think abstractly.

Formal operations allow language to be used to transcend the boundaries of space and time.

Language learning, according to Piaget, is determined by increasingly sophisticated thought or cognitive growth resulting from physical or biological maturation. Cognitive growth is not driven or facilitated by using language, but rather oral language only mirrors the fact that cognitive growth has occurred. Piaget's views lend some support to current theories regarding the development of reading and writing in young children. Encouraging children to read and write authentic texts and stories early in the schooling process allows them the opportunity of exploring, manipulating, and experiencing meaning in language. Piaget's views also support providing both actual and vicarious experiences to build children's background experiences in preparation for successful reading. Finally, Piaget's views support using children's language and experiences to create reading and writing materials in the classroom.

Contributions of Vygotsky: Social Interaction

Vygotsky (1896–1934), a famous Russian psychologist and educator, believed that an individual's range of cognitive abilities were in large part predetermined by heredity. Contrary to Piaget's beliefs, Vygotsky (1962, 1978) believed that cognitive development was very much affected by language learning and its use with other human beings in society (Tomasello, 1996). In short, Vygotsky believed that language meaning is determined as it is used in society. As children practice using spoken and written language, they gain expertise in using words as a tool for expressing their thoughts.

Piaget (1955) believed that thought originated first within the child, then was expressed through language. Vygotsky (1962), however, maintained that thought and language in the mind of a child grows out of interactions with others. In short, when children find themselves in social situations, they use language as a tool for exploring their world. Using language pushes cognitive development forward rather than waiting for cognitive development to push language learning forward.

When Piaget observed children in his research studies, he assessed their cognitive development in terms of how they could solve a problem *without* intervention or assistance from a teacher. From these findings and theories, Piaget maintained that there was no point in trying to teach children to perform a particular task until they reached a certain stage of cognitive development when the solution to the task or problem was readily understood. Conversely, Vygotsky assessed cognitive development in terms of how well a child could perform a specific task in collaboration with others. The difference between what a child can do alone and in collaboration with others is what Vygotsky called the **zone of proximal development** (ZPD).

Frank Smith (1988) described the zone of proximal development (ZPD) this way: "Everyone can do things with assistance that they cannot do alone, and what they can do with collaboration on one occasion they will be able to do independently on another." (pp. 196–197) For a ZPD to be created, there must be a joint task that creates a learning situation for this learner/expert interaction. The "expert" (one who has more experience and skill doing the assigned task) can then use different strategies to help the learner succeed in the learning situation (Tharpe & Gallimore, 1988). Instead of withholding certain tasks from a child until a particular stage of cognitive development is reached, as suggested by Piaget (1955), Vygotsky (1978) recommended that once the zone of proximal development was identified, a teacher, parents, or more advanced peers could help a learner perform a task she would not be capable of doing alone.

Vygotsky also differentiated between school and nonschool learning. *Spontaneous concepts* (e.g., hot vs. cold, parent vs. pets) are learned outside of the school environment and are fairly concrete. On the other hand, *scientific concepts* are usually somewhat abstract and are learned primarily in the school environment. Scientific concepts are most effectively learned when they are built on or connected to spontaneous concepts. With time and instruction, scientific concepts become spontaneous concepts, thus continuing the cycle of concept building (Driscoll, 1994). Because Vygotsky valued the role of language use and social interaction as a means for pushing cognitive growth forward, tasks that are challenging or abstract would not be withheld from children in early schooling experiences. Instead, Vygotsky viewed language use and social interaction as the very vehicles that support the child through the learning process, lifting them to higher plains of understanding and performance.

Vygotsky (1978) emphasized that learners *internalize* language activities, like reading and writing, by going through a three-stage process. **Internalization,** as

Unlike Piaget, Vygotsky believed cognitive growth was the product of increasingly sophisticated language use.

The meaning of language is the result of a social negotiation and agreement.

*The **zone of proximal development** is working with a child to accomplish a task he or she cannot yet complete independently.*

Vygotsky viewed social interaction among learners as a primary force for developing cognitive abilities.

Vygotsky called it, begins with the learner watching others as they perform a language task; for example, notice a child who continually asks for the same book to be read aloud again and again by another experienced reader. She is studying what the reader is doing and learning some of reading's most basic structures. The next stage of internalization begins when the learner mimics the language task—like a child pretending to read a book aloud when she is really only looking at the pictures and repeating what was read aloud to her on previous occasions. The third stage of internalization comes when a learner, after benefiting from a great deal of skillful instruction, is able to perform a specific reading task without further help. An example of this stage of internalization is shown in the developmental reading and writing descriptions found later in this chapter. These examples show how the activities of a more experienced reader or writer are studied and internalized by a less experienced learner.

Internalization and the zone of proximal development are depicted in Figure 2.2. The notion that social interaction plays a significant role in developing a child's cognitive growth and language ability is extremely relevant to current trends in reading

Figure 2.2   Teaching model based on Vygotsky's theory

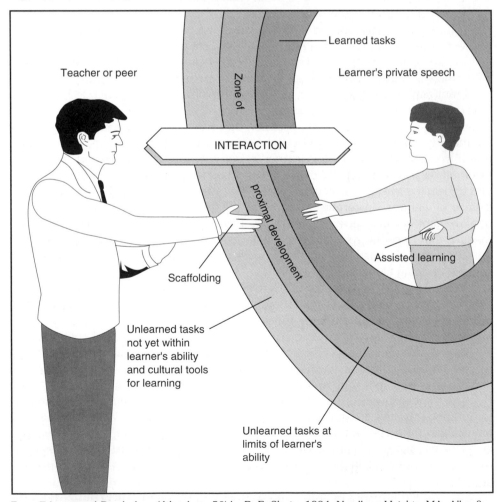

From *Educational Psychology* (4th ed., p. 50) by R. E. Slavin, 1994. Needham Heights, MA: Allyn & Bacon. Reprinted by permission.

instruction. If children are immersed in reading and writing early in their schooling experience and receive support from peers and adults while they are learning, they will begin to internalize certain reading and writing behaviors. Put into practice, Vygotsky's theory, which advocates a child-centered and activity-oriented reading curriculum, enables children to negotiate the meaning of language while using language as an exploratory tool in a supportive learning environment.

Affect: Motivation and Engagement

Several aspects of the reading process combine to influence whether children will choose to read and how much effort they will give to learning to read. Wigfield (1997) articulated an in-depth view of motivation, or *engagement theory,* related to reading that includes the following elements:

- Reading Efficacy
- Reading Challenge
- Reading Work Avoidance
- Reading Curiosity
- Involvement
- Importance of Reading
- Reading for Recognition
- Reading for Grades
- Competition in Reading
- Social Reasons for Reading
- Reading Compliance

Affective aspects of reading include attitudes, motivation, interests, beliefs, feelings, and values.

Attitudes, interest, beliefs, feelings, and values make up the *affective* aspects of the reading process. By comparison, desires, persistence, and motivation constitute what is known as the *cognative* aspects of the reading process (Baker, Dreher, & Guthrie, 2000; Mathewson, 1994; Raven, 1992; Wigfield, 1997b, 2000).

Asher (1980) and Corno and Randi (1997) found that reading comprehension, not surprisingly, was positively affected when children were interested in the reading material. Interest was also shown to be a compensatory factor in reading. For example, some children may struggle with recognizing simple words like *the, at, and,* and *it.* On the other hand, these same children may have no difficulty reading words like *dinosaur* and *tyrannosaurus rex* when they are interested in the material. Interest can also compensate for a child's lack of reading ability (Spangler, 1983; Sweet, 1997). One way to ensure children's interest in a reading selection is to begin by enthusiastically reading aloud or discussing parts of the selection. Another way is to show children how to self-select books or stories for reading.

Young children can often read books about dinosaurs but have trouble reading words like the, this, *and* that.

Children who have had positive experiences with learning to read will more likely continue to derive enjoyment from reading. Conversely, children who have had negative experiences with learning to read may have found the cost of learning to read too high in relation to the perceived benefit. Children who have had positive experiences with reading at home come to school expecting to learn to read. Parents who read to their children and discuss books with their youngsters create a positive attitude toward reading. Children are also highly motivated by the examples they see: If parents are seen reading and enjoying reading, they can help mold positive reading attitudes.

When schools offer a caring and supportive atmosphere for exploring language, children form positive attitudes toward reading (Ruddell & Unrau, 1997). Sensitive

Parents and teachers should help students have positive initial reading experiences.

teachers can do much to positively affect children's attitudes toward reading. Reading aloud stories, books, poems, riddles, and jingles and singing songs together can immerse children in fun and supportive language activities. Providing time each day to explore, read, and talk about books children selected can also support the development of positive attitudes toward reading (Guthrie & McCann, 1997). Schools and families should provide multiple opportunities for children to (1) express their feelings and emotions verbally and through writing, (2) read and discuss stories that offer abundant opportunities to discuss emotional responses, and (3) better understand how others think and feel (Novick, 2002).

The format or physical features of reading materials can also influence children's reading attitudes. Print size or style, the presence or absence of pictures, and the type of cover (soft or hard binding) in books all have been shown to influence children's reading attitudes and habits (Lowery & Grafft, 1967; Reutzel & Fawson, 2002; Reutzel & Gali, 1998; Samuels, 1970).

Attitudes toward reading have also been found to influence reading comprehension. Henk and Holmes (1988) and Reutzel and Hollingsworth (1991a) found that negative and positive attitudes toward the content of reading selections among adults and children can influence reading comprehension. Consequently, teachers should actively monitor children's attitudes and interests in reading so that *affectively appropriate* selections can be chosen for classroom instruction (Cooter, 1994; Santa, 1997).

Grade level and gender have also been shown to influence reading attitudes. Girls tend to exhibit more positive attitudes for reading than boys in grades 1 to 6 (Parker & Paradis, 1986). Alexander (1983) reported positive attitudes toward reading through the end of grade 3, but attitudes toward reading showed sharp negative changes between grades 4 and 5 in the elementary school (Brown, Engin, & Wallbrown,1979). Parker and Paradis (1986) found that positive changes in attitude between grades 4 and 5, where they were found, were related to recreational, library, and general reading materials. It appeared that allowing for student self-selection of reading materials in the intermediate and upper elementary grade levels may play an even greater role than previously thought.

Children who have feelings of inadequacy or inability may be afraid to take the risks associated with learning to read for fear they will fail. Students who are constantly corrected by the teacher or who are the object of pointed humor by peers when reading aloud are much more likely to develop a poor reading self-image. Children with positive self-images, on the other hand, attack new and uncertain situations in reading with poise and confidence. These students expect to learn (F. Smith,1988)!

What Teachers Can Do to Improve Student Motivation

Teachers can do much to avert the development of poor reading attitudes. First, they should seek to understand and respect children's interests and preferences. Second, they can make reading easy by making reading easy (F. Smith, 1983). This means that children can begin reading with very simple, yet complete books like Mercer Mayer's (1976a, 1976b) *Hiccup* and *Ah-Choo* or with leveled reading materials (Fountas & Pinnell, 1996, 1999; Pinnell & Fountas, 2002; Szymusiak & Sibberson, 2001). Appropriately challenging books provide complete and enjoyable story lines while simultaneously controlling the unfamiliar or difficult parts of a text (i.e., new words, concepts, writing genres). Allowing children to choose their own books and having a supply of these appropriately challenging books available can do much to

Think of a time when you selected a book to read. What physical characteristics influenced your choice?

Allowing time for students to choose their own reading materials appears to be increasingly important in the intermediate and upper elementary grades.

bolster young readers' confidence in their ability to successfully tackle the reading puzzle.

Young children should be supported in accomplishing what they are trying to do (Gambrell & Marinak, 1997; F. Smith, 1988). This kind of teaching is at the heart of Vygotsky's belief about teaching in the learner's *zone of proximal development,* as was discussed earlier. Read-along tapes, shared reading of big books, interactive reading with older children, parents, and grandparents, and choral reading can do much to support unsure readers while shielding them from criticism and comparison. The use of flexible grouping schemes can also help alleviate the problem and stigma attached to membership in a "low reading group" (Opitz, 1998)—the *Eagles, Bluebirds,* and *Buzzards* scenario. In learning to read, all children should be helped to feel like eagles.

UNDERSTANDING LANGUAGE

Standards Note
Standard 2.4: The reading professional will understand the phonemic, morphemic, semantic, syntactic, and pragmatic systems of language and their relation to the reading and writing process. As you read this next section, make a listing of definitions for phonemes, graphemes, morphemes, syntax, semantics, and pragmatics.

Language is a mutually or socially agreed on symbol system that represents the full range of human knowledge, experience, and emotions. Children and adults use language as a tool for getting needs met, for thinking, for solving problems, and for sharing ideas and emotions. Language can be both expressive and receptive. *Expressive language* is used when the sender of a message encodes his or her thoughts into the symbol system of the language. Encoded language typically takes the form of oral speech or print. *Receptive language* is used when the receiver of a message decodes the symbol system (oral speech or print) of the language into meaning.

Language study is often divided into at least four major fields of study:

1. *Linguistics* is the study of language structure and how it is used to communicate. In linguistics, language is grouped into four categories: phonemes, morphemes, syntax, and semantics.
2. *Psycholinguistics* is the study of how language is used and organized in the mind. This branch of study is mainly concerned with how language relates to thinking and learning.
3. *Sociolinguistics* is the study of how language relates to human and societal behaviors and interactions. It is concerned primarily with the social and cultural settings in which language is used, such as regions of the country, churches, or schools, and also how levels of education and social class affect language use.
4. *Language acquisition* is the study of how infants learn and use language to meet their needs and express their ideas.

Linguistics *is the study of language structure and how it is used by people to communicate.*

Psycholinguistics *is the study of how language is used and organized in the mind.*

Language acquisition *is the study of how infants learn and use language to meet their needs and express their ideas.*

For the purposes of studying reading, the English language can be divided into three language cueing systems: semantics (the meaning of language), syntax (grammar, or the word order of language), and visual-graphophonics (the visual, letter symbol-speech sound system).

The Semantic Cueing System in Language

Constructing meaning is the central reason for engaging in the act of reading or writing. The *semantic language-cueing system* relates to the reader's background experience, knowledge, interests, attitudes, perspectives, and present context or situation in reading. R. C. Anderson and P. D. Pearson (1984) point out that constructing meaning from print depends in large measure on a reader's prior knowledge and experience with the content of the text. These prior experiences and knowledge are stored together in the mind in something researchers and theoreticians call *schemata,* or *schemas* (anglicized). Schemas are defined as mental packages of related concepts, events, or experiences. Rumelhart (1980) explains that schemas are the foundation of our ability to think and comprehend. Readers use schemas to interpret their world, experiences, and print. Each new concept or event we encounter in life is stored in the brain and used to help us make sense of our world.

Schemas, or the lack thereof, can affect the construction of meaning from a text in many ways. First, readers may have knowledge about the content of a text, but be unable to recover or remember that knowledge. Read the following passage from an experiment conducted by J. C. Bransford and Johnson (1972):

> If the balloons popped the sound wouldn't be able to carry since everything would be too far away from the correct floor. A closed window would also prevent the sound from carrying, since most buildings tend to be well insulated. Since the whole operation depends upon a steady flow of electricity, a break in the middle of the wire would also cause problems. Of course, the fellow could shout, but the human voice is not loud enough to carry that far. An additional problem is that a string could break on the instrument. Then there could be no accompaniment to the message. It is clear that the best situation would involve less distance. Then there would be fewer potential problems. With face to face contact, the least number of things could go wrong. (p. 719)

Did you experience difficulty in fully understanding the text? If you did, you are not alone. J. C. Bransford and Johnson's (1972) experimental subjects experienced great difficulty assigning the content of this passage to a particular topic. Pause for a moment and try to make a mental note of your best guess of what this passage was about. Now turn to page 35 and look at Figure 2.3. Reread the passage.

Were you able to recognize that the passage was a modernized version of the Romeo and Juliet serenade? Did you think the passage was about physics or electricity? Were you thinking about someone making a phone call? Although the word order or syntax was correct and you could pronounce all the words in the text, there was not enough information to allow you to interpret what you read accurately. Once you were able to retrieve the correct schema, however, you were able to interpret the obscure meaning of the text. Even when the information in a text is relatively familiar, readers often access the most likely schema or knowledge base and later modify their choice as they gain more knowledge from the text.

Now, read the following sentences and stop and think about what you see in your mind.

> John was on his way to school.
>
> He was terribly worried about the math lesson.

Next read the following sentences, and notice what happens as you process the new information.

> He thought he might not be able to control the class again today.
> It was not a normal part of a janitor's duties.
> (Sanford & Garrod, 1981, p. 114)

Did you notice a change in the schema accessed to interpret the text? Did your schema change from that of a young boy on his way to school worried about his math class and lesson to that of a concerned teacher and then . . . to that of a concerned janitor?

Semantics is the study of meaning.

Schemas are defined as packages of related concepts, events, or experiences. For example, on reading the word furniture, *readers often activate their knowledge related to furniture.*

Learning can be inhibited if text information is incompatible with information held in a specific schema.

Figure 2.3 The Romeo scene

Not only do schemas help readers interpret what they read, but the text can also influence the schema a reader selects. This back-and-forth influence of text on schema and schema on text is known as an *interaction*.

Researchers have found that the more you know about a topic or event in text, the more comprehensible the text becomes (Pearson, Hansen, & Gordon, 1979).

They have also found that schemas that contain information that is contrary to the information found in a text can result in decreases in comprehension. Suppose a text was written to persuade you that the world was flat rather than round; you might tend to dismiss that information as incorrect. Thus, texts that are contrary to or refute a reader's prior knowledge can present comprehension difficulties (Alvermann, Smith, & Readence, 1985; Gambrell, & Pressley, 2002; Collins-Block & Pressley, 2002; Hollingsworth & Reutzel, 1990; Lipson, 1984; Reutzel & Hollingsworth, 1991a).

Finally, the perspective of the reader can influence what is recalled from reading a text. Goetz, Reynolds, Schallert, and Radin (1983), for example, found that people who read a text passage from the perspective of a burglar recalled distinctly different details than those who were instructed to read it from the perspective of a burglary victim.

It is clear, then, that our expectations, experiences, and perspectives help us anticipate and interpret meaning and relate it to our existing knowledge. The more we experience, both directly and vicariously, the more our schemas grow, allowing us greater ability and flexibility in interpreting what we read.

The Syntactic Cueing System in Language

The *syntactic cueing system* concerns knowledge about word order in language. Proper use of the syntactic system results in grammatically acceptable phrases and sentences in speech and writing. In short, a knowledge of syntax is an understanding of how language is ordered and how language works. Using accepted word order in language is important because it relates to how meaning is constructed. Suppose a reader picks up a book and reads the following:

> a is saying individual the is our aloud ability our in rarely purposes respond reader the silently only skill upon our is word of called conducted reading reading it Most by is private fluent that for element of to to use course one each to. (Chapman & Hoffman, 1977, p. 67)

Although each word can be read one by one, the meaning is unclear because the word order was scrambled. When correct word order is restored, the meaning of the passage becomes easier to construct.

> The ability to respond to each individual word by saying it aloud is, of course, only one element in reading. It is a skill that the fluent reader is rarely called upon to use. Most of our reading is conducted silently for our own private purposes. (Chapman & Hoffman, 1977, p. 67)

Syntactic, or grammatical, knowledge enables readers to predict what comes next in a sentence or phrase. Syntax helps them avoid overreliance on the print to construct meaning. For example, read the following sentence.

> Hopalong Hank is the name of my green pet _____.

Even young children will fill in the blank with a noun. Although children may not be able to state a grammatical rule that accounts for the fact that a noun follows an adjective in a phrase, they are competent enough to know that only certain kinds of words are allowed in the blank. Moffett (1983) states that by the time children enter school, they have mastered the contents of an introductory transformational grammar text. This commentary underscores the fact that young children have to a large

Syntax is an understanding of how language is ordered and how language works.

extent mastered the grammar or syntax of their native tongue when they begin formal schooling; and they can, if allowed, use this knowledge in learning to read.

The Visual-Graphophonic Cueing System in Language

The *visual-graphophonic cueing system* is about how printed language works (directionality, the concept of *word,* word *versus* letter, and the relationship between letters and the sounds the letters are intended to represent). *Graphemes,* or letters, are mutually agreed on symbols for visually representing the sounds of spoken language. Some graphemic systems use an alphabetic principle (sounds and symbols relate to one another such as /b/ represents the "buh" sound), whereas others represent unified concepts or events (words or phrases). For example, English uses a graphemic system that is alphabetic, but Chinese uses a logographic system that represents entire concepts (words) or events (phrases) with pictures or logos.

A *phoneme* as defined by linguists is an abstract unit of speech that roughly approximates the smallest distinct unit of spoken language (Piper, 1993). A *grapheme* is defined as a printed symbol intended to represent a phoneme or an idea. The English graphophonic system is *alphabetic* and as such is composed of 26 letters (graphemes) and approximately 44 sounds (phonemes). Opinions on the number of phonemes we use in English vary among scholars in the field. Ruddell and Ruddell (1995) state that English is composed of 21 consonant sounds, 3 semivowels, 8 unglided vowels, and several levels each for pitch, juncture, and stress—the commonly used and understood prosodic features of spoken language. This brings the total to 44 phonemes. In addition to conventional forms of language study, other forms of sending messages involve using facial expressions, gestures, actions, and so on. In written language, punctuation (i.e., periods, commas, exclamation marks, quotation marks, etc.) is a means of graphically representing pitch, juncture, and stress found in speech.

Pragmatics

As children interact with their environment and with significant others in their social circles, they discover that language is power! They learn that they can control the responses and behaviors of others through language. They learn that language can be used to get what they want and need. In short, they learn that language serves a wide variety of communicative purposes.

The study of how language is used in society to satisfy the needs of human communication is called *pragmatics.* Hymes (1964) described pragmatics as knowledge about language functions and its uses in one's culture. In other words, children's and adults' language-related knowledge, habits, and behaviors are directly influenced by the culture or society in which they live and interact.

M. A. K. Halliday (1975) described three aspects of pragmatic language functions in our day-to-day lives: (a) ideational, (b) interpersonal, and (c) textual. F. Smith (1977) expanded Halliday's teachings into 10 purposes for which language may be used:*

1. *Instrumental:* "I want." (Getting things and satisfying material needs.)

*From "The Uses of Language" by F. Smith, 1977, *Language Arts, 54*(6), p. 640. Copyright 1977 by the National Council of Teachers of English. Reprinted with permission.

A **phoneme** is defined by linguists as the minimal or smallest unit in a spoken language. A **grapheme** is defined by linguists as a printed symbol representing a phoneme. The **graphophonic system** is composed of 26 letters (graphemes) and approximately 44 sounds (phonemes).

Pragmatics is knowledge of how, why, when, and where language is used in acceptable ways within a given society.

2. *Regulatory:* "Do as I tell you." (Controlling the attitudes, behaviors, and feelings of others.)
3. *Interactional:* "Me and you." (Getting along with others, establishing relative status.) Also, "Me against you." (Establishing separateness.)
4. *Personal:* "Here I come." (Expressing individuality, awareness of self, pride.)
5. *Heuristic:* "Tell me why." (Seeking and testing world knowledge.)
6. *Imaginative:* "Let's pretend." (Creating new worlds, making up stories, poems.)
7. *Representational:* "I've got something to tell you." (Communicating information, descriptions, expressing propositions.)
8. *Divertive:* "Enjoy this." (Puns, jokes, riddles.)
9. *Authoritative/contractual:* "How it must be." (Statutes, laws, regulations, and rules.)
10. *Perpetuating:* "How it was." (Records, histories, diaries, notes, scores.)

Once children understand the many uses for language in their lives, they readily recognize the purposes and meaning found in written language. In fact, success in reading depends very much on the degree to which the language children encounter in their early speaking and reading experiences mirror one another (Watson, 2001). Thus, experiences with quality literature, extended discussions about literature, and opportunities to write and respond to literature become integral to success in early reading (Morrow & Gambrell, 2001). It is in this setting that children begin to make the critical connections between oral and written language uses. When texts support and relate to children's oral language experiences, children readily discover that written and oral language are parallel forms of language that serve similar purposes for communication.

Oral Language Acquisition

Standards Note
Standard 1.6: The reading professional will understand the major theories of language development, cognition, and learning. As you read this section, make a compare-and-contrast chart showing how the four language acquisition theories discussed are similar and different.

After the birth of a child, parents anxiously await baby's first words. In the months that precede this event, parents talk to baby, to each other, and to other individuals in their environment. The thought of withholding speech until their infant masters the mechanics of speech production never crosses the parents' minds. When baby utters the first intelligible speech sounds, only the parents or those most closely associated with her understand. Not until many weeks and months later will these utterances mean anything to the casual observer. Several theories have been proposed in an attempt to explain how infants acquire an ability to speak their native tongue. Perhaps the first theory attempting to explain how oral language develops was from the behaviorist tradition in the field of psychology.

Behaviorist Theory

Behaviorists believe that oral language is learned through a process of conditioning and shaping that involves a stimulus, a response, and a reward. Other human role models in an infant's environment provide the stimuli and rewards. Parents' or other caregivers' speech acts as the *stimulus* in the speech environment. And when baby imitates the sounds or speech patterns of the adult models, praise and affection are given as a *reward* for her attempts to learn language. Thus, the **behaviorist theory** of language acquisition states that infants learn oral language from other human role models through a process involving imitation, rewards, and practice.

However, behaviorist theories of language development fail to explain a number of important questions associated with children's language acquisition. For example,

Behaviorists believe that oral language is acquired through a process of conditioning and shaping that involves a stimulus, a response, and a reward.

if a parent is hurried, inattentive, or not present when the child attempts speech, then rewards for the desired speech responses are not always systematically provided. Thus, if baby's language learning were only motivated by rewards, speech attempts would cease unless there were regular and systematic rewards.

Another problem with the behaviorist theory of oral language acquisition centers on the fact that young children do not simply imitate other human speech. Imitation implies that when mother says, "Baby, say Mama," baby would imitate or echo the mother by saying, "Baby, say Mama." Anyone who has raised children knows this is not the case. In fact, baby may not say anything at all! But one thing is clear—children are not mere echo chambers. They are processing language meaning and sorting out the relevant from the irrelevant. Behaviorist language acquisition theories fail to account for this kind of cognitive processing.

Behaviorist language acquisition theories also do not account for speech terms invented by infants. For example, one girl used to call a sandwich a *weechie* even though no one in her home called a sandwich by any such name. Another case in point is the jargon language that is often developed between identical twins. Although behaviorist theories may explain to some extent the role of the social environment and the importance of role models in shaping children's language acquisition, the explanation offered by this theory is at best incomplete and at worse erroneous. There are several cases against behaviorist language acquisition theories (Piper, 1993):

- Evidence of regression in pronouncing sounds and words previously pronounced correctly
- Evidence of novel forms of language not modeled by others
- Inconsistency of reinforcement or rewards provided
- Learning the use and meaning of abstract words
- Uniformity of language acquisition in humans
- Uniqueness of human language learning

Innatist Theory

A second theory pertaining to oral language acquisition among children is called the **innatist theory.** Innatist theorists believe that language learning is natural for human beings. In short, babies enter the world with a biological propensity, an inborn device as it were, to learn language. Lenneberg (1964) refers to this human built-in device for learning language as the *language acquisition device* (LAD). Thus, the innatist theory explains to some degree how children can generate or invent language they have never heard before.

N. Chomsky (1974, 1979) maintained that children use this LAD to construct an elaborate rule system for generating and inventing complex and interesting speech. Or put another way, just as wings allow birds to fly, LAD allows infant humans to speak. Although the innatist theory provides what appears to be a plausible explanation for some aspects of oral language acquisition, researchers have failed to supply satisfactory supporting evidence. Menyuk (1988) wrote, "Despite the apparent logic of this position, there is still a great deal of mystery that surrounds it." (p. 34) There are several cases against innatist language acquisition theories (Piper, 1993):

- The timing of language learning varies greatly within cultures
- Feedback from other language users affects language acquisition
- Environment shapes the language learned and how much language is learned

Innatist theorists
believe that language
learning is natural for
human beings.

Cognitive Theory

A third theory, known as the **cognitive theory,** appears to be a compromise between behaviorist and innatist theories of language learnings. Cognitivists believe that many factors affect an infant's ability to acquire oral language (i.e., social, cultural, linguistic, biological, cognitive). Cognitivists believe that not only do cognitive and maturational factors influence language acquisition, but also the process of language acquisition itself may in turn affect cognitive and social skill development (Luria & Yudovich, 1971). Although children may be born to learn language, as the innatists propose, the language role models available largely determine the language that is eventually learned. Put another way, innatist theory explains why babies learn language in the first place, and the behaviorist theory explains why babies born to English-speaking parents learn to speak English rather than Spanish. Of the three theories discussed thus far, cognitive theories appear to explain a greater proportion of language acquisition questions because it blends elements of both innatist and behaviorist theories.

*The **cognitive theory** appears to be a compromise between the behavioristic and innatist theories of language acquisition.*

Social Interactionist Theories

A fourth theory, known as the **social interaction theory,** assumes that language acquisition is influenced by the interaction of a number of factors—physical, linguistic, cognitive, and *social*. Social interaction theory shares certain assumptions and explanations with behaviorist, innatist, and cognitive theories. It shares the notion that environment is important with behaviorism theories. It shares the idea that language learning is a unique achievement with innatist theories. And it agrees with cognitive theories that language learning is a complex cognitive accomplishment involving active cognitive engagement on the part of the language learner. While some may consider his work to be cognitive, we have placed Vygotsky's writings within this theory of language acquisition because of his emphasis on the importance of social interaction with other people in learning language.

   M. A. K. Halliday (1975) is another who believes that language acquisition grows out of an active need to use language to function in society. Thus, infants learn language to survive, express themselves, and have their needs met. Holdaway (1979, 1984) discussed *approximation* with regard to how children learn to speak. He says that approximating means that infants respond to speech stimuli in their environment by producing a rough, rather than an exact, reproduction of the speech stimulus. Over time, these crude attempts begin to resemble more closely the speech they hear modeled until an acceptable reproduction is achieved. Holdaway (1984) also makes special note of the fact that parents not only tolerate approximations in oral language learning, but reward children's attempts with appreciation and affection.

Parents interpret infants' early language rather than recognize it.

Stages of Oral Language Development

Teachers should become aware of the stages and average rates of oral language development. Bear in mind that oral language developmental rates may vary radically among children.

Parents' Baby Talk: One Way of Getting Attention

Many parents use a special type of speech commonly called *baby talk* with their infants up to about 24 months of age (Stern & Wasserman, 1979). Characteristics of baby talk include higher pitch and special intonation patterns. Studies have shown that infants respond best to high-pitch levels and to varied rhythms in speech (Kearsley, 1973; Kessen, Levine, & Wendrich, 1979). Other research has shown that the ways in which infants react to adult speech affects the subsequent speech and behavior of their adult caretakers. In fact, adults usually use shorter speech patterns with significant periods of pausing to encourage the infant to respond (Gleason, 1989). Thus, it appears that parents and adult caregivers are intuitively intense kid watchers (Y. M. Goodman, 1986). They seem to structure their speech demonstrations carefully in response to their child's responses and suspected needs (Harste, Woodward, & Burke, 1984). In conclusion, parents and adult caregivers change their normal speech structures during interactions with their infants to encourage verbal interaction.

Across languages and cultures, adults use baby talk with their infants.

The First 12 Months: A Time for Hope

During the first 2 months of life, babies cry to indicate their need to be fed, changed, or otherwise attended to in some manner. Because their tiny mouths are almost entirely filled with the tongue, and the vocal cords are still quite high in the throat, children at this age are unable to produce much variation in vocalization. The growth of the head and neck later on allows infants to vary their vocalizations to produce sounds already responded to and experienced in the environment. During this early stage of speech development, young infants also make what linguists call *vegetative sounds,* such as burps, coughs, and sneezes.

Infant speech development begins with vegetative sounds.

From about 2 to 5 months of age, babies begin to coo, much like the sound made by pigeons, although during this period, they may also begin to vary the consonant sounds attached to the pure "oo" vowel sound typical of cooing. These cooing sounds, along with sustained laughter, typically seem to occur during social and speech interactions with caregivers in the environment. Cooing and laughter, however, may also occur when baby is alone or even asleep. D'Odorico (1984) has discovered that during this period, babies develop three distinct types of crying: (1) a need for comfort, (2) a call for attention, and (3) a rescue from distress. All of these speech developments seem to provide great pleasure and even a sense of relief and encouragement for parents and caregivers.

From 6 months to 1 year of age, babies enter a period of oral language development called *vocal play and babbling.* This stage of development is marked by the ability to utter single syllables containing a consonant sound followed by a prolonged vowel sound, such as "Maa Maa." Although many other syllables (e.g., "Laa Laa") may be uttered during this period of development, only a few of these syllables will be retained into the next stage (e.g., "Ma Ma" and "Da Da"). These syllables are retained primarily because their use seems to bring a quick and delightful reaction from parents or adult caregivers. It is also during this period of speech development that children begin to use single words or *holophrases,* sounds, or invented words to represent complete ideas (Au, Depretto, & Song, 1994; Gleason, 1989). For example, while riding down the road, an infant of this age may point to a cow and squeal in delight "mooooo!" Or this same infant may point at the sink and say, "wa wa," indicating that he or she wants a drink of water.

Cooing, crying, and babbling are all means of the developing infant communication with others.

From 1 to 2: By Leaps and Bounds

Language expands rapidly during the second year of development. Children continue to approximate the speech of their parents to the point of duplicating their gestures

Infants experiment with oral language and delight in the reaction they receive from parents and other caregivers.

and intonation patterns. Children in this stage continue to make hypotheses about the rules that govern language use, and they try out and refine these rules as they use language. During this year, toddlers achieve a significant linguistic milestone when they begin to put two words together. These words are typically selected from the large open classes of words known as nouns, verbs, and adjectives. Because these two-word utterances sound much like the reading of a telegram, linguists have called this stage of speech development *telegraphic speech*. Typical utterances of the telegraphic type include "Mommy down!" or "Go potty?" One recognizes readily the ability of these two-word, cryptic speech patterns to communicate an entire complex idea or need.

Infants use two-word utterances called **telegraphic speech** *to express their ideas and needs.*

From 2 to 3: What Does It Mean When I Say *No?!*

Oral language development continues to progress rapidly during the third year. The broken and incomplete nature of telegraphic speech begins to give way to more complex and natural forms of speech. The use of descriptives such as adjectives and adverbs dramatically increases (Fields & Spangler, 2000; Glazer, 1989; Morrow, 2001). One linguistic discovery made by the 2-year-old is the effect of negation. For many years, baby has heard the expression "No, no." Although over time he or she has learned what this expression implies for his or her own behavior, the child has not yet come to understand what the term *no* means when applied to the behavior of others. When asked, "Does baby want an ice cream cone?" baby quickly responds, "No!" But when baby discovers that the ice cream cone (to which he or she had said

"No") is now denied, she begins to cry. Over time, the 2-year-old learns what "No" means and how it affects the behavior of others. In a sense, children at this age begin to establish their own identity—separate from others in their environment—and the "No!" response is evidence of this. Using the words *no* and *not* is an important change in young children's language development.

From 3 to 4: The *Why* Years

By age 3, children begin using complex sentences that include the use of prepositions, pronouns, negatives, plurals, possessives, and interrogatives. Children at this age have a speaking vocabulary of between 1,000 and 1,500 words (Morrow, 2001). Also at this age, children begin to use analogical substitutions in their speech. An **analogical substitution** is the overgeneralization by analogy of a language rule, which often results in using an incorrect substitute word in speech. For example, a child may say, "Mom, will you put my boots on my *foots?*" In this case, the child has over-generalized the rule for pluralizing nouns by adding an -*s* to the irregular noun *foot*. Another example of an analogical substitution is the overgeneralization of the language rule for changing verbs to their past-tense form. For example, Lee rushes into the house and yells, "Daddy, come quick. I *digged* up that mean bush with flowers and thorns on it!" Language "errors" such as these reveal the language rules children have been internalizing and how they go about refining their language hypotheses.

During this fourth year of oral language development, children begin to transform basic sentence structures into interrogative sentences (questions). Before this time, these same children indicated that a question was being asked by making a statement followed by a rising intonation pattern. Thus, questions were framed without the use of interrogatives or by transforming basic sentence structures. However, by the time the child is 3, parents have become well acquainted with the interrogative "Why?"

For statements that appear to be perfectly obvious to adults, the 3-year-old will begin the typical line of questioning with "Why, why, why?" After several answers to this question, parents realize they are trapped in a linguistic situation that is nearly impossible to escape with dignity. Bill Cosby once offered a simple solution that we tried with our own 3-year-old children with reasonable success: You ask why first! Regardless of the questioning nature of the 3-year-old, language development during the third to fourth year is an exciting experience for parents and caregivers.

From 4 to 6: Years of Growth and Refinement

At 4 years of age, children seem to have acquired most of the elements of adult language (Morrow, 2001). Vocabulary and syntactical structures continue to increase in variety and depth. Children at this age possess a vocabulary of about 2,500 words, which by age 6 will have grown to 6,000 words (Clark, 1993; D. D. Johnson, 2001; Norton & Norton, 2003). Some children at age 4 or 5 continue to have trouble articulating the /r/ and /l/ sounds and the /sh/ at the end of words, although the vast majority of children are 90–100% intelligible by age 4.

A son of one of the authors, Cody, has provided many examples of imaginative and generative language. One day Cody had purchased with his hard-earned money several plastic clips for his belt. With these he could hang his flashlight and plastic tools on his belt and make believe he was a workin' man. When his father first saw

*An **analogical substitution** is the overgeneralization by analogy of a language rule although small children rarely receive any formal instruction in these rules.*

At 4 years of age, children seem to have acquired most of the elements of adult language.

these clips on his belt, he inquired, "Cody, what are those things on your belt?" He responded, "Those are my *hookers,* Dad!"

On entering the world of school, kindergarten children often discover a genre of speech known as *toilet talk* and *curse words.* One day, a young boy overheard his kindergarten teacher reprimanding some other boys for using inappropriate language. Sometime later during the day, his teacher overheard him remark regarding the subject of taboo words, "She means those words your Daddy uses when he gets real mad!" According to Seefeldt and Barbour (1986), adults find the way in which children of this age group use language imaginative and amusing. We certainly concur with these observations!

Understanding the development of oral language among children can be a source of increased enjoyment for parents and teachers. Knowing how children develop language helps adults recognize and appreciate the monumental achievement of learning to speak—especially when it occurs so naturally and in a space of just six short but very important years.

DEVELOPMENT OF READING BEHAVIORS

As explained earlier in this chapter, the emergent literacy model views reading acquisition as a gradual process of development: Children pass through certain stages of reading development on the literacy continuum toward becoming independent and skilled readers, much as they do in acquiring oral language. Although the reading readiness model also describes reading development in stages, the emergent literacy model does not view the beginning of reading as a point or threshold on the literacy continuum, but rather as a continuous journey along the continuum.

Under the emergent literacy view of learning to read and write, children are never thought of or talked about as non-readers or non-writers.

Some years ago, two teachers had a discussion about what they meant by "he is a beginning reader." These teachers began to gather data to support the construction of a reading development continuum, shown in Figure 2.4 (Cochrane, Cochrane, Scalena, & Buchanan, 1984). They divided the development of reading into two overarching categories: (a) *preindependent reading* and (b) *independent reading.* Within each of these categories, they describe three more subdivisions. Within the **preindependent reading** category are three subordinate divisions: (a) the magical stage, (b) the self-concepting stage, and (c) the bridging stage. Within the **independent reading** category are three subordinate divisions: (a) the takeoff stage, (b) the independent reading stage, and (c) the skilled reading stage.

The Mystery of Reading: The Magical Stage

Long before children enter school, they begin noticing print in their environment and learn that printed language stands for words they have heard others use or that they have used themselves. Preschool children spontaneously learn to recognize billboards displaying their favorite TV channel logo. They can recognize a favorite soda brand logo or pick out their favorite cereal at the local supermarket. Although they may not be able to read the print exactly on each of these objects, when asked to tell someone what the soda can says, they may respond with "soda" or "pop."

Magical stage *readers readily recognize print in their environment.*

Children at this stage of reading development love to have books read to them. In quiet moments, these children may crawl up into a large comfortable chair to hold, look at, and tell a story from the pictures of their favorite books. Jeremy, when he

Figure 2.4   Reading development continuum

A.   PREINDEPENDENT READING STAGES
   1.   MAGICAL STAGE
   - Displays an interest in handling books.
   - Sees the construction of meaning as magical or exterior to the print and imposed by others.
   - Listens to print read to him for extended periods of time.
   - Will play with letters or words.
   - Begins to notice print in environmental context (signs, labels).
   - Letters may appear in his drawings.
   - May mishandle books—observe them upside down. Damage them due to misunderstanding the purpose of books.
   - Likes to "name" the pictures in a book, e.g., "lion," "rabbit."

   2.   SELF-CONCEPTING STAGE
   - Self-concepts himself as a reader, i.e., engages in reading-like activities.
   - Tries to magically impose meaning on new print.
   - "Reads" or reconstructs content of familiar storybooks.
   - Recognizes his name and some other words in high environmental contexts (signs, labels).
   - His writing may display phonetic influence, i.e., *wtbo = Wally, hr = her.*
   - Can construct story meaning from pictorial clues.
   - Cannot pick words out of print consistently.
   - Orally fills in many correct responses in oral cloze reading.
   - Rhymes words.
   - Increasing control over nonvisual cueing systems.
   - Gives words orally that begin similarly.
   - Displays increasing degree of book handling knowledge.
   - Is able to recall key words.
   - Begins to internalize story grammar, i.e., knows how stories go together, e.g., "Once upon a time," "They lived happily ever after."

   3.   BRIDGING STAGE
   - Can write and read back his own writing.
   - Can pick out individual words and letters.
   - Can read familiar books or poems that could not be totally repeated without the print.
   - Uses picture clues to supplement the print.
   - Words read in one context may not be read in another.
   - Increasing control over visual cueing system.
   - Enjoys chants and poems chorally read.
   - Can match or pick out words of poems or chants that have been internalized.

B.   INDEPENDENT READING STAGES
   1.   TAKEOFF STAGE
   - Excitement about reading.
   - Wants to read to you often.
   - Realizes that print is the base for constructing meaning.
   - Can process (read) words in new (alternate) print situations.

From *Reading, Writing, and Caring* (pp. 44–46) by O. Cochrane, D. Cochrane, D. Scalena, and E. Buchanan, 1984, New York: Richard C. Owen Publishers. Copyright 1984 by Richard C. Owen Publishers. Reprinted by permission.

Figure 2.4   *continued*

- Aware of and reads aloud much environmental print (signs, labels, etc.).
- Can conserve print from one contextual environment to another.
- May exhibit temporary tunnel vision (concentrates on words and letters).
- Oral reading may be word-centered rather than meaning-centered.
- Increasing control over the reading process.

2. INDEPENDENT READING
   - Characterized by comprehension of the author's message by reader.
   - Readers' construction of meaning relies heavily on author's print or implied cues (schema).
   - Desires to read books to himself for pleasure.
   - Brings his own experiences (schemata) to the print.
   - Reads orally with meaning and expression.
   - May see print as literal truth. What the print says is right (legalized).
   - Uses visual and nonvisual cueing systems simultaneously (cyclically).
   - Has internalized several different print grammars, i.e., fairy tales, general problem-centered stories, simple exposition.

3. SKILLED READER
   - Processes material further and further removed from his own experience.
   - Reading content and vocabulary become a part of his experience.
   - Can use a variety of print forms for pleasure.
   - Can discuss several aspects of a story.
   - Can read at varying and appropriate rates.
   - Can make inferences from print.
   - Challenges the validity of print content.
   - Can focus on or use the appropriate grammar or structuring of varying forms of print, e.g., stories, science experiments, menus, diagrams, histories.

was 2 years old, enjoyed the naming of each animal in his favorite picture book. After naming each picture, he enthusiastically made the sounds of each, the roar of a lion or the crowing of a rooster. Parents and teachers of readers who find themselves journeying through the magical stage of reading development may see children who hold books upside down, turn the pages from the back to the front, and even tear out a page unintentionally.

Although these actions may concern parents on one level, children who behave in these ways evidence a need for exposure to and understanding of the purpose of books. Withholding books from these children because they do not know how to handle them or read them at this stage would most certainly prove to be detrimental.

Children in the magical reading developmental stage develop a marked preference for a single or favorite book. Willing adults are often solicited into reading this book again and again. Although parents and others may tire rapidly of this book, the affection and familiarity increases with each reading for the child. Favorite books are often repeatedly read to the point where the child memorizes them. Some parents even try to skip pages or sentences in these books, thinking their child will not notice, but they soon learn their child has internalized these books, and the unsuspecting adult will be caught every time.

The reading of entire contexts such as those found on product logos and in books constitutes evidence that young children prefer to process printed language from the whole to the parts. Young children prefer reading the entire context of a sign or label and memorizing an entire book long before they want or need to focus on the details and parts of printed language.

Favorite books are requested to be read aloud again and again, indicating how young children want to practice learning to read.

"Look, Mom, I'm Reading": The Self-Concepting Reading Stage

The self-concepting reading developmental stage describes children who have come to view themselves as readers. Although these children may not yet be able to read exactly what the print says, they are certainly aware of printed language and their own progress toward breaking the literacy barrier. Children in this stage will try to read unfamiliar books by telling the story from the pictures and from their own imaginations. Selected words are readily recognized, such as their own name, favorite food labels, and signs on bathroom doors. These children evidence an increasing awareness of words and sounds. They often ask questions about how words begin and about rhyming words. If given a chance, these children can also fill in the rest of a sentence when asked to do so. For example, while reading the "Three Little Pigs," a teacher may say, "And the Big Bad Wolf knocked at the door and said, 'Little Pig, Little Pig'. . . . " Children at this stage will immediately fill in the hanging sentence with "Let me come in."

*Children in the **self-concepting stage** view themselves as readers.*

Spanning the Gap: The Bridging Stage

Children at the bridging stage of reading development can pick out familiar words and letters in familiar contexts and books. However, they often cannot pick these same words out of an unfamiliar book or context when asked. Children in the bridging stage can reconstruct stories from books with greater precision than can children in the previous stage. In fact, children in the bridging stage can no longer reconstruct the story completely without using the print, although they will continue to use picture clues to augment their growing control over the print system.

Children in the bridging stage can also read back what they have written. It has long been a disappointment for us when teachers and parents fail to count these early behaviors as real reading by brushing them aside as cute. Parents or teachers will often remark, "She's not reading. She's got that book memorized." Only by understanding that reading is a developmental process and that memorizing favorite print and books is universal among children will parents and teachers be able to enjoy, recognize, and support the progress their children make toward conventional reading behaviors and skills.

Some parents and teachers discount memorizing books as an unimportant step in learning to read.

Blast Off!: The Takeoff Stage

If you are an unoccupied adult, look out for kids in the takeoff stage. They are excited about reading and will perform for any reluctantly willing audience. In fact, they want to demonstrate their emerging ability as frequently as others will allow. Children at this stage of reading development have a clear understanding that print forms the basis for reading the story and constructing meaning. Words read in one book or context are now recognized in new or unfamiliar contexts. Signs and environmental print are subjects of intense interest among take-off readers. It seems as if print has a magnetic appeal for these children.

One autumn evening in a parent-teacher conference while one of the authors was teaching first grade, a parent said that her son, Curt, had requested new breakfast cereals. When his mother asked why, Curt responded, "There's not enough to read on these boxes." Mother bought him a box of cereal that seemed to contain enough print to satisfy his appetite.

Oral reading during the takeoff stage may become word or letter centered. Although oral reading before this time may have failed to perfectly represent the print on the page, it was smooth, fluent, and filled with inflection. The fact that words and letters have been discovered at this stage of development may lead to a situation where children appear to regress temporarily in their reading development. Children in this stage need to focus on print details, which lead to less fluent and inflected oral reading for a time. With sustained opportunities to read and gain control over the reading process and print system, fluency and inflection will soon return.

"I Can Do It by Myself!": The Independent Stage

Takeoff readers want an audience, but independent readers take great pride in reading books to themselves for pleasure. The independent reader has developed control over the entire reading process and cueing systems. Reading is now carried on with simultaneous use of the author's printed clues and the reader's own schema for the topic. Fluency and inflection have returned to oral reading. In fact, children now read chunks or phrases fluently instead of laboring over single words. The independent reader is predicting ahead of the print and using context to construct meaning, not just as an aid to decoding (Stanovich, 1980). The ability to critically analyze print, however, has not yet been achieved. Thus, these readers may believe everything they read or may exhibit a tendency toward seeing anything in print as literal, truthful, and absolute.

Reaching the Summit: The Skilled Reader

The skilled reader not only understands print, but also uses print to support and extend thinking. Although this is the final stage of reading development, it is not the end of the process. Becoming skilled in reading is a lifelong journey. The journey to skilled reading involves processing print that is further and further removed from one's own experiences and knowledge. In other words, print is now used increasingly as a means to acquire new and unfamiliar information. The variety of printed media that skilled readers process increases from narratives and textbooks to magazines, newspapers, TV guides, tax forms, and so on. Skilled readers can talk about different types of text organizations, make inferences from print, use print to substantiate opinions, challenge the surface validity of printed materials, and vary their reading rate according to the personal purposes for reading, such as skimming and scanning.

Although more research is needed to corroborate the descriptions offered by Cochrane et al. (1984) in the reading development continuum, this model provides a useful framework for parents, teachers, and scholars through which they can view the becoming of a reader with increased understanding and a good deal less anxiety.

Take-off stage read-ers may sound like worse readers than chil-dren in earlier stages because they are focus-ing so intently on the print.

The **independent reader** has developed control over the entire reading process and cuing systems.

Independent readers lack critical analysis skills.

Think of a time when you used print to sup-port or extend your own thinking. What were you aware of at that time?

DEVELOPMENT OF STORYBOOK READING BEHAVIORS

A more scholarly description of reading development is described in the work of Sulzby (1985). In her study, Sulzby researched and tested a classification scheme for describing children's emergent reading of storybooks (Figure 2.5).

Picture-Governed

In the earliest stages of storybook reading, children's behaviors seem to be largely governed by pictures. Children's earliest **picture-governed** behaviors often included labeling, commenting, pointing, or even slapping at the pictures. Some children in this earliest stage also became so caught up in the action of the pictures that it was as though the story were happening at the moment. For example, such a child

Figure 2.5 Emergent storybook reading behaviors
Based on E. Sulzby (1985).

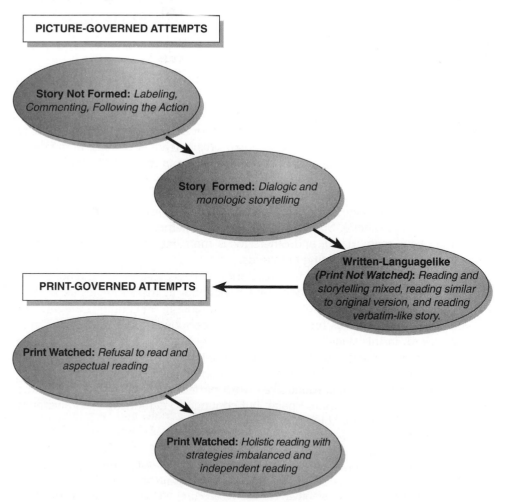

PICTURE-GOVERNED ATTEMPTS

Story Not Formed: *Labeling, Commenting, Following the Action*

Story Formed: *Dialogic and monologic storytelling*

Written-Languagelike (Print Not Watched): *Reading and storytelling mixed, reading similar to original version, and reading verbatim-like story.*

PRINT-GOVERNED ATTEMPTS

Print Watched: *Refusal to read and aspectual reading*

Print Watched: *Holistic reading with strategies imbalanced and independent reading*

might say, "See, there he goes. He's getting away, and they don't even see him!" Later in this stage, children's storybook readings become better suited or formed to the story in the book. Children engage in dialogic and monologic storybook reading. In *dialogic* storybook reading, children either create a "voice" for the characters in the story, or they tell the story by making comments directed to a listener of the story. Characters are lived as if the child is in the story, or the child tells the story for the benefit of the listener. "And she woke up! That's cuz the handsome prince kissed her," might signal this type of storybook reading. In any case, these story readings are often disjointed and difficult to follow. When children shift to *monologic* story-tellings, a complete story is told and understood. The story is also told with a story-telling intonation rather than a reading intonation (Sulzby, 1985, p. 468).

After children reach the monologic storybook reading stage, they begin to tell well-formed stories that approximate written language. Children's written-language-like reading attempts fall into three subcategories: (a) reading and storytelling mixed, (b) reading similar-to-original story, and (c) reading virtually verbatim. Once children enter into these storybook reading behaviors, they tend to focus their attention partially on the print as a means for governing their reading. Consequently, they move into Sulzby's (1985) second category of storybook reading behaviors, **print-governed** attempts at reading.

*Notice two main categories of Sulzby's storybook reading behaviors **picture-governed** and **print-governed.***

Print-Governed

Within this second category of storybook reading behaviors, children often engage in three initial responses to storybook print: (a) refusal, (b) aspectual reading, and (c) holistic reading. In the first stage, *refusal,* children refuse to try to read as they learn that print carries the story rather than the picture. For example, a child might remark, "I don't know the words. I can't read yet. I can't really read—I was just pretending." The child is now aware of the important role of decoding letters into words and refuses because she is afraid to make a mistake. With positive support and skilled instruction, they continue their development.

In the *aspectual* stage, children focus on one or two aspects of the print (often to the exclusion of others). Some children focus on memory of certain words (sight words they have memorized), and others focus more intently upon specific letter-sound combinations for sounding out words.

The final category, *holistic,* is divided into two subcategories: (a) reading with strategies imbalanced, and (b) reading independently. In the strategies-imbalanced stage, children might read a storybook by over-depending on certain strategies such as substituting known words for unknown words or sounding out every letter in an unknown word. In this stage, children have not yet become skilled in the selection and use of reading strategies during reading. In the *independent stage,* children have learned to balance the use of decoding and comprehension strategies during reading. These youngsters sometimes sound like "word perfect" readers and at other times make deviations from the printed page, but continue to demonstrate an awareness and control of the process of reading.

Sulzby (1985) remarked in summary,

Finally, and most important, the development that was observed in these studies appears to make sense in light of theoretical ideas about general and language development and the findings of other current research. . . . These discoveries about literacy development appear to challenge traditional assumptions about the nature of young children—assumptions built upon a conventional model. (p. 479)

Emergent views of reading development do in fact challenge the more conventional views of the past.

DEVELOPMENT OF WRITING BEHAVIORS

Laura, a 3-year-old neighbor girl, sat quietly on the couch next to her parents with four unlined, white 3- by 5-inch index cards and an old, teeth-marked pencil in her hands as her parents visited in the living room with a neighbor. After about 10 minutes, Laura slipped down from the couch and walked over to the visitor. Timidly, she approached, clutching one index card behind her back. Then, impulsively, she thrust the card from behind her back into the waiting hand of the visitor. He studied the marks Laura had made on the card. "Wow! Laura," he exclaimed, "You are writing!" Laura's face broadened into a smile that stretched from ear to ear, "I really writed, didn't I!" Young children discover that writing has meaning before they know how to write real words. Laura demonstrated her developing understanding that writing is a system for recording thoughts and feelings on paper to share with others. She had come to this understanding without formal spelling and writing instruction. By carefully watching others in her environment, Laura had taken the risk to act like a skilled writer and try out her tentative hypotheses about how printed language functions.

Many of us have seen children attempting to solve the printed language puzzle through drawing and scribbling. Just as with reading, however, one may be tempted to dismiss these early attempts at writing as cute, but certainly not *real* writing, as

Young children discover that writing has meaning before they know how to write real words.

Figure 2.6   Laura's scribbles

Writing can also be a system for developing thoughts and feelings.

shown in Figure 2.6. This attitude may be as dangerous as rooting out a flower in the early stages of growth because the roots do not look much like the flower.

Through careful study over a period of decades, researchers have discovered that young children pass through certain developmental stages in their writing and spelling similar to those discussed with respect to oral language and reading development. An understanding of these stages helps teachers recognize the "roots" of writing and spelling development and, as such, enable them to help nurture the roots of scribbling and drawing into the flower of writing.

Scribbling and Drawing Stage

Scribble writing *is as important to writing development as babbling is to oral language development.*

When young children first take a pencil or crayon in hand, they use this instrument to explore the vast empty space on a blank sheet of paper. In the earliest stages, children's writing is often referred to as scribbling by adult observers (Bear, Inverizzi, Templeton, & Johnston, 2000; Clay, 1987; Temple, Nathan, Burris, & Temple, 1993).

Figure 2.7 Laura's scribbles as exploration

These random marks are the wellsprings of writing discovery. As shown in Figure 2.6, Laura's scribbles appeared to be the result of acting on the paper just to see what happens, without any particular intent. Her scribbles do not evidence much of what adults normally consider to be conventional or even purposeful writing. In Figure 2.7 Laura began to evidence an exploration of alternative forms to her previous scribbles. Circles, curved lines, and letterlike forms begin to appear as a part of Laura's writing exploration.

Sometime later, Laura's scribbles begin to look more and more like adult cursive writing. Note in Figure 2.8 that Laura's scribbles have become linear, moving from left to right. When questioned, Laura could tell what she meant with each of her scribbles. Unlike Figure 2.6, Laura's scribbling represented her meaning in a more conventional way. Because this writing sample was produced near Christmastime, Laura revealed that these scribbles represented a "Christmas Wish List." Often, letter-like writing or shapes, as shown in Laura's Christmas list, are used repeatedly in early writing attempts. Clay (1987) calls the tendency to reuse and repeat certain scribblings and drawings *recursive writing*. The purpose behind recursive writing seems to be a need for comfort and familiarity as children prepare to move into the next levels of writing development.

Weeks later, Laura produced the writing found in Figure 2.9. Note in this example that drawings have begun to be used to carry part of the intended message. In addition, directly above the head of what appears to be a drawing of a young girl, one can clearly see the emergence of letter-like forms etched in broken detail. When queried about the intent of these letter-like forms, Laura responded, "That says Laura!" Evidently, Laura had discovered at this point in her development as a writer that drawings can supplement the message and that writing is different from drawing.

In another example, Toby, a 4-year-old child, produced the writing found in Figure 2.10. Toby used humanlike forms to represent members of his family in his

Children soon discover that drawing and scribbling are alternate forms of written expression.

Figure 2.8 Laura's scribble cursive writing: Christmas list

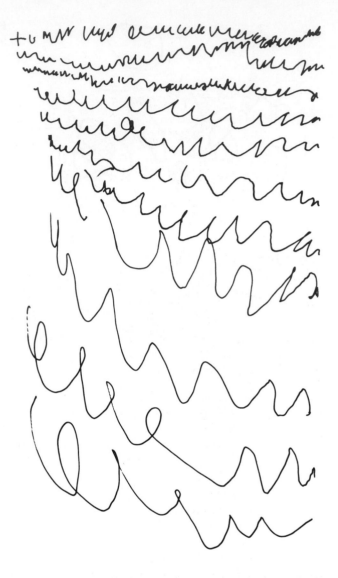

thank-you letter. One sees the use of letter-like symbols randomly scattered about the page. Near the center, Toby signed his name. By looking carefully, one can see the upside-down letter *b* and what looks like a letter *y,* which Toby chose to represent his name. Thus, one can see that during this initial stage of writing development, Laura and Toby used scribbling, drawing, and disconnected letter-like forms to explore and record their meaning on paper. These children had likewise discovered that writing can be used to communicate meaning and that although drawing and writing are complementary processes, they are not the same.

Prephonemic Stage

The next stage of writing and spelling development among young children is often called the **prephonemic stage** (Temple, Nathan, Burris, & Temple, 1993). At this stage of writing development, children begin to use real letters, usually capital letters, to represent their meaning; letters do not represent their phonemic or sound values.

Figure 2.9 Laura's self-portrait

Rather, they use letters as placeholders for meaning, representing anything from a syllable to an entire thought. For example, Chaundra, a kindergartner, produced the writing in Figure 2.11. Note Chaundra's use of letters to represent her meaning. Only by asking the child to explain the meaning can one readily discern that she used letters as meaning placeholders and not to represent their phonemic values.

Clay (1975) points out that children in the prephonemic stage of writing development will usually produce a string of letters and proudly display them to a parent while asking, "What does this say?" or "What did I write?" We can remember our children doing this with the magnetic letters we have on our refrigerator doors; they would meticulously arrange a string of letters and then ask what they had written.

Early Phonemic Stage

During the next stage of writing development, the **early phonemic stage** (Temple et al., 1993), children begin to use letters, usually capital consonant letters, to represent words. Children at this stage of writing development have discovered

*In the **prephonemic stage,** children begin to use real letters, usually capital letters, to represent their meaning; letters do not represent their phonemic or sound values.*

Figure 2.10   Toby's thank-you letter

Figure 2.11   Chaundra's pre-phonemic writing

Figure 2.12 Samantha's early phonemic writing: A house

that letters represent sound values. Children write words represented by one or two consonant letters—usually the beginning or ending sounds of the word. In Figure 2.12, Samantha uses only the consonant letters to represent the word *house* in her message.

Temple et al. (1993) suspect that the tendency for children in the early phonemic stage to represent a word with only one or two letters is due to an inability to "hold words still in their minds" while they examine them for phonemes and match these to known letters. (p. 101) Although this may be true, it is also possible that children at this stage are continuing to learn certain letters of the alphabet. It may also be true that writers in this stage of development have not developed the ability to segment more than the initial or final sounds in a word. Certainly, these possibilities would lead to the incomplete representation of words as found in the early phonemic stage of writing development. This is an area needing much more investigation (Teale, 1987; Templeton, 1995).

*In the **early phonemic stage,** children begin to use letters, usually capital consonant letters, to represent words.*

Letter-Naming Stage

The **letter-naming stage** of writing development is a small but important jump from the early phonemic stage. This stage is recognized by the addition of more than one or two consonants with at least one vowel used by young writers to represent the spelling of words (Temple et al., 1988). Chris, a kindergartner, produced an example of the letter-naming stage writing in response to his teacher's urgings to write about the rainbow he had seen the day before (see Figure 2.13).

*The **letter-naming stage** is recognized by the addition of more than one or two consonant letters used by young writers to represent the spelling of words.*

Figure 2.13 Chris's letter-naming stage writing: Rainbow

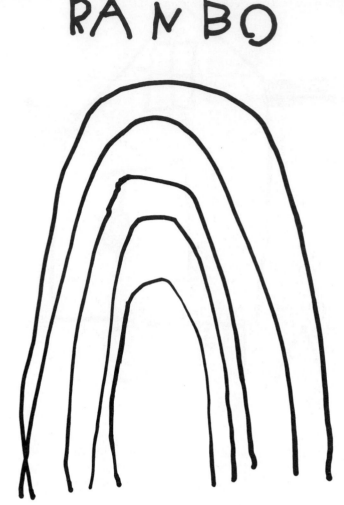

Although Chris continues to use capital letters exclusively, vowel letters have begun to appear in his writing. He had clearly discovered that words are made up of phonemes, both vowels and consonants; that these phonemes occur in an auditory sequence; and that these phonemes are properly represented in printed form from left to right. Although Chris was not yet reading independently, he had made important discoveries about print that nurtured his acquisition of reading; and his acquisition of reading will inform his acquisition of conventional spellings. With continued experiences in reading, Chris's writing will rapidly become more closely aligned with standard spelling and lead to the final stage of writing development—the transitional stage.

Transitional Stage

Figures 2.14 and 2.15 illustrate the **transitional stage** of writing and spelling. Writing produced by youngsters in this stage looks like English, but the words are a mix of phonetic and conventional spellings. Typically, these writers neglect or overgen-

Figure 2.14　Devin's Halloween story

eralize certain spelling generalizations. For example, the final silent *e* is sometimes omitted by these writers; familiar phonic elements are substituted for less familiar phonic elements; and double consonants are typically neglected.

Devin, a first grader, wrote the story shown in Figure 2.14 during October. He demonstrates not only some of the substitutions and omissions mentioned previously, but also a top-to-bottom arrangement for his story.

Figure 2.15 shows a note that Candice wrote to her parents during the fall of her second-grade year. Notice the spellings of *parents, hurting, guys,* and *special.* Some of the spellings are unconventional, but the writing of this child looks very much like English and communicates the message well. Candice's writing is also a good example of the characteristics of transitional writing mentioned previously—the mix of standard and nonstandard spellings. Note also that transitional writers have discovered the use of other features of standard writing such as possessives, punctuation, and the standard letter- or note-writing format.

These examples demonstrate the progression of children's writing along a developmental continuum, originating with their early attempts to make meaning on paper through scribbling and drawing to later refinements including the use of conventional spelling, grammar, and mechanics.

Transitional stage
writings look like English, but the words are a mix of phonetic and conventional spellings.

Figure 2.15   Candice's note to her parents

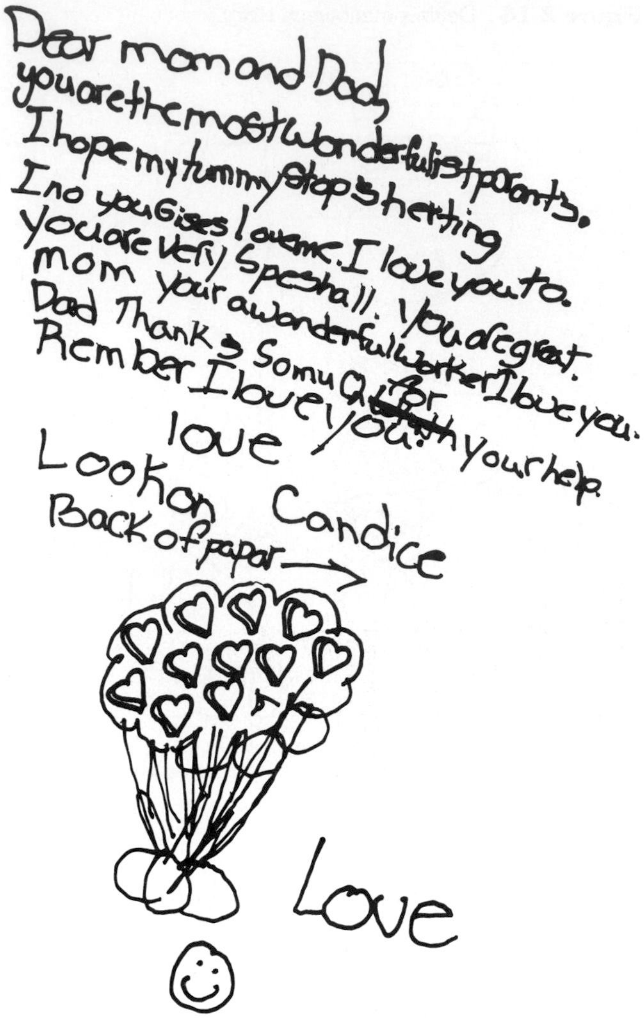

Dear mom and Dad,
you are the most wonderfullist pornts.
I hope my tummy stops herting
I no you Giges I ovemc. I love you to.
You are very Spesha ll. You are great.
mom your a wonderfull worker I luvc you.
Dad Thanks Somuch for your help.
Rember I love you

love

Look on   Candice
Back of paper →

Love

One note of caution should be sounded at this point: Although we may discuss oral language, writing, and reading development in terms of stages through which children pass, we want to emphasize to teachers that they should not use this information to try to hasten development or to expect that children will, or even should, pass through each stage of development in the order described. Rather, teachers should use this information as a basis for understanding and supporting children's language learning by providing an environment rich in print and print use, gentle guidance, and enthusiastic encouragement as children struggle to solve the language and literacy puzzle. Just as children learned to speak within a nurturing home environment filled with supportive oral language users, they will develop into readers and writers within print-rich school and home environments filled with the support and encouragement of other competent and caring readers and writers. Figure 2.16 integrates information about oral language, reading, and writing development to show that these modes of language learning are developmentally similar.

Notice at least two ways young children can be helped to develop into readers and writers.

Figure 2.16 Development across the language modes of oral language, reading, and writing

Oral Language Acquisition	Reading Development Stages	Writing Development Stages
Sounds, cooing, babbling	Picture-governed attempts: Story not formed	Scribbling and drawing
Holophrases and telegraphic speech	Picture-governed attempts: Story formed	Prephonemic
Vocabulary growth and negation language structures	Picture-governed attempts: Written language like—print not watched	Early phonemic
Vocabulary growth and interrogative structures	Print-governed attempts: Print watched	Letter-naming
Vocabulary growth, analogical substitutions, and passive language structures	Print-governed attempts: Strategies imbalanced	Transitional
Adult-like language structures, continuing vocabulary growth, and the ability to articulate all the sounds of the language	Print-governed attempts: Independent reading	Conventional

DEVELOPING A SENSE OF STORY

In 1966, Durkin found one characteristic common to the homes of early readers—parents who read books aloud to their children. Although we knew from Durkin's research that reading aloud to children seemed to be related to their becoming readers, we did not fully understand how reading aloud facilitated learning to read. During the 1970s, cognitive psychologists began to study the dimensions of how stories and narratives were constructed as well as how children developed a sense of story (Applebee, 1979; Graesser, Golding, & Long, 1991). Out of this research grew the realization that authors seemed to be writing stories by following a set of implicitly held rules or schemas for how stories should be constructed. Thus, researchers developed a generalized set of rules to describe how narratives were composed. These rules were compiled and resulted in the development of several story grammars (Mandler & Johnson, 1977; Stein & Glenn, 1979; P. N. Thorndyke, 1977).

Story Grammar Elements

The elements found in a **story grammar** roughly parallel the description of the parts or plot of a story. A story typically begins with a description of the setting or location, the introduction of the main characters, and the general time frame of the events in the story. Stories may be composed of a single episode; however, complex stories may contain several episodes. Within each story episode, a series of events has been labeled by story grammarians. The labels may differ from one story grammar to another,

Experience with books and stories has no reasonable substitute for helping children acquire a sense of story.

but the elements generally include (a) a setting, (b) an initiating event, (c) an internal response, (d) goals, (e) attempts, (f) outcomes, and (g) a resolution.

The setting is described as a location, time, and the introduction of the characters. The initiating event or problem essentially starts the story action. This is followed by the reaction of the main character(s) to the initiating event, usually called an *internal response to the initiating event*. Next, the main character may devise some plan(s) to solve the problem set up in the initiating event, which is a process of setting goals to be achieved by the main character. Next, the main character makes one or more attempts to achieve the goals or solve the problem. Finally, the outcome of the attempts is made known, and describing the results of the character's success or failure in achieving the desired outcomes concludes the story.

One question raised subsequent to the development of story grammars centered on how adults had come to know and use a story grammar for writing stories. It was originally hypothesized that adult writers had learned the structure or grammar for stories by reading or hearing narratives throughout their lives. As a consequence, several researchers began to investigate whether or not young children had begun to develop a sense of story. Nurss, Hough, and Goodson conducted a study of particular interest in 1981 with a group of preschool children attending a local day-care center. These researchers concluded that preschool children had not yet developed a complete sense of story structure. Other studies (Olson & Gee, 1988; Stein & Glenn, 1979) demonstrated that older children recalled stories more completely and could reorder scrambled pictures and story parts with greater precision than younger children. Thus, a concept of story structure appeared to be developmental in the sense that older children possessed more complete story structure knowledge than did younger children. One reason for this may be that older children had more experience with stories and as a result had more elaborate schemas for stories than did their younger counterparts.

Some researchers attempted to directly teach story grammar in the hopes that a sense of story would be imparted more effectively to young children; however, these attempts met with disappointing results (Golden, 1992; Muth, 1989). Consequently, few, if any, reading experts now endorse such an approach (Vacca, Vacca, Gove, Burkey, Lenhart, & McKeon, 2003). Instead, most researchers recognize that direct experience with books and stories is important for helping children acquire a sense of story. D. Taylor and Strickland (1986) recommend that parents read aloud regularly to their children to help them develop a sense of story. Nurss et al. (1981) suggest that story reading and discussion become an integral part of any preschool, nursery, or kindergarten program to help these children develop a concept of story structure. Morrow (1984) found that having children retell stories to other children or adults can significantly aid their development of a sense of story. Thus, the results to date indicate that children acquire a sense of story structure developmentally, over time, through reading or from hearing stories read aloud frequently.

UNDERSTANDING PRINT CONCEPTS AND THE LANGUAGE OF INSTRUCTION

Making sense of the purposes and symbols of reading and writing is a monumental task for young children. Research has demonstrated that children begin to attend to print at very young ages and come to school already having learned a great deal about the forms and functions of printed language (Y. M. Goodman & Altwerger, 1981;

Harste et al., 1984). In our view, children must experience the meaningfulness of printed language before they can make sense of school-based instructional practices (Lomax & McGee, 1987; B. Roberts, 1992). Thus, it is important for teachers to study how children develop an understanding of printed language to be able to effectively assist children through their learning experiences with printed language.

Environmental Print Studies

Reading **environmental print** involves reading printed language on signs, displays, billboards, and labels found in the environmental context of everyday living. In 1967, Ylisto conducted a print-awareness study involving some 200 4-, 5-, and 6-year-old children. They were presented with 25 printed word symbols taken from traffic signs and cereal boxes that progressed in difficulty through six steps—from a highly contextualized setting (in a natural setting or photograph) to a more abstract setting (a page of a book or a word card). The youngest of these children were able to identify some of the symbols through each of the six steps.

Romero (1983) and Y. M. Goodman and Altwerger (1981) conducted studies to investigate the print awareness of Anglo, African-American, Mexican-American, and Papago children ages 3, 4, and 5. These researchers found that 60% of 3-year-old children and 80% of 4- and 5-year-old children could read some environmental print. Harste et al. (1984) found that 3-year-old children could correctly identify environmental print or make a semantically acceptable "best guess." Hiebert (1978) found that children made significantly more errors recognizing words when they were presented without the environmental context. In other words, children seemed to be reading the entire context—not just the print. For example, if the word on a stop sign were transcribed onto a box of cereal, younger children would read the word *stop* as the cereal name about 38% to 50% of the time (Dewitz, Stammer, & Jensen, 1980). Thus, according to J. M. Mason (1980), children's early reading of environmental print is highly context dependent.

In another study that supported Mason's (1980) belief, Masonheimer, Drum, and Ehri (1984) found that young readers' errors increased when the unique print associated with a logo was removed from a full context. Even greater increases in errors were found when the unique print associated with a logo was replaced with conventional print. From these results, many researchers believed that children failed to devote attention to graphic detail; rather, children were reading the entire context. McGee, Lomax, and Head (1988) assessed 81 children, ages 3 to 6, for word reading and letter identification ability prior to having children read environmental print items. They found that children attended to graphic detail more when reading functional print items (*TV Guide,* newspapers, maps, books, coupons, telephone book, etc.) than environmental print items (product wrappers, containers, signs, billboards, etc.). Although expert word readers paid greater attention to graphic detail than did novice word readers, even prereaders paid some attention to graphic detail when responding to functional print items.

Because research uncovered the importance of a phonological route to word recognition, Stahl and Murray (1993) investigated the influence of students' phonological awareness on environmental print recognition using blending, segmenting, phoneme isolation, and phoneme deletion tasks. They examined the ability of 113 kindergarten and first-grade children to recognize 16 black and white environmental print items in context and out. They asserted that children learn little about the recognition of words through exposures to words in environmental context.

Environmental print is described as printed language on signs, displays, billboards, and labels found in the environmental context of everyday living.

Reading environmental print has been shown to be highly dependent on the context of the print.

Cronin, Farrell, and Delaney (1999) found that recognizing words in environmental print created an advantage for learning those same words in isolation. Instructing children using environmental print is seen as an important means for introducing children to the world of written language (Aldridge & Rust, 1987; Kuby, Kirkland, & Aldridge, 1996; McGee & Richgels, 2000; Orellana & Hernandez, 1999; Proudfoot, 1992; Rule, 2001; Wepner, 1985).

Student Perceptions of Reading

When a young girl attending an elementary school was asked what she could do to become a better reader, she responded, "I would study my vowel rules and my phonics a lot because that's mostly reading." (DeFord & Harste, 1982, p. 592) Jerry Johns (1986) recalled a time when a second-grade boy was asked, "What do you think reading is?" He responded, "Stand up, sit down!" By this he meant that when he read his teacher requested that he stand, then sit when he was finished. These are just a few of the perceptions students have about the purposes of reading.

In his ground-breaking study, Reid (1966) investigated the understanding of the purposes of reading held among 5-year-old children in a classroom in Edinburgh, Scotland. The children were asked, "What is reading?" Their answers indicated that they had a very vague notion about what reading was and how it was to be done. Some children, Reid reported, were unsure about whether one read the pictures or the marks on the page.

In a similar study, Weintraub and Denny (1965) found that children came to school with widely disparate perceptions about reading and that 27% of them could not verbalize anything intelligible about the reading process. Johns and Johns (1971) supported this result with their own research finding that 70% of students from kindergarten through grade 6 gave vague, irrelevant answers or no response at all to the question of "What is reading?"

In a later and much larger study involving 1,655 students in grades 1 through 8, Johns and Ellis (1976) found that 69% of these students gave essentially meaningless responses to the question of "What is reading?" Nearly 57% of the responses to the question "What do you do when you read?" were judged to be meaningless. In answer to the question "If someone didn't know how to read, what would you tell him that he would need to learn?" 56% of the respondents indicated something that had to do with pronouncing or decoding words and letters. Canney and Winograd (1979) replicated this study showing that most children believed that their reading could be improved by learning to decode better rather than to learn to comprehend, read fluently, or even develop a disposition to read.

Children's perceptions about reading are closely tied to their teachers' beliefs and attendant instructional practices.

An interesting insight into young readers' perspectives about reading was found in the work of Reutzel and Sabey (1996). They examined how first-grade student perspectives about reading were influenced by their teachers' beliefs about how children learn to read. Children were given the *Burke Reading Interview* (Burke, 1987), and teachers completed the *Theoretical Orientations to Reading Profile* (DeFord, 1985). Responses of students and teachers were examined and found to be highly related to one another. Hence, students' perceptions of the act of reading seemed to be subject to the influence of their teachers' beliefs about reading instruction.

From these studies, one may conclude that young readers have only vague notions about the purposes and mechanics of the reading process. Additionally, children's perceptions of the purposes and functions of the reading act are influenced by the beliefs their teachers hold about reading instruction. Finally, as children gain more experience with print, they are able to refine and better articulate their concepts about reading and are more likely to view reading as a meaning-seeking or constructive process.

UNDERSTANDING CONCEPTS ABOUT PRINT

As children have opportunities to interact with print through reading signs, learning the alphabet, or reading books, they begin to pay closer attention to the details of printed language. **Print concepts** typically embrace an understanding of some of the following:

- Directionality (left to right, top to bottom)
- The difference between a word and a letter
- The meaning and use of punctuation marks
- The match between speech and print on the page
- Many other technical understandings about how print and books work

Day and Day (1979) found that 80% of 51 first graders they studied had mastered book orientation and directionality by the end of first grade. However, only a small percentage could recognize incorrect words or letter sequences in a line of print or could explain the use of quotation marks. Downing and Oliver (1973) found that young children could not differentiate reliably between a word and a letter. Johns (1980) found that above-average readers evidenced greater print awareness than did below-average readers. Yaden (1982) concluded that even after a full year of reading instruction, some beginning readers' concepts about printed language remained incomplete and uncertain. B. Roberts (1992) and Lomax and McGee (1987) found that an understanding of print concepts is an important precursor of reading development among young children.

In view of these findings, Johns (1980) and N. E. Taylor (1986) cautiously recommended that print concepts and the language of reading instruction be explicitly taught to young readers. Other researchers believed children would learn printed language concepts as well in a print-rich environment where they interacted on a consistent basis with meaningful printed materials (Ferreiro & Teberosky, 1982; Hiebert, 1981; Holdaway, 1979; McCormick & Mason, 1986).

Research reported by Reutzel, Oda, and Moore (1989) showed that kindergartners learned as much about print concepts and word reading in a print-rich environment as they did with the addition of direct instruction on specific print concepts. Thus, it appeared that children learned print concepts as well in a print-rich environment with plenty of opportunities for interaction in meaningful ways with printed materials as with the addition of isolated, systematic print concept instruction.

Reutzel, Fawson, Young, Morrison, and Wilcox (2003) conducted a more recent study of the effects of *concepts-about-print* knowledge on 4- to 7-year-old children's ability to read environmental print displays under five different conditions, ranging from the original display to a display with errors embedded in block style black and white print (MxPonalds instead of McDonalds). This study showed that other than word recognition ability, concepts-about-print knowledge played an important role in helping young children read environmental print under a variety of circumstances. They concluded that children do need, however, to be taught to use their decoding knowledge to read environmental print items; they do not spontaneously do so. This means that children try to read environmental print holistically—without breaking it

Very young students rarely perceive reading to be an act associated with constructing meaning for personal purposes.

Young children learn as much about print concepts and word reading in a print-rich environment as they do with the addition of direct instruction on specific print concepts.

down beyond the visual or graphic features. Hence, environmental print items may be used to provide some of children's early phonics instruction.

Summary

In many respects, the acquisition of reading and writing parallels the acquisition of oral language acquisition seen in infants and young children. Children process print and speech from whole to parts to whole again within the context of supportive and socially interactive language environments. They begin by crudely approximating demonstrations of speech, reading, and writing behaviors and refine these attempts over time with the help of others to become more like the people they attempt to emulate. Other language users play a critical role in youngsters' speech, reading, and writing acquisition. But when children enter schools, informed teachers can do much to support youngsters in their efforts to become independent, skilled readers and writers. Armed with a knowledge of how children develop as speakers, readers, and writers, teachers can provide the conditions and instruction necessary to move children forward as well as to help parents understand the critical role they continue to play in their children's progress as readers and writers.

Check your understanding of chapter concepts by using the self assessment for Chapter 2 on our Companion Website at www.prenhall.com/ reutzel.

Concept Applications

In the Classroom

1. Using the information about children's writing development, describe Vygotsky's concept of ZPD and explain where a teacher's intervention could be most beneficial to a learner. Then describe what intervention would be most beneficial to the student at that stage of development.
2. Using information about children's reading development, construct a diagram describing reading developmental attributes one might expect to see during each of Piaget's stages of cognitive development.

In the Field

1. Visit with two children of about the same age for about 15 minutes each. Record your visit on audiotape. Write a short essay about the features of spoken language that these children had learned well and those speech features where they may need further demonstrations to support their learning.
2. For 1 week (1 hour per day), visit a kindergarten classroom. Make a listing of invented language used by children at this age. Publish your findings for the other members of the class.
3. Interview two parents about their young children's reading development. Ask them what their children are doing with books and print. Describe in writing the results of the interviews. Which stage(s) of reading development would best describe these two children's reading behaviors? Why?
4. Collect five samples of kindergarten or first-grade children's writing. Label each according to a stage of writing and spelling development described in this chapter. Explain your reasons for categorizing each.
5. Show a child at least 10 food product labels and ask him or her to read them. Record each answer. Ask the child to explain how he or she arrived at these answers. In writing, discuss each answer with respect to how the child answered and why.

6. Ask a child to tell you a story. Record the story on audiotape. Analyze the telling using story grammar. Describe in writing the parts of the story included and excluded in the telling. What can you conclude about this child's sense of story development?

7. Hand two kindergarten or first-grade children a book by the spine and upside down. Ask each child to:
   a. Show you where to begin reading.
   b. Show you which way your eyes should progress along the print.
   c. Show you a letter.
   d. Show you a word.
   e. Show you the end of the book.

   In writing, discuss your findings for each child. Describe what each child knows and does not yet know about printed language concepts.

8. Ask three young children what they think reading and writing are. Record their responses on audiotape or in writing. Explain the perceptions these children have of reading and writing in a separate essay or as an entry in your learning log.

9. Ask a young child to read a book to you. After recording the event, reread the description of emergent storybook reading behaviors in Figure 2.5 (based on Sulzby, 1985). Where does this child fit within the developmental stages of storybook reading development?

Recommended Readings

Clay, M. M. (1998). *By different paths to common outcomes.* York, ME: Stenhouse.

Dixon-Krauss, L. (1996). *Vygotsky in the classroom: Mediated literacy instruction and assessment.* New York: Longman.

Fosnot, C. T. (1996). *Constructivism: Theory, perspectives, and practice.* New York: Teachers College Press.

McGee, L. M., & Richgels, D. J., (2003). *Literacy's beginnings: Supporting young readers and writers* (4th Ed.). Needham Heights, MA: Allyn & Bacon.

Snowball, D. & Bolton, F. (1999). *Spelling K–8: Planning and Teaching.* York, ME: Stenhouse.

Temple, C., Nathan, R., Burris, N., & Temple, F. (1993). *The beginnings of writing* (3rd Ed.). Boston, MA: Allyn & Bacon.

Vygotsky, L. S. (1978). *Mind in society.* Cambridge, MA: Harvard University Press.

Theoretical Roots of Reading Instruction

Focus Questions

When you are finished studying this chapter, you should be able to answer these questions:

1. What can be said about the need for reading in our society today and in the future?

2. Why do teachers need to study and understand the reading process?

3. How do theories of the reading process relate to instructional practices?

4. Which of the instructional practices for teaching reading do you believe are most effective, and why?

5. Why do you think educators call comprehensive reading instruction *comprehensive*?

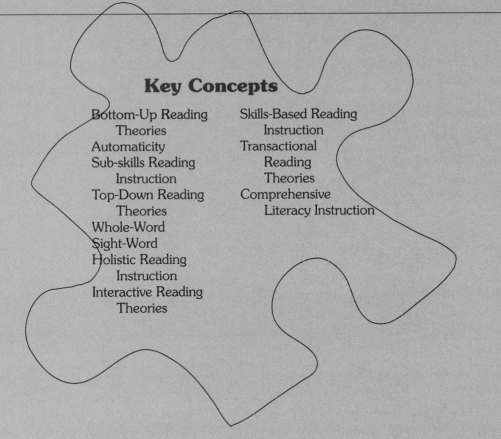

Key Concepts

Bottom-Up Reading
    Theories
Automaticity
Sub-skills Reading
    Instruction
Top-Down Reading
    Theories
Whole-Word
Sight-Word
Holistic Reading
    Instruction
Interactive Reading
    Theories

Skills-Based Reading
    Instruction
Transactional
    Reading
    Theories
Comprehensive
    Literacy Instruction

Fundamental knowledge for every teacher of literacy includes understanding theories of the reading process and the variety of instructional models that spring from these theories. Throughout the history of reading instruction a debate has and continues to rage around a) whether reading instruction should focus on helping learners recode symbols into sounds and put sounds together to make words, or b) whether reading instruction should focus on helping learners extract or construct meaning from the print as a primary emphasis of instruction. New and experienced teachers are less likely to be persuaded to believe that extreme positions on either side of the reading debate are realistic when contextualized in the elementary classroom. In this chapter, we describe the nature of the debates around reading instruction and the need for understanding theory and reading instructional models.

THE NEED FOR UNDERSTANDING HOW CHILDREN LEARN TO READ

Children learn to read from many people, but most children learn to read from teachers who know and use effective reading instructional practices in classrooms.

On several occasions, we have been asked by exasperated teachers just what we would do if we had to teach 30 youngsters to read. As former classroom teachers, our responses to such a question usually lead to a discussion of the role and importance of teachers, teacher knowledge, and teacher skills. Recently, the National Education Association's Task Force on Reading 2000 report declared, "It is not the method that makes the difference, it is the teacher!" (2000, p. 7). Teacher knowledge and competence form the foundation for effective reading instruction. Teachers of young children must come to know and understand: (1) reading theories, (2) best practices in reading instruction, (3) the structure and elements of language, and (4) how children develop into successful readers and writers.

Young children learn to read from people who know and use effective instructional practices. Despite what many publishers claim, the overwhelming evidence shows that teachers make the difference in children's reading achievement, not published and/or purchased reading programs! Evidence has been mounting for years that adopting a new published reading program is not the answer to the problems of providing effective reading instruction. In fact, published reading programs typically have very limited effects on students' reading achievement. In the 1985 *Becoming a Nation of Readers Report,* it was concluded that adopting a new reading program influences students' reading achievement scores by only 3% whereas the competence of the teacher influences student reading achievement scores by 15%—five times more than programs.

Visit Chapter 3 of our Companion Website at www.prenhall.com/reutzel to look into the chapter objectives, standards and principles, and pertinent web links associated with Theoretical Roots of Reading Instruction.

To clarify the contrast between knowledgeable teachers and reliance upon published reading programs, we turn to a metaphor about carpenters and their tools. It is a well-accepted fact that a skilled, master carpenter can produce excellent quality work with access to only marginally adequate hand tools. Admittedly, access to better tools makes such carpenters more efficient as well as effective. However, an unskilled, novice carpenter is likewise capable of turning out poor quality craftsmanship even when he or she has access to the finest and newest power tools and technology. In the end, it is the knowledge and skill of the carpenter that makes the difference in the quality of the product, not the tools. So it is with teaching children to read. It is the touch of the master teacher's hand that makes the real difference—not the program.

Standards Note
Standard 2.11: The reading professional will know relevant reading research from general education and how it has influenced literacy education. As you read this chapter, record in a personal study notebook how each reading theory connects to research on how to teach young children to read and write.

You may recall a television commercial advertising a specific brand of picante sauce in which the cowpokes seated around the campfire requested a new bottle of picante sauce from the cook. They were disappointed when it was not their usual brand and remarked disparagingly, "This stuff's made in New York City!" Well, a similar response is often heard about published reading programs—this program is made in New York City. Reading programs developed in New York City cannot appropriately anticipate the needs of students and teachers in the far reaches of Mississippi, Montana, or Minnesota. Although many published programs promise success for all children, they typically only deliver success for some without the thoughtful use and adaptation of a competent classroom teacher.

Knowledgeable teachers produce excellent results regardless of the programs found in the classroom. On the other hand, we recognize that the best of all possible worlds puts a highly knowledgeable and skilled teacher with a rich array of reading materials, programs, and resources in every classroom so that all children can enjoy optimal conditions for learning to read.

THEORIES OF THE READING PROCESS

Unfortunately, the mere mention of the word *theory* causes some teachers to go into near apoplexy, dismissing complex explanations of the reading process as *impractical*. In defense of the practicality of reading theories, Moffett and Wagner (1976) asserted that nothing is so practical as a good theory. All teachers have in-the-head theories to guide their reading instructional decisions (DeFord, 1985; Gove, 1983). On the other hand, we have also found that few teachers can clearly or explicitly articulate the theories from which they make decisions about reading instruction.

Theories of the reading process offer explanations about how children become proficient readers. By definition, a theory is "a system of ideas, often stated as a principle, to explain or to lead to a new understanding" (T. L. Harris & Hodges, 1981, p. 329). The reading process is defined as "what happens when a person processes text to obtain meaning" (T. L. Harris & Hodges, 1995, p. 212). Thus, theories of the reading process offer, through the articulation of a system of ideas, new understandings about what happens when a person processes text to obtain meaning.

Reading theories are alternative explanations of the complex process of learning to read. Theories are neither proven nor unproven. They are neither true nor false. They are neither right nor wrong. They can be viewed, however, as more or less complete. This means that some reading theories do a better job of explaining the complex nature of the reading process than do others. Also, theories of the reading process have led researchers and teachers to propose a variety of successful instructional practices for helping children develop into successful, flexible, and strategic readers.

Before leaving this section, stop and list two reasons why knowing reading theories will help you know how to help children learn to read more effectively. This can

Standards Note

Standard 1.5: The reading professional will perceive reading as the process of constructing meaning through the interaction of the reader's existing knowledge, the information suggested by the written language, and the context of the reading situation. As you read this chapter, notice how each of the four reading theories and the accompanying reading instructional approaches address the issues of constructing meaning, readers' prior knowledge, and the context of the reading situation in how young children learn to read and write.

Focus on several ways theory can be practical.

Developing a belief system about how students learn to read and write begins with putting theories into practice.

List two reasons why knowing reading theories helps teachers know how to help children more effectively.

help you to establish a purpose for learning about the upcoming four types of reading theories and the instructional practices developed by teachers and researchers in response to these reading theories.

In the sections that follow, we describe four reading theories: (1) bottom-up, (2) top-down, (3) interactive, and (4) transactional. We show how these theories have influenced the production of curriculum materials and reading programs, and influence teachers' choices about effective teaching practices. We believe by making the link between *theory* and *practice* explicit, we can help all teachers, novice and expert alike, come to realize that all reading instructional choices are derived from personally held *theories* about the reading process. We also believe that in making these connections explicit, teachers can discover that no single theory of the reading process in and of itself provides a complete explanation. Teachers who know how theory and practice relate are better able to see and understand connections between various explanations of the process of learning to read and the multitude of potential instructional choices for teaching children to read.

Bottom-Up Theories of the Reading Process

Notice some weaknesses associated with two of the earliest models representing the bottom-up theoretical position.

Bottom-up theories hypothesize that learning to read progresses from children learning the *parts* of language (letters) to understanding *whole* text (meaning). Much like solving a jigsaw puzzle, bottom-up models of the reading process say that the reading puzzle is solved by beginning with an examination of each piece of the puzzle and then putting pieces together to make a picture. Two bottom-up theories of the reading process remain popular even today: *One Second of Reading* by Gough (1972) and *A Theory of Automatic Information Processing* by LaBerge and Samuels (1974).

Gough's (1972) *One Second of Reading* model described reading as a sequential or *serial* mental process. Readers, according to Gough, begin by translating the parts of written language (letters) into speech sounds, then piece the sounds together to form individual words, then piece the words together to arrive at an understanding of the author's written message.

*The term **automaticity** suggests that readers have limited attention capacity that can be shifted rapidly between the parallel processes of decoding and comprehension.*

In their reading model, LaBerge and Samuels (1974) describe a concept called automatic information processing or **automaticity.** This popular model of the reading process hypothesizes that the human mind functions much like a computer and that visual input (letters and words) is sequentially entered into the mind of the reader. Almost without exception, humans have the ability to perform more than one task at a time (computer specialists sometimes call this "multitasking"). Because each computer, and by comparison, the human mind, has a limited capacity available for multitasking, attention must be shifted from one job to another. If one job requires a large portion of the available computer's attention capacity, then capacity for another job is limited. The term "automaticity" implies that readers, like computers, have a limited ability to shift attention between the processes of decoding (sounding out words) and comprehending (thinking about the meaning of the author's message in the text). If readers are too bogged down in decoding the text, they will not be able to focus on the job of comprehending the author's message.

An example of automaticity in action can be seen in the common skill of learning to ride a bike. Novice bike riders focus so intently on balancing, turning the handlebars, and pedaling that they sometimes fail to attend to other important tasks like direction and potential dangers. Similarly, a reader who is a poor decoder focuses so much of his attention on phonics and other sounding out strategies, he has little brainpower left for comprehending. When this happens, the reading act, like an overloaded computer, "crashes." In contrast, children who are accomplished bike riders can ride

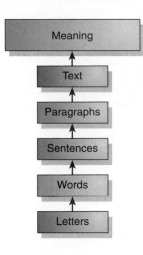

Figure 3.1 Bottom-up theories of the reading process

without hands, carry on a conversation with a friend, dodge a pothole in the road, and chew gum at the same time. Like the accomplished bike rider, fluent readers can rapidly focus on the author's message because decoding no longer demands the lion's share of their attention capacity. In summary, the LaBerge and Samuels (1974) model predicts that if reading can occur automatically, without too much focus on the decoding process, then improved comprehension will be the result. A bottom-up theory of the reading process is represented in Figure 3.1. Important features of this reading theory are summarized in the left-hand column of Figure 3.3 (see p. 75).

Teachers who believe that bottom-up theories fully explain how children become readers often teach sub-skills first: they begin instruction by introducing letter names and letter sounds, progress to pronouncing whole words, then show students ways of connecting word meanings to comprehend texts. Although bottom-up theories of the reading process explain the decoding part of the reading process rather well, there is certainly more to reading than decoding. To become readers, students *must* compare their knowledge and background experiences to the text in order to understand the author's message. Truly, the whole purpose of reading is comprehension.

The Relationship of Bottom-Up Reading Theories to Phonics-First Reading Instruction

Sub-skills, also called "phonics-first" reading instruction, may be thought of as a pyramid with sound/symbol relationships (the parts of language) at its base and comprehension (constructing the meaning) as the capstone (Weaver, 1988, 1994). Chall (1979, 1983), a strong proponent of the phonics-first instructional model, characterized decoding as the first stage of learning to read.

> The essential aspect of *Stage One* is learning the arbitrary set of letters and associating these with the corresponding parts of spoken words [phonics]. . . . The qualitative change that occurs at the end of this stage is the insight gained about the nature of the spelling system of the particular alphabetic language used. (Chall, 1979, p. 39)

Phonics-first teachers, whether they realize it or not, base their instruction on bottom-up theories of the reading process (see Figure 3.2). Why? Because they typically focus instruction on teaching children letter-sound relationships during the earliest stages of reading instruction. Although comprehension is also important in a

Phonics is the foundation of reading in the sub-skills model with comprehension as the capstone.

Figure 3.2 Sub-skills or phonics-first reading instruction

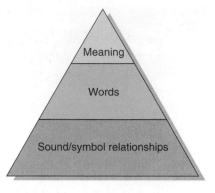

phonics-first instructional approach, this approach assumes that efficient decoding leads directly to comprehension.

Instruction using a sub-skills model begins with the letters of the alphabet and the sounds these letters represent.

As you might expect, phonics-first teachers assume the primary cause some readers struggle is the inability to decode. Therefore, they believe that children must be taught phonics first via the letters of the alphabet and the sounds these letters represent *before* beginning to read books independently. Flesch (1955, 1979), among others, cautioned that allowing children to attempt to read words or books without knowing the 26 letters and the 44 speech sounds they represent could lead to reading failure and frustration. Thus, letter names and letter sounds become the basic building blocks of reading within a sub-skills or phonics-first instructional approach.

The use of supplemental phonics programs, along with the exclusive use of phonically controlled (decodable) readers, often characterizes the components of a sub-skills or phonics-first instructional approach. *Decodable books* are usually made up of words that follow phonic generalizations or patterns children have been taught, such as short vowel word families like *can, man, fan.* The rationale for having children read decodable books is well illustrated in the *Becoming a Nation of Readers* report statement: "The important point is that a high proportion of the words in the earliest selections children read should conform to the phonics they have already been taught" (R. C. Anderson et al., 1985, p. 47). This argument has recently surfaced again in calls for the production and use of "decodable texts," or phonics readers, in states like California and Texas (Allington, 1997, 2002).

Sub-skills models assume the primary cause of reading difficulty to be the inability to decode.

As you examine Figure 3.3, notice the clear connection to phonics-first instruction. Phonics-first teachers begin reading instruction by teaching each of the parts of language (letters) as a prerequisite to reading words, sentences, and stories. Notice how beginning reading passages (decodable texts) use words that are phonically regular and follow specific phonic generalizations. Finally, notice it is assumed that if a child masters decoding, then comprehension will automatically follow in this instructional model.

Top-Down Theories of the Reading Process

Top-down reading theories place primary emphasis on the role of a reader's prior knowledge rather than on the print on the page.

Top-down theories of the reading process are rooted in Gestalt psychology, a school of thought that became popular in America in the early 1960s. To gain insight into Gestalt psychology, consider the classic example shown of Rubin's vase in Figure 3.4.

Gestalt psychology asserted that learners respond to physical stimuli such as images, letters, or drawings. This means that learners *act* upon what they see using

Figure 3.3   Connecting bottom-up and sub-skills and phonics-first reading instructional practices

Bottom-Up Theories of the Reading Process

• During reading and learning to read, language is processed from the parts to the whole, as in building a structure from blocks one at a time.
• Learning to read is based on Stimulus–Response chains posited by behaviorists.
• Learning to read is accomplished by reducing the skill of reading to its smallest parts to be mastered one at a time.
• Repetition in reading is focused on practicing the parts of the complex skill of reading to a level of overlearning or automaticity.
• Language stimuli for reading are carefully controlled to represent consistently identified language rules or patterns to be learned.
• Mastery of the smallest parts of reading is assumed to lead to competent understanding and performance of the whole act of reading.
• Automatic decoding of the smallest parts of language is a prerequisite to reading and comprehending connected texts or books.
• Correctness is expected; mistakes are to be corrected.
• Pronouncing words provides access to one's speaking vocabulary to enable comprehension.
• Comprehending words provides access to new vocabulary words and comprehension of text.

Sub-Skills or Phonics-First Reading Instructional Practices

• Reading instruction is begun by learning the 26 letters and the 44 sounds.
• Instruction proceeds to demonstrate the association(s) between the 26 letters and the 44 sounds.
• Blending the sounds represented by the letters in a word from left-to-right in temporal sequence or "sounding out" phonically regular words is taught.
• A limited number of high-frequency sight words are taught.
• Texts composed of carefully controlled words that are either known sight words or are phonically regular words are introduced to children for reading practice.
• More phonic patterns, rules, and generalizations are taught and learned.
• Texts are controlled to include new words as application for the patterns, rules, or generalizations learned.
• Control over text is gradually released, allowing phonically irregular words.
• Comprehending text is a direct outgrowth from the ability to pronounce words.

Figure 3.4   The Rubin vase

their own knowledge and experiences. As you viewed the Rubin Vase in Figure 3.4, what did you see? Did you see the vase? Or did you see two people facing each other? How did you decide to attend to one or the other interpretation of the picture? Did you notice that the picture did not change, but your perception of the picture changed? Did you see the vase first because it was named "Rubin's vase"? What if it had been named "Rubin's *faces*"? Perhaps you would have noticed the faces first, and the vase second.

Gestaltist psychology does not view the reading act as passive. Readers are seen as actively responding to the stimuli presented in print and texts.

According to Gestalt psychology, what is seen, such as pictures, words or letters, is processed from the whole image to its parts (Otto, 1982). First, the whole of a picture is perceived (see Figure 3.4). After determining the nature of the image, one perceives the parts (i.e., shape, contours, identity). Once you decided the picture in Figure 3.4 was a vase, you perceived the base, the top, and the shape of the vase. However, had you seen the other interpretation of the picture, two people facing each other, then you would have noticed the neck, the chin, the nose, and the heads of two people.

Because you already knew this was a picture of a vase, your perceptions of the picture were affected by that perception. Gestalt psychologists explain that learners *actively* organize and interpret visual stimuli rather than *passively* taking in the visual image without interpretation. Because the *whole* of a stimulus, such as a picture, influences the perception of its *parts,* Gestaltists were often heard to say, "the whole is greater than the sum of its parts."

Since learning to read involves visual stimuli, it is conceivable, according to the Gestalt school, that reading begins with a visual check of "whole" first (text, sentences), then proceeds to identification of the smaller parts (words, letters, and letter features). Reading goes beyond the visual (e.g., cognitive, affective, and linguistic factors). For example, when one reads, the words do not have meaning; rather, the reader brings personal meaning to the text from background experiences and collected knowledge.

Gestalt psychological thought led to the development of *top-down* theories of the reading process. In top-down theories, the knowledge and experiences the reader brings to the print influence, shape, and direct comprehension, rather than the print on the page. Reading begins with the reader's knowledge, not the print. Top-down theories of the reading process suggest that reading is a meaning-construction process first and foremost, not merely a process of carefully attending to visual clues in print. A top-down theory of the reading process is represented in Figure 3.5.

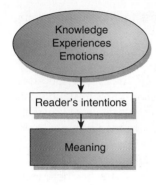

Figure 3.5 Top-down theories of the reading process

To understand at a practical level how reading can be influenced by a reader's background knowledge and experience, read a few lines from the well-known poem "Jabberwocky," by Lewis Carroll (1872).

'Twas brillig, and the slithy toves
Did gyre and gimble in the wabe;
All mimsy were the borogoves,
And the mome raths outgrabe.
Beware the Jabberwock, my son!
The jaws that bite, the claws that catch!
Beware the Jubjub bird, and shun
The frumious Bandersnatch!

It is obvious, that you cannot read or understand this poem by simply pronouncing the words on the page or by attending more carefully to the visual stimuli (words, letters, etc.) displayed on the page. As readers, we use our knowledge about the animal kingdom—jaws, claws, and birds—to deduce that the Jabberwock is some kind of creature. We also use our experience with grammar and language to determine that the Jabberwock is a thing, not an action or a description. In spite of the intuitive appeal of top-down reading theories, it is clear that at some point in the reading process all readers *must* attend to the print in order to know which aspects of their knowledge and background experiences to apply in understanding the author's message.

It is clear readers cannot "read" text without attending to the details of the print. Consequently, there can be no purely "Top-down" models of the reading process in any real application.

The Relationship of Top-Down Reading Theories to Whole-Word Reading Instruction

In the mid-1880s, a German researcher at the University of Leipzig named James M. Cattell published a paper entitled, "The Time Taken Up in Cerebral Operations," in which he found that adult readers could recognize words as rapidly as letters. Students were shown letters and words with a device called a *tachistoscope*—a piece of equipment that used a tiny shutter as found in many cameras to expose words and letters to a viewer at various speeds and for varying amounts of time. From these early experiments, coupled with results of research in the mid-1920s and early 1930s showing that many children were failing first grade because they were not learning to read successfully, a new approach to teaching reading called the **whole-word method** was born in the late 1930s.

It was thought that children could be taught to recognize whole words by sight, without any analysis of letters or sounds. Learning to read words would not only be more interesting and motivating for young children, but as was shown in Cattell's

Nineteenth century research found that adult readers could recognize short words as quickly as they could recognize individual letters.

research, could be done without the dull, boring, and needless trek through learning letter names and letter sounds.

As a part of the **whole-word** or **sight-word approach** to teaching reading, researchers undertook studies of "word frequency" (i.e., how often words appear in most writing) in printed texts. Lists of the most frequent words in the English language were developed. The most frequent words in English were taught first to young children. Words like *the, and, a,* and *look* were taught using word lists displayed on walls and in little reading books. Children practiced reading these words until they were memorized. Some of the most famous of these early reading books were known at the *New Basic Readers* or the *Dick and Jane* readers, originally published in 1941.

Once children learned to recognize the frequent words by sight, teachers were to teach children to "discover" how the sounds and letters within known words worked. In so doing, children could then figure out unknown words. So, once a whole word was recognized, then the parts of the word could be studied to determine how the parts contributed to the whole (see Figure 3.6). Can you see how these instructional practices relate to top-down theories of the reading process?

A more recent variation on the whole-word instructional approach was an approach to teaching reading called *whole language* reading instruction (Heymsfeld, 1989). With *whole language,* teachers and researchers believed that students would learn to read as naturally as they had learned to speak. The central unit of meaning, the sentence, was thought to be the smallest unit of meaning for teaching children to read in whole language approaches. Children were immersed in print-rich classrooms where they would hear stories read aloud, and they would repeatedly read the same story or poem, typically within the pages of a "big book" or on large chart paper, again and again with the assistance of the teacher. All of this was to proceed without invasive, meaningless drills and skills and the use of decodable texts often associated with phonics-first instruction (Goodman, 1986; Rayner, Foorman, Perfetti, Pesetsky, & Seidenberg, 2002). Notice how top-down theories of the reading process influenced whole language reading instruction by examining the information in Figure

Children were taught to recognize on sight the most "highly frequent" words in the language during the whole word reading movement.

Whole language emphasized that the smallest unit of meaning for teaching reading was a phrase or sentence which led to the use of patterned or predictable texts.

Figure 3.6 Whole-word, sight-word, or holistic reading instruction

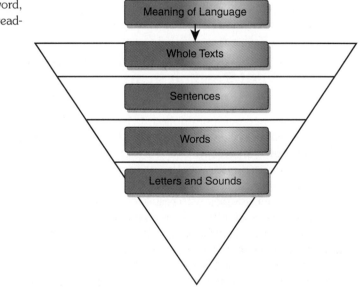

Figure 3.7 Connecting top-down theories of the reading process and whole-word reading instructional practices

Top-Down Theories of the Reading Process

- During reading and learning to read, language is processed from the whole to the parts, as in taking a completed jigsaw puzzle apart.
- Learning to read is based on "the whole is greater than the sum of its parts," as asserted by Gestalt psychology.
- Learning to read is accomplished naturally and holistically through immersion in print-rich and language-rich environments.
- Repetition in reading is focused on practicing phrases, sentences, or stories again and again until the text elements are internalized.
- Language stimuli in beginning reading materials are not controlled but represent naturally occurring patterns of language such as "run, run as fast as you can. . . ." in the "Gingerbread Man" story.
- Learning how to read stories, sentences, or phrases is assumed to lead to a perception of the parts and their relationship to the whole text and meaning.
- Repeated readings of authentic books of interest with help or independently are assumed to lead to an ability to read fluently with comprehension.
- Mistakes or miscues are seen as positive indicators of students' willingness to take risks.
- Having a large oral language base gives students access to printed language.
- Comprehending texts provides access to new vocabulary words and increased insights into how the sound-symbol system works for decoding unknown words.

Whole-Word, Sight-Word, or Holistic Reading Instruction

- Reading instruction begins by engaging children in an abundance of stories and books read aloud to and with children.
- Instruction proceeds to demonstrate during the reading of various sizes and types of books how good readers sound when they read.
- Guessing the identity of a word based on the pictures, the meaning of the text, or the first letter clue (minimal cues) is encouraged so as to leave large amounts of attention capacity available for meaning or comprehending.
- Children are encouraged to learn many words by sight without further decoding or analysis. Using letter-sounds to unlock unknown words is seen as the strategy of last resort.
- Children are taught to read with patterned books and authentic children's literature stories to optimize the chance that children will have something to read of worth and something that will make sense. Controlling the language too strictly is viewed as having a detrimental effect on the comprehensibility of the language.
- Children practice reading a story again and again to internalize the language, structure, and meaning of stories. Analyzing story language too closely (sound-to-letter blending) is viewed as unnecessary to produce skilled, fluent readers.
- Control over the reading of the stories or books is gradually released from the teacher model to the children.
- Decoding ability is the product of language insights gained as children construct the meanings of a variety of texts and text patterns.

3.7. Do you see the connection between first comprehending the whole, whether it was a word, a sentence, or a text, and then interpreting the parts of the whole?

Before continuing this discussion of reading theories and reading instruction, we want to alert you to the fact that as a teacher you will probably experience these extreme theories of the reading process—bottom-up and top-down, and their attendant instructional practices (phonics first and whole-word/whole language). These extreme views have and continue to provoke heated debates, "reading wars," and political mandates. Whether it was the adoption of phonics-first reading instruction in the 1960s, 1970s, and 1980s or the turn to whole language from the 1980s into the 1990s, these extreme instructional approaches are never likely to be as effective as approaches in which these extremes are combined (Rayner et al., 2002). Attempts

Extreme bottom-up or top-down models of the reading process exclude elements of the reading process necessary for children to learn to read.

__Interactive theories__ of reading place an equal emphasis upon emphasis on the print or text and the reader's prior knowledge.

Interactive theories of reading are drawn from cognitive psychology and represent a combination of bottom-up and top-down theories.

to combine these theoretical extremes have resulted in *interactive theories* of the reading process.

Interactive Theories of the Reading Process: Resolving the Weaknesses and Combining the Strengths of Bottom-Up and Top-Down Reading Theories

As theorists came to better understand the reading process, it became clear that neither top-down nor bottom-up theories adequately explained the complexity of the reading process. As a consequence, **interactive reading theories** were created that combined the strengths of both top-down and bottom-up explanations of reading while minimizing weaknesses associated with either theory alone (see Figure 3.8).

Interactive theories of the reading process explain that readers apply what knowledge is needed to understand a text, while simultaneously decoding print. Put another way, readers must process an array of information sources from the print (context, clues, sentences, sounding out unknown words, etc.) and from their background knowledge to understand the author's message.

Interactive processing of print requires that readers take on what some reading experts call active and passive roles (J. L. Vacca et al., 1995). For example, if a reader possesses a great deal of prior knowledge or experience about spiders and the text is about spiders, then the reader will be more likely to use her knowledge about spiders and not need to focus much attention on the print. This kind of reader involvement is considered *active processing.* On the other hand, if readers know very

Figure 3.8 Interactive theories of the reading process

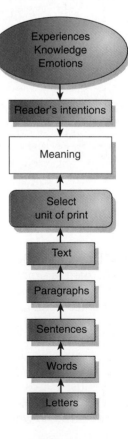

little about spiders, then they may take on a more *passive print processing* role—relying more heavily on the information on the printed page to understand the author's message.

To better demonstrate active and passive print processing, consider the following two examples. Many of us will have little or no trouble reading the first passage below about Cody's birthday surprise because we possess a good bit of prior knowledge of and experience with birthday parties. We are able to *actively* process the text and predict ahead of the print to move the reading process forward.

CODY'S BIG DAY

Today was Cody's birthday. He was 5 years old, big enough to go to kindergarten this fall. His mother had planned a sledding party up the canyon on the gently sloping foothills of the rugged mountains above. The sun shone brightly that day, and all the children had fun riding their sleds down the slopes. After the sledding party, Cody and his friends played games and opened presents. To top off the party, the boys and girls ate pizza, ice cream, and cake. That night Cody went to bed as happy as any little boy could be.

Now, read the next passage about syntactical structures in language. Because only a few people, linguists for example, know much about this topic, readers cannot predict ahead of the print and must depend more heavily on the print to understand the author's message. In this situation readers construct meaning *passively* by relying on the print to direct their selection of prior knowledge or experiences—if indeed the readers are able to understand the author's message at all. In some cases an author may assume too much prior knowledge, leaving too many gaps in necessary information for readers to construct meaning.

SYNTACTICAL STRUCTURES

. . . we must be careful not to exaggerate the extent to which a behavioral reinterpretation of intuition about form will clarify the situation. Thus suppose we found some behavioral test corresponding to the analysis of "John finished eating". . . . Or, to choose a more interesting case, suppose that we manage to develop some operational account of synonymy and significance. (N. Chomsky, 1975, p. 102)

Interactive theories of reading suggest that readers use what is necessary, either text information or background knowledge, to achieve the goal of making sense of text. Teachers who subscribe to interactive models of the reading process will probably adopt a *skills-based instructional approach* for teaching children to read.

Readers must integrate an array of information sources from the text and from their background to construct a valid interpretation of the author's message.

The Relationship of Interactive Theories of the Reading Process to Skills-Based Reading Instruction

Skills-based reading instruction includes three important instructional components: comprehension, vocabulary, and decoding. These components are important because skill-based teachers believe that children need to be given instruction that helps them activate and use their background knowledge, vocabulary, and experiences

*The **skills model** is composed of three major skill areas: comprehension, vocabulary, and decoding.*

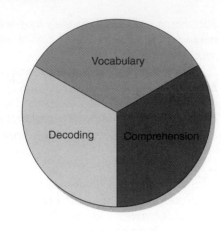

Figure 3.9 Skills-based reading instruction

to construct meaning or comprehend text along with applying decoding skills/strategies to figure out the pronunciation of unknown words.

Children are taught to use their background knowledge and remember new vocabulary words the teacher has just introduced, before reading a new story or text. After students finish reading and discussing a story, three separate skill lessons are taught—one each on comprehension, vocabulary, and decoding (see Figure 3.9, Weaver, 1988).

Notice that in skills-based reading instruction, decoding knowledge is not shown as the foundation of the reading instructional process as it was in the sub-skills or phonics-first instructional model, but rather as an equal part of the reading instructional process. This is because students are taught the skills of decoding text and text comprehension simultaneously. Children do not learn to decode and then learn to comprehend. Rather, in skills-based reading instruction, children are expected to integrate their knowledge of decoding and their background knowledge, vocabulary, and experiences as needed to construct the meaning from text.

Skills-based reading instruction has been one of the most commonly used approaches for providing reading instruction in schools. The reason for the popularity of skills-based reading instruction is related to the fact that the basal reader (i.e., reading textbooks) *teacher's editions* (TE) typically provide teachers with a carefully prescribed "script" to follow. Prior to reading a story, teachers are helped to activate students' background knowledge through discussion and pre-teach new vocabulary words. After reading a story, teachers are provided with skill or strategy lessons on vocabulary, comprehension, and decoding skills that children need to learn at each level of development.

In many basal reader teachers' editions (TE), the reading skills to be taught are found in a *scope and sequence chart.* The scope and sequence of reading skills is typically organized around three major components of reading instruction—decoding, comprehension, and vocabulary. Skills-based reading instruction treats the teaching of comprehension as a set of separate skills to be taught: such as predicting outcomes, getting the main idea, summarizing, understanding cause/effect, and so forth. The same can be said of the teaching of vocabulary and decoding skills. Each skill is to be learned one at a time and applied in a reading selection.

Several assumptions are associated with skills-based reading instruction. First, reading ability is achieved by learning a skill + a skill + a skill. Second, skills-based reading instruction is designed so that each of the language-cueing components—

After students read a story, three skill lessons are typically taught—one each on comprehension, vocabulary, and decoding.

The skills model treats comprehension as a set of discrete skills.

decoding, context, and meaning—is taught simultaneously with the other two categories of reading instruction. Third, each skill is usually taught in a self-contained lesson and must later be applied by the reader in a reading selection. Finally, readers must independently integrate, using all the skills taught in the three reading components of decoding, vocabulary, and comprehension.

In Figure 3.10, the connection between interactive theories and skills-based reading instruction is summarized. It is important to understand that interactive theories emphasize a blending of the elements of print (bottom-up) and the reader's knowledge and experiences (top-down). As such, interactive theories or explanations of the reading process influence skills-based teachers' instructional practices. Skills-based teachers place emphasis on developing reading skills by helping students use their prior knowledge, vocabulary, and experiences to comprehend text.

Texts for reading instruction are developed that (presumably) match students' backgrounds, speaking vocabulary, and world knowledge levels. The validity of this claim can be questionable in urban schools, however, since so many children come to our schools as English language learners (ELL). There is also an attempt to control text difficulty based on the number of words, size of words, and the length of sentences. Familiar and unfamiliar words are taught from a vocabulary list before reading each passage. Next, a *purpose* (reason) for reading the selection is discussed, such as "Let's read to find out why Charlotte the spider is trying to help her friend, the pig." Comprehension is checked after reading each selection, typically through a question and answer session with the students. The most notable practice in skills-based reading instruction is that after reading a story in the basal reader, three skill lessons are taught: (a) decoding, (b) vocabulary, and (c) comprehension. By examining interactive reading theories as shown in Figure 3.9, one can see the theory that equal emphasis on using background knowledge and the features of the print leads to skills-based reading instruction.

*Since **interactive theories** of reading emphasize a balanced emphasis on text and prior knowledge and skills instruction, notice how these influence the teaching of decoding, vocabulary, and comprehension skills.*

Transactional Theories of the Reading Process

Transactional theories of the reading process are an *elaboration of interactive theories.* **Transactional reading theories** include all of the beliefs found in interactive, but also factor in how a reader's knowledge and experiences can influence the way an author's message is understood. As with some of the recent cognition theories that take into consideration students' intentions when they read and how that can affect understanding (Kirshner & Whitson, 1997), transactional theories explain that reading comprehension can be altered by influences within the reader. Figure 3.11 shows how transactional theories contain the full interactive model, but it is embedded within the social and situational context of the reading event.

Transactional theories of the reading process originated with the early work of Dewey and Bentley (1949) and show us that the reader, the text, and the social or situational setting are linked during the reading event. You may think of the reading transaction in many ways, but perhaps it is best understood by using the metaphor of a real estate transaction.

Let us say two individuals meet in an attorney's office for the purpose of purchasing and selling a home. The seller cannot be present for the event, so she gives her real estate agent power of attorney to complete the transaction in her behalf. Each person brings the documents, papers, checks, and such necessary to complete the transaction. When the transaction is completed, neither individual's circumstance

***Transactional theories** of the reading process are an elaboration of interactive theories.*

Transactional theories of the reading process suggest that there is an interdependency between individuals and their environment.

Figure 3.10   Connecting interactive reading theories and skills-based reading instructional practices

Interactive Theories of the Reading

• During reading and learning to read, language is processed by balancing the features of the print with the reader's prior knowledge, culture, and background experiences.

• Learning to read is thought to be the *construction of meaning* through emphasizing information gained from the print and from the reader's prior knowledge.

• Learning to read is accomplished by placing a balanced emphasis on mastering three skill areas: decoding, vocabulary, and comprehension.

• Language stimuli for reading practice are carefully controlled to represent words that are familiar to the child's background and used frequently in the language.

• Mastery of the skill areas of reading, decoding, vocabulary, and comprehension is assumed to lead to competent understanding and performance of the whole act of reading.

• A balanced emphasis on isolated lessons in each of the three skill areas of decoding, vocabulary, and comprehension is assumed to be integrated by each learner.

• Integration of the three skill areas is assumed to enable skilled, independent reading.

• Correctness is expected, although varying interpretations for meaning based on background knowledge are accepted.

Skills Reading Instructional Approach

• Reading instruction focuses on three skill areas in isolated lessons: decoding, vocabulary, and comprehension.

• Instruction begins in all three areas:
  - Decoding: Learning the 26 letters and 44 sounds.
  - Vocabulary: Learning high-frequency sight words in lists, e.g., *the*, *and*, *me*, *look*, etc.
  - Comprehension: Listening to stories read aloud for the main idea, sequence, or details.

• Instruction continues in the three skill areas in connection with the introduction of simple stories in books called "pre-primers."
  - Decoding: Letter–sound associations learned along with some blending and the sounds letters represent in selected sight words.
  - Vocabulary: New high-frequency sight word lists are learned along with attention to new conceptual knowledge focused around word meaning categories.
  - Comprehension: Simple comprehension skills related to short stories in the teacher's edition focus on main ideas and noting details.

• Instruction progresses to the use of a student's anthology of stories (some use controlled text, some use literature-based stories) and instruction in the three skill areas continues throughout the elementary years.
  - Decoding: Prefixes, suffixes, context clues, etc.
  - Vocabulary: Unfamiliar words, multiple meaning words, word categories, synonyms, antonyms, etc.
  - Comprehension: Sequencing, literary devices, following directions, etc.

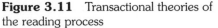

Figure 3.11 Transactional theories of the reading process

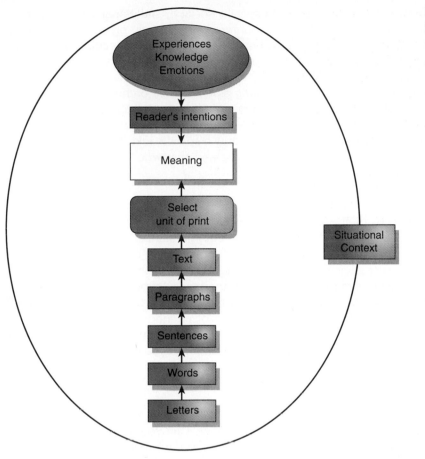

is the same as before. One is hopefully wealthier, or at least free from a mortgage obligation; the other is the proud owner of a piece of real estate. Furthermore, our real estate transaction is likely to occur in specific situations or places, such as a title company, attorney's office, or mortgage company—one would not expect to conduct a real estate transaction in a swimming pool or a bakery.

A reading transaction can be compared to this real estate transaction. Two people have agreed to come together to share a reading event. The author or writer cannot be present at the event, so she sends her representative—the text. The reader brings her life experiences, language background, and reading skills to make sense of the writer's text. Upon successful completion of the reading transaction, neither the reader nor the text is quite the same as before the event. The text delivered by the writer has been interpreted, reconstructed, and stored in the mind of the reader in a unique, personalized manner. In a way, the text is no longer an exact duplicate of the text sent by the author. The reader's knowledge structures and experiences have also been changed in the transaction. She is now the proud owner of a new piece of knowledge or experience because of the reading transaction. As a result, both the text and the reader's knowledge structures have been changed during the reading event.

Reading transactions also occur in specific social or situational settings. For example, in a kitchen the texts to be encountered are typically procedural text types such as lists, food ads, coupons, directions, or recipes. This specific situation, the kitchen, causes the reader to adopt a particular purpose and use appropriate strategies for reading kitchen-related texts.

Transactional theories of the reading process are well represented in Rosenblatt's transactional theory of the literary work.

L. Rosenblatt (1978) described reading as a carefully orchestrated relationship between reader and text in a social situation. Situational conditions, such as *time, location, mood, pressures, reasons, intents,* and *purposes* influence a reader's *stance* for selection of reading strategies when reading a specific text. Rosenblatt described two stances or purposes for reading—*efferent* and *aesthetic.*

Efferent Stance

*When readers focus their attention on information to be remembered and used from reading a text, they are taking an **efferent stance.***

When readers focus their attention on information to be gathered, retrieved, or remembered from reading a text, they take an efferent stance. For example, reading the driver's license manual in preparation for an upcoming driving examination exemplifies an efferent stance toward a text. Reading a novel for the purpose of writing a book report to summarize the plot is another example of taking an efferent stance toward a text. Also, when readers assume an efferent stance toward reading a novel as an assignment in school, the focus of attention is on remembering or gleaning information from the text to pass a test rather than reading for recreation. Obviously, then, there is a need to account for another type of *transactional stance* or motivation for reading a text—an aesthetic stance.

Aesthetic Stance

*Think of a time when you took an **aesthetic stance.** Can you recall the book and the emotions evoked as you read?*

Think of a time when you took an aesthetic stance. Can you recall the book and the emotions felt as you read? When reading aesthetically, the learner draws on past experiences, connects these experiences to the text, savors the beauty of the literary art form, and becomes a participant in the unfolding events of the text. For example, when a teacher reads Wilson Rawls's (1961) story, *Where the Red Fern Grows,* a feeling of reverence and sensitivity grows with the reading of the story. The teacher's voice may break a little bit toward the end of a read-aloud session, which deepens the emotions for the children. The listeners wonder how love could sacrifice itself so tenderly, so completely, and yet so sadly that a red fern would grow. When the teacher closes the book, there is silence in the room, and many eyes are filled with tears. This is the silence of reverent reflection—a silence in which readers ponder the significance of the experience they have had through reading.

Transactional theories hold that the social and situational context for reading influences the kinds of reading tasks to be completed. Context, or reasons for reading, influence the types of texts to be read, the purposes of the reader, and the strategies selected by to the reader (see Figure 3.11).

The Relationship of Transactional Theories of the Reading Process to Comprehensive Literacy Instruction

Transactional theories seem to best align with approaches to teaching known as **comprehensive literacy instruction.** The elements associated with comprehensive reading instruction have been carefully defined in several recently published and nationally disseminated reading research reports. Several of these reports are listed below:

- *Preventing Reading Difficulties in Young Children* (Snow, Burns, & Griffin, 1998).
- *Starting Out Right: A Guide for Promoting Children's Reading Success* (Burns, Griffin, & Snow, 1999).
- *Report of the National Reading Panel* (National Reading Panel, 2000).
- *Putting Reading First: The Research Building Blocks for Teaching Children to Read* (Armbruster, Lehr, & Osborn, 2001).
- *Every Child a Reader* (California Reading Task Force, 1998).

It is important to note that comprehensive reading instruction is firmly grounded in scientifically researched elements of effective reading instruction. Recommended teaching practices include, but are not limited to, the following (Reutzel & Cooter, 2003):

Transactional reading theories are best related to comprehensive literacy instruction.

Explicit, Direct, Systematic Instruction of
- Comprehension
- Phonemic Awareness
- Phonics
- Vocabulary
- Fluency

Comprehension Instruction
- Story Structure
- Self-Monitoring
- Prediction
- Clarifying
- Making Inferences
- Summarizing
- Activating Background Knowledge
- Text Structures
- Questioning (Self, Author, Differing Types)
- Imagery

Early Reading Instruction
- Oral Language Development
- Concepts of Print
- Letter Recognition and Production
- Phonemic Awareness
- Phonics
- Common Spelling Patterns
- High Frequency Sight Words

ESL and Bilingual Instruction
- If resources are available, teach reading in the first language

Book Reading and Literature Study
- Use discussion groups, i.e., book clubs, literature circles
- Read a variety of text types and genres
- Provide time and practice reading books
- Provide an independent reading program
- Establish a print-rich classroom
- Promote out-of-school reading programs

Quality Reading Instruction for All Grades
- Teach strategy lessons
- Design consistent, focused, and cohesive instruction
- Teach the purposes of reading and writing
- Read aloud to students
- Use guided reading, especially for younger children
- Give students oral feedback on decoding, meaning, and fluency of their reading

Writing Instruction
- Provide time for writing extended texts
- Teach children grammar, handwriting, spelling, and conventions
- Publish children's writing

Comprehensive literacy instruction focuses on helping children learn to read using essential components of instruction within a framework of reading and writing TO, WITH, and BY children.

Best practices for teaching reading cited in the national reading research reports are shown in Figure 3.12.

The success of comprehensive reading instruction is dependent upon the teacher's knowledge of these research-based practices *and* the ability to use them effectively with all children. Some teachers and researchers summarize the use of best

Figure 3.12   Best practices associated with comprehensive literacy instruction
Based on *The Foundations of Literacy* by D. Holdaway., Copyright © 1979 by D. Holdaway. Reprinted by permission of Scholastic Australia.

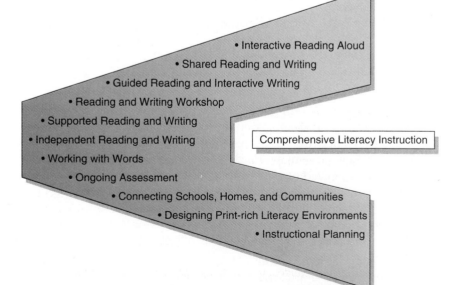

reading instructional practices using three prepositions—TO, WITH, and BY. Comprehensive reading instruction involves teachers and children in daily reading of texts where the teacher reads TO children, works WITH children individually and in groups, and provides time and proper conditions for reading practice BY children (Fountas & Pinnell, 1996; Mooney, 1990). A comprehensive reading program begins with a careful and ongoing assessment of each child's reading development. This assessment helps the teacher know where to begin to meet the diverse needs of each learner.

In comprehensive reading classrooms, teachers read aloud *to* and interact *with* children about books regularly, knowing that this helps them see, understand, and develop appropriate reading skills. The classroom environment is rich with print from the everyday lives and learning of the children. Learning activities are designed to provide stimulating opportunities for children to read and write for differing purposes and for children to experience a variety of text types and in a variety of purposes. Favorite storybooks are read and reread in a structured setting that supports children as they make sense of print with expert help and guidance from a skilled teacher.

Early in the process, children's attempts to make sense of print are often assisted with sensitive demonstrations and intentional, explicit skill or strategy instruction while reading a text in a whole class setting or in small reading groups. Direct, explicit, and systematic instruction is provided in the areas of phonemic awareness, concepts-of-print, letter identification, phonics, vocabulary, comprehension, and fluency. Reading skills are practiced and applied daily while reading a variety of texts.

Teachers who subscribe to comprehensive literacy instruction use a variety of reading materials such as decodable texts, pattern texts, leveled texts, stories, and information books. Children are taught to use reading skills and strategies in books carefully selected to present children with just the right amount of reading challenge. Guided reading instruction provides teachers with a structure with which to guide, teach, model, and assist children in developing and applying essential skills. Finally, children are provided with abundant reading materials and time to read personally selected, challenging, and varied reading materials.

Similar practices in writing are incorporated into comprehensive literacy programs. Teachers demonstrate and reveal to children the many ways in which writing can be used (Calkins, 1994; Graves, 1983): to tell the stories of our own lives, to organize and record ideas, to manage our time (or the time of others). Children are also helped to understand the form, features, and functions of the various writing styles. This is done via demonstrations of writing strategies during carefully planned writing activities. Children are shown how to use strategy/skill lessons in grammar, handwriting, punctuation, and spelling to improve their own writing. Children are given time to write each day. They are encouraged to keep notebooks, lists, and journals.

In summary, teachers implementing the elements of comprehensive reading instruction put transactional reading theory into practice by teaching reading and writing skills using a diversity of text types, for a variety of purposes, and in a variety of social and situational settings found in school and out. For example, comprehensive literacy teachers may design a science laboratory learning center complete with information books, materials for conducting experiments, lab manuals, directions, a computer for online research, experimenter's notebooks, etc. In this example, children learn to perform various reading and writing tasks, for the purposes scientists use literacy, in a specific place or situation in which the literacy occurs in a real world context.

The connection between transactional theories of the reading process and comprehensive reading instruction is shown in Figure 3.13.

Think of two ways in which transactional theories of the reading process connect with comprehensive literacy instruction.

Comprehensive literacy instruction attends to all of the components of effective literacy instruction as well as the context in which reading instruction takes place.

Figure 3.13 Connecting transactional theories of the reading process and comprehensive reading instructional practices.

Transactional Theories of the Reading Process

• During reading and learning to read, readers process language by constructing meaning using the print and their own experiences and knowledge as conditioned by their intentions, purposes, and the situational context.

• Learning to read is thought to be an event where a reader's response to a text is conditioned by sound-symbol, grammatical, and meaning cues appropriate to the print, the people, the physical environment, the cultural expectations of the situation, and each individual's experiences, knowledge, skills, and strategies for processing text.

• Reading materials should include a variety of types of books and levels to meet the needs of all children.

• Children approximate the demonstrations of fluent reading and writing with significant guidance from a competent, well-prepared teacher.

• Teachers and children carefully study reading materials to understand text structure, language patterns, challenges, tricky words, and other print features that may influence the ability to successfully process the print.

• Mistakes are expected in learning to read and are viewed as "risk taking" and indicators of progress among young children.

• Teacher demonstrations and modeling of fluent reading and writing are integral for children to learn how to construct meaning from print that is appropriate to the text and the situational context.

Comprehensive Reading Instructional Practices

• Instruction focuses on teaching children oral language, phonemic awareness, letter recognition and production, concepts-about-print, phonics, spelling, writing conventions, vocabulary, text comprehension, and fluency using a variety of text types and levels of challenge.

• Instruction in processing the print uses a whole-to-part-to-whole approach.

• Because instruction focuses on the end goal of constructing meaning, instructional activities are based on best practices substantiated in scientifically-based reading research such as interactive read aloud, shared reading, guided reading, independent reading, shared writing, interactive writing, guided writing, and independent writing.

• A print-rich, active, and well-organized classroom is considered to be an integral part of comprehensive reading instruction.

• Because oral language is considered the basis of all language learning, talking, discussing, and interacting about texts is integral to comprehensive reading instruction.

• Reading information trade books in science, social studies, math, art, etc., is a part of integrating comprehensive reading instruction with other curricular areas of study.

• Children receive guidance and opportunity on a regular basis to choose books and write for personal and authentic reasons.

• Classrooms are busy language-learning workshops filled with literacy tools, books, and print and lively interactions around these resources in a variety of learning centers and situations.

Transactional reading theories suggest that children learn to actively construct meaning from encounters with texts using their own experiences, along with information available on the printed page. Children are assisted in their learning by competent teachers providing explicit instruction on essential reading and writing skills. Teachers provide real stories and poems to be read; design learning centers and practice areas where children can try out their literacy skills in a variety of real-world situations; present exemplary models of reading and writing behaviors; offer sensitive and helpful guidance about how to apply reading skills and strategies; and create a learning environment and specific classroom situations that provide children with motivation to read and write.

Transitions in Reading Instruction Change Model

Because so many children are falling between the cracks and failing to become literate, especially in our urban schools, teachers often feel pressured to make the transition to comprehensive reading instruction almost overnight. Yet our research clearly suggests that transitions toward comprehensive reading instruction may take several years to accomplish.

The primary goal of using comprehensive reading instruction is to help all children become fluent readers in the early years. Once children learn to read fluently, teachers help them to expand and refine their literacy skills throughout their schooling. The *seven principles for comprehensive reading instruction* shown in Chapter 1 provide the framework for comprehensive literacy instructional programs.

> The **transitional instructional model** *is discussed in Chapter 1 and affirms that most teachers make professional growth and approximations over time toward implementation of comprehensive literacy instruction.*

1. Understand **language learning and literacy development**
2. **Assess learner needs** to plan appropriate instruction
3. Construct **well-organized and vibrant learning environments**
4. Implement comprehensive, **research-proven instruction**
5. Accommodate **learners with special needs**
6. Involve the **family, school, and community**
7. Show children how to **apply literacy skills** in all areas of study

Transitions begins with an understanding of (a) theory that leads to the development of an articulate definition of the reading process, and then to (b) an understanding of best practices in reading instruction. Developing this knowledge base helps teachers consistently select appropriate strategies to assess where students are in their reading development and choose teaching and learning activities targeted to specific student needs.

Along this transitions pathway, teachers often find elements within each of the various reading theories presented in this chapter with which they agree (Heymsfeld, 1989). That's fine. Comprehensive reading instruction, though a very clear and consistent perspective, is not an absolute, all-or-nothing model (Routman, 1988, 1996, Pressley, 2002). Rather, a transitions change model suggests that teachers are moving deliberately toward expertise in developing well-articulated, research-based, and comprehensive reading instructional practices.

Summary

A cursory survey of reading habits among the American population today revealed significant problems for teachers, children, families, and schools. Increasing numbers of young children are not learning to read on grade level by third-grade. Recent reports suggest that the achievement gap rather than narrowing is widening. Although not all indicators are negative, today's teachers need to understand that now, more than *ever*, the ability to read is necessary to survive and prosper in a rapidly progressing technological and information-oriented society and economy. The goal of producing able readers simply is not sufficient for today's schools.

For teachers to achieve the objectives associated with high-quality comprehensive reading instruction, they must study children and understand how they learn to understand and process printed language as discussed in Chapter 2. They must also clearly comprehend the way language is used by humans to communicate and learn. What is more, they must have a working knowledge of dominant reading theories and how these theories connect to or drive instructional decisions and classroom instructional practices. It is equally important to understand one's own beliefs about how children learn to read and how reading should be taught.

Check your understanding of chapter concepts by using the self assessment for Chapter 3 on our Companion Website at www.prenhall.com/ reutzel.

Concept Applications

In the Classroom

1. Conduct a poll in your college classes about the numbers of trade books (excluding college textbooks) read by each person in the last year. Then find out how much time each person spends reading narrative versus information texts. What proportion of the time is spent reading for information purposes?

2. After reading this chapter, write a brief description of how your current beliefs about teaching reading and writing have been changed. Then, as you read the remainder of the book, keep a log of information you learn that may cause you to further rethink your initial beliefs about reading instructional practices.

3. List the major assumptions and characteristics of the bottom-up, top-down, interactive, and transactional models of the reading process, and summarize each in writing.

4. List the major assumptions and characteristics of the four approaches to reading instruction—sub-skills or phonics first, whole word, sight word or holistic, skills-based, and comprehensive reading instruction—and summarize each in writing.

5. List three major connections between theories of the reading process and instructional practices used to teach reading in classrooms.

In the Field

1. Visit a kindergarten or first-grade classroom. Describe in detail how children are being engaged in learning to read and write. You may also be able to gather some writing samples to photocopy and return to the children. Make a list of the types of books you saw them reading. Which of the major models of the reading process best explains what you saw? Why?

2. Ask a teacher to tell you about his or her reading instructional beliefs. Visit the teacher's classroom, and determine if these beliefs are reflected in his or her classroom instruction. Describe what you saw and how it related to one of the four reading instructional approaches.

3. Visit children in several grade levels. Interview them using questions based on the *Burke Reading Interview* (Burke, 1987). Ask them:
   a. What is reading?
   b. Who do you think is a good reader in your class? Why?
   c. What would you do to teach someone how to read?
   d. How did you learn to read?
   e. What might you do to become a better reader?

   Record the responses for the different grade levels and compare. How do children's understandings of reading differ from grade to grade? Discuss your findings with a peer in your class. Did the two of you notice similar differences?

Recommended Readings

Armbruster, B. B., Lehr, F., & Osborn, J. (2001). *Put reading first: The research building blocks for teaching children to read.* Washington, DC: The Partnership for Reading—NIL, NICHHD, and U.S. Department of Education.

Birdshaw, D., Burns, S. Carlisle, J. F., Duke, N. K., Garcia, G. E., Hoffman, J.V. et al. (2001). *Teaching every child to read: Frequently asked questions.* Ann Arbor, MI: Center for the Improvement of Early Reading Achievement.

Blair, S. M. and Williams, K. A. (1999). *Balanced reading instruction: Achieving success with every child.* Newark, DE: International Reading Association.

Burns, M.S., Griffin, P., & Snow, C. E. (1999). *Starting out right: A guide to promoting children's reading success.* Washington, DC: National Academy Press.

Cooter, R. B. (Ed.) (2004). *Perspectives on rescuing urban literacy education: Spies, saboteurs, & saints.* Mahwah, NJ: Erlbaum.

Fielding, L., Kerr, N., & Rosier, P. (1998). *The 90% reading goal.* Kennewick, WA: The National Reading Foundation.

Fitzgerald, J. (1999). What is this thing called "balance"? *The Reading Teacher, 53*(2), 100–115.

Gambrell, L. B., Morrow, L. M., Neuman, S. B., and Pressley, M. (1999). *Best practices in literacy instruction.* New York: Guildford Press.

Pressley, M. (2002). *Reading instruction that works: The case for balanced teaching,* 2nd Ed. New York: Guildford Press.

Rayner, K., Foorman, B. R., Perfetti, C. A., Pesetsky, D., & Seidenberg, M. S. (2001). How psychological science informs the teaching of reading. *Psychological Science in the Public Interest, 1*(2), 31–74.

Rayner, K., Foorman, B. R., Perfetti, C. A., Pesetsky, D., & Seidenberg, M. S. (2002). How should reading be taught? *Scientific American,* (March), 85–91.

Reutzel, D. R, & Cooter, R. B. (2003). *Strategies for reading assessment and instruction: Helping every child succeed,* 2nd Ed. Upper Saddle River, NJ: Merrill/Prentice Hall.

Routman, R. (2003). *Reading essentials: The specifics you need to teach reading well.* Portsmouth, NH: Heinemann.

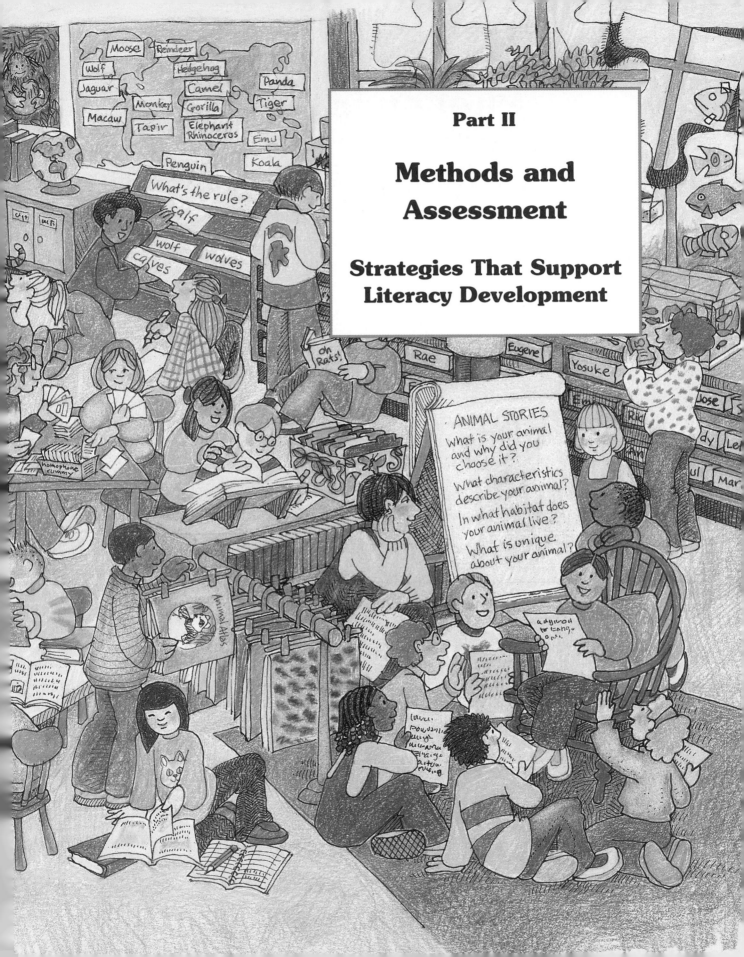

Part II

Methods and Assessment

Strategies That Support Literacy Development

chapter 4

Phonemic Awareness and Phonics Instruction

Focus Questions

When you are finished studying this chapter, you should be able to answer these questions:

1. Does instruction in *phonemic awareness* help children succeed in reading?

2. How is phonemic awareness (PA) developed in children? Why is PA such an important skill to be acquired?

3. What is the *alphabetic principle?*

4. Does phonics instruction improve reading achievement?

5. What is the value of teaching onsets and rimes?

6. What is meant by *structural analysis?*

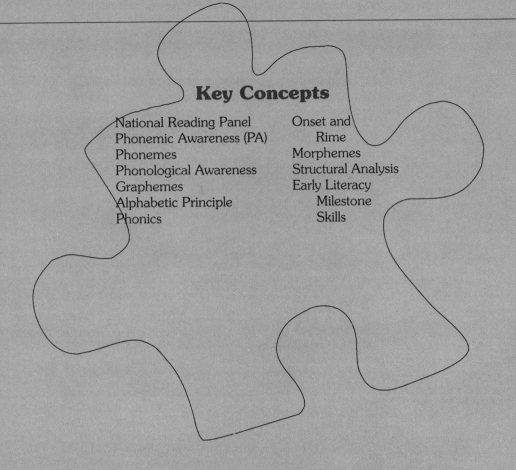

Key Concepts

National Reading Panel
Phonemic Awareness (PA)
Phonemes
Phonological Awareness
Graphemes
Alphabetic Principle
Phonics

Onset and
  Rime
Morphemes
Structural Analysis
Early Literacy
  Milestone
  Skills

In 1950s America, children loved to discover a "secret decoder ring" inside their Cracker Jack box. It was fun to think about encripting messages for others to discover and, even more thrilling, *decoding* secret communiqués from neighborhood friends. Without the secret decoder ring, though, you were locked out of all communications.

Teaching children to translate written symbols into words is foundational to reading. After many years of debate as to how this decoding process can best be developed, several new research reports were issued that brought a good bit of clarity to the field of reading education. At the heart of these studies were findings related to two specific areas: phonemic awareness and phonics.

Visit Chapter 4 of our Companion Website at www.prenhall.com/ reutzel to look into the chapter objectives, standards and principles, and pertinent web links associated with Phonemic Awareness and Phonics Instruction.

Nearly 100 years of research indicates that alphabet knowledge and phonemic awareness are the two best predictors of beginning reading success (Adams, 1990a).

Teaching children to translate written symbols into words is foundational to reading. After many years of debate on how this decoding process can best be developed, several new research reports have brought a good bit of clarity to the field of reading education. At the heart of these studies are findings related to two specific areas: phonemic awareness and phonics. In this chapter we summarize these findings and describe in some detail the specific skills that must be learned by young readers; what we sometimes refer to as the *"what"* of teaching. Later, in Chapter 11, we go into great detail as to *how* these skills can be taught in stimulating ways.

RESEARCH ON EARLY READING

Important research on beginning reading by Marilyn Jager Adams (1990a, 1990b), published in the 1990s, began a chain reaction in the field. Based on a review of nearly 100 years of reading research, Adams concluded that the two best predictors of beginning reading success are *alphabet knowledge* and *phonemic awareness* (i.e., the understanding that spoken words are made up of individual speech sounds). These findings contributed to a major swing in the reading education pendulum toward *evidenced-based* solutions to current reading issues. The *Report of the National Reading Panel* (2000) also had a major impact.

Report of the National Reading Panel

In 1997, the United States Congress asked the director of the National Institute of Child Health and Human Development (NICHD) and the Secretary of Education to convene a national panel to assess the status of research-based knowledge on reading instruction. The **National Reading Panel,** as it came to be known, issued its report in April 2000 (available free online at www.nationalreadingpanel.org).

The *Report of the National Reading Panel* included a call for improved classroom instruction in several key areas: *alphabetics* (phonemic awareness and phonics instruction), *fluency* (reading rate, accuracy, and intonation), *vocabulary knowledge,* and *text comprehension.* The panel found that effective teachers (a) understand how reading develops in each of these critical areas, (b) have the ability to quickly and efficiently assess each of their students to learn which skills are already known and which are still developing, and (c) use assessment information to plan instruction targeting student needs.

While some have challenged several of the findings of the report, few would question its impact on current policy at the national level and on related federally funded intiatives.

Other Scientific Research on Reading Instruction: Common Findings

In addition to the *Report of the National Reading Panel,* several other important research reports have appeared in recent years describing effective reading instruction. They include:

- Snow, C. E., Burns, M. S., and Griffin, P. (1998). *Preventing Reading Difficulties in Young Children.* Washington, DC: National Academy Press.

- American Federation of Teachers (1999). *Teaching Reading Is Rocket Science: What Expert Teachers of Reading Should Know and Be Able to Do.* Washington, DC: Author.
- National Education Association. (2000). *Report of the National Education Association's Task Force on Reading 2000.* Washington, DC: Author.
- California Reading Task Force. (1998). *Every Child a Reader.* Ann Arbor, MI: Center for the Improvement of Early Reading Achievement.
- Flippo, R. F. (2001). *Reading Researchers in Search of Common Ground.* Newark, DE: International Reading Association.

Reutzel and Cooter (2003) sorted the instructional and programmatic recommendations into categories in order to better understand the elements of a comprehensive reading program.

Following is a summary of essential skills and recommended classroom practices (where applicable) drawn from the research reports cited above (see Figure 4.1).

Teachers Make the Difference

There was one clear finding across all of the recent research reports—*In the end, it is teachers, not programs, that make the critical difference whether students achieve and succeed in reading.* Linda Darling-Hammond, executive director of the National Commission on Teaching and America's Future, in a report entitled *What Matters Most: Teaching for America's Future* (1996), concluded, "What teachers know and do is the most important influence on what students learn. Competent and

Figure 4.1 Evidenced-based reading skills and practices[*]

"Alphabetics" (Using Direct Instruction [DI] Methods)

   -**Phonemic awareness**

   -**Alphabetic Principle**

   -**Phonics**

Concepts of print (Grades EC–1; Direct Instruction [DI] methods)

Oral reading fluency (DI methods)

Independent reading practice (Structured "Buddy Reading")

Exposure to a variety of reading materials/genre

Comprehension strategies (DI methods)

Vocabulary (DI methods)

Oral language development (DI methods)

Spelling and word study (DI methods)

Interactive read aloud (Structured)

Technology-assisted reading instruction

Integrated reading, writing, and language instruction

Adequate time for daily reading/writing instruction and practice

[*]Note: These recommendations are *minimal* and do not speak to the many other needs of students, such as family involvement or adapting the curriculum to meet the needs of exceptional children.

caring teaching should be a student right." (p. 6) Likewise, nearly two decades ago the seminal report *Becoming a Nation of Readers* (Anderson, Scott, Hiebert, & Wilkinson, 1985) found that teacher ability was at least five times more important than the adoption of new published reading materials.

> An indisputable conclusion of research is that the quality of teaching makes a considerable difference in children's learning. Studies indicate that about 15 percent of the variation among children in reading achievement at the end of the school year is attributable to factors that relate to the skill and effectiveness of the teacher. In contrast, the largest study ever done comparing approaches to beginning reading found that about 3 percent of the variation in reading achievement at the end of first grade was attributable to the overall approach of the program." (Anderson et al., 1985, p. 85)

Optimal word-identification instruction requires a knowledgeable teacher with expertise in assessment to decide which children need which skills, grouping according to student needs, and best teaching strategies.

A more recent study, *Preventing Reading Difficulties in Young Children,* asserted a similar conclusion about the significant contribution of teacher competence to children's achievement in reading (Snow, Burns, & Griffin, 1998). The National Education Association's Task Force on Reading 2000 summarized this critical point well, "The teacher, not the method, makes the real difference in reading success." (2000, p. 7)

In other words, the solution for meeting the literacy needs of all children is a knowledgeable and skilled classroom teacher. To that end, in this chapter we review the most potent research currently available on helping students acquire word-identification skills, as well as ways of helping children acquire these important skills within a context of rich language and literature.

AN EVIDENCE-BASED SEQUENCE OF INSTRUCTION

One of the continuing challenges for practicing teachers is how to unravel and apply myriad research findings in reading to their classroom teaching. This task has been especially daunting of late in the areas of phonemic awareness, alphabetic principle, and phonics. We are frequently asked to define each of these terms and answer questions like these: Aren't phonics and phonemic awareness basically the same? (Answer: No.) Does it matter when you offer instruction in these three areas? (Answer: Yes!) Is it appropriate to teach all children phonemic awareness and phonics skills *every day* in grades K–2? (Answer: No, it is *not* appropriate. The *only* thing we recommend for *all* children is good oral hygiene!)

R. Cooter, D. R. Reutzel, and K. Cooter (1998) developed a simple instructional model to help teachers interpret the research on sequencing phonemic awareness, alphabetic principle, and phonics instruction. Figure 4.2 shows the development of children from the emergent reading stage toward fluent reading, at least in terms of word identification.

Notice the three developmental areas are depicted as a developmental staircase progressing from (a) the most basic level of **phonemic awareness** (an exclusively oral language activity), to (b) **alphabetic principle** development (matching elemental sounds and the letters that represent them), and ultimately to (c) **phonics** (decoding written symbols to speech sounds). This progression from exclusively speech/sound activities to eventually understanding how to decode symbols back to speech sounds is at the heart of recent breakthroughs in reading research.

Figure 4.2 Phonemic awareness, alphabetic principle, and phonics: Developmental and instructional progression

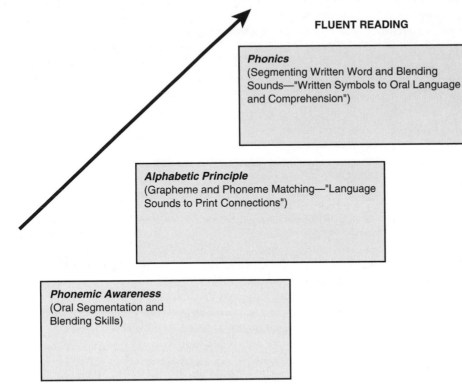

FLUENT READING

Phonics
(Segmenting Written Word and Blending Sounds—"Written Symbols to Oral Language and Comprehension")

Alphabetic Principle
(Grapheme and Phoneme Matching—"Language Sounds to Print Connections")

Phonemic Awareness
(Oral Segmentation and Blending Skills)

EMERGENT READING

From *Sequence of Development and Instruction for Phonemic Awareness* by R. B. Cooter. Jr., D. R. Reutzel, and K. S. Cooter, 1998, unpublished paper.

In the remainder of this chapter, we take a much closer look at phonemic awareness and phonics instruction.

PHONEMIC AWARENESS

An Anticipation Guide on Phonemic Awareness

To begin the study of this topic, please complete the anticipation guide (see Figure 4.3) to discover the extent of your own prior knowledge about phonemic awareness. After reading this section, you should complete the anticipation guide again to see if your opinions and understandings have changed. You may want to use this technique as a tool in future teaching situations as a kind of "action research" experiment.

*Complete the phonemic awareness "anticipation guide" **before** reading further, then retake the quiz **after** reading to see if your prereading assumptions were accurate.*

Research on Phonemic Awareness

Phonemic awareness (PA) refers to the understanding that spoken words are made up of individual speech sounds (Burns, Griffin, & Snow, 1999; Pikulski & Templeton, 1997). For example, "no" and "she" each have two speech sounds, or

Figure 4.3   Phonemic awareness

Anticipation Guide

Directions: Read each statement and decide if it is **TRUE** or **FALSE.** Write your response in column A. After reading this part of the chapter on Phonemic Awareness, reread the statements and respond in column B. Discuss the differences in your responses with a fellow student (or the instructor if you are taking a college course).

A		B
_____	1. At least 80% of all children require instruction in phonemic awareness in order to be successful in learning to read.	_____
_____	2. Phonemic awareness refers to a child's awareness of sounds that make up words.	_____
_____	3. Measures of phonemic awareness have been found to predict success in early reading as well as measures of intelligence, general language development, and listening comprehension.	_____
_____	4. Phonemic awareness has nothing to do with writing.	_____
_____	5. Children who are low in reading performance rarely score low in phonemic awareness.	_____
_____	6. Instruction in phonemic awareness alone is not enough to prevent and correct reading problems.	_____
_____	7. If children have acquired phonemic awareness then they also understand the alphabetic principle.	_____
_____	8. Individual sounds are easier to hear than syllables, so they should be taught first.	_____
_____	9. Phonemic awareness is the same thing as phonics.	_____
_____	10. Blending sounds to produce words is one of the easiest phonemic awareness skills.	_____
_____	11. Research indicates a particular sequence for teaching phonemic awareness.	_____
_____	12. Matching letters to the speech sounds they represent is an appropriate phonemic awareness activity.	_____

Standards Note
Standard 11.5: The reading professional will be able to interpret research finds related to the improvement of instruction and communicate these to colleagues and the wider community. After you read more on evidence-based practices, develop a concise, succinct jargon-free summary of "best practice" regarding letter-sound instruction for colleagues as well as a wider public audience.

Phonemic awareness refers to the understanding that spoken words are made up of individual sounds or **phonemes.**

phonemes. Phonemes are not the same as letters, by the way; letters *represent* phonemes in the spelling of words. Before children learn to read print, they need to become aware of how the sounds in words work and, as mentioned, that spoken words are made up of phonemes (Armbruster, Lehr, & Osborn, 2001; National Reading Panel, 2000).

When most children begin their schooling, they come equipped with a sizable vocabulary and a fairly well developed knowledge of syntax. However, many lack phonemic awareness. For instance, the word *dog* is known to many 4- and 5-year-olds only as a domestic animal that walks on four legs. They usually lack the awareness that *dog* is composed of three sound units or phonemes, /d/, /o/, and /g/.

Phonemic awareness is an important factor in beginning reading success, and in learning to spell (Lyon, 1997; National Reading Panel, 2000; Snow et al., 1998). About 20% of students lack phonemic awareness (Adams, 1990a), a problem that can be easily resolved through classroom instruction. Numerous studies have shown that while phonemic awareness is an important factor, it is not sufficient alone to ensure reading success (G.R. Lyon, 1997). Rather, instruction in phonemic awareness should be viewed as an important element of a comprehensive reading program in the early elementary grades.

Researchers have identified eight essential phonemic awareness abilities for students to acquire. Can you name them?

What Scientifically Based Research Tells Us About PA Instruction

In phonemic awareness instruction, teachers help children develop the ability to notice, think about, and work with the individual sounds in spoken words. Numerous studies have now confirmed the kinds of teaching activities that help children develop phonemic awareness. These types of activities will help those of your students who come to school without phonemic awareness fill in that gap and become better readers (Adams, 1990a; Blevins, 1997). Further, these activities will pave the way for all of your students to become better spellers (National Reading Panel, 2000). Here are the research-based categories for you to use in selecting teaching and learning activities:

- *Phoneme isolation*   Recognizing individual sounds in words.

    Teacher: What is the first sound in *boy?*
    Student: The first sound in *boy* is /b/.

- *Phoneme identity*   Hearing the same sound in different words.

    Teacher: What sound is the same in *boy, bake,* and *butter?*
    Student: The first sound /b/ is the same.

- *Phoneme categorization*   Recognizing a word having a different sound in a group of three or four words.

    Teacher: Which word doesn't belong? *Run, rake, toy.*
    Student: *Toy* doesn't belong because it begins with /t/.

- *Phoneme blending*   Children listen to phonemes spoken separately, then blend them together to form a word.

    Teacher: What is this word? /m/ /a/ /k/
    Student: /m/ /a/ /k/ is *make.*

- *Phoneme segmentation*   Breaking a spoken word into its separate phonemes while tapping or counting on their fingers each sound.

    Teacher: Say the sounds you hear in the word *cup* slowly.
    Student: cccccccc uhhhhhhhh pppppppp.
    Teacher: How many sounds did you count in *cup?*
    Student: *Cup* has three sounds.

- *Phoneme deletion*   Recognizing that a phoneme can be removed from a spoken word, and that part of the word remains.

    Teacher: If I take away the sound /b/ in the word *brook,* what word is left?
    Student: *Brook* without /b/ is *rook.*

- *Phoneme addition*   The ability to create a new word by adding a phoneme.

  Teacher: If I add the sound /s/ to the word *tree,* what new word would I have?
  Student: *Tree* with /s/ added to the end would be *trees.*

- *Phoneme substitution*   Exchanging a phoneme for one in a spoken word to create a new word.

  Teacher: The word is *run.* Change /n/ to /t/. What's the new word?
  Student: The new word is *rut.*

Some Misunderstandings About Phonemic Awareness

Phonics is not the same as phonemic awareness; on the contrary, it is the understanding that letters and letter combinations represent phonemes that can be blended to create spoken words.

One of the most common misunderstandings about phonemic awareness is that it is the same as *phonics.* It's not. As we learned earlier, phonemic awareness is the understanding that *spoken words* are made up of individual speech sounds called phonemes. Phonics, on the other hand, is the understanding that letters and letter combinations *represent* phonemes that can be blended to create spoken words (of course, words that are "sounded out" using phonics are not actually spoken when we read to ourselves, but you see what we mean).

One thing is certain: having children learn phonemic awareness will help them acquire phonics later on, as you will see later in this chapter. The reason is simple, really. When students are phonemically aware and can hear individual sounds (phonemes) in spoken words, then learning that alphabet letters or letter combinations *represent* these same speech sounds makes perfect sense—there is a one-to-one relationship between sounds and letters. The introduction of phonics becomes the next logical step in learning to read. Phonics knowledge helps children reverse the process and translate written symbols back into phonemes or speech sounds; hence, the age-old term "sounding out."

Phonological Awareness

Phonological awareness includes identifying and manipulating larger parts of spoken language, such as words, syllables, onsets and rimes, rhyming, and alliteration.

Another misunderstanding is the belief that phonological awareness and phonemic awareness are synonymous terms. Again, this is not so. Phonological awareness is a broader term that goes beyond simple awareness and manipulation of speech sounds; phonemic awareness is only one part of phonological awareness. **Phonological awareness** includes identifying and manipulating larger parts of spoken language such as words, syllables, onsets and rimes (discussed later in this chapter), rhyming, and alliteration (Armbruster et al., 2001; National Reading Panel, 2000).

As with phonemic awareness, children can demonstrate their phonological awareness in a number of ways (Armbruster et al., 2001), including

- *identifying and making rhymes orally*
  "Hickory, dickory **dock,**
  The mouse ran up the **clock.**"
- *identifying and working with syllables in spoken words*
  "I can tap out the sounds in *kindergarten:* **kin-der-gar-ten!**"
- *identifying and working with onsets and rimes in spoken syllables or one-syllable words.* Note: An *onset* is the part of a syllable that comes before the vowel; the *rime* is the rest (Adams, 1990b, p. 55).
  The first sound in *tall* is **/t/,**
  and the last part is **-all.**

Figure 4.4 Sequence of development and instruction for phonemic awareness

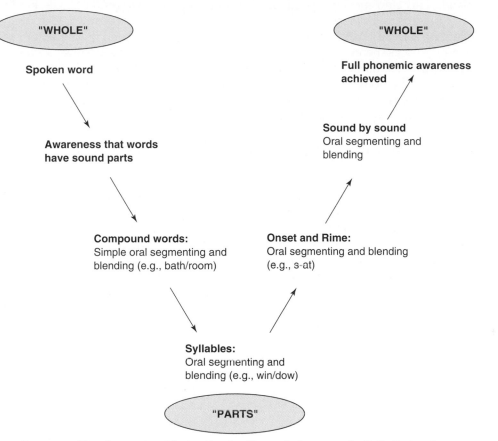

From *Sequence of Development and Instruction for Phonemic Awareness* by R. B. Cooter, Jr., D. R. Reutzel, and K. S. Cooter. 1998, unpublished paper.

- *identifying and working with individual phonemes in spoken words*
  The first sound in *dog* is **/d/.**

The Instructional Sequence for Phonemic Awareness

In all instruction, teachers should move from the simplest, most basic concepts toward the more complex. Figure 4.4 shows that the most basic starting point is helping students understand that spoken words are made up of individual speech sounds. Word stretching activities such as "word rubber banding" can help students begin to hear individual speech sounds or phonemes. Once this most basic level of awareness begins to emerge, teachers should help students begin to develop simple segmenting and blending skills using compound words. For example, children are able to catch on quickly that simple compound words like *airport, bloodhound, clothespin,* and *rainbow* are just two smaller words "glued" together. They can hear and segment the two spoken words easily! If the compound words are chosen so that each word part is a one-syllable word that carries a meaning students easily understand, both the sound and meaning connections can be understood at once by most students. Learning simple segmenting and blending with compound words is the first major jump into phonemic awareness.

Describe how "word rubber banding" activities can help students learn to hear speech sounds.

Phonemic awareness instruction tackles the segmenting and blending of simple compound words first.

Segmenting and blending syllables moves students into the realm of dividing words by sound units.

Syllables are the next speech sound unit for students to orally segment and blend. This step moves students from simply segmenting smaller words in compound words to dividing words by sound units that *seem* more abstract. Clapping or counting syllables heard in words like *window* and *kindergarten* helps them to segment sound elements (i.e., win-dow, kin-der-gar-ten). Blending activities such as: "I will say the first part of a word, then the rest of the word. Say the word as a whole. /sha/ . . . dow. What is the word? (*shadow*)" help students further develop phonemic awareness.

The next phonemic awareness level calls for segmenting and blending *onsets and rimes.* As noted earlier, an onset is the part of a syllable that comes before the vowel; the rime is the rest (Adams, 1990b, p. 55). For example, in the word *sat,* "s" is the onset and "-at" is the rime. Similarly, in the first syllable of the word *turtle,* "t" is the onset and "-ur" is the rime. This activity is easily done in the context of poetry (teaching rimes with *rhymes*).

Segmenting spoken words sound-by-sound is the next and most abstract level of phonemic awareness and is a necessary forerunner of letter-by-letter sounding out in phonics. The difference here is that we segment, then blend, individual *sounds* in spoken words. This final stage of phonemic awareness development helps children use phonemic segmentation and blending in more sophisticated and fun ways. Now your students will be ready for such activities as phonemic categorization, deletion, addition, and substitution tasks, described earlier.

Some Tips for Planning Instruction in Phonemic Awareness

What are some of the more important tips for planning phonemic awareness instruction offered by Blevins (1997)?

Blevins (1997, pp. 7–8) has summarized some useful points on phonemic awareness that are important for teachers in kindergarten through grade 2 to keep in mind as they plan for instruction.

- *Phonemic awareness is not related to print.* Oral and aural (listening) activities are what phonemic awareness teaching and learning are all about. Once children can name and identify the letters of the alphabet, they are ready to move into learning the *alphabetic principle.*
- *Many, if not most, poor readers in the early grades have weak phonemic awareness skills.* Thus, phonemic awareness may be an important issue (on a limited basis) for teachers well beyond the K–2 years. Indeed, phonemic awareness training may well be indicated throughout K–12 education for students considered "remedial" readers.
- *Model, model, model!* Children need to see their teacher and other students actually doing the phonemic awareness activities you offer.

Several other recommendations have been suggested (National Association for the Education of Young Children, 1986; Yopp, 1992) for the selection of phonemic awareness activities.

- *Learning activities should help foster positive feelings toward learning through an atmosphere of playfulness and fun.* Drill activities in phonemic awareness should be avoided, as should rote memorization.
- *Interaction among children should be encouraged through group activities.* Language play seems to be most effective in group settings.

- *Curiosity about language and experimentation should be encouraged.* Teachers should react positively when students engage in language manipulation.
- *Teachers should be prepared for wide differences in the acquisition of phonemic awareness.* Some children will catch on quickly, whereas others will take much longer. Teachers should avoid making quick judgments about children based on how they perform in phonemic awareness activities.

*REMINDER: Now that you have finished reading about phonemic awareness, go back and complete the **anticipation guide** in Figure 4.3.*

ALPHABETIC PRINCIPLE

A **grapheme** is the smallest part of *written* language that represents a phoneme in the spelling of a word. A grapheme may be just one letter, such as b, d, f, p, s, or several letters, such as ch, sh, th, -ck, ea, -igh (Armbruster et al., 2001, p. 4). When phonemic awareness is combined with letter-sound knowledge, students can attain a new level of understanding called the *alphabetic principle* (Byrne & Fielding-Barnsley, 1989).

The **alphabetic principle** is the knowledge that a specific letter or letter combination represent each of the speech sounds (phonemes). Discovery of the alphabetic principle is thought to be necessary for students to progress in their reading development, particularly in learning phonics. Thus, primary-level teachers actively seek out activities that help students learn (a) the alphabet letters and the sounds they represent, (b) that speech is made up of individual sounds that can be represented by specific letters and letter combinations, and (c) that the spellings of words remain generally constant across the various books or texts children encounter (i.e., the word *book* is written using the same letters every time you see it in print). In Chapter 11, we suggest a number of ways teachers can introduce the alphabetic principle to early readers.

*A **grapheme** is the smallest part of written language that represents a phoneme in the spelling of a word.*

__Alphabetic principle__ is the knowledge that a letter or letter combination represents each of the phonemes, or speech sounds.

How might the interaction among children develop their language skills?

The Phonics Quick Test*

1. For the word *sparkle,* it is divided between _____ and _____. The a̲ has an _____ controlled sound, and the e̲ _____.

2. In the word *small,* *sm-* is known as the *onset* and *-all* is known as the _____.

3. Ch̲ in the word *chair* is known as a _____.

4. The letter c̲ in the word *city* is a _____ sound, and in the word *cow* is a _____ sound.

5. The letters bl̲ in the word *blue* are referred to as a consonant _____.

6. The underlined vowels in the words *au̲thor, sprea̲d,* and *blue̲* are known as vowel _____.

7. The words *tag, run, cot,* and *get* have which vowel pattern? _____

8. The words *glide, take,* and *use* have the _____ vowel pattern.

9. The single most powerful phonics skill we can teach to emergent readers for decoding unfamiliar words in print is _____ sounds in words. We introduce this skill using consonant or vowel(?) (choose one) sounds because they are _____.

10. The word part *work* in the word *working* is known as a _____.

11. The word part *-ing* in the word *working* is known as a _____.

12. Cues to the meaning and pronunciation of unfamiliar words in print are often found in the print surrounding the unfamiliar—which is to say, in the _____.

*Answers to the *Phonics Quick Test* are found at the end of this chapter.

PHONICS INSTRUCTION IN COMPREHENSIVE READING CLASSROOMS

A Phonics Prereading Quiz

Surveys conducted by the International Reading Association (IRA) found that phonics is one of the most talked about subjects in the field of reading education (second only to comprehensive reading instruction). Reutzel and Cooter (2003) have developed a kind of phonics "quick test" so that you can see just how much you already know about the subject. Please complete the preceeding exercise *before* reading further. (The results may surprise you!) As with the anticipation guide on phonemic awareness, you may benefit from retaking the *Phonics Quick Test after* you have finished reading this section.

Phonics: What We Know from Research and Practice

Phonics instruction emphasizes how spellings are related to speech sounds in systematic and predictable ways.

Phonics instruction emphasizes how spellings are related to speech sounds in systematic and predictable ways (Burns & Snow, 1999; Reutzel & Cooter, 2003). Research confirms that systematic and explicit phonics instruction is more effective than non-systematic or programs that ignore phonics (National Reading Panel, 2000). When delivered as part of a comprehensive reading program—one that includes expansive vocabulary instruction, reading practice in great books, and writing development, all delivered by a skillful teacher—phonics instruction can help children become enthusiastic lifelong readers.

Marilyn Jager Adams (1990b), in her exhaustive review of phonics and other factors essential to word identification in *Beginning to Read: Thinking and Learning About Print,* found that approaches in which systematic code instruction was included with the reading of meaningful connected text resulted in superior reading achievement overall, for both low-readiness and better prepared students (p. 125). Adams also noted that these conclusions seem to hold true regardless of the instructional approach by which reading is taught. However, it should be noted that very few, if any, studies have been conducted comparing comprehensive reading strategies with more traditional skills instructional models—or even basal readers. Nevertheless, one cannot deny that there is a compelling need to include systematic phonics as an important part of a comprehensive reading program.

Approaches to Phonics Instruction

Several approaches to phonics instruction have found support in the research (National Reading Panel, 2000). These approaches are sometimes modified or combined in reading programs.

Synthetic Phonics Instruction—Traditional phonics instruction in which students learn how to change letters or letter combinations into speech sounds, then blend them together to form known words, i.e., sounding out.

Onset and Rime Instruction—Teaching students to recognize and pronounce the letter(s) coming before the vowel in a one-syllable word (onset) as well as the vowel and what goes with it (rime). For example, in the word *ran,* **r** is the onset and *-an* is the rime.

Analogy-Based Phonics—A variation of onset and rime instruction, this approach has students use their knowledge of word families to identify new words that have that same word part. For example, students learn to pronounce *light* by using their prior knowledge of the *-ight* rime from three words they already know—*right, might,* and *night.*

Analytic Phonics Instruction—A variation of the previous two approaches, students study previously learned whole words to discover letter-sound relationships. For example, *Stan, steam,* and *story* all include the **st** word element (*st* is known as a consonant blend).

Phonics Through Spelling—Students segment spoken words into phonemes and write letters that represent those sounds to create the word in print. For example, *rat* can be sounded out and written phonetically. This approach is often used as part of a *process writing* program.

Arguments *For* and *Against* Intensive Phonics Instruction

Those who support the use of intensive phonics instruction in beginning reading have traditionally cited several benefits of this practice (Chall, 1967; Flesch, 1955, 1981). One argument is that English spelling patterns are relatively consistent; therefore, phonics rules can aid the reader in approximating the pronunciation of unfamiliar words. As a result, phonics rules can assist the reader in triggering meaning for unfamiliar words if they are in the reader's listening and speaking vocabulary. It is felt that when phonics rules are applied in conjunction with semantic

Standards Note
Standard 6.2: The reading professional will be able to use phonics to teach students to use their knowledge of letter/sound correspondence to identify sounds in the construction of meaning. Juel, Biancarosa, Cohen, and Deffes (2003) espouse *anchored word instruction,* so that children are taught letter-sound knowledge and vocabulary meaning. They state, however, that current visitations found most teachers focusing on phonological awareness and decoding skills without attention to meaning. Where do you stand? Are you over-correcting? Can we have it both ways?

List some approaches to phonics instruction.

(meaning) and syntactic (grammar) cues in the passage, the reader can positively identify unknown words in most elementary-level reading materials.

Those opposing intensive phonics instruction cite a number of justifications for their position as well. The chief complaint is that the English language is *not* all that regular and that phonics generalizations often have many exceptions (A. J. Harris & Sipay, 1990). Focusing on ambiguous details in words, to the exclusion of such comprehension-based strategies as using context clues, can cause some children to miss appropriate meaning and word clues.

Another problem with overreliance on phonics cues is the time factor for processing the author's message. When engaged in the act of reading, the reader stores the author's message—as represented by each word, sentence, and paragraph—in the reader's short-term memory. As thoughts are constructed from the text, they are processed and become part of long-term memory. If a reader who encounters an unknown word spends too much time trying to figure out the identity of a single word, then she risks forgetting (or losing from short-term memory) that earlier part of the message already processed. That is why many teachers tell children to "skip" unknown words and let the context of the passage "do the work for them." When considering how many phonics rules and generalizations exist, it is not hard to see why some teachers feel that overreliance on phonic analysis, to the exclusion of context, is not helpful to emerging readers.

Another criticism of heavy skill-and-drill phonics programs has to do with what are known as *decodable texts*. Decodable texts offer children only those words that they have been taught the phonics skills to sound out. Richard Allington (1997), in an amusing research-proven commentary, described his objections to decodable texts this way:

> The decodable texts displayed at the recent meeting of the International Reading Association reminded me of nothing so much as the 1960s' "Nan can fan Dan" and "Nat the rat" readers.
>
> I submit that there is not a single well-designed study that supports the exclusive use of decodable texts in beginning reading (or remedial instruction). . . . There *is* research support for providing children with "manageable" texts—texts they can read without too much difficulty. (p. 15)

Other studies have indicated that decodable texts are not more effective teaching beginners to read than other kinds of texts (Hiebert, 1999). Thus, the question of which type of text is best for beginning readers seems to be somewhat open. We suggest you use some decodable texts along with high-quality children's books for a comprehensive approach. Selections for early readers should include simple predictable texts, nonfiction texts, decodable texts, easy readers, and authentic literature (Brown, 2000).

The question in building a comprehensive reading program is not whether one should teach phonics strategies. Rather, we need to ask *which phonics skills should be taught* and *how we should teach them*. The next section partially answers the "which phonics skills" question.

List some problems with using phonics instruction.

Scope and sequence guides help coordinate instruction across states, which can be especially helpful in maintaining continuity for highly mobile students.

Some Important Phonics Generalizations to Teach

Most states and local school districts have developed their own "scope and sequence" guides to help teachers know which reading skills should be taught at each grade level. The primary value of these scope and sequence guides is that they help coordinate instruction across the state, which can be especially helpful in maintaining continuity in learning for highly mobile students. Texas, California, Mississippi, Kansas, and Oklahoma are just a few of the states that have developed their own curriculum guides. Eventually, there is likely to be a national curriculum detailing the essential knowledge and skills to be learned by students at each grade level.

Following are a few research-proven phonics skills that seem to be included in virtually all curriculum guides.

Beginning Consonant Sounds in Words

Arguably the single most efficient phonics generalization to teach is *beginning consonant sounds in words.* When used in conjunction with context clues and the readers background knowledge, beginning consonant sounds can help students identify up to 90% of words typically found in elementary reading materials through grade 2 or grade 3. This is because consonant sounds tend to be the most constant or reliable, as compared to vowels, which account for much (but not all) of the variance in English.

The C Rule

The letter *c* is an irregular consonant letter that has no phoneme of its own. Instead, it assumes two other phonemes found in different words, *k* and *s*. In general, when the letter *c* is followed by *a, o,* or *u,* it will represent the sound we associate with the letter *k,* also known as the *hard c* sound. Some examples are the words *cake, cosmic,* and *cute.*

On the other hand, the letter *c* can sometimes represent the sound associated with the letter *s*. This is referred to as the *soft c* sound. The *soft c* sound is usually produced when *c* is followed by *e, i,* or *y*. Examples of the *soft c* sound are found in the words *celebrate, circus,* and *cycle.*

The G Rule

G is the key symbol for the phoneme we hear in the word *get* (Hull, 1989, p. 35). It is also irregular, having a *soft* and a *hard g* sound. The rules remain the same as they are for the letter *c*. When *g* is followed by the letters *e, i,* or *y,* it represents a *soft g* or *j* sound, as with the words *gently, giraffe,* and *gym.* If *g* is followed by the letters *a, o,* or *u,* then it usually represents the *hard* or regular sound as with the words *garden, go,* and *sugar.*

The CVC Generalization

When a vowel comes between two consonants, it usually has the short vowel sound. Examples of words following the CVC pattern include *sat, ran, let, pen, win, fit, hot, mop, sun,* and *cut.*

Vowel Digraphs

When two vowels come together in a word, the first vowel is usually long and the second vowel silent. This occurs especially often with the *oa, ee,* and *ay* combinations. Some examples are *toad, fleet,* and *day.* A common slogan used by teachers, which helps children remember this generalization, is "when two vowels go walking, the first one does the talking."

You will find a Safety Net Lesson for struggling readers on Short Vowel Sounds and the CVC Pattern in Chapter 4 on the Companion Website at www.prenhall.com/ reutzel.

The VCE (Final E) Generalization

When two vowels appear in a word and one is an *e* at the end of the word, the first vowel is generally long and the final *e* is silent. Examples include *cape, rope,* and *kite.*

The CV Generalization

When a consonant is followed by a vowel, the vowel usually produces a long sound. This is especially easy to see in two-letter words such as *be, go,* and *so.*

R-Controlled Vowels

Vowels that appear before the letter *r* are usually neither long nor short but tend to be overpowered or "swallowed up" by the sound. Examples include *person, player, neighborhood,* and *herself.*

Other Important Phonics Terms and Skills

Even though the phonics generalizations seem to be the most useful, most basal reading programs focus attention on many others. Following are several more terms, definitions, and examples of other phonics skills related to consonants and vowels not already discussed in this chapter.

- *Consonant digraphs*—Two consonants together in a word that produce only one speech sound *(th, sh, ng).*
- *Consonant blends or clusters*—Two or more consonants coming together in which the speech sounds of all the consonants may be heard *(bl, fr, sk, spl).* Vowels
- *Vowel digraphs*—Two vowels together in a word that produce only one speech sound *(ou, oo, ie, ai)*
- *Schwa*—Vowel letters that produce the *uh* sound (*a* in *America*). The schwa is represented by the upside-down *e* symbol: ə
- *Diphthongs*—Two vowels together in a word that produce a single, glided sound *(oi* in oi*l, oy* in *boy).*

Onset and Rime

Onset *is the part of the syllable that comes before the vowel.*

Rime *is the part of the syllable that starts with the vowel.*

Adams (1990b) notes that linguistic researchers have proposed an instructionally useful alternative form of word analysis known as *onsets* and *rimes.* As was pointed out earlier, an **onset** is the part of the syllable that comes before the vowel; the **rime** is the rest (Adams, 1990b, p. 55). Although all syllables must have a rime, not all will have an onset. The following list gives a few examples of onsets and rimes in words:

Word	Onset	Rime
A	—	A
in	—	in
aft	—	aft
sat	s-	-at
trim	tr-	-im
spring	spr-	-ing

One may wonder what the usefulness of onset and rime is in the classroom, at least as far as word identification instruction is concerned. First, some evidence indicates that children are better able to identify the spelling of whole rimes than of individual vowel sounds (Adams, 1990b; Barton, Miller, & Macken, 1980; Blevins, 1997; Mustafa, 1997; Treiman, 1985). Second, children as young as 5 and 6 years of age can transfer what they know about the pronunciation of one word to another that has the same rime, such as *call* and *ball* (Adams, 1990b). Third, although many traditional phonics generalizations with vowels are very unstable, even irregular phonics patterns seem to remain stable within rimes. For example, the *ea* vowel digraph is quite consistent within rimes, with the exceptions of *-ear* in *hear* compared to *bear*, and *-ead* in *bead* compared to *head* (Adams, 1990b). Finally, there appears to be some utility in children learning rimes. Nearly 500 primary-level words can be derived through the following set of only 37 rimes (Adams, 1990b; Blachman, 1984):

-ack	-at	-ide	-ock
-ain	-ate	-ight	-oke
-ake	-aw	-ill	-op
-ale	-ay	-in	-or
-all	-eat	-ine	-ore
-ame	-ell	-ing	-uck
-an	-est	-ink	-ug
-ank	-ice	-ip	-ump
-ap	-ick	-ir	-unk
-ash			

The application of onset and rime to reading and word identification seems obvious. Students should find it easier to identify new words in print by locating familiar rimes and using the sound clue along with context to make accurate guesses as to the words' pronunciation. Spelling efficiency may also increase as rimes are matched with onsets to construct "invented" spellings (we prefer to call them "temporary" spellings so that children and parents understand that we intend to develop correct spellings).

One teacher recently remarked that the easiest way to teach rimes is through *rhymes!* She was exactly right. Children learn many otherwise laborious tasks through rhymes, songs, chants, and raps. Any of these that use rhyming words can be very useful to teachers. For example, a teacher may wish to use an excerpt like the one shown below from the book *Taxi Dog* by Debra and Sal Barracca to emphasize the *-ide* and *-ill* rimes. The rimes are noted in bold type for easy identification by the reader.

Rhymes, songs, and raps are fun ways to teach onsets and rimes.

> It's just like a dream,
> Me and Jim—we're a team!
> I'm always there at his s**ide**.
> We never stand st**ill**,
> Every day's a new thr**ill**—
> Come join us next time for a r**ide**! (1990, p. 30)

Structural Analysis: An Important Next Step

Another way readers decode unfamiliar words in print is called *structural analysis.* Rather than attacking words on the letter-phoneme level, this kind of word identification uses a reader's knowledge of meaning "chunks" in words. Here's how it works. A reader encounters a word that is unknown to him in print (that is, the word is known

Structural analysis uses a reader's knowledge of meaning "chunks" in words to identify familiar elements.

As children become more proficient using word-identification strategies and context clues, they become more confident in "attacking" unknown words in print.

Comprehending pre-fixes, suffixes, and root words is a structural analysis skill.

to him when he hears it, just not familiar in print)—let's say the word is *unbelievable*. Our reader in this example has heard the word part *believe* dozens of times in con-versations and seen it in print (e.g., in sentences like, "Yes, I believe you," or "I believe that all children should have a nice birthday party."), and immediately recognizes it. The prefix *un-* is likewise very familiar to the reader from other words he has learned, such as *untie, unreal,* and *unhook.* He is able to infer from his prior knowledge of words that *un-* means something like "not" or "to reverse." Finally, the reader's mind focuses briefly on the suffix (and word), *-able,* and its obvious meaning also deduced from his prior knowledge of words like *workable*. In our example, then, the reader has found a new way of decoding words at something larger than the sound-symbol level. He progressed from the root word (**believe**), to the prefix (**un-**), to the suffix (**-able**). Furthermore, it was the meaning of these word parts that led to successful de-coding. Structural analysis takes phonological awareness to a new and higher level.

How Structural Analysis Works

__Morphemes__ are the basic meaning unit of words.

The two classes of mor-phemes are __bound__ and __free.__

Words are made up of basic meaning units known as **morphemes.** Morphemes may be divided into two classes—*bound* and *free. Bound morphemes* must be attached to a *root word* (sometimes called a *base word*) to have meaning. Prefixes and suf-fixes are *bound* morphemes (e.g., *pre-, un-, dis-, en-, inter-, extra-, -ed, -ies, -er,*

-*ing*). *Free* morphemes *(base words* or *root words)* are meaning units that can stand alone and have meaning. The word *replay* has both a bound and free morpheme: *re-,* the bound morpheme (prefix) meaning "again," and *play,* the free morpheme that has meaning on its own. Sometimes two free morphemes combine to form a new compound word, such as dog*house,* out*doors,* play*ground,* and to*night.* Studying words to identify familiar word elements is known as **structural analysis.**

Teachers can help children begin to practice structural analysis in the same ways as for onset and rime. The idea to get across to students is that whenever a good reader comes to a word she cannot identify through context and phonics alone, she sometimes looks within the word for a recognizable base (root) word and its accompanying prefix, suffix, or endings (Durkin, 1989; Lass & Davis, 1985). In other words, we are telling our students to "look for something you know within the word."

The following selected examples of affixes are adapted from *The Reading Teacher's Book of Lists* (Fry, Polk, & Fountoukidis, 1984).

Prefixes

Prefix	Meaning	Example	Prefix	Meaning	Example
intro-	inside	introduce	ad-	to, toward	adhere
pro-	forward	project	para-	beside, by	paraphrase
post-	after	postdate	pre-	before	predate
sub-	under	submarine	per-	throughout	pervade
ultra-	beyond	ultramodern	ab-	from	abnormal
dis-	opposite	disagree	trans-	across	transatlantic

Suffixes

Suffix	Meaning	Example	Suffix	Meaning	Example(s)
-ant	one who	servant	-ee	object of action	payee
-ist	one who practices	pianist	-ary	place for	library
-ence	state/quality of	violence	-ity	state/quality of	necessity
-ism	state/quality of	baptism	-ette	small	dinette
-s, -es	plural	cars	-ard	one who	coward
-kin	small	napkin	-ing	material	roofing

Standards Note
Standard 6.1: The reading professional will be able to teach students to monitor their own word identification through the use of syntactic, semantic, and grapho-phonic relations. This chapter focuses on one of the three major cueing systems. After reading, prepare notes on how you'd teach children to best self-monitor word identification. Be specific as to what they'll need to do at the word level when repair strategies are needed.

Putting It All Together: A Sequence of Word Identification Skills

Based on the research summarized thus far in this chapter, it is now possible for us to suggest a general listing of *early literacy skills* that directly relate to word identification. This sequence of *early literacy milestone skills* (see Figure 4.5) proceeds from emergent levels of phonemic awareness through phonics and other decoding skills. Children who become proficient in these abilities and practice them regularly in pleasurable reading will attain a high degree of fluency.

Summary

Recent research has confirmed the necessity of teaching children phonemic awareness, the alphabetic principle, and phonics skills explicitly. In this chapter we have described a research-supported sequence for teaching phonemic awareness skills, moving from a simple understanding that spoken words are made up of sound parts to the most abstract level of sound by sound segmentation, blending, and

Figure 4.5 Early literacy milestone skills

Stage 1:   Phonemic Awareness
Simple awareness that spoken words have individual sound parts
Compound words: simple oral segmenting and blending
Syllables: oral segmenting and blending
Onset and rime: oral segmenting and blending
Individual sound by sound: oral segmenting and blending
Advanced phonemic awareness skills: oddity tasks and sound
     manipulation

Stage 2:   Alphabetic Principle
Alphabet learning
Sound/symbol associations (awareness of phoneme/grapheme
     relationships)

Stage 3:   Reading: Phonics and Decoding Strategies Development*
Context clues (as a meaning-based word attack strategy)
Context clues plus the structural analysis skills
• compound words (segmenting and blending)
• syllabication (segmenting and blending)
• onset and rime (segmenting and blending)
Context clues plus letter-by-letter analysis (segmenting and blending)
• beginning sounds in words, plus . . .
• ending sounds in words, plus . . .
• medial sounds in words

*Note: Ways of assessing whether students have reached these and other literacy milestones
are discussed in Chapter 9, Assessing Literacy Learning.

sound manipulation. As competence in phonemic awareness is reached, students are helped to gain an understanding that the sounds in spoken words can be symbolically represented by letters (alphabetic principle). This level of understanding brings students to the point of development where they are ready to acquire basic phonics skills.

After basic phonics skills have been learned, readers are ready to learn an even higher level of word identification called structural analysis. Here the reader uses his prior knowledge of word parts and their meaning to both pronounce and understand unfamiliar words in print. Thus, a great deal of this chapter presented a practical sequence of instruction leading to fluent level word identification. In later chapters we present research-proven strategies teachers can use to teach each of these important reading skills.

Check your understanding of chapter concepts by using the self assessment for Chapter 4 on our Companion Website at www.prenhall.com/reutzel.

Concept Applications

In the Classroom

1. Using the information summarized on the National Reading Panel findings, develop an informal test you can use with kindergarteners to assess their current phonemic awareness abilities. It should include activities in each of the following areas:

• Phoneme isolation
• Phoneme identity

The Phonics Quick Test Answer Key

1. The word *sparkle* is divided between r and k. The *a* has an r-controlled sound, and the *e* is silent.

2. In the word *small*, sm- is known as the "onset" and -*all* is known as the rime. (See Chapter 8 for a full explanation.)

3. *Ch* in the word *chair* is known as a consonant digraph.

4. The letter *c* in the word *city* is a soft sound, and in the word *cow* it is a hard sound.

5. The letters *bl* in the word *blue* are referred to as a consonant blend.

6. The underlined vowels in the words *author*, *spread*, and *blue* are known as vowel digraphs.

7. The words *tag, run, cot,* and *get* have which vowel pattern? Consonant — vowel — consonant (CVC)

8. The words *glide, take,* and *use* have the vowel — consonant — "e" vowel pattern.

9. The single most powerful phonics skill we can teach to emergent readers for decoding unfamiliar words in print is beginning sounds in words. We introduce this skill using consonant sounds first because they are the most constant (or "dependable" or "reliable').

10. The word part "work" in the word *working* is known as a root (for " base" or "unbound morpheme") word.

11. The word part "-*ing*" in the word *working* is known as a suffix (for "bound morpheme").

12. Cues to the meaning and pronunciation of unfamiliar words in print are often found in the print surrounding the unfamiliar—which is to say, in the context.

Grading Key for Teachers

Number correct	Evaluation
12	Wow, you're good! (You must have had no social life in college.)
10–11	Not too bad, but you may need a brush-up (i.e., read this chapter).
7–9	Emergency! Take a refresher course, quick (i.e., read this chapter)!
0–6	Have you ever considered a career in telemarketing?! (Just kidding, but read this chapter . . . right away!)

- Phoneme categorization
- Phoneme blending
- Phoneme segmentation
- Phoneme deletion
- Phoneme addition
- Phoneme substitution

2. Conduct a library and Internet search for books that could be used to help you introduce the *alphabetic principle* to emergent readers. After locating and reading each, prepare an annotated bibliography to share with a group of your colleagues in class. If at least five persons share their annotated bibliographies, you will each have a marvelous resource for your future teaching.

3. Go online and find the Web page for your state's education department. Locate and print out the scope and sequence of recommended skills in

the areas of phonemic awareness, the alphabetic principle, and phonics. Compare this list to the curriculum guide from the school district in which you plan to have your internship (student teaching). Prepare a "Comprehensive Decoding Checklist" to use in profiling each child's decoding abilities. This will be useful to you later when we discuss reading assessment. More importantly, you have created a valuable tool to inform your teaching.

In the Field

1. Using one of the recommended resources below, develop and teach to a small group of children several lessons for the following phonemic awareness skills:
   - Simple oral segmenting and blending of compound words
   - Oral segmenting and blending of syllables
   - Oral segmenting and blending of onsets and rimes
   - Sound-by-sound oral segmenting and blending

2. Now, take advantage of the work you accomplished in Activities #1 and #3 of the In the Classroom section above. Arrange to work one-on-one with several emergent readers in kindergarten or grade 1. Administer the informal assessment you created for Activity #1 to determine each child's level of phonemic awareness. Then, using the Comprehensive Decoding Checklist you created for Activity #3, chart each student individually using your findings. Share your results with the cooperating classroom teacher who has these students in her room to see to what extent your findings are in agreement with her perceptions. (Note: Remember that the classroom teacher has spent much more time with these children and may have some different perceptions. Sometimes it's a bit like comparing a snapshot with a color movie—the teacher's is a much more comprehensive viewpoint.)

Classroom Resources for Teachers

Blevins, W. (1997). *Phonemic awareness activities for early reading success.* New York: Scholastic.

Blevins, W. (1998). *Phonics from A to Z.* New York: Scholastic.

Fox, B. J., & Hull, M. A. (2002). *Phonics for the teacher of reading,* 8th Ed. Upper Saddle River, NJ: Merrill/Prentice Hall.

Fry, E. B., Kress, J. E., & Fountoukidis, D. (2000). *The reading teacher's book of lists.* New York: Jossey-Bass.

Reutzel, D. R., & Cooter, R. B. (2003). *Strategies for reading assessment and instruction: Helping every child succeed,* 2nd Ed. Upper Saddle River, NJ: Merrill/Prentice Hall.

Texas Education Agency. (2003–2004). *Texas primary reading inventory* (TPRI). Austin, TX: Author. Available online, in both English and Spanish, on the Web site for the Texas Education Agency: Reading Initiative at **http://www.tea.state.tx.us/reading/**.

Wilson, R. M., Hall, M. A., Leu, D. J., & Kinzer, C. K. (2001). *Phonics, phonemic awareness, and word analysis for teachers: An interactive tutorial,* 7th Ed. Upper Saddle River, NJ: Merrill/Prentice Hall.

Recommended Readings

American Federation of Teachers. (1999). *Teaching reading is rocket science: What expert teachers of reading should know and be able to do.* Washington, DC: Author.

Armbruster, B. B., Lehr, F., & Osborn, J. (2001). *Put reading first: The research building blocks of teaching children to read.* Jessup, MD: National Institute for Literacy.

Brown, K. J. (2000). What kind of text—For whom and when? Textual scaffolding for beginning readers. *The Reading Teacher, 53*(4), 292–307.

Burns, M. S., Griffin, P., & Snow, C. E. (1999). *Starting out right: A guide to promoting children's reading success.* Washington, DC: National Academy Press.

California Reading Task Force. (1998). *Every child a reader.* Ann Arbor, MI: Center for the Improvement of Early Reading Achievement.

Flippo, R. F. (2001). *Reading researchers in search of common ground.* Newark, DE: International Reading Association.

National Reading Panel. (2000). *Report of the National Reading Panel: Teaching children to read.* Washington, DC: National Institute of Child Health and Human Development. Available online at: **www.nationalreadingpanel.org**.

Snow, C. E., Burns, M. S., and Griffin, P. (1998). *Preventing reading difficulties in young children.* Washington, DC: National Academy Press.

chapter 5

Increasing Vocabulary and Word Knowledge

Focus Questions

When you are finished studying this chapter, you should be able to answer these questions:

1. What are the four acquired vocabularies?

2. What are the three levels of vocabulary learning?

3. What are the "evidence-based" principles of scientific research on vocabulary learning listed in this chapter?

4. Which words are worth teaching?

5. Why are some words more difficult to learn than others? What strategies can teachers use to help children learn them?

6. How can we help English language learners (ELL) acquire new vocabularies for reading, writing, and speaking?

7. How does the study of various word functions enable students to better communicate and understand others?

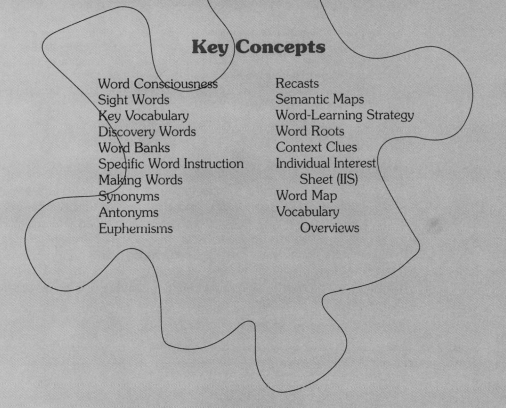

Key Concepts

Word Consciousness
Sight Words
Key Vocabulary
Discovery Words
Word Banks
Specific Word Instruction
Making Words
Synonyms
Antonyms
Euphemisms

Recasts
Semantic Maps
Word-Learning Strategy
Word Roots
Context Clues
Individual Interest
   Sheet (IIS)
Word Map
Vocabulary
   Overviews

Recognizing and understanding written vocabulary is essential to reading. Indeed, unless children are able to understand word meanings as they read, the process is reduced to mindless decoding (Fountas & Pinnell, 1996). Children who come to school with thousands of "words in their head"—words they can hear, understand, and use in their daily lives—are already on the path to learning success (Allington & Cunningham, 1996). Similarly, children who have small listening, speaking, and reading vocabularies—from what could be termed "language deprived backgrounds"—must receive immediate attention if they are to have any real chance at reading success (National Research Council, 1998; Johnson, 2001).

On the importance of building vocabulary knowledge, Reutzel and Cooter (2003) have written the following:

✦ *Visit Chapter 5 of our Companion Website at www.prenhall.com/ reutzel to look into the chapter objectives, standards and principles, and pertinent web links associated with Increasing Vocabulary and Word Knowledge.*

Words are the symbols we use to express ideas; *captions,* you might say, that describe our life experiences. Vocabulary development is a process that goes on throughout life and can be enhanced in the classroom through enticing learning experiences. Except for economically deprived or children with disabilities, most acquire a vocabulary of over 10,000 words during the first five years of their lives (Smith, 1987). Most school children will learn between 2,000 and 3,600 words per year, though estimates vary from 1,500 to more than 8,000 (Nagy, Herman, & Anderson, 1985; Clark, 1993; Johnson, 2001).

WHERE AND HOW DO STUDENTS ACQUIRE NEW VOCABULARY?

The truth is, there are many sources for learning new words and some of them may surprise you—at least, just a bit. Students learn a great deal of their new vocabulary from conversations, independent reading, and even from the media. However, they do not learn new words from each source equally, nor is each source of equal value in expanding their vocabularies. To illustrate the point, here are some selected statistics revealing the sources of rare words (i.e., *new* or *unfamiliar* words) found in various language and text forms that are commonly accessed by children and adults (A. E. Cunningham & Stanovich, 1998; Rasinski, 1998):

Source	Number of rare (uncommon) words per 1,000
Adult speech (expert testimony)	28.4
Adult speech (college graduates to friends)	17.3
Prime time adult television	22.7
Mister Rogers and *Sesame Street*	2.0
Children's books—Preschool	16.3
Children's book—Elementary	30.9
Comic books	53.5
Popular magazines	65.7
Newspapers	68.3
Adult books	52.7
Scientific article abstracts	128.0

Were you surprised by any of these findings? How about the number of rare words used by college graduates in their conversations with friends compared to the number commonly found in comic books! Or, for that matter, the number of uncommon words found in comic books compared to elementary children's books? Perhaps there is a case to be made for daily reading for children in self-selected books—including comics and popular magazines!

In this chapter we take a careful look, an *evidence-based* look, at how children learn new words, the kinds of vocabulary they should learn, and the ways in which new vocabulary should be taught. As you will *see,* vocabulary knowledge is an essential building block of reading and writing processes.

RESEARCH ON VOCABULARY LEARNING

In reviewing recent research on vocabulary learning and its role in reading, one conclusion becomes crystal clear: Reading and writing activities, obviously, are dependent on words. Indeed, all good readers have a large store of high-frequency words they can read and spell instantly and automatically (Allington & Cunningham, 1996). So what do we know about vocabulary learning? To partially answer this question, we discuss key findings supported by recent research (Guthrie, 1982; Nagy, Herman, & Anderson, 1985; Stahl & Fairbanks, 1986; Stahl & Jacobson, 1986; Adams, 1990a; Stahl, Hare, Sinatra, & Gregory, 1991; Krashen, 1993; Allington & Cunningham, 1996; National Research Council [NRC], 1998; Burns, Griffin, & Snow, 1999; Johnson, 2001; Partnership for Reading, 2001).

Vocabulary Is Built Through Language Interactions

Children who are exposed to advanced vocabulary through conversations learn words needed later on to help recognize and comprehend while reading. Burns, Griffin, and Snow (1999) explain it this way.

> Vocalization in the crib gives way to play with rhyming language and nonsense words. Toddlers find that the words they use in conversation and the objects they represent are depicted in books—that the picture is a symbol for the real object and that the writing represents spoken language. In addition to listening to stories, children label the objects in books, comment on the characters, and request that an adult read to them. In their third and fourth years, children use new vocabulary and grammatical constructions in their own speech. Talking to adults is children's best source to exposure to new vocabulary and ideas. (p. 19)

Reading and being read to also increase vocabulary learning. Books give us challenging ideas, colorful descriptive words and concepts, and new knowledge and information about the world in which we live. Conversely, children who come to school with limited vocabularies, either due to second language learning or the effects of poverty (Cooter, 2003), struggle to take even their first steps in reading and understanding texts. Burns, Griffin, and Snow (1999) ask "How can they understand a science book about *volcanoes, silkworms,* or *Inuits?* What if they know nothing of *mountains, caterpillars,* or *snow* and *cold climates?*" (p. 70) As teachers, we must make sure that no child is left behind due to weak vocabulary development. We do this in myriad ways, as you will discover in this chapter and throughout the remainder of our book.

Children from disadvantaged backgrounds where frequently books and language-oriented games are not part of their daily lives are at greater risk for reading failure.

The Four Types of Vocabulary

Though we often speak of vocabulary as if it were a single thing, it is not. Human beings acquire four types of vocabulary. They are, in descending order according to size, listening, speaking, reading, and writing. *Listening vocabulary,* the largest, is made up of words we can hear and understand. All other vocabularies are subsets of our listening vocabulary. The second largest vocabulary, *speaking vocabulary,* is comprised of words we can use when we speak. Next is our *reading vocabulary,* words we can identify and understand when we read. The smallest is our *writing vocabulary,* words we use in writing. These four vocabularies are continually nurtured in the effective teacher's classroom.

The four types of vocabulary are listening, speaking, reading, and writing.

Levels of Vocabulary Learning

The truth is, words are *not* either known or unknown. As with most new learning, new vocabulary words and concepts are learned by degree. The Partnership for Reading (2001), in summarizing conclusions drawn by the National Reading Panel,

Be sure to go to the National Reading Panel Web site on the Internet at www.national readingpanel.org for a free copy of their conclusions.

Figure 5.1   Levels of vocabulary learning (Partnership for Reading, 2001)

Level of Word Knowledge	Definition
Unknown	The word is completely unfamiliar, and its meaning is unknown.
Acquainted	The word is somewhat familiar; the student has some idea of its basic meaning.
Established	The word is very familiar; the student can immediately recognize its meaning and use the word correctly.

described three levels of vocabulary learning: *unknown, acquainted,* and *established.* Definitions for each are presented in Figure 5.1.

Bear in mind that these levels or degrees of learning apply to each of the four vocabulary types—listening, speaking, reading, and writing—so helping children build strong reading and writing vocabularies can sometimes be a formidable task indeed.

If you think about it, sometimes we learn new meanings to words that are already known to us. The word *race,* for example, has many different meanings (to run a race, a group of people, etc.). One of the most challenging tasks for students can be learning the meaning of a new word representing a completely unknown concept. According to the research:

> Much of learning in the content areas involves this type of word learning. As students learn about *deserts, hurricanes,* and *immigrants,* they may be learning both new concepts and new words. Learning words and concepts in science, social studies, and mathematics is even more challenging because each major concept often is associated with many other new concepts. For example, the concept *deserts* is often associated with other concepts that may be unfamiliar, such as cactus, plateau, and mesa. (Partnership for Reading, 2001, p. 43)

WHAT RESEARCH TELLS US ABOUT *TEACHING* VOCABULARY

Most vocabulary is learned indirectly, but some vocabulary *must* be taught directly. The following conclusions about indirect vocabulary learning and direct vocabulary instruction are of particular interest and value to classroom teachers (National Reading Panel, 2000).

Children learn the meanings of most words indirectly, through everyday experiences with oral and written language.

Children learn most of their vocabulary indirectly by having conversations with others, being read to, and while doing their own reading.

There are typically three ways children learn vocabulary indirectly. First, they participate in oral language every day. Children learn word meanings through conversations with other people, and as they participate in conversations, they often hear words repeated several times. The more conversations children have, the more words they learn!

Another indirect way children learn words is by being read to. Reading aloud is especially powerful when the reader pauses during reading to define an unfamiliar word and, after reading, engages the child in a conversation about the book. Conversations about books help children to learn new words and concepts and to relate them to their prior knowledge and experience (Partnership for Reading, 2001).

The third way children learn new words indirectly is through their own reading. This is one of many reasons why many teachers feel that a daily DEAR time (Drop Everything and Read) of 10–20 minutes is so critical (Krashen, 1993). Put simply, the more children read on their own, the more words they'll learn.

From evidenced-based reading research, we can conclude that students learn vocabulary indirectly when they hear and see words used in many different contexts. Conversations, read aloud experiences, and independent reading are essential.

Students learn vocabulary when they are taught individual words and word-learning strategies directly.

Direct instruction helps students learn difficult words (Johnson, 2001), such as words that represent complex concepts that are not part of the students' everyday experiences (National Reading Panel, 2000). We also know that when teachers *preteach* new words that are associated with a text the students are about to read, better reading comprehension results.

As mentioned above, direct vocabulary instruction should include specific word learning, as well as teaching students word-learning strategies they can use on their own.

Developing word consciousness can boost vocabulary learning.

Word consciousness learning activities stimulate an awareness and interest in words, their meanings, and their *power*. Word-conscious students enjoy words and are zealous about learning them. In addition, they have been taught how to learn new and interesting words.

The key to capitalizing on word consciousness is through wide reading and use of the writing process. When reading a new book aloud to students, call their attention to the way the author chooses her words to convey particular meanings. Imagine the fun you can have discussing some of the intense words used by Gary Paulsen (1987) in his book *Hatchet,* Shel Silverstein's (1974) clever use of rhyming words in his book of poetry *Where the Sidewalk Ends,* or the downright "magical" word selection employed by J. K. Rowling (1997) in *Harry Potter and the Sorcerer's Stone.* Encourage your students to play with words, such as with puns or self-created raps. Help them research a word's history and search for examples of a word's usage in their everyday lives.

Vocabulary instruction results in an increase in word knowledge and reading comprehension.

The most effective methods of vocabulary instruction include (a) information about word meanings, (b) showing vocabulary in a variety of contexts, and (c) multiple exposures of the new word.

PRINCIPLES OF EFFECTIVE VOCABULARY INSTRUCTION

From the research cited previously, as well as that conducted by Stahl (1986) and Rasinski (1998), we have developed a list of principles for effective vocabulary instruction for teachers to consider.

Principle 1:   Vocabulary is learned best through *direct,* hands-on experience.

Context helps readers choose the correct meaning for multiple-meaning words. The old adage that "experience is the best teacher" is certainly true in vocabulary learning. The next best way to learn new vocabulary is through indirect, vicarious experiences from daily reading in interesting and varied texts (Rasinski, 1998). Marilyn Jager Adams (1990a) put it this way:

> The best way to build children's visual vocabulary is to have them read meaningful words in meaningful contexts. The more meaningful reading that children do, the larger will be their repertoires of meanings, the greater their sensitivity to orthographic structure, and the stronger, better refined, and more productive will be their associations between words and meanings. (p. 156)

Principle 2:   Teachers should offer both *definitions* and *context* during vocabulary instruction.

As children learn new words, they do so in two ways. First, students learn basic definitions or information that helps determine the connections of the new word to known words (i.e., elaboration). This step can be accomplished by simply providing the definition, building with students semantic maps linking the known with the new, and through other comparisons such as synonyms, antonyms, classification schemes, word roots, and affixes.

Second, context information has to do with knowing the basic core definition of a word and how it varies, or is changed, in different texts. For example, the word *run* is generally thought of as a verb meaning "to move swiftly." When looking for this simple word in the dictionary, one quickly realizes that the word *run* has approximately 50 definitions! There is the word *run*, as in "running a race"; "a run of bad luck"; or the "run" women sometimes get in their hosiery. Context helps the reader know which definition the author intends. In fact, without context, it is impossible to say with certainty which meaning is intended. Thus, it is important for teachers to help students understand both the *definitional* and *contextual* relations of words. Vocabulary instruction should include both aspects if reading comprehension is to benefit.

Principle 3:   Effective vocabulary instruction must include a depth of learning component as well as a breadth of word knowledge.

Deep processing connects new vocabulary with students' background knowledge. Depth of learning, or "deep processing" of vocabulary, has two potential meanings: relating the word to information the student already knows (elaboration) and spending time on the task of learning new words (expansion). Stahl (1986) defines three levels of processing for vocabulary instruction:

1. *Association processing:* Students learn simple associations through synonyms and word associations.
2. *Comprehension processing:* Students move beyond simple associations by doing something with the association, such as fitting the word into a sentence blank, classifying the word with other words, or finding antonyms.
3. *Generation processing:* Students use the comprehended association to generate a new or novel product (sometimes called *generative comprehension*). This process could involve a restatement of the definition in the student's own words, creating a novel sentence using the word correctly in a clear context, or comparing the definition to the student's personal experiences. One caution relates to the generation of sentences by students: Sometimes students generate sentences without really processing the information deeply, as with students who begin each sentence with "This is a . . . . " (Pearson, 1985; Stahl, 1986).

Memorizing long lists of isolated words is a relatively ineffective way to teach new vocabulary. In fact, students learn new vocabulary some 10 times faster by reading than through intensive vocabulary instruction with word lists (Nagy, Herman, & Anderson, 1985; Krashen, 1993).

Principle 4: Students need to have *multiple exposures* to new reading vocabulary words.

Notice that multiple exposures to new vocabulary improve comprehension. Vocabulary learning requires repetition. To learn words thoroughly, students need to see, hear, and use words many times in many contexts (Rasinski, 1998). Providing students with multiple exposures in varied contexts appears to significantly improve reading comprehension. The amount of time spent reading these new words also seems to be a relevant factor for improving comprehension.

WHICH WORDS SHOULD WE TEACH?

M. McKeown and Beck (1988) have addressed an important issue in their research: *Which vocabulary should be taught in elementary classrooms?* They point out that one problem with traditional vocabulary instruction in basal readers has been the equal treatment of all categories of words. As an example, a mythology selection in a basal reader about *Arachne,* who loved to weave, gives the word *loom* as much attention as the word *agreement.* McKeown and Beck point out that although the word *loom* may be helpful in understanding more about spinning, it is a word of relatively low use compared to the word *agreement,* which is key to understanding the story and of much higher utility as students move into adult life.

Not all words are created equal, especially in terms of difficulty in elementary classrooms. As McKeown and Beck (1988) explained:

> The choice of which words to teach and what kind of attention to give them depends on a variety of factors, such as importance of the words for understanding the selection, relationship to specific domains of knowledge, general utility, and relationship to other lessons and classroom events. (p. 45)

Why You Shouldn't Try to Teach *ALL* Unknown Words

There are several good reasons why you should not try to directly teach *all* unknown words. For one thing, the text may have too many words that are unknown to your students, far too many for direct instruction. You'll want to limit your vocabulary teaching time to not more than 5 to 10 minutes so that they can spend the bulk of their time actually reading. Most of your students will be able to handle a fair amount of new words, up to 5 percent, simply by using context clues in the passage. Also, your students *need* many opportunities to *practice* and *use* the word-learning strategies you are teaching them for learning unknown words on their own.

Words You *Should* Teach

Realistically, you will probably be able to teach thoroughly only a few new words (8 to 10) per week, so you need to choose the words you teach carefully. Focus your energies on high utility words and words that are important to the meaning of the selections you will be reading in class. A logical place to begin vocabulary instruction is the teaching of *sight words.*

Sight Words

Sight words occur frequently in most texts and account for a majority of written words. Understanding text relies in part on the immediate recognition of these high-

When selecting new words to teach, consider the importance of the word to understanding the selection.

Sight words *are high frequency words that students recognize immediately by sight.*

frequency words. Studies of print have found that just 109 words account for upwards of 50 percent of all words in student textbooks, and a total of only 5,000 words accounts for about 90 percent of the words in student texts (J. B. Carroll, Davies, & Richman, 1971; Adams 1990b). Knowledge of high-frequency sight words, logically, can help readers manage text in a more fluent way. Many of these words, such as *the, from, but, because, that,* and *this,* sometimes called *structure words,* carry little meaning but do affect the flow and coherence of the text being read. The actual meaning of the text depends on the ready knowledge of less frequent, or *lexical words,* such as *automobile, aristocrat, pulley, streetcar, Martin Luther King,* and *phantom.* Adams and her colleagues (1991) concluded that:

> While the cohesion and connectivity of English text is owed most to its frequent words (e.g., *it, that, this, and, because, when, while*), its meaning depends disproportionately on its less frequent words (e.g., *doctor, fever, infection, medicine, penicillin, Alexander, Fleming, melon, mold, poison, bacteria, antibiotic, protect, germs, disease*). (p. 394)

It is critical that you, the teacher, make sure that all of your students learn to instantly recognize sight words, so you should have a reliable list of these words as a resource. Figure 5.2 presents the Fry (1980) word list of the 300 most common words in print. The Fry list is widely regarded as the best-researched list of sight words in the English language.

Sight Words for Bilingual Classrooms (Spanish)

Just as the most common sight words have been identified in English, high-frequency words have also been identified for Spanish (Cornejo, 1972). This popular word list is divided by grade and presented in Figure 5.3.

Key Vocabulary

Silvia Ashton-Warner, in her classic book *Teacher* (1963), described **key vocabulary** words as "organic," or *lexical words* that come from within the child and his or her own experiences. Ashton-Warner states that key vocabulary words act as "captions" for important events in life that the child has experienced.

Here's how the process works. Children come to the teacher individually at an appointed time, or during a group experience, and indicate which words he or she would like to learn. For instance, the teacher may ask, "What word would you like to learn today?" The child responds with a lexical word—perhaps a word like *police, ghost,* or *sing.* Once the child has told the teacher a word she would like to learn, the teacher writes the word on an index card or a small piece of tag board using a dark marker. The student is then instructed to share the word with as many people as possible during the day. After the child has done so, the word is added to her writing folder or *word bank* for future use in writing.

Ashton-Warner found that the most common categories of key vocabulary words children wanted to learn were *fear words* (*dog, bull, kill, police*), sex (as she called them) or *affection words* (*love, kiss, sing, darling*), *locomotion words* (*bus, car, truck, jet*), and a *miscellaneous* category that generally reflects cultural and other considerations (*socks, frog, beer, Disneyland, Dallas Cowboys*).

Figure 5.2 Fry new instant word list

The first 10 words make up about 24% of all written material, the first 100 words about 50% of all written material, and the first 300 about 65%.

1. the	44. each	87. who	130. through	173. home	216. never	259. walked
2. of	45. which	88. oil	131. much	174. us	217. started	260. white
3. and	46. she	89. its	132. before	175. move	218. city	261. sea
4. a	47. do	90. now	133. line	176. try	219. earth	262. began
5. to	48. how	91. find	134. right	177. kind	220. eyes	263. grow
6. in	49. their	92. long	135. too	178. hand	221. light	264. took
7. is	50. if	93. down	136. means	179. picture	222. thought	265. river
8. you	51. will	94. day	137. old	180. again	223. head	266. four
9. that	52. up	95. did	138. any	181. change	224. under	267. carry
10. it	53. other	96. get	139. same	182. off	225. story	268. state
11. he	54. about	97. come	140. tell	183. play	226. saw	269. once
12. was	55. out	98. made	141. boy	184. spell	227. left	270. book
13. for	56. many	99. may	142. following	185. air	228. don't	271. hear
14. on	57. then	100. part	143. came	186. away	229. few	272. stop
15. are	58. them	101. over	144. want	187. animals	230. while	273. without
16. as	59. these	102. new	145. show	188. house	231. along	274. second
17. with	60. so	103. sound	146. also	189. point	232. might	275. later
18. his	61. some	104. take	147. around	190. page	233. close	276. miss
19. they	62. her	105. only	148. form	191. letters	234. something	277. idea
20. I	63. would	106. little	149. three	192. mother	235. seemed	278. enough
21. at	64. make	107. work	150. small	193. answer	236. next	279. eat
22. be	65. like	108. know	151. set	194. found	237. hard	280. face
23. this	66. him	109. place	152. put	195. study	238. open	281. watch
24. have	67. into	110. years	153. end	196. still	239. example	282. far
25. from	68. time	111. live	154. does	197. learn	240. beginning	283. Indians
26. or	69. has	112. me	155. another	198. should	241. life	284. really
27. one	70. look	113. back	156. well	199. American	242. always	285. almost
28. had	71. two	114. give	157. large	200. world	243. those	286. let
29. by	72. more	115. most	158. must	201. high	244. both	287. above
30. words	73. write	116. very	159. big	202. every	245. paper	288. girl
31. but	74. go	117. after	160. even	203. near	246. together	289. sometimes
32. not	75. see	118. things	161. such	204. add	247. got	290. mountains
33. what	76. number	119. our	162. because	205. food	248. group	291. cut
34. all	77. no	120. just	163. turned	206. between	249. often	292. young
35. were	78. way	121. name	164. here	207. own	250. run	293. talk
36. we	79. could	122. good	165. why	208. below	251. important	294. soon
37. when	80. people	123. sentence	166. asked	209. country	252. until	295. list
38. your	81. my	124. man	167. went	210. plants	253. children	296. song
39. can	82. than	125. think	168. men	211. last	254. side	297. being
40. said	83. first	126. say	169. read	212. school	255. feet	298. leave
41. there	84. water	127. great	170. need	213. father	256. car	299. family
42. use	85. been	128. where	171. land	214. keep	257. miles	300. it's
43. an	86. called	129. help	172. different	215. trees	258. night	

Ashton-Warner (1963) referred to key vocabulary as "one-look words" because one look is usually all that is required for permanent learning to take place. The reason that these words seem so easy for children to learn is that they usually carry strong emotional significance and, once seen, are almost never forgotten. This process helps children begin to build a significant cadre of lexical sight words.

Figure 5.3   Cornejo's high-frequency word list for Spanish (graded)

Pre-Primer	Primer	1st	2nd	3rd	4th	5th
a	alto	bonita	ayer	amar	árbol	amistad
azul	flor	arriba	aqui	aquí	bandera	azucar
bajo	blusa	fruta	año	debajo	abeja	contento
mi	ella	globo	cerca	familia	escuela	corazón
mesa	ir	estar	desde	fiesta	fácil	compleaños
pan	leche	café	donde	grande	fuego	edad
mamá	más	letra	hacer	hermana	hacia	escribir
lado	niño	luna	hasta	jueves	idea	felicidad
la	padre	luz	hijo	lápiz	jardín	guitarra
papá	por	muy	hoy	miércoles	llegar	estrella
me	si	noche	leer	once	manzana	igual
no	tan	nombre	libro	quince	muñeca	invierno
esa	sobre	nosotros	martes	sábado	naranja	orquesta
el	sin	nunca	mejor	semana	saludar	primavera
en	tras	ojo	mucho	silla	sueño	recordar
cuna	color	pelota	oir	sobrino	señorita	respeto
dos	al	porque	papel	vivir	tierra	tijeras
mi	día	rojo	paz	zapato	traer	último
de	bien	té	quien	tarde	ventana	querer
los	chico	taza	usted	traje	queso	otoño

Discovery Words

During the course of a typical school day, students are exposed to many new words. These words are often discovered as a result of studies in the content areas. Words such as *experiment, algebra, social, enterprise, conquest, Bengal tiger, spider,* and *cocoon* find their way into students' listening and speaking vocabulary. Every effort should be made to add these **discovery words** to the word bank as they are discussed in their natural context. Such words often appear in new student compositions. Developing vocabulary in content areas can help children discover words in their natural context.

Which Words Are the Most Difficult to Learn?

Here are some examples of words that can be especially difficult for your students (National Reading Panel, 2000):

Some of the most difficult words to learn are words with multiple meanings and idiomatic expressions.

• *Words with multiple meanings* are quite challenging for students. They sometimes have trouble understanding that words with the same spelling and/or pronunciation can have different meanings, depending on their context. For example, note the different uses of *run* in the following sentences: "Molly complained when she found a *run* in her hose," versus "Jeff Johnston plans to *run* for Congress." Or, again, note the different uses and pronunciation of the word *read* in the following sentences: "I will *read* the story later today," versus "I *read* the story yesterday." Words with multiple meanings and/or pronunciations can be confusing for students. When they notice in the dictionary that a number of different definitions are possible, choosing the context-specific definition can be confusing.

• *Idiomatic expressions* also can be especially difficult for language deficient students in inner city settings and for students who are English language learners (ELL) (Cooter, 2003). Because idiomatic expressions do not match literal meanings of the words used, you may need to explain to students expressions such as "chocolate moose," "gorilla war," "airplane hangers," or "get the picture." A great book to use as a catalyst for discussing idioms is Fred Gwynne's (1999) *A Chocolate Moose for Dinner.*

COMMON STRATEGIES USED IN VOCABULARY INSTRUCTION

An important question for teachers is this, *How can we help students increase their vocabulary knowledge?* In this section we present a few of the most common and successful methods. In later chapters we add to this methodological base for each grade level range. We begin this discussion with *word banks,* a tool with which we have had much success.

Word Banks

Word banks are used to help students collect and review sight words. They can also be used as personal dictionaries. A word bank is simply a student-constructed box, file, or notebook in which newly discovered words are stored, reviewed, and used in their writing. In the early grades, teachers often collect small shoeboxes from local stores for this purpose. Children at the beginning of the year decorate the boxes to make them their own. In the upper grades, more formal-looking word banks are used to give an adult appearance; notebooks or recipe boxes are generally selected.

Alphabetic dividers can also be used at all levels to facilitate the quick location of word bank words. Alphabetic dividers in the early grades help students rehearse and reinforce knowledge of alphabetical order. Figure 5.4 shows an example of a word bank.

Word banks help students collect and use new words for reading and writing.

Specific Word Instruction

Specific word instruction can deepen students' knowledge of word meanings and, in turn, help them understand what they are hearing or reading (Johnson, 2001). It also can help them use words accurately in speaking and writing. Three ways of providing specific word instruction have been drawn from the research evidence (National Reading Panel, 2000; Partnership for Reading, 2001): *preteaching vocabulary, extended instruction,* and *repeated exposures.*

What Specific Word Instruction Looks Like in the Classroom

The Partnership for Reading, a federally funded collaborative effort of the National Institute for Literacy, the National Institute of Child Health and Human Development, and the U.S. Department of Education, in 2001 published the booklet *Put Reading*

Figure 5.4   A word bank

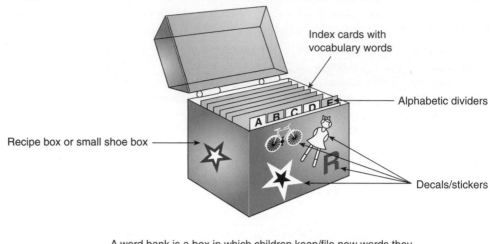

Index cards with vocabulary words

Alphabetic dividers

Recipe box or small shoe box

Decals/stickers

A word bank is a box in which children keep/file new words they are learning. The words are usually written in isolation on one side of the card, and in a sentence on the back of the card (usually with a picture clue).

Example:

Front

bicycle

Back

Jason rode his bicycle to school.

First: The Research Building Blocks for Teaching Children to Read. This document was constructed to help disseminate data from the 2000 report of the National Reading Panel and covers the topics of phonemic awareness instruction, phonics instruction, fluency instruction, vocabulary instruction, and text comprehension instruction. In order to help you better understand what each of the three specific word instruction components might look like in the classroom, we include examples from *Put Reading First* after each definition.

> *Preteaching Vocabulary: Before students read, it is helpful to teach them specific words they will see in the text for the first time. Teaching vocabulary before reading helps students learn new words and comprehend the text.*

You can obtain Put Reading First: The Research Building Blocks for Teaching Children to Read *(2001) online free at* www.nifl.gov. *The report of the National Reading Panel,* Teaching Children to Read: An Evidence-Based Assessment of the Scientific Research Literature on Reading and Its Implications for Reading Instruction, *is likewise available online at* www.nationalreadingpanel.org.

AN EXAMPLE OF CLASSROOM INSTRUCTION:

Preteaching Vocabulary[*]

A teacher plans to have his third grade class read the novel *Stone Fox* by John Reynolds Gardiner. In this novel, a young boy enters a dogsled race in hopes of winning prize money to pay the taxes on his grandfather's farm. The teacher knows that understanding the concept of taxes is important to understanding the novel's plot. Therefore, before his students begin reading the novel, the teacher may do several things to make sure that they understand what the concept means and why it is important to the story. For example, the teacher may:

- engage students in a discussion of the concept of taxes; and/or
- read a sentence from the book that contains the word taxes and ask students to use context and their prior knowledge to try to figure out what it means.
  To solidify their understanding of the word, the teacher might ask students to use taxes in their own sentences.

"From *Put Reading First: The Research Building Blocks for Teaching Children to Read* (2001). Noncopyrighted material published by the National Institute for Literacy. Available online at www.nifl.gov.

> *You will find a Safety Net Lesson for struggling readers on Building Vocabulary from Books in Chapter 5 on our Companion Website at www.prenhall.com/reutzel.*

Extended instruction: *Students should be saturated (marinated!) with word learning activities spread over an extended period of time. These should be activities that actively engage students (as opposed to passive learning tasks).*

AN EXAMPLE OF CLASSROOM INSTRUCTION:

Extended Instruction[*]

A first grade teacher wants to help her students understand the concept of **jobs,** which is part of her social studies curriculum. Over a period of time, the teacher engages students in exercises in which they work repeatedly with the meaning of the concept of jobs. The students have many opportunities to see and actively use the word in various contexts that reinforce its meaning.

The teacher begins by asking the students what they already know about jobs and by having them give examples of jobs their parents have. The class might have a discussion about the jobs of different people who work at the school.

The teacher then reads the class a simple book about jobs. The book introduces the idea that different jobs help people meet their needs and that jobs either provide goods or services. The book does not use the word **goods** and **services,** rather it uses the verbs **makes** and **helps.**

The teacher then asks the students to make up sentences describing their parents' jobs by using the verbs **makes** and **helps** (e.g., "My mother is a doctor. She helps sick people get well.")

Next, the teacher asks students to brainstorm other jobs. Together, they decide whether the jobs are "making jobs" or "helping jobs." The job names are placed under the appropriate headings on a bulletin board. They might also suggest jobs that do not fit neatly into either category.

The teacher might then ask the students to share whether they think they would like to have a making or a helping job when they grow up.

The teacher next asks the students to talk with their parents about jobs. She tells them to try to bring to class two new examples of jobs—one making job and one helping job.

As the students come across different jobs throughout the year (for example, through reading books, on field trips, through classroom guests), they can add the jobs to the appropriate categories on the bulletin board.

[*]From *Put Reading First: The Research Building Blocks for Teaching Children to Read* (2001). Noncopyrighted material published by the National Institute for Literacy. Available online at www.nifl.gov.

Repeated exposures to vocabulary: You will find that the more students use new words in different contexts, the more likely they are to learn the words permanently. When children see, hear, and work with specific words, they seem to learn them better.

AN EXAMPLE OF CLASSROOM INSTRUCTION:

Repeated Exposures to Vocabulary*

A second grade class is reading a biography of Benjamin Franklin. The biography discusses Franklin's important role as a scientist. The teacher wants to make sure that her students understand the meaning of the words **science** and **scientist,** both because the words are important to understanding the biography and because they are obviously very useful words to know in school and in everyday life.

At every opportunity, therefore, the teacher draws her students' attention to the words. She points out the words **scientist** and **science** in textbooks and reading selections, particularly in her science curriculum. She has students use the words in their own writing, especially during science instruction. She also asks them to listen for and find in print the words as they are used outside of the classroom—in newspapers, magazines, at museums, in television shows or movies, or the Internet.

Then, as they read the biography, she discusses with students in what ways Benjamin Franklin was a scientist and what science meant in his time.

*From *Put Reading First: The Research Building Blocks for Teaching Children to Read* (2001). Noncopyrighted material published by the National Institute for Literacy. Available online at www.nifl.gov.

Standards Note
Standard 6.5: The reading professional will be able to teach students to recognize and use various spelling patterns in the English language as an aid to word identification. As you learn about "making words", list on a T Chart the advantages and disadvantages of onset and rime teaching, as opposed to traditional letter-sound relationships.

Word Play is a wonderful Internet site that links to many sites featuring fun with words. You can visit these sites in Chapter 5 of our Companion Website at www.prenhall.com/ reutzel.

Making Words

Making Words (Cunningham & Cunningham, 1992) is an excellent word learning strategy that helps children improve their phonetic understanding of words through invented or "temporary spellings" while also increasing their repertoire of vocabulary words they can recognize in print (Reutzel & Cooter, 2003). Making Words will be a familiar strategy for anyone who has ever played the popular crossword board game *Scrabble!*

Making Words begins when students are given a number of specific letters with which to make words. They begin by making two- or three-letter words using the letters during a set amount of time, then progress to words having more letters until they finally arrive at a specific word that uses all the letters. This final word is usually the main word to be taught for the day, but the other words discovered may be new for some students. By manipulating the letters to make two-, three-, four-, and more letter words using temporary or "transitional" spellings, students have an opportunity to practice their phonemic awareness skills. Making Words is recommended as a 15-minute activity when used with first and second graders. In the following tables (see Tables 5.1 and 5.2) we summarize and adapt the steps in planning and teaching a Making Words lesson suggested by Cunningham and Cunningham (1992).

Table 5.3 gives the details necessary for two more Making Words lessons suggested by Cunningham and Cunningham (1992), which may be useful for helping students learn the procedure.

Examples of Making Words activities, as well as another Cunningham favorite, *word walls,* are demonstrated further in Chapters 10 through 12.

Table 5.1 Planning a making words lesson

1. Choose a word to be the final word to be emphasized in the lesson. It should be a key word that is chosen from a reading selection to be read by the class, fiction or non-fiction, or may be of particular interest to the group. Be sure to select a word that has enough vowels and/or one that fits letter–sound patterns useful for most children at their developmental stage in reading and writing. For illustrative purposes, we will use the word *thunder* in these instructions, which was suggested by Cunningham and Cunningham (1992).

2. Make a list of shorter words that can be spelled using the main word to be learned. For the word *thunder,* one could derive the following words: *red, Ted, Ned/den/end* (note: these all use the same letters), *her, hut, herd, turn, hunt, hurt, under, hunted, turned, thunder.*

From the words you were able to list, select 12–15 words that include such aspects of written language as (a) words that can be used to emphasize a certain kind of pattern, (b) big and little words, (c) words that can be made with the same letters in different positions (as with Ned, end, den), (d) a proper noun, if possible, to remind them when we use capital letters, and especially (e) words that students already have in their listening vocabularies.

3. Write all of these words on large index cards and order them from smallest to largest words. Also, write each of the individual letters found in the key word for the day on large index cards (make two sets of these).

4. Reorder the words one more time to group them according to letter patterns and/or to demonstrate how shifting around letters can form new words. Store the two sets of large single-letter cards in two envelopes—one for the teacher, one for children participating during the modeling activity.

5. Store the word stacks in envelopes and note on the outside the words/patterns to be emphasized during the lesson. Also note clues you can use with the children to help them discover the words you desire. For example, "See if you can make a three-letter word that is the name of the room in some people's homes where they like to watch television." (*den*)

Function (Four-Letter) Words

Many words are very difficult for students to learn because they carry no definable meaning. Words in this category include *with, were, what,* and *want.* Referred to as *structure words* (also known as *functors, glue words,* and *four-letter words*), these words are perhaps the most difficult to teach because they cannot be explained in a concrete way for children. Imagine trying to define or draw a picture of the word *what!*

Patricia Cunningham (1980) developed the *drastic strategy* to help teachers solve this difficult instructional problem. Here is her six-step process.

*The drastic strategy is useful for teaching **function words,** or those that have no meaning, for example, what, with, and that.*

Step 1: Select a function word, and write it on a vocabulary card for each child. Locate a story for storytelling, or spontaneously create a story in which you use the word many times. Before you begin your story, ask the children to hold up their card every time they hear the word printed on their card. As you tell the story, pause briefly each time you come to the word in the text.

Step 2: Ask children to volunteer to make up a story using the word on their card. Listeners should hold up their card each time they hear their classmate use the function word.

Table 5.2   Teaching a making words lesson

1. Place the large single letters from the key word in a the pocket chart or along the chalkboard ledge.

2. For modeling purposes, the first time you use Making Words, select one of the students to be the "passer" and ask that child to pass the large single letters to other designated children.

3. Hold up and name each of the letter cards and have students selected to participate in the modeling exercise respond by holding up their matching card.

4. Write the numeral 2 (or 3, if there are no two-letter words in this lesson) on the board. Next, tell the student "volunteers" the clue you developed for the desired word. Then, tell the student volunteers to put together two (or three) of their letters to form the desired word.

5. Continue directing the students to make more words using the clues provided and the letter cards until you have helped them discover all but the final key word (the one that uses all the letters). Ask the student volunteers if they can guess what the key word is. If they cannot, ask the remainder of the class if anyone can guess what it is. If no one is able to do so, offer them a meaning clue (e.g., "I am thinking of a word with ___ letters that means. . . .").

6. Repeat these steps the next day with the whole group as a guided practice activity using a new word.

Table 5.3   Making words: Additional examples

Sample Making Words Lessons (Cunningham & Cunningham, 1992)
Lesson using one vowel:
Letter cards: u k n r s t
Words to make: us, nut, rut, sun, sunk, runs, ruts/rust, tusk, stun, stunk, trunk,
            trunks (the key word)
You can sort for . . . rhymes, "s" pairs (run, runs; rut, ruts; trunk, trunks)

Lesson using big words:
Letter cards: a a a e i b c h l l p t
Words to make: itch, able, cable, table, batch, patch, pitch, petal, label, chapel,
            capital, capable, alphabet, *alphabetical* (the key word)
You can sort for . . . el, le, al, -itch, -atch

Step 3:   Ask the children to study the word on their card. Next, go around to each child and cut the word into letters (or have the children do it for themselves). Have the children try to arrange the letters to make the word. Check each child's attempt for accuracy. They should mix up the letters and try to make the word again several times, Each child should be able to do this before moving on to the next step. Put the letters into an envelope and write the word on the outside. Children should be encouraged to practice making the word during free times.

Step 4:   Write the word on the chalkboard and ask children to pretend their eyes are like a camera and to take a picture of the word and put it in their mind. Have them close their eyes and try to see it in their mind. Next, they should open their eyes and check the board to see if they correctly imagined the word. They should do this three times. The last activity is for them to write the word from memory

Developing vocabulary in content areas can help children discover words in their natural context.

after the chalkboard has been erased, then check their spelling when it is rewritten on the chalkboard. This should be done three times.

Step 5: Write several sentences on the board containing a blank in the place of the word under study. As you come to the missing word in the sentences, invite a child to come to the board and write the word in the blank space provided.

Step 6: Give children real books or text in which the function word appears. Ask them to read through the story, and whenever they find the word being studied, they should lightly underline (in pencil) the new word. When they have done this, read the text to them, and pause each time you come to the word so the students can read it chorally.

We recommend one final step to the drastic strategy: Add the word under study to the child's word bank for future use in writing.

There is one drawback to the drastic strategy—*time*. Sometimes it is not necessary to teach *every* step in the drastic strategy for all words. A careful assessment of your students' vocabulary knowledge and needs, coupled with years of classroom experience, will help you decide when certain steps can be omitted.

Teaching Word Functions and Changes

Synonyms

Synonyms are words that have similar, but not exactly the same, meanings (D. D. Johnson & Pearson, 1984). No two words carry exactly the same meaning in all situations. Thus, when teaching children about new words and their synonyms,

Can you find examples of interesting reading materials that might be used to teach synonyms?

teachers should provide numerous opportunities for students to see differences as well as similarities. As with all reading strategies, this is best done within the natural context of real books and authentic writing experiences.

One very productive way to get children interested in synonyms in the upper elementary grades is to teach the use of a thesaurus with their writing. Children can begin to see how using a thesaurus can spice up their writing projects. This tool is best used during revising and editing stages of the writing process when children sometimes have problems coming up with descriptive language in their writing. For example, let's say a character in their story was tortured by hostile savages (sorry to be so violent in our example!), but the child writes that the victim felt *bad*. If this word is targeted for thesaurus research, then the child may come up with synonyms for *bad* such as *in pain, anguished, in misery, depressed,* or *desperate*.

Following are several common words that children overuse that could be researched using a thesaurus.

good	big	thing
pleasant	vast	object
glorious	grand	item
wonderful	enormous	like
delightful	huge	organism

One way to get children involved with synonyms is to take text from some of their old-favorite books and revise selected words. Teachers might want to develop a modified cloze passage, deleting only certain kinds of words, and then let the children use synonyms to complete the blanks. Take, for example, the following excerpt from a book well suited for this purpose with early to intermediate grade readers, *The Grouchy Ladybug* (Carle, 1986):

"Good morning," said the friendly ladybug.

"Go away!" shouted the grouchy ladybug. "I want those aphids."

"We can share them," suggested the friendly ladybug.

"No. They're mine, all mine," screamed the grouchy ladybug.

"Or do you want to fight me for them?"*

*From *The Grouchy Ladybug* by E. Carle, 1977/1986, New York: HarperCollins. Reprinted by permission.

One option is to delete words following a statement (e.g., *said, shouted, suggested, screamed*) and put them in a list on the chalkboard with possible synonyms, such as *hinted, greeted, growled, yelled, reminded, mentioned, pointed out,* and *offered.* The resulting rewrites may look something like the following:

"Good morning," *greeted* the friendly ladybug.

"Go away!" *growled* the grouchy ladybug. "I want those aphids."

"We can share them," *hinted* the friendly ladybug.

"No. They're mine, all mine," *yelled* the grouchy ladybug.

"Or do you want to fight me for them?"

Class discussions might relate to how the use of different synonyms can alter meaning significantly, thus showing how synonyms have similar meanings, but not the exact same meanings. For example, if we took the sentence

"Go away!" shouted the grouchy ladybug.

and changed it to read

"Go away!" hinted the grouchy ladybug.

it would be easy for children to understand how the author's message had been softened considerably. This cross-training with reading and writing experiences helps synonyms to take on new relevance as a literacy tool in the hands of children.

Antonyms

Antonyms are word opposites or near opposites. *Hard–soft, dark–light, big–small* are examples of antonym pairs. Like synonyms, antonyms help students gain insights into word meanings. When searching for ideal antonym examples, teachers should try to identify word sets that are mutually exclusive or that completely contradict each other.

Word opposites, or near opposites, are ***antonyms.***

Several classes of antonyms have been identified (D. D. Johnson & Pearson, 1984) that may be useful in instruction. One class is called *relative pairs,* or *counterparts.* Examples include *mother–father, sister–brother, uncle–aunt, writer–reader,* because one term implies the other. Other antonyms reflect a complete opposite or reversal of meaning, such as *fast–slow, stop–go,* and *give–take.* Complementary antonyms tend to lead from one to another such as *give–take, friend–foe,* and *hot–cold.*

Antonym activities, as with all language-learning activities, should be drawn from the context of familiar books and student writing samples. By using familiar text with clear meanings, it is easy for children to see the full impact and flavor of differing word meanings. Remember, in classroom instruction involving minilessons, teaching from whole text to parts (antonyms in this case) is the key. Thus, if the teacher decided to develop an antonym worksheet for students, then the worksheet should be drawn from a book that has already been shared (or will be shared) with the whole class or group. One example of a fun book for this exercise is *Weird Parents* by Audrey Wood (1990), which could yield sentences like the following (in the space provided, students write in antonyms for the underlined words):

1. There once was a boy who had underline weird ( ) parents.
2. In the morning ( ), the weird mother always walked the boy to his bus stop.
3. At 12 o'clock when the boy opened ( ) his lunch box, he'd always have a weird surprise.

Another possibility is to ask children to find words in their writing or reading for which they can think of antonyms. A student in sixth grade reading *A Wrinkle in Time* (L'Engle, 1962) might create the following list of book words and antonyms:

Wrinkle Words/Page No.	Antonyms
punishment/13	reward
hesitant/63	eager
frightening/111	pleasant

If a student in third grade had written a story about his new baby sister, he might select some of the following words and antonyms:

Baby Story Words	**Opposites**
asleep	awake
cry	laugh
wet	dry

One way to assess students' ability to recognize antonyms is through multiple-choice and cloze exercises. The idea is to choose sentences from familiar text and let students select which word is the correct antonym from among three choices. The choices may include one synonym, the correct antonym, and a third choice that is a different part of speech. Following are two examples taken from the book *The Glorious Flight* (Provensen & Provensen, 1983):

1. Like a great swan, the *beautiful* (attractive, homely, shoots) glider rises into the air. . . .
2. Papa is getting *lots* (limited, from, loads) of practice.

Of many possible classroom activities, the most profitable will probably be those in which students are required to generate their own responses. Simple recognition items, as with multiple-choice measures, do not cause children to go within themselves nearly as deeply to find and apply new knowledge.

Euphemisms

*Learning **euphemisms** (words or phrases used to soften language to avoid harsh or distasteful realities) can improve students' writing versatility and reading comprehension.*

According to Tompkins and Hoskisson (1991, p. 122), **euphemisms** are words or phrases that are used to soften language to avoid harsh or distasteful realities (e.g., *passed away*), usually out of concern for people's feelings. Euphemisms are certainly worth some attention because they not only help students improve their writing versatility but also aid in reading comprehension.

Two types of euphemisms are *inflated* and *deceptive* language. Inflated language euphemisms tend to make something sound greater or more sophisticated than it is. For example, *sanitation engineer* might be an inflated euphemism for *garbage collector.* Deceptive language euphemisms are intentional words and phrases meant to intentionally misrepresent. Children should learn that this language often is used in advertisements to persuade an unknowing public. Several examples of euphemisms based on the work of Lutz (cited in Tompkins & Hoskisson, 1991, p. 122) follow:

Euphemism	**Real Meaning**
dentures	false teeth
expecting	pregnant
funeral director	undertaker
passed away	died
previously owned	used

senior citizen   old person
terminal patient   dying

Onomatopoeia and Creative Words

Onomatopoeia is the creation of words that imitate sounds (*buzz, whir, vrrrrooom*). Some authors, such as Dr. Seuss, Shel Silverstein, and others, have made regular use of onomatopoeia and other creative words in their writing. One instance of onomatopoeia may be found in Dr. Seuss's book *Horton Hears a Who!* (1954) in the sentence "On clarinets, *oom-pahs* and *boom-pahs* and flutes." A wonderful example of creative language is found in Silverstein's (1974, p. 71) poem "Sarah Cynthia Sylvia Stout Would Not Take the Garbage Out" in the phrase "Rubbery *blubbery* macaroni. . . . "

Children can be shown many interesting examples on onomatopoeia and creative words from the world of great children's literature. The natural extension to their own writing comes swiftly. Children may want to add a special section to their word banks for onomatopoeia and creative words to enhance their own written creations.

Onomatopoeia is the creation of words that imitate sounds, like zzzoooom, buzz, vrrrroooom.

Shared Reading Experiences and Vocabulary Learning

M. Senechal and Cornell (1993) studied ways vocabulary knowledge can be increased through *shared reading experiences* (where adults and children read stories together). The methods investigated included reading the story verbatim (read alouds), asking questions, repeating sentences containing new vocabulary words, and what has been referred to as *recasting* new vocabulary introduced in the selection.

Recasts build directly on sentences just read that contain a new word the teacher (or parent) may want to teach the child. Verbs, subjects, or objects are often changed to recast the word for further discussion and examination. Thus, if a child says or reads, "Look at the *snake,*" the adult may recast the phrase by replying, "It is a large striped *snake.*" In this example, the same meaning of the phrase was maintained, but adjectives were added to enhance understanding of the word *snake.*

Interestingly, Senechal and Cornell concluded that teacher questioning and recasts were about as effective as reading a book aloud to a child as a word learning tool. Thus, reading passages aloud to students can often be just as potent as direct teaching strategies. We need to do both: read aloud regularly *and* discuss passages containing new vocabulary with students in challenging ways.

MEETING THE NEEDS OF ENGLISH LANGUAGE LEARNERS (ELL)

A growing percentage of students in our schools are learning to read in a second language—*English.* According to the National Center for Educational Statistics (1999), about 17 percent of all students are classified as Hispanic (14 percent) or Asian/Pacific Islander (3 percent). Many of these students speak a language other than English as their native tongue. As it was in the earliest days of our country for most newcomers, learning to read and write in English can be a formidable challenge, but one that must be successfully addressed if all of our students are to reach their potential. *Literacy is, in so many ways, the gateway to social equity.*

English Language Learners (ELL) often need assistance with unfamiliar vocabulary encountered while reading.

One of the common needs of English language learners (ELL) is assistance with unfamiliar vocabulary they encounter while reading. Peregoy and Boyle (2001), in their book *Reading, Writing, & Learning in ESL,* recommend some guidelines for vocabulary development.

- First, select words to emphasize that you consider important to comprehending each assigned passage.
- Next, create several sentences loaded with context using these target words. This will give them an opportunity to use context to predict the meaning of the target words.
- Teacher modeling of prediction strategies using context is a must for students to grasp this strategy.
- Follow these modeling and guided practice sessions with discussion using excerpts from the text they will be assigned in which the target words appear.

Two vocabulary development activities are highly recommended for ELL students (Peregoy & Boyle, 2001; May & Rizzardi, 2002; Reutzel & Cooter, 2003)—the *Vocabulary Cluster Strategy* and *Semantic Maps.*

Using the Vocabulary Cluster Strategy with ELL Students

It is especially important that ELL students who struggle with reading use the context of the passage, their background knowledge, and the vocabulary they know to understand new words in print. This is true whether English is their second language or their first (as is the case with children from language-deprived backgrounds). English language learners (ELL) and students who have language deficiencies due to poverty are two large groups of students who benefit from direct instruction of this kind (Peregoy & Boyle, 2001). With the Vocabulary Cluster strategy, students are helped to read a passage, gather context clues, and then predict the meaning of a new word targeted for learning by you, the teacher. Here's how it works.

First, you will need to gather multiple copies of the text students are to read, an overhead transparency and projector, and erasable marking pens for transparencies. Select vocabulary you want to teach from the text you will use; it could be a poem, song, excerpt from a chapter book (novel), or non-fiction textbook. Gather your students around the overhead projector and draw their attention to the transparency you have prepared. The transparency should contain an excerpt from the text with sufficient context to help students predict what the unknown word might be. The target word(s) should have been deleted and replaced with a blank line, much the same as with a cloze passage. In Figure 5.5 you will see a passage prepared in this way along with a Vocabulary Cluster supporting the new word to be learned. This example is based on the book *Harry Potter and the Prisoner of Azkaban* (Rowling, 1999). Through discussion you will lead students into predicting what the unknown word might be. If the word is not already in students' listening vocabulary, as with ELL students or those with otherwise limited vocabularies, then you will be able to introduce the new word quite well using the context and synonyms provided in the vocabulary cluster.

Semantic Maps

Semantic maps are essentially a kind of "schema blueprint" in which students sketch out or map what is stored in their brain about a topic. Semantic maps help ELL students relate new information to schemata and vocabulary already in the brain,

Semantic maps are useful in tying together new vocabulary with prior knowledge and related terms (Johnson & Pearson, 1984; Monroe, 1998; Reutzel & Cooter, 2003).

Figure 5.5 "Vocabulary Cluster" based on *Harry Potter and the Prisoner of Azkaban:* Target word "irritable"

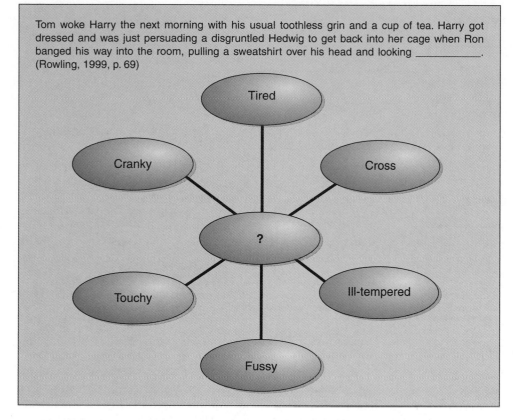

> Tom woke Harry the next morning with his usual toothless grin and a cup of tea. Harry got dressed and was just persuading a disgruntled Hedwig to get back into her cage when Ron banged his way into the room, pulling a sweatshirt over his head and looking _____. (Rowling, 1999, p. 69)

From *Strategies for Reading Assessment and Instruction: Helping Every Child Succeed,* 2nd Ed., D.R. Reutzel & R.B. Cooter, 2003. Upper Saddle River, NJ: Merrill/Prentice Hall. Used with permission.

integrate new information, and restructure existing information for greater clarity (Yopp & Yopp, 2000). For students having learning problems, using semantic maps prior to reading a selection has also proven to promote better story recall than traditional methods (Sinatra, Stahl-Gemake, & Berg, 1984). Writing materials are the only supplies needed.

There are many ways to introduce semantic mapping to students, but the first time around you will want to use a direct instruction approach with a lot of teacher modeling, guided practice, and independent practice.

One way is to introduce semantic maps through something we call "wacky webbing." The idea is to take a topic familiar to all, such as the name of one's home state, and portray it in the center of the map. Major categories related to the theme are connected to the central concept using either bold lines or double lines. Details that relate to the major categories are connected using single lines. Figure 5.6 shows a semantic map for the topic "Tennessee."

Semantic maps can also be constructed that relate to a story or chapter book the students are reading. In Figure 5.7 we use an example (Reutzel & Cooter, 2003) of a semantic map from a story in the book *Golden Tales: Myths, Legends, and Folktales from Latin America* (Delacre, 1996).

Figure 5.6 Tennessee semantic web

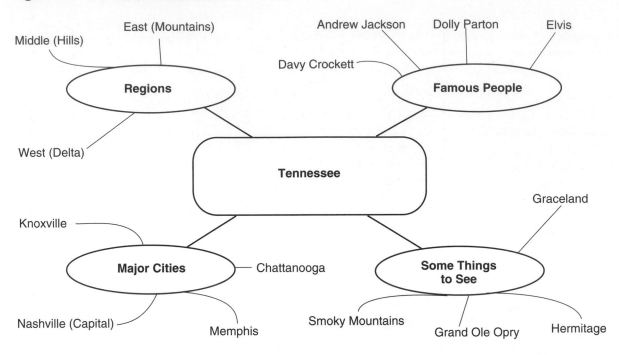

From *Strategies for Reading Assessment and Instruction: Helping Every Child Succeed,* 2nd Ed., D.R. Reutzel & R.B. Cooter, 2003. Upper Saddle River, NJ: Merrill/Prentice Hall. Used with permission.

Figure 5.7 ""Guanina" semantic map

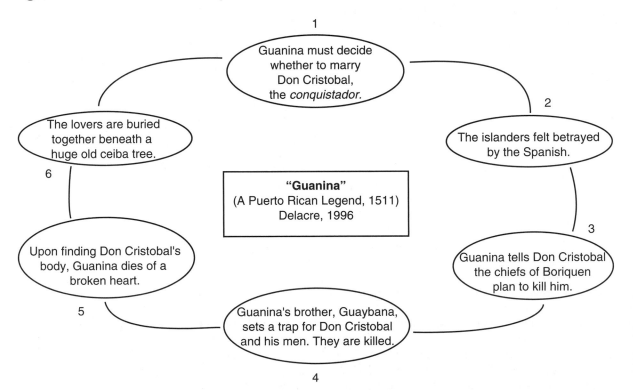

From *Strategies for Reading Assessment and Instruction: Helping Every Child Succeed,* 2nd Ed., D.R. Reutzel & R.B. Cooter, 2003. Upper Saddle River, NJ: Merrill/Prentice Hall. Used with permission.

144

Certainly, any of the strategies found in this chapter can be adapted for ELL students, so long as you are direct and explicit in your teaching. Direct instruction helps ELL students create mental scaffolding for support of new vocabulary and concepts.

Linking Multicultural Experiences with Vocabulary Development

Vocabulary development in spoken and written English is at the heart of literacy learning (Wheatley, Muller, & Miller, 1993). Because of the rich diversity found in American classrooms, teachers need to consider ways of adapting the curriculum so that all children can learn to recognize and use appropriate and descriptive vocabulary. In this section, we consider three possible avenues proven to be successful in multicultural settings.

1. *Linking vocabulary studies to a broad topic or novel.* We know that there is a limit to the number of words that can be taught directly and in isolation. K. Au (1993) tells us that students in multicultural settings learn vocabulary best if the new words are related to a broader topic. Working on vocabulary development in connection with students' exploration of content area topics is a natural and connected way to learn new words and explore their various meanings. In Chapter 13 we go into further detail about how vocabulary instruction can be conducted in content units, including the use of special computer-assisted programs.

2. *Wide reading as a vehicle for vocabulary development.* Reading for enjoyment on a daily basis helps students increase their vocabulary knowledge, not to mention myriad other reading abilities. Teachers can help students become regular readers by assessing their reading interests (see Chapter 9), then locating books that fit the reader. Matching books and students is a simple way of encouraging the kinds of reading behaviors that pay dividends. Helping students learn how to choose books on their developmental level (see "Rule of Thumb" in Chapter 12) is an important way students can learn to independently select books.

3. *The Village English activity.* L. Delpit (1988) writes about a method of teaching Native Alaskan students new vocabulary that works well in many multicultural settings. This *Village English activity* respects and encourages children's home languages while helping them see relationships between language use and social/professional realities in the United States (Au, 1993).

The Village English activity begins with the teacher writing "Our Language Heritage" at the top of half a piece of poster board and "Standard American English" at the top of the second half. The teacher explains to students that in America people speak in many different ways and that this makes our nation as colorful and interesting as a patchwork quilt. For elementary students, we think this would be a good time to share *Elmer* by David McKee (1990), a book about an elephant of many colors (called a "patchwork elephant") and how he enriched his elephant culture.

The teacher explains that there are many times when adults need to speak in the same way so they can be understood, usually in formal situations. In formal situations, we speak Standard American English. When at home or with friends in our community, we usually speak the language of our heritage. It is like the difference between a picnic compared to a "dressed up" formal dinner. On the chart, then, phrases used in the native dialect can be written under the heading "Our Language Heritage" and comparative translations are noted and discussed on the side labeled

"Standard American English." These comparisons can be noted in an ongoing way throughout the year as part of a special *word wall.* The Village English activity can be an interesting way to increase vocabulary knowledge while also valuing language differences.

HELPING STUDENTS ACQUIRE NEW VOCABULARY INDEPENDENTLY

The ultimate task for teachers is to help students become independent learners. The ongoing learning of new vocabulary throughout life is unquestionably a key to continued self-education. In this section, we feature ways students can become independent learners of new words.

Word Learning Strategies

Students must determine the meaning of words that are new to them when these words are discovered in their reading. The key is to develop effective **word-learning strategies,** such as how to use *dictionaries and other reference aids,* how to use *information about word parts* to figure out the meanings of words in text, and how to use *context clues* to determine word meanings.

Using Dictionaries and Other Reference Aids

Students must learn how to use dictionaries, glossaries, and thesauruses to help broaden and deepen their knowledge of words. In preparation for using these tools, students must learn such things as alphabetical order, ordinal language (i.e., first, second, third. . . .), and about *guide words.* The most helpful dictionaries and reference aids include sentences providing clear examples of word meanings in context.

Using Information About Word Parts

Students can use their knowledge of word parts—affixes (prefixes and suffixes), base words, and word roots—to figure out unfamiliar words in print.

In Chapter 4, we learned that *structural analysis* involves the use of word parts, such as *affixes* (prefixes and suffixes) and *base words,* to figure out the meaning of new words in print. Students can likewise use structural analysis skills independently as a meaning-based, word-learning tool just as effectively as they would as a decoding strategy. For example, learning the four most common prefixes in English (*un-, re-, in-, dis-*), can provide helpful meaning clues for about two-thirds of all English words having prefixes. Prefixes are relatively easy to learn because they have clear meanings (for example, un- means not and re- means again); they are usually spelled the same way from word to word. Suffixes can often be a bit more challenging to learn than prefixes. For one thing, quite a few suffixes have confusing meanings (e.g., the suffix -*ness,* meaning "the state of" is not all that helpful in figuring out the meaning of *tenderness*).

The four most common prefixes in English, un-, re-, in-, and dis-, provide helpful meaning clues for about two-thirds of all words having prefixes.

Students should also learn about **word roots,** or words having their origins from other languages. About 60 percent of all English words have Latin or Greek origins (Partnership for Reading, 2001, p. 39). Latin and Greek word roots are common to the subjects of science and social studies and also form a large share of the new words for students in their content-area textbooks. Teachers should teach the highest frequency word roots as they occur in the texts students read.

Using Context Clues to Determine Word Meanings

Context clues are meaning cues found in the words, phrases, and sentences that surround an unknown word. It is not an overstatement to say that the ability to use context clues is fundamental to reading success. This is because most word meanings will be learned indirectly from context. Following is another classroom example from the publication *Put Reading First* (2001), this time demonstrating the use of context clues as a word-learning strategy.

AN EXAMPLE OF CLASSROOM INSTRUCTION:

Using Context Clues[*]

In a third grade class, the teacher models how to use context clues to determine word meanings as follows:

> **Student** *(reading the text):* When the cat pounced on the dog, the dog jumped up, yelping, and knocked over a lamp, which crashed to the floor. The animals ran past Tonia, tripping her. She fell to the floor and began sobbing. Tonia's brother Felix yelled at the animals to stop. As the noise and confusion mounted, Mother hollered upstairs, "What's all that **commotion?**"

> **Teacher:** The context of the paragraph helps us determine what **commotion** means. There's yelping and crashing, sobbing, and yelling. And then the last sentence says, "as the **noise** and **confusion** mounted." The author's use of the words *noise* and *confusion* gives us a very strong clue as to what **commotion** means. In fact, the author is really giving us a definition there, because **commotion** means something that's noisy and confusing—a disturbance. Mother was right; there was definitely a **commotion!**

[*]From *Put Reading First: The Research Building Blocks for Teaching Children to Read* (2001). Non-copyrighted material published by the National Institute for Literacy. Available online at www.nifl.gov.

Encouraging Wide Reading

Reading is a cognitive skill that in some ways mirrors physical skill development. As with physical skills, the more one practices reading, the more reading ability increases. In our work with at-risk students, over the years, we have come to realize that if we can simply get children to read every day for at least 15 to 20 minutes, their reading ability will increase quickly and exponentially. In one study, Reutzel and Hollingsworth (1991c) discovered that allowing children to read self-selected books 30 minutes every day resulted in significantly improved scores on reading comprehension tests. These children performed as well as students who had received 30 minutes of direct instruction on the tested reading comprehension skills. Their results suggest that regular daily reading is probably at least as effective as formal reading instruction, and the children can do it on their own! Encouraging children to read books that match their interests can motivate them to read independently and grow their vocabulary.

What Are Some Ways Teachers Can Encourage Wide Reading?

How can teachers encourage children to read independently on a regular basis? The answer lies in helping children become aware of their own interests and in finding books they can read. The interest issue can be resolved in two steps. First, the

Standards Note
Standard 6.3: The reading professional will be able to teach students to use context to identify and define unfamiliar words. Telling students to use context to figure out new words is not sufficient. Develop five specific examples of context clues, using specific vocabulary to illustrate it.

Wide reading is a powerful way for students to build vocabulary knowledge independently.

Surveying student interests with an individual interest sheet (IIS) helps teachers select free-reading materials.

teacher should administer an *interest inventory* to the class at the beginning of the year (see Chapter 9 for ways of assessing student interest) to determine what types of books are indicated for classroom instruction. These results, however, could be taken a little further: As the second step, we suggest that the teacher start an **individual interest sheet (IIS)** for each child based on these results and present them to children during individual reading conferences (discussed more in later chapters). The IIS simply lists topics that appear to be of interest to the child and suggests books available in the school library. Over time, the children can list additional topics they discover to be of interest and can look for books in those areas. The principle is much the same as having children keep a list of topics they would like to write stories about. Figure 5.8 shows a sample IIS, with new interests written in by the student.

Figure 5.8   Sample individual interest sheet (IIS)

> ***Individual Interest Sheet***
>
> **Mrs. Harbor's Sixth Grade**
>
> **Sunnydale School**
>
> Name: Holly Ambrose
>
> Things I am interested in knowing more about, or topics that I like . . .
>
> | **Topics** | **Books to consider from our library** |
> | --- | --- |
> | horses | *The Red Pony* (J. Steinbeck) |
> | getting along with friends | *Afternoon of the Elves* (J. Lisle) |
> | romantic stories | *The Witch of Blackbird Pond* (E. Speare) |
> | one-parent families | *The Moonlight Man* (P. Fox) |

Encouraging children to read books that match their interests can motivate them to read independently and grow their vocabulary.

A useful reference for teachers attempting to match children's interests with quality literature is Donna Norton's (2002) book *Through the Eyes of a Child: An Introduction to Children's Literature.* Most high-interest topic areas are discussed in this text and are matched to several possible book titles. Book suggestions include brief descriptions of the main story line to help in the decision-making process.

Computer-Assisted Vocabulary Learning

As computers become more accessible to students and teachers, the question arises: Can some of the new computer applications available help students learn new vocabulary? Reinking and Rickman (1990) studied the vocabulary growth of sixth grade students who had computer-assisted programs available to them. They compared students who read passages on printed pages accompanied by either a standard dictionary or glossary (the traditional classroom situation) with students who read passages on a computer screen. These computer-assisted programs provided either *optional* assistance (on command) for specific vocabulary words or *mandatory* (automatic) assistance. Two very interesting things were learned from their research. First, students reading passages with computer assistance performed significantly better on vocabulary tests that focused on the words emphasized than did students in traditional reading groups. Second, students receiving automatic computer assistance with the passages also outperformed the more traditional reading group on a passage comprehension test relating to information read in the experiment. These results suggest that computer programs that offer students passages to read with vocabulary assistance can be helpful. Further, they suggest to us another possible advantage of the computer: teaching students to use what might be termed a *vocabulary enhancer,* such as a thesaurus program, with their writing, which could help students discover on their own new synonyms and antonyms for commonly used words. Most word processing programs, such as *Microsoft Word,* have a thesaurus program already installed for easy use.

Name and describe two ways teachers can enhance vocabulary learning.

Computer-assisted vocabulary instruction can provide motivational word-learning instruction in a classroom learning center.

Vocabulary Overview

Vocabulary overviews help students decide which words they will learn. In classroom settings teachers can usually anticipate vocabulary that may be troublesome during reading and teach these words through brief mini-lessons. But when children read independently, they need to find ways to learn new words on their own. One activity that serves this purpose is the vocabulary overview. **Vocabulary overviews** help students select unfamiliar words in print, then use context clues and their background knowledge to determine word meaning.

One way of helping students develop their own vocabulary overviews is Haggard's (1986) *vocabulary self-selection strategy* (VSS). Our version of the VSS begins with a small-group mini-lesson to learn the process. Students are asked to find at least one word they feel the class should learn. Next, they define the word to the best of their ability based on context of clues and any clues from their own background knowledge. On the day the words are presented, each child takes turns explaining (a) where each word was found, (b) his or her context-determined definition for the word, and (c) reasons why the class should learn the word.

Word Maps

A **word map** (Schwartz & Raphael, 1985) is a graphic rendering of a word's meaning. It answers three important questions about the word: *What is it? What is it like?*

Word maps *help students tap schema connections to understand word meanings.*

Figure 5.9   Word map

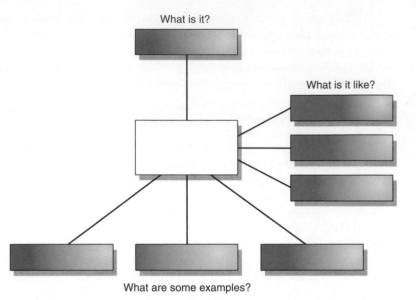

What are some examples? Answers to these questions are extremely valuable because they help children link the new word or concept to their prior knowledge and world experiences, a process known to have an effect on reading comprehension (Stahl et al., 1991). An example of a word map is shown in Figure 5.9.

Introducing this vocabulary-acquisition strategy to students is a relatively easy task. First, the teacher presents the idea of using this kind of graphic organizer to understand new word meanings, and models the word map as one example. Next, students work with the teacher in a guided practice format to organize familiar information using the three key questions used in the word map.

Simple concepts should be used in initial guided practice exercises to help students learn how to use the map. For example, a practice map might be constructed using the word *car.* Answers for each of the story map questions that might be offered by elementary students follow:

> Word: *car*
>
> What is it? (transportation, movement)
>
> What is it like? (four wheels, metal, glass, lights, moves, steering wheel)
>
> What are some examples? (Honda, station wagon, Thunderbird, convertible)

After working through several examples with the whole group or class, teachers should give students opportunities to practice using the word map. In the beginning, whole-class practice works best, followed by independent practice using narrative and expository texts of the students' or teacher's choosing.

Summary

In this chapter we have gained some important insights into ways children can be helped to expand their vocabulary knowledge. First, we know that word knowledge is essential for reading comprehension. Evidence-based research tells us that vocabulary instruction should utilize activities (like the ones found in this chapter) that link word learning to concept and schema development. We should also teach specific word learning strategies to our students as well as strategies they can use on their own to understand unfamiliar words in print.

Wide reading should be encouraged and made possible in the classroom. Literally thousands of words are learned through regular and sustained reading. Time should be set aside each day for this crucial learning activity. As an example, Johnson (2001) advocated the use of a program called Read-a-Million-Minutes, which was designed to foster wide reading throughout Iowa. All students set their own in-school and out-of-school reading goal that contributes to the school's goal.

Direct instruction should be used to teach words that are necessary for passage comprehension. Considering how critical some words are for comprehending a new passage, teachers should not leave vocabulary learning to incidental encounters, but rather plan regular direct instruction lessons to make sure that essential words are learned. Active learning activities yield the best results. According to research conducted by Stahl (1986), vocabulary instruction that provided only definitional information (i.e., dictionary activities) failed to improve comprehension significantly. Active learning opportunities, such as creation of word webs, playing word games, and discussing new words in reading groups or literature circles, are far more effective in cementing new knowledge and improving comprehension.

We also know that students require a good bit of repetition to learn new words and integrate them into existing knowledge (schemas). In some cases, students may require as many as 40 encounters to fully learn new vocabulary. To know a word well means knowing what it means, how to pronounce it, and how its meaning changes in different contexts. Repeated exposures to the word in different contexts is the key to successful learning.

Students should be helped to develop their own strategies for word learning from written and oral contexts. This includes the use of context clues, structural analysis (word roots, prefixes, suffixes), and research skills (use of the dictionary, thesaurus, etc.).

Finally, parents can help their children succeed in expanding concept and vocabulary knowledge by exposing them to new experiences and helping them to read about and discuss new ideas in the home.

Concept Applications

In the Classroom

1. Design a lesson plan introducing a chosen word learning strategy to third grade students. You should be certain that the lesson includes rich literature examples, teacher modeling, and ample guided practice for students.
2. Create a Deceptive Language bulletin board that shows various uses of euphemisms in advertising aimed at children as consumers. Create a second board showing how these same tactics are used on adults through advertising (and perhaps by political leaders!).
3. Prepare a lesson plan for second-year (*not* the same as second *grade*) ELL students introducing one of the vocabulary learning strategies provided in this chapter. You will need to identify the age of the students and their first language and consider the background knowledge they might have to help them use the new strategy. As always, be certain that the lesson includes rich literature examples, teacher modeling, and ample guided practice for students.

Check your understanding of chapter concepts by using the self assessment for Chapter 5 of our Companion Website at www.prenhall.com/reutzel.

In the Field

1. Do an interest inventory with five students in a local elementary school. Next, prepare an IIS that matches at least four of their interests to popular children's literature. Ideas for the books should be recommended by the school librarian or drawn from D. Norton's (1998) book *Through the Eyes of a Child: An Introduction to Children's Literature.* Finally, present the IIS forms to each child, and explain how they are to be used. Copies of both forms should be turned in to your college instructor, along with a journal entry explaining how each child reacted.
2. Prepare and teach a mini-lesson demonstrating the VSS for multicultural classes. Develop a simple handout for the students with helpful hints about collecting new words for investigation.
3. Locate an elementary classroom in which the writing process (discussed fully in Chapter 12) is practiced. Working with two child-volunteers, prepare a mini-lesson on synonyms and antonyms using samples they permit you to borrow from their writing folders.

Recommended Readings

Allen, J. (1999). *Words, words, words: Teaching vocabulary in grades 4–12.* Portland, ME: Stenhouse.

Beck, I. L., McKeown, M. G., & Kucan, L. (2002). *Bringing words to life: Robust vocabulary instruction.* New York: Guilford Press.

Cunningham, P. M., & Cunningham, J. (1992). Making words: Enhancing the invented spelling-decoding connection. *Reading Teacher, 46*(2), 106–115.

Fry, E. B., Kress, J. E., Fountoukidis, D. L. (1993). *The reading teacher's book of lists,* (3rd Ed.). Paramis, NJ: Prentice Hall.

Ganske, K. (2000). *Word journeys: Assessment-guided phonics, spelling, and vocabulary instruction.* New York: Guilford.

Johnson, D. D. (2001). *Vocabulary in the elementary and middle school.* Boston: Allyn & Bacon.

Peregoy, S. F., & Boyle, O. F. (2001). *Reading, writing, & learning in ESL.* New York: Longman.

6 Improving Reading Comprehension

Focus Questions

When you are finished studying this chapter, you should be able to answer these questions:

1. What is the difference between *teaching* and *testing* reading comprehension?

2. How do readers' prior experiences or schemas influence their comprehensions?

3. What comprehension strategies can be taught to students to help them distinguish narrative and expository text structures?

4. What are some types of metacognitive training lessons described in this chapter?

5. What are some strategies suggested for knowledge- and experience-based comprehension instruction?

6. What strategies are discussed in this chapter to make questioning reading comprehension more effective?

7. What are the four parts of a reciprocal teaching lesson?

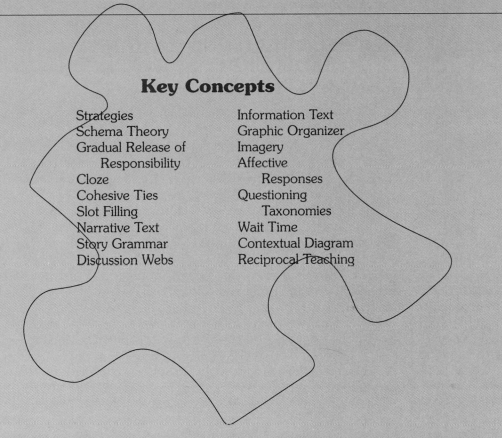

Key Concepts

Strategies
Schema Theory
Gradual Release of
    Responsibility
Cloze
Cohesive Ties
Slot Filling
Narrative Text
Story Grammar
Discussion Webs

Information Text
Graphic Organizer
Imagery
Affective
    Responses
Questioning
    Taxonomies
Wait Time
Contextual Diagram
Reciprocal Teaching

Reading comprehension is the very heart and soul of reading (Keene & Zimmerman, 1997; Collins-Block, Gambrell, & Pressley, 2002; Collins-Block & Pressley, 2002). Although learning to recognize letters, learning to connect letters with sounds, and then blending these elements into words is extremely important (Pressley, 2000; Johnson, 2001), teachers must never lose sight of the ultimate goal of reading instruction—comprehending the text! From their very first encounters with print, teachers should help children discover meaning from print by providing effective comprehension instruction (Pearson & Duke, 2002).

Visit Chapter 6 of our Companion Website at www.prenhall.com/ reutzel to look into the chapter objectives, standards and principles, and pertinent web links associated with Improving Reading Comprehension.

ISSUES IN TEACHING READING COMPREHENSION

Instruction *or* Assessment?

During the late 1960s and throughout the 1970s, reading comprehension was largely taught by asking students questions following reading or by assigning skill sheets as practice for reading comprehension skills such as getting the main idea, determining the sequence, following directions, noting details, and cause and effect relationships. In 1978, Dolores Durkin reported findings from reading comprehension studies conducted in public school classrooms. After observing a variety of "expert" teachers engaged in reading instruction in both reading and social studies classrooms, Durkin concluded that these teachers spent very little time actually teaching children how to understand texts. *In fact, less than 1 percent of total reading or social studies instructional time was devoted to the teaching of reading comprehension.* Unfortunately, many researchers conclude that the situation in today's schools has not improved appreciably over the last 25 years (Collins-Block, Gambrell, & Pressley, 2002).

So, what is happening in America's classrooms with respect to comprehension instruction? Durkin (1978) provided insights into that question as well. Teachers, she said, do not teach comprehension skills, but only "mention" or "question." Durkin defined a *mentioner* as a teacher who says "just enough about a topic [e.g., unstated conclusions] to allow for a written assignment to be given" (Durkin, 1981a, p. 516). Furthermore, attention to new vocabulary words was often brief, even "skimpy" (p. 524). Basal reader teacher's manuals were usually consulted for only two purposes: (a) to study the list of new vocabulary words and (b) to ask the comprehension questions following the reading of a selection. Worksheets, in reality nothing more than informal tests, dominated classroom reading comprehension instruction.

Durkin (1978) observed that less than 1% of total reading or social studies instructional time was devoted to the teaching of reading comprehension.

Durkin conducted a second study (1981b) in which she investigated the comprehension instruction found in five nationally published basal reading series. Her conclusions in this study essentially supported her earlier study: Publishers, like teachers, failed to understand the differences between teaching and testing reading comprehension. Basal reader teachers' manuals offered little or no help for teachers about *how to teach* children to comprehend text. Instead, the main resources were reading comprehension worksheets mislabeled as instruction. Durkin concluded that teachers often have difficulty telling the difference between *teaching* and *testing* when it comes to reading comprehension.

Basal teacher's manuals offered little or no help for teachers about how to teach children to comprehend text.

If mentioning and questioning are not the qualities of effective comprehension instruction, then what is? Durkin (1978) suggested that effective comprehension instruction includes helping, assisting, defining, demonstrating, modeling, describing, explaining, providing feedback, thinking aloud, and *guiding* students through learning activities. Simply asking students to respond to a worksheet or to answer a list of comprehension questions does nothing to develop new comprehension skills. Research has shown that reading comprehension improves when teachers provide explicit comprehension strategy instruction (Morrow, 1985, Bauman & Bergeron, 1993; Brown, Pressley, Van Meter, & Schuder, 1996; Dole, Brown, & Trathen, 1996) and when they provide instructional activities that support students' understanding of the texts they will read (Eldredge, Reutzel, & Hollingsworth, 1996; Hansen, 1981; Tharp, 1982; Dowhower, 1987; Reutzel, Hollingsworth, & Eldredge, 1994). The key to success is for teachers to design and deliver carefully structured learning activities that lead students to higher levels of comprehension.

Teaching Comprehension in the Primary Grades

Most of early literacy research recently has been directed toward the issues of word identification, particularly phonemic awareness and phonics instruction (Snow, Burns, & Griffin, 1998; National Reading Panel, 2000; RAND Reading Study Group Report, 2001). This is so much the case that, "The terms *comprehension instruction* and *primary grades* do not often appear in the same sentence" (Pearson & Duke, 2002, p. 247). But more recently leading reading authorities, corporately sponsored study groups such as the RAND Reading Study Group, and federal government agencies concluded that young children can and should be taught reading comprehension strategies from the onset of reading instruction.

In many classrooms the idea that children learn to read before reading to learn is evidenced in a lack of comprehension instruction in the primary grades.

Teaching Comprehension in the Information Age

Information text (nonfiction) presents different kinds of comprehension obstacles for younger readers. Unlike stories (fiction), information texts are written to explain new concepts, historical events, and previously unknown vocabulary. Text organizations used by authors (e.g., cause/effect, comparison/contrast, problem/solution, description, listing) help structure their ideas depending on their purpose (Alexander & Jetton, 2000). These structures are used extensively in the areas of mathematics, the sciences, historical texts, and the social sciences. Many young readers have trouble following these organizational structures, which can lead to knowledge deficits in critical areas and a widening achievement gap among young children (Neuman, 2001).

In spite of the growing need for content knowledge in the Information Age, the vast majority of reading materials in grades K–3 are *narrative* or story in form. Duke (2000) took a closer look at the reading instruction of children in 20 first-grade classrooms from very low and very high socioeconomic-status school districts (i.e., school districts having a lot of poor families versus districts with a lot of upper-class families). She found very few informational texts in any of these classrooms, particularly the low socioeconomic-status schools. The most startling finding was children in low socioeconomic classrooms, "poor kids," in other words, were asked to read information books only about 3.6 minutes per day on average. Clearly, teachers must spend much more time helping children read and understand nonfiction informational text if they are to excel. Similarly, reading researchers need to devote more energy to this critical topic (Pearson & Duke, 2002).

There is little time spent teaching comprehension strategies using information texts in the primary grades.

Comprehension Strategy Instruction: Single Strategies or Multiple Strategies?

Pressley (2002b) pointed out another vexing issue concerning comprehension instruction. In his *Turn of the Century Status Report* on comprehension strategy instruction. Teachers are increasingly aware that they need to explicitly teach comprehension strategies to children. But *which strategies,* taught in *what order?* Should they be taught singly or in combination? In one approach to teaching comprehension strategies, Keene and Zimmerman (1997) in their book *Mosaic of Thought* encouraged teachers to teach children single comprehension strategies, one at a time, from a list of seven research validated strategies. These single strategies are to be taught in separate "mini-lessons" in which the teacher demonstrates the use of the strategy and gradually releases the application of the strategy to the students. Later, students are taught ways of applying the strategy in other reading situations.

Research has yet to determine whether teaching comprehension strategies singly or as a set of multiple strategies is most effective for young children.

Another approach for teaching comprehension strategies has been described in Palincsar & Brown's (1984) *Reciprocal Teaching* and Pressley's (2002) *Transactional Strategies Instruction.* Here children practice using *multiple* comprehension strategies as a set or *package* as they read, then discuss what they've learned in small groups with teacher support. The idea is to teach children a "routine" for working through texts using a specific set of comprehension strategies. Research has yet to determine if teaching a combination of comprehension strategies as a set is preferable to teaching a series of single strategies. One thing is certain: children need to be taught comprehension strategies continuously.

COMPREHENDING TEXT: SCHEMA THEORY

Schema theory explains how knowledge is stored in the mind. A *schema* (the plural is *schemata* or *schemas*) can be thought of as a mental file folder of categorical knowledge *(chairs, birds, ships),* events *(weddings, birthdays, funerals),* emotions *(anger, frustration, joy, pleasure),* and roles *(parent, judge, teacher)* drawn from the reader's life experiences (Rumelhart, 1981). Schemas do not exist in the mind in any tangible form. Rather schemas are abstract representations of how knowledge is structured in the mind.

If schemas are like file folders for different concepts, then each concept "folder" has parts inside; these are called *semantic features.* For example, the semantic features associated with the concept of *bird* may include examples, such as *eagles, robins,* and *blue jays;* attributes of birds, such as wings, feathers, and beaks; and a category in which a particular bird belongs—such as *pets* or *birds of prey.* Hence, schemas are organized in our minds by *associations, categories, examples,* and *meaning;* and each are found in our memory much like looking up a topic in an encyclopedia. For example, when looking up the topic of *birds* in an encyclopedia, one typically encounters information about birds, including attributes, categories, and examples of birds.

Schemas are also linked together when there are related meanings (A. M. Collins & Quillian, 1969; Lindsay & Norman, 1977; Anderson & Pearson, 1984; Reznitskaya & Anderson, 2002). Each schema is connected to another related schema, forming a vast interconnected network of knowledge and experiences within the mind of the individual. The size and content of each schema are influenced by past experiences. Thus, younger children predictably possess fewer, less well-developed schemas than mature adults. For example, consider Figure 6.1, which represents a first-grader's schema about birds; then in Figure 6.2, compare the first grader's bird schema with that of a freshman high school student just completing a biology class.

Because individuals have their own unique life experiences stored in memory, teachers must not assume that all children in a classroom possess identical knowledge for a given concept, event, or experience. Although readers' schemas often have common features, as shown in Figures 6.1 and 6.2, the first grader's schema, for ex-

*A **schema** is a package of knowledge containing related concepts, events, emotions, and roles experienced by the reader.*

*Each **schema** contains a set of defining attributes or semantic features, such as wings and feathers associated with a bird schema.*

Notice how researchers have represented schemas.

Figure 6.1　First grader's bird schema network

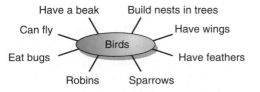

Figure 6.2 High school student's bird schema network

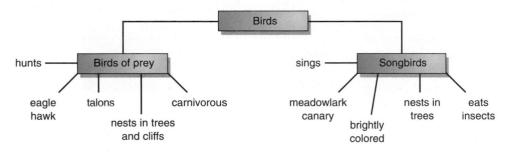

ample, is less developed than the high school student's. Schemas are never complete; they simply provide a flexible place (a mental "file folder") for storing new information. One concept fundamental to schema theory is the idea of adding new information to a schema through a process called **slot filling.** In conclusion, a schema can be thought of as a flexible and growing cognitive framework with slots that can be filled in by the personal and vicarious experiences of a reader.

Pearson, Hansen, and Gordon (1979) found that children who already know a great deal about a given topic before reading about that topic, such as *spiders* prior to reading a text on spiders, remembered more from their reading than did children who knew little or nothing about the topic. This study demonstrates that teachers must be as concerned about building children's knowledge across a wide variety of topics at the same time they are helping students gain control over comprehension strategies. In this way we can close both the knowledge gap and the reading achievement gap (NAEP, 2000; Neuman, 2001).

Younger readers generally possess less well-developed schemata than older readers.

*Adding new information to an incomplete schema is called **slot filling.***

COMPREHENDING TEXT: A PROCESS OVERVIEW

Comprehending text is a complicated process. Based on schema theory, we see comprehension as a five-stage model that includes *searching, selecting, applying, evaluating,* and *composing.*

1. *Searching* for an appropriate schema, a specific "mental file folder," by paying attention to meaning clues taken from the text (i.e., words, sentences, and paragraphs).
2. *Selecting* an appropriate schema based on the clues found in the text.
3. *Applying* the information in that mental file folder (schema) to help the reader figure out the author's message.
4. *Evaluating* whether the schema chosen was the correct one or if it should be discarded and replaced with another schema that seems to make more sense.
5. *Composing* a new or revised understanding (memory) that is added to the existing schema or used to create a new schema.

***Comprehending** can be thought of as a five-step process: searching, selecting, applying, evaluating, and composing.*

This process is illustrated in Figure 6.3.

When readers begin reading a text, they bring along all of their schemas to help them get meaning from the print. What readers expect to find when they begin reading a selection, in terms of content, vocabulary, and format, is influenced by two factors: (a) the *function* of the reading materials, such as labels, road signs, bus

Figure 6.3   A schema-based explanation of processing text information

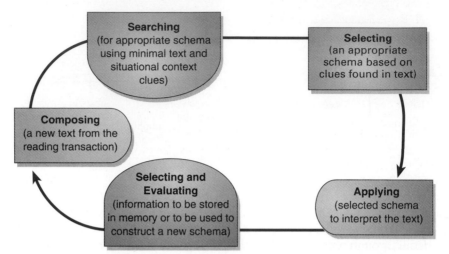

Schemas guide the construction of each word meaning as well as the meaning of the entire text.

schedules, books, or newspapers, and (b) the *situational context* in which the act of reading takes place, such as a supermarket, a car, a bus terminal, a bookstore, or an easy chair at home. In this way, context factors—*function* and *situation*—help readers efficiently select a tentative schema for interpreting the print.

As an example, consider the following. Imagine that you are going to a local laundromat to wash your clothes for the first time. Since you are new at this, you will probably look around the laundromat for information to help you accomplish the task. On a nearby wall, you see a large sign posted above the washing machines. The text reads as follows:

> The procedure is actually quite simple. First you arrange the items into different groups. Of course, one pile may be sufficient, depending on how much there is to do. If you have to go somewhere else due to lack of facilities, that is the next step, otherwise you are pretty well set. It is important not to overdo things. It is better to do too few things at once than too many. In the short run this may not seem important, but complications can easily arise. A mistake can be expensive as well. At first, the whole procedure will seem complicated. Soon, however, it will become just another facet of life. It is difficult to foresee any end to the necessity for this task in the immediate future, but then, one never can tell. After the procedure is complete, one arranges the materials into different groups again. Then they can be put into their appropriate places. Eventually they will be used once more and the whole cycle will then have to be repeated. However, that is part of life. *(J. D. Bransford & Franks, 1971, p. 719)*

If you had not read these directions on a sign in a laundromat, you may have had greater difficulty limiting your search for the correct schema to interpret the sign to the act of washing clothes. Thus, the function of a sign and the situational context of reading, in this case the laundromat, helped you limit your search to the most likely schema—washing clothes.

Once the most likely schema is selected for interpreting a text, it is applied. In the laundromat scenario, you would interpret the word *procedure* in the text to mean *the act of,* or *steps involved in,* washing clothes. If you had selected a postmaster schema by mistake, then the word *procedure* may have been interpreted as the act of, or steps in, sorting letters into post office boxes. Thus, the selected schema can be used to guide the interpretation of each word in the text as well as the collective meaning of all the words in the text.

Schemas also provide a framework for absorbing new information found in the text. Empty slots in a novice's laundry schema are filled in using information found in the sign. Connections are also made between existing knowledge about doing laundry and the new information learned in the sign. By contrasting new information to already known schemas, readers automatically decide which information is important to remember for future use.

During this ongoing process, readers create a newly revised schema that includes new information learned; in this case, new knowledge gained from reading the laundry sign. In a way, comprehending text is a bit like creating a *new* text (Tierney & Pearson, 1983). In other words, one change resulting from the reading "transaction" above is that the reader is changed—he now possess greater knowledge about doing the laundry than he did before reading the sign on the wall. The sign on the wall has changed, in a sense, because it has been transformed in the mind of the reader. Hence, the act of comprehending a text can be thought of in terms of a dialogue between reader and author that takes place in a specific situational context.

COMPREHENSION DIFFICULTIES

Comprehension difficulties can be traced to four schema-related problems (Rumelhart, 1984). Each of these problems is discussed with examples to help you gain an understanding by experiencing firsthand the difficulties students may encounter in comprehending.

• *Difficulty 1: Students may not have the necessary schema to understand a specific topic. Without a schema for a particular concept, they simply cannot understand the text.*

In the passage below, for example, readers not having the needed schema cannot understand individual word meanings and have trouble comprehending the overall text.

A—Machine-baste interfacing to WRONG side of one collar section 1/2 inch from raw edges. Trim interfacing close to stitching. B—Clip dress neck edge to stay stitching. With RIGHT sides together, pin collar to dress, matching centers back and small dots. Baste. Stitch. Trim seam; clip curve. Press seam open. *(Gibson & Levin, 1975, p. 7)*

Although individuals with a sewing schema readily interpret this passage, those who don't possess a sewing schema experience greater difficulty making sense of certain specialized words *(baste, interfacing)* in the text and the text as a whole.

• *Difficulty 2: Readers may have well-developed schemas for a topic, but authors may fail to provide enough information or clues for readers to locate or select a given schema.*

In some cases a reader may already know a great deal about the topic to be read. However, the author may fail to provide enough information in the text that connects with the reader's schema. For example, read the following text to see if you can locate your schema on this well-known topic.

> Our hero bravely defied all scornful laughter that tried to prevent his scheme. "Your eyes deceive," he had said, "An egg not a table correctly typifies this planet." Now three sturdy sisters sought proof, forging along sometimes through calm vastness. *(J. C. Bransford & Johnson, 1972)*

The authors failed to include explicit clues in the text such as *explorer, ships,* and *America,* making the selection of a *Christopher Columbus* schema much more difficult. Without these important clues being placed in the text, it will be hard for readers to call up specific "slots" (associations) found in the Columbus schema.

> • *Difficulty 3: Readers may hastily select a schema for interpreting a text, only to discover later that the text information does not match the known information for that schema.*

When this comprehension difficulty occurs, readers usually shift from using the first schema to the appropriate one to correctly comprehend the text. You may recall the following example from Chapter 2. Read this scenario again and think how your schema changes with new information.

> John was on his way to school.
>
> He was terribly worried about the math lesson.
>
> He thought he might not be able to control the class again today.
>
> It was not a normal part of a janitor's duties.
>
> *(Sanford & Garrod, 1981, p. 114)*

Did you experience several shifts to select the appropriate schema to interpret the text? Not only do schemas help readers interpret what they read, but also the information found in the text helps readers decide which schemas are selected.

> • *Difficulty 4: The cultural and experiential background of readers may affect their perspective when selecting a schema to interpret a text. This sometimes leads to an "understanding" of the text but a misunderstanding of the author.*

To illustrate this comprehension difficulty, Lipson (1983) conducted a study showing that Catholic and Jewish children comprehended texts better when they were compatible with their own religious beliefs than when the texts went against their religious schemas. Other studies (Read & Rosson, 1982; Alvermann, Smith, & Readence, 1985; Reutzel & Hollingsworth, 1991a) have also shown that students' schemas that are based on their prior knowledge, attitudes, and experiences have a strong influence on how well students comprehend and *remember* information from their readings.

To illustrate this difficulty further, R. C. Anderson, Reynolds, Schallert, and Goetz (1977) asked people in a study to read the following paragraph:

> Tony slowly got up from the mat, planning his escape. He hesitated a moment and thought. Things were not going well. What bothered him most was being held, especially since the charge against him had been weak. He considered his present situation. The lock that held him was strong but he thought he could break it. He knew, however, that his timing would have to be perfect. Tony was aware that it was be-

cause of his early roughness that he had been penalized so severely—much too severely from his point of view. The situation was becoming frustrating; the pressure had been grinding on him for too long. He was being ridden unmercifully. Tony was getting angry now. He felt he was ready to make his move. He knew that his success or failure would depend on what he did in the next few seconds. (p. 372)

Most people in the study thought the passage described a convict planning his escape. There *is,* however, another possible interpretation. When physical education majors in this study read the passage above, they thought it was about wrestling. Thus, the experiential background of the readers influenced their understanding of what they read.

Students may need assistance to help them locate and use their schemata to comprehend text. For example, sometimes a picture can be very helpful.

A MODEL FOR EFFECTIVE COMPREHENSION INSTRUCTION

Gradual Release of Responsibility Instruction Model

Pearson and Gallagher (1983) designed a model for effective comprehension instruction called the **gradual release of responsibility.** In Figure 6.4, the diagonal line from the upper left-hand corner extending downward toward the lower right-hand corner represents varying degrees of responsibility teachers and children *share* in learning and using comprehension strategies or completing comprehension tasks. The upper left-hand corner in Figure 6.4 shows teachers carrying the major share of the responsibility for comprehension task completion, and the lower right-hand corner shows students carrying the major share of the responsibility.

The concept of *gradual release* shown in this instructional model can be used as a planning guide for any of the comprehension strategy lessons presented in the remainder of this chapter.

*The **gradual release of responsibility model** depicts the idea that responsibility for comprehension tasks should be shifted gradually over time from the teacher to the student.*

Figure 6.4 The Gradual Release of Responsibility model of instruction

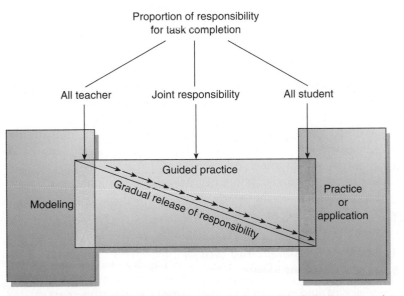

Source: From "The Instruction of Reading Comprehension" by P. D. Pearson and M. C. Gallagher, 1983, *Contemporary Educational Psychology, 8*(3), pp. 317–344. Copyright 1983 by Academic Press. Reprinted by permission.

It is important at this point to recall again Vygotsky's (1962) *zone of proximal development,* which reminds us that children need to be helped to do those things they cannot yet do independently.

How Gradual Release of Responsibility Works in the Classroom: The Teacher's Job

It is assumed that, before any kind of comprehension skill lesson is planned, the teacher has assessed her students to find out which strategies are needed. This is what we refer to as *class profiling,* and is discussed in-depth later in Chapter 9 titled *Assessing Literacy Learning.* The teacher then sets about planning learning activities for each strategy.

The first step, as indicated in Figure 6.4, is for the teacher to *model* how the skill is used in a reading situation. Modeling involves repeated examples where the teacher, as a master-user of the new strategy to be learned, demonstrates how the strategy "looks" when she uses it. Modeling should be done until the teacher is reasonably sure that the student(s) have an understanding of what is expected of them.

Teachers need to model the use of comprehension strategies using think alouds.

In the early stages of the next phase, *guided practice,* the teacher continues to model how the strategy is used in reading situations, but she now invites students to try it themselves. Thus, in the early stages of guided practice, as the model in Figure 6.4 indicates, most of the responsibility for using the strategy still rests with the teacher, but it is becoming a "joint responsibility." Students are starting to "get their hands dirty" as they try out the strategy with the help of the teacher. You might say that the teacher is shifting from serving as a *model* to being a supportive *coach.* You will need to plan for numerous practice activities during the guided practice stage; one or two lessons will not be enough.

As guided practice continues and the students gain confidence in using the new strategy, teachers begin to slowly phase out their direct support. Practice sessions can be planned in which students, working in pairs, practice using the strategy. Students only call upon the teacher now when they have a problem they cannot solve for themselves. This allows you to move about the classroom making "house calls" as needed, and to conduct informal assessments of their learning.

One caution for new teachers: be sure and have students *over-learn* the new strategy. One of our teacher friends calls this "marinating" students in the new knowledge (i.e., have them over-learn until the new knowledge is "soaked to the bone"). Teachers tend not to provide enough guided practice on new skills, which can result in only temporary or short-term learning. "Marinating" takes care of this problem.

In the final stage of the gradual release of responsibility model, students use the strategy independently—with little or no support. Activities planned now are essentially "all student" in nature. Again, much practice is needed to make sure the new skill has *crystallized* in students' minds. Before moving on and starting instruction on a new comprehension skill, the teacher ends the way she began—by assessing whether students are now proficient in using the skill.

How Gradual Release of Responsibility Works in the Classroom: The Student's Job

Much of what is expected of students can be inferred from the description above, but let's take a few moments to clarify their role. It may be helpful if you think of students in learning situations as *apprentices* and you yourself as a skilled craftsman.

At the beginning of a comprehension strategy lesson, when the teacher is busy modeling (demonstrating) the new strategy to be learned, the student's job is to *observe*. Learners should attend to the teacher demonstration and ask questions to clarify as necessary. During the guided practice phase, the student's job is to *experiment* with the new strategy.

In the final stages of learning, independent practice, students *demonstrate* for teachers how they can now use the newly acquired strategy on their own. New comprehension abilities are best demonstrated by students using language (Benson & Cummins, 2000): post-reading discussion, written summaries (e.g., reading response journals), oral retellings, and construction of graphic organizers that show key concepts and vocabulary, just to name a few possibilities. Student-generated language responses help teachers get a closer look at thinking processes that have been developed as a result of the learning activities.

Students need to assume responsibility for using comprehension strategies with teacher guidance and support.

COMPREHENSION INSTRUCTION: PHRASES AND SENTENCES

Comprehension instruction proceeds from an understanding of individual words in context to comprehending phrases and sentences. In this section of the chapter, we discuss how teachers can help children derive the meaning of individual words in text and "chunk" into meaningful phrases and sentences.

Standards Note
Standard 7.1: The reading professional will provide direct instruction and model when and how to use multiple comprehension strategies, including retelling. After reading each of the comprehension strategies presented, plan a direct instruction lesson for one comprehension strategy that includes gradually releasing responsibility for using the strategy to a group of children.

"Clozing" in on Comprehension: Deriving the Meaning of Words in Text

One of the more potent ways of teaching children how to use the context of a sentence to guess the identity of an unknown word is a teaching method known as *cloze*. The **cloze** procedure is "the use of a piece of writing in which certain words have been deleted and the pupil has to make maximum possible use of context clues available in predicting the missing words." (Bullock Report, D.E.S., 1975, p. 93). According to Rye (1982), the cloze procedure is a useful instructional strategy because "the human mind has a tendency to complete incomplete patterns or sequences." (p. 2) When cloze was first introduced by W. L. Taylor in 1953, it was proposed as a means of measuring reading ability. Since that time, a variety of instructional uses have been developed using cloze to improve children's ability to comprehend word meanings in text. Here are several instructional uses of cloze.

The most familiar version of cloze involves an *every nth*-word deletion pattern. Typically, every 5th or 10th word in a passage of 250 words is deleted and left for students to complete using the context, or surrounding familiar words, in the sentence. Look at the following example, which uses an every 5th-word deletion pattern.

The most familiar version of cloze involves an every nth-word deletion pattern.

Many scientists believe that there are other forms of intelligent life somewhere in space. These forms may not _____ the way we do. _____ often show life forms _____ space with silly-looking _____ . Movies often show them _____ frightening monsters. But have _____ ever wondered what those _____ life forms might think _____ us?

Primary-aged children experience greater success with an every 10th-word deletion pattern because children are given more context clues to use before encountering the next deletion.

Watson and Crowley (1988) describe another approach using the cloze procedure called *selected deletions.* The advantage to this approach is that teachers can delete selected words depending on their instructional goals and the needs of their students. For example, different categories of words may be selected for deletion: words signaling the sequence of text *(first, second, next, before, after),* words referring back to or ahead to other words in the text *(he, she, this, those, which),* words showing location *(behind, on, under, next to),* words signaling an explanation *(thus, because, so, therefore, as a result),* words signaling comparisons *(but, yet, although, similarly),* and words signaling an example *(such as, for example, that is, namely).* Here is one example of selected deletions:

Many scientists believe that there are other forms of intelligent _____ somewhere in space. These _____ may not look the way we do. Movies often show life _____ from space with silly-looking _____ .
_____ often show them as frightening monsters. But have you ever wondered what those other _____ forms might think of us?

*With **selected deletions,** teachers delete selected words depending on their instructional goals and the observed needs of their students.*

Phrasing for Comprehension: "Chunking" and "Readers' Theater"

To comprehend well, students must be able to mentally *chunk* words into meaningful phrases. Chunking develops best when children are given multiple opportunities to practice reading a text several times with increasing fluency (Irwin, 1996). We have also found that wide reading of easy materials across a variety of genre (e.g., mysteries, information texts, biography, poetry, short stories) is very useful—particularly information texts.

Students can practice *chunking* in a number of ways. One method is to rewrite a passage into chunks. An example taken from the book *The World of Matter* by Ron Cole (1997) is found in Figure 6.5.

Readers' theatre is another great task for practicing phrasing and fluency. In reader's theatre, children practice reading from a script in preparation for sharing an oral performance with classmates and selected audiences (Sloyer, 1982; Hill, 1990b). Unlike a play where students memorize lines, practice actions, and use elaborate stage sets to make their presentation, emphasis is placed on presenting a dramatic oral reading of a text for an audience who imagines setting and actions.

Typically, readers' theatre works best when easy texts are selected for practice. Information texts such as *The Popcorn Book* (dePaola, 1978) and *The Magic School Bus Lost in the Solar System* (Cole, 1990) may be used effectively as readers' theatre practice scripts (Young & Vardell, 1993). Also, scripts based on quality narratives,

One way to practice "chunking" is to rewrite a passage into visual chunks for fluency practice.

Readers' theater is a very useful task for practicing phrasing and fluency.

Figure 6.5   Chunking an information text

Big or small/ hot or cold/ shiny or dull/ visible or invisible/ every living thing/
And nonliving thing/ in our universe/ is made up of the stuff/ we call **matter.**/
Matter can be defined/ as anything that takes up space. (p. 1)

stories, and poems are good choices. Readers' theatre selections should be packed with action, contain an element of suspense, and include an entire meaningful story or episode. A few examples of such texts are Martin and Archambault's (1987) *Knots on a Counting Rope,* Viorst's (1972) *Alexander and the Terrible Horrible No Good Very Bad Day,* and Barbara Robinson's (1972) *The Best Christmas Pageant Ever.*

Hennings (1974) describes a simple procedure for preparing readers' theatre scripts for classroom performance. First, the text to be performed is read silently by the individual students. Second, the text is read again orally, sometimes using choral reading in a group. After the second reading, children either choose their parts, or the teacher assigns parts to the children. (We suggest that students be allowed to select their three most desired parts, write these choices on a slip of paper, and submit them to the teacher, and that teachers do everything possible to assign one of these three choices.) The third reading is also an oral reading with students reading their parts with scripts in hand. Students may have several rehearsal readings as they prepare for the final reading or performance in front of the class or a special audience.

COMPREHENSION INSTRUCTION: CONNECTING INFORMATION AND MAKING INFERENCES

An important part of reading comprehension involves the ability to make connections between words and ideas in text. This leads to the ability of making inferences or "reading between the lines" (Hollingsworth & Reutzel, 1988; Keene & Zimmerman, 1997; Pearson & Duke, 2002). Drawing inferences requires readers to link words and ideas between sentences, then, connect key ideas found in several sentences. Therefore, let's first take a look at the *connectives* that link ideas between sentences. Next, we will discuss what are called *slot-filling* inferences—those that connect ideas across several sentences.

*Words that link sentences together are called **cohesive ties.***

Connecting Ideas Among Sentences

Important ideas between sentences are "glued" together by words known as *cohesive ties* (Moe & Irwin, 1986). Some examples of these "glue words" or cohesive ties follow:

Cohesive Ties (categories)	Example
Reference	
Includes many pronoun types, location words, and time words.	Austin went to the park. He climbed the slide. "Mom, look at that car! Can we go over there?"
Substitution	
Replacing a word or phrase with another.	"My dress is old. I need a new one." "Do you know him?" "No, do you?"
Ellipsis	
Omitting a word or phrase resulting in an implied repetition.	"Were laughing?" "No, I wasn't." "Dylan wears expensive sneakers. His look nicer."

Conjunction

Connects phrases and sentences using additive, adversative, causal, and temporal ties.

"Denver ate ice cream after dinner. He didn't eat fish *because* he dislikes them."

Lexical

Using synonymous or category terms to establish ties in text.

The bear went fishing. This large mammal likes to eat fish.

Some students struggle with comprehension because they do not understand cohesive ties. As always, you should assess your students to see who may be having trouble understanding cohesive ties. We suggest beginning your assessment with referential ties (see previous text—especially common pronouns.)

Teaching Cohesive Ties

Here are some tips for effective cohesive ties lessons. (Note an example lesson is shown in Figure 6.6 inspired by Pulver, [1986] and Baumann and Stevenson, [1986].

- Directly explain each cohesive tie and give examples of how it works in text (Reutzel & Morgan, 1990).
- Think aloud by describing your own thought processes as a reader on how a cohesive tie works in text.
- Ask questions to encourage discussion and description of students' thoughts about each cohesive tie.
- Practice each cohesive tie during group activities.
- Practice each cohesive tie during independent activities.

Drawing Inferences: Making Connections Across Sentences in Text

As children read a text, they must often fill in information that the author did not include; this is called *drawing inferences* or *making an inference*. Missing information in texts are like empty slots left by the author to be filled in by the reader (Fillmore, 1968; Kintsch, 1974; Trabasso, 1980). These slots can be filled in by identifying relevant clues from the sentence context and answering questions like:

Instigator = Who did it?
Action = What was done?
Object = To whom or what was it done?
Location = Where was it done?
Instrument = What was used to do it?
Result = What was the result or goal?

Other slot filling inferences are shaped by the situation including the character's motivation, cause and effect factors, and time/space relationships.

Hollingsworth and Reutzel (1988a) developed an approach for helping students learn to make a variety of *slot filling inferences* called GRIP (Generating Reciprocal Inferences Procedure). To begin a GRIP lesson, the teacher models how a par-

Figure 6.6 Example cohesive ties lesson—Reference ties

Purpose for Learning the Strategy: This strategy will help you make connections between words and ideas in sentences. By using this strategy, you will improve your understanding of text information.

Objective: Learn to identify pronouns that refer back to another person, place, thing, or idea.

Teacher Explanation & Modeling: This strategy begins preparing several pairs of sentences that show a pronoun replacing a noun in another sentence. For example:

Carter jumped on the bunk bed.
He was playing like Spiderman.

Place these sentences and others you have prepared on an overhead transparency.

Read the first pair of sentences aloud. Underline the word 'he' and ask aloud, "I wonder what the word 'he' refers to in this other sentence? Does 'he' refer to the bunk bed? No, that doesn't make sense. Maybe 'he' refers to Carter. That makes sense. I guess the "he" refers to another person, place, thing, or idea in a neighboring sentence."

Draw an arrow showing the backward reference of "he" to Carter

Carter jumped on the bunk bed. He was playing like Spiderman.

Guided Application: Now let's try these next sentences together. Underline the word "she" in the second sentence. Ask, "I wonder what word in the other sentence the word 'she' is telling us about? Can anyone help me?" (Allow the children to pick out the referenced term, Candice.)

Invite a student to come forward and draw an arrow between the words "she" and "Candice."

Candice liked to ride horses. She dreamed one day of riding in a parade.

Continue with another example set of sentences. This time invite students to find the word to underline, "They." Next ask them to find the referenced term. Then invite a student to come and draw the arrows between the referenced ties.

Individual Application: "Now I want you to finish this handout in pairs. Begin by underlining the words that are referencing each other and then draw an arrow between the words. When you are finished, I want you to come up here record and your work on the overhead transparency. I will number you off into pairs. Remember your number because that is the number of the sentence pair you will record on the overhead transparency up here. So, if your pair number is '6,' you and your partner will come up and complete sentence pair number 6. Do you all understand?"

Assessment: After the children complete their handouts and the numbered item on the overhead, bring the group together. Project the overhead transparency, and invite pairs to come forward and explain how they identified the reference terms.

ticular type (Instigator, Action, Object, etc.) of *slot filling inference* is made. She starts by reading aloud and highlighting key words in the text, as highlighted in the example below:

The *elevator ride* was great fun. Now Kathy and Becky *looked down* through the wire fence as the wind whistled in their ears. The *people* and the *cars on the street looked* just like *tiny* toys. Although they were *very high up*, the girls were not frightened. It was exciting to *see the whole city* spread out before them.

This passage helps readers understand "location" inferences. Where were Kathy and Becky? The teacher, in her modeling, makes the inference that Kathy and Becky were on a high building, perhaps a skyscraper, overlooking a city—the location. Next, the teacher thinks aloud and explains how she used the underlined clue words in the passage to justify the inference she made.

Notice how teachers model the process of making an inference in the first stage of the GRIP strategy.

To gradually release the responsibility for making an inference from the teacher to the students, the GRIP lesson continues using at least four more paragraphs. In the second paragraph, the teacher highlights the words, the children make the inference, and the teacher justifies the inference the students made. In the third paragraph, the children highlight the key words, the teacher makes the inference, and the students justify the inference—the roles have now reversed. In the fourth and final passage, students highlight the key words, make the inference, and justify the inference; the teacher assesses whether they are now proficient in the skill.

To *crystallize* this new knowledge children have gained from the GRIP method, a final step could be to have them *generate* their own reciprocal inferences. This is done by having students, working in pairs, create a list of five or more key words and write their own text. You will need to model how a writer can insert the clues into a text without giving away the inference to be made. After writing their texts, students exchange texts, mark key words, make an inference, and justify their inferences to the peer authors. Another variation to this approach involves a game board activity (Figure 6.7) with directions for playing the game (Figure 6.8).

In the second stage of the GRIP strategy, students compose inferential text for peers to make inferences.

Figure 6.7   Generating Reciprocal Inferences Procedure (GRIP) game board

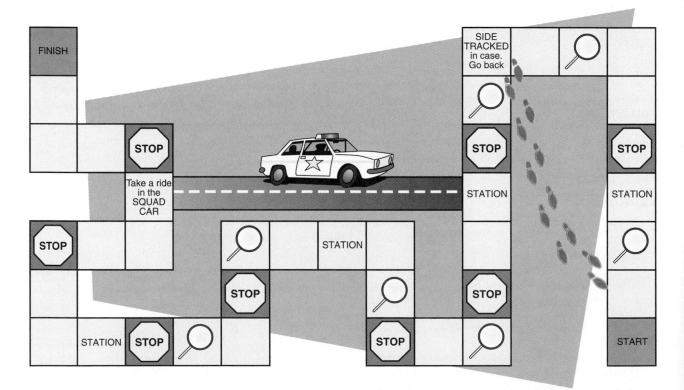

Source: From "Get a GRIP on Comprehension" by P. M. Hollingsworth and D. R. Reutzel, 1988, *Reading Horizons, 29*(1), p. 78. Copyright 1988 by Reading Horizons. Reprinted by permission.

Figure 6.8 Directions for Generating Reciprocal Inferences Procedure (GRIP) game board

Children play the GRIP board game in pairs. Before the game begins, each child needs to understand the rules for playing the game and follow them carefully. We begin by discussing the game rules with the children:

1. Requires two players to play the game.
2. Write four sentences that go together to make a story. Underline the clue words in each sentence.
3. Select a marker.
4. Place marker on START.
5. Throw the die, letting the highest start the game.
6. Each player moves his/her marker the number of spaces shown on the die.
7. If you land on STATION, have the other player read a sentence.
8. If you land on MAGNIFYING GLASS, move to the nearest STATION, have the other player read a sentence.
9. A different sentence is read at each STATION.
10. You must be on STATION to guess, and you get only one guess.
11. If you land on STOP SIGN, go back to the space from which you started your turn.
12. You can be on the same space as the other player.
13. If you land on SIDETRACKED, follow the feet.
14. If you land on SQUAD CAR, follow the road.
15. Whoever guesses what the story is about is the winner, and the game is over.

When the GRIP board game is introduced, play the game with one child while the other children in the classroom watch. This makes the transition from discussing the rules to playing the game easier.

Source: From "Get a GRIP on Comprehension" by P. M. Hollingsworth and D. R. Reutzel, 1988. *Reading Horizons, 29*(1), pp. 76–77. Copyright 1988 by Reading Horizons. Reprinted by permission.

COMPREHENSION INSTRUCTION: TEACHING STUDENTS ABOUT TEXT STRUCTURES

Understanding Stories: Narrative Text Structure

Understanding the way in which authors organize and structure their ideas in texts is key to good reading comprehension (Simmons & Kameenui, 1998; Pressley, 2000; Pearson & Duke, 2002). One of the most important aspects of teaching young children to comprehend narrative texts is to teach them story structure (Vallecorsa & Bettencourt, 1997). The elements of story structure have been captured in a system of rules called **story grammars** (Thorndyke, 1977; Mandler & Johnson, 1977; Stein & Glenn, 1979). Story grammars are the rules, necessary elements to make a story, and the expected sequence for these elements. Researchers generally agree on the following elements and sequence of elements in a story grammar: *setting, problem, goal, events,* and *resolution.*

Developing a sense of how stories are written and organized helps readers predict what is coming next with greater skill, store information in schemas more efficiently, and recall story elements with increased accuracy and completeness. Several

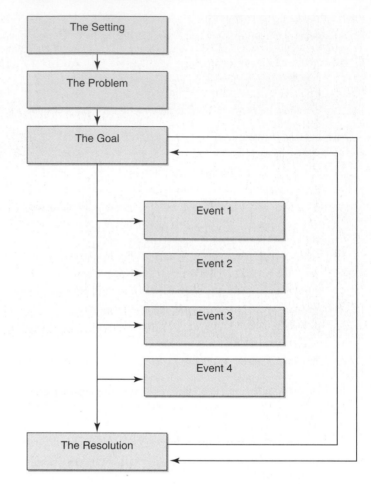

Figure 6.9 Story grammar map

researchers have described effective teaching procedures for developing readers' story grammar knowledge (Gordon & Braun, 1983; Hagood; 1997).

Story schemas can be enhanced by teaching students the major structural elements of stories.

1. Instruction in story structure is most effective when it makes use of well-formed stories such as *Jack and the Beanstalk, Cinderella, The Three Billy Goats Gruff,* and *The Little Red Hen.* Visual organizers can be used to guide the introduction of the concept of story structure (see Figures 6.9 and 6.10). For the first story used in story structure instruction, read the story aloud, stop at key points in the story, and discuss the missing information needed to fill in the empty parts of the story grammar map or story structure clothesline. For stories read after introducing the concept of story schema, use visual organizers to introduce and elicit predictions about the story before reading. During and after reading, the visual organizer such as a story map (shown later in this chapter) can be used to guide a discussion.

2. Set the purposes for reading by asking questions related to the structure of the story. Questioning designed to follow the story's structure will focus students' attention on major story elements.

3. After questioning and discussing story structure, specific questions about the story content can be asked.

Figure 6.10 Clothesline

4. For continued instruction, gradually introduce less well-formed stories so that students will learn that not all stories are "ideal" in organization.
5. Extend this instruction by encouraging children to ask their own questions using story structure and to apply this understanding in writing their own stories.

Another effective method for developing story structure awareness is asking children to read stories and talk about the story structure in small discussion and cooperative learning groups (Mathes, 1997; Simmons & Kameenui, 1998; Gersten, Fuchs, & Williams, 2001). In the following sections, we describe several instructional strategies shown to improve comprehension of narrative text.

Narrative Graphic Organizers: Story Maps, Frames, and Discussion Webs

Story Maps. Story maps are diagrams that show the elements (title, setting, problem, events, resolution) and sequence of story events. According to Reutzel (1985b, 1986c), story maps help teachers accomplish two major comprehension goals. First, by creating story maps, teachers become involved in thinking about the structure of stories and how story elements are related to one another. Such involvement in making story maps leads to increased planning and better organization of comprehension instruction. Second, when story mapping is used, students are helped to understand the important parts of stories as well as how these parts relate to one another.

To design a story map, Reutzel (1985b) lists the following steps:

1. Preread the story. Construct in sequence a listing of the major elements that make up the plot of the story.
2. Place the title of the story in the center of the story map.

Story maps help teachers and students think about the important elements of stories and visualize the story structure.

Story maps can be used before, during, and after reading to improve comprehension by helping children visualize the organization of a story.

Figure 6.11   Story Map of *The Paper Bag Princess* (Munsch, 1980).

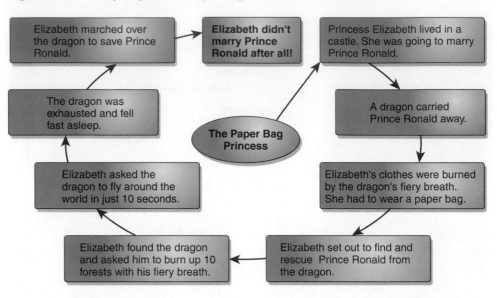

3. Draw enough ties projecting out symmetrically from the center of the map to accommodate the major elements of the story's plot (setting, problem, goal, events, and resolution).
4. Attach information from the summary listing to each of the ties in clock-wise rotation around the story map.

After creating a story map as shown in Figure 6.11 for the *Paper Bag Princess* (Munsch, 1980), introduce children to the story by viewing a copy of the story map on an overhead projector, large chart paper, or at the board. While pointing to the center of the story map, ask children, "What do you think the story will be about today?" Children focus their attention on the title of the story at the center of the story map to guide their predictions and discussion. Next, move the pointer to the setting circle and ask students to predict details in the story map such as "Who do you think the characters are in the story, or what can we tell about the characters in the story." After discussing the setting, move the pointer to the circle where the story problem is shown. Ask students to read the information in the story map and ask them why they think this may be a problem for the characters in the story. Move the pointer around the story map discussing the information found in each story element tie. Children read the story after the discussion of the story map to see if their predictions were accurate.

During reading, children will often reference the unfolding story against the information contained in the story map (Reutzel, 1985b). In this way, the story map acts as a meta-cognitive aid to help students determine whether or not they comprehend the elements and sequence of the story events as well as the relationship among these events. After reading, students are asked to write (for older students) or dictate (for younger students) a summary of the story without the story map. They can also be asked to fill in the details in an incomplete story map handout.

Story maps may be used before, during, and after reading a text to make predictions, discuss story elements, or review the sequence of events in a story. By visually representing the major elements of the story plot and the relationships among

Story maps can be used with a variety of ages, text structures, and reading strategies to improve reading comprehension.

those elements, teachers plan and implement more purposeful, focused reading lessons, which lead to increased student memory for and comprehension of text.

Discussion Webs. Discussion plays an important part in guiding students' comprehension and interpretation of reading selections (Alvermann, Dillon, & O'Brien, 1987; Gambrell & Almasi, 1996). Children are encouraged during discussions to examine more than one point of view as well as to refine their own comprehension of a text. **Discussion webs** are an adaptation of the cooperative teaming approach by McTighe and Lyman (1988) known as *Think–Pair–Share*. The aim of using discussion webs is to encourage children to adopt a listening attitude, to think individually and critically about ideas, and to involve typically less verbal children in the ongoing discussion of a reading selection.

The aim of using discussion webs is to encourage children to discuss issues from more than a single point of view.

Alvermann (1991) describes a five-step process for using discussion webs:

1. Begin by preparing students to read a selection by activating their background for the selection, introducing unfamiliar vocabulary terms and concepts, and setting a purpose for reading. An example may be based on the story *Tales of a Fourth Grade Nothing* (Blume, 1972), as shown in Figure 6.12.

Notice five steps for using discussion webs.

2. After reading the selection, students are introduced to the discussion web. Students are placed in pairs and asked to discuss the pros and cons of the question in the center of the web, "Was Fudge really a bad kid?" Children take turns jotting down reasons for the yes and no continuum of the web.

3. Once children have had sufficient time to discuss the question in pairs and jot their ideas down on the web, one pair of students is placed with another pair of students. This group of four students discusses and shares its thinking around the central question in the discussion web. Children are told to keep an open mind and to listen carefully during this part of the sharing. They are also reminded that it is appropriate to disagree with others in appropriate ways. The children work as a group toward a concluding statement that can be placed in the web.

4. When each group of four has reached a conclusion, a spokesperson is selected to represent the conclusion during the general group discussion. Spokespeople are encouraged to represent dissenting points of view as well as the group's majority conclusion.

Figure 6.12 Discussion web based on *Tales of a Fourth Grade Nothing* (Blume, 1972)

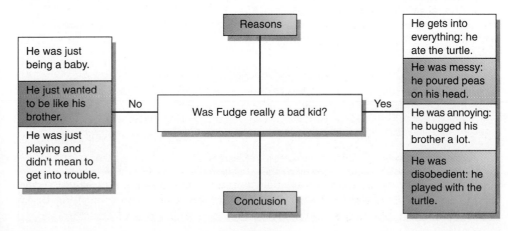

5. As a follow-up, children are asked to complete their own discussion webs by filling in their own ideas as well as those of the groups with whom they participated. These individual responses in the discussion webs should be prominently displayed in the classroom when completed.

Discussion webs help teachers lead students to deeper understandings of characters, story outcomes, how two sides of an issue may be considered, and using critical thinking strategies to make reasoned judgments.

Schema Stories. D. Watson and Crowley (1988) describe a strategy lesson called schema stories where children use what they know about story structure to reconstruct cut-apart elements of a story. The key to this lesson is to select text that contains highly predictable structures such as "once upon a time" and "they lived happily ever after." After selecting a well-formed story, such as *Elbert's Bad Word* (Wood & Wood, 1988), prepare the lesson by photocopying the text, then physically cutting the story into sections (each of which is long enough to contain at least one main idea). One or two paragraphs will usually be sufficient in length to accomplish this purpose. To begin the lesson, each section of text is distributed to a small group of students (five to eight students).

A student is selected in each group to read the text aloud. The teacher asks for the group that thinks it has the beginning of the story to raise their hands. Members of the group must explain why they believe they have the requested part of the story. A consensus must be reached by the class before proceeding to a discussion of the next text segment. This procedure continues as described until all of the segments of the text have been put in order. An example of a schema story lesson is found in Figure 6.13.

Schema story lessons make excellent small-group or individual comprehension lessons that can be placed into a center or station devoted to comprehension strategies. All of the segments of a text can be placed into an envelope and filed in the center. Two children, or individuals, can come to the center and select an envelope and

Schema stories are used to teach children to predict and confirm story predictions.

Figure 6.13 Schema story using text from *Elbert's Bad Word*

- "Come with me young man!" Elbert's mother said with a frown. In the lavatory Elbert's mother handed him a bar of soap.
- One afternoon at an elegant garden party, young Elbert heard a word he had never heard before.
- Elbert knew something had to be done.
- He ran down a cobbled path and knocked at the gardener's cottage. The gardener, who was a practicing wizard, opened the door.
- He baked the words into a little cake. Elbert ate every last crumb.
- Soon the trouble began anew.
- Then with a terrible thud, the mallet landed on Elbert's great toe.
- "My stars! Thunder and lightning! Rats and blue blazes! Suffering cats! Blistering hop toads! Zounds and gadzooks!" he shouted.
- Everyone breathed a sigh of relief and gave Elbert three rousing cheers.
- He saw something that looked like a little spider scurry down a dark hole, and disappear.
- Forgetting about it, the boy went on his way. But the word waited patiently.
- Then with a terrible thud, the mallet landed on Elbert's great toe. Elbert opened his mouth to scream, but the bad word sprang out, bigger and uglier than before.
- Opening his desk, the gardener pulled out a drawer filled with words that crackled and sparkled. Use these words, and perhaps you won't get into trouble.

work on reconstructing the story. A key for self-checking can be included to reduce the amount of teacher supervision.

Accessing Information: Information Text Structure

Nearly 85 percent of all adult reading is with information texts (i.e., nonfiction). Information texts contain facts, details, descriptions, and procedures that are necessary to understand concepts and events in the world around us. Authors structure information texts using several well-known text patterns or structures. Armbruster and Anderson (1981) and Meyer (1979) researched text patterns most used by authors of information texts. These include: time order (putting information into a chronological sequence); cause and effect (showing how something occurs because of another event); problem and solution (presenting a problem along with a solution to the problem); comparison (examining similarities and differences among concepts and events); simple listing (registering in list form a group of facts, concepts, or events); and descriptions.

Simply put, readers who understand an author's organizational pattern recall more from reading information texts than readers who do not (Bartlett, 1978; Meyer, Brandt, & Bluth, 1980). Research has also shown that poor or struggling readers are less likely to be able to identify and use an author's organization of text to recall information. Thus, teachers need to teach children how to identify the author's organizational pattern or text structure and use this knowledge.

Information text structures include time order, cause and effect, problem and solution, comparison, simple listing, and descriptions.

Using Background Knowledge to Comprehend Information Texts

Elaborative interrogation is an intervention especially well suited to information text comprehension. By using "why" questions to promote active processing of factual reading materials (Wood, Pressley, & Winne, 1990), students are encouraged to activate their prior knowledge and experiences and use these to create relationships linking facts together from text. Facts linked together into a network of relationships improve students' understanding and memory for text information.

It is important that "why" questions be asked in such as way as to orient students to activate prior knowledge supporting the facts they need to learn—otherwise such questions will not enhance comprehension and memory for text. We describe the Elaborative Interrogation strategy using the trade book *My Picture Book of the Planets* (Krulik, 1991), in a model lesson shown in Figure 6.14.

Menke and Pressley (1994) state that, "*Answering why questions is as good as constructing images to boost memory for facts, providing the questions are well focused.*" (p. 644) The Elaborative Interrogation strategy has been validated to improve readers' comprehension of factual material ranging from elementary school ages to adult. It is recommended that teachers use Elaborative Interrogation when they train struggling students to access relevant prior knowledge in situations where they typically do not do so spontaneously to improve information text comprehension.

Asking "why" questions helps students process information text more effectively resulting in better understanding and memory.

Information Text Graphic Organizers: Highlighting Text Structure

Instruction in higher-level text organization not only enhances students' retention of major ideas in text, it also improves their retention of lower-level text details in information texts (Williams, Brown, Silverstein, & deCani, 1994). Dickson, Simmons, & Kameenui (1998) describe a six-principle instructional framework for providing effective text structure strategy instruction: (1) introduce the big ideas, (2) explicit instruction

Figure 6.14   Example lesson on elaborative interrogation

Purpose for Learning the Strategy: This strategy will help you relate your own experiences and knowledge to the facts you read in books and other information texts. By using this strategy, you will improve your understanding of and memory for text information.

Objective: Learn to respond to statements in text as if they were stated as "why" questions.

Teacher Explanation & Modeling: This strategy begins by reading a section of text. For example, *My Picture Book of the Planets,* I would begin by reading the title. Then, I might ask myself, "Why would someone write a book about the planets?" My answer might include such ideas as the author wanted to teach others and me about planets as compared with stars, or I might wonder if other planets can support life like on Earth, etc. Next, I read about the first planet, Mercury, in the book. "Mercury is the planet closest to the sun. It is very hot and dry" (Krulik, 1991). I might ask myself the why question, "Why is Mercury so hot?" I read on, "Because it is so close to the sun, Mercury takes the shortest amount of time of any of the planets to circle the sun." I ask myself, "Why is closeness to the sun related to a shorter time needed to circle the sun?"

Guided Application: Now let's try this strategy together. Mariann, come read this statement aloud for the class. After she has read this statement, I will make a "why" question from the statement. O.K. read this statement. Mariann reads, "Mercury is gray and covered with craters." My question is, "Why would Mercury be gray and covered with craters?" Students are invited to use their knowledge and background to answer this "why" question.

Now let's reverse the roles. I will read aloud the next statement and you make this statement into a "why" question. Teacher reads aloud, "Some of Mercury's craters are bigger than the whole state of Texas!" Children raise their hands. Benji is called upon. He asks, "Why are the craters on Mercury so big?" A discussion ensues to potentially answer these "why" questions.

Individual Application: Now I want you to read the rest of this book. When you get to the end of each page, pick one statement to write a "why" question in your notebooks. Next, see if you can answer the question from your own knowledge or experiences. If not, try using the book to answer your question. If neither source can answer your question, save it for our discussion of the book when we are all finished reading. Now, go ahead and read. If you forget what I want you to do, look at this poster for step-by-step directions. The teacher displays the following poster at the front of the room on the board.

Using the Elaborative Interrogation Strategy
- Read each page carefully.
- Stop at the end of each page and pick a statement.
- Write a "why" question for the statement you pick in your reading notebooks.
- Think about an answer to the "why" question using your own knowledge and experiences.
- If you can, write an answer to your "why" question.
- Read the pages again looking for an answer. Read on to another page to look for the answer.
- If you can, write an answer to your "why" question.
- If you can't write an answer to your "why" question, save it for our group discussion after reading.

(continued)

Source: From "Hitting the Wall: Helping Struggling Readers Comprehend" in C. Collins-Block, L. B. Gambrell, and M. Pressley (eds.) by D.R. Reutzel, K. Camperell, and J. A. Smith, 2002, *Improving Comprehension Instruction: Advances in Research Theory, and Classroom Practice,* pp. 321–353, San Francisco, CA: Jossey-Bass.

Notice the six instructional principles for providing highly effective text structure instruction with information texts.

of strategies, (3) mediated scaffolding, (4) strategic integration, (5) primed background knowledge, and (6) judicious review cycles.

The first principle for helping students identify and use text structure is understanding the "big ideas." Two "big ideas" associated with teaching text structure are:

Figure 6.14 *continued*

Assessment: After the children read, hold a discussion where children are asked to share their "why" questions and answers. Ask children to hand in reading notebooks with their "why" questions and answers. Examine these notebooks to determine the success of using this strategy. Unanswered "why" questions can be placed into a "question" web for further reading and research. The web may look something like the one shown below:

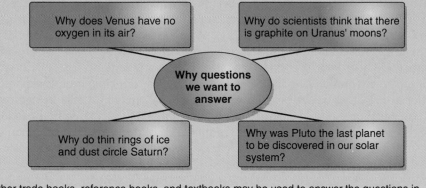

Other trade books, reference books, and textbooks may be used to answer the questions in this "why" question web.

Planned Review: In about one week, plan to review the use of the "Elaborative Interrogation" strategy by using trade books or textbooks with other curricular subjects such as health, social studies, or with math word problems.

(1) the physical presentation of text, and (2) text structures. The physical presentation of text deals with how well the physical presentation of text highlights importance of information and the relationship among various levels of information within the text. Physical text features affect the comprehensibility of text. When authors write, they use a variety of typographic features. Comprehension instruction about the physical presentation of text should include attention to headings, sub-headings, signal words, topic sentences, and paragraph organization. Aside from these text features, authors will sometimes use italics, bolded text, bullets, or boxes to highlight text features and make text more reader-friendly. We suggest that teachers draw attention to these features during group readings to heighten students' awareness of their presence and functions in text.

The higher-level structure of text deals with well-organized patterns that establish the flow, organization, and relationship of information within an entire text, i.e., descriptive structure, listing structure, sequential structure, compare/contrast structure, problem/solution structure, or a collection of explanations structure, etc. Identifying and using higher-level text structure helps all readers, good and poor, more effectively organize their recall of important ideas and details in text.

To make comprehension strategies explicit as described in instructional principle two, teachers need to define and explain the strategy components, inform students about when and why the strategies are helpful as well as the expected benefits of using the strategies, model the strategy use, ask students to verbalize the strategy, and provide feedback, coaching, and guidance during the learning process. Teachers will explicitly teach students various patterns of text organization; tell students how learning these patterns will help them understand and remember text; model how to identify text patterns; and provide them written prompts or lists to help them identify text patterns in their reading materials.

Principle three, mediated scaffolding for teaching information text structure, is focused on two types or targets of scaffolding: (1) controlling the difficulty of the content and task, and (2) controlling the difficulty of the reading materials. Mediated content and task scaffolding occurs when teachers structure the learning to proceed from easy to more difficult content or tasks. Mediated material scaffolding guides students' thinking as they work through a task or new content base within a leveled text. Using guidance and leveled texts is best exemplified in practices associated with guided reading (Fountas & Pinnell, 1996, 2001). When providing mediated scaffolding of text structures, teachers use "think alouds," lists of procedures, graphic organizers, and structured questions to elicit and focus attention on the text's top-level structure.

Strategic integration of comprehension strategies, principle four, means pulling together a collection or set of related strategies and applying these in natural and novel settings. For example, instruction on information text structure is applied in actual texts to be read by students under the guidance of the teacher rather than using these strategies only in adapted texts or text "snippets" during whole class strategy lessons. Maximum transfer for automatic, student-initiated strategy use has been demonstrated to occur when natural, novel settings are (1) scheduled in different subject areas and (2) at different periods in the school day outside of the traditional literacy instructional block (Block, 1993; Block & Mangieri, 1995/1996).

Principle five, priming background knowledge, refers to activating students' prior knowledge about the content and the structure of a text to be read in order to facilitate comprehension of text. Teachers may use graphic organizers to show the relationship between main ideas and the parts of a story. We remind you that using the Elaborative Interrogation strategy is an effective strategy to prime background knowledge and experience as well.

Judicious review, the sixth and final principle for providing effective comprehension text structure strategy instruction, refers to closely spaced and shorter reviews where students apply strategy instruction to a variety of text structures and organization. We provide a model lesson on teaching text structure in Figure 6.15. We continue using the information picture book *My Picture Book of the Planets* in order to demonstrate how teachers can not only increase students' factual recall of the text, but also increase their awareness of the text structure used by the author to organize the text.

Experience-Text-Relationships (E-T-R): Discussing Information Texts

Tharp (1982) developed Experience-Text-Relationships (E-T-R) as a structure for lessons to improve comprehension of information text. An E-T-R lesson is organized around three steps. First, student experiences related to the text to be read are discussed. *How are caterpillars and butterflies related? Which comes first, the caterpillar or the butterfly?* Second, information text requires special instructional attention because it contains heavy concept and vocabulary loads, placing unusual demands on the reader. To help with this task, an E-T-R lesson uses reading and questioning. Students read to assigned points in the text and stop to discuss questions posed by the teacher and/or the students. *What is the difference between a cocoon and a chrysalis?* Third, information text structure is less familiar for young readers than narrative text, prompting comprehension difficulties (Pearson & Duke, 2002). To help younger readers to make connections between their own experience and the text, a discussion following the reading of the text focuses on making the connections

Figure 6.15   Using graphic organizers to teach information book text structure

Purpose for Learning the Strategy: This strategy will help you recognize the pattern(s) authors use to organize their ideas when they write stories, books, or other printed materials.

Objective: To learn to use the knowledge of text structures to organize study, note taking, and memory for reading a variety of texts.

Teacher Explanation & Modeling: When I read, I try to think about how the author has organized the information so that I can remember it better. In *My Picture Book of the Planets* (Krulik, 1991), the author presents a list of planets in the solar system from the planet nearest the sun to the planet farthest from the sun. I also notice that with each planet the author writes a description of the planet with several interesting facts. So, I have drawn a graphic organizer to show how this author has written the book. Look at what I have drawn up here on the board.

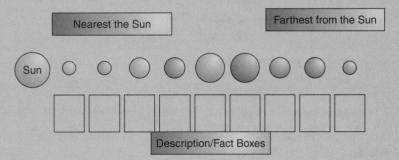

By using this text structure/ graphic organizer strategy, I can read, take notes, and remember how this book works much better.

Guided Application: Let's look through our copies of the book to see if the graphic organizer on the board properly shows the order of the book's organization. What is the first planet that is closest to the sun? Mercury. Is that the planet shown first in the graphic organizer? Yes. Good. What is the second planet in the graphic organizer at the board? Venus. Is that the second planet in the book? Yes. Good. Now look through the rest of the book and check to see if the graphic organizer properly shows the author's organization.

Individual Application: I am giving each of you a copy of the graphic organizer for *My Picture Book of the Planets* (Krulik, 1991). As you read about each planet, write down two to three facts about each planet in the descriptive box underneath each planet in the graphic organizer to help you remember what you have read. Please notice that the author has organized the book to be a "collection or list" of descriptions about each planet.

Assessment: Ask students to turn in their completed graphic organizers. Check to see what they have done and how they have used the graphic organizer. Also, you may want to give them a blank organizer to fill in after the discussion of the book. This will help them and you to see how this strategy creates a mental organizer for the book's structure and the facts about each planet.

Planned Review: In about one week, plan to review the use of the "Text Structure-Graphic Organizer" strategy by using trade books or textbooks with other curricular subjects, such as health, social studies, or with math word problems.

Source: From "Hitting the Wall: Helping Struggling Readers Comprehend," by D. R. Reutzel, K. Campbell, and J. A. Smith, 2002, in C. Collins-Block, L. B. Gambrell, & M. Pressley (eds.), *Improving Comprehension Instruction: Advances in Research Theory, and Classroom Practice,* pp. 321–353, San Francisco, CA: Jossey-Bass.

explicit. *So what did you learn from reading this text about butterflies that you will think about the next time you see a butterfly or a caterpillar?*

An E-T-R lesson is composed of four stages: (a) planning, (b) concept assessment and development, (c) guided reading of the text, and (d) application, during which the teacher helps students draw relationships between the text information and their own

Notice the three steps of an E-T-R lesson.

Figure 6.16   To structure a lesson based on the E-T-R strategy, a teacher might create a visual organizer such as this one for *The Life of the Butterfly* (Drew, 1989)

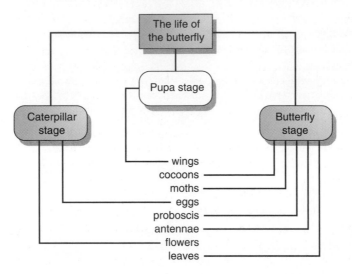

background experiences. To clarify the E-T-R lesson structure, a lesson as well as a graphic organizer based on the book *The Life of the Butterfly* (Drew, 1989) is presented in Figure 6.16.

Planning an E-T-R Lesson

To plan an E-T-R lesson, the teacher follows three steps. First, preread the information book to determine the major concepts and main ideas in the text. Second, look for major points to bring up during the discussion, formulate attention-focusing questions, and note important vocabulary concepts that may need to be pre-taught. When planning an E-T-R lesson, we have found it useful to plan the lesson around a graphic organizer like the one found in Figure 5.16. The final step in planning involves thinking about ways information in the text about the life of a butterfly can be shared, used, and extended into other related curriculum areas.

Eliciting Student Knowledge and Experience

Tharp (1982) explains that capturing children's interest and activating their prior knowledge and experience at the outset of the lesson are critical to success. This can be accomplished by asking questions that invite students to engage in dialogue about their own background experiences in interesting and imaginative ways. For example, while teaching an E-T-R lesson using *The Life of the Butterfly* (Drew, 1989), you might begin the lesson with the following introduction and questions.

> **Teacher:** (while holding the book up for the children to see) In this book, we will learn about how a caterpillar becomes a butterfly. Can you tell me what you know about caterpillars and butterflies?

After this initial discussion, subsequent questions could focus attention on critical or potentially unfamiliar concepts and vocabulary related to butterflies and caterpillars. For example, children may need to learn the vocabulary terms *spiracles, pupa, antennae,* and *proboscis.*

Text Reading and Study

At this point in the lesson, the teacher moves into guided reading of predetermined parts of the text. Through questioning and discussion, teacher and children negotiate a purpose for reading each segment of the book. The lesson proceeds by alternating purpose setting, silent reading, and discussion for each segment of the text. A visual organizer plays a central role in the alternating activities of purpose setting, reading, and discussion. By displaying an organizer, the teacher directs reading and discussion toward filling in the organizer. So, for each cycle of the lesson, the teacher fills in the organizer with additional information until it is complete. The lines are drawn in after the discussion to show which of the items previously discussed belonged with the phases of the life of a butterfly. In this way, the teacher represents the author's structure for conveying the information in the text. Thus, the text information is mapped onto the organizer, which visually depicts the organization and content of the information the author presented in the text.

Again, we encourage you to look for opportunities to teach other useful concepts and vocabulary not presented in the text. Teachers should remain alert to opportunities to build or elaborate on children's existing butterfly schemas; for example, explaining that moths build cocoons and butterflies develop in a chrysalis is a topic with which the text deals only briefly.

Application

After the entire text has been read, help students draw relationships between the text and their own background knowledge. By using the graphic organizer, students may be encouraged to synthesize and summarize the information discussed throughout the lesson. On another occasion, students may become involved in other research and extension activities. These may range from something as simple as illustrating their favorite butterfly to something as complex as building a three-dimensional diorama of collected and labeled butterflies. By following the steps in Elaborative Interrogation and E-T-R lessons coupled with text structure lessons using graphic organizers, students will experience quality comprehension instruction for processing information texts on a variety of topics and levels of reading challenge.

COMPREHENSION INSTRUCTION: INTERPRETATION AND ELABORATION

Activating students' background knowledge in preparation for reading is critical for promoting reading comprehension. In fact, many teacher's guides and editions contain a section entitled "Building Background for the Story," or "Building Background Knowledge." One well known and highly useful strategy is called K-W-L. Ogle (1986), the originator of K-W-L, asserts that this strategy is best suited for use with information texts.

K-W-L

Step K: What I Know

K-W-L strategy lessons begin with step K, *what I know*. This step is composed of two levels of accessing prior knowledge: (a) brainstorming and (b) categorizing information. Ask children to brainstorm about a particular topic (in the case of a narrative, brainstorm a particular theme or message). For instance, you might ask children what they know about bats. A list of associations is formed through brainstorming. When students make a contribution, Ogle (1986) suggests asking them where or how they got their information to challenge them to use higher levels of thinking.

Next, ask students to look for ways in which the brainstorming list can be reorganized into categories of information. For example, you may notice that the brainstorming list shows three related pieces of information about how bats navigate. These can be reorganized into a "navigation" category. Encourage children to look at the list and think about other categories represented in the brainstorming list.

Notice three steps for using K-W-L.

Step W: What Do I Want to Learn?

During step W, students recognize gaps, inaccuracies, and disagreements in their prior knowledge to decide what they want to learn. You, the teacher, can play a central role in pointing out these problems and helping students frame questions for which they would like to have answers. Questions can be framed by using the stem "I wonder." After children generate a series of questions to be answered from the reading, they are to write down personal questions for which they would like answers. These are often selected from those questions generated by the group.

Step L: What I Learned

After reading, ask students to write down what they learned. This can take the form of answers to specific questions they asked or a concise written summary of their learning. These questions and answers may be discussed as a group or shared between pairs of students. In this way, other children benefit from the learning of their peers as well as from their own learning. In summary, K-W-L has been shown to be effective in improving reading comprehension by causing students to activate, think about, and organize their prior knowledge as an aid to reading comprehension (Dewitz & Carr, 1987).

Imagery: Elaborating the Meaning of Text

When students make visual images about what they read, they make mental "movies." Making visual images within the mind as one reads provides an effective framework for organizing, remembering, and constructing meaning from text (Wilson & Gambrell, 1988; Sadoski & Quast, 1990). Struggling readers do not spontaneously create mental images as they read. As a consequence, struggling readers often miss out on the comprehension-monitoring boost that mental imagery can give them (Gambrell & Bales, 1986). Wilson and Gambrell (1988) indicate specific ways to instruct children in how and when to apply *imagery* as a comprehension tool in Figure 6.17.

Since research on visual imagery indicates that some students do not spontaneously use visual imagery, but can when directed to do so, teachers need to provide guidance and practice in the use of imagery during reading. Wilson and Gambrell (1988) recommend the following considerations when selecting materials to be used to encourage visual imagery:

1. For modeling and teacher-guided practice activities, select brief passages of about paragraph length.
2. Choose passages that have strong potential for creating "mental movies" (i.e., those that typically contain rich descriptions of events and objects).

Figure 6.17   Hints for making visual images during reading

1. Inform students that making pictures in their minds can help them understand what a pas-
    sage is about. Specific directions, depending on whether the text is narrative or information
    text, may be helpful. For example, "Make a picture in your mind of the interesting charac-
    ters in this story." "Make pictures in your mind about the things that happened in this story."
    "Make a picture in your mind of the human skeleton with each of the bones labeled." Using
    visual imagery in this manner encourages students to integrate information across the text
    as they engage in constructing the meaning.
2. Inform students that, when something is difficult to understand, it sometimes helps to try to
    make a picture in their minds. Using visual imagery can help students clarify meaning, and
    it encourages them to think about whether they comprehend or not.
3. Encourage students to make visual images about texts they want to remember. Tell them
    that making pictures in their minds can help them remember. As a follow-up to story time or
    silent reading, invite students to think about the visual images they made and encourage
    them to use their images to help them retell the story to a partner. This activity will help stu-
    dents realize the value of using visual imagery to enhance memory.

Point out that not all text material is easy to visualize—especially when the material is about unfamiliar and abstract concepts. Tell students that in those instances
they should select another strategy that would be easier to use and more helpful (be
prepared with suggestions that better fit some of the text types they are likely to encounter). With minimal guidance and practice, students can learn and enjoy using visual imagery to enhance their reading experiences.

Affective Responses: Interpreting and Elaborating Meaning

Discussion and dialog are critical aspects of effective comprehension instruction
(Gambrell & Almasi, 1996). One widely recognized and recommended approach to
discussion and dialog about text is called *reader response,* which invites students to
take a much more active role (Bleich, 1978; Rosenblatt, 1978, 1989). Reader response theories suggest there are many possible meanings in a text, depending upon
the reader's background and reaction to the text. Rosenblatt's (1978) *transactional
theory* described reading and literature study as a carefully orchestrated relationship
between reader and text (Clifford, 1991).

Rosenblatt (1978) describes two stances—efferent and aesthetic—in discussing
how readers may choose to focus their attention during reading. When readers focus their attention on information to be remembered from reading a text, they are
taking an *efferent stance.* When readers adopt an aesthetic stance, they draw on
past experiences, connect these experiences to the text, often savor the beauty of
the literary art form, and become an integral participant in the unfolding events of
the text.

Discussion of or dialog about texts in small groups is often called a *literature circles* or *book clubs* that lead students into *grand conversations* about books (Peterson & Eeds, 1990; Daniels, 1994; McMahon & Raphael, 1997; Raphael, Pardo,
Highfield, & McMahon, 1997; Tompkins, 2003). Grand conversations about books
motivate students to extend, clarify, and elaborate their own interpretations of the
text as well as learn to consider alternative interpretations offered by peers (see
Chapter 13, Reading Workshop).

Figure 6.18   Alternative affective responses to books

1. Prepare a condensed or simplified version of the text to read aloud to younger readers.
2. Draw a map of the journey of characters in a story.
3. Talk to your teacher or a peer about the book.
4. Make a wanted poster for a character in the text.
5. Make an information poster for an information book.
6. Select a part of the book to read aloud to others.
7. Send a letter to your parents, a friend, or your teacher telling about a book and why they should read it.
8. Write a classified newspaper ad for a book.
9. Rewrite a story or part of a story as a readers' theatre.
10. Make transparencies about the story to use on the overhead projector.
11. Make a power point slide computer presentation about an information book.
12. Make a character report card on your favorite character.
13. Make a passport application as your favorite character.
14. Write a "Dear Abby" column as your favorite character.
15. Write a missing persons report about a story character.
16. Draw a part of the book and ask others to tell about what part of the story is illustrated.
17. Write a newspaper headline for a book or story.
18. Write a newspaper report for a story character or about information you have learned in an information book.
19. Write to the author to describe your responses to a book.
20. Illustrate a book using a variety of art mediums or techniques.
21. Write a letter to the librarian suggesting why he or she should or should not recommend a book to someone.
22. Study about the author and write a brief biography.
23. Compose a telegram about the book to tell someone why he or she must read this book.
24. Make a TV commercial and videotape it.
25. Plan a storytelling session for kindergarten children.
26. Interview a story character and write the interview.
27. Compare and contrast characters, settings, or facts in a book using a Venn diagram.
28. Construct a game of Trivial Pursuits using facts in an information book.
29. Construct a game of Password using clues about characters or events in a story.
30. Compose an imaginary diary that may be kept by a book character.

There are many ways to invite students to respond to text to increase comprehension.

There are many ways to invite students to respond to texts they read. One of the most common is to ask children to write in a response journal (Parsons, 1990). We have developed a listing of affective responses to text that represent both aesthetic and efferent stances as described by Rosenblatt (1978) in Figure 6.18.

STRATEGIES FOR EFFECTIVE QUESTIONING

Asking questions is not enough; teachers must help students learn how to answer questions.

Questions are an integral part of life both in and out of school. From birth, we learn about our world by asking questions and then by testing our answers against the realities in our environment. In school, teachers ask questions to motivate children to become involved in learning and to assess the quality of their learning. Because questions are so much a part of the schooling process and can affect the quality of children's comprehension, teachers must know how to effectively use questioning to deliver quality reading comprehension instruction.

Figure 6.19 Illustrations to explain question–answer relationships (QARs) to students

In the Book QARs

Right There
The answer is in the text, usually easy to find. The words used to make up the question and words used to answer the question are **Right There** in the same sentence.

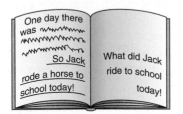

**Think and Search
(Putting It Together)**
The answer is in the story, but you need to put together different story parts to find it. Words for the question and words for the answer are not found in the same sentence. They come from different parts of the text.

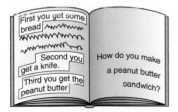

In My Head QARs

Author and You
The answer is *not* in the story. You need to think about what you already know, what the author tells you in the text, and how it fits together.

On My Own
The answer is *not* in the story. You can even answer the question without reading the story. You need to use your own experience.

Source: Figure from "Teaching Question Answer Relationships, Revisited" by Taffy E. Raphael. *The Reading Teacher,* February 1986. Reprinted with permission of Taffy E. Raphael and the International Reading Association.

Question–Answer Relationship

Raphael (1982, 1986) describes four question–answer relationships (QARs) to help children identify the connection between the type of question asked and the information sources necessary and available for answering questions: (a) right there, (b) think and search, (c) author and you, and (d) on my own. Figure 6.19 shows examples of each of these four types of QARs.

Instruction using QARs begins by explaining to students that when they answer questions about reading there are basically two places they can look to get information: *in the book* and *in my head.* This concept should be practiced with the students by reading aloud a text, asking questions, and having the students explain or show where they found their answers. Once students understand the two-category approach,

QARs help students learn to identify types of questions asked and where to get information necessary to answer questions.

expand the *in the book* category to include *right there* and *putting it together.* The distinction between these two categories should be practiced under the guidance of the teacher with several texts, gradually releasing responsibility to the students. For older students, Raphael (1986) suggests that students be shown specific strategies for locating the answers to *right there* questions. These include looking in a single sentence or looking in two sentences connected by a pronoun. For *putting it together* questions, students can be asked to focus their attention on the structure of the text, such as cause–effect, problem–solution, listing–example, compare–contrast, and explanation.

Next, instruction should be directed toward two subcategories within the *in my head* category: (a) *author and me,* and (b) *on my own.* Here again, these categories can be practiced as a group by reading a text aloud, answering the questions, and discussing the sources of information. To expand this training, students can be asked to identify the types of questions asked in their basal readers, workbooks, content area texts, and tests as well as to determine the sources of information needed to answer these questions. Students may be informed that certain types of questions are asked before and after reading a text. For example, questions asked before reading typically require that students activate their own knowledge. Therefore, questions asked before reading will usually be *on my own* questions. However, questions asked after reading will make use of information found in the text. Therefore, questions asked after reading will typically focus on the *right there, putting it together,* and *author and me* types of questions.

Using the QARs question–answering training strategy is useful for at least two other purposes. First, it can help teachers examine their own questioning with respect to the types of questions and the information sources students need to use to answer their questions. Second, some teachers may find that by using QARs to monitor their own questioning behaviors they are asking only *right there* types of questions. This discovery should lead teachers to ask questions that require the use of other information sources. Students can use QARs to initiate self-questioning before and after reading. Children may be asked to write questions for each of the QARs categories and answer these questions. Finally, a poster displaying the information in Figure 5.19 can heighten children's and teachers' awareness to the types of questions asked and the information sources available for answering those questions.

Raphael and Pearson (1982) provided evidence that training students to recognize these question–answer relationships resulted in improved comprehension and question–answering behavior. In addition, evidence also shows that teachers find the QARs strategies productive for improving their own questioning behaviors.

Questioning the Author

Research has shown that many young readers construct very little meaning from the information they read in textbooks. Several features in the text combine to create a number of obstacles for young children's comprehension of information text. These include: (1) incoherence, (2) lack of clear descriptions and explanations, (3) unrealistic assumptions on the level of background knowledge, (4) the objective nature of the language used, and (5) the "authority" that places it above criticism (McKeown, Beck, & Worthy, 1993). These "inconsiderate" features of a textbook's organization and content inhibit comprehension, and the textbook's authority causes students to attribute these difficulties to their own inadequacies. As a result, younger readers feel reluctant to persist in using their natural "problem-solving" abilities in the face of these perceptions (Anderson, 1991; Schunk & Zimmerman,1997).

A *Questioning the Author* lesson attempts, "in a sense to 'depose' the authority of the textbook through actualizing the presence of an author." (McKeown, Beck, & Worthy, 1993, p. 561) Children are taught that the information in textbooks is just someone's thoughts written down and that sometimes these ideas are not written as well or as clearly as they might be. Next, the teacher prompts the children as they read a text using a series of questions such as:

- What is the author trying to tell you?
- Why is the author telling you that?
- Is that said clearly?

Asking children to search out answers to these questions encourages them to actively engage the ideas in the text. As children encounter difficulties in understanding the text, they are encouraged, again through teacher questioning, to recast the author's ideas in clearer language. Questions used for this purpose include:

- How could the author have said the ideas in a clearer way?
- What would you want to say instead?

Asking children to "revise" the author's ideas and writing causes them to "grapple" with the ideas and problems in a text. In this way, children engage texts in ways that successful readers use to make sense of complex ideas and texts.

Recent research has shown that *Questioning the Author* results in increased length and complexity of recalled ideas from text and answers to comprehension questions as compared with other forms of book discussions (Sandora, Beck, & McKeown, 1999).

COMPREHENSION INSTRUCTION: MONITORING AND SELF-REGULATION

Metacognition and Fix-Up Strategies

In addition to activating, elaborating, or modifying prior knowledge to improve comprehension, readers must learn to monitor and self-regulate the status of their own ongoing comprehension and know when comprehension breaks down. The act of monitoring one's unfolding comprehension of text is called metacognition, or sometimes *metacomprehension*. The ability to plan, check, monitor, revise, regulate, and evaluate one's unfolding comprehension is of particular importance in reading. If a child fails to detect a comprehension breakdown, then she will take no action to correct misinterpretations of the text. However, if a child expects the text to make sense and has the ability to strategically self-correct comprehension problems, then reading can progress as it should.

To help students develop the ability to monitor their own comprehension processes, H. K. Carr (1986) suggested a strategy called "click or clunk." This strategy urges readers to reflect at the end of each paragraph or section of reading by stopping and asking themselves if the meaning or message "clicks" for them or goes "clunk." If it clunks, what is wrong? What can be done to make sense of it?

Although the ability to detect when comprehension breaks down is important, it is equally important to know which *fix-up* strategies to select in repairing broken comprehension and when to use these strategies. Consequently, students may know

Questioning the Author prompts students to "depose" the authority of text by asking the author questions as if the author were present.

Metacognition involves readers in checking the status of their own understanding and taking steps to repair failing comprehension when necessary.

that they need to take steps to repair comprehension but may not know which steps to take or when to take them. As a consequence, children should be introduced to the options available to them for repairing broken comprehension. A. Collins and Smith (1980) suggest the following fix-up or repair strategies for use by readers who experience comprehension failure.

An online Reading Instructional Handbook has wonderful material on monitoring comprehension. Link to this site from Chapter 6 on our Companion Website at www.prenhall.com/ reutzel.

- Ignore the problem and continue reading.
- Suspend judgment for now and continue reading.
- Form a tentative hypothesis using text information and continue reading.
- Look back or reread the previous sentence.
- Stop and think about the previously read context; reread if necessary.
- Seek help from the environment, reference materials, or other knowledgeable individuals.

To help students develop a sense for when to select these strategies for repairing failing comprehension, teachers may consider using a think-aloud modeling procedure. Begin a think aloud by reading part of a text aloud. Comment on your own thinking as the teacher. By revealing to students your thinking, the hypotheses you form for the text, and anything that strikes you as difficult or unclear, you demonstrate for the students the processes successful readers use to comprehend a text. Next, remind students of the click or clunk strategy. Gradually release the responsibility for modeling metacognitive strategies to the children during follow-up lessons. It also helps if you display the fix-up repair strategies on a poster prominently placed in the classroom to draw students' attention to these strategies throughout the year.

For students needing additional help with metacognitive strategy development, we recommend Baumann, Jones, and Seifert-Kessell's (1993) think-aloud lessons. In think-aloud lessons, students are explicitly taught what the strategies of metacognition are through definition, description, and examples. Next, children are told why learning these strategies is important for helping them become better readers. Finally, students are taught how to use these strategies through a sequence of instruction using (a) verbal explanation, (b) teacher modeling, (c) guided practice, and (d) independent practice. The think-aloud lesson centered on the following topics:

- Self-questioning
- Sources of information (see question–answer relationships, QARs, previously in this chapter)
- Think-aloud modeling introduction (see GRIP, previously in this chapter)
- Think-aloud review and extension (see GRIP)
- Predicting, reading, and verifying
- Understanding unstated information
- Retelling a story (see retellings in Chapter 10)
- Rereading and reading on (see fix-up strategies)
- Think-aloud/comprehension-monitoring application

We recommend this procedure because it brings together in an integrated fashion all of the elements of excellent, research-based metacognitive reading instruction, which has been shown to be very effective in helping students acquire a broad range of metacognitive strategies.

Figure 6.20 Situational context diagram

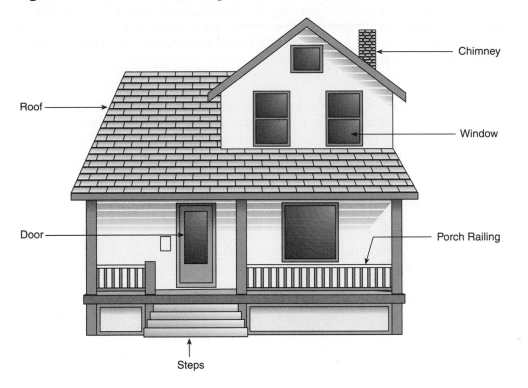

COMPREHENSION INSTRUCTION: MEETING THE NEEDS OF SECOND LANGUAGE LEARNERS

Contextual Diagrams: Labeling the Situational Context

For many second language learners, pictures or diagrams of social or situational settings wherein objects and actions are labeled are of significant help for acquiring ability to speak, listen, read, and write in a largely unfamiliar language (Freeman & Freeman, 2000). The purpose of contextual diagrams, such as the one shown in Figure 6.20, is to allow students to learn language for settings outside the school classroom. Diagrams of the kitchen, bedroom, or bathroom at home can help students begin to learn and associate second language terms with familiar or even somewhat unfamiliar objects in another setting. Diagrams of stores, libraries, mechanic shops, or hospitals wherein objects and actions are labeled can move students' potential for language comprehension well beyond the physical and social confines of the school classroom. Hence, diagrams of whole, meaningful, and naturally occurring situations serve a purpose of expanding the language learning contexts of English as second language (ESL) and limited English proficiency (LEP) students in schools.

COMPREHENSION INSTRUCTION: MEETING THE NEEDS OF STRUGGLING READERS

Palincsar and Brown (1985) designed and evaluated an approach to improve the reading comprehension and comprehension monitoring of students who scored two years below grade level on standardized tests of reading ability and reading compre-

Contextual diagrams allow LEP students to learn needed vocabulary before entering an unfamiliar societal setting.

Reciprocal teaching is a useful strategy for helping students who have difficulties with comprehension and monitoring.

hension. Their results along with many others (Rosenshine & Meister, 1994; Loranger, 1997) suggest a teaching strategy that is useful for helping students who have difficulties with comprehension and comprehension monitoring called *reciprocal teaching*. Essentially, this strategy involves teachers and students in exchanging roles, which increases student involvement in the lesson.

The reciprocal teaching lesson is composed of the following four phases or steps:

1. *Prediction:* Students are asked to predict from the title and pictures the possible content of the text. The predictions are recorded by the teacher.
2. *Question generation:* Students generate purpose questions after reading a predetermined segment of the text, such as a paragraph or page.
3. *Summarizing:* Students write a brief summary for the text by starting with "This paragraph was about. . . ." (p. 299) Summarizing helps students capture the gist of the text.
4. *Clarifying:* Students and teacher discuss a variety of reasons a text may be difficult or confusing, such as difficult vocabulary, poor text organization, unfamiliar content, or lack of cohesion. Students are then instructed in a variety of comprehension fix-up or repair strategies (as described earlier in this chapter).

Once teachers have modeled this process with several segments of text, the teacher assigns one of the students (preferably a good student) to assume the role of teacher for the next segment of text. The teacher may also, while acting in the student role, provide appropriate prompts and feedback when necessary. When the next segment of text is completed, the student assigned as teacher asks another student to assume that role.

Teachers who use reciprocal teaching to help students with comprehension difficulties should follow four simple guidelines suggested by Palincsar and Brown (1985). First, assess student difficulties and provide reading materials appropriate to students' decoding abilities. Second, use reciprocal teaching for at least 30 minutes per day for 15 to 20 consecutive days. Third, teachers should model frequently and provide corrective feedback. Finally, student progress should be monitored regularly and individually to determine whether the instruction is having the intended effect.

Hoyt (1999) describes a process using cards for teaching children the four interrelated processes of *Reciprocal Teaching*. Prepare children to use *Reciprocal Teaching Cards* by modeling the process with several segments of text. Next, have students use the cards shown below in small groups. The group leader shows the cards.

Card #1: Please get ready to read to _____ .

Card #2: I predict this part will be about _____ . (Leader speaks.)

Card #3: Does anyone else have a prediction? (Group members speak.)

Card #4: Please read silently to the point we selected.

Card #5: Are there any words you thought were interesting? (Group.)

Card #6: Are there any ideas you found interesting or puzzling? (Group.)

Card #7: Do you have comments about the reading? (Group.)

Card #8: Summarize (in 2 or 3 sentences): This was about _____ . (Discussion Leader.)

Palincsar and Brown (1985) and many others (Rosenshine & Meister, 1994; Loranger, 1997) have reported positive results for this intervention procedure by demonstrating dramatic changes in students' ineffective reading behaviors. While reciprocal teaching was originally intended for use with information text, this intervention strategy may be used with narrative texts by focusing discussion and reading on the major elements of stories.

With minor changes, reciprocal teaching can be used with narrative as well as expository texts.

Summary

Teaching comprehension, unlike assessing comprehension, involves teaching behaviors such as modeling, explaining, thinking aloud, demonstrating, and defining. Teachers must not assume they are teaching children to comprehend text when they mention or assign comprehension skill practice sheets. Comprehension instruction in the early grades is both inconsistent and infrequent (Taylor, Pearson, Clark, & Walpole, 2000). In fact, comprehension instruction in the early grades is often neglected in favor of developing automatic decoding abilities in young children. Also, there is considerable concern that children are learning *about* comprehension rather than acquiring knowledge *through* comprehension (Neuman, 2001). Access in the early years to information texts is also an issue of current concern among researchers (Duke, 2000a & b). And finally, there is considerable debate around whether or not comprehension strategy instruction is best taught as single or multiple strategies.

Schema theory, a theory about one's storehouse of prior knowledge and experience and how these influence the ability to comprehend text, was depicted in the context of a simplified model of text comprehension involving searching, applying, selecting and evaluating, and composing.

The Gradual Release of Responsibility model of instruction was discussed to provide a comprehensive framework for effective comprehension instruction. Other effective instructional strategies for improving comprehension of narrative text and information text as well as focusing on comprehending text parts such as sentences, words, and typographic features were highlighted throughout the chapter.

Finally, readers were shown effective strategies for teaching comprehension at the phrase and sentence levels, making inferences, using text structure to improve comprehension, activating prior knowledge, elaborating and responding to texts, effective questioning practices, self-monitoring and fix-up strategies, helping LEP/ESL students, and assisting readers with comprehension difficulties.

Check your understanding of chapter concepts by using the self assessment for Chapter 6 on our Companion Website at www.prenhall.com/ reutzel.

Concept Applications

In the Classroom

1. Pick a favorite story. Describe the story grammar parts of your selection. Make a story map, a schema story lesson, or design a story grammar questioning map.
2. Select a chapter from an elementary science, health, math, or social studies text. Identify the organizational pattern used by the authors. Make a graphic organizer.
3. Choose a literature or basal textbook selection. Design two metacognitive monitoring lessons of the 10 possible lessons described by Baumann et al. (1993) in this chapter. Be sure to include each of the lesson parts, that is, (a) verbal explanation, (b) teacher modeling, (c) guided practice, and (d) independent practice.

4. Take a 250-word passage from a story or an information text. Show how you could use two cloze techniques on this passage by preparing two cloze lessons.
5. Make some group response cards or boards for use in your classroom to respond to questions.
6. Evaluate the recommendations for background building in a basal reader. If necessary, describe how you would alter the recommendations.

In the Field

1. Make arrangements to visit a public school classroom. Carefully observe and record the time devoted to teaching versus testing reading comprehension.
2. Visit with a classroom teacher about the skills she thinks are important for helping students become skilled readers. Summarize these views in a brief essay.
3. Devise a lesson to train children to use *Questioning the Author* with an information book or content textbook. Try it out in an elementary school classroom. Reflect on this experience by making an entry in your professional journal.
4. Prepare a reciprocal teaching lesson using the reciprocal lesson cards. Make arrangements to visit a local resource or Title I classroom to teach your lesson.
5. Prepare a situational context diagram. Make arrangements to work with LEP or ESL students in an elementary school classroom. Use your diagram to teach a language lesson and report on your findings.

Recommended Readings

Alexander, P. A., & Jetton, T. L. (2000). Learning from text: A multidimensional perspective. In M. L. Kamil, P. B. Mosenthal, P. D. Pearson, and R. Barr (Eds.), *Handbook of reading research* (Vol. 3, pp. 285–310). Mahwah, NJ: Erlbaum.

Anderson, R. C., & Pearson, P. D. (1984). A schema-theoretic view of basic processes in reading. In P. D. Pearson (Ed.), *Handbook of reading research* (pp. 255–292). New York: Longman.

Collins-Block, C., Gambrell, L. B., & Pressley, M. (2003). *Improving comprehension instruction: Advances in research, theory, and classroom practice*. San Francisco, CA: Jossey-Bass.

Collins-Block, C., & Pressley, M. (2002). *Comprehension instruction: Research-based best practice*. New York: Guilford Press.

Keene, E. O., & Zimmermann, S. (1997). *Mosaic of thought: Teaching comprehension in a reader's workshop*. Portsmouth, NH: Heinemann.

Pearson, P. D., & Duke, N. (2002). Comprehension instruction in the primary grades. In C. Collins-Block & M. Pressley (Eds.), *Comprehension instruction: Research-based best practices* (pp. 247–258). New York: Guilford Press.

Pressley, M. (2000). What should comprehension instruction be the instruction of? In M. L. Kamil, P. B. Mosenthal, P. D. Pearson, & R. Barr (Eds.), *Handbook of Reading Research*, Vol. 3. Mahwah, NJ: Erlbaum.

Simmons, D. C., & Kameenui, E. J. (1998). *What reading research tells us about children with diverse learning needs: Bases and basics*. Mahwah, NJ: Erlbaum.

Taylor, B. M, Graves, M. F., & Van den Broek, P. (2000). *Reading for meaning: Fostering comprehension in the middle grades*. New York: Teachers College Press.

Developing Reading Fluency

Focus Questions

When you are finished studying this chapter, you should be able to answer these questions:

1. What are the characteristics of fluent reading according to evidence-based research?

2. Is there a relationship between fluency and reading comprehension? Explain.

3. Describe the grade level expectations for reading fluency.

4. How is reading fluency developed?

5. What is the Fluency Formula for organizing classroom instruction? How are repeated readings and guided oral reading incorporated in this plan?

6. What is *guided reading* instruction (Fountas & Pinnell, 1996), and how is it organized?

Key Concepts

Reading Fluency
Automaticity
Quality
Rate
The Fluency Formula
Fluency Pyramid
Decodable Text
Orthography
Guided Oral Reading
Guided Reading
Guided Reading
    Strategy

Leveled Books
Choral Readings
Partner Reading
Neurological Impress Method
Book Buddies
Repeated Readings
Sustained Silent
    Reading (SSR)
Performance
    Reading
Readers' Theatre

Storytelling was the life's blood of communications in the early history of our country, a time when many could neither read nor write. Then, as literacy trickled down the socioeconomic pyramid, stories kept alive for generations were written down. Some 20 years ago we discovered Donald D. Davis, an enthralling storyteller from North Carolina. Davis had recorded a splendid video in which he told a story, the *Crack of Dawn,* about wonderful life lessons learned from his Aunt Laura Henry, "...the oldest living thing I'd ever seen." Later, his book *Listening for the Crack of Dawn* was released. Amazingly, the story he had told on the video and the written version were virtually identical! We then realized that our favorite storyteller was not only a great teller of tales verbally, but also a fluent *reader.* He had READ the tale on the video so fluently we thought it must be extemporaneous! No... Donald Davis is a fluent reader. He knows when to slow down or add voice intonations, and reads with such automaticity it seems like natural speech.

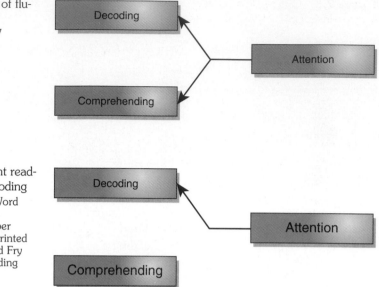

Figure 7.1   A model of fluent reading
Adapted from Chall, 1967

Figure 7.2   Less fluent readers focus mostly on decoding
From "The New Instant Word List," by Edward Fry, The Reading Teacher, December 1980, pp. 284–289. Reprinted with permission of Edward Fry and the International Reading Association.

 *Visit Chapter 7 of our Companion Website at www. prenhall.com/reutzel to look into the chapter objectives, standards and principles, and pertinent web links associated with Developing Reading Fluency.*

Fluent readers are better able to comprehend the author's message.

WHAT IS READING FLUENCY?

Reading fluency involves the ability to read text smoothly and at a reasonable rate. When fluent readers read aloud, they do so effortlessly with speed, accuracy, and proper expression as though they are speaking. Because of the "automatic" nature of their reading, fluent readers are able to focus their attention on the ideas in the text and comprehend the author's message. In Figure 7.1 we present a model reflecting the *automaticity* of fluent readers.

On the other hand, less fluent readers struggle along through text in a very labored, word-by-word way. They must focus most of their attention on decoding the words, so comprehension suffers. Figure 7.2 shows how comprehension can be virtually ignored when readers must devote most of their mental energies on decoding. Thus, fluency is important because it provides a kind of bridge between word recognition and reading comprehension (Rasinski, 1985; Reutzel & Hollingsworth, 1993; National Reading Panel, 2000).

What Skills Do Fluent Readers Possess?

There seems to be agreement among researchers as to the skills one must develop to become a fluent reader (Juel, 1991; Richards, 2000; National Reading Panel, 2000; Allington, 2001). They include the following:

- **Automaticity** involves translating letters-to-sounds-to-words effortlessly and accurately.
- **Quality** refers to the reader's ability to use proper intonation or expression (i.e., "prosodic features"—pitch, juncture, and stress) in one's voice.
- **Rate** involves attaining appropriate reading speed according to the reader's purpose or the type of passage. What is an appropriate rate? Figure 7.3 presents some suggested guidelines.

Figure 7.3 Oral reading fluency end-of-year goals for grade levels 1–5: Words per minute (wpm)—Instructional level (adequate) text

Grade Level	*Minimum* Words per Minute* (wpm)	Fluent Oral Reading (wpm)
Grade 1	60 wpm	80 wpm
Grade 2	70 wpm	100 wpm
Grade 3	80 wpm	126 wpm**
Grade 4	90 wpm	162 wpm**
Grade 5	100 wpm	180 wpm

*Adapted from *Texas Essential Knowledge and Skills,* 2002, at the Texas Education Agency Web site http://www.tea.state.tx.us/.
**Source: *Listening to Children Read Aloud.* Washington, D.C., U.S. Department of Education, National Center for Education Statistics. 1995, 1/p. 44.

Figure 7.4 Fluency benchmark standards*

Kindergarten:
"Reads" familiar texts emergently, i.e., not necessarily verbatim from the print alone.

Grade 1:
Reads aloud with accuracy any text that is appropriately designed for the first half of grade 1.

Grade 2:
Accurately decodes orthographically regular multisyllable words and nonsense words.
Accurately reads many irregularly spelled words and such spelling patterns as diphthongs, special vowel spellings, and common word endings.

Grade 3:
Reads aloud with fluency any text that is appropriately designed for grade level.

*Criteria derived for the research by the Committee on the Prevention of Reading Difficulties in Young Children. Snow, C. E., Burns, M. S., & Griffin, P. (Eds.). (1998). *Preventing reading difficulties in young children.* Washington, D.C.: National Academy Press.

Armed with these three abilities, a fluent reader can decode words in a text accurately, with correct phrasing and intonation, and at a rate that facilitates text comprehension.

Reading Fluency "Standards"

In 1998, the federally sponsored Committee on the Prevention of Reading Difficulties in Young Children conducted an exhaustive study of evidence-based reading research. Included in its report *Preventing Reading Difficulties in Young Children* (Snow, Burns, & Griffin, 1998) were desired "benchmarks accomplishments" for kindergarten through third grade in reading and writing. Figure 7.4 presents excerpts that pertain to reading fluency from the report. They help us to better understand what we hope to achieve in our teaching of normally developing children at each of these grade levels.

Fluent readers have learned the following skills: automaticity, quality, and rate.

Fluency Is Sometimes Ignored in Basal Reading Programs

Basal reading programs often ignore the need to develop reading fluency.

Standards Note
Standard 4.3: The reading professional will be well versed in individual and group instruction and interventions targeted toward those students in greatest need or at low proficiency levels. Basal programs rarely address fluency, and fluency is a major problem for struggling readers. Pick one good fluency builder (e.g., readers' theatre) and develop specific plans for your present or future class, meeting the range but targeting your struggling readers.

For many years reading fluency has been acknowledged as an important goal in becoming a proficient and strategic reader (Allington, 1983, 1984, 2001; Rasinkski & Padak, 1996; Opitz & Rasinski, 1998; Klenk & Kibby, 2000; National Reading Panel, 2000; Rasinski, 2000). But as important as fluency is to reading success, it is often neglected in basal reading programs (i.e., published series adopted by each state—more on basal readers is found in Chapter 8). In fact, an analysis of basal programs during the 1990s (Stein et al., 1993) concluded that very few programs emphasized the development of reading fluency (Snow, Burns, & Griffin, 1998). Since many teachers rely heavily on basal readers as the foundation for their instructional program, particularly in the first five years of their career, fluency instruction can be virtually overlooked. This is unfortunate, concluded the National Reading Panel (2000), because

> If text is read in a laborious and inefficient manner, it will be difficult for the child to remember what has been read and to relate the ideas expressed in the text to his or her background knowledge. Recent research on the efficacy of certain approaches to teaching fluency has led to increased recognition of its importance in the classroom and to changes in instructional practices. (p. 11)

Our recent visits to many elementary school classrooms likewise reveal little attention to reading fluency in daily instruction. As we continue in this chapter, we offer some important insights from the very best research as to how you can help all students become more fluent readers and, in turn, better *comprehenders*.

DEVELOPING READING FLUENCY

How Readers Develop Fluency

Fluency instruction must be well organized and consistently delivered. Several researchers (Allington, 1983, 2001; Rasinski, 1989; Rasinski & Padak, 1996; Richards, 2000) have identified classroom practices that help most students develop the ability to read fluently. Here are the practices they identified.

Provide Direct Instruction Using Guided Oral Reading

Students need structure and support in new learning. When the National Reading Panel (2000) conducted its review of research in the area of fluency, it concluded that guided oral repeated reading procedures

> that included guidance from teachers, peers, or parents had significant and positive impact on word recognition, fluency, and comprehension across a range of grade levels. These studies were conducted in a variety of classrooms in both regular and special education settings with teachers using widely available instructional materials. (p. 12)

When students practice a single text repeatedly, their oral reading becomes fluent. Supporting students using such strategies as choral reading, buddy or dyad reading, and computer-assisted reading can be most effective in a well-conceived reading fluency program. We will take a closer look at these and other strategies later in the chapter and throughout the remainder of the book.

Use a Good Deal of Modeling

Being exposed to rich and varied models of fluent reading helps many children. In this case, parents or siblings spend significant amounts of time reading aloud to these children. Through this process of modeling fluent reading, children learn the behaviors of fluent readers. Other researchers have documented the significant impact of modeling upon the acquisition of fluent reading (Durkin, 1966, 1974; Amarel, Bussis, & Chittenden, 1977). Observing, listening to, and imitating fluent reading models help students learn how to become fluent readers themselves. Modeling fluent reading for students and pointing out specific behaviors as texts are read aloud, as well as providing constructive feedback, can also help students become fluent.

Students Need Massive Amounts of Practice

The more we can help students spend significant time reading—on their own with books of high interest, "buddy reading" with a classmate, and in guided oral reading—the greater their fluency will become. The research on this point is clear: Proficient readers spend more time reading silently than do students having reading problems (Allington, 1980; NAEP, 2000).

Good readers are given more opportunities to read connected text and for longer periods of time than are students having reading problems. This dilemma leads Allington (1977) to muse, "If they don't read much, how they ever gonna get good?"

Struggling readers usually benefit more from paired or "buddy reading" than reading on their own.

Provide Students with Access to Easy Reading Materials

Proficient readers spend more time reading easier texts than students having reading problems (Gambrell et. al., 1981). Reading easy books may help proficient readers make the transition from word by word reading to fluent reading, while poorer readers spend more time reading materials that are relatively difficult. This practice denies students with reading problems access to reading materials that could help them develop fluent reading abilities.

ORGANIZING FOR INSTRUCTION: THE FLUENCY FORMULA

Careful planning is always crucial for successful teaching. In fluency instruction, as with most reading skill areas, the teacher must choose a "balanced diet" of reading materials for practice exercises (i.e., stories, nonfiction materials, poetry) and provide adequate teacher modeling, student practice with peers, and independent practice.

The Fluency Formula (summarized in Figure 7.5), developed for Title I reading teachers in Kansas, is an effective model for organizing fluency instruction that includes these elements (R. Cooter & K. Cooter, 2002). Sample lesson plan forms are shown in Figure 7.6 for your own uses. In the description that follows, you will see how important research-based elements have been included. While you may not wish to use the Fluency Formula in its entirety, its components should be strongly considered as you make transitions toward comprehensive reading instruction.

*The **Fluency Formula** (R. Cooter & K. Cooter, 2002) contains all of the essential ingredients of research-based fluency instruction. Try incorporating its components as you are making transitions toward comprehensive reading instruction.*

Planning for Instruction

An effective teacher always maps out her teaching plan well before reaching the school house; none of this *shooting from the hip* or *random acts of teaching* for us! Lesson planning always begins with the decision about an appropriate objective.

Figure 7.5   The fluency formula

Planning for Instruction
A. Identify Instructional Standards (Objectives)
B. Selection of Passages for Modeling and for Guided Oral Reading (Fluency Pyramid)
C. Develop Lesson Plans

Step I: Passage Introduction & Modeling
A. Introducing the Passage & Concepts
  • Introduce Vocabulary
  • Introduce New Concepts
  • Introduce the Fluency Skill to Be Learned
B. Teacher Modeling of the Targeted Fluency Skill

Step II: Guided Oral Reading Practice
A. Guided Oral Reading Strategies: *Teacher with Kids*
  • Guided Reading Strategy (Fountas & Pinnell, 1996)
  • Choral Reading
B. Peer Supported Practice: *Kids Helping Kids*
  • Partner or "Buddy" Reading
  • Neurological Impress Method (NIM)
  • Book Buddies

Step III: Independent Practice Reading
  • Repeated Readings
  • Sustained Silent Reading or DEAR Time

Step IV: Performance Reading for Fluency Assessment
  • Readers' Theatre
  • Evening Newscast
  • Radio Reading
  • Dialog Retellings

Objectives for fluency instruction, as with anything else in the curriculum, should be drawn from three sources:

1. A careful review of grade levels expectations and state *standards*
2. An assessment of each child's abilities and *individual needs* relative to the standards
3. A collation of all students' needs into a classroom profile to better understand more universal group needs

Identifying Standards for Fluency Instruction

Standards for fluency have been developed by most states for each grade level and by the U.S. Department of Education. Figures 7.3 and 7.4 are examples of these kinds of standards. In Chapter 9, Assessing Literacy Learning, we discuss ways of developing both individual and group objectives from assessment data. Standards almost invariably pertain to one of three principle areas: automaticity, quality, and reading rate. These three areas are described later in the description of step 1 of the Fluency Formula.

Selecting Reading Materials: Varying Literary Genre

The primary goal in the first part of fluency instruction is to model fluent reading behavior for students.

Once you have selected a fluency objective, reading materials should be selected for (1) reading aloud (modeling), and (2) for instruction (guided oral reading). Your primary goal in the first part of fluency instruction should be to *model* fluent reading be-

Figure 7.6 Lesson planning form: The fluency formula

Fluency Standard or Objective to be taught (i.e., state standard; Automaticity, Quality, or Rate):
_____

Passage(s) to be used:
_____

Step I: Passage Introduction & Modeling
Goal: Share a new passage modeling fluent reading behavior.
A. **Vocabulary and Concepts to be introduced:**

   Method of Instruction (for A)

B. **Methods for Introducing and Modeling the New Fluency Skill:**
   1. **Teacher Input:** (Preteaching—State in your own words the skill/task you expect students to perform.)
   2. **Modeling:** (Specify which part of the reading selection you will use to model this aspect of fluency, and how you will model it.)

Step II: Guided Oral Reading Practice
A. **Guided Oral Reading Strategies:** *Teacher Helping Kids*
   1. **Strategy to be used:**
   2. **Procedures for teaching** (step-by-step):
   3. **Materials Needed:**
   4. **Assessment Strategies** (Specific standards-based criteria for how you will know when learning occurs):
B. **Peer-Supported Practice:** *Kids Helping Kids*
   1. **Strategy to be used** (e.g., buddy reading, NIM, etc.):
   2. **Student assignments/pairings** (Attach assignment sheet):
   3. **Procedures for teaching** (step-by-step):
   4. **Materials Needed:**
   5. **Assessment Strategies** (Specific standards-based criteria for how you will know when learning occurs):

Step III: Independent Practice Reading
Specify the strategy and texts to be used for each Fluency Group:
Group: _____
Strategy (Repeated readings, SSR, Assisted-SSR, etc.): _____

Text: _____
Group: _____
Strategy (Repeated readings, SSR, Assisted-SSR, etc.): _____

Text: _____
Group: _____
Strategy (Repeated readings, SSR, Assisted-SSR, etc.): _____

Text: _____
Step IV: Performance Reading for Fluency Assessment
Specify the fluency performance task the students will use, when ready: _____
_____
_____
_____

havior. As the teacher, you are theoretically the *best* reader in the room and your young charges want to see and hear what fluent reading behavior is like. Because you will have a wide range of reading ability represented in your class, you will want to think about modeling for students in two venues—whole class and small groups based on reading level (i.e., guided reading groups).

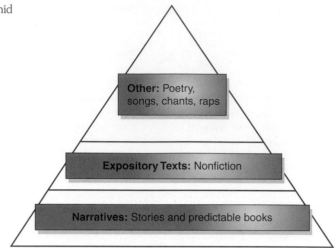

Figure 7.7 Fluency pyramid for passage selection and modeling: Grades K–2

For whole group modeling, remember the "balanced diet" idea mentioned above: *model reading from a variety of genre in children's literature.* In reality, the selection of reading passages may not be all that balanced (sorry to throw you a curve ball). Here's what we mean. Think of the balanced diet at each grade level as more like the famous food pyramid.

In grades K through 2, the bottom of the **fluency pyramid** (i.e., where most of the emphasis is placed) has narrative selections or stories. Thus, much of your oral reading to the class for modeling should come from high quality books like *The Polar Express, Alexander and the Terrible, Horrible, No Good, Very Bad Day* (Viorst, 1987); and *When Lightening Comes in a Jar* (Polacco, 2002). At the center of the pyramid for grades K–2 should be interesting nonfiction books that not only provide a medium for modeling fluency, but also help children develop an understanding of new concepts and vocabulary. Notice that expository text examples are almost equal in proportion to narrative texts. At the top of the pyramid, less frequent in comparison to the first two types, is some extra spice for their fluency diet: songs, poetry, chants, and raps. Figure 7.7 shows a fluency pyramid scheme for passage selection in the early grades.

In grades 3 through 6, the pyramid changes significantly. Nonfiction or *expository text* becomes the staple for modeling and practice. This should not be a return to the narrative forms of the early grades, but selections that bridge between nonfiction information and the creative images of novelists. Historical fiction is perhaps the clearest example of these kinds of narratives for modeling and practice. For example, Linda Sue Parks (2001) won the 2002 Newbery Medal for her book *A Single Shard.* It is a book set in 12th-century Korea and talks about how the central character, Tree-ear, an orphan who lives under a bridge, becomes involved with a community of pottery makers. This book makes for fine modeling and will have your students crying out for you to continue when your time for modeling each day has expired. Along the way they will also learn more about another culture, art, and enjoy a good bit of drama. Figure 7.8 shows our conception of a fluency pyramid for grades 3 through 6.

Just as children get a balanced diet from the offerings on the food pyramid, the fluency pyramid offers a balanced selection of narratives, expository texts and miscellany such as poetry, songs, chants, and raps.

Selecting Reading Materials: Readability and Target Word Frequency

Passages *only* read aloud by the teacher during modeling can be at reading levels well above the abilities of the listeners. In these cases, the teacher is simply demonstrating how a passage can be read with proper intonation and rate. But when passages

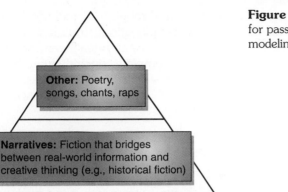

Figure 7.8 Fluency Pyramid for passage selection and modeling: Grades 3–6

are selected for children to read themselves, whether with the teacher or with another student, then the passages should conform to certain guidelines.

- *Use selections within the decoding range of the learner*—95 percent or better accuracy in decoding. A good rule of thumb is that the range of readers in a classroom is usually equal to plus or minus the grade level designation. For example, in second grade classrooms there can be a range of readers from a preprimer level to fourth grade. In a fourth grade classroom there can be struggling readers at emergent or first grade levels and some students reading at an eighth grade level.

- *Text type and your objective should be a good match*—The objective of your lesson, depending on the needs of your student, will fall within the domain of either automaticity, quality, or reading rate. If your purpose is to practice automaticity, then you may want to choose what is called **decodable text.** Decodable texts are usually short books that use common spelling patterns, or **orthography.** If, on the other hand, your objective is to help readers adjust their reading speeds according to their purpose or type of text, then you may want to choose a variety of text samples, such as stories, mathematics word problems, history readings, and poetry, for demonstration and practice sessions.

- *Word overlap*—New vocabulary to be emphasized should appear multiple times.

- *Target rates*—Have been identified using benchmarks for the grade level as minimums.

- *A variety of literary genre*—Should be used and in appropriate proportions for the grade level (see the Fluency Pyramid in Figures 7.7 and 7.8).

Develop Your Lesson Plan

Once you have completed the above tasks, lesson planning begins. Using the template for planning provided in Figure 7.6, you will be able to map out in some detail the flow of fluency instruction to be offered. It is important that new teachers work through this process so that instruction is presented in a seamless way. *Scaffolding*

A good rule of thumb for anticipating the range of reading ability in a classroom is that the range is usually equal to plus or minus the grade level designation. Thus, a fifth grade classroom can have struggling readers at emergent or first grade levels and fluent readers at the tenth grade level.

Decodable texts *are written using common spelling patterns, or* **orthography** *(such as are found in words like call, ball, tall, wall). Words containing the pattern(s) being emphasized appear throughout decodable text to help readers develop automatic and rapid decoding.*

of instruction is used to help students work through their individual zones of proximal development. Verbal instructions and explanations to students make sense, and nothing important is omitted. Even long-time veteran teachers who are new to fluency instruction should fully complete the template, since they are first-time teachers in this area. Once you get your sea legs with this model, lesson planning can become less detailed in terms of language, but the steps should always be followed to insure comprehensive instruction.

Step I: Passage Introduction and Modeling

The Fluency Formula (R. Cooter & K. Cooter, 2002) begins in earnest with the teacher introducing the selection much like a *book talk*. Start off by showing the book jacket, telling a little about the author, and explaining why you chose this selection. Children should be feel enticed and even excited about hearing the selection.

Introduce Important Vocabulary

Next, introduce any new vocabulary that may not be familiar to the students. There are actually three levels of vocabulary knowledge (National Reading Panel, 2000): unknown words, acquainted, and established. *Unknown* words are completely unfamiliar to students whether they hear or attempt to read the word. *Acquainted* words are those students have some familiarity with, but need some kind of review. *Established* words are known to students when they hear them spoken or see them in print. Unknown and acquainted words that are important in the selection you plan to model are the ones you will need to introduce before reading aloud. In Chapter 5, which deals with vocabulary instruction, there is much more detail on this point.

Introduce the Targeted Fluency Skill

Finally, before reading the text, draw students' attention to the fluency skill you plan to emphasize—whether they are seeing it for the first time or as a review. As noted earlier, the three main areas of fluency delineated in scientifically based reading research are automaticity, quality, and reading rate. Name and describe the fluency skill you will be modeling before reading, then return to the skill after reading. Reread short portions of the selection "thinking out loud" how you are using the fluency strategy. Thinking out loud for students is the essence of modeling. You should use many examples, *saturating* students, if you will, with examples drawn from your reading.

For instance, one of the fluency skills you will want to develop is the ability to "chunk text"—read in meaningful phrases. *Scooping* (Hook & Jones, 2002) is a strategy for helping students learn to chunk phrases as a means of attaining good fluency in reading. On the following page is a description of moving the activity from teacher modeling to independent reading.

Step II: Guided Oral Reading Practice

This phase of the Fluency Formula (R. Cooter & K. Cooter, 2002) provides students with repeated and monitored oral reading experiences. These **guided oral reading** sessions are at the heart of the Fluency Formula and are based on the very best reading research. In the summary of the *Report of the National Reading Panel* (2000), the authors noted:

Standards Note
Standard 5.1: The reading professional will be able to create a literacy environment that fosters interest and growth in all aspects of literacy. List four activities for your present or future classroom that promote fluency—be general, but cite titles that you'll use.

Scooping is a strategy for helping students to learn to "chunk," or read in meaningful phrases as a means for attaining good fluency in reading.

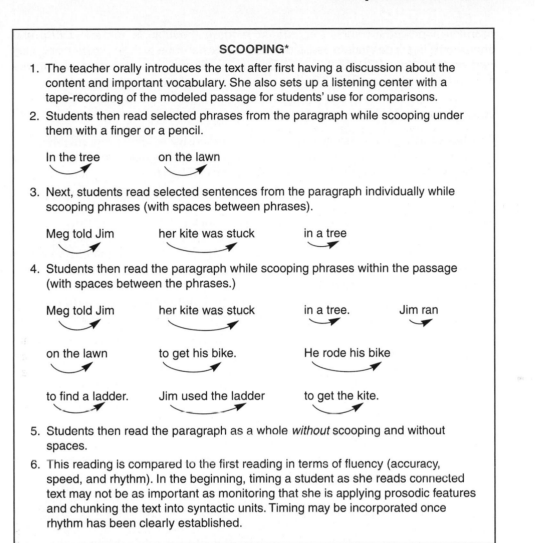

SCOOPING*

1. The teacher orally introduces the text after first having a discussion about the content and important vocabulary. She also sets up a listening center with a tape-recording of the modeled passage for students' use for comparisons.

2. Students then read selected phrases from the paragraph while scooping under them with a finger or a pencil.

    In the tree   on the lawn

3. Next, students read selected sentences from the paragraph individually while scooping phrases (with spaces between phrases).

    Meg told Jim   her kite was stuck   in a tree

4. Students then read the paragraph while scooping phrases within the passage (with spaces between the phrases.)

    Meg told Jim   her kite was stuck   in a tree.   Jim ran

    on the lawn   to get his bike.   He rode his bike

    to find a ladder.   Jim used the ladder   to get the kite.

5. Students then read the paragraph as a whole *without* scooping and without spaces.

6. This reading is compared to the first reading in terms of fluency (accuracy, speed, and rhythm). In the beginning, timing a student as she reads connected text may not be as important as monitoring that she is applying prosodic features and chunking the text into syntactic units. Timing may be incorporated once rhythm has been clearly established.

Adapted from Hook & Jones (2002). *Perspectives.*

[Guided oral reading] encourages students to read passages orally with systematic and explicit guidance and feedback from the teacher. . . . On the basis of a detailed analysis of the available research that met NRP methodological criteria, the Panel concluded that guided repeated oral reading procedures that included guidance from teachers, peers, or parents had a significant and positive impact on word recognition, fluency, and comprehension across a range of grade levels. These studies were conducted in a variety of classrooms in both regular and special education settings with teachers using widely available instructional materials. . . . These results also apply to all students—good readers as well as those experiencing reading difficulties. (p. 12)

Two kinds of guided oral reading are provided in Step II of the Fluency Formula. The first is done with the aid and guidance of the teacher. The second involves repeated readings with a peer. In each case, the student has ample practice rereading texts for fluency and for getting feedback from a more fluent reader.

In the following sections, we highlight some of the most successful strategies used for guided oral reading practice. In the realm of teacher-assisted instruction, we will

Two kinds of effective guided oral reading are repeated readings with a peer and reading with the aid of a teacher.

examine a procedure known as *guided reading* (Fountas & Pinnell, 1996) and *choral reading*. The student-assisted strategies we describe include *partner* or buddy reading (Greene, 1970; Eldredge & Quinn, 1988) and the *Neurological Impress Method* (Heckelman, 1966, 1969).

Guided Reading

The major purposes of guided reading are to develop reading fluency strategies and to move children toward independent reading.

Guided reading is an essential part of a comprehensive reading program (Mooney, 1990; Fountas & Pinnell, 1996). The major purposes of guided reading are (a) to develop reading fluency strategies and (b) to move children toward independent reading. Children are grouped by developmental levels that reflect a range of competencies, experiences, and interests. The strategy centers on developing the child's ability to successfully process text with limited teacher guidance and interaction.

Guided reading groups typically include four levels of children's reading development: (a) early emergent, (b) emergent, (c) early fluency, and (d) fluency. Guided reading groups are composed of six to eight children who work together for a period of time under the direct guidance of the teacher.

It is important to note that the membership of guided reading groups changes as children progress during the year. This is a crucial point because failure to modify groups as students progress can result in static ability groups much like the "Eagles, Bluebirds, and Buzzards" as practiced in earlier days. The static nature of these ability groups caused children to suffer self-esteem damage and have lowered academic expectations, particularly struggling readers left in the "lower" developmental groups.

Leveled Books

Offering fluency instruction for students hinges on their being correctly placed in books on their reading level. Thus, the notion of **leveled books,** books categorized according to their difficulty so that they can be matched to students at that level, is an important one for fluency instruction. Before a guided reading group is begun, the teacher must take great care to match the levels of text with the identified needs of a group of children to insure that the group can enjoy and control the story throughout the first reading. Texts chosen for each leveled group should present children with a reasonable challenge, but also with a high degree of potential success.

Please see the listing of criteria typically used for leveling books for guided reading instruction on page 209. In Table 7.1 we include a useful reading level cross-referencing guide comparing grade levels to guided reading levels, to Reading Recovery levels (a popular remedial reading program for first grade students), and to the stages of reading.

Lesson Planning for Guided Reading

The basic lesson pattern employed in guided reading lessons consists of seven phases, which are listed and explained in Figure 7.9.

Teacher Feedback During Instruction

Understanding the nature, quantity, and quality of teacher feedback during guided oral reading, as well as in other "coaching" situations, is a crucial part of helping students become fluent readers. The self-assessment questions on the bottom of page 211 for teachers are provided to assist in this process.

Levels 1–4 (A–D)

- Repeating language patterns.
- Illustrations that match and explain most of the text. Actions are clearly presented without much in the way of extraneous detail that might confuse the reader.
- Whole meaning or story that is likely to match the experiences and conceptual knowledge common to most beginning readers.
- The language of the text developmentally matches syntax and organization of most young children's speech for whom the text is intended.
- Sentences and books themselves are comparatively short (e.g., 10–60 words).
- Print is carefully laid out so that it consistently appears on the same place on the page throughout each book.

Assumption at this level:

That when students encounter an unknown word in print they can easily use context from known words and illustrations along with language pattern cues and early word analysis skills for successful decoding.

LEVELS 5–8 (D–E)

- One often sees predictable, repetitive language patterns, but without allowing the same pattern to dominate the entire text.
- There is now more variation of language patterns, as opposed to one or two word changes, for example.
- Words and phrases may appear to express different meanings through varying sentence structures.
- By the end of these stages, the syntax is more typical of written or "book" language. Illustrations provide minimal support for readers determining exact language.

LEVELS 9–12 (E–G)

- Variation in sentence patterns is now the norm.
- Longer sentences with less predictable text.
- Written language styles and genre become more prominent, including the use of some verb forms not often used by young children in oral settings.
- The average sentence length in texts increases (double that found in levels 5–8).
- Events in a story may continue over several pages.
- Illustrations provide only moderate support to the meaning of the stories.

LEVELS 13–15* (G–H)

(*Consider these characteristics as enhancements to the description for levels 9–12.)
- There is a greater variety of words and the inclusion of more specialized vocabulary.
- Pictures provide some support for the overall meaning of the story, but cannot be used by the reader to interpret the precise message.

LEVELS 16–20 (I–K)

- Now there are longer stories or sequences of events.
- Story events are developed more fully than texts at lower levels.
- Vocabulary is progressively more rich and varied.
- Illustrations are used to help to create the atmosphere and setting, rather than to specifically depict the content of the text.
- It is now common to have full pages of print.

General Explanation of Criteria for Determining the Reading Levels of Texts: Levels 1–20 (A–K) The language of the text developmentally matches syntax and organization of most young children's speech for whom the text is intended.

Table 7.1 Guided Reading Leveling Comparisons
Here is a handy guide to help you translate books from publishers using Guided Reading ratings to leveling systems common in one-to-one tutorial programs (i.e., Reading Recovery, Cooter & Cooter's *BLAST* program, etc.).

Grade Level (Basal)	Guided Reading Level (Fountas-Pinnell)	One-to-One Tutoring Level	Stages of Reading
Kindergarten	A	A	Emergent
	B	1	
		2	
Pre-Primer	C	3	
	D	4	
	E	6–8	
Primer	F	10	Early
	G	12	
1st Grade	H	14	Transitional
	I	16	
2nd Grade	J–K	18–20	
	L–M	24–28	
3rd Grade	N	30	Fluent/Extending
	O–P	34–38	
4th Grade	Q–R	40	
5th Grade	—	44	
6th Grade	—	—	

Figure 7.9 Guided reading lesson overview

Picture Talk • Walk through a new book by looking at the pictures. Ask children, "What do you see?"

First Reading • Depending on the students' developmental levels, the first reading is initially done by the teacher with children following the lead. Later, the teacher gradually releases responsibility for the first reading to the children by sharing the reading role and then fading into one who encourages children to try it on their own.

Language Play • In this phase of the guided reading lesson, the teacher carefully analyzes the text to find specific elements associated with written language to teach children how language works. For early emergent readers, this may mean letter identification, punctuation, or directionality. In the fluency stage, children might identify text genre or compound words.

Rereading • Children read the text again with the assistance of the teacher, a peer, or a mechanical device such as a computer or tape. Novice readers are encouraged to point to the text as they read, whereas fluent readers are encouraged to "read the text with your eyes" or silently.

Retelling • Children retell what they have read to their teacher or to their peers. Typically we say, "Can you tell me what you've read?" Sometimes we probe children's retellings with other questions to prompt recall.

Follow-up • The most effective follow-up activity to a guided reading lesson is to invite children to take guided reading books home for demonstrating their ability to parents and siblings. This provides needed practice time and promotes increased confidence and self-esteem among young readers.

Extensions • Extending books through performances, murals, artwork, and even music helps children deepen their understandings and increase their interpretations of text.

1. Am I more often telling the word than providing a clue?
2. What is the average self-correction rate of my students?
3. Do I assist poor readers with unknown words more often than good readers? If so, why?
4. Am I correcting miscues even when they do not alter the meaning of the text? If so, why?
5. Does one reader group tend to engage in more self-correction than other groups? If so, why?
6. Does one reading group have more miscues that go unaddressed than other groups?
7. What types of cues for oral reading errors do I provide, and why?
8. What is *my* ultimate goal in reading instruction?
9. How do I handle interruptions from other students during oral reading? Do I practice what I preach?
10. How does my feedback influence the self-correction behavior of students?
11. Does my feedback differ across reader groups? If so, *how* and *why*?
12. Would students benefit more from a form of feedback different from that which I normally offer?
13. Am I allowing students time to self-correct (3–5 seconds)?
14. Am I further confusing students with my feedback?
15. Do I digress into "mini-lessons" mid-sentence when students make a mistake? If so, why?
16. Do I analyze miscues to gain information about the reading strategies students employ?
17. Does the feedback I offer aid students in becoming independent, self-monitoring readers? If so, how?
18. Do I encourage students to ask themselves, "Did that make sense?" when they are reading both orally and silently? If not, why not?
19. Do students need the kind of feedback I am offering them?

Source: Adapted from "Teacher Interruptions During Oral Reading Instruction: Self-Monitoring as an Impetus for Change in Corrective Feedback," by M. Shake, *Remedial and Special Education, 7*(5), pp. 18–24.

Choral Reading

Choral reading can be done in three ways: unison reading, echo reading, and antiphonal reading.

Choral readings of text can be done in at least three ways. Wood (1983) recommends *unison reading* and *echo reading*. Unison reading is where everyone reads together. Echo (sometimes called *echoic*) reading has the teacher or a student read a passage aloud, then everyone else "echoes" by repeating it. A third method we have found useful is *antiphonal* reading. Derived from ancient monastic traditions, antiphonal reading has two groups. The first reading group reads a passage aloud (usually a sentence or two), and the second group echoes the reading.

Student-Assisted Strategies: Partner or Buddy Reading

In **Partner reading** *a more fluent reader, or sometimes a reader of equal fluency, reads aloud with a "buddy."*

Partner reading or buddy reading has a student reading aloud with a more fluent partner or, sometimes, a reader of equal fluency. The partner provides the model of fluent reading in place of the teacher, provides useful feedback, and helps, when needed, with word recognition.

Usually the partners take turns reading an assigned passage aloud to one another, with the more developed reader reading first, thus providing the model for fluent reading. Then, the second reader rereads the passage in the same way as the first. The more fluent reader offers feedback on how his partner can read the passage more fluently, and the less fluent reader rereads the passage until he can do so independently.

Readers of about the same ability are sometimes paired for this exercise. The difference is that both readers first hear the teacher reading the passage as the model, then the two buddies take turns reading to each other and offering feedback until they can each read the passage fluently.

Student-Assisted Strategies: Neurological Impress Method

The **neurological impress method** *involves a student and a more fluent reader in reading the same text aloud simultaneously.*

The **neurological impress method** (NIM) involves the student and a more fluent reader in reading the same text aloud simultaneously (Heckelman, 1966, 1969). Unlike other partner reading examples described before, NIM has the student and more fluent model reading in unison at the same volume at first, and then the model's voice gradually fades as the student becomes more confident.

The use of multiple sensory systems associated with using NIM is thought to "impress" the fluent reading patterns of the teacher onto the student through direct modeling. It is assumed that exposing students to numerous examples of texts (read in a more sophisticated way than struggling readers could achieve on their own) will enable them to achieve automaticity in word recognition more naturally. This assumption stands to reason when viewed in light of more recent advances in learning theory, especially those espoused by Vygotsky (1978).

Each NIM session is aimed at reading as much material as is possible in 10 minutes. Reading material selected for the first few sessions should be easy, predictable, and make sense for the reader. However, other more challenging materials that are on the student's normal guided reading level can be used rather quickly.

The neurological impress method has been shown to be very effective in helping struggling readers develop fluency.

To use the NIM, the student sits slightly in front and to one side of the teacher as they hold the text. The more fluent reader moves her finger beneath the words as they are spoken in near-unison fashion. Both try to maintain a comfortably brisk and continuous rate of oral reading. The more fluent reader's role is to keep the pace when the student starts to slow down. Pausing for analyzing unknown words is not permitted. The more fluent reader's voice is directed at the student's ear so that the words are seen, heard, and said simultaneously.

Since many struggling readers have not read at an accelerated pace before, their first efforts often have a mumble-like quality. Most struggling readers typically take time to adjust to the NIM; however, within a few sessions they start to feel more at ease. Many struggling readers say they enjoy the NIM because it allows them to read more challenging and interesting material like "good readers."

At first, the more fluent reader's voice will dominate the oral reading, but in later sessions it should be reduced gradually. This will eventually allow the student to assume the vocal lead naturally. Usually three sessions per week are sufficient to obtain noticeable results. This routine should be followed for a minimum of 10 consecutive weeks (Henk, 1983).

The NIM can also be adapted for group use (Hollingsworth, 1978). Here the teacher tape-records 10 minutes of his or her own oral reading in advance. Individual students can read along with the tape while following the text independently, or the tape can be used in a listening center to permit the teacher to spend individual time with each student as others participate in reading with the tape. Despite the advantages of the prerecorded tape format, teachers' or more fluent peer's one-to-one interactions with individual students result in a better instructional experience.

Book Buddies

In the **book buddies** strategy, students improve reading fluency with the help of a classroom volunteer tutoring in a one-to-one setting (Invernizzi et al., 1997). The four-part lesson uses *repeated readings* of a familiar text, *word study* (phonics and structural analysis), *writing for sounds,* and reading a new book.

In the word study portion of the lesson, students principally focus on beginning consonants, middle and ending consonant sounds, and finally on vowel sounds. This program leads students to a better understanding of "speech to print" concepts for improved automaticity and the beginning of a sight vocabulary (Snow, Burns, & Griffin, 1998).

Research on book buddies has been very positive indeed. In one study (Invernizzi et al., 1997), three groups of 358 first and second grade students participated. First graders who scored in the bottom quartile of the Title I referral list were assigned tutors using this method. University faculty members provided the assessments and lesson plans for the tutors. Results were very positive for developing automaticity, in fact, on a par with coaching by professionally trained teachers.

Book buddies enlists the aid of a volunteer classroom tutor in a one-on-one setting with a student.

Step III: Independent Practice

Developing students as readers is in some ways like a coach developing an Olympic swimmer. There are numerous skills to be developed and learned to the point of automaticity. If the student, or swimmer, is to become proficient, then there must be many hours of practice. You might say, then, that independent practice is intended to provide students with ample opportunities to become *Olympic readers*—strong, capable, and fluent. Two of the more productive strategies for independent practice are repeated readings (Samuels, 1979; Dowhower, 1991) and sustained silent reading.

Repeated Readings

Repeated readings engage students in reading interesting passages orally over and over again to enhance students' reading fluency (Samuels, 1979; Dowhower, 1987). Although it might seem that reading a text again and again could lead to boredom, it can actually have just the opposite effect.

Repeated readings help improve students' comprehension, vocabulary recognition, and oral reading performance.

In the beginning, texts selected for repeated readings should be short, predictable, and easy. When students attain adequate speed and accuracy with easy texts, the length and difficulty of the stories and poems can gradually be increased.

Repeated readings help students by expanding the total number of words they can recognize instantaneously and help improve students' comprehension and oral elocution (performance) with each succeeding attempt. Improved performance quickly leads students to improved confidence regarding reading aloud and positive attitudes toward the act of reading. Additionally, because high-frequency words (e.g., *the, and, but, was, etc.*) occur in literally all reading situations, the increase in automatic sight word knowledge developed through repeated readings transfers far beyond the practiced texts.

Research indicates that repeated readings are most effective when students are supported during independent reading. Audiotapes, tutors, or peer feedback are supports shown to be most effective during repeated reading practice sessions (National Reading Panel, 2000). For example, try providing a tape-recorded version of the story or poem to be practiced. Students can read along with an audiocassette tape to develop fluency similar to the model on the tape (probably your voice). Also, students can tape record their oral reading performance as a source of immediate feedback. If two audiocassette tape players are available, ask students to listen and read along with the taped version of the text using headphones. At the same time, use the second recorder for recording the student's oral reading. The child can then replay his version simultaneously with the teacher-recorded version to compare or simply listen to his own rendition alone. Either way, the feedback can be both instant and effective.

You may use taped recordings of repeated readings for further analysis of each reader's improvement in fluency and comprehension. Also, using a tape recorder frees the teacher to work with other students, thereby conserving precious instructional time and leaving behind an audit trail of student readings for later assessment and documentation. On occasion, teachers should listen to the tape with the reader present. During this time the teacher and student can discuss effective ways of reducing word recognition errors and increasing reading rate.

Sustained Silent Reading

Sustained silent reading (SSR), or *Drop Everything and Read Time (DEAR Time), works by allowing students to choose a book that interests them and orchestrating timed periods each day for them to read said book.*

Sustained silent reading (SSR), also known as *DEAR Time* (Drop Everything And Read) is a very popular method of independent reading practice in our schools. The way it works is simple. Students first self-select a book of interest to them from the library, then check to make sure it won't be too hard for them using a strategy known as *rule-of-thumb* or ROT. Here are the steps in rule-of-thumb (ROT):

Rule-of-Thumb Strategy for Choosing "Just Right" Books

1. Choose a book that looks interesting.
2. Open the book to any page that has lots of words on it.
3. Begin reading aloud or silently. When you come to a word you don't know, hold up your small finger.
4. If you come to another word you don't know, hold up your next finger. If you use up all of your fingers on one hand (and come to your thumb) on one page, then the book is *too hard* and you should put it back. Just find another book you like just as well and repeat the ROT exercise to make sure it's just right for you.

Once students have chosen their books, they are ready for DEAR Time. The goal is for students to read a total of 20 minutes per day in a self-selected book. For younger students you may need to have several 5-minute periods for DEAR Time. Teachers will usually set an egg timer for the amount of time they wish, then *everyone* reads (including the teacher). Some principals even have daily schoolwide DEAR Time.

The research on SSR or DEAR time has been somewhat inconclusive. There is no real question that students must have a good deal of practice if they are to become fluent readers. The question really is—what kind of practice? For struggling readers in particular, SSR may not be very effective. If a struggling reader is truly *struggling* with basic word recognition skills, for instance, sitting alone and staring at a book he is unable to decode will do little to develop his fluency.

In many cases, SSR will be far more effective if a form of buddy reading is used rather than having students reading in isolation. This is especially so with emergent readers in the early grades who have not yet mastered the alphabetic principle and/or basic decoding skills and with struggling readers (National Reading Panel, 2000).

A teacher in Kansas once remarked, "I've been an ice skater all my life. I recently had a chance to go see Dorothy Hamill in the *Ice Capades*. You know, just being around Dorothy Hamill won't make me as good an ice skater as Dorothy Hamill. Its like struggling readers during SSR if they don't have any support; just being around great readers won't make them great readers . . . it takes much more."

Another exception has to do with the teacher's role during SSR. While it is certainly a desirable goal for teachers to participate in SSR themselves by reading and modeling their enjoyment of reading, it may not always be in some students' best interest. For example, some struggling readers lack initiative or a desire to read. In these cases, a teacher may need to intervene during SSR and give the student a motivating purpose to read or a task to fulfill. Some examples might include:

"I'd like you to draw me a picture of your favorite character when you finish reading this story."

"Find five _____ (e.g., color, describing, number, etc.) words for me as you read."

"I will want you to act out one of the characters when you finish, and I'll see if I can guess which one it is!"

Step IV: Performance Reading for Fluency Assessment

Performance reading has students reading aloud for the teacher and/or an audience so that the teacher can monitor each student's fluency growth. Students prepare for the exercise, regardless of format, by orally rereading the text to be performed until they can read it with maximum fluency. There are several ways this can be done that have found support in evidence-based research. Before we get to those, we should first examine a very well-known approach that you should *not* use—"round-robin reading."

Long ago teachers commonly relied on an activity commonly known as *round-robin reading* as a means of listening to students read aloud. Students would sit in a circle. The teacher would call on a child to begin reading from a story in the basal reader, and the other children would follow along. After the first student read a paragraph or two, the teacher would stop her, call on the next student to the first one's right, and ask her to continue reading. This process was repeated until *every* child in the circle had a chance to read.

Sustained silent reading (SSR) is most effective with readers who have mastered basic word recognition skills. Emergent and struggling readers will benefit most from SSR when they can participate in a paired-reading format.

Round-robin reading is not an effective method to use in your classroom for fluency development.

Though the simplicity of round-robin is very appealing, research has revealed it to be far less effective than other available strategies for monitoring fluency development, and it can even have a negative impact on some children (Eldredge, Reutzel, & Hollingsworth, 1996). Round-robin fails to give children adequate opportunities for repeated readings before performing, defeats comprehension (i.e., when a student realizes the paragraph he'll be asked to read is three ahead of the current student in the "hot seat," he'll tend to look ahead and start silently reading his passage feverishly hoping that he won't "mess up" when it's his turn), and causes some students embarrassment when they are unable to read their paragraph fluently. Our advice? Please don't use round-robin in your classroom; there are better alternatives that will help you monitor fluency development, improve student development, and protect fragile egos in the process. There are effective alternatives that can be used for performance reading.

Readers' Theatre

Perhaps the most successful performance reading strategy, in terms of the research (Sloyer, 1982; National Reading Panel, 2000; Partnership for Reading, 2001) is readers' theatre. **Readers' theatre** involves rehearsing and performing a script that is rich with dialogue before an audience. The script itself may be one from a book or, in the upper elementary or middle school grades, could be developed by a group of students working in collaboration as part of a literature response activity (Cooter & Griffith, 1989).

Stayter and Allington (1991) tell about a readers' theatre activity for which a group of heterogeneously grouped seventh graders spent five days reading, rehearsing, and performing short dramas. After a first reading, students began to negotiate about which role they would read. More hesitant students were permitted to opt for smaller parts, but everyone was required to participate. As time passed, the students critiqued each others' readings and made suggestions as to how they should sound (e.g., "You should sound like a snob"). The most common response in this experience was how repeated readings through drama helped them better understand the text. One student said,

> The first time I read to know what the words are. Then I read to know what the words *say* and later as I read I thought about how to say the words. . . . As I got to know the character better, I put more feeling in my voice. (Stayter & Allington, 1991, p. 145)

Literature selected for readers' theatre is often drawn from tales from the oral tradition, poetry, or quality picture books designed to be read aloud by children. However, nonfiction passages can also be adapted and written to be more like a documentary. Selections should, whenever possible, be packed with action, have an element of suspense, and comprise an entire, meaningful story or nonfiction text. Also, texts selected for use in readers' theatre should contain sufficient dialogue to make reading and preparing the text a challenge and involve several children as characters. A few examples of narrative texts we have seen used include Martin and Archambault's *Knots on a Counting Rope* (1987), Viorst's *Alexander and the Terrible, Horrible, No Good, Very Bad Day* (1972), and Barbara Robinson's *The Best Christmas Pageant Ever* (1972).

Here is an easy procedure to follow. If a story is selected for reading, students should be assigned to read characters' parts. If poems are selected for a readers' theatre, students may read alternating lines or groups of lines. Readers' theatre in-the-round, where readers stand around the perimeter of the room and the audience is in the center surrounded by the readers, is a fun and interesting variation for both performers and audience.

Students will often benefit from a discussion prior to reading a readers' theatre script for the first time. This discussion helps students make connections between their own background experiences and the text to be read. Also, struggling readers usually benefit from listening to a previously recorded performance of the text as a model prior to their initial attempts at reading the script.

Hennings (1974) described a simplified procedure for preparing readers' theatre scripts for classroom performance. First, the text to be performed is read silently by the individual students. Second, the text is read again orally, sometimes using choral reading in a group. After the second reading, children either choose their parts or the teacher assigns parts to the children. We suggest that students be allowed to select their three most desired parts, write these choices on a slip of paper, and submit them to the teacher and that teachers do everything possible to assign them one of these three choices. The third reading is also an oral reading with students reading their parts with scripts in hand. There may be several rehearsal readings as students prepare for the final reading or performance in front of the class or a selected audience.

Readers' theatre offers students a unique opportunity to participate in reading along with other, perhaps more skilled, readers. Participating in the mainstream classroom with better readers helps students with reading problems feel a part of their peer group, provides them with ready models of good reading, and demonstrates how good readers, through practice, become even better readers. Working together with other readers fosters a sense of teamwork, support, and pride in personal and group accomplishment.

There are numerous variations on readers' theatre that possess all of the effective elements. Here are three that you may want to try.

• **Evening Newscast** The evening newscast activity offers maximum opportunity for students to practice their roles using the kind of intonation characteristics used by newscasters. Teachers may want to encourage students to adopt and adapt the particular style of a famous personality, such as "Katie Curtsy" or "Bryant Gum-ball."

• **Radio Plays** *Radio plays* is an adaptation of something called "radio reading" (Searfoss, 1975), a procedure for developing oral reading fluency in a group setting, a process which shields students having reading problems from the sometimes harsh emotional consequences from peers due to their limited reading abilities.

Developing a radio play involves virtually the same process as any other student drama and uses a purely oral–aural (i.e., speaking–listening) delivery. Students first write a one-act play based on their book as described in the preceding section. Next, materials are gathered for the purpose of creating needed sound effects (police whistles, recorded train sound effects, door opening/closing, etc.), and different human sounds are practiced (such as a girl's or boy's scream, tongue clicking noise, and throat-clearing). After thorough rehearsal of the script with sound effects, the radio play is taped on a cassette recorder and played over the school's public address system into the classroom.

Teachers may want to obtain recordings of old radio shows, such as *The Shadow,* to help students better understand the concept. A more current source is Garrison Keillor's radio program *A Prairie Home Companion,* which airs every Saturday night on National Public Radio stations and usually has several radio dramas each week.

• **Dialogue Retellings** We recommend that students create *dialogue retellings* by first writing a script retelling the key information and/or dialogue from their

Research shows that Readers' Theatre is one of the most successful performance reading strategies.

You will find a Safety Net Lesson for struggling readers on developing fluency and making words in Chapter 7 of our Companion Website at www. prenhall.com/reutzel.

selection and then prepare a puppet show for younger students. Participants should rehearse their parts until they are perfectly fluent and should solicit suggestions from other peers before the day of performance. A book like *The Lion, the Witch, and the Wardrobe* by C. S. Lewis (1961) makes a great example for teachers to use in explaining this option. Walley (1993) recommends the use of cumulative stories, those having a minimum of plot and a maximum of rhythm and rhyme, in early elementary grades. Jane Yolen's (1976) *An Invitation to a Butterfly Ball* is one such example.

Summary

Fluency is the ability to read a text accurately with appropriate intonation and phrasing and at a good speed according to the text's purpose. Fluency instruction, since it helps readers achieve automatic decoding, is critical for comprehending the author's message.

Reading fluency can be developed by teacher modeling of fluent behaviors and by having students participate in guided oral repeated reading sessions. It can be further strengthened by massive amounts of practice (i.e., practice reading). Struggling readers and, in fact, all others benefit most from practice reading that provides feedback and direction.

Monitoring and evaluating the development of reading fluency is an important teacher activity. Various forms of the readers' theatre were discussed that can be both motivational and informative for teachers and students alike. Careful analysis of students' oral reading in these sessions can help teachers in setting instructional goals.

Concept Applications

In the Classroom

1. In groups of four in your college class, or in a small group of teachers from your school, perform the following tasks for a selected grade level:
   a. Identify your state's standards for fluency instruction for the selected grade. These can usually be located on the state's department of education Web site on the Internet.
   b. For each form of reading fluency (automaticity, quality, rate), determine which of these areas are addressed in the state standards, and which are not.
   c. Outline the strategies named in this chapter that would be appropriate for improving reading fluency at this level, and match each to one of the state standards.
   d. If you are using this book as part of a college class, present your findings for the above to the group. Be sure to provide your classmates with a copy of your findings for future reference in the field.
   e. If you are a small group of teachers from a school working through this exercise, share your findings with another grade level team and your principal. Determine together whether a renewed emphasis on reading fluency is warranted based on current classroom practices.

In the Field

2. Develop a unit of study using the Fluency Formula presented in this chapter, then teach it to a small group of students (or the class if you al-

---

Standards Note
Standard 5.4: The reading professional will be able to provide opportunities for learners to select from among a variety of written materials, to read extended texts, and to read for authentic purposes. Create several text sets for your present grade level, leveled appropriately for the readability range.

Check your understanding of chapter concepts by using the self assessment for Chapter 7 of our Companion Website at www.prenhall.com/ reutzel.

ready have your own classroom). Be sure to pretest students before planning your unit (see Chapter 9 for additional assessment tips) so that you will know which fluency area to emphasize. Also, compare your students' needs to the state's standards for reading fluency, and clearly identify in your lesson plan which skill is being addressed.

3. Identify a struggling reader who needs help developing greater fluency. The classroom teacher in charge should easily be able to help you find a good candidate. After determining through assessment or from class records the reading level of the student, select appropriately leveled texts that you can use to plan a Neurological Impress Method (NIM) lesson. Work with this student on a selected passage for a minimum of three sessions per week (about 10–15 minutes each time) until s/he can read at least two passages fluently. Keep a log of your daily lesson plans and results. It is a good idea to tape record these sessions so that you can replay them later to help add detail to your journal reflections.

Recommended Readings

Fountas, I., & Pinnell, G. S. (1996). *Guided reading.* Portsmouth, NH: Heinemann.

Mooney, M. E. (1990). *Reading to, with, and by children.* Katonah, NY: Richard Owen.

Opitz, M. F., & Rasinski, T. V. (1998). *Good-bye round robin: 25 effective oral reading strategies.* Portsmouth, NH: Heinemann.

Park, L. S. (2001). *A single shard.* New York: Clarion.

Sloyer, S. (1982). *Reader's theatre: Story dramatization in the classroom.* Urbana, IL: National Council of Teachers of English.

Materials and Programs for Literacy Instruction: Basals and Beyond

Focus Questions

When you are finished studying this chapter, you should be able to answer these questions:

1. How have basal readers changed over the years?

2. What are the major components associated with basal readers?

3. What are five strengths and five weaknesses of basal readers?

4. How are basal readers produced and organized?

5. What are at least two ways in which teachers can maximize their use of basal teacher's editions?

6. What are three nationally recognized reading programs for teaching children to read?

Key Concepts

Basal Readers
Teacher's Edition
Scope and Sequence Chart
Decodable Text
Instructional Management
   System
Basal Reader Adoption
Themed Units
Literature-Based Basals

Basal Reader Adoption
Reconciled Reading Lesson
ReQuest (Reciprocal
   Questioning)
Reading Recovery
Success for All
Four Blocks
Early Steps

Basal readers in one form or another have played an integral role in American reading instruction for centuries and are likely to continue to do so well into the future (McCallum, 1988; Reutzel, 1991; Giordano, 2001; Hoffman, 2001; Robinson, in press). According to *The Literacy Dictionary*, a basal reading program is "a collection of student texts and workbooks, teacher's manuals, and supplemental materials for developmental reading and sometimes writing instruction, used chiefly in the elementary and middle school grades." (T. L. Harris & Hodges, 1995, p. 18)

UNDERSTANDING THE BASAL READER

A basal reading program is a set of commercially prepared and marketed resource materials for providing classroom reading instruction in elementary and middle schools. Research indicates that basal readers are used daily in 92 to 98 percent of primary classrooms in the United States (Flood & Lapp, 1986; Wade & Moje, 2000). More recent data suggest that 85 percent of intermediate grade classrooms continue to rely on basal reader instruction to some degree (Shannon & Goodman, 1994; Wade & Moje, 2000). These data clearly demonstrate the integral role that basal reader instruction has played and continues to play in contemporary American reading instruction.

Current basal readers have descended from a long ancestry of basal readers. The first in this line of predecessors was the hornbook, the earliest reading instructional material widely used and recorded in American history (N. B. Smith, 1986). A cursory examination of the hornbook clearly illustrates the strong religious underpinnings of early American reading instruction (Figure 8.1). Another ancestor of the modern basal published during this era of reading instruction was the New England Primer (Figure 8.2). Rooted deeply in the religious freedom movement of the American colonists, early reading instruction was aimed at helping children learn the necessary theology to work out their salvation. This goal could be accomplished only by reading the Bible.

McCallum (1988) pointed out that as the American citizenry moved away from government by the church to civil government, moral character, national interests, and patriotism for a new nation influenced both the aims and the content of basal readers. Consequently, the McGuffey Eclectic Readers (Figure 8.3) were introduced to the educational community in the 1830s by William H. McGuffey (Bohning,

---

Check your understanding of chapter concepts by using the self assessment for Chapter 8 on our Companion Website at www.prenhall.com/reutzel.

Basal readers are used daily in 9 of 10 primary classrooms in the United States.

The hornbook clearly illustrated the strong religious underpinnings of early American reading instruction.

The New England primer was aimed at not only teaching children to read but also to help them work out their salvation.

Figure 8.1   A hornbook with the alphabet, a syllabary, and the Lord's Prayer

Photo courtesy of The Horn Book, Inc.

Figure 8.2 A page from *The New England Primer*

1986). In 1912, the Beacon Street Readers were published by Ginn & Co., located on Beacon Street in Boston. These readers reflected a strong emphasis on phonics, complete with elaborate articulation drills and diacritical markings (Aukerman, 1981; Smith, 1986; Robinson, in press).

The New Basic Readers (Figure 8.4), affectionately known as the "Dick and Jane" readers, principally authored by William S. Gray and Marion Monroe, were originally published by Scott, Foresman and Company in 1941. The Dick and Jane readers conveyed the stereotypic American dream pervasive in the United States during and following World War II and the Korean Conflict. The family depicted in the Dick and Jane basals owned a spacious, white, two-story home in a well-cared-for suburban neighborhood. Mother stayed home while Father worked at a successful career, providing for the family's needs. A car and a pet dog and cat also adorned the dream of the American family portrayed in this series. For those who remember the Dick and Jane readers fondly and wish to update their acquaintance, we suggest a modern humorous satire written by Marc Gallant (1986), entitled *More Fun with Dick and Jane*.

The McGuffey Eclectic primer was intended to inculcate young children with moral character.

Observe the language in Figure 8.4.

Figure 8.3   Sample pages from *McGuffey's Eclectic Primer,* Revised Edition
New York: Henry H. Vail, 1909.

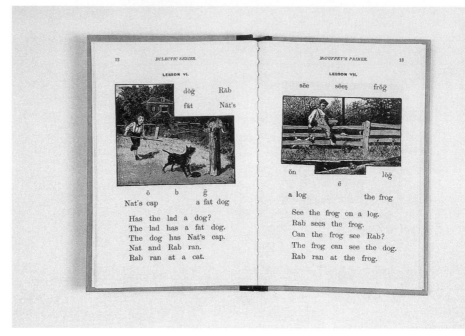

Figure 8.4   Sample pages from the Dick and Jane Readers

From *The New We Look and See* by W. S. Gray, M. Monroe, A. S. Artley, and M. H. Arbuthnot, 1956, Chicago: Scott Foresman. Copyright 1956 by Scott Foresman.

The basal readers produced during the mid-1960s and through the early 1970s reflected a serious-minded response to a perceived threat to national security by the successful launching of Russia's Sputnik into space. This perception prompted a quick return to basic and rigorous academics in American schooling. The publication of Flesch's 1955 book *Why Johnny Can't Read* added fuel to the fire for the hasty return to phonics and basic skill instruction in reading. One well-known basal reading program originally published during this era evidencing the return to basic skills and phonics in reading instruction was *Reading Mastery: DISTAR.*

The basals of the late 1970s into the mid-1980s reflected a continued emphasis on a basic skills approach to reading instruction but was accompanied by a major shift in the composition and content of basal readers. The stereotypic portrayal of men and women in basals was attacked and, as a consequence, revised. The failure of basal readers to represent ethnic minorities fairly was assailed by basal critics. Thus, compilers of the basals of this era reacted by attempting to represent the increasing complexity of modern American society while maintaining a continuing emphasis on back to basics and accountability (Aukerman, 1981).

The basals of the late 1970s and early 1980s reflected an emphasis on back to basics and accountability.

Reading selections found in basal readers of the 1990s and early twenty-first century reflected the influence of the literature-based reading instruction movement of the late 1980s. These basal readers include a substantial number of selections from classical and contemporary children's literature (Reutzel & Larsen, 1995).

The value and the role of the basal reader continue to be the focus of debates (Wade & Moje, 2000). Shannon (1989b, 1992, 1993) asserts that basal readers have contributed to a deskilling of teachers' expertise and decision making related to reflective and thoughtful reading instruction. Baumann (1992, 1993, 1996) asserts on the other hand, that teachers who are otherwise capable and intelligent decision makers are not falling prey to a mindless adherence to basal teacher's editions as Shannon indicates. He says that teachers who otherwise think and make decisions do not stop making decisions when they approach basal reading instruction (Durkin, 1984).

The value and role of the basal reader continue to be debated among reading professionals.

In 1992, the National Assessment of Education Progress (NAEP) surveyed U.S. fourth grade classroom teachers about their primary resource for providing reading instruction. This survey found that 36 percent of fourth grade teachers relied solely on basal readers, 49 percent relied on a combination of basal readers and trade books, and 15 percent relied on materials other than basal readers. Researchers have determined that the use of trade books to teach reading steadily decreased with each grade level from 75 percent in kindergarten to 25 percent in grade five (Fractor, Woodruff, Martinez, & Teale, 1993).

Because of the continued widespread and pervasive use of basal readers in American schools as the core for providing basic reading instruction (Shannon, 1983; Flood & Lapp, 1986; Shannon & Goodman, 1994; Wade & Moje, 2000), it is imperative that preservice and in-service teachers learn to use the basal reader with judgment and skill. The purpose of this chapter is to provide teachers with the information necessary for taking control of their basal reader teacher's editions. Teachers who are in control of reading instruction are empowered to make informed instructional decisions about how, when, and why to use basal readers for providing reading instruction.

Teachers and administrators need to understand the basal reader to make informed instructional decisions.

ANATOMY OF THE BASAL READING APPROACH

Basal readers are typically composed of a set of core materials. These include: (1) a student's text, (2) a teacher's edition, (3) a student's workbook, (4) a teacher's edition workbook, (5) supplemental practice exercises, (6) enrichment activities (usually both of these are in the form of masters that can be duplicated), (7) big books, (8) leveled readers, (9) phonic or decodable readers, and (10) end-of-unit or end-of-book tests. Other supplemental materials can be acquired at additional cost—picture cards, picture with letter cards, letter cards, word cards for display on word walls, pocket charts,

Focus on the core materials that compose basal readers.

Figure 8.5   A basal reading program usually includes a teacher's edition, a student edition, workbooks, and an array of supplemental materials

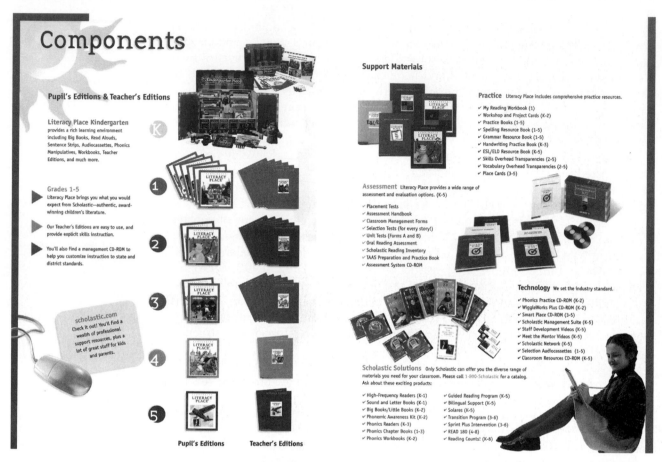

From *Scholastic Literacy Place: Problem Patrol* (p. R88) 2000, New York: Scholastic. Copyright 2000 by Scholastic, Inc. Reprinted by permission.

classroom trade-book libraries, big books, and technology, including videotapes, CD-ROMs, DVDs, and publisher World Wide Web sites on the Internet. In addition, many basal reading series provide a system for record keeping, management of the reading skills taught and mastered, and assessment. Figure 8.5 shows core components available for Scholastic's *Literacy Place* basal program for grades 3–6. Because many teachers will employ a basal series in a school reading program, we will describe each of the most basic basal components along with examples.

The Basal Teacher's Edition

For teachers, perhaps the most important part of the basal reading program is the **teacher's edition** because it contains instructional guidance and support (see Figure 8.6). For many new teachers, the basal teacher's edition is the most important source of initial professional development.

Within the pages of the teacher's edition, one usually finds three important features: (a) the scope and sequence chart of the particular basal reading program, (b) a

A scope and sequence chart describes in detail the range of concepts and skills to be taught in the basal program as well as the order in which these concepts and skills are to be presented.

Figure 8.6 Example of a 2000 teacher's edition for *Scott Foresman Reading* basal series

From *Scott Foresman Reading: Take Me There* (Teacher's ed., Grade 1, Volume 5), 2000, Glenview, IL: Scott Foresman Company. Copyright 2000 by Scott Foresman Company. Reprinted by permission.

reduced version of the student's text, and (c) lesson plans (see Figures 8.7 and 8.8). A **scope and sequence chart** describes in great detail the range of skills and/or concepts to be taught in a basal program as well as the sequence in which these are to be presented during the school year. The entire student's text, shown as a reduced facsimile, is included for convenience in the teacher's edition. To save the teacher preparation time, lesson plans are included. Current basal readers typically design reading lessons around a modified sequence of the Directed Reading Thinking Activity (Stauffer, 1969).

It is important that teachers and administrators understand that the teacher's edition is a resource to be used with discrimination, not a script to be followed rigidly. Teachers and administrators should not allow the basal teacher's edition to dictate the reading program. Rather, teachers should be encouraged to decide what is and what is not appropriate in the teacher's edition for use with a particular group of children.

Most basal reader programs design reading lessons using a modified lesson framework known as the Directed Reading Thinking Activity.

Figure 8.7   A scope and sequence chart showing the range of skills to be taught in a basal program

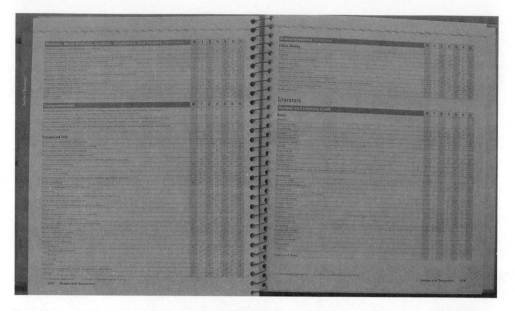

From *Scott Foresman Reading: Take Me There* (Teacher's ed., Grade 1, Volume 5, pp. 228–229), 2000, Glenview, IL: Scott Foresman Company. Copyright 2000 by Scott Foresman Company. Reprinted by permission.

Figure 8.8   Example of the internal pages from a 2002 teacher's edition for *SRA Open Court Reading* basal series

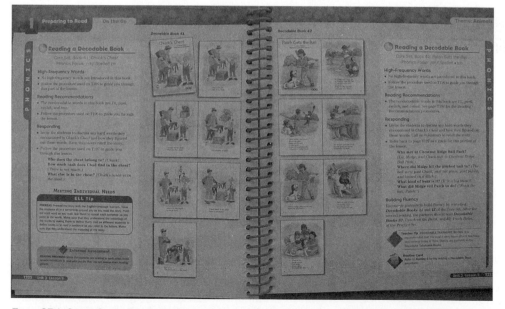

From *SRA Open Court Reading: Things that Go* (Teacher's ed., Level I, Unit 3), 2002, Columbus, OH: SRA/McGraw-Hill. Copyright 2002 by SRA/McGraw-Hill. Reprinted by permission.

The Student's Basal Text

The student's basal text is an anthology of original contemporary and classic stories, poems, news clips, and expository text selections. Some basal student selections have been created expressly for inclusion in the student's basal reader. Other selections have been adapted from contemporary and classic children's literature or trade books. High-quality artwork generally accompanies the selections. Interspersed throughout the student's text, one may also find poetry selections, jokes, riddles, puzzles, informational essays, and special skill and/or concept lessons. Some basal student texts contain questions children should be able to answer after reading the stories. Upper-level basal readers often contain a glossary of words that students can refer to when decoding new words or so that students can look up the meaning of new words found in the text.

Changes in basal student texts have resulted in a "more engaging basal" than those of two decades ago as judged by students, teachers, and reading experts (Hoffman et al., 1994; McCarthey et al., 1994).

Authentic Trade Literature

A close examination of quality children's literature included in the more recent basal reader revisions reveals few, if any, alterations of the authors' language or word choice. However, one disturbing publishing practice relates to cropping or cutting original artwork in children's picture book stories. Because of costs involved in the reproduction and permission for use of original artwork, basal publishers have engaged in cutting or moving the beautiful artwork that supports and sustains the text in many children's books (Reutzel & Larsen, 1995). The practice of cropping or cutting support artwork may be even more damaging than altering the text for young, emergent readers who may rely more heavily on the pictures for support throughout their initial readings of a new or unfamiliar text at early stages of reading development.

Information Texts

N. Duke (2000, pp. 205) defined *information texts* as evidencing several features, including (a) a function to communicate information about the social or natural world; (b) factual content; (c) technical vocabulary; (d) classificatory or definitional material; (e) graphical elements like maps, graphs, and diagrams; (f) varying text structures, for example, cause and effect, problem and solution, compare and contrast, etc.; and (g) repetition of topical themes. Duke (2000) went on to investigate the experiences offered to children in 20 first-grade classrooms selected from very low and very high socioeconomic-status school districts with reading information texts. She found a scarcity of informational texts available in these classrooms—particularly in low socioeconomic-status schools. To compound the scarcity of information texts found in the classrooms, there were relatively few informational texts available in school libraries and on classroom walls and other display surfaces in the schools. As a result, young children in low socioeconomic classrooms read information texts 3.6 minutes per day on average.

In a more recent study, Moss and Newton (2001) investigated the amount of information text available in current second, fourth, and sixth grade basal reading series. These researchers found that 16 to 20 percent of all selections in current basal readers could be classified as information texts. The preponderance of selections found in current basal readers continue to contain narrative or fiction (66 percent).

Notice what is included in the student's basal text.

Standards Note
Standard 5.2: The reading professional will use texts and trade books to stimulate interest, promote reading growth, foster appreciation for the written word, and increase the motivation of learners to read widely and independently for information, pleasure, and personal growth. As you read about the different types of reading materials in school reading programs, make a list of five things you can do with such a rich variety of resources to stimulate and motivate children and adolescents to read.

Although many basal readers include well-regarded children's literature, publishers continue to modify or adapt children's books in various ways for inclusion in basal readers.

Information texts need to play a larger role in beginning reading instruction.

Beginning Reading Texts

Controlling Word Difficulty and Frequency

Control over word difficulty in beginning reading texts presumably allows for the systematic introduction of a predetermined number of unfamiliar words in each new story (Hiebert, 1999; Hoffman, 2001). Control of word difficulty is usually achieved by using simpler words, or words with fewer syllables, in place of longer words and by shortening sentences. Basal publishers have for many years controlled the language of beginning reading texts by using simple, one-syllable words. Town and Holbrook (1857) in the *Progressive Reading* basal reading series are among the earliest educators to explain the use of controlled texts in beginning reading texts:

> The authors, satisfied that the most simple language is best adapted to the class of pupils for whom this Reader is designed, have adhered, as strictly as possible, to the one-syllable system. They have departed from it only when necessary to avoid any stiffness of style, or weakness of expression, which might arise from too closely following it in every instance. (p. 3)

Compare the text from the following 1865 and 2000 basal reader beginning text as shown below:

1865

John stands by his father.

"I will be a good boy, father. . ."

2000

Bob went to the barn for Dad

Dad asked Bob to feed the pigs

Controlling the difficulty of words encountered in basal reader stories supposedly renders text less difficult to read. However, research by Pearson (1974) challenged the idea that shorter sentences are easier to read. Pearson found that short, choppy sentences are actually more difficult to read because explicit connecting or sequencing words such as *because, and, so, then, before,* and *after* are deleted from the text and consequently need to be inferred by the reader to comprehend the text.

Controlling Decoding Difficulty

In some basal reader programs, the earliest books, or *primers,* often contain reading selections known as **decodable text** (Adams, 1990a, 1990b; Beck, 1997; Grossen, 1997; Foorman, Francis, Fletcher, Schatschneider, & Mehta, 1998; Hiebert, 1999). Decodable texts are designed to reinforce the teaching of particular phonic elements such as short *a* by using highly controlled vocabulary in their stories (*Nan* and *Dan*). Decodable texts are frequently sold as supplemental books to school districts to augment basal reader instruction. A decodable text example is shown in the following excerpt (*Scholastic,* Book 14, Phonics Readers, pp. 2–7; Schreiber & Tuchman, 1997):

The Big Hit

Who hid? Pig.
Who had a mitt? Pig.

Many beginning reading texts are designed to control for word difficulty and frequency.

Decodable beginning reading texts are designed to provide texts for practicing previously taught phonics lessons.

Who did not sit?
Who did hit?
Up. Up. Up.
Who had a big hit? Pig.
Who slid? Pig did!

Although decodable texts can be useful for teaching phonics, children seldom encounter such contrived texts outside of school. As a consequence, the practice of controlling vocabulary to this extent continues to be questioned on the grounds that it tends to result in senseless or inconsiderate texts and tends to cause children to think that reading is primarily a decoding task rather than a search for meaning (Armbruster, 1984; Allington, 1997; Hiebert & Martin, 2001). The lack of real content or presence of a discernable story line in these decodable texts is suspected of causing children to quickly lose interest in reading if overused.

Controlling Language Patterns in Texts

Predictable texts are characterized by the repetition of a syntactic unit that can range from a phrase to a group of sentences, e.g., "run, run, as fast as you can, you can't catch me, I'm the Gingerbread man." Perhaps the best known examples of patterned trade books are those authored and advocated by Bill Martin (1967), who wrote books such as *Brown Bear, Brown Bear, What Do You See?* These books have been found to decrease the control over new or unique words as well as adding the presence of engaging illustrations.

Other patterned books are published as part of a total reading program. For example, those published by the Wright Group, but originally from New Zealand, have been well accepted in the U.S. (Literacy 2000). Books in the *Sunshine Series* begin with simple repetitious phrases accompanied by strong picture or illustration supports, as in the story *"Look."*

Predictable texts control for language patterns at the phrase and sentence levels.

Look said the birds, cats.
Look said the birds, dogs.
Look said the birds, bread.
Look said the birds, children.

You can clearly see that the difficulty of the language found in patterned beginning readers is still controlled, as in the past. The major difference is that the control is exerted at larger levels of text—phrases and sentences. This approach to beginning reading has produced some interesting research findings. Children who read patterned texts learned a group of sight words as quickly as children who read controlled word difficulty and frequency texts (Bridge, Winograd, & Haley, 1983). However, more recently, Johnston (1998) found that learning new words in first grade was improved when words were learned separate from the text, rather than in the context of predictable texts. It seems that controlling text patterns also presents some limitations in providing the texts needed for effective beginning reading instruction.

Leveling Texts

With the availability of enormous varieties of beginning reading texts today (high frequency words, decodable texts, children's authentic literature, and patterned texts), many teachers are in search of a way to provide a systematic and gradual introduction to beginning reading. Fountas and Pinnell (1999) in their book *Matching Books*

Many classroom teachers now use books leveled from A–Z to provide beginning reading instruction.

to Readers: Using Leveled Books in Guided Reading, K–3 describe the need for a way to level the collection of beginning reading materials in the classroom. Based on their work and that of others (e.g., Reutzel & Cooter, 2003; Flynt & Cooter, 2004), we present a guide titled Selecting Books for Reading Instruction: Reading Level Translations (see Table 8.1).

Many teachers in the primary grades rely heavily on a system for leveling books such as the one shown above to match students with texts that meet their instructional needs. Although leveled books can be an enormously helpful tool in beginning reading instruction, Szymusiak and Sibberson (2001) in *Beyond Leveled Books: Supporting Transitional Readers in Grades 2–5,* warn against the dangers of a "steady diet" of reading in leveled books. They say "When student's reading diet is exclusively a leveled one, their purpose for reading disappears. They read for us. They become eager to reach the next level, instead of being eager to learn more from what they are reading." (p. 15–16) We know the leveling mania has gone too far when children must read from only leveled materials, when teachers will only purchase materials for reading based on levels, and when children and teachers no longer seek the goal of independence in reading through instruction in self-selection of appropriately challenging and interesting reading materials!

On the other hand, to abandon some controls on text difficulty seems to be, as Holdaway (1979) puts it, "sheer madness." Holdaway reminds us that many children continue to struggle to read authentic texts that are far too difficult for them to handle independently. It is clear that basal readers need to provide a balance of text types, including decodable, leveled, patterned, informational, and authentic story texts, in quantities that allow teachers to choose what works best with each child at various levels of reading development. And finally, Hiebert (1999) makes an impassioned call for authors to produce a new kind of beginning reading text modeled after the creations of Dr. Seuss in books such as *Green Eggs and Ham.* She states:

Dr. Suess' books are still viewed by many as the best model texts for engaging beginning readers.

> Over a decade ago, Anderson and others (1985) called for inventive writers to use Dr. Seuss as a model for creating engaging texts for beginning readers. This call needs to be extended again but, this time, with a clearer mandate—one that derives from a strong vision of what beginning readers need to learn. Such texts require thought to word density ratios and to the repetitions across as well as within texts of words that share phonetic elements." (p. 565)

The Workbook

In years past, the most used part of any basal reading series was the workbook (Osborn, 1985). In fact, if any part of the basal reading lesson was neglected, it was seldom the workbook pages (J. Mason, 1983; Durkin, 1984). Although clearly less the case today, workbook exercises remain firmly entrenched in many classrooms. It appears that some teachers, administrators, and publishers, as evidenced by the continued inclusion of workbook pages or worksheets as part and parcel of basal reading series, still see seat work as the real "work" of the school literacy program (Allington & Cunningham, 1996). (See Figure 8.9.)

Workbooks are one instructional tool that can assist or inhibit children's reading progress.

Workbook exercises aren't intended to supplant time for structured, well-planned reading instruction or independent reading. Rather, workbook exercises were intended for use by teachers and students to independently practice skills, strategies, and literary understandings previously instructed by the teacher. Also, workbook exercises are often used as a type of formative or ongoing "paper and pencil" assess-

Table 8.1 Selecting Books for Reading Instruction: Reading Level Translations*

Reading Levels (Traditional Designations)	Guided Reading (GR) Levels (extrapolated from Fountas & Pinnell, 1996, 2001)	Common Text Attributes	Exemplar Books & Publishers (Using GR levels)	Approximate Level of Reading Development
Preschool-Kindergarten (Readiness)	A	Wordless picture books	**A**= *Dog Day!* (Rigby)	Emergent
	B	Repeated phrases, text-picture matching, experiences common to readers, short (10–60 words)	**B**= *Fun with Hats* (Mondo)	
PP (Preprimer)	C D E	Same as above for B, but repeating phrases don't dominate the book, more language variation, by level E syntax becomes more like regular "book language"	**C**= *Brown Bear, Brown Bear* (Holt) **D**= *The Storm* (Wright Group) **E**= *The Big Toe* (Wright Group)	Emergent → Early
P (Primer)	F G	Longer sentences/less predictable text, new verb forms appear, story grammar elements continue over multiple pages, pictures provide only a little support	**F**= *A Moose Is Loose* (Houghton Mifflin) **G**= *More Spaghetti I Say* (Scholastic)	Early
Grade 1 Grade 1 (late in the year)	H I	As with F and G but there is a greater variety of words and content vocabulary, pictures provide very little to gaining meaning	**H**= *A Zoo Party* (Wright Group) **I**= *There's a Nightmare in My Closet* (Penguin)	Early → Transitional
Grade 2 (early) Grade 2 Grade 2 (late)	J K L M	Longer stories with more complicated story grammar elements, varied vocabulary with rich meanings, common to have whole pages of text, more content (nonfiction) selections are in evidence	**J**= *The Boy Who Cried Wolf* (Scholastic) **K**= *Amelia Bedelia* (Harper & Row) **L**= *Cam Jansen and the Mystery of the Monster Movie* (Puffin) **M**= *How to Eat Fried Worms* (Dell)	Transitional → Fluent
Grade 3	N-P	Fewer illustrations, more complex nonfiction, complex sentences and challenging vocabulary, higher order thinking begins here	**N**= *Pioneer Cat* (Random House) **O**= *Whipping Boy* (Troll) **P**= *Amelia Earhart* (Dell)	Fluent (Basic)

Table 8.1 *continued*

Reading Levels (Traditional Designations)	Guided Reading (GR) Levels (extrapolated from Fountas & Pinnell, 1996, 2001)	Common Text Attributes	Exemplar Books & Publishers (Using GR levels)	Approximate Level of Reading Development
Grade 4	Q-S	Few illustrations, more complex language and concept load, higher order thinking is deepened, appearance of metaphor, topics are farther from student experiences, historical fiction is common, complex ideas are presented	**Q**= *Pony Pals: A Pony for Keeps* (Scholastic) **R**= *Hatchet* (Simon & Schuster) **S**= *Story of Harriet Tubman, Conductor of the Underground Railroad* (Scholastic)	**Fluent →** **Extending to** **Content Texts**
Grade 5	T-V	Fantasy, biographies, historical fiction, and realistic fiction are common; technical figures are used; plots and subplots in fiction, print is smaller (200-300 words per page	**T**= *Harry Potter and the Sorcerer's Stone* (Scholastic) **U**= *Crocodilians* (Mondo) **V**= *The Riddle of the Rosetta Stone* (Harper)	**Fluent →** **Extending to** **Content Texts**
Grade 6	W-Z	Increasing book length and complexity; science fiction requires more technical knowledge; satire, irony, and higher-order thinking texts sometimes deal with required regularly, content controversial subjects	**W**= *Maya Angelou: Greeting the Morning* (Millbrook) **X**= *Where the Red Fern Grows* (Bantam/Doubleday) **Y**= *The Giver* (Bantam/Doubleday) **Z**= *The Watcher* (Simon & Schuster)	**Fluent →** **Extending to** **Content Texts**
Grade 7	—	Progressively increasing concept load, complexity, and sentence length	*Holes* (Farrar Straus & Giroux)	**Fluent →** **Extending to** **Content Texts**
Grade 8	—	Progressively increasing concept load, complexity, and sentence length	*The House of the Scorpion* (Atheneum)	**Fluent →** **Extending to** **Content Texts**

*Adapted from *The Flynt/Cooter Reading Inventory for the Classroom, 5th Edition*, by E.S. Flynt and R.B. Cooter, 2004, Upper Saddle River, NJ: Merrill/Prentice Hall, and *Strategies for Reading Assessment and Instruction: Helping Every Child Succeed*, 2nd Ed., by Reutzel, D.R., & Cooter, R.B. (2003). Upper Saddle River, NJ: Merrill/Prentice-Hall. [E TB.08.001]

Figure 8.9 Many basal reading programs still integrate workbook, seatwork, and practice sheets devoted to skill practice into the basal reading program

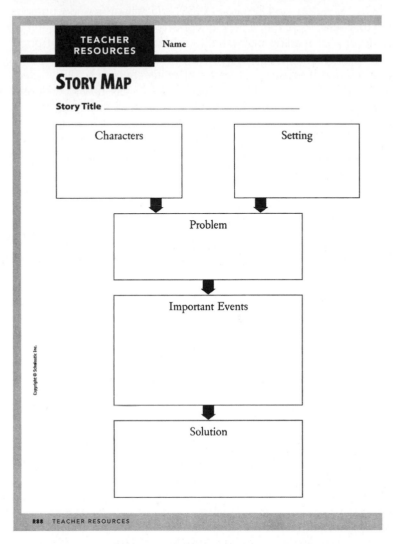

From *Scholastic Literacy Place: Problem Patrol* (p. R88), 2000, New York: Scholastic. Copyright 2000 by Scholastic, Inc. Reprinted by permission.

ment. In addition to these twin purposes, many teachers also use workbook exercises to manage, direct, or focus student activity in independent learning centers when the teacher is actively working with small groups of children in teacher-guided reading groups. Thus, used in these ways, workbook exercises play at least three distinct roles in classrooms—practice, assessment, and management.

Past research revealed that students spend up to 70 percent of the time allocated for reading instruction, or 49 minutes per day, in independent practice or completing worksheets, like those found in workbooks, whereas less than 10 percent of the total reading instructional time, or about 7 to 8 minutes per day, is devoted to silent reading in the primary grades. In fact, publishers indicate that there is an insatiable demand for worksheets (R. C. Anderson, Hiebert, Scott, & Wilkinson, 1985). More

The subject of testing and evaluation will be discussed in depth in Chapter 9.

recent studies indicate that many teachers assign or provide time for only small amounts of real reading and writing, in some cases less than 5 minutes per day (Knapp, 1991)! Jachym, Allington, and Broikou (1989) and Allington and Cunningham (1996) reported that seat work, that is, using worksheets, is displacing many of the more important aspects of reading instruction, such as the acquisition of good books and time spent reading. Based on these findings, it seems obvious that workbooks have been misused and overused. However, when teachers judiciously select workbook exercises to support and reinforce concepts and skills provided during teacher-guided instruction, students benefit from valuable practice and feedback on their progress in relation to specific reading skills, strategies, and literary understandings. Dole, Osborn, and Lehr (1990, p. 8–15) provided six guidelines for assessing the worth of workbook and worksheet-type reading tasks in the *Workbooks* subtext for the *Basal Reading Programs: Adoption Guidelines Project*.

To determine the value of workbook tasks, notice the six principles for evaluating workbook tasks.

Some Guidelines for Workbook Tasks:

1. When analyzing *the content of workbook tasks,* look for tasks that:
   - Are integrated with the lessons in the teacher's manual and with the student textbook
   - Relate to the most important (and workbook-appropriate) instruction in the lessons
   - Are based on the reading selections
   - Use vocabulary that is from current or previous lessons
   - Increase in difficulty as grade level increases
2. When analyzing the *content of workbook task design,* look for tasks that require:
   - Students to read all possible choices before selecting an answer
   - Student responses that can be judged correct or incorrect
   - Student responses that indicate to the teacher what the student knows
   - Students be able to successfully complete part two of the task without successfully completing part one
3. When analyzing the *practice and review* tasks, look for tasks that provide:
   - Sufficient practice
   - Independent practice
   - Extra practice
   - Systematic review
4. When analyzing *instructional language,* look for tasks that:
   - Use language consistent with the rest of the program
   - Are accompanied by brief explanations of purpose or explanatory titles that students understand
   - Have clear and easy-to-follow instruction, with attention to consistency, sentence length, and directional steps
5. When evaluating *reading and writing responses,* look for tasks that:
   - Provide opportunities for students to respond in their own words
   - Provide opportunities for students to apply several comprehension strategies or decoding skills in one task
6. When evaluating the *considerateness to students,* look for:
   - Repeated use of task formats
   - Consistent responses
   - Occasional tasks that are fun
   - Few or no nonfunctional tasks

Workbooks can be a valuable resource for teachers and students when used correctly. On the other hand, when they are overrelied upon or misused, workbook exercises can be a debilitating deterrent to students' reading progress.

Assessment

Although workbook exercises can be used for formative assessment of reading skill, strategy, and literary understandings development, most basal reading series provide end-of-unit or end-of-book tests for summative evaluation of student learning. These tests are generally criterion-referenced tests, which means that the items measured on these tests are directly related to the specific skills, strategies, or literary concepts taught in that unit, level, or book. Most basal readers now provide suggestions for designing individual assessment portfolios for each student, including the use of running records. Teachers who want to present students' reading demonstrations to parents as evidence for a reading portfolio will need to obtain audiotapes of students' reading and analyze them using something like "running records" analysis (see Chapter 9, Assessing Literacy Learning) for the foreseeable future. As the stakes are raised higher and higher for performance of standardized assessment measures, many current basal readers are correlating skills, strategies, and literary understanding taught with nationally published standardized tests (see Figure 8.10).

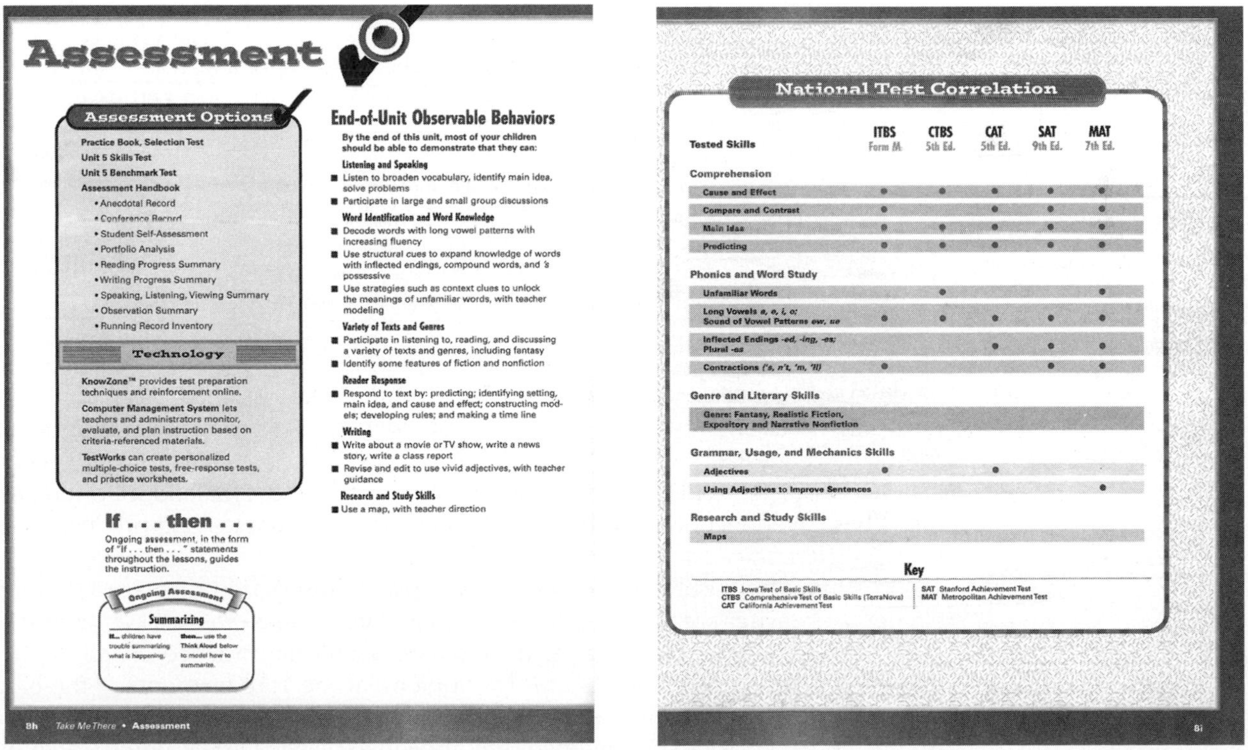

Figure 8.10 Many basal teacher's editions show how program elements correspond with nationally published standardized tests

From *Scott Foresman Reading: Take Me There* 2000, (Teacher's ed., Grade 1, Volume 5, pp. 8h–8i), Glenview, IL: Scott Foresman Company. Copyright 2000 by Scott Foresman Company. Reprinted by permission.

Tests are instruments or tools for examining student progress. Such tools can be properly or improperly used and interpreted.

Just as workbook exercises can be abused, so it is with tests. Tests should provide teachers information about the quantity and quality of children's literacy learning to inform, shape, and direct future instructional choices and selection of interventions. Test results should not be used to label children or embarrass teachers. Two poignant examples of the misuse of test data are found in the books *First Grade Takes a Test* (Cohen, 1980) and *Testing Miss Malarkey* (Finchler, 2001). No single test score should ever form the basis for making important decisions about children's learning or their teachers' competence. Administrators and teachers must be extremely cautious in the use and interpretation of single literacy (reading and writing) test scores.

Record Keeping

An **instructional management system** allows teachers to keep accurate records from year to year regarding each child's progress through the adopted basal reading program's scope and sequence of skills. Maintaining records to document teaching and learning is an important part of accountability. Most basal reading series provide a means for keeping records on children's progress through the skills outlined in the scope and sequence chart of the basal. Most often, the methods of assessment specified are paper-and-pencil testing or worksheet administration. The scores obtained on these exercises are entered into a master list or record available today in CD-ROM form, which follows the children throughout their elementary years. Such a skills-management system allows teachers to keep accurate records from year to year regarding each child's progress. Unfortunately, some teachers spend inordinate amounts of time keeping records of this kind, which leads to a most undesirable condition, captured by Pearson in 1985:

Most basal reading series provide a means for keeping records on children's progress.

A skills-management system allows teachers to keep accurate records from year to year regarding each child's progress through the adopted basal reading program's scope and sequence of skills.

> The model implicit in the practices of [this teacher] was that of a manager—[a] person who arranged materials, texts, and the classroom environment so learning could occur. But the critical test of whether learning did occur was left up to the child as s/he interacted with the materials.
>
> Children practiced applying skills; if they learned them, fine; we always had more skills for them to practice; if they did not, fine; we always had more worksheets and duplicating sheets for the same skill. And the most important rule in such a mastery role was that practice makes perfect, leading to the ironic condition that children spent most of their time on precisely that subset of skills they performed least well. (p. 736)

To this we would like to add the comment that, disturbingly, teachers under this model spent the bulk of their time running off worksheets, assigning, correcting, and recording rather than guiding, demonstrating, or interacting with children or books. Although increasingly elegant with the addition of CD-ROM technology, record keeping should go well beyond keeping track of worksheet evaluation. Fortunately, many basal readers now recognize this fact and include process and product measures of children's reading and reading habits.

Basal reading series are typically composed of three elements: a teacher's edition, student text, and student workbooks.

In summary, basal reading series are typically composed of a core of three elements—teacher's edition, student text, and workbooks—as well as a host of available kits, charts, cards, tests, technology, additional practice exercises, and assessment/record-keeping systems to supplement the core elements of the basal series. In an effort to compete with trade-book publishers, basal publishers are also producing big books to complement the already expansive list of purchasable options listed previously. Teachers should be careful not to accept these new "basal" big books without careful examination. In some cases, big books published by basal companies are not big books at all—they are big basals!

Although the basal reader approach offers a resource for helping teachers provide systematic and sequenced reading instruction throughout the elementary and middle grades, teachers must nonetheless be careful to supplement this core program with trade books, silent reading time, group sharing, extensions of reading into writing, speaking, drama, music, and so on, and to provide individual assessment of children's reading progress, behaviors, and attitudes. When this goal is understood and achieved, basal readers can provide valuable literacy tools and resources to schools, administrators, teachers, and children. In addition, basals provide a safety net for many teachers, novice and experienced, because they help teachers make personal and professional growth toward implementing balanced, comprehensive reading instruction.

Notice how teachers can supplement the basal reader core program.

PRODUCTION AND ORGANIZATION OF BASAL READERS

Basal reading series are owned by large, diversified business corporations and are produced by a variety of publishing houses from coast to coast. A chief editor oversees the production of a basal reader with the assistance of a senior author team, a group of individuals in the field of reading who are known and respected as experts (see Figure 8.11).

Basal reading programs are often recognized and known by the name of the publishing house that produces the basal. Over the last 20 years, the number of basal publishing companies that have survived the intense business competition, demanding and sometimes invasive state standards, and the vicissitudes of change have dwindled from over 20 companies to half a dozen or less by the time this book was published.

Basal reading programs are typically known by the name of the publishing house that produces the basal.

Harcourt Brace
SRA McGraw-Hill
Houghton Mifflin
Scholastic
Scott Foresman

Minor revisions of basal readers occur every few years; major revision cycles occur every five or six years. Major revisions are usually slated for completion during the same year Texas and California consider basal readers for statewide adoption. Consequently, the "Texas and California" effect is known to exert considerable influence on the content and quality of new basal readers (Keith, 1981; Farr, Tulley, & Powell, 1987). In reading circles, one often hears the axiom, "as Texas and California go, so goes the nation."

Strengths and Weaknesses of Basal Readers

Although basal readers continue to be the mainstay of reading instruction in American schools, the basal reader approach to reading instruction has not gone unscrutinized. Criticisms of basal readers have ranged from the cultural to the literary, from

Figure 8.11 Title page showing basal authoring team names

TEACHER'S EDITION

SCHOLASTIC
LITERACY PLACE®

UNIT 2

Problem Patrol

LITERACY PLACE AUTHORS

CATHY COLLINS BLOCK
Professor, Curriculum and Instruction, Texas Christian University

LINDA B. GAMBRELL
Professor, Education, University of Maryland at College Park

VIRGINIA HAMILTON
Children's Author; Winner of the Newbery Medal, the Coretta Scott King Award and the Laura Ingalls Wilder Lifetime Achievement Award

DOUGLAS K. HARTMAN
Associate Professor of Language and Literacy, University of Pittsburgh

TED S. HASSELBRING
Co-Director of the Learning Technology Center and Professor in the Department of Special Education at Peabody College, Vanderbilt University

ADRIA KLEIN
Professor, Reading and Teacher Education, California State University at San Bernardino

HILDA MEDRANO
Dean, College of Education, University of Texas-Pan American

GAY SU PINNELL
Professor, School of Teaching and Learning, College of Education, Ohio State University

D. RAY REUTZEL
Provost/Academic Vice President, Southern Utah University

DAVID ROSE
Founder and Executive Director of the Center for Applied Special Technology (CAST); Lecturer, Harvard University Graduate School of Education

ALFREDO SCHIFINI
Professor, School of Education, Division of Curriculum Instruction, California State University, Los Angeles

DELORES STUBBLEFIELD SEAMSTER
Principal, N.W. Harllee Elementary, Dallas, Texas; Consultant on Effective Programs for Urban Inner City Schools

QUALITY QUINN SHARP
Author and Teacher-Educator, Austin, Texas

JOHN SHEFELBINE
Professor, Language and Literacy Education, California State University at Sacramento

GWENDOLYN Y. TURNER
Associate Professor of Literacy Education, University of Missouri at St. Louis

From *Scholastic Literacy Place: Problem Patrol*, 2000, New York: Scholastic. Copyright 2000 by Scholastic, Inc. Reprinted by permission.

the linguistic to the instructional. Because basal readers are used in over 90 percent of American classrooms, most teachers will inevitably have occasion to make use of the basal reader approach to reading instruction (Flood & Lapp, 1986; Zintz & Maggart, 1989; Baumann, 1993; Hoffman, et. al., 1994; McCarthy, et al., 1994; Wade & Moje, 2000). To make instructional decisions about how, when, and why to use the basal, teachers and administrators must know the strengths and weaknesses of the basal reader approach to reading.

Basal readers contain an organized and systematic plan for teachers to consult in planning reading instruction.

In defense of basal reading series, it must be said that basals possess certain positive qualities that contribute to their enduring popularity in American classrooms. For example, basal readers contain an organized and systematic plan for teachers to consult. Basal readers published more recently often provide teaching suggestions from which comprehensive literacy teachers make decisions about when and how to teach skills that are important to authentic reading-related behaviors. In addition, basal readers are sequenced from grade to grade, thus providing for continuous reading instruction throughout the elementary school years and for continuity both within grades and across grade levels.

The readily available tests and practice exercises found in the workbooks save teachers enormous amounts of time in materials preparation. Reading skills are gradually introduced, practiced, and reviewed through the plan provided in the scope and sequence of the basal. The lesson plans found ready-made in the teacher's editions also save teachers much preparation time. A variety of literary genres is available to teachers and students in current basal readers. The structure provided in basal readers is often very reassuring for novice or beginning teachers. Administrators can manage and provide accountability evidence more easily by adopting and using basal reading series. In short, basal readers possess several characteristics that teachers and administrators find helpful and worthwhile.

Readily available tests and practice exercises found in the basal workbooks save teachers enormous amounts of time in materials preparation.

Advantages of the Basal Reader Approach*

- A sequenced curriculum of instruction is provided by grade level and across grade levels. Instruction is arranged to provide for both initial instruction and a systematic review of skills taught.
- A continuous arrangement of instructional skills and concepts from grade to grade is supplied.
- To save teachers time, a completely prepared set of stories, instructional directions and activities, instructional practice materials, and assessment and management devices is available.
- Student texts are arranged in ascending difficulty.
- Reading skills are gradually introduced and systematically reviewed.
- Teachers are provided lesson plans.
- Students are exposed to a variety of literary genres.
- Organization and structure of basal readers are helpful to beginning teachers just learning about the reading curriculum.
- A variety of beginning reading texts and books are typically available, including trade book libraries, big books, leveled books, and decodable books.
- Organization and structure of basal reading programs are reassuring to administrators and school patrons that important reading skills are being taught.

Limitations of the Basal Reader Approach

- Some new decodable and leveled selections are dull and repetitious.
- Cropping illustrations from original children's trade books renders selections less engaging for readers of all ages.
- Skill instruction is rarely applied in or related to decoding the text or comprehending the selection's content.
- The basal lesson design in teacher's editions very often fails to relate one part of the lesson, such as vocabulary introduction, to subsequent parts of the reading lesson, such as story comprehension discussion.
- Stories often do not relate to students' interests.
- The format of basal readers (hard bound and thick book) is often less appealing than the format of trade books (soft bound and thin book).
- Censorship by special interest groups leads to the selection of content that contain little real subject matter content, that deals with few real-life applications, or that presents little content that advocates ethical living in society.
- Teacher's editions seldom contain useful directions on how to teach/model reading comprehension strategies.

Although popular, basal readers are not without significant deficiencies.

*Based on "Understanding and Using Basal Readers Effectively" by D. R. Reutzel in *Effective Strategies for Teaching Reading* (p. 259), edited by B. Hayes, 1991, Needham Heights, MA: Allyn and Bacon. Copyright 1991 by D. R. Reutzel. Reprinted by permission.

- A rigid adherence to the basal reader leaves little room for teacher creativity and decision making.
- The grading or leveling of basal readers promotes the use of static homogeneous grouping strategies.
- Management demands of the basal program can become so time consuming that little time remains for teachers to reflect on the quality of reading instruction and for students to self-select reading materials.
- Use of the basal reader approach has traditionally been associated with the use of "round robin" reading and ability grouping. Insisting that all children simultaneously attend to the same selection while another child reads orally encourages such practices.

Although popular, basal readers are not without significant deficiencies. Many of the objections voiced about the stories found in the basal readers can be traced to publishers' efforts to produce decodable texts or leveled books.

Basal readers have improved significantly in recent years.

Basal readers have improved significantly in recent years. Although in the past narrative selections in students' basal readers tended in the early grades to be repetitive and boring, recent basal readers have included more high-quality children's literature. However, some are concerned that high-quality literature is beyond the ability of many students to handle independently (Holdaway, 1979). Thus, recent trends have included demands for decodable and leveled texts (Allington, 1997). Although the variety of selections found in basal readers may be considerable, some educators are concerned with what appears to be genre and topic flitting in basal readers. Because of this criticism, most recently published basal readers now organize their selections into similar genres, topic/text pairs (fiction and information), or themed units. Recent basal readers have included more generous exposure to information, nonfiction, or expository selections in comparison to those of generations past.

Basal readers have also been criticized for poorly representing societal groups and concerns. This problem is often attributable to the censorship of various special interest groups that enter into the **basal reader adoption** process, particularly in states that adopt statewide (Marzano, 1993/1994). Basal teacher's editions continue to be assailed for poor instructional design and content (Ryder & Graves, 1994; Wade & Moje, 2000). Durkin (1981a) found that many teacher's editions contained an abundance of questions and evaluative activities mislabeled as instructional activities. What was labeled as instruction was often found to be nothing more than an assessment exercise. Reutzel and Daines (1987a) found that basal reading skills lessons seldom supported or even related to the selections to be read in the basals. These conclusions supported J. Mason's (1983) findings that teacher's reading instruction was, more often than not, unrelated to the text that children would be asked to read. In another study the same year, Reutzel and Daines (1987b) reported that even the parts of the reading units had little relation to one another. Although these conditions have improved somewhat in the newer generations of basal readers, with stories that are generally more engaging (Hoffman, et.al, 1994), problems persist.

Despite limitations, basal reader programs can provide a foundation for classroom reading instruction.

Despite these limitations, the basal "baby" simply cannot be thrown out with the bath water (McCallum, 1988; Winograd, 1989; Baumann, 1993). Basal readers have filled an important niche for many teachers and will likely continue to do so well into the future. As they await continued improvements in the basal, teachers armed with an understanding of their strengths and weaknesses, as described here, can enjoy their benefits while overcoming or avoiding their weaknesses.

Organization of the Basal Reader

Basal readers are designed to take children through a series of books, experiences, and activities toward increasingly sophisticated reading behaviors. Each basal series typically provides several readers or books of reading selections at each level. For example, the *Scott Foresman: Reading* (2000) basal provides the following books organized by theme for each grade level:

Grade 1:   *Good Times We Share*
            Take a Closer Look
            Let's Learn Together
            Favorite Things Old and New
            Take Me There
            Surprise Me!
Grade 2:   *You + Me = Special*
            Zoom In!
            Side by Side
            Ties Through Time
            All Aboard!
            Just Imagine
Grade 3:   *Finding My Place*
            The Whole Wide World
            Getting the Job Done
            From Past to Present
            Are We There Yet?
            Imagination.kids
Grade 4:   *Focus on Family*
            A Wider View
            Keys to Success
            Timeless Stories
            Other Times, Other Places
            Express Yourself!
Grade 5:   *Relating to Others*
            My World and Yours
            A Job Well Done
            Time and Time Again
            Traveling On
            Think of It!
Grade 6:   *Discovering Ourselves*
            The Living Earth
            Goals Great and Small
            The Way We Were—The Way We Are
            Into the Unknown
            I've Got It!

Important features to be found in current teacher's editions are: (1) philosophical statements, (2) skills overview for the unit, (3) classroom routines, (4) accommodating special needs, (5) assessment ties to national standards and tests, (6) technology information, (7) themes, (8) projects, (9) assessment benchmarks, (10) glossary,

(11) bibliography, and (12) a scope and sequence chart. The scope and sequence chart is a year-by-year curricular plan, usually in chart form, that includes the instructional objectives and skills associated with a specific basal reading program. Objectives and skills are arranged in the scope and sequence chart by categories and grade levels. It is in the scope and sequence chart that teachers learn about the objectives of the basal program and the sequence of lessons designed to accomplish the objectives.

Some contemporary basal readers are organized into themed units.

Most contemporary basal readers are organized into **themed units,** with several selections organized around a selected theme or topic; still others are organized into arbitrarily divided units of instruction. Most basal readers follow a somewhat *modified* version of the Directed Reading Thinking Activity (DRTA) format developed by Stauffer in 1969. This format can be represented in eight discrete parts or steps in the lesson:

1. Activate prior knowledge and building background
2. Skill lessons on phonics, spelling, vocabulary, and comprehension
3. Previewing and predicting
4. Setting the purpose
5. Guiding the reading
6. Confirm predictions
7. Comprehension discussion questions
8. Skill instruction and practice in oral language, writing, grammar, phonics, handwriting, comprehension, and fluency
9. Enrichment ideas and projects

Lessons are arranged for teachers into a daily planner. It is not intended that teachers will use all of the resources of the basal reader teacher's edition, but that they will select those resources on a daily basis that best suit the needs of the children in the classroom. We remind our readers emphatically that basal teacher's editions are *resources* to augment the teacher's knowledge of the reading process and the needs of his/her students, NOT a script to be followed without judgment, skill, and decision making.

A Closer Look at the Anatomy of a Basal Reading Lesson

Activating Prior Experience and Building Background

Notice what teachers should focus on when building story background.

Activities intended to activate prior experiences and build background involve the teacher and students in a discussion of the topic and unfamiliar concepts to be encountered in the story. Beck (1986, 1995, 1996) directs teachers to focus discussion on the central problem, a critical concept, or an interview with or questioning of the author (see Chapter 6) or to give voice to the story characters. This segment of the basal lesson plan provides students with the necessary lead-in experiences, discussion, and knowledge to facilitate comprehension of the story content. Because comprehension of a story is at least partially dependent upon owning the meaning of specific unfamiliar words, teachers are often encouraged in basal reading lessons to focus on activities designed to help students understand how new vocabulary words will be used in the context of the story.

Skill Lessons

This part of the basal reading lesson is designed for teaching selected lessons on phonics, vocabulary, or comprehension skills to prepare students to read the theme selection successfully. If a phonics lesson is provided, it will focus on a new phonics element that is necessary to strengthen students' understanding of sound–symbol relationships to facilitate the development of automaticity in decoding. Likewise, if a vocabulary lesson is provided, the teacher will help children anticipate unfamiliar vocabulary terms to be encountered in the upcoming text. And if a comprehension lesson is provided, it will help children anticipate the structure of the upcoming text and any potential challenges or obstacles that may interfere with understanding the selection.

Skill lessons are provided in most contemporary basal readings for each of the essential elements of reading instruction.

Previewing and Predicting

This segment of the basal lesson focuses on helping children develop the ability to survey a text before reading it to determine how the author has arranged and presented the information or story. Typically, the teacher will guide children through the text by reading the story title, heading, subheadings, and looking at the pictures. Students are often encouraged to make predictions from the title, the subheads, and the pictures.

Basal reader lessons also provide teachers guidance for previewing, predicting, setting purposes for reading, guiding reading of selections, confirming predictions, discussing selections, and integrating the basal reader with other themes, topics, or content areas.

Setting the Purpose for Reading

This part of the basal reading lesson is devoted to developing a goal or objective for reading and is intended to provide motivation and purpose for reading the story. Teachers are directed to help students read to find the answer to a specific question. Such questions can emanate from (a) the teacher, (b) the student, or (c) both. Many current basal teacher's manuals provide teachers hints on how to help children develop their own, self-questioning competencies. Some basal teacher's editions also provide information to teachers about how to develop students' abilities to "talk back to the text" or "question the author," as described more fully in Chapter 7.

Guiding the Reading of the Selection

During this phase of the basal reading lesson, students read to a predetermined point in the selection. The students are to answer questions or to confirm their predictions. Many teacher's editions suggest that the reading be silent reading. Some teachers, however, especially primary grade teachers, ask that children read stories orally to assess word-decoding abilities and use of decoding and comprehension strategies.

Confirm Predictions

Students review personal or class predictions with the teacher. During this part of the basal lesson, students may be asked to reread portions of the text to justify their predictions. Once the entire selection has been read, a comprehension discussion ensues.

Comprehension Discussion Questions

After reading, students discuss the basal selection by answering questions posed by the teacher. Questions for conducting comprehension discussions are found interspersed throughout and following the story in most teacher's editions.

Skill Instruction and Practice

Skill instruction, application, and practice focus on developing readers' skills in several areas of the reading curriculum: (a) decoding, (b) vocabulary, (c) grammar, (d) writing, (e) handwriting, (f) spelling, (g) fluency, (h) oral language, and (i) comprehension. Individual skill lessons from each of these areas are usually found following the story in the teacher's edition. After instruction and practice, students practice the skills on black line masters or workbook sheets.

Theme Projects

Theme projects bring closure to the topic of study and focus students' efforts on research or creative projects that help them synthesize the information they have gleaned from reading into a personally meaningful product. For example, if children are studying about families, they may be guided into taking an oral history of their grandparents or other senior citizens. They would tape record, transcribe, revise, edit, illustrate, and share the stories of these elderly significant others in their lives and communities.

INSTRUCTIONAL PLANS FOR MORE EFFECTIVELY USING THE BASAL TEACHER'S EDITION

As stated previously, basal readers were never intended to displace the teacher's instructional decision making in the classroom or to supplant opportunities for students to read a wide range of literary genres (Winograd, 1989). Rather, basal readers were intended as an instructional resource to help teachers provide basic, sequenced reading instruction for a wide range of student abilities (Squire, 1989). Although some teachers are content to sample or follow the teacher's edition, effective reading teachers are aware of alternative and research-based reading lesson frameworks for modifying the basal teacher's edition. Because this is often difficult for novice and some experienced teachers, we offer detailed examples of how you can plan reading lessons using a variety of reading lesson frameworks within the familiar confines of the basal reader teacher's edition.

Reconciled Reading Lesson

The reconciled reading lesson (RRL) reverses the traditional basal lesson instructional sequence.

Most teachers recognize the importance of activating personal experiences and building adequate and accurate background knowledge to prepare readers to successfully process text. The **reconciled reading lesson** (RRL) (Reutzel, 1985a, 1991) is useful for this purpose. (However, with texts for which students already possess adequate background knowledge, RRL may unnecessarily postpone reading the selection. In this case, we recommend using the DRTA.) The RRL recommends that teachers begin the basal lesson with the information at the end of most lessons—the language enrichment and curriculum extenders—and then work backward to vocabulary assessment as the last element in the lesson (Reutzel, 1985a). To begin an RRL, turn to the language enrichment and extension section of the reading lesson in the basal teacher's edition. The activities suggested in this part of the lesson are often excellent for building background knowledge and discussing unfamiliar concepts. In one major basal reader, for example, a lesson on the story "Stone Soup" (M. Brown, 1947) suggested that teachers make stone soup and have children write a recipe from their experience. Although these ideas could be used as excellent extensions of the story, the activities may be just as appropriate for background building before reading rather than for enrichment after reading.

The second modification that the RRL proposes for the basal lesson sequence centers on the place of reading skill instruction. The RRL recommends teaching reading skills before reading and then relating reading skill instruction to the selection to be read. If this is not possible, teachers should select an appropriate reading skill that relates to the selection. By relating skills to the stories, teachers help children understand that reading skills are to be applied during reading. For example, the vocabulary skill of categorizing words was to be taught with the story in one reading lesson in a major basal reader; however, the words selected for the vocabulary-categorizing activity were unrelated to the words in the story. One must ask the question, why teach this vocabulary skill in relation to a contrived list of words or using an instructional text snippet (Pearson, 1989a) when the skill could more aptly be applied to words taken from the story itself?

The RRL recommends teaching reading skills before reading and relating them to the selection to be read.

The decoding skill lesson associated with another basal story dealt with teaching children the vowel digraph /oa/. A quick glance over the text revealed that only one word in the entire text contained that vowel digraph. Even worse, the stories preceding and following the story in the lesson contained no words with the /oa/ vowel digraph. This is just one demonstration of the findings that basal lessons seldom relate skill instruction to the selections children are expected to read (Reutzel & Daines, 1987b). Because of this failure on the part of some publishers, the teacher may often need to make explicit the relation between the skills taught and how (or if) these skills can be applied during the reading.

If the story does not lend itself to the reading skills to be taught, then adapt skill instruction to the story. For example, for the story *Good Work, Amelia Bedelia* by Peggy Parish (1963), an appropriate comprehension skill to select for instruction would be understanding figurative or idiomatic expressions. If the teacher's edition did not direct teachers to focus on this skill, the professional decision could be made to teach the prescribed skill lesson—such as getting the main idea—later in the year and to teach figurative or idiomatic expressions with this story. Instructional decisions such as these are characteristic of transitional teachers' taking control of their teacher's editions. In summary, the RRL recommends that skill instruction be taught before reading and be explicitly related to and applied in reading.

If the story does not lend itself to the reading skills to be taught, then adapt skill instruction to the story.

The third step in the RRL involves a discussion of the story intended to foster comprehension. The typical organization of the basal reader teacher's edition provides for comprehension discussion through a list of comprehension questions following the selection in the teacher's edition. The RRL recommends that guided questioning, discussion, and prediction be included as an integral part of the prereading phase of the reading lesson. Questions usually discussed after reading may be discussed before reading. Children are encouraged to predict answers to the questions before reading and then to read to confirm their predictions. Such a practice can help students selectively focus their attention during reading.

Research has shown that the RRL significantly increased students' comprehension and recall of text over the traditional DRA as well as other alternative lesson frameworks.

The remainder of the RRL should be very brief. Students read the selection in the basal. Postreading activities focus primarily on assessment of comprehension and skill application. Questions can be asked, such as, Did the students comprehend? How well did students predict answers to the prequestions? Did students revise their predictions as a result of the reading? Do the students understand the meanings of the new vocabulary words as they were used in the context of the story? In short, assessment is the primary purpose for postreading activities in the RRL. Prince and Mancus (1987) and Thomas and Readence (1988) reported that using the RRL significantly increased students' comprehension and recall of text over the traditional DRA and other alternative lesson frameworks.

Reciprocal Questioning

ReQuest, or **reciprocal questioning,** developed by Anthony Manzo in 1969, is a structure for presenting reading lessons in which teachers and children silently read parts of a text and exchange the role of asking and answering questions about that text. The ReQuest procedure can be used with individuals or with groups. The process begins with the teacher and students reading a preassigned portion of a text silently. Both the teacher and the students close the book after reading. Next, the students ask the teacher questions about the text, and the teacher answers these questions clearly and accurately. By answering the students' questions first, the teacher can demonstrate for students effective question-answering behaviors. Next, the teacher and students reverse roles. The teacher and students begin by reading the next part of the text and then close their books. At this point, students try to answer the questions the teacher asks. At some point in the lesson, usually predetermined by the teacher, students are asked to predict the potential events and outcome of the remainder of the text to be read. A list of predictions is constructed through discussion and shown at the board. Students read the remaining text to confirm or correct their predictions. After reading, the teacher leads a discussion to reconsider the original predictions. (See Figure 8.12.)

ReQuest, or reciprocal questioning, is a structure for presenting reading lessons in which teachers and children silently read parts of a text and exchange the role of asking and answering questions about that text.

Because children are encouraged to construct their own questions for reading, they become active readers to the extent that they (a) select their own purposes for reading and (b) engage in a proven reading strategy involving sampling, prediction, and reading to confirm or correct predictions. ReQuest involves teachers and students equally in the roles of participant and observer in the lesson rather than allowing children spend their time looking on as passive observers. As a result, ReQuest helps children to learn how to compose and answer questions about text through active observation and participation in the reading lesson.

CONTRASTING DIFFERING PHILOSOPHICAL EMPHASES IN PUBLISHED BASAL READING SERIES

Although current basal readers are alike in many surface respects, they often differ with respect to authoring teams' and publishing/corporate beliefs about how children should be taught to read. Some basal readers, for example, emphasize the acquisition and development of early, automatic decoding skills. Basal reading series created from a decoding emphasis focus first on helping children acquire and apply word-

Figure 8.12 Example ReQuest Lesson

Book title: *Franklin in the Dark* (Bourgeois & Clark, 1986).

Read Text: "Franklin could slide down a riverbank all by himself. He could count forwards and backwards. He could even zip zippers and button buttons. But Franklin was afraid of small, dark places and that was a problem because. . . ." (p. 1)
Student 1 question: What's the turtle's name?
Teacher answer: His name is Franklin.
Student 2 question: What are things that Franklin can do?
Teacher answer: Franklin can slide down a riverbank, and button buttons, and zip zippers. Oh, he can also count forward and backward.
Student 3 question: What was Franklin afraid of?
Teacher answer: Franklin was afraid of small dark places.
Teacher question: What kind of animal was Franklin?
Student answer: A turtle.
Teacher question: Why do you think that being afraid of small, dark places can be a problem for a turtle?
Student 1 answer: Because then he wouldn't want to go deep under the water.
Student 2 answer: Because turtles hide in their shells, and if he was afraid of the dark, maybe he wouldn't want to hide in his shell.
Teacher comment: Those are both good answers. Let's read the next page and see why his being afraid is a problem.
Text: "Franklin was a turtle. He was afraid of crawling into his small, dark shell. And so, Franklin the turtle dragged his shell behind him." (p. 2)

After reading the second page of text:

Teacher 1 question: What was Franklin afraid of?
Student answer: He was afraid of getting into his shell because it was dark and small.
Teacher 2 question: What did Franklin do instead of getting into his shell?
Student answer: He had to drag it behind him.
Teacher question: What do you think Franklin could do so that he wouldn't be afraid of hiding in his shell?
Student 1 answer: He could take some medicine that wouldn't make him afraid anymore.
Student 2 answer: He could get a bigger shell so that it wouldn't be so small.
Student 3 answer: He could use a flashlight to light up his shell.
Student 4 answer: He could make a window in his shell so that it wouldn't be so dark.
Teacher comment: You're all really thinking hard about Franklin and his problem. Now let's read on to find out what Franklin does about his fear and see if what we thought was right.

identification skills in decodable texts and then later apply these skills in more authentic texts.

In contrast to a decoding emphasis in basal reading series, other basal reading series emphasize exposure to worthwhile literature and the construction of meaning from text from the very onset of reading instruction. These basal reading series are often referred to as literature-based readers. In literature-based basal readers, children are simultaneously taught sight words, decoding skills, vocabulary skills, and comprehension skills to be applied in the reading of worthwhile children's stories and information selections. Thus, differences in philosophies among basal publishers are typically reflected in both the structure and content of their published basal reading series.

Although basal readers may be alike in many surface respects, they often differ with respect to authors' beliefs about how children learn to read and, consequently, how children should be taught to read.

Decoding Emphasis Basal Reading Series

Basal readers founded on a strong decoding belief place an early and strong emphasis on the development and acquisition of decoding, phonics, or "sounding out" skills. In fact, decoding emphasis basal readers are often classified as "phonics first," explicit, or synthetic phonics basal readers (Flesch, 1955, 1981; R. C. Anderson et al., 1985). Learning the letter sounds and names until a child has mastered the 26 letter names and the 40-plus sounds those letters represent is considered to be a prerequisite to reading words and connected text from this philosophical point of view.

Once children have learned these letter names and sounds, this knowledge will allow them to crack the written code. Next, they are shown how to blend these sounds together to "sound out" words. For example, a child learns the letters *a, t,* and *c.* Blending sounds from left to right produces *c - a - t, cat.* Although all basal readers provide some type of decoding instruction, decoding emphasis basal readers are distinguished by the following features: (a) teaching grapho-phonic relationships as a prerequisite to reading words and text, (b) teaching the blending of letter-sound elements to make words, and (c) initially reading phonically controlled or decodable texts written to conform to specific phonics generalizations.

Decoding basal readers begins with the smallest units of language first and progresses toward larger, more meaningful units of language (Weaver, 1994). Science Research Associates' (SRA) *Reading Mastery Plus* (Engelmann & Bruner, 2002) pictured in Figure 8.13 is considered by many to represent the epitome of a decoding emphasis basal reading series.

Literature-Based Basal Reading Series

Literature-based basal readers, although committed to decoding skill development, go well beyond the preoccupation with pronouncing words and the construction of meaning from print emphasized in decoding emphasis basal readers. Literature-based basal readers attend to issues of vocabulary development and comprehension, the requisite skills for decoding (Weaver, 1994), and exposure to child classics and contemporary children's literature from the very start of instruction. For example, discussions build experiential background, and demonstrations help children draw on prior knowledge rather than simply teaching a list of new vocabulary words to enhance reading preparation. The Scholastic *Literacy Place* program (Block, Gambrell, Hamilton, Hartman, Hasselbring, Klein, Medrano, Pinnell, Reutzel, Rose, Schifini, Seamster, Sharp, Shefelbine, and Turner, 2000) shown in Figure 8.14 is one such example. Literature-based basal readers present comprehension, vocabulary, and phonics skill lessons simultaneously from the very start of reading instruction, whereas decoding basal readers will delay emphasis on these components until word-identification and decoding skills have been mastered. Literature-based basal reading series are predicated on the belief that children must be motivated and engaged by the content of the reading to persist in acquiring and applying reading skills of any kind, decoding or comprehension.

ADOPTING AND EVALUATING BASAL READERS

Few professional decisions deserve more careful attention than that of evaluating and adopting a basal reading series. Because you as a teacher will evaluate one or more basal reading series during your professional career, you need to understand how to

Figure 8.13   Sample page from the SRA *Reading Mastery Plus* program

READING VOCABULARY

Do not touch small letters.

Get ready to read all the words on this page without making a mistake.

EXERCISE 2

Sound out first

a. (Touch the ball for **white**.) Sound it out. Get ready. (Quickly touch **wh, ī, t** as the children say *whwhwhīīt*.)
b. What word? (Signal.) *White*. Yes, **white**.
c. (Repeat exercise until firm.)

steps

EXERCISE 3

Sound out first

a. (Touch the ball for **steps**.) Sound it out. Get ready. (Quickly touch **s, t, e, p, s** as the children say *sssteeepsss*.)
b. What word? (Signal.) *Steps*. Yes, **steps**.
c. (Repeat exercise until firm.)

must

EXERCISE 4

Sound out first

a. (Touch the ball for **must**.) Sound it out. Get ready. (Quickly touch **m, u, s, t** as the children say *mmmuuussst*.)
b. What word? (Signal.) *Must*. Yes, **must**.
c. (Repeat exercise until firm.)

do

EXERCISE 5

Listen, sound out

a. (Point to **do**.) I'll tell you this word. (Pause.) **Do**. What word? (Signal.) *Do*. Yes, **do**.
b. (Touch the ball for **do**.) Sound it out. Get ready. (Quickly touch **d, o** as the children say *dooo*.) (dōōō.)
c. What word? (Signal.) *Do*. Yes, **do**.
d. (Repeat *b* and *c* until firm.)

who

EXERCISE 6

Listen, sound out

a. (Point to **who**.) I'll tell you this word. (Pause.) **Who**. What word? (Signal.) *Who*. Yes, **who**.
b. (Touch the ball for **who**.) Sound it out. Get ready. (Quickly touch **wh, o** as the children say *whwhwhooo*.)
c. What word? (Signal.) *Who*. Yes, **who**.
d. (Repeat *b* and *c* until firm.)

Repeat any troublesome words.

Individual test

(Call on different children. Each child reads a different word.)

EXERCISE 7

ar word

a. (Point to **ar** in **started**.) What do these letters say? (Signal.) *Are*. Yes, **are**.
b. (Touch the ball for **started**.) Read this word the fast way. Get ready. (Signal.) *Started*. Yes, **started**.

EXERCISE 8

Read the fast way

a. Read these words the fast way.
b. (Touch the ball for **doing**. Pause two seconds.) Get ready. (Signal.) *Doing*. Yes, **doing**.
c. (Repeat *b* for **what**.)

what

09   Lesson 100

From *Reading Mastery Plus, Presentation Book C* (Level 1, p. 89) by S. Engelmann and E. C. Bruner, 2002, Columbus, OH: SRA McGraw-Hill. Copyright 2002 by SRA Division of McGraw-Hill Companies. Reprinted by permission.

evaluate and select basal reading programs effectively. Learning about this process will also enable you to help reform, restructure, and strengthen future revisions, editions, and basal reading adoption processes.

Adopting a Basal Reader Program

Twenty-two states have adopted some form of highly centralized, state-level control over the evaluation and selection of basal reading programs. The remaining 28 states and the District of Columbia allow individual districts and schools to select basal reading series at the local level (Table 8.2).

Regardless of whether evaluations and selections occur at the state or local level, the task of decision making is most often placed in the hands of a textbook adoption committee. Farr et al. (1987) indicate that these committees often use a locally produced checklist to evaluate basal readers. Unfortunately, most adoption checklists require the evaluators to determine only the presence, rather than the quality, of certain features in basal reading programs. Follett (1985) estimated that the average amount of time textbook adoption committee members spend evaluating basal reading programs is approximately one second per page, resulting in what Powell (1986) calls a

Because many teachers will evaluate one or more basal reading series during their professional careers, they need to understand how to evaluate and select basal readers effectively.

Figure 8.14   The *Scholastic Literacy Place 2000* basal series draws on contemporary children's literature to build background, preview, and predict.

From *Scholastic Literacy Place: Problem Patrol,* (p. 186–187), 2000, New York: Scholastic. Copyright 2000 by Scholastic, Inc. Reprinted by permission.

"Flip Test" approach to evaluation and selection. Farr et al. (1987) proposed several guidelines for improving the basal reader adoption process (see Figure 8.15). Although many of these recommendations will require major changes, improving the basal reader adoption process can itself contribute much to teachers' understanding of the reading curriculum and, as a result, can enhance the overall quality of reading instruction. Dole, Osborn, and Lehr (1990) at the Center for the Study of Reading developed a comprehensive set of materials for evaluating and adopting basal reader programs entitled *A Guide to Selecting Basal Reading Programs.* From our evaluation of checklist, guidelines, and processes for adopting basal reader programs, the Dole et al. (1990) materials are the most comprehensive, thorough, research-based available today.

Evaluating Basal Readers

Only after teachers are sufficiently well informed about the characteristics of effective basal reader programs can they act to correct or adjust the use of the basal to benefit their students. Although discussions about basal reader evaluations can sometimes

Table 8.2   Textbook adoption policies by state

State Adoption	Local Adoption
Alabama	Alaska
Arkansas	Arizona
California	Colorado
Florida	Connecticut
Georgia	Delaware
Hawaii	District of Columbia
Idaho	Illinois
Indiana	Iowa
Kentucky	Kansas
Louisiana	Maine
Mississippi	Maryland
Nevada	Massachusetts
New Mexico	Michigan
North Carolina	Minnesota
Oklahoma	Missouri
Oregon	Montana
South Carolina	Nebraska
Tennessee	New Hampshire
Texas	New Jersey
Utah	New York
Virginia	North Dakota
West Virginia	Ohio
	Pennsylvania
	Rhode Island
	South Dakota
	Vermont
	Washington
	Wisconsin
	Wyoming

be unpleasant, they are necessary to help teachers become aware of both the strengths and limitations of the basal reader approach. Dole, Rogers, and Osborn (1987) recommended that for the evaluation of basal readers to be improved, those involved should focus on the following:

Notice who is often charged with the responsibility for adopting a new basal reader.

1. Identify the facets of effective reading instruction.
2. Delineate criteria related to effective reading instruction to be analyzed in the basal readers.
3. Provide a means for carefully recording how well basal readers measure up to the established criteria.

Because many reading teachers are concerned with curriculum changes that reflect a decided move toward more evidence-based, or scientifically based comprehensive reading instructional practices in basal readers, we strongly recommend that classroom professionals obtain the materials, worksheets, and procedures found in Dole, Osborn, and Lehr's "Adoption Guidelines Project," in *A Guide to Selecting Basal Reading Programs*. These can be obtained by sending requests to the Center

Figure 8.15   Guidelines for basal reader adoption process

Basic Assumptions

1. The selection of a reading textbook series should not be considered the same as the adoption of the total reading curriculum.

2. Basal reading adoptions should be conducted by school districts rather than by states.

3. The final decision regarding textbook selection should reside with the committee that spends the time and energy reviewing the books.

Selection of Reviewers

1. Reviewers should have the respect of other teachers in the school system.

2. We do not recommend in-service training in the teaching of reading, but we do strongly recommend training for reviewers in the review and evaluation of reading textbooks.

Establishing Criteria

1. The adoption committee's most important task is the determination of the basal reading series factors to be used in evaluating the programs.

2. As the selection criteria are established, the committee must agree on the meaning of each factor.

Procedures in Reviewing and Evaluating Basal Readers

1. Committees must be provided an adequate amount of time to conduct thorough evaluations of reading textbooks.

2. Committees should be organized in ways other than by grade level.

3. Procedures used to evaluate basal programs should be tested before the actual evaluation takes place.

4. Whatever evaluation procedures are used, committee members must do more than make a check mark.

5. Any person who wishes to address the entire adoption committee or any individual committee members should be allowed to do so.

6. Reading adoption committees need to consider carefully how much and what contact to have with publishers' representatives.

7. Pilot studies are useful if they are carefully controlled.

8. When the committee has completed its work, a report of the committee's evaluation procedures and findings should be made public.

From "The Evaluation and Selection of Basal Readers" by R. Farr, M. A. Tulley, & D. Powell, 1987, *The Elementary School Journal, 87*(3), pp. 267–281. Published by The University of Chicago Press. Copyright 1987 by The University of Chicago. Reprinted by permission.

Standards Note
Standard 12.2: The reading professional will adapt instruction to meet the needs of different learners to accomplish different purposes. Make a T chart with *same* and *different* as the column heads. Compare selected effective reading programs of national significance.

for the Study of Reading, University of Illinois—Guide, P.O. Box 2121, Station A, Champaign, IL 61825-2121.

Selected Effective Reading Programs of National Significance

In 1998, J. Pikulski reviewed the effectiveness of several national reading programs designed to prevent reading failure. Although basal readers remain the predominant form of reading instruction in most classrooms, several of these national programs are worth noting here, especially (1) Reading Recovery, (2) Success for All, (3) Four Blocks, and (4) Early Steps.

Reading Recovery

Reading Recovery, developed by clinical child psychologist, Marie Clay, is an early intervention program design to reduce reading failure in the first grade for the lowest performing 20 percent of students. The aim of the program is to help low-achieving children catch up to the level of their age-related peers. Reading Recovery was imported from New Zealand to the United States by faculty at the Ohio State University (Allington, 1992). Reading Recovery (RR) trained teachers enroll in a year-long course of graduate studies with regular follow-up professional development seminars to keep training current and approved (Lyons & Beaver, 1995). Teachers trained in RR must receive training from an approved RR teacher trainer and at one of several approved sites throughout the nation.

Reading Recovery is an effective program for training teachers to help struggling readers succeed.

The average RR student is recovered from below grade level performance in an average of 12 to 14 weeks. Discontinued children show normal development after release from the program. Students in New Zealand and in the United States demonstrate the substantial positive effects this invention has on young children's reading and writing development (Clay, 1990; DeFord, Lyons, & Pinnell, 1991; Pinnell, DeFord, & Lyons, 1994).

Children selected for the RR program receive one-on-one, intensive daily reading instruction for 30 minutes. During this 30-minute daily instructional period, teachers and children engage in five major activities in a sequenced and structured format. First, is the rereading of at least two familiar books or "familiar rereads" of books they have read previously with the assistance and guidance of the RR teacher. Second, the RR teacher takes a daily "running record" of the student's oral reading of the new book introduced the previous day. During the running record the teacher notes which words are read accurately or inaccurately and analyzes the inaccuracies for the cue system the student used or didn't use to inform upcoming instructional emphasis and planning.

Third, the teacher and students work with letters and words. A typical experience is "making words" using plastic magnetic letters on a cookie sheet. The teacher may show a child the word "ran" and ask the child to blend the sounds to pronounce the word. Then the teacher may remove the "r" and substitute "f" and ask the child to blend the new sound to get the word "fan."

Fourth, the child dictates a sentence or two called a "story" in RR terminology. Then the teacher helps the child write the "story" by stretching words with the child, encouraging him/her to write the letter for each sound to get each word. After each word is written, the teacher asks the student to reread the previous word(s) until the entire sentence is written. After reading the entire sentence, the teacher will cut the sentence into word strips and ask the student to re-order the word strips into the sentence.

The fifth and final activity in an RR lesson is the introduction of a new story. The teacher has preread the story and noted challenges and obstacles the child might face in reading this book. The teacher will walk the student through the "pictures," introducing new vocabulary, sounding out tricky words with the student, often using a small, white board and marker, and discussing any unfamiliar concepts or language prior to the children reading the book with the careful guidance, support, and feedback of the teacher.

Some educators have suggested that RR may be too expensive to implement on a wide scale in the United States where the reading failure rate exceeds 20 percent. However, over 80 percent of children in RR move to discontinuance and grade level performance in less than a semester of intensive instruction, with continuing acceptable progress. Reductions in referrals to special education services and lowered retention rates indicate that RR is substantially more cost effective than are many of the commonly tried options, including special education, for addressing the needs of low-performing children (Dyer, 1992).

Some critics of Reading Recovery regard this program as too expensive for wide-spread adoption and use.

Success for All

Success for All (SFA) is a total school reform program for grades K–3. The goal of the SFA program is to have all children reading on grade level by third grade, with no retentions and referrals to special education for reading problems. Dr. Robert Slavin, Director of the Center for Research and Effective Schooling for Disadvantaged Students at Johns Hopkins University, and his colleagues developed the SFA program. The SFA program is grounded in three premises. First, the primary grade classroom is the best place to work on ensuring children's school success. Second, provide needed additional instruction to students as soon as they are identified as needing it. And third, think creatively about the use of school resources, personnel, and instructional time.

Success for All focuses on providing high quality literacy instruction and supplementary tutoring in grades K–3.

SFA focuses on providing quality reading instruction in grades K–3 as well as providing supplementary support in the form of individual tutoring sessions. Children are placed into heterogeneous classroom groupings for most of the day, but when the 90-minute reading instructional block begins, children are regrouped into "ability" groups of 15 to 20 students across the three grade levels 1–3. Regrouping according to reading levels allows whole-group, direct instruction of children and is intended to eliminate the overreliance upon seat work and worksheets found in many classrooms.

For students who are not responsive to whole-class instruction in their reading groups, supplementary individual tutoring for 20 minutes per day is provided in the SFA program. Tutoring sessions focus on the same strategies and skills taught in the whole-class sessions, and where possible, the classroom teacher is freed up by the use of classroom aides to provide the tutoring sessions. SFA also recommends that children attend a half-day preschool and a full-day kindergarten to accelerate progress in learning to read successfully. Multiple program evaluations have shown that SFA is an effective program for reducing referrals to special education and grade level retentions. However, in most of the studies, SFA has not achieved the goal of helping every child read on grade level by the end of third grade (Slavin et al., 1990, 1992, 1996).

Four Blocks

The Four Blocks program integrates basal reading programs with time spent writing, working with words, and independent reading.

The **Four Blocks** (FB) program implemented in Winston-Salem, North Carolina, by P. Cunningham is a program of first grade reading instruction. The FB program organizes daily reading instruction around four 30-minute blocks of instruction: (1) Basal Block, (2) Writing Block, (3) Working with Words Block, and (4) Self-Selected Reading Block. During the Basal Block, the teacher and children selectively use materials and suggestions provided in the school or district's adopted basal reading program. This means that children read stories, essays, articles, etc., found in the anthology (student's text) of the basal reader program and that the instructional activities found in the basal reader are used during this instructional time.

During the Writing Block, the teacher typically begins with a 5- to 10-minute mini-lesson on a writing convention, style, or genre. Following the mini-lesson children engage in individually selected writing projects, taking these projects through the typical stages and activities of a writer's workshop—drafting, revising, editing, and publishing. The Working with Words Block consists of reading words from the *word wall* and *making words*. Word wall words are high frequency, phonically irregular words posted on a wall for children to learn to read and spell by sight rather than through pattern analysis or decoding. The making words activities consist of using groups of letters to make as many words as possible. The teacher will usually give children a clue on words that can be made by using two or more of the letters in various combinations. This activity concludes with using all of the letters in the group to make a single word known as the *secret word*. The final 30-minute time block, Self-Selected Reading, has students read books of their own choosing, including information books, and complete projects and responses to the books they read to share their experiences and knowledge with other children. Results reported by Cunningham, Hall, and Defee (1998) indicate that the program has been successful with children having a wide range of literacy levels without using ability grouping or leveled grouping.

Early Steps

Early Steps, developed by Darrell Morris (Morris, Shaw, & Perney, 1990), is an early intervention program designed to reduce reading failure in the early years. Children selected for the Early Steps (ES) program receive one-on-one, intensive daily reading instruction for 30 minutes. During this 30-minute daily instructional period, teachers and children engage in four major activities in a sequenced and structured format. To begin a lesson, the children reread familiar leveled books read during a previous day's lesson for 8 to 10 minutes.

Second, for 5 to 6 minutes the tutor takes the student through a series of word sort activities. This is done by the teacher placing three words, such as *hat, man, cap,* horizontally across the table or desktop. After demonstrating the task of sorting several of the words in the pile of words for the student, the student completes the task. Sorting tasks focus initially on sorting words according to "phonograms, word families, or rimes."

For the next 5 to 8 minutes of the lesson, the child writes a sentence from his or her own experience. After a short dialog with the tutor, the child writes by saying aloud each word, stretching the word, and recoding the letter for each sound segmented from the stretched word. After the child is finished writing, the tutor writes the sentence on a sentence strip and cuts it apart for the child to put together and reread.

Early Steps is an effective "tutoring" program for struggling readers.

The fourth and final step in the lesson is the introduction of a new book the child is expected to read the next day without much help. The books are selected in ascending levels of difficulty, thus pushing the child's reading progress forward. Before reading, the tutor helps the child look at the pictures, talk about the unfamiliar vocabulary words, and situate the book in a meaningful frame of reference. During the reading, the tutor coaches the child to use strategies and self-correct. Once this book is completed, it is used the next day for the familiar rereading.

In many ways, Early Steps is very much like Reading Recovery, only with a more systematic approach to the teaching of phonic decoding strategies. Research by Santa and Hoien (1998) showed Early Steps intervention in grades one and two helped the most at-risk students to approach the average performance level of their peers within one academic year of instruction. Early Steps not only boosted scores on decoding but also on measures of spelling, word recognition, and comprehension.

HELPING STUDENTS WITH SPECIAL NEEDS SUCCEED WITH BASAL READER INSTRUCTION

Historically, the basal reader has not been very successful as a tool for reading remediation—for several reasons. First, some teachers find the stories in basal readers to be bland and uninviting, especially for problem readers. What is needed most is literature that turns on the turned-off learner—an order too tall for many basals to fill. Second, if a child is failing to achieve success using one approach to reading instruction, in this case the basal reader, then common sense tells us that what is needed is an alternative strategy—not just more of the same. Finally, basal reader systems frequently do not allow students enough time for real reading. The multifarious collection of skill sheets and workbook pages tends to be so time consuming that little time is left for reading. In Chapter 1, we discussed principles for encouraging literacy, some of which are most pertinent when using basal readers to help students with special needs. Three direct applications of these principles are especially useful.

Notice three ways to support students with special needs by using the basal reader.

Reading the Basal Straight Through

Teachers working with special needs students recognize that what these children need most is regular and sustained reading. We suggest that skill sheets and workbook pages be used judiciously or even avoided to allow for more time spent reading. Children should be allowed to read basals straight through as an anthology of children's stories. The teacher may wish to skip stories that offer little for the reader in this setting.

Repeated Readings

In repeated readings, the teacher typically introduces the story as a shared book or story experience, then students attempt to read the book alone or with a friend (Routman, 1988). If the story has rhyme or a regular pattern, it may be sung or chanted. Repeated readings of stories help children achieve a sense of accomplishment, improve comprehension, and build fluency.

Supported, or Buddy, Reading

The Internet School Library Media Center (ISLMC) Multicultural Page is a meta site which brings together resources for teachers, librarians, parents, and students. You can link to this resource from our Companion Website at www.prenhall.com/ reutzel.

Many times, at-risk readers are very reluctant to become risk takers. Teachers simply must find ways of breaking the ice for them and create classroom safety nets. Supported, or buddy, reading allows students to read basal stories aloud together, either taking turns or in unison. By rereading these supported selections, students' fluency and comprehension improve. Another variation is for teacher–student combinations to read together. Similar to the procedure known as neurological impress (P. M. Hollingsworth, 1978), the student and teacher read aloud in unison at a comfortable rate. For first readings, the teacher usually assumes the lead in terms of volume and pace. In subsequent repeated readings, the student is encouraged to assume the lead.

Chapter 9 provides more insights into how teachers can enhance the reading and writing environment as they begin making the transition from basal-only teaching to more balanced literacy perspectives and practices. In the process, we will discover numerous opportunities for assisting students with special needs within the elementary classroom.

HELPING STUDENTS WITH DIVERSE CULTURAL OR LANGUAGE NEEDS SUCCEED WITH BASAL READERS

Students who do not possess reading and writing ability in a first language should be taught to read and write in their native or first language to support and validate them as worthwhile individuals. In addition, reading instruction in the first language helps students capitalize on what they already know about their primary languages and cultures to build concepts that can facilitate the acquisition of English (Krashen & Biber, 1988; Freeman & Freeman, 1992). In any case, teachers must be sensitive to these students' special needs, which include (a) a need for safety and security, (b) a need to belong and be accepted, and (c) a need to feel self-esteem (Peregoy & Boyle, 1993).

Teachers should help English as a second language (ESL) or limited English proficiency (LEP) students feel at ease when they arrive in the classroom by assigning them a personal buddy who, if possible, speaks the language of the newcomer. This buddy is assigned to help the new student through the school day, routines, and so on. Another approach is to avoid changes in the classroom schedule by following a regular and predictable routine each day, which creates a sense of security. To create a sense of belonging, assign the student to a home group for an extended period of time. A home group provides a small social unit of concern focused on helping the newcomer adapt to everyday life as well as provides a concerned and caring peer group. Finally, self-esteem is enhanced when an individual's worth is affirmed. Opportunities for the newcomer to share their language and culture during daily events in the classroom provide a useful way to integrate them into the ongoing classroom culture.

To help ESL or LEP students succeed in classrooms where basal readers are the core of instruction, Law and Eckes (1990, p. 92) recommend the following:

- Supplement the basal as much as possible with language experience stories (as discussed previously in this chapter).
- Encourage extensive reading: Gather basal textbooks from as many different levels as possible. Also acquire easier textbooks in content areas as well as trade books to encourage a wide range of reading topics.
- Expose children to the many different types of reading available in the "real" world, such as magazines, *TV Guide,* newspapers, product labels, signs.

> *Describe three things that can be done to support second language learners when using a basal reader.*

Summary

Basal readers over the past two centuries have become a veritable institution in American reading instruction. As social and political aims have changed over the years, basal reader content and structure have been altered to reflect these changing conditions. Modern basal readers are typically composed of several major components, including a teacher's edition, a student's reader, workbooks, assessment, supplementary literature, and technology. For teachers, basal readers represent a structured approach to teaching reading, which can save enormous amounts of preparation time. On the other hand, basal readers can in some instances displace teacher judgment to the degree that the basal becomes the reading program rather than a tool to be used to support the reading program. Large, national commercial publishers produce basal readers. Senior authors on basal series are usually individuals known and respected nationally or internationally in the field of reading.

Adopting a basal reader for use in schools is a task most teachers will probably face in the course of their professional careers. Hence, it is important for teachers to understand how basal readers have been adopted in the past and know how the adoption process may be improved.

Although basal readers can be useful tools for providing reading instruction, some teachers need to make conscious efforts to take control of their basal teacher's editions by changing the way in which they provide instruction. Suggestions in this chapter included using the balanced reading program, RRL and ReQuest. Other selected, nationally known reading programs that are not considered basal reading programs were also discussed—Success for All, Reading Recovery, Four Blocks, and Early Steps.

Finally, readers with special needs who may be struggling can be helped by reading the basal straight through, allowing repeated readings of self-selected basal stories, and providing buddy or other forms of supported reading. ESL and LEP students can be helped to feel at home as newcomers in a school environment. The teacher can also take steps to supplement and extend basic basal reader text for these students.

Visit Chapter 8 of our Companion Website at www.prenhall.com/ reutzel to look into the chapter objectives, standards and principles, and pertinent web links associated with Materials and Programs for Literacy Instruction: Basals and Beyond.

Concept Applications

In the Classroom

1. Go to your local school district or university curriculum materials library. Locate two basal readers. Locate the following items in the teacher's edition: (a) the scope and sequence chart, (b) the parts of a directed reading lesson, (c) the skill lessons, (d) the workbooks, and (e) the book tests or assessment materials. Compare the instructional approaches and contents of each using a compare/contrast T chart.

2. Compare the contents of a current basal reader to the contents of the Dick and Jane or McGuffey basal readers. Write a brief essay on the differences you note.

3. Select a basal reader lesson and story. Redesign this lesson on your own by changing it to make use of (a) the RRL, (b) the LEA, (c) ReQuest, or (d) DRTA.

4. Plan Block 1 using the basal reader in the Four Block reading program. Design how you would use the basal for a week for 30-minutes per day.

5. Select a leveled book. Go through the parts of a Reading Recovery lesson, and write a plan about how you would introduce this as a new book to a struggling reader.

In the Field

1. Interview a teacher in the field about the strengths and weaknesses of the basal. Find out why this teacher uses or does not use the basal.

2. Visit a classroom in a local elementary school where Success for All is used. Observe a teacher teaching reading. Which parts of the SFA program did the teacher use? Which parts did the teacher omit? Write an essay about your observations.

3. Prepare a basal reading lesson to be taught in the schools. Secure permission to teach this lesson in a local grade-level appropriate classroom. Write a reflective essay on the experience, detailing successes, failures, and necessary changes.

4. Select a basal reading lesson in a teacher's edition. Adapt the lesson in the teacher's edition by rewriting it using a balanced reading program, RRL, ReQuest, or Four Blocks. Secure permission to teach this lesson in a local grade-level appropriate classroom. Write a reflective essay on the experience detailing successes, failures, and necessary changes.

Recommended Readings

Baumann, J. F. (1992). Basal reading programs and the deskilling of teachers: A critical examination of the argument. *Reading Research Quarterly, 27*(4), 390–398.

Cheney, L. V. (1990). *Tyrannical machines.* Washington, DC: National Endowment for the Humanities.

Dole, J. A., Osborn, J., & Lehr, F. (1990). *A guide to selecting basal reading programs.* Urbana, IL: Center for the Study of Reading.

Duke, N. K. (2000). 3.6 minutes per day: The scarcity of informational texts in first grade. *Reading Research Quarterly, 35*(2), 202–224.

Fountas, I. C., & Pinnell, G. S. (1999). *Matching books to readers: Using leveled books in guided reading, K–3,* 83–91. Portsmouth, NH: Heinemann.

Hiebert, E. H. (1999). Text matters in learning to read. *The Reading Teacher, 52*(6), 552–66.

Hoffman, J. V., McCarthey, S. J., Abbott, J., Christian, C., Corman, L., Curry, C., Dressman, M., Elliott, B., Matherne, D., & Stahle, D. (1994). So what's new in the new basals? A focus on first grade. *Journal of Reading Behavior, 26*(1), 47–73.

McCarthey, S. J., Hoffman, J. V., Christian, C., Corman, L., Elliott, B., Matherne, D., & Stahle, D. (1994). Engaging the new basal readers. *Reading Research and Instruction, 33*(3), 233–256.

Moss, B., & Newton, E. (2001). An examination of the information text genre in basal readers. *Reading Psychology, 23*(1), 1–13.

Perspectives on basal readers. [Special issue]. *Theory Into Practice, 28*(4), 1989.

Reutzel, D. R., & Larsen, N. S. (1995). Look what they've done to real children's books in the new basal readers. *Language Arts, 72*(7), 495–507.

Robinson, A. (2002). *American reading instruction,* Rev. Ed. Newark, DE: International Reading Association.

Shannon, P. (1992). *Becoming political: Readings and writings in the politics of literacy education.* Portsmouth, NH: Heinemann.

Smith, N. B. (1986). *American reading instruction.* Newark, DE: International Reading Association.

Winograd, N., Wixson, K. K., & Lipson, M. Y. (Eds.). (1989). *Improving basal reader instruction.* New York: Columbia Teachers College Press.

9

Assessing Literacy Learning

Focus Questions

When you are finished studying this chapter, you should be able to answer these questions:

1. What are the principles of effective classroom reading assessment?

2. How do traditional assessment procedures differ from comprehensive reading assessment procedures?

3. What are some examples of commercial reading tests available for classroom use?

4. Name five reading assessment strategies that can be used to inform instruction.

5. What is *profiling?* How is profiling used to form needs-based reading groups?

6. How can teachers derive grades from comprehensive reading assessment strategies?

7. What are some of the current issues in reading assessment?

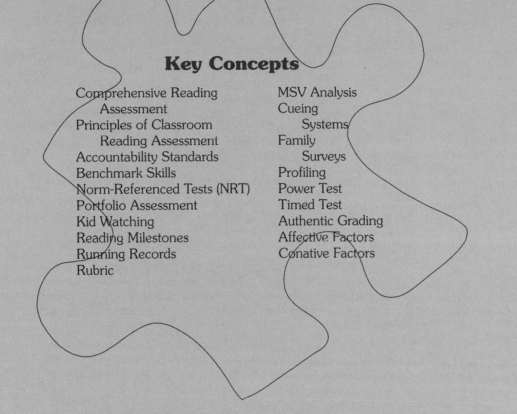

Key Concepts

Comprehensive Reading
    Assessment
Principles of Classroom
    Reading Assessment
Accountability Standards
Benchmark Skills
Norm-Referenced Tests (NRT)
Portfolio Assessment
Kid Watching
Reading Milestones
Running Records
Rubric

MSV Analysis
Cueing
    Systems
Family
    Surveys
Profiling
Power Test
Timed Test
Authentic Grading
Affective Factors
Conative Factors

Reading assessment is intended to inform teaching. **Comprehensive reading assessment** strategies satisfy this purpose and are typically informal, analyze reading using real books, provide natural experiences with text, and are aimed at carefully analyzing student growth.

Differences between traditional assessment and comprehensive reading assessment perspectives can be likened to the differences between a black-and-white photograph and a color movie: Traditional assessment, at best, provides teachers and administrators with a limited view of readers (like a black-and-white "snapshot" of a child), whereas comprehensive reading assessment provides teachers with a much clearer and more complete view of the learner (like a color movie).

In this chapter, we describe traditional and comprehensive reading assessment strategies and examples of each. First, we explore some basic principles of classroom reading assessment.

Visit Chapter 9 of our Companion Website at www.prenhall.com/ reutzel to look into the chapter objectives, standards and principles, and pertinent web links associated with Assessing Literacy Learning.

Assessment begins with an understanding of grade level expectations described in the state's standards.

PRINCIPLES OF CLASSROOM ASSESSMENT

The following **principles of classroom assessment** are intended to help teachers decide which strategies should be adopted to improve their classroom instruction. They are based on our own classroom experiences, research in the field, and opinions expressed to us by classroom teachers.

Principle 1: Assessment Should Inform and Improve Teaching

When considering whether or not to perform any sort of reading assessment, the teacher should ask, "Will this procedure help me make important educational decisions regarding this student's reading needs?" The procedure should yield rich insights as to materials and ways of offering instruction (e.g., skills to be learned next, grouping based on student needs, etc.) that can positively affect students' reading growth. The process begins with an understanding of required state standards and a careful survey of what is known about the students using available information (home surveys, cumulative records, informal assessments, student self-assessments, etc.).

Next, the teacher forms hypotheses about where each student is in his or her reading development (Bintz, 1991). The task is to select assessment procedures that will help the teacher better understand student abilities and confirm or reject earlier hypotheses. Armed with the information obtained from these processes, the teacher teaches lessons aimed at helping students develop further in their individual *zones of proximal development.* Figure 9.1 depicts this assessment-teaching process.

Principle 2: Assessment Procedures Should Help Teachers Discover What Children *Can* Do, Not Only What They Cannot Do

Reading assessment in recent decades has usually followed what has been termed a *medical* or *clinical model.* The clinical model was used to cloak reading assessment in the robes of science and precision. A thinly veiled assumption was that children getting off to a rough beginning must have something organically wrong slowing their reading development. The idea was that whenever a teacher discovered a student

Figure 9.1   Assessment-teaching process

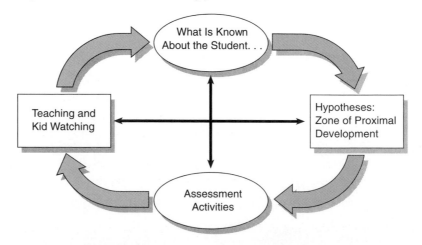

having difficulty with reading, a "diagnosis" of the child's problem areas would be developed using various reading tests. From this diagnosis of strengths and, more importantly, weaknesses, a "prescription" or remediation program was developed. After several decades of following this medical model and the establishment of federally sponsored remedial programs to support them (such as Title I Reading and Special Education), very little impact has been registered with students struggling in reading (Mullis, Campbell, & Farstrup, 1993).

A new perspective in assessment seems warranted. Rather than spending precious classroom time trying to identify what students *cannot* do, many teachers are finding that their time is much better spent finding out what students *can* do. Once teachers understand student abilities, it becomes much easier to decide which new learning experiences should be offered to help them develop further. Later in this chapter, we describe the reading milestones through which students progress to help you better judge where they are in their reading development and what they may be able to learn next.

Principle 3: Every Assessment Procedure Should Have a Specific Purpose

It is easy for teachers to fall into the habit of giving tests simply because of tradition. For example, at a school where one of the authors taught, it was common practice to give a battery of tests to all struggling readers who were referred for assessment by the classroom teacher. Such a battery today might include formal tests like the:

- *Woodcock Reading Mastery Tests—Revised* (Woodcock, Mather, & Barnes, 1987)
- *Brigance® Comprehensive Inventory of Basic Skills—Revised* (Brigance, 1999)
- *Slosson Intelligence Test* (Slosson, 1971)
- *Comprehensive Test of Phonological Processing* (CTOPP) (1999)
- *Comprehensive Test of Nonverbal Intelligence*

The problem with this shotgun approach to assessment is that all children receive the same battery of tests without regard to their known abilities or anticipated needs.

Because reading assessment can be somewhat stressful to students, we should be careful to administer only those formal tests that are absolutely necessary; informal, less stressful procedures should be used when possible. This practice will most likely provide the necessary information to begin instruction, which will then lead to a better understanding of the student's ability.

"Shotgun" approaches to assessment waste valuable time and resources and they are stressful to students.

Principle 4: Classroom Assessment Should Be Linked to *Accountability Standards* and Provide Insights Into the *Process* of Reading

With the passage of the No Child Left Behind Act and other state and federal legislation in reading education has come an even greater emphasis on classroom assessment. **Accountability standards** established by the states and professional organizations, such as the International Reading Association (IRA) and the National Council of Teachers of English (NCTE), describe evidence-based reading skills that are typically mastered by the end of each school year. These **benchmark skills,** as they are often referred to, should be directly measured regularly to determine where students are in their reading development, and thus provide teachers with needed data for planning instruction.

Reading is a complex process that involves such important areas as skill development in print awareness, decoding, vocabulary knowledge, interest-related factors, and command of oral language. Good reading assessment mirrors this understanding and uses a variety of tools to create student profiles. Clay (1985), for instance, developed a primary level tool known as the *Concepts About Print Test,* which assesses the print awareness of emerging readers and can be used to assess what they know about fundamental print concepts (Heathington, 1990). Clay has also suggested the use of running records for assessing reading ability more authentically. These and other comprehensive reading assessment procedures are discussed later in this chapter.

Principle 5: Assessment Procedures Should Help Identify *Zones of Proximal Development*

Balanced literacy assessment helps teachers understand which reading skills should be introduced next.

Earlier in the book we discussed Vygotsky's (1962, 1978) notion of a *zone of proximal development,* or the area of potential growth in reading that can occur with appropriate teacher and peer intervention. To identify students' zones of proximal development, teachers need to determine accurately what children can already do and thus which new skills they may be ready to learn next. For example, in a kindergarten or first-grade classroom, children who can create story lines for wordless picture books, and who have been doing so for some time, should be ready for books containing simple and predictable text.

Teachers also need to watch for any problem areas students may have. Whether only one student or many students seem to have the same reading problem, the teacher should offer a mini-lesson to help them over the hurdle. In other words, the reading curriculum should be responsive and flexible according to students' demonstrated needs and patterns of ability.

Principle 6: Assessment Strategies Should Not Supplant Instruction

State- and locally-mandated testing sometimes seems to overwhelm the teacher and take over the classroom. In Texas, for example, a state that has had high-stakes testing since the early 1980s, many principals complain that some teachers virtually stop teaching from January until April in order to drill students on practice tests. If a teacher loses sight of the purpose of classroom assessment, namely, to inform and influence instruction, then he or she may well move into the role of *teacher as manager* rather than *teacher as teacher* (Pearson, 1985). The assessment program should complement the instructional program and grow naturally from it.

Principle 7: The Most Valid Assessment Is Individual Assessment

Whole-group assessment only provides gross estimates of reading program effectiveness. Teachers must know how to watch, listen, and interact with students, one at a time, to develop clear understandings of their abilities and plan instruction for the entire class.

In the remainder of this chapter, we survey effective reading assessment practices. We begin with an analysis of traditional reading assessment procedures that remain prevalent in American school districts. Later, we take a more in-depth look at comprehensive reading assessment options and related issues.

TRADITIONAL READING ASSESSMENT

Traditional reading assessment in the United States typically provides districtwide and national comparisons of children using commercial reading tests. Informal reading inventories, group reading tests, individual diagnostic reading tests, formal achievement tests, and commercially available kits are common examples. Though these assessments only provide a partial picture of student learning, they are widely used and should be understood by teachers.

In this section, two questions regarding traditional reading assessment are briefly addressed. First, what types of commercial reading tests are commonly available to teachers? Second, what problems are sometimes encountered with these types of reading assessments?

Traditional assessment typically fails to inform instruction adequately.

Informal Reading Inventories

An informal reading inventory (IRI) is typically individually administered (though some can be given to groups of children) and often has graded word lists and story passages. Emmett A. Betts is generally considered to be the first developer of the IRI; however, several other individuals contributed to its development as far back as the early 1900s (Johns & Lunn, 1983).

IRIs typically have passages more like authentic books than most other commercial tests.

The Teacher's Guide to Reading Tests (Cooter, 1990) cites several advantages and unique features of IRIs that help to explain why teachers continue to find them useful. One advantage is that IRIs provide for authentic assessments of the reading act. An IRI more closely resembles real reading. Students are better able to "put it all together" by reading whole stories or passages. Another advantage of IRIs is that they usually provide a systematic procedure for studying student miscues or errors (see the discussion of running records later in this chapter for examples of miscues).

IRIs are rather unusual when compared to other forms of reading assessment. First, because they are informal, no norms, reliability data, or validity information is usually available. This is often seen as a disadvantage by some public school educators, especially when assessing students in special education classes where reliability data are needed. Second, IRIs offer information that is often quite helpful to teachers in making curricular decisions, especially teachers who place students into needs-based or guided reading groups (Fountas & Pinnell, 1996). IRIs provide an approximation of each child's ability in graded or "leveled" reading materials, such as basal readers and books used for guided reading. These approximations, or reading levels, are interpreted as independent level (easy or recreational), instructional level, or frustration level (failure or difficult). A third characteristic is that the various IRIs available tend to be quite different from each other. Beyond the usual graded word lists and passages, IRIs vary a great deal in the subtests offered (e.g., silent reading passages, phonics, interest inventories, concepts about print, phonemic awareness, auditory discrimination) and in the scoring criteria used to assess miscues. Finally, some argue that the best IRIs are those constructed by classroom teachers themselves using reading materials from their own classrooms (a form of content or curricular validity).

Several examples of IRIs now used in many school systems follow.

Standards Note
Standard 10.1: The reading professional will be able to develop and conduct assessments that involve multiple indicators of early literacy learner progress. Having read the seven principles of reading assessment, list and consider the multiple indicators of early literacy progress that you currently use or would like to use so that you have a truly informative "color movie."

• *The Flynt/Cooter Reading Inventory for the Classroom, Fifth Edition* (Flynt & Cooter, 2004). *The Flynt/Cooter Reading Inventory for the Classroom* is a modern version of the traditional IRI concept. The authors incorporate current research on comprehension processes, running records, fluency, and miscue analysis into a more effective authentic reading assessment. They included such research-based procedures as unaided/aided recall and story grammar comprehension evaluation, high-interest selections, appropriate length passages, both expository and narrative passages, and a time-efficient miscue grid system for quick analyses of running records.

*The English * Español Reading Inventory incorporates recent assessment research and high-interest passages in both Spanish and English.*

- *DRA* (Beaver, 2001). An informal reading inventory offering graded reading passages for students to read, rubrics for evaluating students' oral reading, and a handy box in which to store student portfolios.

- *The Flynt/Cooter English * Español Reading Inventory* (Flynt & Cooter, 1999). This easy-to-use tool offers complete informal reading inventories for prekindergarten through grade 12 students in both Spanish and English. The Spanish passages were carefully developed and field-tested with the aid of native Spanish-speaking teacher-researchers from the United States, Mexico, and Central and South America to avoid problems with dialect differences and to maximize their usefulness in U.S. classrooms.

Group Reading Tests

Sometimes it is necessary to quickly assess the reading abilities of children in group settings and gather norm-referenced information. **Norm-referenced tests** compare student performance to a cross section of students at that same grade level or age in other parts of the country who were administered the same test. In this way, students are compared to the average performance of other students taking the same test. Group reading tests described in this section feature norm-referenced data and also offer a few other benefits. For example, these tests are usually available in different versions or *forms* (e.g., Form A, Form B), allowing school systems to measure learning at the beginning of the school year and again at year's end. Group reading tests usually have several levels available, allowing learners to be matched to a test of appropriate difficulty.

The major disadvantage of group reading tests is that they provide little or no usable information for modifying the classroom teacher's curriculum (i.e., informing instruction). Most information yielded by these tests tends to numeric and general (i.e., stanines, percentile rankings, and grade equivalents). In more recent years, educators have begun to turn away from such statistics as grade equivalents in favor of the more meaningful *normal curve equivalents* (NCE) or *stanines*. An example of a group reading test follows.

- *Gates-MacGinitie Reading Tests, Third Edition* (MacGinitie & MacGinitie, 1989). A most popular instrument with school systems and reading researchers, the Gates-MacGinitie assesses children ranging from prereading levels through grade 12. The prereading level, readiness level, and level 1 (kindergarten to 1.9 grade levels) have only one form available, but levels 2 through 10/12 (grades 1.5 to 12.9) have two forms each (Aaron & Gillespie, 1990). Levels 2 through 10/12 have essentially two measures of reading: vocabulary and comprehension.

Individual Diagnostic Reading Tests

Teachers sometimes feel it is necessary to assess an individual student's reading ability using norm-referenced measures. This often happens when new students move

Standardized tests have traditionally been used to assess literacy progress.

into a school district without their permanent records, or when struggling readers are being considered for extra assistance programs such as Title I or special education classes. Following is an example of a commonly used test:

Individual diagnostic tests can be helpful in assessing new students for whom prior assessments or permanent records are not yet available.

• *Woodcock Reading Mastery Tests—Revised* (Woodcock et al., 1987, 1997). The *Woodcock Reading Mastery Tests—Revised* (WRMT-R/NU) is a battery of six individually administered subtests intended to measure reading abilities from kindergarten through adult levels. Subtests cover visual-auditory learning, letter identification, word identification, word attack, word comprehension, and passage comprehension. Its design reveals a skills perspective of reading, and divides the assessment into two sections according to age and ability levels: *readiness* and *reading achievement.* The WRMT-R/NU reports norm-referenced data for both of its forms, as well as insights into remediation. Results may be calculated either manually or using the convenient scoring program developed for personal computers (PCs). This WRMT-R/NU is frequently used by teachers in special education and Title I reading programs.

Other Reading-Related Tests

Finally, many tests, though they may not all be reading tests per se, provide classroom teachers with insights into children's reading behavior. Several examples follow:

• *Fox in a Box* (CTB McGraw-Hill, 2000). An informal criterion-referenced test that provides teachers with a sketch of students' abilities in a number of early reading areas. *Fox in a Box* includes assessment "strands" in phonemic awareness, phonics (alphabet recognition, writing, spelling, decoding), sight word knowledge, and oral reading fluency. The "fox" is a puppet in the kit that can be used to hold students' attention during assessments.

The K-TEA/NU is an individually administered achievement test.

• *Kaufman Test of Educational Achievement* (K-TEA/NU) (Kaufman & Kaufman, 1997). Sometimes teachers require norm-referenced data to determine how a child is progressing compared to other children nationally, such as when teachers are working with a population of students who are performing at atypically high or low levels. That is, working with either struggling readers or gifted students over a long period of time may give teachers a distorted view of what "normal" achievement looks like. The Kaufman Test of Educational Achievement (K-TEA/NU), available in both English and Spanish forms, can provide useful insights in these situations.

The K-TEA/NU is a norm-referenced test yielding information in the areas of reading, mathematics, and spelling. Intended for students in grades 1 to 12, the K-TEA/NU is available in a *brief form* for quick assessments (when only standardized data are needed) and a *comprehensive form* (provides both standardized data and insights into classroom remediation). Alternate forms are not available, but the authors suggest that the two versions may be used as pretest–posttest measures.

• *Woodcock-Muñoz Language Survey* (WMLS), English and Spanish Forms (Woodcock & Muñoz-Sandoval, 1993). Teachers, particularly in urban centers, often have a large number of students who are learning English as a second language (ESL). The extent to which students have acquired a listening and speaking vocabulary in English is an important factor in reading instruction because reading (a) is a language skill, and (b) depends on learners having a fairly strong English vocabulary. The WMLS is a widely respected instrument used throughout the United States that takes about 20 minutes to administer. It features two subtests: Oral Language and Reading/Writing.

• *Peabody Picture Vocabulary Test, Third Edition* (PPVT-III) (Dunn & Dunn, 1997). Growth in reading ability is directly related to the student's vocabulary knowledge. In fact, one can only read and understand words that are already known. The PPVT-III is a quickly administered test (11–12 minutes) that indicates how strong a student's vocabulary knowledge is compared to other students of the same age nationally. Results can help the teacher better understand the needs of students in terms of formal and informal vocabulary instruction.

• *Test de Vocabulario en Imágenes Peabody* (TVIP), (Dunn, Lugo, Padilla, & Dunn, 1986). This test is an adaptation of an early version of the previously described *Peabody Picture Vocabulary Test* for native Spanish speakers. It takes about 10 to 15 minutes to administer and measures Spanish vocabulary knowledge.

Problems with Many Traditional Reading Tests

In this section, we have examined some of the traditional reading tests prevalent in many American schools. The primary strength of these instruments is their usefulness for documenting general reading performance. When compared to more *authentic* comprehensive reading assessment methods, which are discussed in the next section, traditional assessments sometimes seem woefully inadequate. Following is a discussion of a few of the specific problems or shortcomings of traditional tests.

Traditional assessments are often based on incomplete views of the reading process.

• *Traditional tests often mirror limited views of the reading process.* Although reading research has confirmed the balanced nature of the reading act, traditional reading assessment has remained in the relative dark ages of skills-only teaching. Traditional reading assessment stubbornly clings to the notion that reading can be conveniently divided into constituent pieces and discrete elements such as phonics knowledge, hierarchical comprehension elements, and reading and study skills. Although these factors are, of course, essential, they ignore other important elements such as the student's background knowledge, language development, motivation to read, family support factors, learning environment, and writing connections. In short, traditional reading assessment can be very limited and simplistic in nature.

• *Traditional reading assessment fails to help teachers improve instruction.* Traditional assessment all too often yields information of little help for improving classroom teaching. Because their purpose is to provide national comparisons for schools and school districts, not to chart the progress of students in reading development, many traditional assessments, such as norm-referenced tests, fall short in helping the teacher plan instruction.

• *Traditional reading assessment fails to use authentic reading tasks.* Children are frequently assessed using only snippets of real reading passages, words and sounds in isolation, and multiple-choice formats. Reading assessment, when it is good classroom assessment (Valencia, 1990), looks like real reading. We should use different forms of text including stories, informational text, poetry, and environmental print. Our assessments should have students reading for different purposes and in different contexts.

• *Traditional reading tests provide incomplete appraisals of reading ability.* Most traditional assessments are paper-and-pencil tests that focus only on a few aspects of the reading act. Important parts of reading—such as interest, motivation, and the ability to decode unfamiliar words when reading self-selected books—are not investigated. Developing powerful learning opportunities for students is difficult with such limited information.

• *Traditional assessments, especially standardized tests, are commonly viewed negatively by classroom teachers for a number of important reasons.* Many teachers have found that standardized tests create a negative feeling in their classrooms and often hinder learning. Two classroom teachers (Nolan & Berry, 1993) summed up the feelings of many on this point in a published interview:

> [We] resented how the district's standardized tests intruded on class time, created an atmosphere of anxiety, and failed to reflect the complexity of [reading] learning, the quality and presentation of the text, or the conditions of collaboration and discussion that are valued in [a thriving] classroom. (p. 606)

There are legitimate needs for traditional assessment in our schools, particularly to satisfy mandated state and local accountability requirements. However, the needs of the classroom teacher go well beyond what traditional testing can satisfy. The day-to-day needs of classroom teachers—the need for data that inform instruction—are more effectively addressed in *comprehensive reading assessment,* the subject of the next section.

Many teachers feel that excessive traditional testing common in most school districts creates stress and negative effects in students.

COMPREHENSIVE READING ASSESSMENT

Traditional reading assessment is often termed *formal* or *product assessment.* That is, much of the information yielded from these assessments (except for *informal reading inventories*) is oriented toward bottom-line numerical comparisons of children and offers the classroom teacher very little that informs instruction (Cambourne

Comprehensive reading assessments focus on "authentic" reading tasks to gauge literacy development in students.

& Turbill, 1990; Clay, 1990). On the other hand, **comprehensive reading assessment** includes some traditional measures, but is generally much more *process-oriented* (i.e., uses real reading or *authentic* tasks as the context for assessment). Comprehensive reading assessments survey student development in reading and writing processes based on developmental theory and scientific research.

Teachers who develop high-quality comprehensive reading assessments frequently have several purposes in mind. The central purpose is to inform their teaching decisions for improved student learning (Fountas & Pinnell, 1996). Teachers have a fundamental need to know where students are in terms of their reading development and to create a record of their progress. Another need is to discover what students can do in reading.

Comprehensive reading assessments assist teachers in another primary responsibility: reporting student progress to parents, administrators, school board members, and other stakeholders (Fountas & Pinnell, 1996). Finally, comprehensive reading assessments help teachers learn more about the reading process itself and how children can be assisted in becoming fluent readers.

Portfolio Assessment Schemes: An Approach for Collecting Information

Portfolio assessment schemes are a popular and extremely effective vehicle for authentically assessing reading development (Valencia, McGinley, & Pearson, 1990; Farr, 1991; Tierney, Carter, & Desai, 1991; Glazer & Brown, 1993). The reading

Comprehensive literacy assessment tools, including *portfolios,* allow teachers to "see" the processes individual children use when they read and write.

portfolio is both a *philosophy,* or way of viewing assessment, and a *place* for gathering pieces of evidence indicating student growth and development in reading (Valencia, 1990). Cooter and Flynt (1996) explain that the *philosophy* of portfolios suggests that we should consider all factors related to reading when assessing students.

Portfolios are consistent with newer curriculum designs (Farr, 1991, p. 2) that emphasize the integration of the language arts (listening, speaking, reading and writing). They focus on the processes of constructing meaning, use of quality literature and other information aids, problem solving and application skills, and student collaborations. Therefore, portfolios are a means for dynamic and ongoing assessment (Tierney, 1992). (p. 42)

Portfolios also represent a *place* for collecting student work samples that provide "windows" on the strategies used by students when reading and writing (Jongsma, 1989; Farr, 1991; Tierney, 1992; Farr & Tone, 1994). File folders, storage boxes, hanging files, and notebooks are a few of the common portfolio containers used to hold daily samples or "evidence" of student learning.

Two sets of portfolios are often maintained in the classroom (Cooter & Flynt, 1996): *student portfolios* and *file portfolios.* Student portfolios are kept in the possession of students and may be added to by either the student or the teacher. File portfolios are year-long files kept by the teacher on each student. They include representative samples of student development over time.

A portfolio approach places the responsibility and control for reading assessment back into the hands of those most affected by it—teachers and students (Valencia, 1990) and provides the foundation for teacher/student conferences (Farr, 1991). Portfolio assessment schemes develop a vivid picture of how students are progressing from one reading developmental milestone to the next. They are certainly not the *only* way to conduct reading assessments, but they are an effective mode for many teachers.

Portfolio assessment is both a philosophy and a place for gathering student data.

List some of the process and product features of portfolio assessment.

Kid Watching: Classroom Observations of Children and Reading

For many teachers, the most basic assessment strategy is systematic observations of children engaged in the reading act, or **kid watching.** Clay, in her classic book *The Early Detection of Reading Difficulties* (1985) explains her philosophy concerning observations:

> I am looking for movement in appropriate directions. . . . For if I do not watch what [the student] is doing, and if I do not capture what is happening in records of some kind, Johnny, who never gets under my feet and who never comes really into a situation where I can truly see what he is doing, may, in fact, for six months or even a year, practice behaviours that will handicap him in reading. (p. 49)

In kid watching, we are looking for positive "movement" in literacy learning (Clay, 1985).

Thus, observation is a critical tool at the teacher's disposal for early assessment of students and their abilities.

There seems to be consensus among reading experts regarding the critical features of observation (Holdaway, 1979; Clay, 1985; Rhodes & Dudley-Marling, 1988). A summary of these important points and additional points we recommend follows:

• *Begin with a knowledge of reading standards and "reading development milestones."* The teacher must fully understand the state's grade level standards, as

Teachers must have a thorough understanding of how reading develops for kid watching to be instructive.

Think of ways that you could make kid watching a regular part of your teaching schedule.

Observations should be tied to the reading standards adopted by the school district.

well as the stages of reading development, to be an effective observer. These standards and stages of learning, or *reading development milestones,* are described in some detail in the next section of this chapter.

• *Adopt an attitude of researcher.*   When making observations, it is important to step out of the usual directive role of teacher into a more investigative role. As teachers, we need to observe, reflect on what we have seen, and then plan appropriate next steps in learning.

• *Make multiple observations over time (longitudinal).*   Teachers should look at reading behaviors over time to detect *patterns* of ability and/or needs. One-shot observations tend to be unreliable indicators of where students are in their development and can lead to inaccurate conclusions. By making numerous observations over time, the teacher will be able to document growth and identify areas needing further development. In general, the younger the child or the poorer the reader, the more time the teacher will need to spend both observing and pondering observations (Clay, 1985).

• *Observe real reading in varied situations.*   Most commercial reading tests require students to read in very artificial situations. The text may be boring, use stilted language, or be limited to narrative (story) compositions. Children should be observed reading self-selected materials as well as district-required reading materials. In addition, it is important to observe students reading in varied settings (whole-class readings, teacher–student conferences, small reading group).

• *Document observations with regularity and clarity.*   Observations should be recorded promptly and regularly. All entries should be easy to read and tied to the reading standards agreed upon in the school or district. In fact, any other teacher in the school district should be able to read and interpret a student's reading portfolio without difficulty. In addition to written records, many teachers now include observation guides and videotape or audiotape recordings of student observations in their assessment portfolio.

Reading Milestones

One semester a young student teacher was busily making notes on a clipboard as she watched second graders working away. The students were engaged in activities such as reading, planning writing projects, working at a computer station, listening to books on tape while following along in small books, and several other reading-learning tasks. When the student teacher was asked by the visiting college supervisor what she was working on, she said, "I'm noting what the children are doing as part of their reading portfolio." The supervisor responded, "That's great! How do you know what to watch for?" After a few moments of the student teacher appearing bewildered, the supervisor said, "If you have time later, I'd like to share with you information about reading milestones. They are observable learning stages that can be noted as part of your assessment profiling system." She quickly accepted the offer and seemed to welcome the information enthusiastically.

To be an effective kid watcher, the teacher must gain an understanding of the stages of reading development through which children grow. In this section, we share basic information about the early developmental stages of reading according to the latest research. Knowing which of these skills students have and have not acquired will help you construct a classroom profile and plan whole-class, small-group, and individualized instruction.

In the latter part of the 1990s, a major urban school district set out to identify what they called "end-of-year benchmark reading skills" for kindergarten through third grade (R. Cooter, 2003). With the benefit of a major grant, they established a team composed of notable reading researchers, master teachers, and distinguished school administrators to review the latest reading research and develop a list of the reading skills that, if acquired by the end of third grade, would likely result in children reading fluently. R. Cooter and K. S. Cooter (1999) have adapted that list, adding the skills their own research indicates are essential for this range of students. They have also included reading skills required by most states as part of their accountability systems, thus giving this list a degree of national validity. Be sure to note that the use of grade level indicators for their **reading milestones** (see Figure 9.2) is only an approximation, because children develop at differing rates. We recommend that you carefully consider these skills as you attempt to assess young or otherwise emerging readers.

The end-of-the-year benchmark reading skills resulted from research started in a major urban school district.

Comprehensive reading assessment begins with an understanding of these reading milestones. It is essential that teachers come to know these observable behaviors and abilities well in order to describe where students are in their development, and to aid in planning future instruction fitted to the students' respective zones of proximal development.

METHODS FOR ASSESSING READING DEVELOPMENT

Once teachers have a clear understanding of reading learning milestones, they are ready to use this knowledge to selectively gather information on individual students. The goal: to plan instruction based on the needs of individual children. As this information is gathered and sorted, you will be able to plan instruction for large groups when most of the children have a demonstrated need for a particular reading skill, small-group instruction when only a few students need a given skill, or individualized instruction when only a single child needs a particular reading skill to continue his or her growth.

Classroom assessment methods should be easy to implement and reasonably quick to administer, and should reveal the needs of individual students.

In this section, we present a variety of effective ways to gather data on student reading development. Of course, it is only a partial list, because of the limitations of a general reading textbook. However, these are arguably the most effective and commonly used strategies in use by master reading teachers. We urge you to pay particular attention to ways of administering running records, as they are incredibly helpful in planning instruction, especially up through grade 3. As you gain complete competence in each of these strategies, we encourage you to read further in a more specialized text (see Reutzel & Cooter, 2003, listed at the end of this chapter) and also to consider taking an advanced graduate course in reading assessment to increase your knowledge of assessment methods.

Running Records

From the earliest days of formal reading instruction, the ability to decode words in print has been viewed as essential (Reutzel & Cooter, 2003). In 1915, for example, William S. Gray published the Standardized Oral Reading Paragraphs for grades 1 through 8, which focused on oral reading errors and reading speed exclusively. In the 1930s and 1940s, Durrell (1940) and Betts (1946) discussed at length the value of

Running records are a preferred method for assessing oral reading.

Figure 9.2 Reading Milestones for Grades K–3

Kindergarten Literacy Milestones (English and Spanish)

Book and Print Awareness

K.BA.1	Knows parts of a book and their functions
K.BA.2	Follows print word by word when listening to familiar text read aloud

Phonemic Awareness

K. PA.1	Simple awareness that spoken words have individual sound parts
K. PA.2	Orally segmenting and blending simple compound words
K. PA.3	Orally segmenting and blending simple two-syllable words
K. PA.4	Orally segmenting and blending simple onsets and rimes
K. PA.5	Orally segmenting and blending sound by sound
K. PA.6	Oddity tasks and sound manipulation
K. PA.7	Produces a rhyming word when given a spoken word

Decoding and Word Recognition

K. D.1	Recognizes and names all uppercase and lowercase letters (an alphabetic principle component)
K. D.2	Knows that the sequence of written letters and the sequence of spoken sounds in a word are the same (an alphabetic principle component)
K. D.S.1	Applies letter sound knowledge of consonant-vowel patterns to produce syllables (Spanish only)

Spelling and Writing

K.S.1	Writes independently most uppercase and lowercase letters
K.S.2	Begins using phonemic awareness and letter knowledge to create simple "temporary" (invented) spellings

Oral Reading

K.OR.1	Recognizes some words by sight, including a few common "environmental print" words

Language Comprehension and Response to Text

K.C.1	Uses less new vocabulary and language in own speech
K.C.2	Distinguishes whether simple sentences do or don't make sense
K.C.3	Connects information and events in text to life experiences
K.C.4	Uses graphic organizers to comprehend text with guidance
K.C.5	Retells stories or parts of stories
K.C.6	Understands and follows oral directions
K.C.7	Demonstrates familiarity with a number of books and selections
K.C.8	Explains simple concepts from nonfiction text

First Grade Literacy Milestones (English and Spanish)

Decoding and Word Recognition

1.D.1	Can segment and blend simple compound words
1.D.2	Can segment and blend simple two syllable words
1.D.3	Can segment and blend a one-syllable word using its onset and rime
1.D.4	Decodes phonetically regular one-syllable words and nonsense words accurately

276

Figure 9.2 *continued*

1.D.5	Uses context clues to help identify unknown words in print
1.D.6	Uses context clues plus beginning, medial, and ending sounds in words to decode unknown words in print
1.D.7	Decodes two-syllable words using knowledge of sounds, letters, and syllables including consonants, vowels, blends, and stress (Spanish only)

Spelling and Writing

1.D.1	Spells three- and four-letter short vowel words correctly (English only)
1.D.2	Uses phonics to spell simple one- and two-syllable words independently (temporary and correct spellings)
1.D.3	Uses basic punctuation (periods, question marks, capitalization)
1.D.4	Uses simple graphic organizers to plan writing with guidance
1.D.5	Produces a variety of composition types such as stories, descriptions, and journal entries
1.D.S.1	Recognizes words that use specific spelling patterns such as r/rr, y/ll, s/c/z, q/c/k, g/j, j/x, b/v, ch, h, i/y, gue, and gui (Spanish only)
1.D.S.2	Spells words with two syllables using dieresis marks, accents, r/rr, y/ll, s/c/z, q/c/k, g/j, j/x, b/v, ch, h, and i/y accurately (Spanish only)
1.D.S.3	Uses verb tenses appropriately and consistently (Spanish only)

Oral Reading

1.OR.1	Reads aloud with fluency texts on his/her independent reading level
1.OR.2	Comprehends any text that is on his/her independent reading level
1.OR.3	Uses phonic knowledge to sound out unknown words when reading text
1.OR.4	Recognizes common, irregularly spelled words by sight

Language Comprehension and Response to Text

1.C.1	Reads and comprehends fiction and nonfiction that is appropriate for the second half of grade one
1.C.2	Notices difficulties in understanding text (early metacognition skills)
1.C.3	Connects information and events in text to life experiences
1.C.4	Reads and understands simple written directions
1.C.5	Predicts and justifies what will happen next in stories
1.C.6	Discusses *how, why,* and *what* questions in sharing nonfiction text
1.C.7	Describes new information in his/her own words
1.C.8	Distinguishes whether simple sentences are incomplete or do not make sense
1.C.9	Expands sentences in response to *what, when, where,* and *how* questions
1.C.10	Uses new vocabulary and language in own speech and writing
1.C.11	Demonstrates familiarity with a number of genres including poetry, mysteries, humor, and everyday print sources such as newspapers, signs, phone books, notices, and labels
1.C.12	Summarizes the main points of a story

Reading Fluency and Rate (Minimum Expectations)

1.F.1	Frequent word-by-word reading
1.F.2	Some two- and three-word phrasing

(continued)

Figure 9.2 *continued*

1.F.3	May reread for problem solving or to clarify (strategic reading)
1.F.4	Shows some awareness of syntax and punctuation
1.F.5	Forty (40) words per minute reading rate (minimum)

Second Grade Literacy Milestones (English and Spanish)

Decoding and Word Recognition

2.D.1	Decodes phonetically regular two-syllable words and nonsense words
2.D.S.1	Decodes words with three or more syllables using knowledge of sounds, letters, and syllables including consonants, vowels, blends, and stress (Spanish only)
2.D.S.2	Uses structural cues to recognize words such as compounds, base words, and inflections such as -mente, -ito, and -ando (Spanish only)

Spelling and Writing

2.SW.1	Spells previously studied words and spelling patterns correctly in own writing (application)
2.SW.2	Begins to use formal language patterns in place of oral language patterns in own writing
2.SW.3	Uses revision and editing processes to clarify and refine own writing with assistance
2.SW.4	Writes informative, well-structured reports with organizational help
2.SW.5	Attends to spelling, mechanics, and presentation for final products
2.SW.6	Produces a variety of types of compositions such as stories, reports, and correspondence
2.SW.7	Uses information from nonfiction text in independent writing
2.SW.S.1	Spells words with three or more syllables using silent letters, dieresis marks, accents, verbs, r/rr, y/ll, s/c/z, q/c/k, g/j, j/x, b/v, ch, h, and i/y accurately (Spanish only)

Oral Reading

2.OR.1	Reads aloud with fluency any text that is appropriate for the first half of grade two
2.OR.2	Comprehends any text that is appropriate for the first half of grade two
2.OR.3	Uses phonic knowledge to sound out words, including multisyllable words, when reading text
2.OR.4	Reads irregularly spelled words, diphthongs, special vowel spellings, and common word endings accurately

Language Comprehension and Response to Text

2.C.1	Reads and comprehends both fiction and nonfiction that is appropriate for the second half of grade two
2.C.2	Rereads sentences when meaning is not clear
2.C.3	Interprets information from diagrams, charts, and graphs
2.C.4	Recalls facts and details of text
2.C.5	Reads nonfiction materials for answers to specific questions
2.C.6	Develops literary awareness of character traits, point of view, setting, problem, solution, and outcome

Figure 9.2 *continued*

2.C.7	Connects and compares information across nonfiction selections
2.C.8	Poses possible answers to *how, why,* and *what-if* questions in interpreting nonfiction text
2.C.9	Explains and describes new concepts and information in own words
2.C.10	Identifies part of speech for concrete nouns, active verbs, adjectives, and adverbs
2.C.11	Uses new vocabulary and language in own speech and writing
2.C.12	Demonstrates familiarity with a number of read-aloud and independent reading selections, including nonfiction
2.C.13	Recognizes a variety of print resources and knows their contents, such as joke books, chapter books, dictionaries, atlases, weather reports, and *TV Guide*
2.C.14	Connects a variety of texts to literature and life experiences (language to literacy)
2.C.15	Summarizes a story, including the stated main idea

Reading Fluency and Rate (Minimum Skills)

2.F.1	Combination of word-by-word and fluent phrase reading
2.F.2	Some expressive phrasing
2.F.3	Shows attention to punctuation and syntax
2.F.4	Fifty (50) words per minute reading rate (minimum)

Third Grade Literacy Milestones (English and Spanish)

Decoding and Word Recognition

3.D.1	Uses context clues, phonic knowledge, and structural analysis to decode words

Spelling and Writing

3.SW.1	Spells previously studied words and spelling patterns correctly in own writing
3.SW.2	Uses the dictionary to check and correct spelling
3.SW.3	Uses all aspects of the writing process in compositions and reports with assistance, including
	3.SW.3.1 Combines information from multiple sources in written reports
	3.SW.3.2 Revises and edits written work independently on a level appropriate for first semester of third grade
	3.SW.3.3 Produces a variety of written work (response to literature, reports, semantic maps)
	3.SW.3.4 Uses graphic organizational tools with a variety of texts
	3.SW.3.5 Incorporates elaborate descriptions and figurative language
	3.SW.3.6 Uses a variety of formal sentence structures in own writing
3.SW.S.1	Writes proficiently using orthographic patterns and rules such as qu, use of n before v, m before b, m before p, and changing z to c when adding -es (Spanish only)

(continued)

Figure 9.2 *continued*

3.SW.S.2   Spells words with three or more syllables using silent letters, dieresis marks, accents, verbs, r/rr, y/ll, s/c/z, q/c/k, g/j, j/x, b/v, ch, h, and i/y accurately (Spanish only)

Oral Reading

3.OR.1   Reads aloud with fluency any text that is appropriate for the first half of grade three

3.OR.2   Comprehends any text that is appropriate for the first half of grade three

Language Comprehension and Response to Text

3.C.1   Reads and comprehends both fiction and nonfiction that is appropriate for grade three

3.C.2   Reads chapter books independently

3.C.3   Identifies specific words or phrases that are causing comprehension difficulties (metacognition)

3.C.4   Summarizes major points from fiction and nonfiction text

3.C.5   Can discuss similarities in characters and events across stories

3.C.6   Can discuss underlying theme or message when interpreting fiction

3.C.7   Distinguishes when interpreting nonfiction text between:

        3.C.7.1   Cause and effect

        3.C.7.2   Fact and opinion

        3.C.7.3   Main idea and supporting details

3.C.8   Uses information and reasoning to evaluate opinions

3.C.9   Infers word meaning from roots, prefixes, and suffixes that have been taught

3.C.10   Uses dictionary to determine meanings and usage of unknown words

3.C.11   Uses new vocabulary in own speech and writing

3.C.12   Uses basic grammar and parts of speech correctly in independent writing

3.C.13   Shows familiarity with a number of read-aloud and independent reading selections, including nonfiction

3.C.14   Uses multiple sources to locate information

        3.C.14.1   Tables of contents

        3.C.14.2   Indexes

        3.C.14.3   Internet search engines

3.C.15   Connects a variety of literary texts with life experiences

Reading Fluency

3.F.1   Very few word-by-word interruptions

3.F.2   Reads mostly in larger meaningful phrases

3.F.3   Reads with expression

3.F.4   Attends consistently to punctuation

3.F.5   Rereads to clarify or problem-solve

3.F.6   Sixty (60) words per minute reading rate (minimum)

Cooter, R. B., Jr. & Cooter, K. S. (1999). *BLAST!: Balanced Literacy Assessment System and Training.* Chicago: Rigby.

studying oral reading errors as a way to inform reading instruction. These and other writings began the development of what we now refer to as informal reading inventories (IRI), in which oral reading errors are analyzed.

Half a century after Gray's test was published, Marie Clay (1967) began publishing landmark research detailing a systematic analysis of oral reading errors of emergent readers. The examination and interpretation of the relative "value" of oral reading errors (i.e., semantic and syntactic "acceptability") by Clay helped usher in a new age of understanding of decoding processes.

Clay (1972), in her manual *The Early Detection of Reading Difficulties,* sought to formalize methodology for teachers conducting decoding assessments. Clay's "running records" for analyzing oral reading errors proved to be functional for most classroom teachers. In the next section, we describe in detail how running records are constructed and used to inform classroom teaching.

*Oral reading errors are known as **miscues.***

Conducting Running Records

Marie Clay (1972, 1985, 2000), a New Zealand educator and former president of the International Reading Association, described the **running record** as an informal assessment procedure with high reliability (.90 on error reliabilities) that informs teachers regarding students' decoding development. The procedure is not difficult, but does require practice. Clay estimates that it takes about two hours of practice for teachers to become relatively proficient at running records. In essence, the teacher notes everything the student says or does while reading, including all the correct words read orally and all miscues (Wiener & Cohen, 1997). Clay recommends that three running records be obtained for each child on various levels of difficulty for initial reading assessment. Her criteria for oral reading evaluation are based on words correctly read aloud:

Independent Level (easy to read)   95–100% correct
Instructional Level (ideal for teaching)   90–94% correct
Frustration Level (too difficult)   80–89% correct

Running records using Clay's method are taken without having to mark a prepared script and may be recorded on a sheet of paper, requiring about 10 minutes to transcribe. Guidelines for administration follow:

1. A sample from the book(s) to be used that is 100–200 words in length is needed. For early readers, the text may fall below 100 words. Allow the student to read the passage one or two times before you take the running record.

2. Sit alongside the student while she reads so that you can both see the page. It isn't really necessary to have your own photocopy of the text; a blank sheet of paper will do. Record all accurate reading by making check marks on a sheet of blank paper for each word said correctly. Errors or "miscues" should be noted using the notations indicated in Figure 9.3. Figure 9.4 shows an example of a running record taken using a passage from *The Flynt/Cooter Reading Inventory for the Classroom* (Flynt & Cooter, 2004) using the marking system.

Understanding Miscues: MSV Analysis

Marie Clay (1985) developed a way of interpreting miscues for use in her widely acclaimed *Reading Recovery* program, commonly referred to as **MSV analysis.** This

Figure 9.3 Notating miscues in a running record

Reading Behavior	Notation	Explanation
Accurate Reading	√ √ √ √ √ √	*Notation:* A check is noted for each word pronounced correctly.
Self-Correction	√ √ √ √ attempt SC ─────────────── word in text	The child corrects an error himself. This is not counted as a miscue. *Notation:* "SC" is the notation used for self-corrections.
Omission	───── ──────────── Word in text	A word or words are left out during the reading. *Notation:* A dash mark is written over a line above the word(s) from the text that has been omitted.
Insertion	Word inserted ──────────── ───── 	The child adds a word that is not in the text. *Notation:* The word inserted by the reader is placed above a line and a dash placed below it.
Student Appeal and Assistance	───── A ──────────── Word from text	The child is "stuck" on a word he cannot call and asks (verbal or nonverbal) the teacher for help. *Notation:* "A" is written above a line for "assisted" and the problem word from the text is written below the line.
Repetition	√ √ √ **R** √ √ √	Sometimes children will repeat words or phrases. These repetitions are not scored as an error, but *are* recorded. *Notation:* Write an "R" after the word repeated and draw a line back to the point where the reader returned.
Substitution	Substituted word ──────────── Word from text	The child says a word that is different from the word in the text. *Notation:* The student's substitution word is written above a line under which the correct word from text is written.

Figure 9.3 *continued*

Teacher Assistance	$\dfrac{}{\text{Word from text}}\Big|$ ___ T	The student pauses on a word for five seconds or more, so the teacher tells him/her the word.
		Notation: The letter "T" is written to the right of a line that follows the word from text. A blank is placed above a cross-line to indicate that the student didn't know the word.

way of thinking enables you to determine whether the student uses three primary **cueing strategies** when she encounters a new word and a miscue occurs: Meaning Cues (M), Syntax Cues (S), and Visual Cues (V). Here is a summary based on the work of Flynt and Cooter (2003).

• *M = Semantic (Meaning—Does it make sense?)* In reviewing each miscue, consider whether the student is using meaning cues in her attempt to identify the word. Context clues, picture cues, and information from the passage are examples of meaning cues used by the reader.

• *S = Structure (or Syntax—Does it sound right?)* A rule system or *grammar,* as with all languages, governs the English language. For example, English is essentially based on a "subject–verb" grammar system. *Syntax* is the application of this subject–verb grammar system in creating sentences. The goal in studying *syntax cues* as part of your miscue analysis is to try and determine the extent to which the student unconsciously uses rules of grammar in attempting to identify unknown words in print. For example, if a word in a passage causing a miscue for the reader is a verb, ask yourself whether the student's miscue was also a verb. Consistent use of the appropriate part of speech in miscues (i.e., a noun for a noun, a verb for a verb, articles for articles, etc.) is an indication that the student has internalized the rule system of English grammar and is applying that knowledge in attacking unknown words.

• *V = Visual (Graphophonic—Does it look right?)* Sometimes a miscue looks a good bit like the correct word appearing in the text. The miscue may begin with the same letter or letters, for example saying the *top* for *toy,* or *sit* for *seat.* Another possibility is the letters of the miscue may look very similar to the word appearing in text (e.g., *introduction* for *introspection*). Use of visual cues is essentially the student's ability (or inability) to apply phonics skills. The extent to which readers use visual cues is an important factor to consider when trying to better understand the skills employed by developing readers when attacking unknown words in print.

Applying MSV thinking is fairly simple once you get the hang of it. In Figure 9.5 we return to the miscues previously noted in Figure 9.4 and conduct an MSV analysis on each. Do you see why each interpretation was made?

Figure 9.4 Running record example

Student _____ _Paco_ ___(Grade 2)_____

Title: **The Pig and the Snake**

One day Mr. Pig was walking to	✓ ✓ ✓ ✓ ✓ ✓ ✓
town. He saw a big hole in the	✓ ✓ sam/saw | sc ✓ ✓ ✓ ✓ ✓
road. A big snake was in the	✓ ✓ —/big ✓ ✓ ✓ ✓ ✓
hole. "Help me," said the snake,	✓ ✓ ✓ OUT/— ✓ ✓ ✓
"and I will be your friend." "No, no,"	✓ ✓ ✓ ✓✓ —/friend | A ✓ ✓
said Mr. Pig. "If I help you get	✓ ✓ ✓ ✓ ✓ ✓ ✓ ✓
out you will bite me. You're	✓ ✓ ✓ R ✓ ✓
a snake!" The snake cried and	✓ ✓ ✓ ✓ ✓ ✓
cried. So Mr. Pig pulled the	✓ ✓ ✓ ✓ popped/pulled
snake out of the hole.	✓ ✓ ✓ ✓ ✓
Then the snake said, "Now I am	✓ ✓ ✓ ✓ ✓ ✓ ✓
going to bite you, Mr. Pig."	✓ ✓ ✓ ✓ ✓ ✓
"How can you bite me after	✓ ✓ ✓ ✓ ✓ —/after | T
I helped you out of the hole?"	✓ ✓ ✓ ✓ ✓ ✓ ✓
said Mr. Pig. The snake said,//	✓ ✓ ✓ ✓ ✓ ✓
"You knew I was a snake	✓ ✓ ✓ ✓ ✓ ✓
when you pulled me out!"	✓ ✓ ✓ ✓ ✓

Source: Flynt, E. S., & Cooter, R. B. (2001). *The Flynt/Cooter Reading Inventory for the Classroom, 4/e.* Upper Saddle River, NJ: Merrill/Prentice Hall. Used with permission of the authors.

Figure 9.5 Running record with MSV analysis

Student: Paco (Grade 2)		
Title: **The Pig and the Snake**	**E** MSV	**SC** MSV
One day Mr. Pig was walking to ✓ ✓ ✓ ✓ ✓ ✓ ✓		
town. He saw a big hole in the ✓ ✓ sam|sc ✓ ✓ ✓ ✓ ✓ saw		Ⓜ Ⓢ Ⓥ
road. A big snake was in the ✓ ✓ —/big ✓ ✓ ✓ ✓ ✓	M S V	
hole. "Help me," said the snake, ✓ ✓ ✓ out/— ✓ ✓ ✓	Ⓜ Ⓢ V	
"and I will be your friend." "No, no," ✓ ✓ ✓ ✓✓ —|A ✓ ✓ friend	M S V	
said Mr. Pig. "If I help you get ✓ ✓ ✓ ✓ ✓ ✓ ✓ ✓		
out you will bite me. You're ✓ ✓ ✓ R ✓ ✓		Ⓜ Ⓢ Ⓥ
a snake!" The snake cried and ✓ ✓ ✓ ✓ ✓ ✓		
cried. So Mr. Pig pulled the ✓ ✓ ✓ ✓ popped/pulled	Ⓜ Ⓢ Ⓥ	
snake out of the hole. ✓ ✓ ✓ ✓ ✓		
Then the snake said, "Now I am ✓ ✓ ✓ ✓ ✓ ✓ ✓		
going to bite you, Mr. Pig." ✓ ✓ ✓ ✓ ✓ ✓		
"How can you bite me after ✓ ✓ ✓ ✓ ✓ —|T after	M S V	
I helped you out of the hole?" ✓ ✓ ✓ ✓ ✓ ✓ ✓		
said Mr. Pig. The snake said,// ✓ ✓ ✓ ✓ ✓ ✓		
"You knew I was a snake ✓ ✓ ✓ ✓ ✓ ✓		
when you pulled me out!" ✓ ✓ ✓ ✓ ✓		

Source: Flynt, E. S., & Cooter, R. B. (2001). *The Flynt/Cooter Reading Inventory for the Classroom, 4/e.* Upper Saddle River, NJ Merrill/Prentice Hall. Used with permission of the authors.

Figure 9.6   Flynt/Cooter running record "grid" system.

	Mispronounce	Substitute	Self-correct	Insertions	Teacher assist	Omissions	Other
Hot Shoes							
The guys at (the) I.B. Belcher						1	
Elementary School ~~loved~~ *lived* (SC) all the			1				
new sport shoes. Some ~~wore~~ *wib* the	1						
" Sky High" model by Nicky.							
Others who *really* couldn't ~~afford~~ *buy* Sky		1		1			
Highs would settle for ~~a lesser~~ *another*		1					
shoe. Some liked the "Street							
Smarts" by Concave, or (the)						1	
"Uptown-Downtown"*s* by Beebop.				1			
The Belcher boys ~~got~~ *go* to the point		1					
with their shoes that they could							
~~identify~~ *impea* their friends just by	1						
looking at their ~~feet~~ *shoes* (SC). But the boy			1				
who was the ~~envy~~ *every* of all the fifth		1					
grade was Jamie Lee. He had a							
pair of "High Five Pump'em Ups"							
by Adeedee. The only thing Belcher							
boys loved as *ll much as their*							
shoes was basketball.							
TOTALS	2	4	2	2	0	2	0

An Alternative Running Records System

Flynt and Cooter (1999, 2004) developed a method of scoring running records that makes the process both time efficient and useful to classroom teachers. Adopted in their informal reading inventories, *The Flynt/Cooter Reading Inventory for the Classroom* (2004) and *The English * Español Reading Inventory* (1999), this system involves the use of what they call a "miscue grid." This system can be extremely effective when used with text selections that are matched to student interests.

In the following excerpt from *The Flynt/Cooter Reading Inventory* (Figure 9.6), you will notice how miscues can be noted on the left side of the grid over the text, then tallied after the student has finished reading in the appropriate columns to the right according to miscue type. This process makes the administration quicker and enables teachers to identify error patterns for each oral reading. The "grid" method can easily be adapted by teachers for use with excerpts from any literature sample.

Teachers should preselect passages on a range of reading levels or have students select the passage(s) to be read a day ahead of the actual reading, so that the first 100 words can be transcribed onto the left-hand side of a blank grid patterned after the one shown in Figure 9.6. During the oral reading, tape-record the session so that the reading can later be reviewed for accuracy of transcription. Miscues should be noted in the left-hand column over the text facsimile, using the symbols described earlier for miscues. After all miscues are noted, examine each miscue and make a final determination about its type (mispronunciation, substitution, insertion, etc.), then make a mark in the appropriate grid box on the right side of the form. Only one hash mark is made for each miscue. Once this process is completed, each column is tallied.

In Figure 9.6, you will note that the reader had two mispronunciations, two insertions, and so on. When the student has read several passages for the teacher over a period of weeks and months, it becomes easy to identify "error patterns"—types of miscues that happen regularly—and to plan appropriate instruction for small-group or individual instruction.

Finally, if you decide to use the grid system, be sure and conduct an MSV analysis on each miscue to better understand which cueing systems the reader is using.

For best results, allow students at least some choice in the books to be read for running records.

The Burke Reading Interview

The Burke Reading Interview (Burke, 1987) provides some initial insights into how students see themselves as readers and the reading task in general. The following questions have been adapted from the Burke procedure.

1. When you are reading and come to a word you don't know, what do you do? What else can you do?
2. Which of your friends is a good reader? What makes him/her a good reader?
3. Do you think your teacher ever comes to a word she doesn't know when reading? What do you think she does when that happens?
4. If you knew that one of your friends was having problems with his or her reading, what could you tell your friend that would help?
5. How would a teacher help your friend with reading problems?
6. How do you think you learned to read?
7. Are you a good reader?
8. What would you like to be able to do better as a reader?

Interest Inventory

Getting to know students is critical if the teacher is to have insights into background knowledge, oral language abilities, and the selection of reading materials that will be of interest. An interest inventory that is administered either one-to-one or in small groups is a great tool for getting to know students, and we offer one example in Figure 9.7.

Concepts About Print

Teachers in the primary grades must understand in some detail what children know about print concepts. The *Concepts About Print* (CAP) test was designed by Marie Clay (1985) to help teachers establish priorities in reading instruction for emergent

Figure 9.7   Interest inventory

Interest Inventory

Student's Name _____

Date _____

Instructions: Please answer the following questions on a separate sheet of paper.

1.   If you could have three wishes, what would they be?
2.   What would you do with $50,000?
3.   What things in life bother you most?
4.   What kind of person would you like to be when you are older?
5.   What are your favorite classes at school, and why?
6.   Who do you think is the greatest person? Why do you think so?
7.   Who is your favorite person? Why?
8.   What do you like to do with your free time?
9.   Do you read any parts of the newspaper? Which parts?
10. How much TV do you watch each day? What are your favorite shows, and why?
11. What magazines do you like to read?
12. Name three of your favorite movies.
13. What do you like best about your home?
14. What books have you enjoyed reading?
15. What kind of books would you like to read in the future?

---

and early readers. Clay's test assesses some 24 basic print awareness elements, including: front of a book, print versus pictures, left-to-right progression, changes in word order, changes in letter order in words, meaning of a period, and location of a capital letter. The assessment is carried out using one of two available books, *Sand, Stones, Follow Me Moon,* and *No Shoes.* The procedure is for the teacher to read one of the books with the student and ask such questions as where to begin reading, which way to go, and where to go next (Fountas & Pinnell, 1996). Results of the CAP test can be especially helpful to kindergarten and first grade teachers who want to establish an initial class profile of strengths and needs. A listing of the concepts about print assessed on the CAP test is shown in Figure 9.8.

Alphabet Knowledge (Early Readers)

Alphabet knowledge is a critical stage of literacy development following phonemic awareness.

Knowledge of the alphabet is essential in early reading instruction: it provides teachers and students with common language for discussing graphophonic relationships. Assessment of alphabet knowledge should occur in two contexts: letters in isolation and letter recognition within words and sentences. We recommend that alphabet knowledge be assessed as part of the print awareness test discussed previously.

Figure 9.8 Selected concepts about print surveyed on the CAP test (Clay, 1985)*

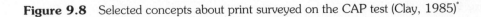

Selected Print Concepts

Front of the book
Knows that print contains the author's message
Knows where to start reading
Knows which way to go when reading
Return sweep to the left
Word by word matching
First and last concept
Bottom of the picture
Left page before right
Notices one change in word order
Notices one change in letter order
Knows the meaning of the question mark (?)
Knows the meaning of the period (.)
Knows the meaning of the comma (,)
Knows the meaning of quotation marks (" ")
Can identify the first and last letter of a word
Can identify one letter and two letters
Can identify capital letters

Note: The learner is asked to identify each of the following within the context of a special book (e.g., *Sand* or *Stones*) developed for this purpose.

Additional Observation Checklists and Scales

Linda Lamme and Cecilia Hysmith (1991) recommend a scale that can be used to identify key developmental behaviors in emergent readers. It describes 11 levels often seen in the elementary school and could be used in tandem with the much more comprehensive reading learning milestones previously discussed. Following is a slight adaptation of that scale:

Level 11: The student can read fluently from books and other reading materials.
Level 10: The student seeks out new sources of information. He or she volunteers to share information from books with other children.
Level 9: The student has developed the ability to independently use context clues, sentence structure, structural analysis, and phonic analysis to read new passages.
Level 8: The student reads unfamiliar stories haltingly (not fluently), but requires little adult assistance.
Level 7: The student reads familiar stories fluently.
Level 6: The student reads word-by-word. He or she recognizes words in a new context.
Level 5: The student memorizes text and can pretend to "read" a story.
Level 4: The student participates in reading by doing such things as supplying words that rhyme and predictable text.

> *The National Research Centers provide many resources on assessment. Link to their site from Chapter 9 on our Companion Website at www.prenhall.com/reutzel.*

Figure 9.9   Diffily's classroom observation checklist

| Student's Name _____ | | | | | Date |

Literacy Development Checklist					
	Seldom				Often
Chooses books for personal enjoyment	1	2	3	4	5
Knows print/picture difference	1	2	3	4	5
Knows print is read from left to right	1	2	3	4	5
Asks to be read to	1	2	3	4	5
Asks that story be read again	1	2	3	4	5
Listens attentively during story time	1	2	3	4	5
Knows what a title is	1	2	3	4	5
Knows what an author is	1	2	3	4	5
Knows what an illustrator is	1	2	3	4	5
In retellings, repeats 2+ details	1	2	3	4	5
Tells beginning, middle, end	1	2	3	4	5
Can read logos	1	2	3	4	5
Uses text in functional ways	1	2	3	4	5
"Reads" familiar books to self/others	1	2	3	4	5
Can read personal words	1	2	3	4	5
Can read sight words from books	1	2	3	4	5
Willing to "write"	1	2	3	4	5
Willing to "read" personal story	1	2	3	4	5
Willing to dictate story to adult	1	2	3	4	5

Gratefully used by the authors with the permission of Deborah Diffily, Ph. D., Alice Carlson, Applied Learning Center, Ft. Worth, TX.

Level 3:   The student talks about or describes pictures. He or she pretends to read (storytelling). He or she makes up words that go along with pictures.

Level 2:   The student watches pictures as an adult reads a story.

Level 1:   The student listens to a story but does not look at the pictures.

Many teachers find that checklists that include a *Likert scale* (a five-point scale) can be useful in student portfolios because many reading behaviors become more fluent over time. One example developed by Diffily (1994) is shown in Figure 9.9.

Fluency Evaluation

Fluency *includes the ability to read at an appropriate rate.*

Reading fluency, as described in Chapter 7, is the ability of students to read at an appropriate speed and with proper phrasing. An informal assessment of fluency through teacher observations is not difficult, but more formal methods can consume a great deal of valuable classroom time. Two effective methods that streamline the process considerably are presented in this section.

Multidimensional Fluency Scale

Zutell and Rasinski (1991) have developed a *Multidimensional Fluency Scale* (MFS), which serves as a useful informal assessment of fluency. The MFS offers a practical measurement of students' oral reading fluency that provides clear and valid information. To administer an MFS, the teacher will collect a student self-selected passage of 200 to 300 words, the Multidimensional Fluency Scale document (see Figure 9.10), and a cassette tape player/recorder with blank tape.

Reutzel and Cooter (2003) recommend that teachers have students rehearse a familiar self-selected word passage (200–300 words) at least three times prior to using the Multidimensional Fluency Scale. It may be informative for teachers also to observe the difference in a student's fluency with a practiced, self-selected, familiar text and with an unpracticed, teacher-selected, unfamiliar text chosen at the child's approximate grade level.

Rubric for Fluency Evaluation

The Rubric for Fluency Evaluation (Fountas & Pinnell, 1996) is recommended as a formal assessment technique. (A **rubric** is a tool for scoring student work; the concept is discussed in greater detail later in the chapter.) Children are asked to read aloud a selection they have read twice before and can read with at least 90 percent accuracy. The oral reading should be taped for analysis purposes (this part could actually be done by students as a center activity or as an activity carried out by an adult volunteer). Listen to the tape and evaluate the oral reading using the Rubric for Fluency Evaluation shown in Figure 9.11, which we have adapted from Fountas and Pinnell (1996).

Cassette recordings of oral reading can help teachers verify the accuracy of their fluency assessments.

Reading Logs

Reading logs are daily records of student reading habits and interests, usually during sustained silent reading (SSR) periods (Cambourne & Turbill, 1990). Students keep these records for the teacher on simple forms kept in their student reading portfolio folder at their desks or another appropriate location. Reading logs list the date, book or text they have read, and page numbers.

Retellings

One of the best ways to find out if a student understands a story he or she has read is through retellings (Gambrell, Pfeiffer, & Wilson, 1985; Morrow, 1985). Retellings can be accomplished in many ways. First, the teacher may wish to use pictures from the story as a memory prompt. As the teacher flashes pictures sequentially from the book or story, the child retells the story from memory. A second option is *unaided recall,* or retelling without pictures or other prompts. We recommend a two-step process, in which the teacher begins by having the student retell everything he or she can remember about the passage. If it is a narrative passage, the teacher can use a record sheet like the one shown in Figure 9.12 to record critical elements of the story grammar the student has recalled. After the student stops retelling the first time, the teacher asks, "What else can you remember?" Usually the student will recall one or more bits of information. The teacher continues to ask the child, "What else do you

Figure 9.10   Multidimensional fluency scale

Multidimensional Fluency Scale (MFS)
(Zutell & Rasinski, 1991)

Use the following scales to rate reader fluency on the three dimensions of phrasing, smoothness, and pace.

A. **Phrasing**

1. Monotonic with little sense of phrase boundaries, frequent word-by-word reading.

2. Frequent two- and three-word phrases, giving the impression of choppy reading; improper stress and intonation that fail to mark ends of sentences and clauses.

3. Mixture of run-ons, mid-sentence pauses for breath, and possibly some choppiness; reasonable stress/intonation.

4. Generally well phrased, mostly in clause and sentence units, with adequate attention to expression.

B. **Smoothness**

1. Frequent extended pauses, hesitations, false starts, sound-outs, repetitions, and/or multiple attempts.

2. Several "rough spots" in text where extended pauses, hesitations, etc. are more frequent and disruptive.

3. Occasional breaks in smoothness caused by difficulties with specific words and/or structures.

4. Generally smooth reading with some breaks, but word and structure difficulties are resolved quickly, usually through self-correction.

C. **Pace** (during sections of minimal disruption)

1. Slow and laborious.

2. Moderately slow.

3. Uneven mixture of fast and slow reading.

4. Consistently conversational.

From "Training Teachers to Attend to Their Students' Oral Reading Fluency," by J. Zutell and T. Rasinski, 1991, *Theory Into Practice, 30*(3), pp. 211–217.

remember?" until he or she cannot remember anything more. Then the teacher refers to the story grammar record sheet for any categories (e.g., setting, characters) not addressed by the student and asks direct questions about the unaddressed areas. This is another form of aided recall.

Story Maps

Story maps (Beck & McKeown, 1981; Routman, 1988) can be used to determine whether a child understands the main parts of a narrative passage. Like the story grammar map previously mentioned in Chapter 7, the same story grammar elements

Figure 9.11 Rubric for fluency evaluation

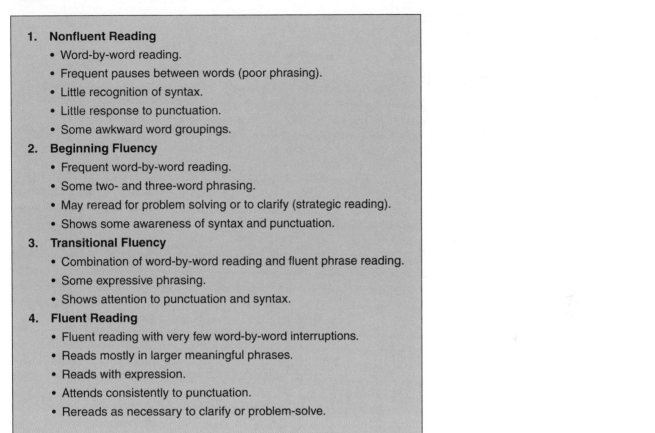

1. **Nonfluent Reading**
   - Word-by-word reading.
   - Frequent pauses between words (poor phrasing).
   - Little recognition of syntax.
   - Little response to punctuation.
   - Some awkward word groupings.
2. **Beginning Fluency**
   - Frequent word-by-word reading.
   - Some two- and three-word phrasing.
   - May reread for problem solving or to clarify (strategic reading).
   - Shows some awareness of syntax and punctuation.
3. **Transitional Fluency**
   - Combination of word-by-word reading and fluent phrase reading.
   - Some expressive phrasing.
   - Shows attention to punctuation and syntax.
4. **Fluent Reading**
   - Fluent reading with very few word-by-word interruptions.
   - Reads mostly in larger meaningful phrases.
   - Reads with expression.
   - Attends consistently to punctuation.
   - Rereads as necessary to clarify or problem-solve.

Adapted from Fountas, I. C., and Pinnell, G. S. (1996). *Guided Reading: Good First Reading for All Children:* Portsmouth, NH: Heinemann.

are used. The task is for students to complete a story map (Figure 9.13) after the completion of a story. A generic format, like the one shown, can be applied to almost any narrative text.

Teacher-Made Cloze Tests

A common assessment strategy is the use of teacher-made cloze tests. Cloze tests ("cloze" is derived from the word *closure*) cause students to use their knowledge of word order (syntax) and sentence meaning (semantics) to guess a missing word in print. A cloze passage is constructed as follows:

Explain how cloze passages could be useful for both assessment and teaching sessions connected to context clue development.

1. Select a narrative or expository passage.

2. Type or scan the passage onto a classroom computer. The first sentence should be typed exactly as it appears in the original text. Beginning with the second sentence, one of the first five words is deleted and replaced with a blank. Then every fifth word is deleted and replaced with a blank.

Figure 9.12   Story grammar retelling record sheet

Student's Name _____ Date _____

Story _____

Source/Book _____

Category	*Prompt Questions (After Retelling)*	*Student's Retelling*
Setting	Where did this story take place?	
	When did this story happen?	
Characters	Who were the characters in this story?	
	Who was the main character(s) in the story?	
	Describe _____ in the story.	
Challenge	What is the main challenge or problem in the story?	
	What were the characters trying to do?	
Events	What were the most important things that happened in the story?	
	What did _____ do in the story?	
Solution	How was the challenge/problem solved?	
	What did _____ do to solve the problem?	
	How did the other characters solve their problems?	
Theme	What was this author trying to tell us?	
	What did _____ learn at the end of the story?	

3. Students then silently read the passage all the way through once before attempting to fill in the blanks.

4. Score the cloze passage using a one-third/one-half formula: If a student correctly guesses *more* than one-half of the deleted words, then the passage is on his independent reading level. If a student correctly guesses *less* than one-third of the missing words, then the passage is too difficult for classroom instruction at this time (the student's frustration level). Scores falling between the one-third to one-half criteria are within the student's instructional level range. With help from the teacher or peers, the student can succeed in this level passage, because it falls within his or her zone of proximal development (see sections in Chapter 3 dealing with the teachings of L. Vygotsky for a review of this concept).

Questioning

Questioning is a most basic and effective means of assessing reading comprehension, and is dealt with at some length in Chapter 6.

Figure 9.13 Story map form

Story Map

Name _____ Date_____

Title _____ Author _____

Setting (Where and when did this story take place?)

Characters (Who were the main characters in this story?)

Challenge (What is the main challenge or problem in the story?)

Events (What were the events that happened in the story to solve the problem/challenge?)

    Event 1.

    Event 2.

    Event 3.

(List all the important events that happened.)

Solution (How was the challenge/problem solved or not solved?)

Theme (What was this author trying to tell us?)

Adapted from *Transitions: From Literature to Literacy* by R. Routman, 1988, Portsmouth, NH: Heinemann.

Family Surveys of Reading Habits

We recently observed a friend of ours who has a heart condition going through his normal daily activities with a small radio-like device attached to his belt. When asked what this gadget was, he indicated that it was a heart monitor. He went on to say that the device constantly measured his heart rate for an entire day to provide the doctor with a reliable account of his normal heart rhythms in the real world of daily activity. Traditional reading assessment has often failed to give teachers such a real world look at students' reading ability by restricting the assessment to school settings. So the question posed here is, "How do we acquire information about a student's

Figure 9.14   Family survey

September 6, 200____

Dear Adult Family Member:

As we begin the new school year, I would like to know a little more about your child's reading habits at home. This information will help me provide the best possible learning plan for your child this year. Please take a few minutes to answer the questions below and return in the self-addressed stamped envelope provided. Should you have any questions, feel free to phone me at XXX–XXXX.

Cordially,

Mrs. Shelley

---

1. My child likes to read the following at least once a week (check all that apply):

Comic books _____	Sports page _____
Magazines (example: *Highlights*) _____	Library books _____
Cereal boxes _____	Cooking recipes _____
T.V. Guide _____	Funny papers _____

Others (please name):

2. Have you noticed your child having any reading problems? If so, please explain briefly.

3. What are some of your child's favorite books?

4. If you would like a conference to discuss your child's reading ability, please indicate which days and times (after school) would be most convenient.

Standards Note
Standard 5.8: The reading professional will be able to implement effective strategies to include parents as partners in the literacy development of their children. Family surveys are a preliminary step in involving parents, who are their children's "first and best" teachers. Study Figure 9.14 and enhance it.

reading habits and abilities away from the somewhat artificial environment of the school?" One way is to assess what is happening in the home using family surveys.

Family surveys are *brief* questionnaires (too long and they'll never be answered!) sent to adult family members periodically to provide teachers insights into reading behaviors at home. Taken into consideration with other assessment evidence from the classroom, family surveys enable teachers to develop a more accurate profile of the child's reading ability. An example of a family survey is provided in Figure 9.14.

EVALUATING YOUR PROGRAM: ASSESSING THE BIG PICTURE

Comprehensive reading assessment implies that teachers look at *all* relevant factors in the teaching and learning process. Teachers should develop a careful analysis of the classroom reading program to determine whether or not it meets the needs of all children. We suggest you begin your analysis by considering the following:

- *Theoretical orientation:* What do you believe about how children learn to read? To which theoretical view of the reading process do you subscribe (see Chapter 3)? To which instructional model do you subscribe (subskills, skills, comprehensive reading, transitional)?

- *Alignment of theory and practice:* How well does your program align with your theoretical beliefs? Are there any elements that do not seem to fit? If so, what can you do to make your beliefs and practices more consistent? *Suggestion:* Review the seven principles in Chapter 1, and compare them to your usual teaching routines to determine which ones may not be consistent with comprehensive reading ideals.

- *Resources:* What resources are available for your program that have not already been tapped (e.g., professional teaching materials at the school, family volunteers, Reading Is Fundamental [R.I.F.] books, support for purchasing learning materials from the PTA, adopt-a-school programs with corporate partners)?

- *Struggling Readers:* What is your procedure for struggling readers? Do you have an intervention program established in your classroom for recovering readers having learning problems?

Evaluating the Classroom Environment

Teachers making transitions toward comprehensive reading instruction often need to consider making adjustments to the classroom environment. This is important because the classroom environment affects student attitudes and, thus, reading performance. Ideally, the classroom environment should approach the comfort level of a home environment if one is to maximize learning potential. Comparing the current classroom environment with those presented in Chapters 10 through 13 will help you determine whether classroom modifications are needed.

Self-Rating Scales

No one knows better than the reader how he or she is doing in reading. A teacher carrying out an assessment agenda should never overlook the obvious: Ask kids how they're doing! Although this is best achieved in a one-on-one discussion setting, large class sizes frequently make it a prohibitive practice. A good alternative to one-to-one interviews for older elementary children is a student self-rating scale, in which students complete a questionnaire tailored to obtain specific information about the reader from the reader's point of view. One example is illustrated in Figure 9.15 for a teacher interested in reading and study strategies used with social studies readings. Whichever reading skills are to be surveyed, remember to keep self-rating scales focused and brief.

Don't forget to ask the obvious: Ask students what they feel are their reading strengths and needs.

Figure 9.15   Self-rating scale: Reading social studies

Reading Social Studies

Name _____ Date _____

1. The first three things I usually do when I begin reading a chapter in social studies are (number 1, 2, 3):

   _____ Look at the pictures.

   _____ Read the chapter through one time silently.

   _____ Look at the new terms and definitions.

   _____ Read the questions at the end of the chapter.

   _____ Read the first paragraph or introduction.

   _____ Skip around and read the most interesting parts.

   _____ Skim the chapter.

   _____ Preview the chapter.

2. What is hardest for me about social studies is . . .

3. The easiest thing about social studies is . . .

4. The thing(s) I like best about reading social studies is (are) . . .

Additional Suggestions for Using Reading Portfolios

Implementing a portfolio-style assessment program can be challenging. In our experience, attention to several details not previously mentioned can lead to a successful experience, including the development of an implementation plan, record-keeping systems, and the use of time management strategies. There are also a few pitfalls to avoid when constructing comprehensive reading assessment programs. In this section, we discuss what we have learned about constructing reading portfolios, as well as other helpful ideas suggested in the professional literature.

Develop a Plan for Constructing Reading Portfolios

Implementation of reading portfolios can often seem overwhelming to many teachers just getting started. Success usually depends on having a simple logic to guide one's choices in this otherwise complex process. Margaret Puckett and Janet Black (1994) have described some key considerations for teachers as they begin to construct a portfolio system. They suggest that teachers (a) decide which basic components will be used, (b) scrutinize information already at hand to decide what additional information may be needed to implement the assessment plan, and (c) decide how portfolios will be used to make teaching decisions and to report progress to families.

Using Rubrics to Improve Reading Analyses

Rubrics are scoring guides or rating systems used in performance-based assessment (Webb & Willoughby, 1993; Farr & Tone, 1994). The intent of rubrics is to assist teachers in two ways: (a) make the analysis of student work samples simpler, and (b) make the rating process more reliable and objective. This is a tall order indeed because any assessment process is rarely objective, value free, or theoretically neutral (Bintz, 1991).

Webb and Willoughby (1993) explain that, once established, "the same rubric may be used for many tasks as long as the tasks require the same skills." (p. 14) Although a rubric may be set up in any number of ways, Farr and Tone (1994) suggest a method that can be used in reading assessment, which we have adapted significantly to reflect current accountability requirements.

Step 1: Begin with your state's reading standards.

Teachers should begin the assessment process with the reading standards established by their state. This knowledge can be applied as one constructs rubrics to insure proper accountability for student learning.

Step 2: Identify anchor papers.

Begin by collecting and sorting all student work samples from the class into several stacks according to quality (e.g., reading response activities, student self-analysis papers, content reading responses). These are known as *anchor papers.* Decide why you feel some work samples represent more advanced development in reading than others and why some work samples cannot be characterized as belonging in the more advanced categories. Be as specific as possible. This will provide you with "range" papers.

Step 3: Choose a scoring scale for the rubric: usually a three-, four-, or five-point scoring system is used.

A three-point scale may be more reliable, meaning that if more than one teacher were to examine the same reading artifacts each would be likely to arrive at the same rubric score (1, 2, or 3). However, when multiple criteria are being considered, a five-point scale may be easier to use. One problem with rubrics is that they imply a hierarchy of skills that may not have been proven through reading research. For example, in the upper grades, is the ability to *skim* text for information a higher or lower level skill than *scanning* text for information? Probably neither.

This brings us to Farr and Tone's (1994) next suggestion on scoring. A rubric is usually scored in a hierarchical fashion. That is, if on a five-point scale a student fulfills requirements for a "3" score, but *not* the criteria for a 4, then even if he fulfills the criteria for a 5, his work would still be ranked as a 3. That system may work fairly well in areas such as mathematics where certain skills can be ranked hierarchically in a developmental sense. For example, for students to progress to the point of performing long division, they will need to be able to do the more basic skills of multiplying, carrying numbers, and subtraction. However, because many reading skills cannot be ranked that clearly, we recommend a slightly different procedure: If a five-point rubric is being used, the

Rubrics are scoring guides that can make your evaluations more objective and consistent.

teacher should survey all five reading skills or strategies identified in the rubric when reviewing artifacts found in the portfolio. If the student has the ability to do four of them, the teacher ranks the student as a 4, regardless of where those skills are situated in the rubric. We hasten to add that this modification may not always be appropriate, especially with emergent readers, among whom clearer developmental milestones are evident.

Step 4: Select reading development work samples for each level of the rubric, and write descriptive annotations.

It is important for teachers to have samples of each performance criterion at hand when attempting to use a rubric. From Step 2, where range papers and anchor were identified, the teacher will have good examples of each reading skill or strategy being assessed. After a careful review of these papers, it is possible to write short summary statements for each level in the rubric.

Figure 9.16 is a sample rubric developed for a fifth-grade class wherein students are to describe (orally and through written response) cause–effect relationships based on in-class readings about water pollution.

Step 5: Modify the rubric criteria as necessary.

Feel free to modify a rubric's criteria as new information emerges. This is another way of maintaining validity in the process.

Figure 9.16   Sample rubric for a fifth grade reading class

Cause-Effect Relationships: Scale for Oral and Written Response

Level 4: Student clearly describes a cause and effect of water pollution, and provides concrete examples of each.

S/he can provide an example not found in the readings.

"We read about how sometimes toxic wastes are dumped into rivers by factories and most of the fish die. I remember hearing about how there was an oil spill in Alaska that did the same thing to fish and birds living in the area."

Level 3: Student describes a cause and effect of water pollution found in the readings.

Student can define "pollution."

"I remember reading about how factories sometimes dump poisonous chemicals into rivers and all the fish die. Pollution means that someone makes a place so dirty that animals can't live there anymore."

Level 2: Student can provide examples of water pollution or effects pollution had on the environment found in the readings.

"I remember reading that having enough clean water to drink is a problem in some places because of garbage being dumped into the rivers."

Level 1: Student is not able to offer voluntarily information about the cause and effects of pollution found in the readings.

GETTING ORGANIZED: PROFILING YOUR CLASS

The assessment ideas presented in this chapter so far provide the means for measuring the development of various reading skills—but that is only one part of the reading teacher's job. Organizing and analyzing the assessment data—first, for each child individually, then for the entire class—are extremely important next steps in instructional planning. Charting the reading skills students have learned and still need to acquire, both individually and as a class, is what we mean by **profiling.**

Profiling is a way of charting the individual and group learning needs of students.

Two Documents Needed for Profiling

The profiling documents teachers use should directly parallel the grade-level reading standards adopted by the school district. Teachers generally need two profiling documents: a *student profile* document to record individual strengths and needs in some detail, and a *classroom profile* document to help organize the entire class's data for the formation of needs-based reading groups.

R. Cooter and K. S. Cooter (1999) developed a system, which includes these two levels of profiling. Figure 9.17 is a portion of their student profiling document. A profiling system should be driven either by the state's reading standards or the school district's scope and sequence skills list (these are usually provided in a curriculum guide to all teachers upon assignment to a school).

Student Profiling Document

In Figure 9.17 you will note that each skill has a blank space to the left; this is for the teacher to note (a) the date she observed the student performing that skill, and (b) the degree to which the student was able to execute the skill. For the latter, a three-point rubric is provided: "E" for students who are just *emerging* with an awareness of the skill, "D" for students who are in the midst of *developing* competency in the skill, and "P" for students who have attained *proficiency* (i.e., mastery) of the skill. These designations are important because they help the teacher differentiate the needs of students in the class. The designations can also be useful for informing parents about how their child is developing as a reader. Note that in the example provided in Figure 9.18, the child has a number of skills at each level of development, as well as some with no designation at all (this means that the child has not yet reached that developmental stage for the skill(s) even at an emergent level). The student profile document should probably be the first contribution a teacher makes to the student's reading portfolio folder.

Classroom Profiling Document

Necessarily accompanying the student profile is the *classroom profile* (*always* have both). This document lists the same reading standards as the student profile only in abbreviated form. In Figure 9.19 is a partially completed classroom reading profile for third grade. Notice that each skill listed matches the same skills found in the student profile. Students' names are written in the blank spaces across the top and the matching designation for how competent the student is with each skill (i.e., the codes *E, D,* or *P*) are transcribed from their individual student profile forms.

Identify Rosa Maria's "emergent" reading skills from this example.

Figure 9.17 A partial student profiling instrument for third grade

Student Profile: **THIRD GRADE LITERACY MILESTONES**
Balanced Literacy Assessment System and Training
(BLAST™)

Student's Name _____

Teacher: Ms. K. M. Spencer

Instructions: Record the date when each milestone skill was observed, and the degree of development (**E** = Emergent, **D** = Developing Skill, **P** = Proficient) in the blank to the left of each skill description.

Decoding and Word Recognition
_____ 3.D.1   Uses context clues, phonic knowledge, and structural analysis to decode words

Spelling and Writing
_____ 3.SW.1   Spells previously studied words and spelling patterns correctly in own writing
_____ 3.SW.2   Uses the dictionary to check and correct spelling
_____ 3.SW.3   Uses all aspects of the writing process in compositions and reports with assistance, including

      _____ 3.SW.3.1   Combines information from multiple sources in written reports
      _____ 3.SW.3.2   Revises and edits written work independently on a level appropriate for first semester of third grade
      _____ 3.SW.3.3   Produces a variety of written work (response to literature, reports, semantic maps)
      _____ 3.SW.3.4   Uses graphic organizational tools with a variety of texts
      _____ 3.SW.3.5   Incorporates elaborate descriptions and figurative language
      _____ 3.SW.3.6   Uses a variety of formal sentence structures in own writing

_____ 3.SW.S.1   Writes proficiently using orthographic patterns and rules such as qu, use of n before v, m before b, m before p, and changing z to c when adding -es (Spanish only)
_____ 3.SW.S.2   Spells words with three or more syllables using silent letters, dieresis marks, accents, verbs, r/rr, y/ll, s/c/z, q/c/k, g/j, j/x, b/v, ch, h, and i/y accurately (Spanish only)

Oral Reading
_____ 3.OR.1   Reads aloud with fluency any text that is appropriate for the first half of grade three
_____ 3.OR.2   Comprehends any text that is appropriate for the first half of grade three

Language Comprehension and Response to Text
_____ 3.C.1   Reads and comprehends both fiction and nonfiction that is appropriate for grade three
_____ 3.C.2   Reads chapter books independently
_____ 3.C.3   Identifies specific words or phrases that are causing comprehension difficulties (metacognition)
_____ 3.C.4   Summarizes major points from fiction and nonfiction text
_____ 3.C.5   Can discuss similarities in characters and events across stories
_____ 3.C.6   Can discuss underlying theme or message when interpreting fiction
_____ 3.C.7   Distinguishes between the following when interpreting nonfiction text:

      _____ 3.C.7.1   Cause and effect
      _____ 3.C.7.2   Fact and opinion
      _____ 3.C.7.3   Main idea and supporting details

Figure 9.17   *continued*

_____	3.C.8	Uses information and reasoning to evaluate opinions
_____	3.C.9	Infers word meaning from roots, prefixes, and suffixes that have been taught
_____	3.C.10	Uses dictionary to determine meanings and usage of unknown words
_____	3.C.11	Uses new vocabulary in own speech and writing
_____	3.C.12	Uses basic grammar and parts of speech correctly in independent writing
_____	3.C.13	Shows familiarity with a number of read-aloud and independent reading selections, including nonfiction
_____	3.C.14	Uses multiple sources to locate information:
		_____ 3.C.14.1 Tables of contents
		_____ 3.C.14.2 Indexes
		_____ 3.C.14.3 Internet search engines
_____	3.C.15	Connects a variety of literary texts with life experiences

Reading Fluency

_____	3.F.1	Very few word-by-word interruptions
_____	3.F.2	Reads mostly in larger meaningful phrases
_____	3.F.3	Reads with expression
_____	3.F.4	Attends consistently to punctuation
_____	3.F.5	Rereads to clarify or problem-solve
_____	3.F.6	Sixty (60) words per minute reading rate (minimum)

To demonstrate how individual student data can be collated into a class profile and help the teacher form reading groups based on needed skills, we provide an example in Figure 9.20. This example is for decoding *and* word recognition, as well as spelling and writing skills assessment. It is easy to see in Figure 9.20 how the teacher can begin forming reading groups based on student needs. For instance, the teacher not only might form a group of students who need to develop skill "Revises and edits," but also recognize that actually two groups are needed—one for those who are emerging in this ability (E-level students), and another for those who are a little further along or "developing" (D-level students).

REPORTING PROGRESS TO FAMILIES: WHAT ABOUT GRADES?

Frequently, teachers become a little perplexed about how to report progress to families and, as they are often required to do, convert assessment information into grades. Some say that while comprehensive reading assessments are more valid than traditional procedures, they are also more difficult to quantify or translate into grades as required by many school districts. We believe the solution to this problem is to learn how to derive traditional grades from comprehensive assessment schemes.

To get started, first distinguish between *graded* assessment measures, which relate to gradable tasks, and *ungraded* measures, which provide developmental information about the student that would be inappropriate to grade. Both ungraded and graded assessment options are included in the umbrella term *comprehensive*

Figure 9.18 Student profiling instrument (partial worksheet of 3rd grade example)

Student Profile: THIRD GRADE LITERACY MILESTONES
Balanced Literacy Assessment System and Training
(BLAST™) (R. Cooter & K. S. Cooter, 1999)

Student's Name _Rosa Maria_

Teacher: Ms. K. M. Spencer

> **Instructions:** Record the date when each milestone skill was observed, and the degree of development (**E** = Emergent, **D** = Developing Skill, **P** = Proficient) in the blank to the left of each skill description.

Decoding and Word Recognition

11/5 D 3.D.1   Uses context clues, phonic knowledge, and structural analysis to decode words

Spelling and Writing

11/12 D 3.SW.1   Spells previously studied words and spelling patterns correctly in own writing

11/19 D 3.SW.2   Uses the dictionary to check and correct spelling

_____ 3.SW.3   Uses all aspects of the writing process in compositions and reports with assistance, including

    10/25 E 3.SW.3.1   Combines information from multiple sources in written reports

    10/18 E 3.SW.3.2   Revises and edits written work independently on a level appropriate for first semester of third grade

    9/3 D 3.SW.3.3   Produces a variety of written work (response to literature, reports, semantic maps)

    9/3 E 3.SW.3.4   Uses graphic organizational tools with a variety of texts

    9/3 E 3.SW.3.5   Incorporates elaborate descriptions and figurative language

    9/25 E 3.SW.3.6   Uses a variety of formal sentence structures in own writing

11/26 D 3.SW.S.1   Writes proficiently using orthographic patterns and rules such as qu, use of n before v, m before b, m before p, and changing z to c when adding -es (Spanish only)

9/14 P 3.SW.S.2   Spells words with three or more syllables using silent letters, dieresis marks, accents, verbs, r/rr, y/ll, s/c/z, q/c/k, g/j, j/x, b/v, ch, h, and i/y accurately (Spanish only)

Oral Reading

11/26 D 3.OR.1   Reads aloud with fluency any text that is appropriate for the first half of grade three

11/26 D 3.OR.2   Comprehends any text that is appropriate for the first half of grade three

Language Comprehension and Response to Text

9/1; 12/10 P/E 3.C.1   Reads and comprehends both fiction and nonfiction that is appropriate for grade three

10/3 P 3.C.2   Reads chapter books independently

12/2 E 3.C.3   Identifies specific words or phrases that are causing comprehension difficulties (metacognition)

12/2 D/E 3.C.4   Summarizes major points from fiction and nonfiction text

Figure 9.19 Partial classroom profiling instrument

CLASSROOM PROFILE (BLAST™): THIRD GRADE LITERACY MILESTONES

Teacher: _____   Date/Grading Period Completed: _____

Instructions: Record the degree to which each milestone skill has been achieved by each student (**E** = Emergent, **D** = Developing Skill, **P** = Proficient) in each box corresponding to the student and skill in the grid.

Decoding and Word Recognition

3.D.1	Context clues, phonic knowledge, and structural analysis

Spelling and Writing

3.SW.1	Uses studied words and spelling patterns
3.SW.2	Uses the dictionary to check spelling
3.SW.3	Uses these aspects of the writing process:
3.SW.3.1	Combines information/multiple sources
3.SW.3.2	Revises and edits
3.SW.3.3	Variety of written work
3.SW.3.4	Graphic organizational tools
3.SW.3.5	Descriptions and figurative language
3.SW.3.6	Variety of formal sentence structures
3.SW.4.S.1	Orthographic patterns and rules (Spanish only)
3.SW.5.S.2	Spells words with three or more syllables using silent letters, dieresis marks, accents, verbs (Spanish only)

Oral Reading

3.OR.1	Reads aloud with fluency

(continued)

305

Figure 9.19 *continued*

Reading Fluency

3.F.1	Very few word-by-word interruptions
3.F.2	Reads mostly in larger meaningful phrases
3.F.3	Reads with expression
3.F.4	Attends consistently to punctuation
3.F.5	Rereads to clarify or problem-solve
3.F.6	Reads sixty (60) words per minute (minimum)

Language Comprehension and Response to Text

3.C.1	Comprehends both fiction and nonfiction on level
3.C.2	Reads chapter books independently
3.C.3	Identifies problem words or phrases
3.C.4	Summarizes fiction and nonfiction text
3.C.5	Similarities: characters/events across stories
3.C.6	Theme or message: interpreting fiction
3.C.7	Nonfiction:
	3.C.7.1 Cause/effect
	3.C.7.2 Fact/opinion
	3.C.7.3 Main idea/details
3.C.8	Evaluation: Uses information/reasoning
3.C.9	Word meaning from roots and affixes
3.C.10	Dictionary: Determine meanings/usage
3.C.11	Uses new vocabulary in own speech and writing
3.C.12	Writing: Basic grammar/parts of speech
3.C.13	Familiar w/read-aloud, indep. reading, nonfiction
3.C.14	Locates information using:
	3.C.14.1 Tables of contents
	3.C.14.2 Indexes
	3.C.14.3 Internet search engines
3.C.15	Connects literary texts with life experiences

Figure 9.20 Needs-based groups

CLASSROOM PROFILE (BLAST™): THIRD GRADE LITERACY MILESTONES

Teacher: K. Spencer

Date/Grading Period Completed: 12 – 14

Instructions: Record the degree to which each milestone skill has been achieved by each student (**E** = Emergent, **D** = Developing Skill, **P** = Proficient) in each box corresponding to the student and skill in the grid.

	Dora	Paula	Ameenah	Jason	Rosa Maria	Harry	James	Dirk	Syporia	Alicia	Johnny	Anna
Decoding and Word Recognition												
3.D.1 Context clues, phonic knowledge and structural analysis	P	P	P	D	D	P	P	D	P	D	P	P
Spelling and Writing												
3.SW.1 Uses studied words and spelling patterns	D	D	E	D	D	D	E	D	P	P	E	P
3.SW.2 Uses the dictionary to check spelling	D	D	D	D	D	D	P	D	D	D	E	P
3.SW.3 Uses these aspects of the writing process:												
3.SW.3.1 Combines information/multiple sources	E	E	E	E	E	E	E	E	E	E	E	E
3.SW.3.2 Revises and edits	D	D	D	E	E	E	E	D	D	E	E	P
3.SW.3.3 Variety of written work	E	D	P	D	E	D	E	E	E	E	E	P
3.SW.3.4 Graphic organizational tools	E	D	E	D	D	P	E	P	E	D	P	D
3.SW.3.5 Descriptions and figurative language	E	E	E	P	E	E	D	P	P	E	P	P
3.SW.3.6 Variety of formal sentence structures	D	D	D	D	D	D	D	P	E	E	D	P
3.SW.4.S.1 Orthographic patterns and rules (Spanish only)	D	P		D	D		D		E	D	D	
3.SW.5.S.2 Spells words with three or more syllables using	P	P		D	P	D						
silent letters, dieresis marks, accents, verbs (Spanish only)												

307

assessment because the teacher uses all of this information to inform and improve instruction. Most of the assessment procedures discussed in this chapter are categorized in the following lists:

Graded Assessment Measures	Ungraded Assessment Measures
Reading logs	Print-awareness tests (CAP, etc.)
Running records	Alphabet knowledge tests
Retellings (unaided and aided recall)	Family surveys
Literature-response projects	Self-rating scales
Cloze passages	Story maps
Questioning	
Evaluation forms	
Fluency assessments	

Ungraded assessment measures provide teachers with background information to help begin instruction during the first few weeks of school. Ungraded assessment measures cannot and should not be viewed as a source for grades. For instance, it would be absurd to "grade" a family survey and use such information to "score" a child's performance at school! Teachers, therefore, use ungraded assessment measures to gain insights into what students already know or have been exposed to in the past.

Grades usually can be derived from the graded assessment measures listed. In the remainder of this section, we discuss ways each of these assessment procedures can yield quantitative scores or grades. As with other examples throughout this book, we offer this information as merely one way of getting the job done, not the only way or even necessarily the best way. An alternative system for reporting called *authentic grading* is also suggested later in the chapter.

Reading Logs

Although some would say that reading logs should be ungraded, it is possible to add a retelling component (*see* p. 291) and thus derive grades. Following is one example usable in a fourth or fifth grade classroom.

A = 4 or more books read along with a reading conference with the teacher

B = 3 books read along with a reading conference with the teacher

C = 2 books read along with a reading conference with the teacher

D = 1 book read along with a reading conference with the teacher

Running Records

Running records should be done with each student about three times per quarter, or about once every three weeks. They are especially helpful through about second or third grade. If running records are to be used as a grading source, grades may be derived from (a) the number of oral reading miscues, and (b) combining the running record information with retellings (discussed next).

Table 9.1 Annie's running record summary

Miscue Category Student: Annie	Baseline (9/12)	1st Rereading (10/3)	2nd Rereading (10/25)	3rd Rereading (11/10)
Book: *If You Give a Mouse . . .*				
1. Word call errors	3	1	0	0
2. Attempted decoding	6	4	3	1
3. Self-correction	2	1	1	1
4. Insertions	4	2	1	1
5. Teacher assistance	6	4	2	2
6. Repetition	4	5	2	1
Totals	**25**	**17**	**9**	**6**

To use the running record for grading purposes, it is necessary to do an initial ungraded reading to be used as a baseline. After several rereadings of the text about three weeks apart, the student's performance can be compared to the baseline performance, then contrasted to a predetermined criterion to establish a grade. For example, earlier in the chapter, we provided a sample passage and analysis taken from *If You Give a Mouse a Cookie* (Numeroff, 1985). Let us assume that, after an initial baseline reading and several subsequent individual reading conferences in a first grade classroom, the student Annie had the results shown in Table 9.1 as she read this popular children's book.

A Sample Criterion for Running Records

If You Give a Mouse a Cookie, approximately 289 words

A = (98% correct oral reading) 6 miscues or fewer

B = (95% to 97%) 9 to 13 miscues

C = (90% to 94%) 17 to 29 miscues

Annie's grade could be computed easily at each of the rereading intervals using the preceding criteria. The criteria in this example are arbitrary and should be adjusted to suit the teacher's belief system. Annie's first reading would place her at the top of the "C" range, her second rereading at the top of the "B" range, and the third rereading at the "A" level. After two or three rereadings for grading purposes, a new book thought to be more challenging would be selected for a new baseline measurement. To assess comprehension, retellings would be used in other books on her instructional reading level.

Retellings

Retellings, as mentioned earlier, are a two-step proposition involving both unaided and aided recall. For grading purposes, we recommend that teachers construct a checklist of important elements from the selection. For narrative selections, the checklist can be generic like the one previously shown in Figure 9.12. As the student retells the story (unaided recall), the teacher records elements remembered relating

A retelling record sheet can be constructed in such a way as to be useful in grading.

to setting, characters, challenge, and so on. After the retelling is complete, the teacher then asks questions from those story grammar categories not addressed during the student's retelling (aided recall). At the conclusion of the retelling process, criteria such as the following (or others established by the teacher) could be used to convert the comprehension performance (combined unaided and aided recall) into a letter grade:

A = 95% recall or better
B = 88% recall
C = 80% recall
D = 75% recall

For students in the upper grades who are reading longer passages or books, we recommend that only a portion of the text be selected for this retelling exercise.

Literature-Response Projects

The literature-response category is perhaps the most subjective for grading. Also, just how much weight literature-response project grades should carry in the overall portfolio will vary according to how much effort and detail were involved. Two very different projects presented here carry different values in the overall portfolio because of levels of difficulty: a literary poster (T. D. Johnson & Louis, 1987) and a group-developed "radio play."

A literary poster has students create a poster around some aspect of a reading selection. The essence of the poster is recalling several important bits of information from the text. Some of the poster types suggested by T. D. Johnson and Louis (1987) are "missing persons," "greatest hero," and "wall of fame." This literature-response activity is done by students as seat work and does not require collaboration with peers. Typically, literary posters require about 20 minutes to complete. To grade such a project, or any other literature-response project for that matter, the teacher must once again decide what is to be measured by naming the criteria. Figure 9.21 shows one possible set of criteria for the upper elementary level book *Fast Sam, Cool Clyde, and Stuff* (Myers, 1975).

Three-way grading is used with radio plays.

A radio play is a drama written by a small group of students (three to five) drawn from a key incident in a book they have all read. The drama, once written, is then read aloud into a tape recorder by the student-actors, complete with sound effects. Radio plays in finished form are usually played for the entire class over the public address system in the school, giving the impression of an actual radio production. Grading for this kind of literature-response activity is often *triangulated,* or three-way. A description of the three grade sources follows:

- *Within-group grade:* Students in the radio play group grade each other. This tends to prevent one or more students from goofing off and still getting full credit for the project.
- *Class evaluation:* All members of the class not associated with the project grade the radio play according to criteria outlined by the teacher. Each of the criteria grades is tabulated by the teacher, and an average or mean grade is calculated based on the overall class evaluation.

Figure 9.21 Criteria for "wall of fame" poster

Criteria for *Fast Sam, Cool Clyde, and Stuff* (Myers, 1975)

"Wall of Fame Poster"

Ms. Holden's Sixth Grade

Directions: To qualify for the grade you want, you must not only have the total number of ideas required but also *have at least one idea from each of the story grammar categories* (setting, characters, challenge, events, solution, theme).

Grade Desired	Requirement
A	12 or more ideas recalled
B	9–11 ideas recalled
C	7–8 ideas recalled
D	6 ideas recalled (one idea from each of the story grammar categories)

• *Teacher grade:* Naturally, the teacher has veto power over any portion of the process if he or she feels the children were not just in their assessment. Additionally, the teacher grades the performance and factors in his or her grade as one-third of the overall group grade. Based on the within-group grade, the teacher then decides if all students in the group get the same grade, or not, based on their contribution.

Cloze Tests

Cloze tests can serve a dual function: as a teaching activity for such reading strategies as using context clues or inferential comprehension development, or for use as an assessment procedure. Typically, most teachers using cloze modify the passage so that specific elements are deleted, such as character names, facts related to setting, and key events in the story. Grading is simply a matter of applying the classroom criteria to the percentage of correct responses (94% to 100% = A, 85% to 93% = B, etc.).

Questioning

Questioning is explained in some depth in Chapter 6 as a tool in comprehension development. For grading purposes, we suggest (a) establishing basic minimum criteria, such as the child must correctly identify at least one element from each of the story grammar criteria during questioning, and (b) applying the overall percentage correct to the classroom grading criteria, as was explained for cloze texts.

Evaluation Forms

Valencia (1990) suggests that good evaluation begins with knowledge of what is to be assessed and how to interpret the performance. Evaluation forms have many different formats reflecting the needs of teachers making transitions. For example, some teachers in early-to-intermediate transitions may elect to use some of the skill

Figure 9.22   Content reading evaluation form.

Name _____   Date _____

Text _____   Pages _____

Content Reading Strategies Practiced After Whole-Group Mini-lessons

1. Follows class instructions given orally
2. Follows written instructions
3. Uses previewing strategy
4. Scans for important information on request
5. Surveys text before reading
6. Completes task on time
7. Can justify inferences drawn from text
8. Distinguishes between relevant and irrelevant facts
9. Other observations

Criteria:

A = Observed competence in this area and was used at appropriate times

B = Observed ability, but missed an opportunity to correctly apply the strategy

C = Used the strategy only once and/or missed obvious opportunities to apply

D = Appears not to fully understand the strategy or when to apply it

Based in part on Kemp, 1987.

sheets supplied by the basal reader as evaluation forms for grading. Why? Because skill sheets tend to focus on discrete, definable reading strategies and easily lend themselves to grading (e.g., 5 of 5 correct = A, 4 of 5 correct = B). For advanced transition teachers, skill sheets may not be an acceptable alternative, because they divorce the reader from more authentic reading activities. These teachers may prefer an evaluation form that is based on teacher observations while the child is reading whole text. Figure 9.22 is one example of an evaluation form that might be used to grade content reading strategies (based in part on Kemp, 1987).

Fluency Measures

Fluency can be graded using a modified rubric.

Fluency is one of the most important indicators of how well students are progressing in their reading development. Parents are usually quite aware, at least in some general sense, of how fluent their child is becoming in reading and care very much about the teacher's assessment of the child's progress.

Evidence-based research (Snow, Burns, & Griffin, 1998) has provided us with a better understanding of fluency development and general benchmark standards at each grade level. In Chapter 7 we presented some of these standards in Figures 7.3 and 7.4. In Figure 9.23 we show a grading scale based on end-of-year standards for fluent oral reading shared in Chapter 7 (Figure 7.3) for fifth grade. It reflects a minimum expectation of 100 words per minute (wpm) by year's end, and 180 wpm as the benchmark for fluent oral reading.

Figure 9.23   Fifth grade criteria for grading reading fluency

Fluency: First Semester Scale	*Fluency: Final Grading Period Scale*
A = Superior fluency achievement (140+ wpm)	A = 180 wpm or better
B = Above average achievement (110–139 wpm)	B = 140–179 wpm
C = Acceptable achievement (90–100 wpm)	C = 100–139 wpm
D = Below acceptable levels (89 wpm or below)	D = Below 100 wpm

POTENTIAL PITFALLS IN COMPREHENSIVE READING ASSESSMENT

In working with teachers making transitions toward comprehensive reading assessment in their classrooms, we have been struck by certain commonalities when they encounter problems. They are in some cases the same problems we have encountered ourselves when trying out new ideas in the classroom. In this section, we alert readers to some of these predictable difficulties.

Overcommitment (by Teachers) to Daily Entries

When teachers discover just how informative reading assessment conferences with students can be, it is natural to want to conduct them more often. We frequently encounter teachers who want to have daily reading conferences with every child. Even though strategies like running records, story retellings, and other assessment ideas are indeed powerful, attempting such regular conferences is not a very reasonable goal to set for oneself. Most teachers find that weekly or bi-weekly reading conferences are quite sufficient.

Teachers must be careful to establish realistic assessment goals.

Spending Too Much Time Managing Portfolios

Trying to manage portfolio assessment systems can become an almost crushing burden when added to the myriad other responsibilities of classroom teachers. Frankly, there is no easy solution to this problem. Many teachers find that using some of the various checklists available by publishers can help organize their observations.

Too Many Contributions by Students

Although we want students to make contributions to their reading and writing portfolios, sometimes they have trouble knowing "how much is too much!" Teachers sometimes notice students putting nearly everything they can think of into their portfolios, making it difficult for teachers to sort and manage them. Whole-group instruction sessions, where the teacher shares the contents of an exemplary portfolio from a previous year or from a student volunteer, can usually help students develop perspective.

Ask a master reading teacher what he or she feels are reasonable weekly expectations for student contributions to their reading portfolios.

OTHER ISSUES IN READING ASSESSMENT

Reading assessment in American education has essentially followed a skills-based medical model since the 1930s, with assessment viewed as the acts of diagnosing strengths and weaknesses and defining which skills are known, to be learned, or remediated. After decades of following this model, many researchers, public officials, and parents feel that gains in reading have been unimpressive. They're right! Results of the National Assessment of Educational Progress (NAEP) conducted over three decades verify that only modest gains in reading have been registered in American schools. Many people concerned with reading development are calling for new approaches to both reading assessment and instruction. In this section, we briefly describe a few of the issues that are presently being debated in reading assessment.

The Notion of Skill Mastery

For decades, educators have discussed the notion of *skill mastery:* the level at which students can automatically and independently perform a given reading skill. In recent years, as reading skills and assessment have become much more politically charged issues (Cantrell, 1999), how teachers go about defining whether or not a skill has been fully learned has become increasingly important. As seen in our earlier discussion on student profiling documents, we favor a rubric system that represents skill attainment as a continuum ranging from *emergent* (E) to *developing* (D) and then on to *proficient* (P). This approach would also seem consistent with the teachings of Lev Vygotsky concerning the zone of proximal development (see Chapter 3).

The Need for a Variety of Reading Contexts in Assessment

Reading is often viewed by test makers as a singular skill. In other words, if a student is given a norm-referenced reading test in seventh grade as part of an overall achievement test, he or she will receive a single reading grade equivalent score or a single percentile ranking. In assessment terms, this is called "reductionist" thinking because it reduces reading, a complex process involving many different skills, to a single number.

Reductionist thinking, when applied to reading, is a flawed practice indeed. Here's why: Different types of texts that one might read (e.g., mystery, poem, song, history, scientific journal article, religious text) all use unique writing styles that require different skills of the reader. Further, a student may be inherently more interested in some text forms and topics than others, which most certainly has an effect on reading performance. Thus, there is a need for a variety of literary forms and contexts in reading assessment to provide an accurate picture of the student's development.

Another casualty of reductionist thinking in reading assessment is precision. For instance, let's say we have a student who, on a norm-referenced test, scores well below grade level expectations. After conducting a more comprehensive assessment, it is discovered that his problem in reading is limited to higher order comprehension, that is, word identification skills, fluency, and vocabulary all seem to be at or above grade level expectations. Unless we conduct comprehensive assessments using a variety of texts and formats, we will be unable to provide all students with appropriate instruction.

Power Tests Versus Timed Tests

A **power test** is one in which the test items are arranged in order of increasing difficulty. There is no time limit on a power test; rather, the student continues until he or she has missed a prescribed number of items or completed the test. A **timed test,** as the name implies, is given for a specific amount of time, and students continue working at the test until the time limit has been reached. Items on a timed test are not usually arranged in any particular order of difficulty.

Each of these tests has its own values and problems. In the best circumstances, a power test, such as the *Peabody Picture Vocabulary Test—Third Edition* (PPVT-III) (Dunn & Dunn, 1997) allows students to reach their own ability level or "ceiling." The same thing is true of an informal reading inventory such as *The Flynt/Cooter Reading Inventory for the Classroom* (Flynt & Cooter, 2004), which is also a kind of power test.

There are some inherent problems with these test types. For example, a student who has a slow reading rate may either run out of time (a problem with timed tests, of course), or run out of mental energy and "fatigue out" on a power test. The problem with running out of time on a timed test is that it causes students to appear particularly weak on skill categories covered in the last part of the test. We have seen this happen on the *Iowa Test of Basic Skills* (ITBS), for example, where at the third grade level the final portion of the reading test measures predominantly higher-order comprehension skills. Thus, a student who only gets to item 15 out of a 21-item subtest may falsely appear weak in higher-order comprehension simply because he or she ran out of time.

Power and *timed tests* yield different results and serve differing purposes.

Norm-Referenced Tests Versus State-Developed Tests

Many states have now developed their own competency tests for reading and other academic areas (e.g., Texas, Kentucky, Tennessee, and Florida). Under the federal No Child Left Behind Act, all other states will soon be required to develop and administer these "high stakes" tests. The intent of state leaders is to establish minimum levels of skill knowledge for students so that school districts have a degree of uniformity.

In addition to the state-developed tests, most school districts also administer **norm-referenced tests** (NRTs) assessing the major academic areas. NRT data allow districts to compare the performance of their students to other students of the same age and grade placement nationally. Valencia and Pearson (1987) note that norm-referenced tests are the most commonly used measures in U.S. schools.

In recent years, some school administrators and state officials have argued that NRTs are no longer necessary because they can get all the data they need from state-developed competency tests. NRT advocates counter that simply passing a minimum competency state reading test, for example, is not the same as actually reading on grade level (something an NRT can reliably indicate). The high mobility of American families, NRT proponents argue, also figures into the need for reliable measures of reading ability. Because maintaining credibility with families, the business community, private foundations, and other stakeholders is an important concern for school administrators seeking bond elections and so forth, this issue will continue to be an important one.

Norm-referenced tests are helpful for making national and program comparisons.

Authentic Grading

Teachers and researchers advocating the use of portfolio assessment in reading are sometimes opposed to grading students. They feel it is inappropriate to grade an area of language development that is so student-specific and that is contradictory to developmental learning theories. Nevertheless, most, if not all, school districts require grades for elementary school reading instruction.

Cooter and Flynt (1996) have proposed a compromise system for reporting grades to families called **authentic grading.** This procedure offers the possibility of satisfying the accountability requirements of many school districts and appeases teachers who seek more valid reporting methods for student reading development. Such a reporting system might contain the following information:

- A letter grade reflecting how well the student has progressed during the grading period (comparing the student to him- or herself).
- A summary paragraph explaining in some detail what the student has achieved during this grading period and what he or she might accomplish next (relates to Vygotsky's zone of proximal development). This information can be derived from a reading learning milestones checklist for each student kept by the teacher as well as other data from the students' portfolios.
- A grade or rating coupled with an explanation that reflects how the student compares to others at his or her level.

These three components would constitute full reporting of student progress and most likely satisfy the requirement to inform parents, students, and school administrators. In Figure 9.24 we offer one conceptualization of an authentic grading report form.

Some advocates of comprehensive reading instruction may object to a system like the one proposed, but the issue of reporting to families in a way that makes use of portfolio learning artifacts is certainly needed. We encourage teachers and school administrators to continue searching for acceptable reporting solutions.

Assessing Affective and Conative Factors in Reading

Consider ways that interest, attitude, and motivation can have powerful effects on reading performance.

One of the most important and multifaceted aspects of reading assessment is the affective domain, which deals with feelings about the reading act (Mathewson, 1985; Wigfield & Guthrie, 1997). Attitude, motivation, interest, beliefs, and values are all aspects of affect that have profound effects on reading development. In the past, affect has been discussed very little in reading assessment and has largely been limited to the administration of interest inventories, observation checklists, and attitude surveys (Walker, 1991). Teachers building comprehensive reading programs require information in student portfolios that provides insights into positive affective aspects that drive the reading process.

Two steps are generally required for teachers to assess **affective factors.** First, teachers must become knowledgeable about affective aspects of reading. Second, teachers need to carefully review each assessment strategy to be used for its potential to probe affective aspects of reading in students. Further discussion and examples of these two points may help the reader begin to discover new ways of focusing on affective dimensions.

What Are the Affective Variables for Reading?

Mathewson (1985) identified four affective variables that drive the reading process: *attitude, motives, feelings,* and *physical sensation.* These variables may affect one's reading by influencing one's decision to read, attention, comprehension, recall,

Figure 9.24   Authentic grading report form

Reading Report Form
Oxford Elementary School

Student's Name_____Grade _____

Teacher _____School _____

Grading Period _____

Part I: **How your child has progressed in reading this grading period.**

   a.   Grade _____

   b.   What your child has learned about reading this grading period . . .

   c.   What we hope your child will be able to do next in reading . . .

   d.   Things you can do at home to help his/her growth in reading . . .

Part II: **How your child compares to other children his/her age or grade level in reading.**

   a.   How your child compares to other students at this grade level:

       _____

Early in Development	Usual Development	Advanced Development

   b.   Comments:

and other factors. Concerning motivation to read, Pintrich and DeGroot (1990) describe motivation constructs that affect students' intrinsic desire to read: readers' beliefs, readers' reasons and purposes for engaging in reading, and readers' affective (emotional) reactions. Cole (2003) has portrayed these three elements graphically, which we have adapted and present in Figure 9.25.

In other research, Mathewson identified eight motives that also appear to affect students' decision to read and reading behavior. With a basic awareness of these affective motivations in reading, one can subjectively analyze various portfolio assessment strategies for their potential to yield insights into students' motivations to read. We have compared Mathewson's eight motives affecting the decision to read

Figure 9.25 Intrinsic motivations to read

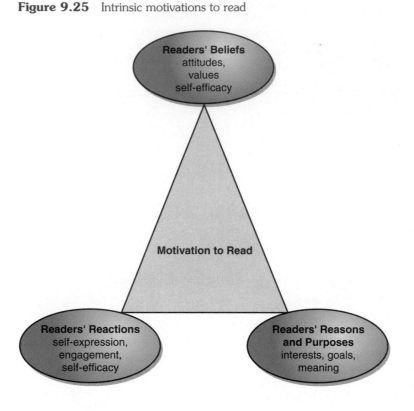

with nine reading activities frequently used as comprehensive reading assessment strategies. Although our specific conclusions (represented in Table 9.2) may be debatable to some, they demonstrate that it may be possible to learn valuable affective reading behavior information through procedures already known and practiced.

What Are Conative Factors for Reading?

Persistence and determination are ***conative factors.***

A related area of research pertains to **conative factors** (Berlak, 1992; Raven, 1992). Conative factors include such aspects of human behavior as determination, persistence, and will. As Berlak (1992) stated in summarizing Raven's work in this area:

> [Students] can enjoy doing something without being determined to see it through, and he or she can hate doing something, but still be determined . . . taking initiative (which would be categorized as an "affective" outcome in Bloom's Taxonomy) is inseparable from intellectual or cognitive functioning, and from action. (p. 17)

These researchers believed that conative factors have been falsely subsumed under the affective label and actually constitute a separate domain of human behavior. R. Cooter (1994) interpreted Raven's (1992) conative research relative to comprehensive reading assessment applications in reading. In so doing, he raised a few questions for further classroom-based research:

> If it is true that [when] teachers and students [are] moving in positive affective/conative directions [it] can result in learning success, what happens when the teacher and student(s) are moving in opposite directions? For example, will a highly motivated student who is determined to learn to read mathematics materials more effectively but

Table 9.2 Motives affecting decision to read that may be discernible through authentic assessment measures

	Belong/ Love	Curiosity	Compe- tence	Achieve- ment	Esteem	Self- actualization	Desire to know	Aesthetic
Reading Logs	X	X	O	X	X	X	X	X
Running Records	O	O	X	X	O	O	O	O
Retellings	X	X	X	O	X	X	X	X
Radio Play	X	X	X	O	O	X	X	X
Wanted Poster	O	X	X	X	O	O	X	X
Burgess Summary	O	O	X	X	O	O	X	O
Diorama	X	X	X	X	O	X	X	X
Schema Map	X	X	X	X	O	O	X	X
Comic Strip	X	X	X	X	X	X	X	X

From "Affective Connections of Selected Naturalistic Assessment Strategies in Reading," by P. H. Werner and R. B. Cooter, May 1991, presented at the 36th Annual Conference of the International Reading Association, Las Vegas, NV. Copyright 1991 by P. H. Werner and R. B. Cooter. Reprinted by permission.

who encounters a teacher disinterested in her students still be able to learn? What about the reverse—where a student is disinterested in an academic task, but who encounters a highly motivated and inspiring teacher? It is difficult to predict in either case whether students will learn. It may be that the answer lies with how strong the affective and conative drives are for students and teachers alike.

Another assessment question relates to affective and conative factors when students read expository versus narrative texts. Classroom experience suggests that interest, motivation, determination, and persistence tend to diminish when students read many expository materials, especially textbooks. Is this less true when using expository trade books (i.e., library books)? Can these feelings be reversed if enticing text response activities are used? (Cooter, 1994, p. 89)

Although answers to these and other questions concerning affective and conative factors are yet to be resolved, they are essential to the effectiveness of any comprehensive reading assessment program. To ignore such factors as interest, motivation, and persistence is to have an incomplete assessment. As Cooter (1994) summarizes, it would be "somewhat akin to a mechanic claiming to have done a complete assessment of an automobile after only checking tire pressures!" (p. 86)

Standards Note
Standard 10.2: The reading professional will be able to use information from norm-referenced tests ... and other indicators of student progress to inform learning. (This standard is exhaustive!) From the listing of "tools" in this standard, list two that you need to enhance or add, and two that you are satisfied with.

Summary

In this chapter, we explored basic principles of classroom reading assessment and described ways of profiling students according to their acquisition of reading skills, key strategies for measuring student growth, and ways that teachers can award grades.

We saw that comprehensive reading assessment carefully analyzes overall student growth in the reading process and helps teachers plan effective instruction.

Differences between traditional and comprehensive reading assessment perspectives were likened to the differences between a black-and-white photograph and a color movie. With traditional models of assessment, the learner's reading abilities are usually estimated using simplistic procedures, such as paper-and-pencil tests, workbook pages, or norm-referenced tests, and look at only a few forms for reading behavior. Comprehensive reading assessment procedures, on the other hand, provide teachers with the clearest and most complete view of the learner. Many aspects of reading are studied using genuine reading situations whenever possible to reveal insights into the learner's zones of proximal development. Running records, home surveys, story retellings, fluency measures, affective surveys, and self-assessment are just a few of the tools available in comprehensive reading assessment.

Current issues in reading assessment seem to be focusing on

Check your understanding of chapter concepts by using the self assessment for Chapter 9 on our Companion Website at www.prenhall.com/ reutzel.

- What is meant by "skill mastery"
- The need for a variety of text forms and contexts in reading assessment
- The proper place of *timed* versus *power* tests in reading
- A growing competition between makers of standardized reading tests and state education agencies developing their own measures of reading
- Reporting progress to families and grading

Other equally perplexing problems in reading assessment relate to the affective domain and conative factors.

Concept Applications

In the Classroom

1. As a review, develop a comparison grid or chart analyzing the differences and similarities between traditional and comprehensive assessment perspectives.
2. Develop a schedule for your classroom (name the grade level) that includes time for the daily assessment of at least four students. What will be the typical assessment "tools" you will probably use during this time? (Name at least four.) Explain and justify why you have selected these particular tools.
3. Develop three evaluation checklist forms that could be used in your classroom, or a grade level you specify, for reading comprehension, word identification, and content reading strategies. Include a suggested rubric with a rationale for each item.

In the Field

Arrange through your college instructor, or in your own classroom, to work with an elementary-age student who is reportedly having difficulty in reading. The following two major assignments can be completed with your student.
Part 1. Complete the following informal assessment procedures:

- A running record and analysis of the miscues using a book chosen by the student

- A commercial informal reading inventory of your choice
- An oral retelling of a book read by the student
- Three classroom observations of the student in various settings, such as reading group, content area materials, and free reading
- An interest inventory, which you have constructed or adapted from the one in this chapter

Part 2. After compiling and summarizing the preceding information, construct a reading profile of the student that includes the following:

- Approximate reading level (instructional)
- Reading skills that appear to be strengths for the child (use your state's standards for this)
- Reading skills that need to be developed

Recommended Readings and Assessment Instruments

Dunn, L., & Dunn, L. M. (1997). *Peabody Picture Vocabulary Test—Third Edition* (PPVT-III). Circle Pines, MN: American Guidance Service.

Dunn, L., Lugo, D. E., Padilla, E. R., & Dunn, L. M. (1986). *Test de Vocabulario en Imágenes Peabody* (TVIP). Circle Pines, MN: American Guidance Service.

Flynt, E. S., & Cooter, R. B., Jr. (1999). *The Flynt/Cooter English * Español Reading Inventory.* Upper Saddle River, NJ: Merrill/Prentice Hall.

Flynt, E. S., & Cooter, R. B., Jr. (2004). *The Flynt/Cooter Reading Inventory for the Classroom,* 5th ed. Upper Saddle River, NJ: Merrill/Prentice Hall.

Reutzel, D. R., & Cooter, R. B. (2003). *Strategies for reading assessment and instruction: Helping every child succeed,* 2nd ed. Upper Saddle River, NJ: Merrill/Prentice Hall.

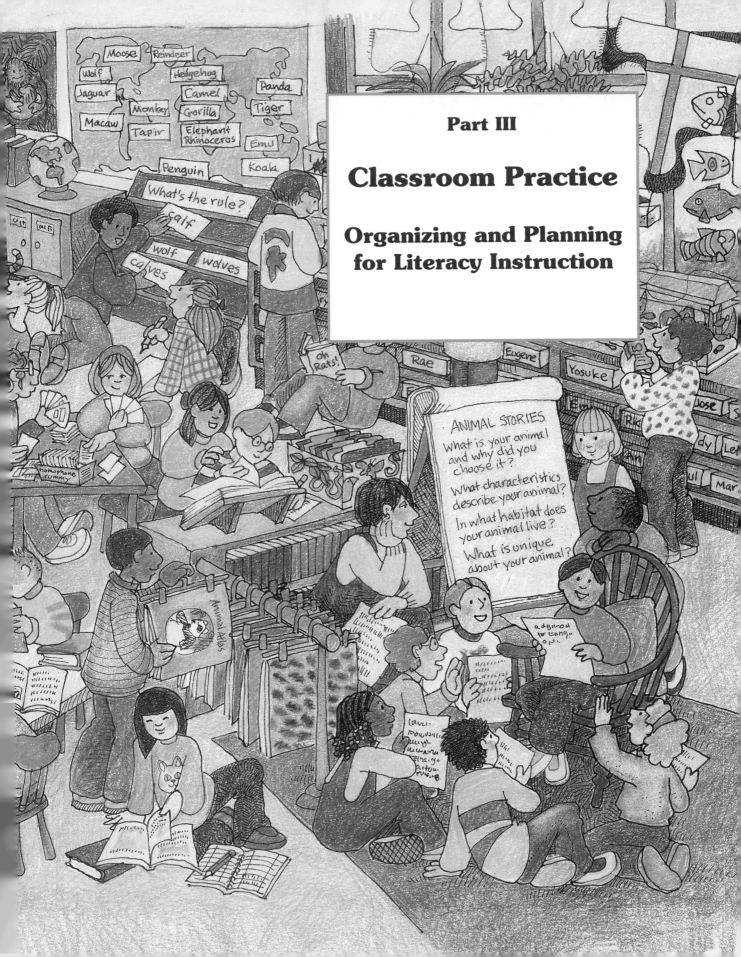

Part III

Classroom Practice

**Organizing and Planning
for Literacy Instruction**

10 Organizing for Reading Instruction: Starting Out Right in Grades K–3

Focus Questions

When you are finished studying this chapter, you should be able to answer these questions:

1. How do you organize whole-class, small-group, learning center, and professional space into a coherent classroom floor plan?

2. What are four literacy learning centers you plan to use in your K–3 classroom?

3. What are six principles for selecting and arranging literacy tools and materials in K–3 classrooms?

4. What are three alternative ways to group students for instruction?

5. What are five things you plan to do to be prepared for literacy instruction on the first day of school?

6. What is a major goal to be accomplished in literacy instruction during the first week of school?

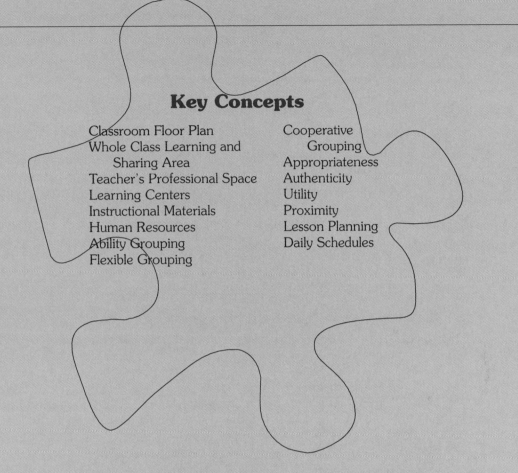

Key Concepts

Classroom Floor Plan
Whole Class Learning and
    Sharing Area
Teacher's Professional Space
Learning Centers
Instructional Materials
Human Resources
Ability Grouping
Flexible Grouping

Cooperative
    Grouping
Appropriateness
Authenticity
Utility
Proximity
Lesson Planning
Daily Schedules

We have learned through many years of professional experience that the old adage, "Those who fail to prepare, prepare to fail," is an indisputable fact when it concerns teaching a classroom full of children! Successful literacy classrooms all have one thing in common—they are well planned, organized, and managed. Whether it is planning the layout of the classroom floor plan, deciding which and how many learning centers to develop, ordering and arranging instructional materials, or organizing the first day and week of instruction, this chapter addresses all of these topics and more. We walk you, the new and experienced teacher alike, through the mental decision making, planning, and organization necessary to be successful on the first day of school and beyond in a K–3 literacy classroom.

WELCOME TO MS. MISKLE'S FIRST GRADE!

Thirty-four bright-eyed and curious first grade children gather around a kidney-bean-shaped table at the back of Ms. Miskle's room on the first day of school. Ms. Miskle places a soda bottle half-filled with white vinegar on the table. "I am going to blow this balloon up with a soda bottle," she says, with a mysterious tone in her voice and a twinkle in her eye. The children giggle and watch intently as Ms. Miskle places a limp red balloon over the lip of the bottle. She pulls the balloon tight over the lip and shakes the balloon back and forth a couple of times. A puff of white powder falls into the vinegar. The liquid inside the bottle begins to foam; at the same time, the balloon begins to fill with air. It grows bigger and bigger and bigger. The children move away from the bottle expecting the balloon to burst at any moment. Just as suddenly as it began, the liquid stops foaming and the balloon stops growing.

"How did that bottle blow up the balloon?" asks Ms. Miskle excitedly. "Hold on to your thoughts, and let's go over to the carpet for a minute. Come over here quietly, and sit down on your assigned square of the carpet. Be sure to keep your hands and feet to yourself by folding your arms and sitting with your legs crossed. I want to write down your ideas on the chart paper." For a few minutes, as they dictate the ideas to her, she writes them down using a new colored marker for each child's contribution to the chart. After writing, Ms. Miskle rereads each idea and asks the children to read it with her as she points to the print.

Once the children's ideas begin to ebb, Ms. Miskle asks them to join her in rereading all of the ideas. After rereading the whole chart paper, Ms. Miskle asks the children if there are just three words they would like to learn to read today from the chart. Children excitedly blurt out the words, blow up, bang, and foam. Ms. Miskle puts these words on cards on the wall. Later in the day, each child receives three small word cards to take home in an envelope. To exit the room that day, children have to reach into the envelope and read the three words on the cards. The children leave first grade that day believing they have achieved the goal of first grade; they have learned to read!

Visit Chapter 10 of our Companion Website at www.prenhall.com/ reutzel to look into the chapter objectives, standards and principles, and pertinent web links associated with organizing for reading instruction.

FIRST STEPS: PREPARING THE ENVIRONMENT FOR EFFECTIVE LITERACY INSTRUCTION

After reading this section on preparing the environment for effective literacy instruction, describe two ways classroom environments are an important part of the total learning experience for elementary school-aged readers.

Each new school year the empty classroom walls and floors call out to the experienced and novice teacher alike, "Welcome Back!" And each new year, you, the teacher, are faced in late summer or early fall with the task of planning, organizing, and preparing a classroom soon to be filled with lively and anxious children. Planning to make effective use of classroom space and other classroom literacy supplies and resources is the first obstacle standing in the way of a successful year of teaching children to read and write.

The physical environment of a classroom exerts a powerful influence on teaching and learning behaviors (Loughlin & Martin, 1987; Reutzel & Wolfersberger, 1996; Roskos & Neuman, 2001; Smith & Dickinson, 2002). Although the environment of the classroom is generally accepted as an important part of literacy instruction, teachers have paid too little attention to how the classroom environment affects children's literacy development. Research has demonstrated a clear relationship between environments in classrooms, homes, and neighborhoods and the acquisition of literacy (Morrow, 1990; Neuman & Roskos, 1992, 1997; Vukelich, 1994; Neuman, 1999; Neuman & Celano, 2000; Dickinson & Tabors, 2001; Roskos & Neuman, 2001).

Spending ample time and expending significant effort prior to the beginning of the school year in preparing the classroom for its eventual occupants, young children, will pay learning and management dividends all year. It is best if you can access literacy instructional tools and materials, such as basal teacher's edition and district curriculum guide, provided by the school *at least three months* prior to the beginning of the school year. This is important so that you can begin thinking about designing (1) the year's curriculum plan and (2) daily lesson plans. It is also critical to get into your classroom *at least one month* prior to the beginning of the school year in order to (1) prepare the environment, (2) assess the classroom supplies for adequacy, and (3) have sufficient lead time to acquire additional supplies, if necessary.

Recent research demonstrates a clear relationship between classroom environments and literacy-related behaviors and learning.

DESIGNING A CLASSROOM FLOOR PLAN

The major reason for carefully designing the physical environment of the classroom is to encourage children to learn from the environment, to interact cooperatively with each other, and to help you, the teacher, efficiently and effectively manage the environment while addressing the diverse learning needs of the children in your care. Decisions about the classroom literacy environment generally focus on three major concerns: (1) how to structure the environment, (2) what to place into the environment, and (3) what activities are to be carried out in the environment.

Our best advice as you begin is—begin simply. Plan a whole-class instructional area along with a few small-group and individual learning areas or centers. As you feel better able to manage a more complex environment, you will probably want to subdivide the classroom into additional, multipurpose learning and instructional spaces.

We suggest that you begin by drawing a **classroom floor plan.** Measure the width and length of your classroom and plot it onto a piece of graph paper. Using graph paper helps you maintain a sense of scale. Think about where and how you want to conduct whole-class instruction and learning activities. Then, survey the remaining space for small-group instruction. Carefully plan where you will place learning centers to reinforce instruction and provide opportunities to practice the skills, strategies, concepts, and processes previously taught.

When designing your first classroom floor plan, begin simply and add complexity as you find yourself managing the children's activities well within the structure you have created.

PLANNING WHOLE-CLASS LEARNING AND SHARING AREAS

A **whole-class learning and sharing area** (see Figure 10.1) is logically located near chalkboards and well away from designated quiet areas in the classroom. A large piece of well-padded carpet can be used to comfortably seat the entire class. Audiovisual equipment needs to be located near the whole-class sharing area. This equipment may include a wall-mounted television, video or DVD player, and overhead projectors; audiocassette or CD players; easels for displaying enlarged print of

Figure 10.1   Whole-class learning and sharing area

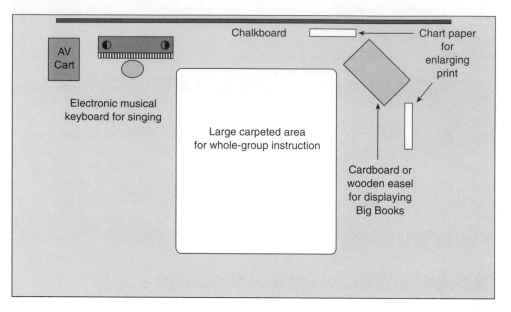

Chalkboard   Chart paper for enlarging print

AV Cart

Electronic musical keyboard for singing

Large carpeted area for whole-group instruction

Cardboard or wooden easel for displaying Big Books

A whole-class learning area is useful for whole-class activities such as singing from a chart, reading a big book, or performing a play.

stories, poems, riddles, songs, or group experience charts; electronic keyboards for music accompaniment; and display easels for reading commercial or child-produced big books. This area should also be clear of obstructions and may occupy up to 25 percent of the total space in the classroom.

When planning the whole-class learning or sharing area, consider such questions as: (1) Where is the best place for the whole group to see and interact with me when I am demonstrating or modeling a literacy skill, concept, process, or strategy? (2) How do I want my children to be seated during whole-group instruction—at their desks, on carpet squares on the floor, at tables? Once you have come to a decision about where and how you want to design the whole-class instructional space, draw it on your classroom floor plan in as much detail as possible.

It is important that you consider details because you should think about your needs as a teacher. Ask yourself questions. Where will I write during whole-class instruction—chalkboard, dry erase whiteboard, large chart paper tablet and easel, hand-held chalkboard or dry erase board, overhead projector? How will I share and display books, poems, song lyrics? Will I need access to a VHS or DVD player, computer, and monitor? Will I need access to a CD or tape player, electronic keyboard or piano? Do I need an easel for big books, pointers, highlight tape, markers, chalk, editing tape, stick-on notes? Think through the types of demonstrations, modeling, and instruction you will offer in this area, make a list of needed supplies, and plan places for storage, and display.

Figures 10.2–10.4 provide three classroom floor plans. They give you ideas, from a simple layout with a very few small learning areas to more complex layouts with a wide variety of classroom learning centers and areas. To add depth and dimension to the classroom floor plan, we also provide you a collage of classroom photos showing floor plans of varying complexity to help you plan and prepare your classroom layout for the beginning of the year.

Figure 10.2   Early transitions, second grade classroom arrangement

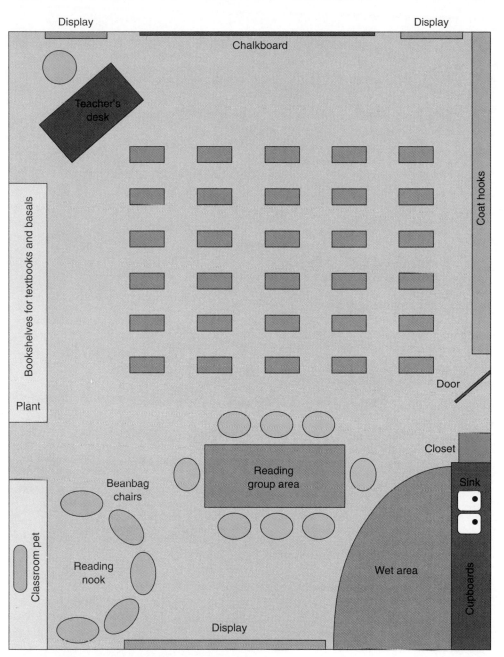

PLANNING THE TEACHER'S PROFESSIONAL SPACE

A next step in designing the classroom floor plan is carefully considering where and how to situate your workspace. In some schools and classrooms, you may actually have a walled off space or office directly adjacent to the classroom. However, in most schools the **teacher's professional space** is integrated into the classroom space—to

Figure 10.3 Intermediate transitions. Second grade classroom arrangement

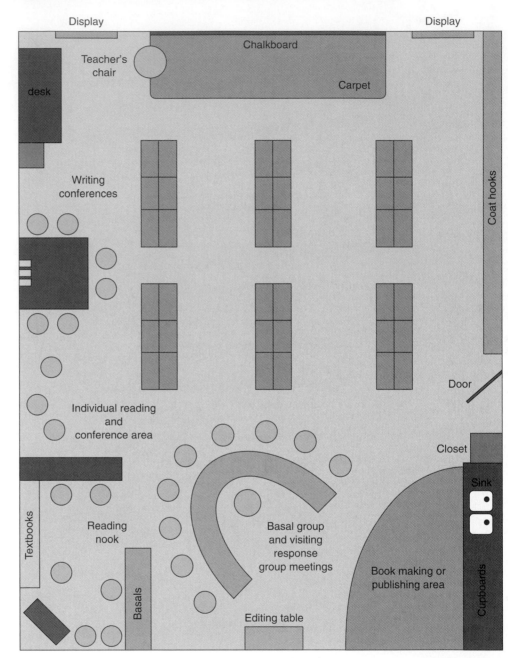

The teacher's professional workspace should not be the dominant focus of the classroom.

encourage high levels of teacher-child interaction. Our advice is that the teacher's workspace should not be the dominant focus in the classroom. We recommend that the teacher's desk be sidelined in a corner of the classroom. Facing the teacher's desk toward the wall discourages you from spending time at your desk when children are in the classroom. Also, having your desk, bookshelf, files, computer, and displays in a corner protects these items from the normal traffic flow of the classroom. We encourage

Figure 10.4 Advanced transitions, first grade classroom arrangement

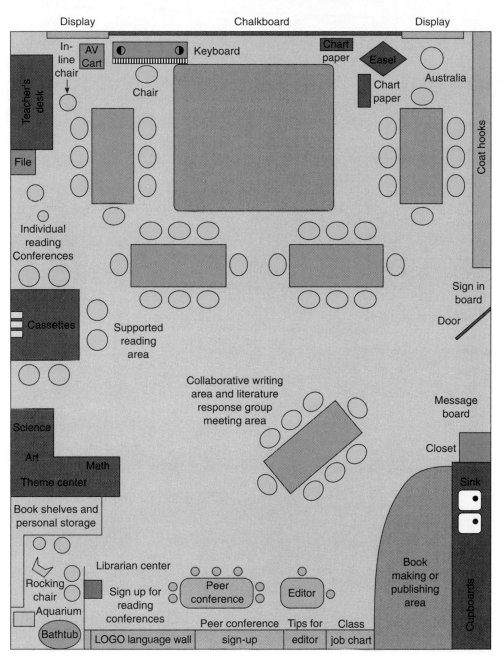

teachers to prominently display their college diplomas and teaching license in this area. These displayed items speak volumes about your professional preparation and qualifications as a teacher: Be sure to have a bookshelf where you can store and display professional books, journals, and reference materials. This, too, speaks to your professionalism. Having thought about how to arrange your personal space in the classroom, draw your workspace into the classroom floor plan (see Figure 10.5).

Classroom arrangement

Classroom arrangement

PLANNING SMALL-GROUP INSTRUCTION AND LEARNING CENTERS

With your professional workspace and the whole-class learning and sharing area designed, you are now ready to plan and design the number and variety of **learning centers,** that is, small-group instructional and learning areas.

Classroom arrangement

Figure 10.5 Teacher's professional space

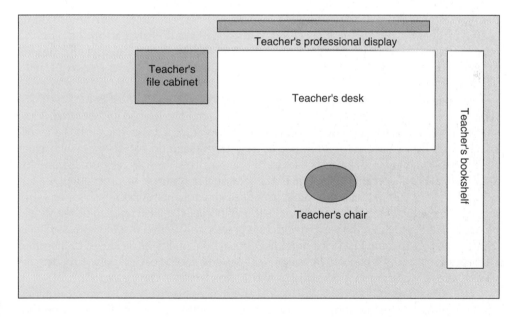

When you begin to plan learning centers in a classroom, there is much to contemplate. First, consider how many you can manage. If you are an inexperienced teacher, have trouble with multitasking, or just feel the need to have a more controlled environment to start the year, then you may not want to have more than two or three learning centers. However, most teachers begin the process of planning learning centers by considering what they want to accomplish in these spaces.

To begin this process, we describe a variety of small-group/learning centers that you may wish to include in your classroom. We have categorized these learning center spaces into three levels of importance for classroom design: (1) critical-standing learning centers, (2) highly recommended standing learning centers, and (3) elective/temporary learning centers.

Critical-Standing Learning Centers

There are five critical-standing learning centers found in many K–3 literacy classrooms: (1) guided reading center, (2) word work center, (3) writing and publishing center, (4) independent reading center, and (5) literacy enriched play center. We classify these learning centers as critical because they are an integral part of a balanced, comprehensive, and research-based reading program: We say standing centers because these spaces are intended to remain a part of the classroom design for the entire school year. If there is to be any sacrifice of learning centers to support early literacy development and acquisition, these critical centers should not be considered expendable.

*There are five critical-standing learning centers in classrooms that use centers:
1) guided reading,
2) word work, 3) writing,
4) independent reading,
and 5) dramatic play.*

The Guided Reading Center

The guided reading center will need individual seating and a table to accommodate up to eight students and the teacher. It is to be designed so that the teacher will be able to assess and guide children's reading of just-right leveled books while providing varying amounts of teacher support as needed. We have found that the use of a kidney- or U-shaped table, eight student-size chairs, and one teacher-size chair work well in relation to the functions to be served in a guided reading area. The teacher is typically seated in the center of the U-shaped table, with her students seated around the perimeter. It is helpful if the guided reading area is located near the classroom library where a selection of leveled books may be found. It is also helpful if the teacher locates a file cabinet where she keeps her assessment folders on individual children near this area.

Locate the guided reading learning center in a quiet place near the classroom library collection where leveled books are stored.

Plastic baskets for holding several sets of leveled books are a must here. These are typically placed on the guided reading area table for students to read while an individual student's reading is assessed by the teacher. It is also helpful if the teacher has a small, roughly 12″ by 12″ white dry erase board, marker, eraser, and cookie sheet with magnetic letters on hand in this center as well. Some teachers like to have a small easel for displaying posters containing information about center routines or procedures, or important information about literacy skills, strategies, or concepts. A pocket chart for working with the sentences, phrases, and words found in leveled guided reading books should be easily within reach. In the second and third grades, the guided reading area facilitates group meetings that begin to look more like those found in literature circles or literature response groups (see Chapter 13). We provide several photos of K–3 guided reading areas to help you envision how the design of this area works in the classroom.

For a much more extensive discussion and description of how to plan for guided reading areas and instruction, we recommend you obtain a copy of Fountas and Pinnell's (1996) *Guided Reading Instruction: Good First Teaching for All Children.*

The Word Work Center

This area of the K–3 classroom can be accommodated in a variety of ways. One may be a small, carpeted corner of the classroom where a small bookshelf, storage bins, or stacked baskets are kept. Another may be a part of the classroom where a table

Guided reading area

or a group of six to eight student desks are clustered together adjacent to a counter top where storage bins or stacked baskets are kept. It may also be a place where a classroom computer is located, for use in studying words by a pair of students while others work on other word work tasks.

This word work center should be located near and have an unobstructed view of the classroom *word wall,* discussed later in this chapter. It should be stocked with magnetic letters, laminated letters, individual-size dry erase boards, markers/erasers, locking plastic packets, pictures for word or letter sorts, and letter trays with plastic letters and letter tiles for making, breaking, and manipulating words and letters. Computer (CD or DVD) programs where children work with words can be provided in this center. Word and letter games, such as letter and word BINGO or letter and word Chutes and Ladders, have a place here as well. This center is expressly designed to *directly reinforce and provide practice* for previous whole-class, explicit, systematic letter, sound, phonemic awareness, spelling, phonics, and sight-word instruction. Each day's activities ought to be designed to (a) reinforce previous learning, (b) encourage exploration and discovery, and (c) provide for accountability through completed daily tasks. If children are asked to make words using the *ick* word family tile, then they should be expected to write on a paper several of the words they made, assuring task completion and providing assessment feedback to the teacher regarding student progress and needs.

For a comprehensive treatment of working with words, we heartily recommend that you get a copy of Bear, Templeton, Invernizzi, and Johnston's (2000) *Words Their Way: Word Study for Phonics, Vocabulary, and Spelling Instruction.*

Word work learning centers are stocked with magnetic letters, cookie sheets, laminated letters, individual-sized dry erase white boards, erasers, markers, pictures for word and letter sorts, letter tiles, and so on.

Figure 10.6   Writing center

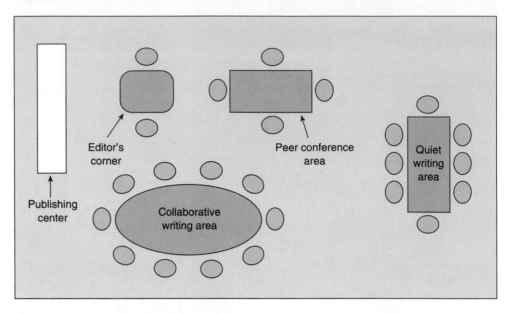

The Writing Center

The **writing center** (see Figure 10.6) often includes three smaller integrated working areas:

- Work area for collaborative writing projects, conferences, and editing
- Quiet area for silent sustained writing
- Publishing area with necessary supplies

A writing center needs to accommodate a variety of activities including drafting, conferencing, editing, and publishing.

The writing area is an integral part of the writing process or writing workshop approach in the K–3 classroom. Because of the nature of the multiple activities in the writing center, it should be located away from the quiet areas designated for silent sustained writing. As part of the writing area, a space for *collaborative writing* is designated for children to interact with teachers and peers about their writing projects—projects that may have been authored by individuals or groups or that may have been coauthored. A *conference area* with table and chairs or just a quiet carpeted corner can function as a location for conducting peer–student or teacher–student conferences about developing writing projects. An *editing area* can be located at a desk or table near the conference area. An older student, the teacher, or an adult volunteer can function as an editor for student-authored works in the classroom. An editor's visor, printer's apron, various writing and marking media, and a poster displaying editorial marks can be located here for the editor's use. The *publishing area* should be stocked with pencils, pens, markers, stapler, and various papers (colors and sizes) for covers. Binding materials also should be available for students to bind or publish their final writing products in a variety of ways. The location for each of the many supplies in this area can be indicated by a printed label or an outline of the object; doing so makes it easier for students to help in keeping the publishing area neat and tidy. Student works published in this area may take the form of big books, shape books,

Figure 10.7 Independent reading center

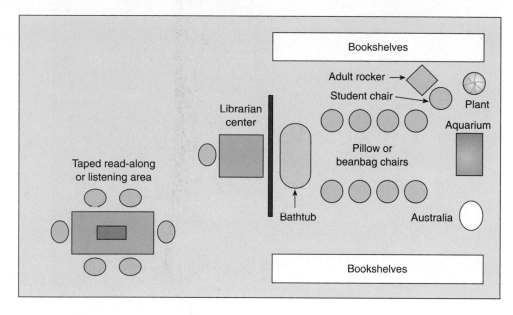

micro-books, accordion books, letters, notes, lists, posters, bulletin boards, and murals (see Figure 10.6).

Independent Reading Center

An *independent reading center* is a quiet, comfortable, inviting niche in the classroom environment designed for enjoying personal reading of a variety of books (narrative and informational, at a minimum) and other print materials at differing levels of challenge. As such, it should be located well away from the mainstream activity of the classroom (see Figure 10.7).

Trade books can be organized into sections for easy reading, early reading, and advanced reading materials. Within each of these categories of reading challenge, books can be organized in alphabetical order by titles or by the author's last name. When multiple copies of a single title are available, old cereal boxes cut in half, covered in contact paper, and displaying the title of the books on the side of the box can be used to store these books as a group.

Big books can be stored in shelves or on hooks, pants hangers, specially made pocket charts, or easels near this area. This location can also be used to store the adopted basal readers. Whether a basal, multiple copies of trade books, or level books are used, this area is ideal for small-group or one-to-one story reading or literature response group meetings. It should be comfortable and well lit. Carpeting, beanbag chairs, a bathtub filled with pillows, pillow chairs, and the like can be used as comfortable places for children to curl up with a favorite book. A large rocking chair can be located here for lap reading with younger children. Plants and aquariums can do much to create a peaceful atmosphere. Accountability for time spent in independent reading is a critical part of assuring that students are in fact reading. To provide for accountability in this center simply and effectively, we used a book time, title, and response log for each child, as shown in Figure 10.8.

The independent reading center needs to provide a comfortable, inviting environment for enjoying books.

Independent Reading Area

Head Start has created a list of recommended books for young readers. Link to this valuable tool for creating your classroom library on Chapter 10 of our Companion Website at www.prenhall.com/reutzel.

Each child records the amount of time in minutes spent reading silently, the title or titles of the books or print materials read that day, and a brief response to what he or she read.

If books or basal readers are to be checked out from this center for out-of-school reading, a librarian's center can be located near the independent reading area for check outs (see Figure 10.7).

A storage container can be kept here for reading backpacks (Cooter, Mills-House, Marrin, Mathews, Campbell, & Baker, 1999) so that take-home books can be protected, accounted for on a regular basis, and sent home daily. Children who serve as librarians keep records on books checked out and those overdue from the class library. All children are asked to be responsible for keeping the classroom library orderly.

We have used a variation of the independent reading center—the Australia Escape Corner. It is based on the book *Alexander and the Terrible, Horrible, No Good, Very Bad Day* by Judith Viorst (1972). When things in the classroom or a student's personal life are just too much to handle at the moment, they may retreat to the Australia Escape Corner, just like Alexander who was always going to Australia, for 10 minutes once a day, no questions asked. If the child needs to remain longer than 10 minutes, she is expected to explain her reasons to the teacher privately. Teachers may also retreat on occasion to Australia. This action alone was found to be one of our best classroom discipline techniques!

Literacy Enriched Play Centers (K–1)

According to Vygotsky (1978) play involves the child in behaviors that are, "beyond his average age, above his daily behavior; in play it is as though he were a head taller than himself. As in the focus of a magnifying glass, play contains all developmental

Figure 10.8   Book title and time log

Name of student _____

Monday—Date _____

Book Titles _____

_____Time in Minutes _____

Tuesday—Date _____

Book Titles _____

_____Time in Minutes _____

Wednesday—Date _____

Book Titles _____

_____Time in Minutes _____

Thursday—Date _____

Book Titles _____

_____Time in Minutes _____

Friday—Date _____

Book Titles _____

_____Time in Minutes _____

tendencies in a condensed form and is itself a major source of development" (p. 102). Vygotsky continues, "At school age play does not die away but permeates the attitude toward reality. . . . It is the essence of play that a new relation is created between the field of meaning and the visual field—that is, between situations in thought and real situations." (p. 104) Play is the child's work, and through it children learn how to engage in literacy tasks demanded in different situations and practice using the more formal language register of book words and language.

Grounded in the research of Neuman and Roskos (1992, 1997) as well as many other early childhood literacy educators (Morrow, 2001, 2002; Rogg, 2001), play centers are a significant part of effective early literacy classrooms. Neuman and Roskos (1992, 1997) found that enriching play centers with a variety of situation-specific literacy tools (artifacts) and materials (props) increased children's use of literacy as a part of their imaginative play. In other words, children incorporated more literate acts and behaviors into their imaginative play when literacy tools were present than when they were not. Also, embedding literacy learning in play centers encourages children to interact and collaborate with peers using language and literacy

Play is the child's work. Every primary-grade classroom should have an area for dramatic, imaginative, or structured play.

as a medium during play. Observations of young children at play have shown that in the presence of literacy tools appropriate to the social situation in the play center, children will engage in attempted and conventional reading and writing acts in collaboration with other children more often (Morrow, 1990; Neuman & Roskos, 1990, 1992, 1997).

Potential play centers appropriate to be considered in K–1 classrooms include:

- Offices—business offices, post offices, doctor's offices, and newspaper offices.
- Businesses—labs, restaurants, bakeries, carpentry shops, art galleries, grocery stores, auto mechanics, and repair
- Travel—airports, airplanes, bus stations, buses, train stations, and trains
- Home—kitchens, home office, school room, and play room
- Drama—plays, readers' theater, puppetry, and creative movement

Play centers should not be limited to the kindergarten classroom but should be a feature of every classroom K–1. A collage of photos provide examples of literacy enriched play centers found in K–1 classrooms.

For play centers to effectively press children into literacy behaviors, literacy tools and materials need to meet certain criteria and be appropriately arranged. Play centers also need to be organized so that literacy interactions between students are encouraged and supported. The play center is typically NOT a quiet place, but rather a very busy place where language and literacy acts are "tried on" for fun and fit. Design principles for organizing literacy tools and materials in the classroom and play centers are discussed in a later section of this chapter.

Literacy enriched play center

Literacy enriched play center

Highly Recommended Standing Learning Centers

Learning centers highly recommended as standing centers in the classroom include: (1) a listening center, (2) a paired/buddy reading center, and (3) an individual assessment/conference center. These centers compliment those centers designated critical but can be, and in some cases are, incorporated into processes found in those centers. There are several other centers which we will describe later that we feel are highly recommended but can be emphasized in grades 2–3, such as a literature circles/response center, fluency development center, and vocabulary development center. But for K–3 classrooms, we feel the centers described here are the most age and stage appropriate.

Listening Center

The *listening center* is a spot where children listen to books read aloud via audiocassette tapes, CDs, and computers. A table, chairs, CD/tape player, books on tape or CD, and six to eight copies of each book title are necessities for beginning a listening center. If possible, each student should be provided a set of headphones for listening. Directions for who is to pass out the books, insert the tape or CD, and operate the CD/tape player must be in place. It is also important that children be given a few questions to answer after reading. For very young readers, these answers can be yes or no or smiling or frowning faces. To encourage the development of good listening habits, it is important that children feel that they will be accountable for time spent in this center and are listening for a purpose. A computer with a CD-ROM or DVD book can be used as another variation on listening centers in K–3 classrooms. We have found that in listening centers where a computer is the means of delivery no more than four children can be seated at a single computer and operate effectively on the print.

If a listening center is used in the classroom, children should be asked to listen for a purpose such as to answer questions or record their feelings in a writing response journal.

Paired/Reading Buddies Center

In this center, a variety of literacy activities that can be pursued in pairs or with reading buddies are made available. Activities for this center may include large display charts of poems, song lyrics, and riddles for buddy reading or singing and pointers to point to the words. A bank of word cards taken from children's language experience charts, big books, basal stories, and other shared reading materials can be located in this center. Large pointers and frames for use with big books can be supplied for children in this center. Words cards can be read together or to each other, or word cards can be matched back into the books, stories, or charts from which they were taken. Pocket charts where children order scrambled sentence strips from books either previously read or yet to be read are another useful activity in this center. In terms of classroom space allocation, we have found that the whole-class learning and sharing area can often double as the *paired/reading buddies center* because these two classroom functions typically do not occur simultaneously in the schedule of the classroom activities.

Younger readers are helped when they are supported as they learn to read by the provision of read-along tapes, buddy readers, or "grandparent helpers" from the community.

Individual Reading Conference Center

The *individual reading conference area* is usually small and quiet (Figure 10.9). It is used for conducting individual reading conferences between teacher and individual students. Students make an appointment to meet with the teacher for an individual reading conference by signing up on the individual reading conference sign-up board (see Figure 10.10). The teacher and an individual student meet together briefly to read and discuss a selected trade book, information text, or story taken from a basal reader. While the student reads, the teacher listens, encourages, records performance, and offers supports.

Individual reading conferences provide an ideal setting for assessing a student's progress in reading, as is discussed in Chapter 9.

Elective-Temporary Learning Centers

These centers come and go when there is a curriculum-based need to learn specific content, processes, or concepts within or across several school subjects, such as science, math, health, social studies, and science. Although we cannot possibly describe all permutations associated with learning centers of this type, we have found that these centers can be identified as requiring specialized equipment, such as a water table, sand table, microscope, incubator, and garden lights. For the most part, the centers we describe below represent in spirit centers we designate as elective-temporary.

Figure 10.9 Individual reading conference area

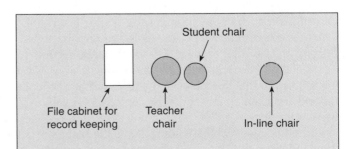

Figure 10.10   Individual reading conference sign-up board

Monday—Date _____

8:00 A.M.

Name _____ Book Title _____

_____ Page Numbers_____

8:10 A.M.

Name _____ Book Title _____

_____ Page Numbers_____

8:20 A.M.

Name _____ Book Title _____

_____ Page Numbers_____

Tuesday—Date _____

8:00 A.M.

Name _____ Book Title _____

_____ Page Numbers_____

8:10 A.M.

Name _____ Book Title _____

_____ Page Numbers_____

8:20 A.M.

Name _____ Book Title _____

_____ Page Numbers_____

Project Approach or Inquiry-Based Learning Center

The *project approach* or inquiry-based study area is designated for in-depth study of a selected topic or theme (Chard, 1998). For example, children may express interest in the topic of magic as a result of having heard *James and the Giant Peach* (Dahl, 1961) read aloud. During the planning of a project focused on *magic,* begin by identifying resources available for investigating *magic.* After brainstorming with the children, design several activities to focus the curriculum on the topic. Children may listen to music about magic in this area or produce art that employs different media that may seem magical, such as crayon-resist drawings or turpentine swirl painting. Geometric puzzles or math problems from *I Hate Mathematics* (M. Burns, 1987) can provide several magical math problems and solutions. Children may read research or information books describing how to perform simple magic tricks. The Harry Potter (J. K. Rowling) series books may also be available in this center for small-group read aloud.

Themed or topical studies help students make cross-curricular connection as well as learn to use reading and writing to learn new and important information.

Be sure to design a way to schedule opportunities for children to use the center and provide a means of record keeping and accountability. An example of a theme center activity log can be found in Figure 10.11. In this log children record the activities they complete each day and write a short essay response to the activities. In the end, children should produce a report, display, or demonstration for sharing and dissemination as evidence of their learning in the project or inquiry center.

Integrated or Content Curriculum Learning Centers

A *content learning center* focuses learning on concepts or processes found in a single curriculum subject, such as mathematics, science, art, music, or social studies. An integrated learning center integrates several subjects and literacy together into a single unit of exploration, discovery, or learning. In an *integrated center,* the center may initially focus on reading a particular book and follow up with several projects, tasks, or assignments. Or, the center may involve children in several projects, tasks, or assignments initially and progress to reading a book to answer questions or add new insights and understandings. For example, children may begin their work in this center by reading William Anton's (1999), *Corn: From Farm to Table.*

During the planning of the project or inquiry center focused on corn, we began by identifying resources available for learning about corn as a part of our life cycles science curriculum. After brainstorming with the children, we designed several activities to focus the curriculum on the life cycle of corn, its uses, and such. Children may look at different kinds of corn seeds under a magnifying glass. They may count how many corn seeds are in a row of seeds on a corncob and represent the numbers using Cuisenaire rods. They may make popcorn the "old fashioned" way with a pot, corn oil, and a burner rather than in a microwave! They could use a semantic feature analysis grid (see Chapter 7 on vocabulary instruction) to compare corn with beans and peas on features such as color, shape, taste, and uses. For exploration at home, children could survey the things that have corn in them or use corn.

In these centers, the object is to integrate literacy learning with other curriculum subjects. As in all other centers, it is critical to design accountability into the daily operation. In the end, children may complete a series of small assignments or tasks related to acquiring knowledge about the content or applying reading strategies.

Content or integrated learning centers help link student learning across time, topics, and subject areas. These centers allow children to explore, express, and elaborate their knowledge.

ORGANIZING CLASSROOM LITERACY TOOLS AND MATERIALS

Based on the literacy environmental research mentioned earlier, Reutzel and Wolfersberger (1996) described six criteria for selecting and arranging literacy tools and materials in K–3 classrooms:

- Appropriateness
- Authenticity
- Utility
- Proximity
- Uses
- Change

Figure 10.11 Research project center activity log

Research Project Activity Log

Student Name _____

Research Topic or Question _____

Monday

Time In: _____

Today I:

Time Out: _____

Tuesday

Time In: _____

Today I:

Time Out: _____

Wednesday

Time In: _____

Today I:

Time Out: _____

Thursday

Time In: _____

Today I:

Time Out: _____

Friday

Time In: _____

Today I:

Time Out: _____

Integrated second grade curriculum unit on Native America

To determine the *appropriateness* of literacy tools or materials, we ask questions. Are the literacy materials developmentally appropriate? Can my children use these tools and materials safely? Can they use these tools and materials in purposeful ways? Can they use these tools and materials in socially meaningful ways to communicate and interact?

Second, we consider the criterion of *authenticity*. We ask, "Are these tools and materials found and used in a variety of settings in school and out?" Third, we consider whether or not literacy tools and materials fit the criterion of *utility*. We ask, "Do these literacy tools and materials serve useful literacy functions found in society?" A partial listing of appropriate, authentic, and useful literacy tools and materials is found in Figure 10.13.

Fourth, we arrange literacy tools so that they are *proximal* to the children and their activities. Children will not use literacy tools as readily if they are stored in a location far from the major area(s) of activity. Fifth, we *suggest possible uses* for literacy tools and materials. For example, we suggest that a message board in the classroom might be used to post announcements, ask questions, or send personal communications. When used in a kitchen play center, a message board may be used to post a grocery list or take telephone messages. In a science center, a message board may be used to list materials needed to conduct an experiment, record the steps of an experiment, or make a diagram for displaying the process or outcome of an experiment.

And sixth, we regularly rotate or *change* the availability of specific literacy tools and materials. Young children, like adults, grow weary of the same old thing. We added to, deleted from, and rotated literacy tools and materials on a regular basis in our K–3 classrooms.

Literacy behaviors increase with the number of literacy props provided in the classroom environment. For example, when children have a message board, they tend to write more often to their peers.

Figure 10.12 Possible literacy props to enrich literacy learning

Books, pamphlets, magazines	Posters of children's books	Appointment book
Ledger sheets	Small drawer trays	Signs (e.g., open/closed)
Cookbooks	Library book return cards	File folders
Labeled recipe boxes	A wide variety of children's books	In/out trays
Personal stationery		Business cards
Grocery store ads/fliers	Telephone books	Self-adhesive notes and address labels
Empty grocery containers	A sign-in/sign-out sheet	
Note cards	ABC index cards	Bookmarks
Pens, pencils, markers	Small plaques/decorative magnets	Post Office mailbox
Trays for holding items		Computer/address labels
Message pads	Assorted forms	Calendars of various types
Envelopes of various sizes	Blank recipe cards	
	Emergency number decals	Posters/signs about mailing
Racks for filing papers		Stamps for marking books
Index cards	Food coupons	
Clipboards	Play money	Typewriter or computer keyboard
Stationery	Small message board	
Stickers, stars, stamps, stamp pads	Notepads of assorted sizes	Telephone
A tote bag for mail	Large plastic clips	Paper of assorted sizes

ORGANIZING INSTRUCTIONAL TOOLS AND MATERIALS FOR EFFECTIVE LITERACY INSTRUCTION

Finding out which literacy tools and materials are available for instruction in your classroom, school building, and district office and then deciding how to arrange and use them is another major decision facing K–3 teachers at the beginning of each year and throughout the school year. Most school districts and schools provide a wide array of commonly available literacy instructional tools and materials for teaching reading and writing. We discuss some of these commonly provided instructional tools and materials so that you can identify them in the district, school, and classroom *and* understand the instructional purposes intended for each.

Trade Books

Trade books by definition are those books typically found in libraries or in bookstores. Trade books vary widely in content as well as length and difficulty. Trade books include wordless picture books, picture books, information books, big books, books with limited print, shape and pop-up books, and books with chapters. In schools, trade books are found in both the school library and classroom libraries.

The size and content of a classroom trade book library vary with the purposes it will serve. For example, if the classroom library is to be used for self-selected, silent reading purposes or in an independent reading program, Veatch (1968) suggests a minimum of three books for each student in the classroom. For the average

Margaret Jensen, of the Cooperative Children's Book Center, University of Wisconsin-Madison, has selected, by topic, appropriate books for young readers. You can link to this valuable resource from Chapter 10 of our Companion Website at www. prenhall.com/reutzel.

classroom, this translates into a range of 75 to 90 books. Stoodt (1989) recommends 10 books per student as a minimum and the International Reading Association (2000) recommends seven titles per child. Using these guidelines, we suggest you strive initially for a classroom library size of between 250 and 300 individual trade book titles. Recognizing the limitations of your personal budget and that of the school, you may reach this number initially by checking out a number of trade books from your school library collection to be housed temporarily in your classroom library.

When you are finished reading this section, write down three ways you can increase your classroom selection of trade books.

Talk with your local PTA representatives. They can often help you acquire more trade books for your library by sponsoring bake sales, by opening school stores where children buy books or other school supplies, and by soliciting donations for books from local merchants and parents. The school librarian can often be a source of trade books. Local thrift and secondhand stores are inexpensive sources. Garage and attic sales are also possible sources. Book auctions, where children bring their own trade books and auction them off to their peers for reading, are an exciting way to provide expanded trade book access for children in schools.

Work in conjunction with your school principal to decide how to use funds allocated for consumable classroom supplies such as workbooks. Sometimes state laws permit the use of these dollars for classroom trade book libraries or multiple copies of paperback books. In addition, encourage children to purchase their own paperback books through book clubs. Typically, for every book purchased by a child in these book clubs, the teacher collects points toward free copies of books. Books for children in low-income communities can also be purchased in site-based managed schools using supplemental federal funds (e.g., Title I, Reading First, and RIF).

Some teachers solicit book donations from parents; used children's books donated by parents whose children have outgrown them are a valuable resource. The PTA can ask parents to donate a book in the name of their child to the classroom or school library rather than sending treats to school on the child's birthday. The possibilities for acquiring a vast supply of trade books for use in schools are limited only by your imagination. It is important, however, that you and your school administrator not relegate the acquisition of trade books for the classroom library to bake sale fund-raisers indefinitely. Rather, you must eventually ensure that acquiring quality trade books becomes a regular line item in local school budgets.

Basal Readers

Because basal readers are used in over 85 percent of schools today, you will not need to look very far to find a basal reading series in your classroom. Contemporary basal reading programs include a greater variety of children's literature and information selections. Many basal reader teacher's manuals encourage the integration of reading, writing, listening, and speaking. Some basal reading programs are also thematically organized, allowing children to explore a topic thoroughly rather than flit from one topic to the next with each subsequent story in the reader (see Chapter 8). T. D. Johnson and Louis (1987) suggest that basal stories can be used in the early grades for extensive modeling and choral readings. In Chapter 11 we will also discuss how basal readers can be used to begin a *guided reading* program (Fawson & Reutzel, 2000).

Workbooks, Worksheets, and Blackline Masters

Workbook pages and blackline masters are a standard component of the reading and writing program in most schools and classrooms. Unfortunately, some teachers use workbook pages unnecessarily or for classroom management purposes (Osborn,

1984; Rupley & Blair, 1987). Children frequently spend as much time completing workbook pages, or pages from blackline masters, as they do interacting with teachers and real books.

Becoming a Nation of Readers (R. C. Anderson, Hiebert, Scott, & Wilkinson, 1985) the report of the commission on Reading, asserted that many children spend up to 70 percent of the time allocated for reading instruction engaged in independent seat work and completing workbooks and worksheets. Although these materials are a necessary part of reading instruction, we encourage you to carefully select and use these practice materials sparingly and never as a substitute for your explicit instruction as a teacher!

Leveled Books

In an increasing number of K–3 literacy classrooms, you will have access in your room or in a central school collection to leveled books for guided reading instruction. Several leveling schemes have been developed and applied to books for emergent and early readers. Reading Recovery® programs use a set of criteria that result in a range of leveled texts from levels 1–20. In today's classrooms, guided reading books are often leveled using a text gradient ranging from levels A–Z (see Chapter 8) found in the writings of Fountas and Pinnell (1996, 2001). Some trade book companies are now using a book leveling process known as Lexiles® producing a range of levels from 200L to 1800L (Stenner, 1996; Stenner & Burdick, 1997). For more about Lexile levels go to www.lexile.com on the World Wide Web. Regardless of the way books are leveled in your school, be sure that you and your colleagues in the school use the same leveling approach. Otherwise, the levels may not match because they have not specifically been equated with one another.

Decodable Books

Decodable books may also be available to you as you inventory your classroom literacy instructional tools and materials. Decodable books are used to teach K–3 students to read by providing text that is consistent in representing words that use specific phonic and spelling patterns (Adams, 1990a, 1990b; Foorman et al., 1997; Lyon, 1998). Decodable books contain text that is controlled to exemplify a particular phonics rule or pattern, such as the one shown here, which you may recall from Chapter 8:

The Big Hit*

Who hid? Pig.
Who had a mitt? Pig.
Who did not sit?
Who did hit?
Up. Up. Up.
Who had a big hit? Pig.
Who slid? Pig did!

*From *Phonics Readers,* Scholastic Book 14, pp. 2–7, by Schreiber & Tuchman. Copyright 1997 by Scholastic, Inc. Reprinted by permission.

Those who advocate the use of decodable texts insist that students must be given sufficient practice in phonically regular texts so that they will develop automatic decoding abilities before they tackle the additional challenges associated with comprehending

Can you think of other reasons that over-reliance on workbooks and worksheets can interfere with young children's desire to learn to read and write?

Leveled books are very popular in today's classrooms. Go to the computer lab and search for sites on the World Wide Web that provide information about leveled books.

The use of decodable books to teach emergent or early readers has recently become popular. The idea is that children will read text that contains phonic elements that the teacher has already introduced in explicit, whole or small group instruction.

more complex written language. On the other hand, some reading experts contend there is no scientific evidence that shows that controlling texts along dimensions of phonics rules and patterns are more effective than other types of beginning reading texts (Allington, 1997; Allington & Woodside-Jiron, 1998; Hiebert, 1999). Furthermore, they assert that controlling book content for phonics patterns or usage renders beginning reading books and stories dry and meaningless. In any case, many national publishing companies are now producing decodable texts for teachers as a part of their classroom reading instruction tools and materials.

Computers and Other Information Technology

Standards Note
Standard 5.7: Use instructional and information technologies to support literacy learning. When using technology, it is important to understand how to select materials that are appropriate for young children. Note in the pages that follow how to evaluate and select age-appropriate hardware and software to support early literacy development.

The children of tomorrow will not just read books. They will use multiple approaches to literacy—especially the Internet and other digital literacy technologies.

The introduction of technology into classrooms has become a priority in school districts around the United States. Internet connections, personal computers (PCs), modems, T-1 (analog) and DS3 (digital) lines, laser printers, software programs, and, of course, technologists to train and maintain computers are absorbing more and more tax dollars. Yet, the benefit to children and literacy learning thus far has been questionable at best in relation to the costs. A recent review of current research by Blok, Oostdam, Otter, and Overmaat (2002) showed that computer-assisted instruction yielded about .2 standard deviation (5–7%) impact on children's learning. Set against the ever-increasing costs of hardware, software, and infrastructure, future studies will need to demonstrate far larger effect sizes to justify continued investment in computer-assisted instruction. So, what should be the role of computers in your classroom environment?

The renowned economist Peter Drucker (1998) stated that when computers and other information technology (IT) came onto the scene in education, the emphasis was (and still is) on the *T* of *technology.* Massive resources have been channeled primarily into purchasing and updating technology hardware and software. Some have estimated that two-thirds or more of these resources have gone into the *T* in IT and less than one-third to training teachers how to use the technology effectively. That ratio is the reverse of how expenditures should be made. This wrongly skewed emphasis has led to a phenomenon we refer to as "invention is the mother of necessity." Too much of our time and resources are spent trying to figure out how to use technology rather than what it is we want to accomplish with it in literacy instruction.

Drucker also suggests that teachers recognize that the emphasis must be on the *I* in IT—*information.* Simply put, our job as teachers is to instill literacy skills to help our young charges search, retrieve, and effectively select information for application and use. In choosing computers and other technology for the classroom, ask yourself these questions:

- Which literacy skills does this group of children need to learn?
- Which activities and methods are the best practices for getting this information across to the students?
- Which of the technologies available could assist me in teaching these skills in an efficient and cost-effective way?

Two other important questions should be considered before making IT selections.

- Are there other, non-technological ways of accomplishing the same tasks with less expense?
- If I am to use technology, is my choice the simplest and least expensive available?

These questions are getting at important principles. One is to choose technologies that are the simplest and cheapest available. For example, if a cassette player and book or buddy reading sessions will help students with fluency practice, then don't feel you need to purchase expensive computers and CD software to do the same task. And if a cloze passage drawn from a popular shared reading activity will suffice, then we shouldn't purchase an expensive program to accomplish the same thing.

On the other hand, some technologies may well be "worth the bucks"! For instance, a program like IBM's *Writing to Read 2000* might be a good choice for some schools to help satisfy students' practice needs in writing. Middle school teachers may decide that Scholastic's *Read 180* computer-based reading program is an appropriate supplement for serving the needs of students with significant reading problems. Some recent research seems to point to motivational benefits for struggling readers who read text online. It suggests that struggling readers may persist in trying to read online text at higher levels because of personal interest and motivation. The central point, as Drucker implies, is that technology should be selected only if it serves the needs of teachers in providing instruction for effective information search, retrieval, and selection as well as other effective reading strategies—and the simpler (least expensive), the better.

MAKING THE MOST OF CLASSROOM DISPLAY AREAS

Immerse K–3 students in an environment of interesting and *functional* print. Display areas can be located almost anywhere in the classroom—walls, windows, floors, doors, and ceilings. Where possible, displays should be student produced rather than teacher produced. A message board for leaving notes is one way teachers and students can communicate with each other. A sign-in board encourages even the very youngest children to write their names at the beginning of the school day. Window writing using pens with water-soluble ink allows students to transcribe their stories, poems, jokes, riddles, and song lyrics onto the window glass. Windows are a fun and novel way to publish writing projects in classrooms. Many children are very intrigued by window-published writing projects.

A logo language wall or environmental print bulletin board can be devoted to print that children bring from home. Logo language is both fun and instructionally useful because it helps even the youngest children to know they can already read. Children bring labels from cans, cereal boxes, old packages, bumper stickers, and newspaper advertisements to display on the wall. This wall can then be a resource for guided reading lessons and whole-group instruction throughout the year. (Be sure to remind children that they must label the contents of a can if they take the label off before it is used!)

Informational displays should be located in prominent places in the classroom. They are used for posting rules, calendars, lunch menus, TV guides, and posters. In addition, informational displays can be used to exhibit information about classroom routines, schedules, hints on successful reading, the writing process, steps and media for publishing writing, lists of words the class knows, songs the class likes, and favorite books.

Scheduling displays can be used for making appointments with peers and teachers for reading and writing conferences as well as editing sessions. Figures 10.13 and 10.14 show examples of such scheduling displays.

Think of a classroom environment where children can use the walls, ceilings, windows, and floor to learn to read and to demonstrate their learning to read. What characteristics are you thinking of in such a classroom?

Figure 10.13   Writing peer conference sign-up board

Monday—Date _____

8:00 A.M.

Name of Author _____ Names of Peers _____

_____

8:15 A.M.

Name of Author _____ Names of Peers _____

_____

8:30 A.M.

Name of Author _____ Names of Peers _____

_____

Tuesday—Date _____

8:00 A.M.

Name of Author _____ Names of Peers _____

_____

8:15 A.M.

Name of Author _____ Names of Peers _____

_____

8:30 A.M.

Name of Author _____ Names of Peers _____

_____

Objects in the classroom may be labeled by even the youngest of children. Children may invent spellings for objects in the classroom and write these on cards. For example, we have seen the following object labels written by young children in kindergarten classrooms: *seling (ceiling), klok (clock), weindos (windows), dr (door), fs (fish),* and *srk (shark).* During subsequent language lessons, children can be alerted to look for these words in their reading and revise them. Many teachers find that within a matter of weeks, invented spellings used to label classroom objects will be revised to reflect conventional spellings (Calkins & Harwayne, 1987). Other areas in the classroom can be used to display helpful reference information, such as numbers, colors, alphabet letters, lunchtime, and classroom helpers. Remember that all classroom displays should be neatly produced so as to set the standard for published works in the classroom.

Figure 10.14 Editing session sign-up board

Monday—Date _____

8:00 A.M.

Name of Author _____Name of Editor _____

_____

8:15 A.M.

Name of Author _____Name of Editor _____

_____

8:30 A.M.

Name of Author _____Name of Editor _____

_____

Tuesday—Date _____

8:00 A.M.

Name of Author _____Name of Editor _____

_____

8:15 A.M.

Name of Author _____Name of Editor ____ _____

_____

8:30 A.M.

Name of Author _____Name of Editor _____

_____

PLANNING AND ORGANIZING NECESSARY STORAGE SPACE

Devote selected areas in the classroom to storage of classroom and student materials. A writing storage area, for children's emerging writing products, is a must. Neatly file author's folders, response journals, and learning logs in corrugated cardboard file boxes. You may wish to store children's writing drafts in three-ring binders on a bookshelf or in another accessible location. A small tablet for recording spelling words can be inserted into the pocket or sleeve of this writing draft binder. Be sure to put each child's name on his/her writing draft binders.

Each child needs a personal storage area in the classroom. We liked using rubber tubs to store children's personal writing materials, pencil boxes, and belongings. They can double as post office boxes with a name and a P.O. box number written on the front of each. These tubs can be stored in specially constructed shelves or along

Storage spaces for young children need to be arranged so that they can care for them independently.

coat racks, the top of bookshelves, and windowsills. Properly cleaned and covered with contact paper, two- to five-gallon ice cream buckets can be stacked along coat racks, cupboards, and windowsills for the same purposes, without incurring the expense of purchasing rubber tubs.

When you arrange publishing materials such as staplers, paper punches, construction paper, and unlined paper for children's daily use, be sure to consider easy accessibility and cleanup. The proper location of each item in the publishing area needs to be labeled to facilitate cleanup and maintenance. We strongly suggest that each item in this center be labeled with both a word and a picture for younger children's use. Also, be sure to properly label sorting baskets or bins to ease the cleanup of this area and improve its appearance. The publishing storage area should also be located near other busy and potentially noisy areas in the classroom.

Book storage areas need to be properly located to facilitate retrieval, cleanup, and accessibility. A reading nook, loft, or corner must be arranged to provide adequate shelf space for a classroom trade book library of at least 300 individual titles. We will discuss more about how to organize the classroom library in Chapter 11. Word cards can be stored in old, labeled shoeboxes on the bookshelves in this area. Child-authored books are to be afforded the same respect as commercially produced books. A library card pocket and a checkout card should be placed in each child-authored book. These books should have a section in the classroom library where they can be read, reread, and checked out. Child-authored big books and charts can be given a prominent display area and/or stored along with other commercially published big books. Plastic pants hangers with clothespins, hooks, or specially designed pocket charts can be used to store or display big books and chart tablets effectively.

Storage for reference materials such as dictionaries, atlases, *The Guinness Book of World Records,* encyclopedias, almanacs, and spellers should be placed near the editing area in the classroom and be accessible to students and the editors. Writing media should be placed near where they are needed in the classroom. Small rubber baskets, boxes, cut-down milk containers, and the like can be used for both storage and sorting of writing materials. Crayons, markers, pencils, pens, erasers, and chalk can be placed in individual containers for storage. In this way, children can easily sort and clean up writing materials scattered during busy writing output times. Other containers should be made available so small quantities of writing media can be moved from large-capacity storage bins to other classroom areas. These small transport containers can be taken to conference areas and collaborative project areas and then returned and sorted for storage and cleanup after use.

MAKING THE MOST OF HUMAN RESOURCES: ORGANIZING FOR EFFECTIVE USE OF PARENTS, VOLUNTEERS, AIDES, AND TUTORS

Schools can and should make reading a community concern by implementing strong literacy volunteer programs that involve businesses, parents, retired teachers, service clubs, and the like.

Many schools have organized or sought funding for school literacy volunteer, aide, or tutoring programs. Title I of the U.S. Elementary and Secondary Education Act (1965) authorized federal funds for reading aides. AmeriCorps is a federally funded program that provides support to school literacy programs by organizing school volunteers, parents, and community groups. America Reads Challenge (1996) was a federally funded program for training school literacy tutors. Regardless of the source of funding or support, schools now have significant access to literacy tutors, volunteers, and aides.

Big book storage

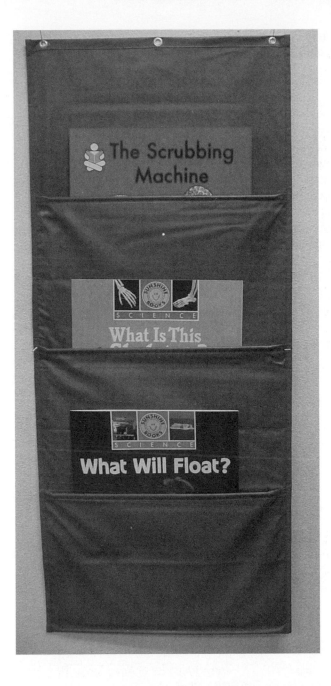

In the National Research Council report *Preventing Reading Difficulties in Young Children* (Snow, Griffin, and Burns, 1998), teachers are strongly cautioned about the use of literacy aides, volunteers, or tutors to provide primary literacy instruction for struggling readers. This report recommends that teachers use volunteers, aides, and tutors to provide reading practice and motivation but not as the primary providers of reading instruction for those who are struggling. This advice makes sense. Why should we give our most needy students to the least prepared individuals?

On the other hand, we also believe that children have a right to learn to read from people! Helping all our children become successful readers and leaving no child

The Help America Read *program is intended to help struggling young readers by providing tutors from the community in local public schools.*

behind ought to be a community concern. Volunteers, aides, and tutors can form a backbone of support for the reading program in schools. All sorts of people can be recruited as volunteers for the classroom reading program. Ervin (1982) suggests using parents, retired teachers, college students, student teachers, high school students involved with Future Teachers of America clubs, and community and government service organizations. Cassidy (1981) suggests using Grey power, or senior citizens, in the classroom as volunteers for tutoring, instructional aides, and producers of instructional materials. More recently, Cooter et al. (1999) have enlisted elderly volunteers in Texas via a group known as "Off Our Rockers"! The Help America Read and I Can Read programs are intended to help struggling young readers by providing tutors from the community in local public schools.

Recruitment of volunteers to support school reading programs can be accomplished in various ways: Announcements made in PTA meetings, notices sent home to parents, pamphlets to community service and religious organizations, and advertisements provided in the local media. Figures 10.15 and 10.16 show volunteer recruitment resources and sign-up forms for volunteers.

Pinnell and Fountas (1997b) offer a wonderful set of materials for training parent volunteers to be part of the U.S. Government's program Help America Read. In their handbook for volunteers, they offer 10 ways that volunteers can help in school classrooms:

- Talking with children
- Reading TO children
- Reading WITH children
- Helping children read on their own
- Writing FOR children
- Writing WITH children
- Helping children write on their own
- Helping children understand phonics, letters, and words
- Making books
- Connecting with children's homes

Organizing, designing, and planning a print-rich, effective classroom literacy environment requires months of thought, study, and preparation. Each and every K–3 classroom should be a busy, purposeful setting for learning to read and write. To accomplish this objective requires extraordinary organization and administrative and

Figure 10.15   Resources for reading program volunteers

- In-school personnel, e.g., principal, secretary, custodians
- Parents
- Grandparents
- Senior citizens
- Local rest homes
- Service clubs, e.g., Kiwanis, Lions, Rotary, Elks
- Government agencies
- Sponsoring businesses
- High school students
- Future Teachers of America
- Scout projects
- Older children in the school
- Church organizations
- News media organizations
- College students
- Student teachers
- Chamber of Commerce
- Reading Is Fundamental groups
- Retired teachers

Figure 10.16 Volunteer sign-up form

Volunteering for the School Reading Program

Children learn to read from other people who can read. Please help children learn to read by volunteering your time.

Name: _____ Street Address: _____

City: _____ Home Phone: _____

Business Phone: _____ Occupation: _____

Grade Level Preference (if any): _____

Teacher Preference (if any): _____

Do you have a child in the school? Yes _____ No _____

Name of child if applicable _____

When can you help? (Please check one)

Daily _____ Weekly _____ Monthly _____

How much time can you give on this basis? _____

Please list available times (e.g., Tuesday/Thursday 8–10 A.M.)

Where would you like to help? (Please check one or more)

_____Classrooms   _____Local library   _____In parents' home

_____Special classrooms _____Day-care center   _____In your own home

_____Library   _____Local businesses

How would you like to help?

(Please indicate your first three preferences with the numbers, 1, 2, & 3)

_____Read to students in a group   _____Give presentations on selected topics

_____Help children with reading   _____Solicit books for class library

_____Help with record keeping and progress evaluation   _____Write with small group of children

_____Produce instructional materials   _____Make puppets

_____Conference with children about their writing projects   _____Give book talks

_____Help children edit writing projects   _____Help children make books

_____Tell stories   _____Help children rehearse a play or other dramatic production

_____Teach children songs   _____Take children's dictation and make little books from dictation

_____Share your own writing

_____Read with individual students

_____I have no particular preference; please place me where I am needed most.

Please list any special talents, abilities, experiences, or knowledge you would be willing to share: _____

management abilities. From designing the classroom floor plan; to designing effective learning centers; to inventorying, purchasing, and arranging literacy instructional tools and materials; to organizing and using the potential of available human resources, you will find that getting ready for school to begin each year is critical to the success of your entire school year, the effectiveness of your literacy instruction, AND your own personal health and well-being!

GROUPING STUDENTS FOR EFFECTIVE LITERACY INSTRUCTION

Ability Grouping

Dividing children into reading groups on the basis of reading ability or achievement, called ability grouping, despite considerable research condemning the practice, continues to be a practice in many classrooms. To form ability groups, rely on standardized, criterion-referenced, or informal reading test scores as a means for assigning children to an ability group, although other factors such as personality attributes, general academic competence, work habits, and home background are also weighed in the decision to assign children to ability groups (Haller & Waterman, 1985). The typical classroom has three levels of ability groups—above average, average, and below average. Groups are very often named to obscure the levels of groups like the *Tigers, Jaguars,* and *Lions.* In some schools, each classroom is an ability group for reading, and children move among teachers at their grade level to the above-average, average, or below-average reading classroom. And, in still fewer schools, some children even move across grade levels to join an ability grouped classroom. Many teachers employ ability, achievement, or homogeneous groups with the intent to meet individual student needs. But, when these ability groups are allowed to remain stagnant for long periods of time, the practice of ability or homogeneous grouping is associated with numerous negative outcomes such as:

Grouping decisions need to be based on benefits for both teachers and children.

- Children in low-ability groups spend more time in oral round-robin reading and reading workbook assignments than do their peers in high-ability groups (Allington, 1983; Leinhardt, Zigmond, & Cooley, 1981).
- Teachers tend to tolerate more outside interruptions in low-ability groups than in high-ability groups (Allington, 1980).
- In the spring of the school year, children assigned to low-ability groups for reading instruction exhibited three times the number of inattentive behaviors exhibited by their counterparts assigned to high-ability groups (Felmlee & Eder, 1983).
- Children in low-ability groups tend to have lowered academic expectations and self-concepts (Eder, 1983; Hiebert, 1983; Rosenbaum, 1980).
- Time devoted to decoding instruction and practice is fully double for low-ability group readers as compared to high-ability groups (Gambrell, Wilson, & Gnatt, 1981)
- Teachers tend to interrupt low readers more often when they miscue while reading than they do high readers (Allington, 1980).

Low-ability group readers receive double the decoding instruction of high-ability group readers.

Weinstein (1976) found that as much as 25 percent of the variation in reading achievement at the end of first grade could be attributed to group assignment. Kulik and Kulik (1982) analyzed the results of 52 studies and determined that (a) ability grouping generally has small effects on achievement, (b) high-ability readers profit from ability grouping in terms of achievement, and (c) the effects of ability grouping on average- and low-ability children's achievement is only trivial. On the other hand, children's friendships tend be increasingly influenced by continuing membership in an ability group (Hallinan & Sorensen, 1985). Eder (1983) showed that even one year in an ability group caused some children to begin to question the reasons underlying their group membership. Although reading achievement may be minimally affected by ability grouping, children's self-images and social circles appear to be profoundly affected (Oakes, 1992). Although ability or homogeneous grouping may be deemed necessary in some instances, it should only be considered on a temporary basis not to exceed one month in duration. Alternative grouping plans such as those suggested in the following discussion should be strongly considered.

Grouping children for instruction is one of the ways in which teachers are able to address individual literacy learning needs in the classroom and manage students' movement and activity when engaged in independent literacy learning center activities. Unlike the classrooms of yesteryear, today's classroom teachers make use of a wide variety of grouping plans, often referred to as *flexible grouping.*

Flexible Learning Groups

In flexible grouping, children are placed into *temporary* groups based on their level of independence as learners and their personal interests. Optiz (1998) says that flexible groups allow "students to work in differently mixed ability groups depending upon the learning task at hand" (p. 10). There are several significant differences that separate ability groups from flexible groups (see Figure 10.17).

Flexible groups are temporary groups that change regularly.

Flexible groups are established and reorganized on the basis of several well articulated principles (Unsworth, 1984, p. 300):

1. There are no permanent groups.
2. Groups are periodically created, modified, or disbanded to meet new needs as they arise.
3. At times there is only one group consisting of all pupils.
4. Groups vary in size from two or three to nine or ten depending on the group's purpose.
5. Group membership is not fixed; it varies according to needs and purposes.
6. Student commitment is enhanced when students know how the group's work relates to the overall program or task.
7. Children should be able to evaluate the progress of the group and the teacher's assessment of the group's work.
8. There should be a clear strategy for supervising the group's work.

Flexible grouping strategies may also be used to accommodate student interests, learning styles, and social needs, such as friendship groups, in addition to meeting instructional needs and goals. The potential for unproductive chaos is high in flexible grouping arrangements if the teacher has not carefully prepared the learning tasks and the environment for success. For flexible grouping to function well in the classroom, the organization, purpose, and tasks must be clearly understood and students well trained to handle the independence and collaboration inherent in the settings, i.e., independent literacy learning centers, for which flexible grouping is particularly well suited. Tasks to be accomplished and how they are to be accomplished must be clearly stated and understood.

Can you think of at least three advantages of flexible grouping over ability grouping?

Figure 10.17   Understanding the differences between ability groups and flexible groups

Ability Groups	Flexible Groups
Assigning Students to Groups	
Tests, Informal Reading Inventories, and Word List Scores	Ability to read leveled books
Duration of Groups	
Static, long term	Dynamic, change regularly
Instructional Expectations	
Dependent upon level of Group, i.e., high or low	High expectations for performance
Forms of Reading Practice	
Oral reading—barbershop Or round robin reading	Guided oral and silent reading
Instructional Materials	
Basal selections chosen by teacher	Basal selections, trade and leveled Books chosen by teacher and students
Modes of Assessment	
Normed or criterion-referenced tests	Observations, informal checklists, performance of authentic reading tasks
Modes of Assessment	
Normed or criterion-referenced tests	Observations, informal checklists, performance of authentic reading tasks

Cooperative Learning Groups

Another grouping strategy for effective reading and writing instruction is called co-operative learning. This grouping strategy makes use of heterogeneous groups ranging from two to five children working together to accomplish a *team task* (Slavin, 1987; Harp, 1989a; Opitz, 1992; Johnson and Johnson, 1999). Harp (1989a) indicates four characteristics of cooperative learning groups. First, each lesson begins with teacher instruction and modeling. Second, the children in the group work together to accomplish a task assigned by the teacher to the group. Third, children work on individual assignments related to a group-assigned task. Each student must be willing to complete his/her part of the group-shared assignment. Finally, a team is recognized by averaging each individual's grade and assigning one grade to the entire group.

Children in cooperative learning groups have consistently shown greater achievement than children who participate in traditional grouping schemes.

Much research indicates that children in cooperative learning groups have consistently shown greater achievement than children who participate in traditional grouping schemes (Johnson, Maruyama, Johnson, Nelson, & Skon, 1981; Stevens, Madden, Slavin, & Farnish, 1987a; Wood, 1987; Slavin, 1988; Webb & Schwartz, 1988; Topping, 1989; Jongsma, 1990; Opitz, 1992; Radencich, 1995). In a synthesis of research on cooperative learning, Slavin (1991) found that cooperative learning not only increased student achievement but also increased student self-concept and social skills.

Manarino-Leggett and Saloman (1989) and Wood (1987) describe several different grouping alternatives that can be applied with the concept of cooperative learning. A few of these group alternatives are briefly described in Table 10.1

Instructional Needs Grouping

Needs groups are determined by careful observation and assessment as teachers work with children in a variety of literacy learning activities. Through the use of various assessment strategies, teachers determine individual student instructional needs. Needs groups are formed when this careful assessment and observation process indicates that several children have similar learning needs. Typically, an instructional needs group will include as few as two students or as many as half the class, 10 to 15 students. The purpose of an instructional needs group is to teach a temporary group of students a particular procedure, literary stylistic device, skill, or strategy they have yet to learn and apply. The vehicle for instruction within these groups is the mini-lesson. Hagerty (1992) describes three types of mini-lessons that may be taught in a needs group setting: (1) *procedural,* (2) *literary,* and (3) *strategy/skill.*

Procedural, literary, and skill/strategy are three different types of potential minilessons.

A procedural reading mini-lesson, for example, might involve the teacher and students learning how to care for new books to be placed into the classroom library or how to repair worn older books. The teacher may demonstrate how to break in a new book's binding by standing the book on its spine and opening a few pages on either side of the center of the book, carefully pressing them down. Cellophane tape and staplers may be used to demonstrate how to repair tears in a book's pages or covers. A heavy-duty stapler can be used to reattach paperback book covers in another demonstration on caring for books.

A strategy/skill mini-lesson might occur during the reading of a big book like *Who's in the Shed?* (Parkes, 1986), with the teacher making note of the fact that many of the words in the book rhyme but that the rhymes are not spelled the same (*shed* and *said.*) Noticing this irregularity in the text, the teacher draws the children's attention to these words and to the fact that these words rhyme but are spelled differently. For example, while rereading the big book the next day, the teacher may cover the words *shed* and *said* with small self-adhesive notes. During the group rereading of the book, the teacher reveals the *covered words.* On subsequent readings, the teacher invites students to join in the reading while emphasizing the target words. Children use the /ed/ rime to produce rhyming words written on cards to be displayed on the word wall. Children add other rhyming words to the word wall as they think of them. Instructional needs groups are formed to meet specific learning outcomes and student needs discerned through careful assessment.

Notice three possible opportunities for teachers to intervene using mini-lessons.

GETTING OFF TO A GOOD START: PLANNING THE FIRST DAY OF SCHOOL

Planning for the first day of school is something that both excites and frightens every teacher, every year, no matter how many years they have taught school. The same thrill and shiver of fear shoots up the spine of every teacher when he or she contemplates that first day of school. Wong and Wong (1998) point out that the critical part of an effective first day is establishing effective classroom management. Wang, Haertel, and Walberg (1994) examined 11,000 research reports to determine factors that most influence student learning in school classrooms. They found there

Table 10.1 Alternative grouping plans for encouraging cooperative learning

Book-Response Pairs
Students interview a peer or partner about a book they have read. After the interview, they write a report on their partner's book.

Cooperative Integrated Reading and Composition (CIRC)
CIRC is a programmatic approach to teaching reading and writing in the intermediate elementary grades (Stevens, Madden, Slavin, & Farnish, 1987a, 1987b). This program consists of three elements: (a) basal-related activities, (b) direct instruction in reading comprehension, and (c) integrated language arts writing.

Composition or Coauthoring Pairs
One of two students explains what he or she plans to write while the other student takes notes or outlines the discussion. Working together, the two students plan the lead-in, thesis, or opening statement. One student writes while the other student explains the outline or notes. They exchange roles as they write a single composition, or they can exchange roles to help each other write their own composition.

Computer Groups
Students work together on a computer to accomplish a given task. Students adopt specific roles such as keyboard operator, monitor, and checker throughout the process. Roles should be regularly rotated to allow each student to experience all three roles.

Drill Partners
Students pair off for drill activities such as working with words from personal or classroom word banks or rereading books to improve fluency.

Dyads
K. D. Wood (1987) assigns roles to each student in a dyad, or pair, of readers. Each student reads silently, or in some cases orally in unison, two pages of text. After reading these two pages, one student acts as recaller. This student verbally recounts what the two had read. The other student acts as listener and clarifier for the recaller. Dyad reading is an effective means for supporting young children's reading development, especially for at-risk readers (Eldredge & Quinn, 1988).

Focus Trios
Children may be randomly assigned or may form social groups of three students for the purposes of summarizing what they already know about a reading selection and developing questions to be answered during reading. After reading, the trio discusses answers to the questions, clarifies, and summarizes answers.

Group Reports
Students research a topic together as a group. Each person is responsible for contributing at least one resource to the report. Written or oral reports must involve all students in the final report.

Group Retellings
Students read different books or selections on the same topic. After reading, each student retells what he or she has read to the other group members. Group members may comment on or add to the retelling of any individual.

Groups of Four
Groups of four are randomly assigned task-completion groups. Each individual is given a responsibility to complete some phase of a larger task. For example, when writing a letter, one student could be the addresser, another the body writer, another the checker, and so on. In this way, all students contribute to the successful completion of the task. Roles should be exchanged regularly to allow students to experience all aspects of task completion.

Jigsaw
Students in a group are assigned to read a different part of the same selection. After reading, each student retells what he or she has read to the others in the group. A discussion usually ensues, during which students may interview or question the reteller to clarify any incomplete ideas or correct misunderstandings. After this discussion concludes, students can be invited to read the rest of the selection to confirm or correct the retellings of other group members.

Table 10.1 *continued*

Metacomprehension Pairs

Have students alternate reading and orally summarizing paragraphs or pages of a selection. One listens, follows along, and checks the accuracy of the other's comprehension of the selection.

Playwrights

Students select a piece of reading they wish to dramatize as a play. Students work together to develop a script, the set, and costumes, and then practice the play with individuals serving in various roles as director, characters, and other necessary functions. The culmination of the group is the performance of the play for a selected audience.

Problem-Solving and Project Groups

Having children work together cooperatively in pairs or small groups to solve reading or writing problems is another effective classroom practice involving the use of other children as a primary resource for enhancing classroom instruction. Problem-solving groups are small groups initiated by children who wish to work collaboratively on a self-selected reading or writing problem. In project groups, children are encouraged to explore a wide variety of possible reading and writing projects, such as plays, puppetry, reader's theater, research, authoring books, poetry, lyrics to songs, notes, invitations, and cards. The products resulting from project groups are to be of publishable quality. Thus, the culmination of a project group is sharing the project or product with an authentic audience.

Reading Buddies

In the lower grades, upper grade children can be selected as reading buddies to assist emergent readers. These buddies can be selected for a short period of time, say a week, then other children can be selected. This allows ample opportunities for upper grade readers to assist lower grade readers. In upper and lower grades, reading buddies can pair off and share a favorite book with a friend by reading exciting parts of the book or just discussing the book.

Strategy Teachers and Concept Clarifiers

Students work together in pairs on reading strategies, such as prediction, sequencing, making inferences, until both can do or explain these concepts or strategies easily.

Test Coaches

As students prepare for a test, a group of students can be given a prototype test. The group can divide the test items into even groups for each individual in the group. Each individual completes a part of the test. The group meets together to review the answers of each of the students, and check, confirm, or correct each answer.

Think-Pair-Share

Lyman (1988) recommends that students sit in pairs as the teacher presents a reading mini-lesson to the class. After the lesson, the teacher presents a problem to the group. The children individually think of an answer, then with their partners discuss and reach a consensus on the answer. A pair of students can be asked to share their agreed-on answer with the class.

Turn-to-Your-Neighbor

After listening to a student read a book aloud, share a book response, or share a piece of published writing, students can be asked to turn to a neighbor and tell one concept or idea they enjoyed about the presentation. They should also share one question they would like to ask the reader or author.

Worksheet and Homework Checkers

When teachers deem it necessary to use worksheets to provide practice for a concept or strategy taught during a reading mini-lesson, students can be organized into groups to check one another's work and provide feedback to each other.

Writing Response Groups

When a writer completes a publishable work or needs help with developing a draft, groups can be organized to listen to the author share his or her work. Afterward, group members can share ideas on how to improve the draft. If the piece is complete, group members should compliment the work and ask the author questions about the presentation.

Adapted from Manarino-Leggett and Saloman (1989) and K.D. Wood (1987).

The first day of school is critical in establishing effective classroom management.

were 28 factors, but the single most important factor governing student learning in classrooms was—classroom management. A teacher who is "grossly inadequate in classroom management skills is probably not going to accomplish much" (Wong & Wong, p. 84).

What is classroom management? It is all of the activities you do as a teacher to organize students, resources, time, and the classroom space so that effective literacy instruction can take place. We have already discussed several issues that relate to effective classroom management—organizing the classroom space, the literacy instructional tools and materials, and the human help available. To bring off a successful first day of school, you must carefully consider the goals and objectives that need to be accomplished in a K–3 classroom on that first day and during the first week of school.

Having said this, we encourage you to contemplate carefully the goals that are important to achieve on the first day of school to get literacy learning off to a good start. We would like to suggest the following goals and activities for your consideration.

Preparing for Success: Goals for Getting Off to a Good Start the First Day

- Before the year begins, send a letter home to each parent and student explaining things that parents and children can do to assist success in early literacy instruction.
- Have the classroom seating, learning centers, instructional spaces, materials, activities, and work planned and ready.
- Enthusiastically greet each child at the door, giving clear directions for what to do to find his/her place in the classroom.
- Prepare the classroom so that each child can find his/her place in the room (seating chart, name tags, labels) and be able to independently put away his/her things in an orderly manner.
- Introduce yourself to the children.
- Get to know something about each child that day.
- Discuss with children your classroom rules and consequences.
- Establish a daily morning routine for getting the day started.
- Prepare a daily schedule and post it where children can see it.
- Encourage "reading and writing" from the first day—giving directions and receiving requests.
- First day literacy activities in K–3: Interactive Read Aloud, Shared Reading, and Language Experience.

Preparing Parents and Students for Success: Making the Initial Contact with a Letter

Each year at least one week before school begins, you should get a copy of your class list from your school principal. Along with this list, ask for the parents' mailing addresses. Even better, if the school secretary can print mailing labels, request these. Compose a letter to parents and to each student. Letters should be welcom-

Figure 10.18 Possible mini-lesson topics

Procedural Mini-lessons	Literary Mini-lessons	Strategy/Skills Mini-lessons
Where to sit during reading time	Differences between fiction and	How to choose a book
Giving a book talk	nonfiction books	Selecting literature log topics
How to be a good listener in a	Learning from dedications	Connecting reading material to
share session	Books that show emotion	your own life
What is an appropriate noise level	Books written in the first, second,	Tips for reading aloud
during reading time	or third person	Figuring out unknown words
What to do when you finish a	Author studies	Using context
book	How authors use quotations	Substituting
What kinds of questions to ask	How the story setting fits the story	Using picture clues
during a share session	Characteristics of different genres	Using the sounds of blends,
Running a small-group discussion	Development of characters, plot,	vowels, contractions, etc.
Self-evaluation	theme, mood	Using Post-its to mark interesting
Getting ready for a conference	How leads hook us	parts
How to have a peer conference	How authors use the problem/	Monitoring comprehension (Does
Where to sit during mini-lessons	event/solution pattern	this make sense and sound
Taking care of books	Differences between a picture	right?)
Keeping track of books read	book and a novel	Asking questions while reading
Rules of the workshop	Titles and their meanings	Making predictions
	Characters' points of view	Emergent strategies
	Examples of similes and	Concept of story
	metaphors	Concept that print carries
	Examples of foreshadowing	meaning
	How authors use dialogue	Making sense
	Predictable and surprise endings	Mapping a story
	Use of descriptive words and	How to retell a story orally
	phrases	Looking for relationships
	How illustrations enhance the	Looking for important ideas
	story	Making inferences
	Secrets in books	Drawing conclusions
		Summarizing a story
		Distinguishing fact from opinion
		Emergent reader skills:
		directionality, concept of "word,"
		sound/symbol relationships

From *Readers' Workshop: Real Reading* (pp. 113–115), by P. Hagerty, 1992, Ontario, Canada: Scholastic Canada Ltd. Copyright 1992 by Patricia Hagerty. Reprinted by permission.

ing, informative, and positive. A sample letter to a first grade parent(s) is shown in Figure 10.19.

A similar letter to each student can be included with the letter to the parents. However, if you can afford it, it is more exciting for each student to receive a letter from you in an individually addressed envelope. A sample letter to a kindergarten student is shown in Figure 10.20.

Communicating with parents helps you, the teacher, to connect with the home to benefit each child in your classroom.

Figure 10.19   Sample letter to parent(s)

Dear Mr. & Mrs. Parents,

   I want to tell you how excited I am to have _____ in my first grade class this next year. First grade is an extraordinary year for all students—they will learn to read and write! Because I know how much you care about your child's success in school, I'd like to offer some simple suggestions that can make a big difference.

- Please ask your child every day what he/she has learned at school. Don't accept the traditional response, *Nothin'*. I can assure you that there will never be a day in our classroom this year when children learn nothing!
- Make time each day to read together.
- Get books in your home for your child to read.
- Point out and discuss print in your daily environment—breakfast cereal boxes, grocery stores, post office, hospital, bus stops, etc.
- Get some magnetic letters for your refrigerator door. Talk about letters and the sounds these letters represent. Make your child's name on the fridge door. Scramble the letters and have them make their name. Play games with these letters to make words.
- Get your child a library card and make a weekly visit to the public or school library together.
- Provide your child with a variety of writing materials, including pencils, crayons, markers, paper, thank you notes, stationery, and recipe cards.
- Encourage your child's efforts to learn to read and write by supporting and praising him/her. Children are motivated if they believe you value their efforts.

   These are just a few things you can do to get your child off to a good start this year. I will send home each week the things we will be learning in class during the next week and a report of what we have learned during the last week. I will also include activities you can do with your child to practice what he or she learned in the last week or prepare your child for what will be learned this next week.

Thank you for trusting me with your most valuable treasure, your child. I pledge to you my very best efforts to make this year a successful and happy year filled with learning for _____.

Warmest regards,

Mrs. Ima Teacher

First Impressions

Make sure that the room is completely ready for the children. Have the classroom floor plan completed. Seating, storage, displays, and furnishing should all be arranged according to the floor plan. Learning areas, centers, and spaces should be clearly marked with signs, posters, and labels. Children's storage areas, seats, cub-

Figure 10.20 Sample letter to a student

Dear Student,

Hi! My name is Mrs. Ima Your Teacher. I will be your teacher this year in kinder-garten. I am so excited that you will be in my class. I expect that you may be a little bit worried or scared about coming to kindergarten. Well, you don't need to be. We are going to have a wonderful time learning, playing, and exploring together. I'll have a place ready for you to put your things when you arrive. I'll have a seat with your name on it and a nametag prepared for you to wear that is just like mine so we can get to know each other.

Will you do me a favor and draw a picture of what you did this summer that you thought was the most fun, the thing you enjoyed the very most? And, be sure to put your name on your picture! We will share the pictures and then put them up on our wall to brighten our room with something from you. I look forward to meeting you on our first day. Don't worry, I'll be right at the door to meet you and to help you get settled.

Warmest regards,

Mrs. Ima Your Teacher

bies, and such should be labeled and ready. You should be wearing a name tag that is the same as the ones you have prepared for the children. Each child's seat or place at a table should have his/her name tag affixed to the desk or table. Also have something the children can do at their seats as they arrive—a puzzle, a counting activity, or a reading/coloring activity.

Be sure to arrive early on the first day. You must be there in plenty of time to be available to children and parents as they arrive. Greet each child with a smile at the door of the classroom. Ask each child for his/her name and then pin a name tag on him/her that matches the one at their seat. Give each child simple directions for what to do after you greet him or her. We had our children in first grade sign their name on the classroom windows using a water-soluble transparency marker. At least have a card or sign-in board where the children see their name or get to write their name to register their presence. The children thought this was an especially engaging way to make their presence known the first day.

Rehearse in your mind how you want your first hour of the first day to play out. Then plan to make the best impression you can on your students and their parents.

Establishing a Plan for Beginning Each School Day

Once the school bell signals the beginning of the school day, you need to establish how you will open each school day from then on. Taking roll or attendance is usually an important part of the opening of the school day, as is taking lunch count. The most efficient way to take roll is to have an attendance board in your room where children indicate they are present by taking a card with their name on it and placing it into a wall chart pocket with their name on it. Pockets without cards indicate to the teacher who is absent that day.

**Attendance
Sign-In**

Another wall chart can be made up for children to indicate if they are eating school lunch or have brought along their own lunch. A simple chart can be displayed with a picture of a lunch pail or bag (Brought My Own Lunch) on one side and a picture of a food tray (Eat School Hot Lunch) on the other side. Children take a clothespin with their name on it and place it on either side of the chart to indicate if they are eating school lunch or eating one they brought from home.

We have a message of the day on a classroom message board posted by the door. We have a classroom environmental print wall where they can bring some environmental print to class and post it on a cork bulletin board using a stapler. We also have a journal at their seats that they can draw or write in as they wait for the day to begin.

Classroom message board

Our point here is that on the first day of school, you need to tell, show, and have selected children demonstrate how each of these things are to be done. You have directions that will be posted just outside the door so that they can be reminded of the things they are to do upon entering the classroom each day.

Establishing a Morning Routine

We began our day with a song illustrated and displayed on a large chart paper. In our first grade classrooms, we sang "Good Morning Says the Sun," to start our morning. We had a calendar chart where we reviewed the day, the days of the week, the month, and the season of the year. We also reviewed the weather for the day—sunny, partly cloudy, cloudy, rain, or snow. We had a school lunch chart displaying the meal to be served that day. We had a daily schedule displayed at the front of the room, which we reviewed each and every morning. We also made daily additions to and discussed an environmental print wall and a word wall. Each morning we would review some words on these walls using a pointer. And we provided a daily time for children to share.

Although many teachers, parents, and administrators question the value of "show and tell" or, as some call it, "bring and brag," we found this time to be especially valuable for learning about our students and giving them a comfortable setting in which to use oral language to express themselves. Typically, we structured this time so as to schedule what to bring and what to do rather than allowing children to bring anything. For the first month of school, we invited one child per day to bring back a box called "All About Me." In this box, they placed special items from home that told us about their interests, where they were born, their favorite food, and the like. We modeled how to do this on the first day of school when introducing ourselves to the children. Our routine is:

Develop a morning routine to give children what they need—security, predictability, structure, and a caring classroom climate.

- Sing a song, such as "Good Morning Says the Sun," together
- Review the Calendar and Weather Chart

- Review the School Lunch Menu
- Review the Daily Schedule Posted in the Pocket Chart
- Review Environmental Print Words and/or Word Wall Words
- Provide Time for Guided Oral Sharing

Making the Classroom Work: Rules and Consequences

Rules are expectations for appropriate student behavior in the classroom. Consequences are the rewards for choices made with respect to honoring the rules in a classroom. We discussed classroom rules and consequences with children on the first day of school. We asked the children to talk with us about what would help us all talk, listen, and get along with each other in order to learn. It is important that even the youngest children have an opportunity to express their needs and ideas related to discipline. We kept our rules to a minimum for younger children. In practical terms, this meant no more than five classroom rules.

Making classroom rules together and displaying them gives every child an equal chance to participate and to understand the expectations for behavior.

Next, we discussed with children the consequences for keeping and breaking classroom rules. We listed and considered potential consequences. We are also free to contribute our thoughts as well. Consequences should address keeping and breaking rules. An example of our classroom rules and consequences is shown in the following:

Classroom Rules
- Raise your hand to ask to speak.
- Listen courteously when others are speaking.
- Keep hands, feet, and objects to yourself.
- Stop anything you are doing when you hear the signal.
- Look and listen carefully to directions.

What Happens If You Choose to Break Our Classroom Rules
- 1st Time—Verbal Warning from the Teacher
- 2nd Time—Lose Morning Recess
- 3rd Time—Lose Morning and Afternoon Recesses
- 4th Time—Call to Parents
- 5th Time—Go to Principal and In-School Discipline Room

Reading from the Start: Getting Attention and Giving Directions

Every child who enters school as a kindergarten student expects to learn to read and write on the first day. Plan to give them the confidence they need on that first day of school.

We started on the first day of school using written direction cards along with our verbal directions. Children were told that after the first week directions for what to do would not be given by talking but rather by using signs. We had produced a series of direction cards on laminated poster board. These cards were rectangular in shape and were placed near a hotel register bell in the middle of the classroom. If for example, we wanted the children to line up, we rang the bell to get their attention. Then, we would hold up a direction sign for them to follow that read, "Please line up quietly at the door." Or, if we wanted them to come to the front of the room where we were seated on a large, divided carpet square for whole group instruction, we would ring the bell and hold up a sign that read "Please sit down quietly on the carpet." This process created an immediate need for children to focus their attention on the print. It was clear from the outset that reading was necessary to function well in this classroom environment.

Figure 10.21 Kindergarten and first grade first day literacy schedule

Half-Day Kindergarten (90 Minutes Literacy)

8:30– 9:00 A.M.:	Greet Children and Parents
9:00– 9:10 A.M.:	Morning Routine (Roll, Lunch Count, Weather, Calendar)
9:10– 9:20 A.M.:	Sharing Time
9:20– 9:35 A.M.:	Interactive Read Aloud
9:35–10:05 A.M.:	Shared Reading and Singing
10:05–10:15 A.M.:	Mini-Lesson Time—Reading/Writing Strategy
10:15–10:30 A.M.:	Recess
10:30–10:45 A.M.:	Science Experiment—Magnets
10:45–11:05 A.M.:	Shared Writing/Language Experience Chart
11:05–11:20 A.M.:	Literacy Enriched Play Centers

First Grade (150 Minutes Literacy)

8:30– 9:00 A.M.:	Greet Children and Parents
9:00– 9:10 A.M.:	Morning Routine (Roll, Lunch Count, Weather, Calendar)
9:10– 9:20 A.M.:	Sharing Time
9:20– 9:35 A.M.:	Interactive Read Aloud
9:35–10:05 A.M.:	Shared Reading
10:05–10:15 A.M.:	Mini-Lesson Time—Reading/Writing Strategy
10:15–10:30 A.M.:	Recess
10:30–10:45 A.M.:	Science Experiment—Vinegar & Soda Gases
10:45–11:10 A.M.:	Shared Writing/Language Experience Chart
11:10–11:30 A.M.:	Word Work—White Board Letter/Word Dictation
11:30–11:50 A.M.:	Word Wall BINGO
11:50–12 Noon:	Phonemic Awareness—Oddity Task, Blending
12:00 Noon–12:45:	LUNCH
12:45– 1:00 P.M.:	Read Aloud Information Book on Gases
1:00– 1:15 P.M.:	Literacy Centers Training—Procedural Mini-Lesson

Literacy Activities on the First Day

Since on the first day we do not know a great deal about children's individual literacy development, activities should be primarily whole-group. Our experiences have shown that the best activities on the first day include: (1) Interactive Read Aloud, (2) Shared Reading, and (3) Language Experience Activities. Since we will discuss each of these as *best practices* in Chapter 11, suffice it to say that each should be a planned part of the first day of literacy instruction. We have found that focusing on a theme, such as, *"What happens when. . . ?"* is a good first day activity. Books read aloud and shared and activities can focus on this theme. We have also found that a science experiment like the one described at the opening of this chapter makes for excellent language development, discussion, and the creation of group *language experience charts,* discussed in Chapter 11. In Figure 10.21 we display sample first-day kindergarten and first grade literacy schedules.

First day literacy activities should be lively, engaging, and involve the whole class.

PLANNING THE FIRST WEEK

Having survived the first day of school, we now turn our attention to planning the first full week of the new school year. The major goal of the first full week of school is to get to know the children and their individual learning needs. This means that you will need time to meet with individual children while managing the whole class. This is not easy and requires careful thought and planning.

Since the goal is to get to know the children's individual learning needs, an assessment plan for the beginning of the year needs to be made. An annual assessment plan for K–3 teachers is described in detail in Chapter 11. Assessment of individual children is best carried out in the *individual reading conference area*. In this area you should have laid out the assessment tools, inventories, and books you will use to assess children in a folder or portfolio.

You will need to call each child from independent individual or group work to the area of the classroom where you conduct individual conferences and assessment. As you begin assessment processes, be sure to put each child at ease about what you are doing. Explain that you want to learn about what they know so that you can know how to help them learn successfully this next year.

Also, you will need to provide meaningful independent seat work and center work for the other children you are not assessing. During the first week of the school year, it is important that you not plan more than one hour per day in kindergarten or two hours per day in first grade for assessment of children. We say this because interaction with the group of children is critically important in establishing a sense of community in the classroom for you and the children. And, we also say this because at this age young children cannot sustain long periods of time without teacher-guided, group interaction. So, the first week is a great time to group children, train them how to complete activities in learning centers successfully, and practice how small groups will rotate through several learning centers each day. We suggest that you try 30 minutes of whole-group seat work assignments followed by two to four learning center rotations of about 15 minutes each depending on grade level—kindergarten (two rotations) and first through third grades (four rotations).

The first week is also a good time to start the practice of writing daily lesson plans. It has been our experience that teachers who take the time to write and reflect on daily lesson plans provide higher quality instruction than those teachers who try to teach from a mere activity mention in a teacher's planning book block or "fly by the seat of their pants" when teaching young children. To put it bluntly, the quality of the outcomes in learning will be directly related to the quality of the teacher's inputs in planning and delivering the instruction. So, to help you get a sense for the detail necessary in a daily lesson plan, we provide a sample lesson plan (Figure 10.22) for a guided reading of an information book in the second-grade.

Make sure you plan adequate time in the first week of school to begin to assess and get to know individual students.

Written lesson plans look like a great deal of work, and they are. But to carefully think through each lesson while planning the materials, information, modeling, explanations, and questions will result in greatly increased learning and confidence in your students. Written lesson plans will give you the satisfaction of knowing you did your best to plan, instruct, reflect on, and improve your teaching. Similar written lesson plans need to be developed daily for each learning center located in the classroom, as well as for group instruction. Careful planning is often the difference between a well-managed classroom and chaos!

After writing daily lesson plans, schedule the time for each literacy lesson and literacy learning center. This can be a rather simple listing of times when you will (1)

Figure 10.22 Written daily lesson plan—second grade

Title of Book *Amazing Water*_____

Objective: *Teach a repertoire of comprehension strategies to successfully process information text for content knowledge.*

Supplies Needed: Amazing Water *big book, ice, water, different shaped containers, hotplate, pan, mirror or piece of clear glass, word cards with pictures, graphic organizer*

Introducing the Book: This is an information book. How is an information book different from a storybook? Let's talk for a moment about some of the differences.

Step 1:—Prompt—What do you see?

Step 2:—Prompt—What do you think the print tells you about the picture?

Step 3:—Read the title of the book to the students while pointing.

Step 4: *Activating Background Knowledge*—Show children the different forms of water.
- Liquid—water and different shaped containers
- Solid—ice cubes
- Gas—steam and then collected onto glass or mirror

Before I read a book, I stop and think about what I know about the book. If the book is about dogs, then I think about what I know about dogs. So, to become better readers, you need to stop and think about what you know about our book today. Now, stop and think about your own experiences with water. What do you think is "amazing" about water? If you have something to share, raise your hand and wait for your turn.

Step 5: Point to and discuss what an author is on the book cover.

Step 6: Open to the Table of Contents—Remind children that information books are different from storybooks. And one of the ways they are different is that they have a TOC at the beginning of the book. The TOC tells you what is in the book and the order or sequence that the information is shared.

Step 7: *Text Structure*—One of the other things that successful readers do is to try and figure out how the author has put the book together. One of the ways I think about how authors put books together is to use a book web. Let's look at the board. I have on the board a book web for our book today, *Amazing Water*. Here in the center of the book web, I have written the title of our book, *Amazing Water*. You also see that I have other picture/word cards on the board. Do you notice that the book web looks kind of like a spider web? That's why we call it a "web."

The author of our book is going to tell us about water by describing each of the things we see in our book web. Having this web helps us see how the author wants us to read the book and how he wants us to remember the information. Let's look at what the author is going to tell us about water and how he wants us to remember it. At the end of the first web strand, we have picture/word cards that say: (1) Liquid. So, the author is going to tell us about water as a liquid. What else is the author going to tell us? Let's look at web strands 2–5: (2) Solid, (3) Gas, (4) Weather, and (5) Forms of Water. Remember, the book web is to help us notice and think about how the author is going to tell us the information in the book.

Step 8: *Predicting*—Now, notice that I have put picture/word cards along the chalkboard tray. Each of these picture/word cards fits underneath one of the five web strands around the title of our book. Let me show you what I mean. *Pick up one picture/word card and think aloud about where and why this picture/word card goes here.* Now, invite individual children to take each picture/word card and predict its place underneath each web strand.

Step 9: *Question Generating*—Before I read, I often think of some questions I'd like to answer as I read. Asking myself some questions helps me focus on important in-

(continued)

Figure 10.22 *continued*

formation and remember it. For example, I might want to ask, "What makes water turn to ice?" Can you think of any questions you would like to ask before we read? Let's put a few up here.

Step 10: Read the big book in a shared reading entitled, *Amazing Water.*

Step 11: *Elaborative Interrogation*—Stop at statements shown below. Mark points in the big book for turning statements into questions with sticky notes showing *?* marks.
    Statements:
        Water is a liquid.
        Ice is a solid.
        Steam, or water vapor, is a gas.
        Lots of different kinds of weather are forms of water.

Step 12: *Imagery*—Stop at points marked with a "closed eye" on a sticky note to make images in the mind.
    Images requested:
        Page 3
        Page 5
        Page 7
        Page 9

Step 13: *Monitoring*—Stop at points with a "Stop Sign" on a sticky note to check comprehension. Review what you have learned so far to see if you are getting it.
    Pages to Stop:
        Page 9
        Page 13

Step 14: *Making Inferences & Confirming*—Discuss the Book
- What new things did you learn about water from this book?
- What things did you feel you didn't understand?
- How could the author have made these ideas clearer? Give the author some advice.
- Who can tell me three different forms of water?
- Let's look at our questions we asked before we read the book. Can we answer any of these? Discuss.
- Let's look at our predictions in the *Amazing Water* book web. How did we do? Let's look closely.

Step 15: *Summarizing*—I am going to scramble our word cards. When we are done, we are going to make a summary. A summary helps us organize what we know using a few big ideas. Let's look at the board again. We are going to make a summary web of what we have learned about *amazing water.* I'm going to put up a sentence strip. It says, The Three Forms of Water. Can anyone tell me what are the three forms of water? Place these around the board drawing a web strand to each. Group the children by using a random method. Give scrambled cards to small, cooperative groups to classify under each category in the web.

New Web—The Three Forms of Water/Liquid, Solid, or Gas

Step 16: *Assessment*—Using "Three Forms of Water" web, list children's names together for each randomly formed group on an observation form you have prepared. Note how well each group of children was able to take the word cards, read the cards, and categorize them into the three forms of water in the web.

Step 17: *Reflection*—Think about where the lesson went well and where there were problems. Adjust the lesson plan to smooth out the problem spots.

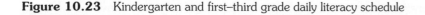

Figure 10.23   Kindergarten and first–third grade daily literacy schedule

---

Half-Day Kindergarten (Up to One Hour of Individual Assessment)

 8:30– 9:00 A.M.: Greet Children and Parents

 9:00– 9:10 A.M.: Morning Routine (Roll, Lunch Count, Weather, Calendar)

 9:10– 9:20 A.M.: Sharing Time

 9:20– 9:35 A.M.: Interactive Read Aloud

 9:35–10:05 A.M.: Group Shared Reading Lesson

10:05–10:20 A.M.: Recess

10:20–10:40 A.M.: Group Seat Work Assignments/Individual Assessment

10:40–10:55 A.M.: Rotation 1 at Learning Centers/Individual Assessment

10:55–11:10 A.M.: Rotation 2 at Learning Centers/Individual Assessment

11:10–11:20 A.M.: Group Counting Lesson

11:20–11:30 A.M.: Classroom Clean Up and Getting Ready to Dismiss

First–Third Grade (Up to Two Hours of Individual Assessment)

 8:30– 9:00 A.M.: Greet Children and Parents

 9:00– 9:10 A.M.: Morning Routine (Roll, Lunch Count, Weather, Calendar)

 9:10– 9:20 A.M.: Sharing Time

 9:20– 9:35 A.M.: Interactive Read Aloud

 9:35–10:05 A.M.: Group Shared Reading and Singing

10:05–10:15 A.M.: Individual Seat Work Assignment—Extension of Shared Reading

10:15–10:30 A.M.: Recess

10:30–10:45 A.M.: Rotation 1 at Learning Centers/Individual Assessment

10:45–11:00 A.M.: Rotation 2 at Learning Centers/Individual Assessment

11:00–11:15 A.M.: Rotation 3 at Learning Centers/Individual Assessment

11:15–11:30 A.M.: Rotation 4 at Learning Centers/Individual Assessment

11:30–11:50 A.M.: Group Seat Work Assignment in Mathematics/Individual Assessment

12:00 Noon–12:45: LUNCH

---

teach a group literacy lesson, (2) assess individual children's literacy development and rotate groups through literacy learning centers, and (3) provide group and independent seat work during the first week. We suggest the general daily schedule for literacy instruction and assessment during the first week of school in K–3 classrooms shown in Figure 10.23.

Summary

This chapter was designed to help you, the novice or experienced teacher, get organized for effective, well-managed literacy instruction in K–3 classrooms. We began with a discussion of how to organize your classroom environment prior to the beginning of the school year. We talked about how to design classroom space; understand,

Written lesson plans are not just for completing college or university assignments. Teachers who teach well go to the work of writing out their lesson plans in sufficient detail to think carefully about what and how they are teaching.

use, and acquire instructional materials and tools; make the most of available human resources; and group children to meet their individual learning needs.

Next, we discussed how to plan for a successful first day of literacy instruction. We provided example letters to parents and students to prepare them for literacy learning in the K–3 years and for the first day of school. We provided examples of how to establish routines for starting each school day with literacy, language, and learning. We also described how important good classroom management is to the success of any K–3 literacy instructional program. We emphasized how establishing rules, consequences, and schedules all help to provide young children with security and structure while fostering choice and independence from the very first day of school. Next we discussed a variety of literacy activities that would be helpful in getting that first day of school off to a good start by creating in children a sense of having learned to read on the first day of school as well as creating a sense of a classroom community through language and literacy activities.

Having helped you prepare for the first day, we discussed what you, the teacher, need to get accomplished during the first week of school in relation to getting ready to begin your K–3 literacy program. We showed you how to make extensive written daily literacy lesson plans and how to schedule time into the days of your first school week to individually assess children's literacy development to guide the construction of your literacy instructional program.

Check your understanding of chapter concepts by using the self assessment for Chapter 10 on our Companion Website at www.prenhall.com/ reutzel.

Concept Applications

In the Classroom

1. Draw a classroom floor plan for how you intend to divide up your classroom space during your first year of teaching. Give a supporting rationale for the design you choose. (Keep in mind the idea of beginning simple and moving to more complex classroom arrangements.)

2. Create a five-year plan for building a classroom library of trade books. Include in your plan a target total number of trade books and relevant target dates for accomplishment of your goals.

3. Prepare a letter to parents and children tailored expressly to the grade level you plan to teach. Take it to a parent you know and discuss it. Allow the parent to give you insights into how or if this letter is helpful.

4. Make a schedule of literacy activities you plan to use on the first day of school. Then, make individual lesson plans like those in this chapter for each of the activities you scheduled.

5. Analyze the cover of this text for qualities of design that are reflected in the research on creating literacy learning environments. What literacy tools and materials are present? How are they arranged? Does this classroom provide for interaction and learning of literacy through demonstrations and engagement? Is the classroom aesthetically pleasing? Does it inform children? Is it divided into functional areas? Has the teacher used personal touches? You might make an analysis grid or evaluation instrument based on these questions for your own classroom.

In the Field

1. Visit at least two public or private school classrooms, and draw a floor plan of the space in the classrooms and how it is used. Be sure to include

display areas and storage areas in your observations. Afterward, interview the teachers. Determine their reasons for the classroom arrangement and use.

2. Discuss with at least two parents the concept of volunteer work in schools. Determine whether or not parents would be willing to give their time to their local school. Invite them to fill out and discuss with you the volunteer sign-up form in Figure 10.16.

3. Visit two school classrooms, and note how teachers and children spend their time. On a separate paper, reflect in writing on your observations. Discuss relative advantages and disadvantages of teacher and student behaviors observed during reading instruction.

4. Interview at least two children in the above-average and below-average ability groups. Ask questions about how they like reading time, completing workbook and worksheet assignments, receiving books for presents, and reading aloud to their peers. Contrast your findings for the above-average and below-average readers.

5. Make arrangements to observe the first day in a K–3 classroom in a local school. Note very carefully the preparation, routines, and schedule of literacy activities. Describe how the teacher uses language and literacy activities on the first day?

Recommended Readings

Bear, D. R., Templeton, S., Invernizzi, M., & Johnston, F. (2000). *Words their way: Word study for phonics, vocabulary, and spelling instruction.* Upper Saddle River, NJ: Merrill/Prentice Hall.

Fountas, I. C., & Pinnell, G. S. (1996). *Guided reading instruction: Good first teaching for all children.* Portsmouth, NH: Heinemann.

Morrow, L. L. (2002). *The literacy center: Contexts for reading and writing,* 2nd Ed. Portland, ME: Stenhouse.

Opitz, M. F. (1998). *Flexible grouping in reading: Practical ways to help all students become better readers.* New York: Scholastic.

Rog, L. J. (2001). *Early literacy instruction in kindergarten.* Newark, DE: International Reading Association.

Wong, H. K., & Wong, R. T. (1998). *How to be an effective teacher: The first days of school.* Mt. View, CA: Harry K. Wong.

11

Providing Effective K–3 Literacy Instruction: Every Child a Reader

Focus Questions

When you are finished studying this chapter, you should be able to answer these questions:

1. What are six characteristics of exemplary primary-grade teachers?

2. How is an annual curriculum plan developed?

3. What are the important components of an annual assessment plan?

4. What are major components of the primary-grades (K–3) reading-writing workshop?

5. What are five ways you learned to foster strong school-family-community partnerships?

Key Concepts

Exemplary Primary Grade
   Literacy Teachers
Literacy Curriculum
Annual Curriculum Plan
Annual Assessment Plan
Norm-Referenced
   (Standardized) Tests
Criterion-Referenced
   (Standards-Based) Tests
Grade Level Outcomes or
   Performance Expectations
Primary Grades Reading-
   Writing Workshop
Read Aloud

Shared Reading
Big Book
Interactive Writing
Language Experience
   Approach
Guided Reading
Independent Reading
Parent–Family–
   Community
   Partnership
Supported Reading
Reading Recovery
Closed Caption
   Television

The most important factor in teaching literacy to young children is the teacher. Effective literacy teachers need to possess three types of knowledge for success in today's classrooms—declarative, procedural, and conditional. Teachers need to know what to teach (declarative knowledge)—the curriculum, the standards, and instructional goals. Next, teachers need to know the "how to" (procedural knowledge) for providing high quality early literacy instruction. And finally, there is that "something" we cannot package fully in any book—conditional knowledge which comes largely through experience in the context of teaching. In this chapter, we provide declarative knowledge necessary for effective K–3 literacy instruction as well as procedural knowledge about how to offer high quality literacy instruction. Throughout, we share elements of our conditional knowledge that have come from years of teaching in and observing early literacy instruction in classrooms.

MS. RIVERA, SECOND GRADE TEACHER:
OBSERVING A MASTER AT WORK

Visit Chapter 11 of our Companion Website at www.prenhall.com/reutzel to look into the chapter objectives, standards and principles, and pertinent web links associated with providing effective K–3 literacy instruction.

It is a warm, summerlike day at Mission Elementary School. We're scurrying down the covered walkways shielding us from the direct sunlight to observe Ms. Rivera's second grade classroom. As we enter Room 6, we are immediately struck with the busy noise we hear from children engaged in activities at several independent learning centers. We scan the room to locate Ms. Rivera. We find her working busily with a small group of children at a word-work center. She is holding a cookie sheet with seven magnetic letters—a, e, i, c, h, l, m—displayed across the top. She asks Tanya to make a two-letter word with the letters while the other students watch. Tanya studies the letters intently. She reaches for the letter m and places it in the center of the cookie sheet. Next, Tanya grabs the letter e and places it in the center of the cookie sheet to make the two-letter word me.

Ms. Rivera asks, "So, Tanya, what word did you make?"

Tanya proudly replies, "ME!"

"Good work, Tanya. Now, Juan can you make another two-letter word?" Juan quickly arranges the letters h and e to make the word he. "Very well done, Juan. I am so proud of you boys and girls. You are terrific at making two-letter words. But now, I have an even harder problem for you. Please take out your white boards and markers." Ms. Rivera intones very seriously, "I think you can solve this problem, but we'll just have to wait and see. Here is the problem. Using our letters," she points to the seven letters, "write as many three-letter words as you can on your white boards. You may work together after you have done your very best to have at least one three-letter word to share with the group."

Ms. Rivera leaves her small group, deeply engaged in their problem, to greet us. She says she is working with this group of children to help them increase their ability to use phonics in their reading and writing. Then, pointing around the room, she shows us her other centers: a reading nook, an integrated curriculum center focused on science content, where children are learning about how different kinds of weather affect rock, a listening center with small books, headphones, and a CD player, and a comprehension strategy center where children are working to complete a categorization task using a graphic organizer of different kinds of rocks under the headings of Sedimentary, Igneous, and Metamorphic.

During this quick visit to Ms. Rivera's classroom, we find children busy talking, reading, listening, and writing. We see children not only reading stories in the reading nook, but also learning content knowledge and new vocabulary and using their new knowledge to solve problems prearranged by this organized and effective second grade teacher. Ms. Rivera's room is a busy place, like so many other primary grade classrooms where children learn about new and interesting things using reading, writing, talking, and listening as the most important tools for getting smarter!

CHARACTERISTICS OF EXEMPLARY PRIMARY GRADE LITERACY TEACHERS

Our purpose in this chapter is to help you become an exemplary literacy teacher in the primary grades. To do this, you must understand the behaviors and knowledge that separate exemplary teachers from less effective teachers of young children. In the last five years, several major research studies have been undertaken with the single objective of describing the practices, beliefs, and knowledge of **exemplary primary grade literacy teachers** (Morrow, Tracey, Woo, & Pressley, 1999; Pressley, Allington, Wharton-McDonald, Collins-Block, & Morrow, 2001; Rogg, 2001; Block, Oakar, & Hurt, 2002). Taken together, these reports reveal the distinctive behaviors of teachers who support exceptional learning and growth in their students' literacy achievement. We share these so that you will understand the characteristics of teachers who are making a difference for children. Classes with high achievement share several common characteristics (Figure 11.1).

In the previous chapter, we showed how to structure a positive, well-ordered, print-rich classroom environment. We also provided information about how to schedule and manage an effective primary grade classroom environment. Now we focus our attention on designing a yearlong curriculum and assessment plan that is based on evidence-based best practices.

Designing a Yearlong Curriculum Plan

For most new teachers (and many experienced teachers as well) perhaps their most difficult task is to create the **annual curriculum plan.** The **literacy curriculum** is defined as a description of the reading and writing skills and strategies children used to learn at a specific grade level. To do this, some of the best sources to begin with are (1) the state's curriculum standards, (2) the school district curriculum guide, and (3) the district-adopted basal reader program's scope and sequence chart. When designing your curriculum plan, it is important to remember that teaching a reading or writing skill or strategy isn't accomplished in one lesson. The curriculum plan also needs to include a schedule for reviewing previously taught lessons.

It would not be practical to describe the specifics of every state's standards, every basal reading program's scope and sequence chart, or every school district's curriculum guide. In helping you design a curriculum plan, we use the guidelines presented in two prominent national reading research reports: *Starting Out Right: A Guide to Promoting Children's Reading Success* (Burns, Griffin, & Snow, 1999) and *Put Reading First: The Research Building Blocks for Teaching Children to Read, K–3.* (Armbruster, Lehr, & Osborn, 2001). In Figure 11.2, we list the research-based building blocks of K–3 literacy curricula. Every K–3 literacy program should include, at a minimum, these elements. As you plan your instructional program, be sure to include each of them.

Scheduling the frequency and depth of literacy skill instruction is another important facet of curriculum planning. We use a template similar to the one shown in Figure 11.3. Here, we show how a kindergarten teacher might go about scheduling her first nine weeks of an evidenced-based literacy curriculum. This template can be expanded to a full year template for planning the literacy curriculum in the primary grades. It is important to remember that these literacy curriculum elements need to be taught *and* scheduled for review during each year.

As you read the characteristics of exemplary primary grade literacy teachers, make note of three areas where you have particular strengths. Also, make note of three areas where you should seek additional learning and experiences to improve your abilities to teach young children well.

As you enter the classroom, be sure to have available the International Reading Association/National Council of Teachers of English Standards, your state or province's standards, school district curriculum guide, and the scope and sequence of your basal reading program to make your annual curriculum plan.

Figure 11.1 Characteristics of exemplary primary grade teachers

- *Instructional Balance*   Teachers integrated explicit skills instruction seamlessly with authentic reading and writing activities.
- *Instructional Density*   Teachers covered many more skills/concepts/strategies per hour of instruction. Every moment, activity in the classroom was oriented toward the goal of promoting learning even lining up for lunch or recess!
- *Instructional Scaffolding*   Teachers provided sufficient support to help children perform literacy tasks without taking over the tasks for children.
- *Understand and Respect Developmental Differences*   Teachers sought to determine each child's zone of proximal development prior to providing instruction and designing learning experiences (see Chapter 2).
- *Encourage Self-Regulation*   Teachers structured the environmental and learning activities so that students understood expectations, behaviors, and outcomes to promote student independence, cooperation, and task completion.
- *Integrate Reading and Writing*   Teachers structured learning so that reading and writing were used in mutually supportive ways. Children learned to "read like writers" and "write like readers."
- *High Expectations*   Teachers expected all children to learn and meet high standards of performance.
- *Good Classroom Management*   The classroom was well organized with clear instruction about the purposes and expectations for each area of classroom space. Instructional routines and procedures were clearly defined, well understood, conspicuously displayed, and consistently applied.
- *Skills/Concepts/Strategies Explicitly Taught*   Teachers taught skills through explanations, demonstrations, modeling, and gradual release of responsibility using the skill or strategy over time. Teachers believed that reading and writing are "taught," not "caught."
- *Access to and Emphasis Upon Books*   Teachers focused classroom learning activities on reading a variety of real texts with children—poetry, songs, environmental print, stories, and information texts. Teachers also recognized the importance of providing access to a large quantity and variety of books of differing levels of challenge.
- *Volume of Reading and Writing*   Teachers structured classroom learning experiences so that every possible moment was focused on authentic reading and writing tasks rather than on completing skill-and-drill sheets.
- *Match the Task Difficulty to Student Competence*   Teachers made every effort to assess and monitor students to assure that the tasks assigned in reading and writing were of sufficient challenge to promote engagement and progress but not to induce frustration and failure.
- *Connect Literacy Across the Curriculum*   Teachers drew no stark boundaries between learning to read and write and reading and writing to learn. Teachers were as comfortable teaching content knowledge to children during reading and writing instruction as they were teaching reading and writing skills as tools for acquiring content knowledge.
- *Postive, Personally Reinforcing Classroom Environment*   Teachers created and maintained a classroom atmosphere of respect, support, and clear expectations. Children were taught to help, support, cooperate, and collaborate in the best interests of others.
- *Work is Play in Kindergarten*   Kindergarten teachers structure multiple play and exploration centers with literacy learning as the focus.
- *Multidimensional Word Recognition Instruction*   Teachers taught children to use letter-sound information, word parts and patterns, and contextual information to identify unknown words.
- *Printed Prompts Prominently Displayed*   Teachers recognized the human tendency to forget rules, routines, and procedures. Such critical information was conspicuously displayed in effective classrooms.
- *Movement Toward Conventional Literacy*   Teachers held high expectations for students to make substantial progress toward use of writing conventions (capitalization, spelling, handwriting, punctuation, form, and appearance) by year's end.
- *Time on Academic Tasks*   Teachers engaged children in a preponderance of reading and writing experiences and activities on a daily basis.

Figure 11.2 Evidence-based K–3 literacy curriculum building blocks[*]

Kindergarten Literacy Curriculum
- Oral Language Development
  - Domain Knowledge—topical, procedural, and thematic concepts
  - Linguistic Knowledge—language and cultural registers (formal, slang, dialect)
- Concepts of Print
  - Front to Back of Book
  - Print Progression
    - Left to Right
    - Right to Left Return Sweep
    - Top to Bottom
  - Concept of Letter
  - Concept of Word
  - One-to-One Correspondence of Words Spoken and Words Written
  - Print Carries the Message, Not the Picture
  - Instructional Language—i.e., beginning, ending, middle, top, bottom, print, sentence, etc.
  - Letter Order
  - Word Order
  - Punctuation
- Alphabet Letters
  - 26 Upper Case Letters
  - 26 Lower Case Letters
- Phonological and Phonemic Awareness
  - Working with words in compound words
  - Working with rhyming sounds (rimes)
  - Working with syllables in words
  - Working with beginning sounds (onsets)
  - Working with phonemes in words
    - Identify the similar sound in words
    - Isolate a specific sound in words
    - Categorize the odd sounding word from a set of words
  - Blending sounds to say words
  - Segmenting sounds in words
  - Manipulating sounds in words (beginning, middle, ending)
- Alphabetic Principle
  - Making a mental connection between letters learned and the sound(s) the letters represent in spoken language
- Motivation and Engagement
  - Voluntary reading and writing
  - Cultivating positive attitudes toward reading and writing
- Writing
  - Letters
  - Phonic Spelling
  - Sight Words
  - Capitalization
  - Phonics through Spelling—Temporary/Invented Spellings

First Grade Literacy Curriculum
- Oral Language Development
  - Domain Knowledge—topical, procedural, and thematic concepts
  - Linguistic Knowledge—language and cultural registers (formal, slang, dialect, etc.)

(continued)

Figure 11.2 *continued*

- Phonics Instruction
  - Vowels (A, E, I, O, U and sometimes Y & W)
  - Consonants (B, C, D, F, G, H, J, K, L, M, N, P, Q, R, S, T, V, X, Z)
  - Vowel Digraphs (ee, ea, ie, ei, oa, etc.)
  - Consonant Digraphs (wh, ch, th, sh)
  - Vowel Diphthongs (oy, oi, ou, ai, etc.)
  - "R" Controlled Vowels
- Fluency Instruction
  - High-Frequency Sight Words
  - Repeated Readings of Text
- Vocabulary Instruction
  - Word meanings
- Comprehension Instruction
  - Activating Background Knowledge
  - Predicting
  - Text Structures
  - Goal or Purpose Setting
  - Imagery
  - Answering Questions
  - Summarizing
- Motivation and Engagement
  - Voluntary reading and writing
  - Cultivating positive attitudes toward reading and writing
- Writing
  - Writes a core of high-frequency words
  - Writes using a mix of conventional and invented word spellings
  - Writes to express meaning in a variety of genre
  - Uses terminal punctuation—period, question mark, exclamation point
  - Uses capitalization at the beginning of sentences

Second Grade Literacy Curriculum
- Phonics Instruction
  - Regularly spelled, multisyllable words and nonsense words
  - Irregularly spelled words and words with diphthongs, special vowel spellings, and common word endings
- Fluency Instruction
  - High-Frequency Sight Words
  - Word Analysis Study: Prefixes, Suffixes, Base Words
  - Repeated Readings of Text
- Vocabulary Instruction
  - New Word Meanings
- Comprehension Instruction
  - Recalls Facts and Details
  - Graphs, Charts, and Diagrams
  - Text Structures
  - Goal or Purpose Setting
  - Imagery
  - Monitoring
  - Compare and Contrast
  - Making Inferences
  - Answering Questions
  - Summarizing
- Motivation and Engagement
  - Voluntary reading and writing of fiction and nonfiction
  - Cultivating positive attitudes toward reading and writing
  - Responding to books

Figure 11.2 *continued*

- Writing
  - Writes a core of high-frequency words
  - Writes using a mix of conventional and invented word spellings
  - Writes to express meaning in a variety of genre
  - Internal punctuation—comma in a series, quotation marks

Third Grade Literacy Curriculum

- Fluency Instruction
  - High-Frequency Sight Words
  - Word Analysis Study: Prefixes, Suffixes, Base Words
  - Repeated Readings of Text
- Vocabulary Instruction
  - Word meanings and "formal or book" register
- Comprehension Instruction
  - Main Idea and Detail
  - Monitoring—can find words that cause problems
  - Cause and Effect
  - Fact and Opinion
  - Making Inferences
  - Answering Questions
  - Summarizing
- Motivation and Engagement
  - Voluntary reading and writing of fiction and nonfiction books
  - Cultivating positive attitudes toward reading and writing
  - Responding to books
- Writing
  - Writes to express meaning in a variety of genre
  - With assistance and modeling uses the writing process, conferencing, editing, and revising, effectively to improve personal writing quality
  - Combines information from multiple sources when writing reports
  - Responds helpfully to other students' writing
  - Independently reviews own work for spelling, mechanics, and presentation

* Based on grade-level accomplishments found in Burns, M. S., Griffin, P., & Snow, C. E. (1999). *Starting Out Right: A Guide to Promoting Children's Reading Success.* Washington, DC: National Research Council.

CREATING AN ANNUAL ASSESSMENT PLAN

"Assessment drives instruction" is often considered a trite, worn-out cliché in American reading instruction. It is nevertheless true, especially now that many states have mandated high-stakes testing in reading and writing in their schools. On the national scene, some have quipped recently that the mantra of the federal legislation No Child Left Behind Act should be retitled to No Child Left **Untested!** In today's classrooms, it is true that accountability and assessment are on the minds of everyone from the federal government to state legislatures, from administrators to parents, and from teachers to the media. It is a time of unprecedented investment in accountability.

The Political Roots of the Current Literacy Emphasis

At no other time in the history of the United States has the federal government invested so heavily—billions of dollars—to improve the reading proficiency of our most disadvantaged, impoverished, and at-risk children and their teachers' abilities to provide

Assessment drives instruction is a maxim in education. Think about why this is true and discuss it with a colleague or classroom teacher.

Standards Note
Standard 12.1: Initiate and participate in ongoing curriculum development and evaluation. As you read the upcoming pages, pay particular attention to the many ways you can develop and evaluate your curriculum and your student's progress in reading and writing through planning and assessment.

Figure 11.3   Annual curriculum planning template—Kindergarten example

Teacher's Name   Mr. Reiden
School Name   Lincoln
Grade Level   Kindergarten   School Year   2004

Week 1
Oral Language Concepts
  Names, First & Last
Concepts of Print
  Book Concepts
Alphabet Letters
  Alphabetic Awareness
Phonological Awareness
  Listening to Rhymes
Motivation
  Read Aloud
Writing
  First Name

Week 2
Oral Language Concepts
  Color Words
Concepts of Print
  L to R Print Direction
Alphabet Letters
  Alphabetic Order
Phonological Awareness
  Rhyming Pairs
Motivation
  Read Aloud
Writing
  Last Name

Week 3
Oral Language Concepts
  Color Words
Concepts of Print
  Top to Bottom
Alphabet Letters
  Aa, Rr, Ss
Phonological Awareness
  Odd Rhyme Out
Motivation
  Take Home Books
Writing
  Word Wall Words

Week 4
Oral Language Concepts
  Names of Basic Shapes
Concepts of Print
  Print Carries the Message
Alphabet Letters
  Ee, Mm, Tt
Phonological Awareness
  Listening to Alliterations
Motivation
  Read Aloud
Writing
  Shared Writing

Week 5
Oral Language Concepts
  Days of the Week
Concepts of Print
  Concept of Word
Alphabet Letters
  Oo, Nn, Ll
Phonological Awareness
  Similar Onsets
Motivation
  Wordless Picture Books
Writing
  Shared Writing

Week 6
Oral Language Concepts
  Days of the Week
Concepts of Print
  Concept of Word
Alphabet Letters
  Ii, Bb, Cc
Phonological Awareness
  Odd Onset Out
Motivation
  Reading Buddies
Writing
  Shared Writing

Week 7
Oral Language Concepts
  Months of the Year
Concepts of Print
  One-to-One Word Matching
Alphabet Letters
  Uu, Pp, Gg
Phonological Awareness
  Odd Word Out
Motivation
  Word Wall Cards
Writing
  Interactive Writing

Week 8
Oral Language Concepts
  Months of the Year
Concepts of Print
  One-to-One Word Matching
Alphabet Letters
  Aa, Hh, Kk
Phonological Awareness
  Odd Sound Out—Beginning
Motivation
  Environmental Print Books
Writing
  Interactive Writing

Week 9
Oral Language Concepts
  Weather Words
Concepts of Print
  Concept of Letter
Alphabet Letters
  Ee, Ff, Jj
Phonological Awareness
  Odd Sound Out—Ending
Motivation
  Make a Recipe with Mom
Writing
  Interactive Writing

high-quality reading instruction based on the latest reading research. This sharp focus on bringing up the bottom quartile of readers has spilled over into increased accountability for all teachers and children.

We think it is important to note that the No Child Left Behind legislation was passed overwhelmingly with bi-partisan votes in the U.S. Congress. While some may suggest that the push for greater literacy in America is solely the work of the Bush administration, the efforts were begun under the Clinton administration as a part of the America Reads Act and the Reading Excellence Act. Therefore, the stimulus for increased accountability isn't the product of party politics, but rather a focus that has emerged from real public concern over our youngsters' ability to compete in a new global economy in which the literacy bar is being raised. *It is not that teachers have failed to teach children to read.* Rather, this new emphasis on literacy is the result of a shifting employment market that demands greater and greater literacy-related abilities.

Using Assessment Data to Improve Instruction

One of the roles, then, of the effective classroom teacher is to understand, plan, and use assessment data to inform instructional choices, intervention selection, and motivational approaches. As we learned in Chapter 9, there are two major types of reading assessments—those designed to make comparisons of children's performances nationally and those designed to determine if children have learned or mastered specific content or processes in reading.

Tests designed to make national, regional, state, district, class, or student comparisons are referred to as **norm-referenced tests** (NRT) or standardized tests. These tests are designed by randomly testing a significant sample population (usually thousands) of children. The results are then plotted graphically and distributed over a *normal curve* of the population; this is where the great majority of children tested fall in the center of what is often a bell-shaped curve with fewer children's scores landing in the tails, or edges of the distribution. These tests are often used to make comparisons of children's individual performance against a national population for comparison and screening purposes.

Tests designed to determine if children have learned or mastered specific content or reading processes as measured against curriculum standards or criteria are referred to as **criterion-referenced tests** (CRT). These tests are constructed to accurately reflect the content or standards associated with teaching the state, district, or school's adopted curriculum.

A third type of testing, informal assessment, is the most useful to teachers. These assessment tools are generally used to diagnose and monitor children's reading progress on a more frequent basis than could be accomplished using NRT or CRT. For more information, please review Chapter 9 on assessment in reading.

As a classroom teacher, you will probably have experience with all of these forms of assessment. Therefore, as you make an **annual assessment plan,** it is important that you schedule time for administering, interpreting, and using data from formal and informal assessment tools to guide your instructional planning and delivery. In Figure 11.4 we offer a sample annual assessment plan that incorporates different forms of assessment at different times. It will help you get a sense of the annual accountability cycle during the school year for grades K–3. Different tests often used in Texas are listed here for illustrative purposes.

Conducting assessment according to the sample plan shown in Figure 11.4 is a futile effort if teachers do not carefully study, analyze, and interpret assessment data. Assessment is not just another task to be completed and checked off the To-Do list. Assessment data should *inform* you, the teacher, about how well your instruction is meeting the learning needs of and expected outcomes for your students. Assessments, particularly informal assessments, should be chosen to help you determine

Why are parents and policy-makers concerned about student reading achievement? Go to http://nces.ed.gov/nationsreportcard and inspect the most recent NAEP Report Card on reading achievement in the U.S.

The most important role of assessment is to inform instructional decisions and selection of instructional interventions.

Think about two major ways that norm-referenced and criterion-referenced tests differ.

Figure 11.4   Sample annual assessment plan—Kindergarten

Sep
NRT—TERA
1. Test of Early Reading Ability
PPVT
2. Peabody Picture Vocabulary Test
CRT—TEKS
3. Texas Essential Knowledge & Skills
IFA
4. Yopp-Singer Phonemic Awareness Test
5. Random Alphabet Display
6. Concepts About Print Test

Oct
IFA
1. Yopp-Singer Rhyming
2. Burke Reading Interview
3. Random Alphabet Display
4. Book Handling Interview

Nov
IFA
1. Yopp-Singer Rhyming
2. Random Alphabet Display
3. Book Handling Interview
4. Sight Word List

Dec
IFA
1. Yopp-Singer Oddity Task
2. Random Alphabet Display
3. Book Handling Interview
4. Sight Word List

Jan
CRT—TEKS
1. Texas Essential Knowledge & Skills
IFA
2. Yopp-Singer Oddity Task
3. Book Handling Interview
4. Sight Word List

Feb
IFA
1. Yopp-Singer Blending Test
2. Random Alphabet Display
3. Concepts About Print Test
4. Burke Reading Interview

Mar
IFA
1. Yopp-Singer Blending Test
2. Random Alphabet Writing Task
3. Book Handling Interview
4. Early Reading Attitude Survey

Apr
IFA
1. Yopp-Singer Segmentation Test
2. Random Alphabet Writing Task
3. Book Handling Interview
4. Sight Word List

May
NRT
1. Test of Early Reading Ability
2. Peabody Picture Vocabulary Test
CRT
3. Texas Essential Knowledge and Skills
IFA
4. Yopp-Singer Battery of Phonemic Awareness
5. Concepts About Print Test
6. Early Reading Attitude Survey
7. Burke Reading Interview
8. Random Alphabet Display & Writing Test
9. Sight Word List

whether grade-level and/or expected outcomes are being achieved. In other words, children should be able to perform certain reading and writing tasks as dictated by curriculum standards.

Discuss with a colleague or teacher why having an annual assessment plan is important.

In Figure 11.5, we bring together the **grade-level outcome or performance expectations** for K–3 students set by the National Research Council. We encourage you to carefully study them. Only after you have done so should you prepare your own annual assessment plan. Each assessment tool you select, as well as those selected for you by the state, should address the relevant expectations for reading and writing instruction at your grade level.

Once you have collected grade-level appropriate data on expectations, you must study these data to see who in your classroom needs further challenges or who is struggling and in need of increased attention and support. Assessment data help

Figure 11.5 Expected literacy accomplishments for K–3 students[*]

Kindergarten Students—Expected Literacy Accomplishments

Oral Language
- Activate background knowledge and use it to understand new information.
- Build conceptual and linguistic domain knowledge—oral vocabulary.
- Model and assess listening comprehension of oral and book language.
- Assist children to understand the purposes and functions of reading and writing.

Reading
- Use playful language activities and games to develop phonological awareness—an awareness of word parts (phonemes, onsets and rimes, see Chapter 4).
- Help children understand book and print concepts.
- Teach children to recognize upper- and lower-case letters.
- Help children make connections between letters and sounds (alphabetic principle, see Chapter 4).
- Help children recognize a few high-frequency words by sight.
- Provide access to books and encourage emergent reading of simple books (memorized and finger-point reading).
- Help children notice when oral or book language doesn't make sense.
- Encourage children to make predictions about stories.

Writing
- Teach children to write upper- and lower-case letters.
- Teach children to write own name.
- Teach children to use invented spellings to express own meaning.
- Teach children to use invented spellings to write teacher-dictated words.
- Help children become aware of the difference between kid writing and conventional writing.

First Grade Students—Expected Literacy Accomplishments

Oral Language
- Use more complex and formal oral language structures.
- Continue to build conceptual and linguistic domain knowledge—oral vocabulary.
- Model and assess comprehension of oral language.

Reading
- Make transition from emergent (memorized and finger-point reading) to reading accurately what is recorded in the text.
- Decode regularly spelled, one-syllable words and nonsense words.
- Accurately read and comprehend any text designed for first half of first grade.
- Use letter-sound knowledge (phonics) to sound out unfamiliar words.
- Has a reading vocabulary of 300–500 sight words and easily sounded-out words.
- Monitor own reading and self-correct using language sense and context when reading fails to make sense.
- Read and comprehend story and information texts appropriate to the grade level.
- Read and comprehend simple written instructions.
- Make predictions and justify predictions for stories.
- Activate background knowledge and use it to understand new information.
- Can count the number of syllables and phonemes in one-syllable words.
- Can blend and segment the phonemes of one-syllable words.
- Can answer simple comprehension questions.
- Engage voluntarily in a variety of reading and writing activities.

Writing
- Spell three- and four-letter short vowel words conventionally.
- Write texts for others to read.
- Write independently using a mix of invented and conventional spellings.
- Use basic, or terminal, punctuation (period, question marks, and exclamation marks) and capitalization.
- Produce a variety of types of compositions and texts, i.e., stories, poems, notes, cards, recipes, journal entries, information texts.

(continued)

Figure 11.5 *continued*

Second Grade Students—Expected Literacy Accomplishments
Oral Language
- Use more formal language registers—book language rather than oral language-like structures.

Reading
- Read and comprehend both fiction and nonfiction books at grade level.
- Accurately decode regular, multisyllable words and nonsense words.
- Use letter-sound knowledge to decode unknown words.
- Accurately decode irregularly spelled words containing diphthongs, special vowel combinations, and common word endings.
- Read voluntarily for interest and own purposes.
- Recall facts and details.
- Read nonfiction to answer specific questions or for specific details.
- Respond creatively to books through dramatizations, fantasy play, or oral presentations.
- Discuss similarities in characters and events across texts.
- Connect and compare information across text selections.
- Pose answers to how, what, why, and what-if questions.

Writing
- Correctly spell previously studied words and spelling patterns in own writing.
- Represent the complete sound of a word when spelling independently.
- Write using formal language patterns in place of oral language patterns at appropriate spots in own writing.
- Make reasonable judgments about what to include in own writing.
- Productively discuss ways to clarify own writing and that of others.
- With assistance, use conferencing, revision, and editing processes to increase quality of own writing.
- Given help, write informative, well-structured reports.
- Attend to spelling, mechanics, and presentation for final products.
- Produce a variety of types of compositions.

Third Grade Students—Expected Literacy Accomplishments
Oral Language
- Use more formal language registers—book language rather than oral language-like structures.

Reading
- Read and comprehend both fiction and nonfiction books at grade level.
- Read aloud with fluency and comprehension any grade-level appropriate text.
- Use letter-sound correspondence knowledge and structural analysis to decode words.
- Read longer fictional selections and chapter books independently.
- Respond creatively to books through dramatizations, fantasy play, or oral presentations.
- Can identify words or phrases causing comprehension difficulties.
- Summarize major points from fiction and nonfiction books.
- Discuss underlying theme in fiction books.
- Ask how, why, and what-if questions in interpreting nonfiction books.
- Use information and reasoning to examine opinions.
- Infer word meaning from previously taught prefixes, suffixes, and base words.

Writing
- Begin to incorporate literacy words and language patterns in own writing, figures of speech, elaborate descriptions.
- Correctly spell previously studied words and spelling patterns in own writing.
- Combine information from multiple sources in writing reports.
- Productively discuss ways to clarify own writing and that of others.
- With assistance, use conferencing, revision, and editing processes to increase quality of own writing.
- Independently review work for spelling, mechanics, and presentation.
- Produce a variety of written work in a variety of formats including multi-media forms.

*Based on grade-level accomplishments found in Burns, M. S., Griffin, P., & Snow, C. E. (1999). *Starting Out Right: A Guide to Promoting Children's Reading Success*. Washington, DC: National Research Council.

you, the teacher, target your instructional planning so that you are effectively working in each child's zone of proximal development where you can be of the greatest assistance.

Communicating with Parents

Parents need to know how their children are progressing beyond the normally scheduled parent-teacher conferences and reporting periods. If you maintain a computer database of your assessments, student records can be made available to parents on the Internet using password protected access processes. This allows parents to check their children's progress at any time of the day or night—a real convenience for today's busy parents. Letters, phone calls, scheduling appointments, and home visits are also important for those students who need extra support. During such times, be sure to reassure parents of your commitment to their child's progress and success. Involve parents in making plans for accelerating their child's reading and writing progress. You may even schedule a time for a seminar, workshop, or home visit to show parents how they can work with their child at home.

We have found that weekly newsletters are greatly appreciated by parents. They should contain a variety of information: (1) what we have learned this week, (2) what we will be learning next week, (3) activities that will help cement last week's learning, and (4) activities that will help prepare me for next week's learning. This helps parents feel that they, too, can make a real difference in their children's education.

List two ways you plan to increase communication with parents about their child's progress in learning to read and write.

__Standards Note__
Standard 11.3: Involve parents in cooperative efforts and programs to support students' reading and writing development. Note four ways you can effectively communicate with parents about their students' reading and writing progress in this section.

PLANNING DAILY INSTRUCTIONAL ROUTINES: READING-WRITING WORKSHOP

The next order of business, once you have assessed your students' reading and writing instructional needs, is to plan daily instructional routines and lessons for the K–3 classroom. Instructional routines and lessons should include best practices and the intensive instruction of curriculum elements supported by scientific research. The **Primary Grades Reading-Writing Workshop** is a daily reading and writing instructional routine designed expressly for the primary grades (K–3). It is a variation on reading and writing workshops for intermediate and middle school grades (Atwell, 1987; Reutzel & Cooter, 1991; Calkins, 1994, 2001; Fountas and Pinnell, 2001). It accommodates several instructional best practices in the primary grades: (1) interactive read aloud, (2) shared reading, (3) guided reading, and (4) independent reading and writing learning centers.

The Primary Grades Reading-Writing Workshop consists of five parts: (1) reading and writing together, (2) learning about words, (3) guided reading, (4) fluency development, and (5) reading and writing learning centers. These five components incorporate elements of scientifically based reading and writing instruction recommended in several recent national reading research reports, including phonemic awareness instruction, decoding instruction, fluency development, vocabulary and comprehension strategy instruction, and guided oral reading feedback and instruction (Snow, Burns, & Griffin, 1998; National Reading Panel, 2000).

The Primary Grades Reading-Writing Workshop is designed to run for 90 minutes per day in kindergarten and 150 to 180 minutes daily in Grades 1–3 during an *uninterrupted* instructional time block. Its structure is outlined in Figure 11.6.

What are the five parts of the Primary Grades Reading-Writing Workshop? Can you see how these parts involve teachers and children in daily TO, WITH, and BY reading and writing experiences?

Figure 11.6   The Primary Grades Reading–Writing Workshop

Reading and Writing Together [T and S]			
(35–40 Minutes Per Day)			
1. Interactive Read Aloud 2. Shared Reading 3. Interactive or Shared Writing			
Working with Strategies [T & S]			
(30 Minutes Per Day)			
1. Decoding and Spelling Instruction 2. Vocabulary & Comprehension Strategy Instruction			
Block 1—15 Minutes	Block 2—15 Minutes	Block 3—15 Minutes	Block 4—15 Minutes
Centers [S]	**Centers [S]**	**Centers [S]**	**Centers [S]**
• Working with Strategies	• Working with Strategies	• Working with Strategies	• Working with Strategies
• Writing/Handwriting	• Writing/Handwriting	• Writing/Handwriting	• Writing/Handwriting
• Reading Response	• Reading Response	• Reading Response	• Reading Response
• Content Study	• Content Study	• Content Study	• Content Study
• Independent Reading	• Independent Reading	• Independent Reading	• Independent Reading
Guided Reading I	**Guided Reading II**	**Guided Reading III**	**Guided Reading IV**
[T & S¹]	[T & S²]	[T & S³]	[T & S⁴]
Fluency Workshop & Assessment			
Fluency Workshop [S]	*(30 Minutes Per Day)*		**Assessment [T & S¹]**
• Repeated Reading Practice		• Reading Accuracy, Fluency & Comprehension Assessment	
• Paired or Buddy Reading Practice		• Spelling, Writing & Handwriting Assessment	
• Performance/Recorded Reading			
Closing Sharing Time *(10–15 Minutes)*			

T = Teacher, S = Students, S with a superscript number = Students in a numbered group.

Reading and Writing Together

During this whole-class, group instructional time (*20 minutes in kindergarten; 35–40 minutes in grades 1–3),* teachers engage young readers in four types of reading and writing experiences: (1) interactive read aloud, (2) shared reading, (3) shared writing, and (4) interactive writing.

Interactive-Read Aloud

Reading aloud and interacting around trade books helps young children become successful readers (Campbell, 1992; Rosenhouse, Feitelson, & Kita 1997; Neuman, 1999; Bennett, 2001; Labbo, 2001). To make reading aloud an optimal instructional experience with younger readers, books need to be read aloud *interactively.* This means stopping to discuss parts of the print, the story line, information, or a picture during the reading. In fact, recent evidence (Dickinson & Tabors, 2001) suggests that interaction is the most important part of making reading aloud effective.

When selecting books to be read aloud to children, you should look for books that not only offer engaging stories and illustrations, but also contribute to children's cognitive development by offering them new concepts, ideas, and experiences. *It is critical that teachers and parents read a balance of books to their children.* Young children are usually the recipients of too much story and narrative text read aloud in schools and homes (Duke, 2000, 2002; Duke, Bennett-Armistead, & Roberts, 2002; Duke & Purcell-Gates, in press). Young children need and enjoy read aloud experiences with information books as well. We have created, based on Trelease's (1995) *The New Read-Aloud Handbook,* a listing of the do's-and-don'ts of read aloud (see Figure 11.7).

How could you plan to train or communicate with parents concerning effective read-aloud strategies?

Figure 11.7 The Do's and Don'ts of reading aloud[*]

> **Do's**
> - Do begin reading to children as early in their lives as they can be supported to sit and listen.
> - Do use rhymes, raps, songs, chants, poetry, and pictures to stimulate their oral language development, listening, and interaction with others.
> - Do read aloud to children at least 10–15 minutes daily, more often if possible.
> - Do set aside a time for daily reading aloud in your curriculum schedule.
> - Do read picture books to all ages, but also gradually move to reading longer books without pictures as well.
> - Do vary the topics and genre of your read-aloud selections.
> - Do read aloud books to children that stretch their intellectual and oral language development.
> - Do allow plenty of time for interaction before, during, and after the reading.
> - Do read aloud with expression and enthusiasm.
> - Do add another dimension to your reading sometimes, such as using hand movements or puppets or dressing up in costume.
> - Do carry a book with you at all times to model your love of books and reading.
>
> **Don'ts**
> - Don't read aloud too fast.
> - Don't read aloud books children can read independently: Give a "book talk" instead!
> - Don't read aloud books and stories you don't enjoy yourself.
> - Don't read aloud books and stories that exceed the children's emotional development.
> - Don't continue reading a book you don't like. Admit it, and choose another.
> - Don't impose your interpretations and preferences on children.
> - Don't confuse quantity with quality.
> - Don't use reading aloud as a reward or punishment.

[*]Based on Trelease (1989).

Figure 11.8 Interactive read-aloud guidelines

> - Designate a legitimate time and place in the daily curriculum for reading aloud.
> - Select quality books.
> - Select literature that relates to other literature.
> - Prepare by previewing the book.
> - Group children to maximize opportunities to respond.
> - Provide a brief introduction.
> - Read with expression.
> - Discuss literature in lively, invitational, thought-provoking ways.
> - Encourage children's responses to the book.
> - Allow time for discussion and interaction about the book.

[*]Based on Teale and Martinez, 1986; Hoffman, Roser, and Battle, 1993.

In 1986, Teale and Martinez (1986) and Hoffman, Roser, and Battle (1993) summarized read-aloud research and developed guidelines for reading aloud to children. We provide a few in Figure 11.8

An interactive read aloud starts with a brief introduction and discussion of the book that helps children activate their background knowledge and personal experiences. If they have little prior knowledge or experience, the effective teacher begins by providing activities, demonstrations, and experiences to build this necessary knowledge. When reading aloud, you should stop at various points in the book to ask children open-ended thinking questions. Invite children to explain concepts they do not understand. Help children make connections between the concepts in books read aloud and their own life experiences. Be sure that adequate time is allowed for discussion during and after the reading. Too often, teachers talk too much, rush through the reading, and don't allow sufficient time for students to express themselves or their ideas during or after the reading. Reading books aloud to children should be an important part of each day's reading instructional time. We recommend, however, that not more than 15 to 20 minutes per day be allocated to interactive read aloud in grades K–1. Though important, reading aloud does not in and of itself help children become independent readers.

Should I Use Grouping for Read Aloud? Most reading aloud to children in school takes place with the entire class. Morrow (1988b) reminds teachers to take advantage of the benefits associated with reading aloud to smaller groups of young children and one-to-one with individuals. Children whose reading development lags behind that of their peers can be helped a great deal by teachers, volunteers, or older peers who take time to read to them in small-group or one-to-one settings.

Shared Reading

Grouping for read aloud allows teachers to assist those students who have had few opportunities to interact around books.

In 1979, Don Holdaway explained that reading bedtime stories was one of the earliest and most significant elements supporting the reading development of young children. **Shared reading,** sometimes called the *shared book experience,* is designed to be used with very young readers to model how readers look at, figure out, and operate on the print. In several scientific research studies, shared reading experiences have been shown to be especially useful with young children (Reutzel & Hollingsworth, 1993; Reutzel, Hollingsworth, & Eldredge, 1994; Eldredge, Reutzel, & Hollingsworth, 1996).

During shared reading, teachers typically use an enlarged text called a **big book.** Big books permit teachers to guide and demonstrate for children how to operate effectively on the print (Barrett, 1982). It is critical when selecting big books for purchase that teachers evaluate the size and legibility of the print from a distance of up to 15 feet away. Many publishers have simply enlarged the print found in traditionally sized books. The result can sometimes be print far too small to be effective with a group of children. The print in big books must be large enough so that the entire group of children can see it as easily as if they were sitting on your knee.

Find strategies and lessons from Pro Teacher on early reading and writing in Chapter 11 on our Companion Website at www.prenhall.com/reutzel.

Shared reading books should have literary merit, engaging and meaningful content, and sustain high interest. Illustrations in shared reading books and stories must augment and expand upon the text. Pictures should tell or support the reading of the story in proper sequence. The proper selection of big books for shared reading experiences hook children on the sounds and patterns of language, engage their minds with meaningful content and knowledge, and make clear the multiple purposes of reading. Big books chosen for shared reading ought to put reasonable demands on younger readers' capabilities. The number of unknown words in relation to known words in a new book selected for shared reading should not overwhelm children. Big books selected for initial shared reading experiences should contain pictures that largely carry the storyline. Print in initial shared reading big books may amount to little more than a repeated line or two underneath the pictures, such as is found in *Brown Bear, Brown Bear* or *Polar Bear, Polar Bear* by Martin (1990, 1991). The print should be consistently placed on the page rather than moving around from page to page.

Figure 11.9 Shared reading in K–3 classrooms

Conducting a Shared Book Experience. To begin a shared book experience, introduce the book to the children. Begin by inviting children to look at the book cover with the prompt, "What do you see?" Allow children to talk about what they see. Ask them, "What do you think the print will tell you about the picture?" Let them study the title carefully and read the title with you. Talk about the front and back of the book and point out certain features of the cover and title page, such as the title, the author, and the illustrator. Next, read the book with "full dramatic punch, perhaps overdoing a little some of the best parts." (F. L. Barrett, 1982, p. 16) While reading the story, invite children to join in on any repeated or predictable phrases or words they recognize or predict. At key points during the shared reading, pause to encourage children to predict what is coming next in the story.

After reading, invite children to share their responses to the book. Ask them to talk about their favorite parts, connect the book to their experiences, and discuss how well they were able to predict and participate. The shared reading book is reread on subsequent days using hand and body movements, simple props related to the book, or rhythm instruments to increase student involvement and activity.

Shared reading is an effective form of oral reading practice.

Once a shared reading book has been reread twice, select something from the print in the book to examine in a close reading. For example, in the big book *The Three Billy Goats Gruff: A Norwegian Folktale* (E. Appleby, 2001), the teacher may decide that students should begin to notice the sight word *the* in the text. To direct students' eyes to the word *the* in the text, the teacher takes stick 'em notes from a pad and cuts several to the size necessary to cover or mask the word *the* in the text. As children and teacher engage in a close reading, they note the masked words. The teacher unmasks the first *the* and asks students to look carefully at the word. What are the letters in the word? Invite a student to come up and copy the word from the book onto a large card. Each time the word *the* is encountered in the close read, it is unmasked and stressed aloud in the reading. After the close reading for *the*, the teacher gives each child a *the* word card. The children are instructed to pick up a pair of scissors from the basket and return to their seats. While at their seats, they cut the card into its three letters and scramble the letters. Each child unscrambles the letters to form the word *the* on their desktops. Each child is given a new index card to write the word *the* to keep in his/her own word collection.

Shared reading is a very effective way to explicitly teach, model, and demonstrate a variety of reading strategies and concepts.

Songs, Raps, Poems, and Chants. An effective and motivating extension of the shared reading experience is to enlarge the lyrics of favorite songs, raps, poems, or chants. Research has demonstrated the positive effects of music on learning language, both oral and written. G. C. Taylor (1981) determined that music-centered language arts instruction resulted in enhanced listening, language awareness, and reading readiness skills. Eastlund (1980) found that music as a medium of language made learning and language acquisition easier for young children. McGuire (1984) reported that children taught music on a daily basis had significantly higher reading growth scores than did children who were not taught music. (Selected resources for songs, poems, chants, and raps to be used in the shared reading are listed in Appendix B.) Reading aloud and shared reading experiences ought to be the primary focus of reading instruction during the first six months of kindergarten and also during the first four to six weeks of first grade reading instruction. Shared reading is gradually replaced in grades 2–3 with more work in guided reading groups.

Shared Writing

Shared writing is an opportunity for teachers and children to share the act of composing a piece of writing. Let's take a look at some highly effective ways you can "share the pencil" with children.

The Language Experience Approach is an excellent way for teachers to help children understand the connection between oral language and written language.

Language Experience Approach. As young children are initially challenged by the transcription demands when writing, many teachers turn to a long-practiced and very useful early writing instructional approach called the language experience approach. The essence of the **language experience approach** is to use children's talk about personal or vicarious experiences as the basis for creating a piece of writing that the children can read. In this approach to writing, children dictate the text and the teacher writes for the children, resulting in the creation of a group language experience chart. This means, of course, that the entire class or group of children need to have shared an experience such as a field trip, a new book read aloud, or the visit of an outside guest. The typical sequence of events associated with the creation of a group language experience chart is:

1. The children participate in a common experience.
2. Teacher and children discuss the common experience.

3. Children dictate the chart, while the teacher transcribes the dictation.
4. Teacher and children share in reading the chart.
5. The chart is used to learn about words and other important language concepts such as punctuation, left-to-right, and sight words.

The selection of an interesting and stimulating experience or topic for children largely determines the success or failure of any language experience activity. Topics and experiences simply must capture the interest of children to provide the necessary motivation. A few examples of ideas for supporting the creation of a group language experience chart include:

- Our mother hamster had babies last night.
- Writing a new version of *The Napping House* (A. Wood, 1984).
- What mountain men did in the old days.
- What we want for our birthdays.
- Planning our Valentine's Day party.
- What did Martin Luther King, Jr., do?
- Sometimes I have scary dreams. Once. . . .
- Once I got into trouble for. . . .
- A classmate is ill; make a get-well card from the class.
- What we want to tell our parents for the open house tomorrow night.

Discuss the experience carefully and completely. Help children assess what they have learned, help them make personal connections, and motivate them to share with others their knowledge, experiences, and personal connections. Be careful not to dominate the discussion. Ask many open-ended questions to promote discussion. Avoid beginning dictation too early in the discussion to prevent a dull, even robotic recounting of the experience.

A Language Experience Example Using *The Polar Express*. Imagine reading aloud *The Polar Express* by Chris Van Allsburg (1985) a few weeks prior to Christmas in a first grade classroom. After inviting children to discuss the book, ask, "If you had been chosen by Santa to receive the first gift of Christmas, what would you have chosen?" Call on individual children to give their ideas. After plenty of discussion, call on children to dictate aloud their best ideas for responding to this question. Record each child's dictation on the chart. With emergent readers, you may wish to record each child's dictation with different colored markers; the colors help children identify their own dictation more easily in the future. Later, you may write the children's names by their dictations. When the chart is complete, read the chart aloud to the children while pointing to each word. After reading the chart aloud, invite the children to read along a second time. Next, ask individual children to read their own responses aloud or invite volunteers to read aloud the responses of other children.

As the teacher, you may wish to read aloud a certain line from the chart and ask for a child to come up to the chart and point to the line you just read aloud. You may copy the lines of the chart on sentence strips and have children pick a sentence strip and match it to the line on the chart. Favorite words on the chart story can be copied onto word cards for matching activities as well. Thus, the text generated by the children for the chart story can be used in subsequent large- and small-group meetings to build the students' sight vocabulary of words on the chart, demonstrate word-recognition strategies, and even help children learn about letter sounds for decoding

You will find a Safety Net Lesson for struggling readers on reading comprehension and analyzing information to make inferences in Chapter 11 on our Companion Website at www.prenhall.com/ reutzel.

Language Experience Group Charts allow an experience shared by the entire class to be recorded and read aloud to practice oral reading or to teach important concepts about print.

purposes. The chart also can be copied onto a regular-size sheet of paper and sent home with each child for individual reading practice.

Morning Message. A morning message is brief, no more than two to six sentences on the level of the children's ability to attend to and produce print (Payne & Schulman, 1998). Topics for the morning message are based on recent or upcoming school or class events and ideas or experiences individual students want to share. Typically, you, the teacher, will write the first sentence of the morning message. It might read, "Good morning, first grade! Today is. . . " or "Wow, yesterday was really special because. . . ." Leads such as this get the students reading and thinking to start the day. Next, read the first sentence of the morning message aloud to the children. While pointing, read it again together. Ask the children if they have anything they would like to write to fill in the next part of the morning message. As children offer suggestions, ask them questions like, "What will we write first?" or "How many sounds do we hear in the first word? Let's clap and count the sounds." By sharing the pen, the teacher and the children write two to six sentences to complete the morning message. In kindergarten and early first grade, some teachers prepare pictures to be used in place of words to keep the writing of the morning message moving along more rapidly. But, by grades 2–3 most children will be able to write their message quite rapidly. Keep the editing tape handy so that you can fix mistakes in spelling, punctuation, and capitalization, as you talk about them. Morning message provides a nice means of sharing the responsibilities for writing between the children and the teacher and is an ideal segue into *interactive writing.*

Morning message is an excellent way to begin interactive writing instruction in the primary grades.

Interactive Writing

An interactive writing session focuses on the teacher writing WITH children, what is sometimes called "sharing the pen." (McCarrier, Pinnell, & Fountas, 1999) Teachers focus an interactive writing lesson on:

- Connecting reading and writing by using literature as a take-off point for writing reproductions, innovations, and new texts
- Developing increasingly sophisticated writing strategies
- Demonstrating saying words slowly and connecting sounds in words to letters and letter combinations
- Expanding children's repertoire of writing genre and forms
- Helping children learn how the spelling process works

The subject and form of interactive writing may vary greatly depending upon the developmental levels of the children and the context of experiences in the classroom. Typically in the early years, the teacher helps children write a sentence, what some call a *story* in New Zealand. As children learn more about the writing process and different types of writing forms and genre, the teacher makes different decisions about how to *share the pen* during interactive writing.

Conducting an Interactive Writing Lesson. There is no one correct way to teach an interactive writing lesson, but based upon the writings of McCarrier, Pinnell, & Fountas (1999), we recommend the following:

In interactive writing, the teacher shares the pen with the children as they compose a piece of writing together as a group.

1. In the early stages of writing, the teacher helps children compose a simple message drawn from literature or from the group's experiences that is repeated sev-

eral times. For example consider this line from *The Very Hungry Caterpillar* (Carle, 1981), *"On Monday he ate through one apple."* If the teacher asked children to innovate on what the caterpillar ate on Monday, a child could offer the following: "On Monday he ate through one *tomato.*" When the teacher asks children to add new words to a line, as she did in the example above, the entire message is reread from the beginning to help children remember how composing proceeds.

2. The teacher and children share the pen as a message is written word by word. When new words are added to a line of text, the children reread the line up to the new or added word. In the earliest stages of writing development, the teacher may write the word for children. With time and development, the teacher shares the pen, inviting children to contribute a letter, several letters, or an entire word.

3. Where appropriate, the teacher encourages the child to stretch the word and say it slowly to predict the letters by analyzing the sounds (see word rubberbanding in Chapter 8). Children may attempt any letter in the word in any order. Working within the child's zone of proximal development a la Vygotsky (1962), the teacher fills in those letters that the child is unable to analyze on his own.

4. A word wall, like those recommended by Cunningham (2000), can be used as a writing resource for children in the classroom. Words can be listed on the wall as Words We Know and Can Write, Words We Almost Know, and Words We Need to Analyze and Write with Help.

5. As teachers and children write interactively, the teacher helps children learn directionality, punctuation, spaces, features of print, and capitalization as they work together to negotiate a text. In this fashion, children learn the mechanics and the authoring processes necessary to produce high-quality writing products.

Interactive writing sessions typically last from five to fifteen minutes depending upon the nature of the text to be produced. The goal of interactive writing is a neat, legible, and sensible text.

Working with Words and Strategies

The purpose of the Working with Words and Strategies instructional block (10 minutes in kindergarten, 30 minutes in grades 1–3) is to develop young readers' decoding/spelling and vocabulary/comprehension strategy awareness, selection, and application. This is a time for explicitly teaching essential elements of the reading and writing curriculum at each grade level K–3. *We cannot emphasize enough the importance of providing students with explicit instruction.* This means that teachers model, explain, demonstrate, guide, and engage students in figuring out new words by applying the strategies taught. We also strongly recommend that daily lessons focus on *both* decoding/spelling instruction and vocabulary/comprehension instruction to provide children a comprehensive, balanced daily reading and writing instructional experience. An explicit making-words lesson based on the work of Cunningham (2000) is presented in Figure 11.10.

Working on letters, sounds, and words is a necessary part of each day's reading, writing, and spelling instruction. Without this consistent and focused attention on letters, sounds, and words on a daily basis, young children do not learn how to decode words accurately and fluently. And without the ability to decode words accurately and fluently, young children will not progress toward strategic, fluent reading for comprehension (Adams, 1990, 2001; Blevins, 1998; Pressley, 2000).

Explicit instruction in the connections between sounds in oral language and the letters of written language is an essential part of a comprehensive reading program.

Think of a way to extend "Word Work" to involve children and parents at home in playful and interesting word learning activities.

Figure 11.10 Teaching children to make words*

1. Display magnetic letters on a cookie sheet or large letters in a pocket chart–*i, o, g, m, n, r.*
2. Pass out lap-size dry erasable white boards, markers, and erasers in zip-lock pouches.
3. Hold up and name the letters–*i, o, g, m, n, r.* Ask children to write the letters on the cookie sheet or in the pocket chart across the top of their white boards.
4. Write a number–*2*–on your teacher white board. This is the number of letters they will need to make the first word.
5. Tell them the first word you want them to make–*nnnnoooo (no).* Ask the children to say the word with you slowly as you s-t-r-e-t-c-h the word so that all the sounds can be heard.
6. Invite the children to write the letters of the word–*no.* Ask them to show you as they finish by holding up their white board toward you. Now, you, the teacher, write the word *(no)* and ask the children to look at your word and check their own writing of the word. IF they did not get it correct, allow time for the children to make the corrections.
7. Continue to make words by giving children clues such as "Change the first letter, the last letter, the middle letter," or "Move all the letters around to get a new word–*go, in,* or *on.*
8. Cue them when they need to use more letters by changing the number on your white board – 3. Ask them to write the word *rrrriiiimmm (rim).* Repeat step 7 with three-, four-, or five-letter words.
9. Ask the children if anyone has figured out how to use all of the letters to make one word–a word Cunningham (2000) calls the secret word. If no one has figured out the secret word, then give children clues to figure out the big word such as "It begins with, It ends with, There is a letter in the middle."
10. Once all the words have been made, take some index cards on which you have written the words and place them one at a time on the table top or in the pocket chart. Have the children say and spell each word. Pick a word and point out a spelling pattern that is used to make other words–beginning letter, ending, rhymes, little words in big words, related words.
11. Send home a take-home sheet with the same letters across the top. Write the letters across the top in large capitals the children can cut apart with their parents and make words to fill in the boxes on the take-home sheet. Provide parents a few simple directions on how they can help work with their children to make words using the same steps and clues you use in class.

*From Patricia Cunningham *Phonics they use: Words for reading and writing.* Copyright © 2000. Published by Allyn and Bacon, Boston, MA. Copyright © 2000 by Pearson Education. Reprinted by permission of the publisher.

You will find a Safety Net Lesson for struggling readers on phonemic awareness and consonant blends in Chapter 11 on our Companion Website at www.prenhall.com/ reutzel.

Working with sounds and letters to make words is fairly grade-level specific. Working to recognize and write letters and to hear and manipulate sounds in oral language are the essential word work components in kindergarten classrooms. Making explicit connections between letters and sounds to make, break, and recognize words is the essential task of first grade classrooms. Extending word work attention to analyzing and understanding word parts such as prefixes, suffixes, affixes, and inflected endings is the focus of word work in second and third grade classrooms.

Reading/Writing Learning Centers

Learning center time is divided into two 15-minute blocks in kindergarten and four in grades 1–3 (30 minutes in kindergarten, 60 minutes in grades 1–3). The structure of the workshop time is fairly rigid in the beginning of the year. Students are trained and reinforced daily for about six weeks to rotate from center to center, use their time wisely in completing center tasks, and manage themselves so as to minimize off-task behaviors. Within each 15-minute block, two major types of activities dominate. The teacher is stationed in the guided reading center, prepared to offer guided reading instruction to at least half the class each day. The children, on the other hand, may participate in a guided reading group or may be assigned to a center rotation group. Centers are teacher selected, designed, and provisioned. We strongly encourage you to use centers that focus young children's attention on decoding, spelling, handwriting, the writing process, content area studies, reader response, word work, and paired- or buddy-reading.

Managing Learning Centers

Management of centers is a primary concern for teachers. Learning centers must be designed so that the activities are clearly understood, independent of teacher supervision, and able to be completed within the time allowed (see Chapter 10 for more on this). It is also important that tasks completed in learning centers have a component of accountability and performance. We show two possible approaches for managing learning center group rotations in Figure 11.11. Managing the workshop is a complex effort for most teachers. Avoid creating too many learning centers to effectively

Learning centers should extend into independent practice those concepts and strategies already explicitly taught by the teacher in whole- or small-group instruction.

Figure 11.11   Center rotation management schemes

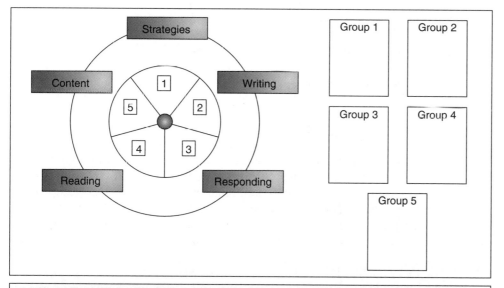

Working with Strategies	Writing	Reader Response	Content Study	Independent Reading
1	2	3	4	5
5	1	2	3	4
4	5	1	2	3
3	4	5	1	2
2	3	4	5	1

Posting a daily schedule or work board allows children and teachers to clearly communicate the behaviors and tasks to be completed each day in learning centers.

Standards Note
Standard 5.4: Provide opportunities for learners to select from a variety of written materials, to read extended texts, and to read for many authentic purposes. Independent reading on a daily basis: provide time, materials, and conditions in the classroom for young learners to select from a wide variety of written materials for extended reading.

Think about whether your students are really independent. If not, you may want to spend this time in supported-practice or teacher-guided instruction rather than establishing an independent learning center for all children in kindergarten or early 1st grade.

monitor and manage. One center rotation can focus on **independent reading** at the K–3 level as a part of the Primary Grades Reading-Writing Workshop. We have come to make this recommendation cautiously in light of recent concerns registered about the value of independent reading, particularly in the early grades where many children are not yet independent readers.

The Role of Independent Reading Time

Recently, the National Reading Panel (NRP) (2000) called into question the value of independent reading time as practiced in the majority of the nation's classrooms, especially in the early grades. Members of this panel indicated that while correlation evidence was clear that time spent reading books independently was related to reading achievement, they could not locate sufficient numbers of well-designed studies to conclude that independent reading was causing reading achievement.

When the NRP (2000) raised this issue, many teachers and researchers could not understand how anyone of sane mind could question the inherent and intrinsic value of independent reading practice. However, upon reflection, some teachers and reading scholars have come to understand that all might not be well with independent reading as practiced in today's classrooms.

Although the National Reading Panel (2000) stopped short of recommending independent reading as "ready for implementation" in the nation's classrooms based on research findings to date, it did not recommend discontinuing independent reading as a part of daily instruction in classrooms altogether. It did, however, assert that without sufficient scaffolding, accountability, and instruction to assure that children were in fact staying on task, independent reading time could end up being time poorly spent. This could be especially true for struggling readers who are not able to read independently.

With teacher guidance and supervision and with the aid of instruction on effective strategies for personally selecting a book, independent reading time can make a significant contribution to a child's gains in reading achievement. To more clearly articulate how this might happen, Reutzel and Fawson (2002) have written *Your Classroom Library,* in which they provide examples of how to teach children to select appropriately leveled books for independent reading practice. One well-accepted approach for structuring independent reading time in classrooms is known as SSR, or *Sustained Silent Reading.*

Sustained Silent Reading (SSR)

If children are going to improve as readers, they must have daily time to read in a variety of texts that engage their interests and are at a reading level they can handle with near perfect accuracy. Hunt (1970) explained that SSR should be a structured activity in which children are given regular, fixed time periods for silently reading self-selected materials on an appropriate level of proficiency.

The purposes of SSR are grounded in the belief that one gets better at anything one regularly practices, known as time on task in the field of education. This is especially true in reading where the practice occurs in materials where success is assured. The more children read, the more they stand to learn about the process of becoming a successful reader. R. Allington (1977) once raised the question, "If they don't read much, how they ever gonna get good?" Other purposes for engaging in SSR include encouraging children to read voluntarily material they have selected for enjoyment or information. To help children derive greater purpose and understanding from SSR, display a poster or chart much like the following (D. Spiegel, 1981).

> We will learn to enjoy reading more and try a variety of reading materials.
> We will learn about new places, new faces, and new ideas.
> We will get better at reading and learn to concentrate while reading.

McCracken and McCracken (1978) describe several positive reasons for implementing an SSR classroom reading-by-children program:

- Reading books is important. Children come to understand what teachers value by taking note of what they are asked to do.
- Anyone can read a book. Readers with special needs do not feel singled out for attention when they engage in reading or looking at a book during SSR.
- Children learn that reading is interacting with an author through sustained engagement with a self-selected text.
- Children develop the ability to remain on task for an extended period of time during SSR.
- Books were meant to be read in large chunks for extended periods of time. Children may get the wrong idea that reading is done during small segments of time and focus on short texts, such as those often found in basal readers.
- Comprehension is improved through SSR activities (Reutzel & Hollingsworth, 1991).
- Finally, children learn to judge the appropriateness of the materials they select for reading during SSR. Reutzel and Gali (1998) found that for most children the hardest part of learning to read was choosing the right book.

Be sure that you have developed clear expectations and rules around SSR. And, don't forget to include some type of response or accountability to assure that the time in SSR has been well spent by students in profitable reading experiences.

Implementing an SSR program is a relatively straightforward process:

1. *Designate a specific daily time for reading.* Allocate no more than 15 minutes per day for SSR. For younger children, teachers might begin with a 10-minute SSR time and lengthen this time throughout the year as children indicate a desire for more time. We have found that a cooking timer with a bell is a welcome addition for younger children so they do not worry about watching the clock.

2. *Hold a procedural mini-lesson to describe the rules of SSR.* To set the stage for successful experiences with SSR, we suggest that teachers conduct a brief lesson on the rules and expectations associated with SSR time. Begin by stating the purposes of SSR shown previously. Second, review with children the rules for participation in SSR. We have found that enlarging these rules and placing them on a chart for the class helps students take responsibility for their own behavior. Finally, explain how students can ready themselves for this time each day. The rules for SSR are shown in Figure 11.12.

3. *Extend the experience through sharing.* Children can be asked to share their books with other students at the conclusion of SSR through a "say something" or "turn to your neighbor" activity. In addition to these informal share sessions, groups of children may organize a response to a book through art, drama, writing, or musical performances to be shared with others. Through sharing, children develop a sense of accountability for the time spent. They come to expect that they will in some way be asked to share what they have been reading during SSR time.

Figure 11.12   The rules for sustained silent reading (SSR)

- Children must select their own books or reading materials.
- Changing books during sustained silent reading (SSR) is discouraged to avoid interruptions.
- Each individual in the classroom is expected to read silently without interruption during the fixed period of time for SSR.
- The teacher and other visitors in the classroom are expected to read silently materials of their own choosing as well.
- Children are not expected to make reports or answer teacher questions about the books they have been reading during SSR.

We offer one last caution with respect to independent reading in the kindergarten and early first grade. During this time, SSR is of questionable value in promoting reading achievement because most children cannot yet process text at the independent level. We do not know, however, whether time spent in the proximity of books, handling books, and looking at books is a motivating factor for younger children to persist in learning to read (Neuman, 1999). This is a question that will have to be decided in the future by research. In the meantime, we do not recommend that children in kindergarten or early first grade spend excessive amounts of time in independent reading since the very idea isn't viable for most children. Perhaps an *enriched library play center* would be an appropriate opportunity for these children to engage books in a playful and purposeful situation, while limiting the time to 10 minutes per day.

Guided Reading

Guided reading instruction is complex and may require extensive study, practice, and time.

Guided reading instruction with feedback to younger students is an essential part of a scientifically or evidence-based K–3 reading instructional program (National Reading Panel, 2000). Guided reading instruction can be conducted in a number of ways, using a variety of formats, schedules, materials, and objectives (Mooney, 1990; Fountas & Pinnell, 1996, 2001; Opitz & Ford, 2001). Guided reading, as we describe it here, focuses on children reading leveled books WITH teacher guidance and instruction and in books that would present too many challenges for them if they were to take full responsibility for the first reading (i.e., the instructional level).

To begin a guided reading program in K–3, you must first understand how to level books. Back in Chapter 8 we included leveling criteria for books adapted from several sources (e.g., Fountas & Pinnell, 1996, 1999; Pinnell & Fountas, 2002; Reutzel & Cooter, 2003; Flynt & Cooter, 2004). These criteria were presented in Table 8.1 on pages 233 through 234. This handy tool can help you level books in your own classroom library, or in a school-wide Literacy Materials Center.

As a minimum, 80–100 guided reading book titles are needed for K–3 guided reading instruction (Fountas & Pinnell, 1999). We have found that many teachers cannot acquire this number within the constraints of a classroom budget. So, many teachers are getting started with guided reading instruction using their basal reader stories. Fawson and Reutzel (2000) provide a listing of leveled basal reader stories for getting reading started if you only have a basal reading program in your school or classroom (Fawson & Reutzel, 2000). If lack of resources constrains your access to

Figure 11.13 Guided reading leveled-book room

guided reading leveled books, we recommend that the entire school combines its book purchases to create a single schoolwide guided reading leveled-book room. This recommendation means, of course, that teachers will need to learn to share. *(This is not always an easy thing for teachers to do!)* A collage of photos showing guided reading leveled-book rooms is shown in Figure 11.13.

After leveling or acquiring sufficient numbers of leveled books (and/or basal reader stories) for the guided reading program, the next task at hand is to assess students for placement into homogeneous, dynamic guided reading groups. Assignment to these groups is based upon the level of guided reading book each child can handle at 90 percent accuracy. This level is sometimes called a just-right book, one that presents children with a reasonable challenge (10 percent), but also with a high degree of potential success (90 percent).

Each year, we begin our guided reading program by assessing children's individual reading of benchmark leveled books. These are reserved for assessment purposes only and are not used for instruction or for independent reading in the classroom.

Learn to level books with your colleagues. Doing so helps you gain a deeper understanding of the criteria that separate books into levels of challenge.

You will need bench-mark books at varying levels to assess children for placement into dynamic, flexible, homogeneous guided reading groups. You may want to go to readinga-z.com to obtain black and white leveled assessment benchmark books.

You may select any guided reading book at different levels as a benchmark. But remember, benchmark books are not to be used for instruction or practice but are used only for assessment to place students in appropriate leveled book reading groups.

During assessment, children are asked to read from different levels of these books until they read with 90 percent accuracy. For example, a first grade teacher may begin assessing children by giving them a Level C book at the first of the year. If they can read this book at 90 percent accuracy, they are placed in this group. If a student reads the book above 90 percent, she is given a Level D book and so on until she reads at 90 percent accuracy. If a student reads the Level C book below 90 percent accuracy, the student is given a Level B book and so on down until she reads at 90 percent. This process continues individually until each and every child has been assessed and placed in a guided reading group where she will receive instruction in an appropriate leveled range of books.

As a result of this assessment, guided reading instruction is provided in small, homogeneous groups of children (3–8 students) who reflect a similar range of competencies, experiences, and interests (Mooney, 1990; Fountas & Pinnell, 1996; Fountas & Pinnell, 2001; Opitz & Ford, 2001). Guided reading instruction is intended to focus on instructing children in their zone of their proximal development (Vygotsky, 1978) or at that point in their literacy development where they can succeed at a task with some expert help but cannot yet succeed on their own.

Guided reading groups are often referred to as dynamic groups because they change on a monthly basis or more often, as children progress through the year. This is a crucial point to understand in implementing guided reading groups. If you, the teacher, fail to modify group composition at least on a monthly basis, these groups can become static *ability* groups, like the Eagles, Bluebirds, and Buzzards seen and practiced in previous decades. The static nature of these old fashioned ability groups caused children, particularly those children in the low ability groups, to suffer documented self-esteem damage and lowered academic expectations.

Teaching the M-S-V Cueing Systems During Guided Reading. In guided reading lessons, teachers lead children to understand that there are three important cueing systems good readers use to unlock unfamiliar text: (1) meaning (M), (2) sentence syntax or organization (S), and (3) the visual-sound system or phonics (V) (Mooney, 1990). To help children use these cueing systems for fluent reading, it is important that you, the teacher, model their application. To develop accurate and fluent decoding, it is important that the teacher encourages children to use their understanding of the visual-sound system as the first approach to an unknown word. After decoding, children should be encouraged to use pictures, the sense of language order (syntax) or meaning to confirm or correct their decoding efforts (Adams, 2001). Fountas and Pinnell (1999) give several examples of prompts teachers might use to direct or guide children to select and apply multiple word solving strategies once decoding has provided an approximate pronunciation of the unknown word (see Figure 11.14).

As you work with children, it is helpful if you use sticky notes pasted on or near your lesson plans to remind you of useful oral reading prompts.

In the earliest stages of guided reading, teachers begin by taking responsibility for the first reading of the text with students. Thus, early guided reading looks in practice much like a shared reading experience; the main differences are the size of the group, the close reading of text with individual guidance, and the use of small, multiple copies of the same title at the just-right level of challenge. Books used for initial guided reading experiences should demonstrate a close match of text and pictures, gradual introduction of unfamiliar concepts and words, as well as sufficient repetition of predictable elements to provide support.

Figure 11.14 Guided reading teacher prompts

Sampling Prompts
- Read this with your finger.
- Do the words you say match with words on the page?
- Try this word. Would that make sense? (M)
- Try this sound. Does that sound right? (S)
- Can you find the word (or) letter?
- Does that make sense? (M)
- Does this sound right to you? (Repeat what the child said.) (S)
- Do you know a word like that?
- What can you do if you don't know a word?

Confirming Prompts
- Were there enough words?
- Read that again.
- Try starting the word at the beginning with the first letter and sound. (V)
- What did you notice?
- Does it start that way? (V)
- Does it end with those letters or sounds? (V)
- You almost got it. Can you find what was wrong?

Self-Correction Prompts
- Why did you stop?
- Check that word again. Does it look right? (V) Sound right? (S)
- Something wasn't quite right. Try it again.

From *Guided Reading: Good First Reading for All Children* by Irene C. Fountas and Gay Su Pinnell. Copyright © 1996 by Irene C. Fountas and Gay Su Pinnell. Published by Heinemann, a division of Reed Elsevier, Inc., Portsmouth, New Hampshire. Used by permission.

During initial guided reading lessons, children are encouraged to use their fingers to finger-point read (Ehri & Sweet, 1991). Finger-point reading involves pointing to the words as they are spoken (Reutzel, 1995). During guided reading lessons, teachers focus children's attention on print concepts such as directionality, i.e., left to right or top to bottom, and on processing text using multiple reading strategies, such as predicting, sampling, confirming, cross-checking, and self-correcting. Following the guided reading of a text, children are asked to engage in summarizing and/or retelling the text. With time and development, children assume more responsibility for the first reading of the text with the teacher taking a supporting role through echoing, coaching, and helping where needed. This gradual release of responsibility generally occurs as we observe that children understand basic print concepts, have acquired a basic sight word vocabulary, select appropriately, and apply reading strategies.

As fluency is demonstrated in oral reading situations during guided reading lessons, teachers gradually help children convert their oral reading to silent reading. As children increase their fluency and comprehension, teachers broaden guidance to include concepts such as studies of genre, reading like a writer (stylistic examinations), text structure, and study/reference skills during guided reading lessons (Opitz & Ford, 2001). Guided reading lessons often consist of the seven parts shown in Figure 11.15.

Guided oral reading instruction is considered an essential best practice within a scientific, research-based reading instructional program (National Reading Panel, 2000). No primary grade (K–3) reading program can be considered functionally complete or comprehensive in nature without providing young children guided oral reading instruction on a daily or, at most, an every-other-day basis. This means you will

Figure 11.15   Seven part guided reading lesson

1. **Familiar Rereading and Assessment**   Children come to the guided reading area of the classroom. They seat themselves and immediately select a book from a basket of previously read leveled books. Each child reads aloud quietly at her own rate. During this time, the teacher chooses one student daily to take a *running record,* as described in Chapter 9 on Assessment.
2. **Introduce the New Book**   To introduce a new book, IT IS CRITICAL that the teacher previously reads and prepares a written plan for introducing a new book. She may plan to point out "tricky words or phrases" in the book, help children decode an important unknown word, draw attention to a new feature in the text such as the print moving across a two-page format. The teacher may engage the children in a picture walk through the book or make predictions. During this part of the lesson, the teacher tries to anticipate problems in applying reading strategies and prepare children for success.
3. **Read the New Book**   Depending on children's experiences with text, the first reading may be done by the teacher, who will gradually release responsibility for the first reading to the children as they develop greater capacity.
4. **Discuss the New Book**   The teacher and children discuss the book, their feelings, any surprises, personal connections with the book, etc. The teacher may ask children to reread parts of the book aloud as a part of this discussion.
5. **Teaching for Strategies**   During this part of the lesson, the teacher asks children to return to the text. She may ask them to find a word by pointing to it. She may ask them, after finding the word, to look at the word and blend the sounds letter by letter as she writes the letters on a small white board. She may spell the word using magnetic letters on a cookie sheet and delete letters or substitute new letters to make and break words. She may ask them to close their eyes and make a picture of a part of the book and then draw it to encourage visual imagery.
6. **Sharing Competence**   Children are encouraged to take guided reading books home to read and share with their parents, caregivers, or siblings. Sharing emerging competence with guided reading texts increases children's self-confidence and motivation.
7. **Extending Meaning**   Children are encouraged to engage in a variety of projects to extend their understanding of guided reading books. They accomplish this through the use of storytelling, puppetry, plays, murals, hand-actions, writing in journals, and making posters.

Be sure to write your guided reading lesson plans so that you are sure you have carefully considered the challenges in the text and how you will explicitly teach and model how to meet these challenges.

need to schedule your reading instructional time to allow meeting with at least half the class of students in guided reading groups on a daily basis.

Many teachers wonder what the other children are doing during guided reading instruction time. The answer is simple; they are engaged in the variety of independent and collaborative learning centers described earlier in this chapter.

Fluency Workshop and Assessment

During the 30-minute Fluency Workshop and Assessment, activities of the teacher and students are different. For the teacher, the bulk of this time is devoted to meeting individually with five students, five minutes each, to hold an individual reading/writing assessment conference. The students are signed up for these conferences by the teacher. Children who are scheduled for one are instructed to bring (1) an assigned benchmark book or text to read aloud for assessment purposes or (2) a book of their own choosing that they have read previously. Benchmark books are used to assess and compare a class of students' reading decoding accuracy, comprehension through an oral retelling, and fluency in terms of words correct per minute rates, phrasing, and intonation. Assessment tools to measure decoding accuracy, oral retellings, and fluency assessment are discussed in Chapters 4, 6, and 7 of this book.

Information garnered in these assessment conferences is used to shape Working with Words and Strategies instruction. Similar conferences to assess writing development can be scheduled periodically to complement the reading assessment described here.

Otherwise, this period is devoted to a variety of center-based activities designed to increase reading fluency. Children engage in repeated readings by going to a listening center where books on audiotapes are available along with multiples copies of a single title. Children can go to the computer center to read a book presented on a CD-ROM. Children may read with a partner by reading around the room, rereading big books together, practicing sight words on word cards in pairs, reading words on the word wall, rereading charts of poems and songs, or rereading sentence strips or interactive writing strips in pocket charts. Still other children will be in a drama center practicing the reading of a play or readers' theater script for performance. Another area of the classroom is stocked with individual audio tapes for children to place into a cassette recorder and record their own reading. After reading into the tape recorder, children rate their own fluency using an adapted student version of the Multidimensional Fluency Scale found in Chapter 7. They may erase the audiocassette recording of their first reading. The repeated reading recording should be rated again, noting any improvements in oral fluency. Each student must come to the final class sharing session from the fluency development period prepared to perform a reading selection for the whole class, a small group, or a peer.

Fluency has been a largely forgotten part of early reading instruction.

Student Sharing Time

As a daily closing activity for the Primary Grades Reading-Writing Workshop, the teacher calls the class together to share a reading selection each child has prepared previously. The idea is to bring closure to the day's work and give children a chance to share their reading with the group or a friend. Children can perform readers' theater productions, their own writing products, puppet shows, individual reading recitations, reader's/author's chair read alouds, and plays. We have found that there is only one problem with sharing time—keeping it to the 10 to 15 minutes time. Once students get used to sharing time, they plan for reading books, scripts, jokes, poems, and even their own writing to share with their friends. As a wrap-up to this discussion, we use a teacher's planning book to show how one teacher scheduled a week of activities in the Primary Grades Reading-Writing Workshop (Figure 11.16).

Trying to keep student sharing time to 5–10 minutes may wind up becoming your greatest challenge in managing the primary-grades reading-writing workshop!

SCHOOL–FAMILY–COMMUNITY PARTNERSHIPS

The evidence continues to mount showing the indispensable nature of the partnership between parents and schools. In schools that serve disadvantaged children in poverty where teachers are teaching and children are learning to read against the odds, a strong school and family partnership is cited as a chief ingredient in the success formula (Taylor, Pearson, Clark, & Walpole, 1999).

It is never too late to start a **school–family–community partnership.** The first step is to just start! Begin by identifying the participants during parent-teacher conferences. Once a group of participants has been identified, determine the time and location of the meetings. If you want to include all parents, it is important that you plan to provide child care, transportation, and other incentives (Vopat, 1994, 1998). We have found that providing a meal as a part of evening parent involvement meetings is a real hit, as are read alouds and free take-home books. Parents need to be willing to sign a commitment form indicating that they are in the project for the duration. In

Figure 11.16   Scheduling/planning reading instruction

Monday	Tuesday	Wednesday	Thursday	Friday
Reading and Writing Together 8:30–9:10 A.M.				
Read Aloud–*Very Hungry Caterpillar* Shared Reading–*On Market Street* Interactive Writing– "And I bought. . . ."	Read Aloud–*Very Quiet Cricket* Shared Reading– Reread Book Masking Sight word "the" Interactive Writing– Cricket Talk	Read Aloud–*Grouchy Ladybug* Shared Reading–*If You Give a Mouse a . . .* Interactive Writing– "If you give a Mouse a cookie he will. . . ."	Read Aloud–*Very Lonely Firefly* Shared Reading– Reread for "en & ill" words Interactive Writing– Word Building	Read Aloud–*Very Busy Spider* Shared Reading– *How Spiders Live* Interactive Writing– "Spiders live. . . ."
Working with Strategies 9:10–9:40 A.M.				
Decoding & Spelling: Phoneme Counting & Spelling–Elkonin Boxes Vocabulary & Comprehension: Listening for Directions	Decoding & Spelling: Building Words– "ake, ick" rimes Vocabulary & Comprehension: Taking a Picture Walk for Predicting	Decoding & Spelling: Pocket Chart Spoonerisms–Initial Consonant Substitution Vocabulary & Comprehension: Insect Semantic Web	Decoding & Spelling: Consonant Riddles Vocabulary & Comprehension: Picture Story Map Prediction of *Three Billy Goats Gruff*	Decoding & Spelling: Sound Search– What's in the middle, beginning, end? Vocabulary & Comprehension: Author Study–Eric Carle
Workshop Time 9:40–10:40 A.M.				
Learning Centers: Paired Language Listening Center Insect Center Word Center Environmental Print Guided Reading Groups: Intro Books– Levels C–E, *Chicken Pox:* F–G, *My Computer:* H–I, *Tents*	Learning Centers: Paired Language Listening Center Insect Center Word Center Environmental Print Guided Reading Groups: Reread for strategies & retell	Learning Centers: Paired Language Listening Center Insect Center Word Center Environmental Print Guided Reading Groups: Reread for language features & extensions	Learning Centers: Paired Language Listening Center Insect Center Word Center Environmental Print Guided Reading Groups: Intro Books	Learning Centers: Paired Language Listening Center Insect Center Word Center Environmental Print Guided Reading Groups: Reread for strategies & retell
Fluency Workshop & Assessment 10:40–11:10 A.M.				
Fluency Centers: Read Around Room Computer Center CD/Tape Reading Record Your Reading Reader's Theater Assessment: Mica & Heather	Fluency Centers: Read Around Room Computer Center CD/Tape Reading Record Your Reading Reader's Theater Assessment: Montage & Mitchell	Fluency Centers: Read Around Room Computer Center CD/Tape Reading Record Your Reading Reader's Theater Assessment: Ginger & Jessica	Fluency Centers: Read Around Room Computer Center CD/Tape Reading Record Your Reading Reader's Theater Assessment: Austin & Sabrina	Class Fluency Development Lesson: *Three Billy Goats Gruff* Assessment:
Closing Sharing Time 11:10–11:25 A.M.				
Turn to Your Neighbor	Reader's Theater Performance	"Today I read. . . ." Interactive Writing	Think, Pair, Share	Fact Web on Spiders

In schools that are beating the odds in teaching children to read, assuring strong school-family-community connections is of key importance!

many cases, it is helpful if parent involvement workshops or seminars can be offered in multilingual formats or different groups to encourage broad participation. Seminars or workshops are best based upon informing and involving parents in the ongoing aspects of the school's programs—thematic units, writing workshops, reading aloud books, and others. Parents want to experience the curriculum and learn ways to help their children succeed in learning to read (Vopat, 1998).

Although an agenda should be planned for workshops or seminars, it is important that the agenda be flexible so that participants can help in building or fleshing-out projects and topics based upon their abilities, interests, and desires. Starting a study group where participants read and discuss important documents, books, and materials together can be most helpful. Also, be sure to include at least one well-selected read aloud book to be shared with parents at each seminar, session, or workshop. Vopat (1998) talks about using a "Roving Parent Journal" that is sent between home and school where teachers and parents can communicate about questions or issues each wants to share with the other party. These journals need to be sturdy and easily identifiable. Also, teachers should remember to photocopy their responses to parents just in case they get lost or misplaced on the way home. . . .

Communicate your learning goals and curriculum clearly to parents and children. Neither the curriculum nor the expected outcomes should come as a secret to parents or children. Projects that target how parents can help their children learn the curriculum and achieve expected outcomes are usually well received. If the method you are using to communicate with parents isn't working, don't give up. Try something you haven't tried, such as phone calls, newsletters, and telephone trees. It is also useful for teachers to provide a space on grade reports for parents to write a response, question, or concern to you.

Family histories are a great way to get parents and children involved in an initial activity that focuses on who they are and their roots. These need to be shared in subsequent parent involvement workshops and seminars as a regular part of the meeting. Remember, most barriers to parent involvement are found within schools and school practices—not within parents.

Start partnerships on day one of the new school year. Start small or large or somewhere in between, but get started. Think of one thing you can do to connect your classroom and school with families and communities, whether it is your first year teaching or your thirtieth. And don't forget to listen to parents; they have much to share because of how much they care (Edwards, 1999).

Making home visits gives teachers insights into student behaviors and learning that are often well worth the extra effort.

Supported Reading: Read-Along Cassettes and Take-Home Books

Parents want to support their children whether they are learning to ride a bicycle or learning to read. **Supported reading** strategies include the use of adult or child volunteers and mechanical support devices, such as computers and read-along cassette tapes. Read-along tapes may be used to effectively support readers through the reading of new or relatively unfamiliar books at all levels. Read-along cassettes and CD-ROM programs are commercially available for a wide variety of fiction and nonfiction beginning reading books. When these tapes are not available, teachers or parent volunteers can record them. Tapes or CD-ROM programs can be color coded for varying text levels and stored in specially designed storage cases.

Take-home books placed into family literacy bags invite parents to actively support and participate in their children's reading growth at home. Take-home books can come from many sources. We suggest that these books come from (1) previously read books in guided reading, (2) a special collection of books just for take-home purposes, (3) the use of published, predictable books, and/or (4) teacher-produced blackline master books produced using published books as patterns. For example, the classic *On Market Street* (Lobel, 1981) uses an alphabet pattern with words and pictures for each alphabet letter. The teacher can innovate upon this book's pattern to

Take-home books and libraries have been found to be widely effective in promoting reading behaviors out of school and between parents and children.

Figure 11.17 Traveling tales backpack

Plain unlined paper	Yarn
Scissors	Watercolors
Lined paper	Wallpaper for book covers
Small stapler	Water-based markers
Staples	Glue stick
Construction paper—multiple colors	Colored pencils
Letter stencils	Pencils
Brass fasteners	Tape
Drawing paper	Paper clips
Card stock	Felt-tip pens
Poster paper	Ruler
Hole punch	Felt-tip calligraphy pens
Crayons	

Writing backpacks are an effective way to involve children and parents in producing and sharing writing products.

produce a new *On Market Street* book with different words and illustrations for each alphabet letter (e.g., alligators, beds). This revised version of the original is copied onto blackline masters and reproduced for each child. To make these copied take-home books more visually attractive, children may wish to color the illustrations at home with the help of their parents. The major purpose of these books is for the child and parents to enjoy reading together at home. Teachers can produce multiple copies of read-along cassette tapes to accompany these take-home books for additional home practice opportunities when parents are unable to assist.

Supported Writing: Traveling Tales Backpack

We have used the traveling tales backpack shown in Figure 11.17 to involve parents and children in collaborative writing projects (Reutzel & Fawson, 1990; Yellin & Blake, 1994; Reutzel & Fawson, 1998; Richgels & Wold, 1998). A traveling tales backpack is filled with writing media and guidelines for parents to work with their children at home to produce a self-selected writing project.

The backpack is sent home with a child for two nights. To maximize involvement and success, parents are contacted by phone or note before the backpack is sent home. Parents and children can choose a variety of ways to respond to their favorite book: They can write shape stories, pocketbooks, accordion books, or cards. Included in the traveling tales backpack is a letter (Figure 11.18) to the parents with guidelines on how to engage their child in the writing process.

After completing the writing project together, parent and child are invited to share their work with the class in the author's chair at school. After sharing, the written product is placed on display for the other children to read and enjoy.

ADAPTING READING INSTRUCTION FOR STRUGGLING READERS

When students in the early elementary grades have trouble with beginning literacy experiences, the effect can be far reaching: The child's self-esteem is usually damaged, life at home is affected, and a cycle of failure may develop. School systems spend

Figure 11.18 Traveling tales parent letter

Dear Parent(s):

Writing activities provided at home can have a great influence on your child's reading and writing development. Traveling Tales is a backpack that includes a variety of writing materials for use by you and your child. As per our conversation, we encourage you to work together cooperatively with your child to create a story that will be shared at school. *Please avoid competition or trying to outdo others.*

Your child has been given this backpack for two nights. If you need more time, please call us at XXX–XXXX. Otherwise, we will be looking forward to you and your child returning the Traveling Tales backpack in two days.

We would like to suggest some guidelines that may help you have a successful and enjoyable Traveling Tales experience with your child.

1.   Help your child brainstorm a list of ideas or topics by asking questions that will invite him or her to express ideas, interests, feelings, etc., about which he or she may wish to write. Stories about personal experiences (factual or fictional), information stories that tell of an area that your child finds interesting, biographies of family members or others, and stories of science or history are possible topics.

2.   After selecting a topic, help your child decide which of the writing materials included in the Traveling Tales backpack he or she will need to use to create his or her story. Suggest that the story may take several different forms. Some ideas include (1) poetry, (2) fold-out books, (3) puppet plays, (4) pocket books, (5) backward books, and (6) shape books.

3.   Help your child think through or rehearse the story before beginning writing. You may wish to write down some of the ideas your child expresses for him or her to use in writing the first draft.

4.   Remember, your child's first draft is a rough draft. It may contain misspellings, poor handwriting, and incomplete ideas. This should be expected. Be available to answer questions as your child works on the first draft. Be careful to encourage him or her to keep writing and not worry about spelling, punctuation, etc. Tell him or her to just do his or her best and both of you can work on correctness later. *This is the idea development stage of writing.*

5.   Once the first draft is completed, try to involve others in the household by asking them to listen to the first draft read aloud. Reading one's writing aloud helps writers determine the sensibleness of the message. Be sure to tell those who are invited to listen to be encouraging rather than critical. Ask questions about ideas that were unclear or were poorly developed. Questions help a writer think about his or her writing without feeling defensive.

6.   Write down the questions and suggestions made by the home audience. Talk with your child about how a second draft could use these suggestions to make the story easier to understand or more exciting. Remember to be supportive and encouraging! Offer your help, but encourage your child to make his or her best efforts first.

7.   After the second draft is completed, your child may wish to read his or her writing to the family group again. If so, encourage it. If not, it is time to edit the writing. Now is the time to correct spellings, punctuation, etc. Praise your child for his or her attempts and tell him or her you want to help make his or her writing the best it can be. Show your child which words are misspelled and why. Do the same with punctuation and capitalization.

(continued)

Figure 11.18   *continued*

8.   With the editing complete, the writing is ready to be revised for the final time. When your child writes the final draft, encourage him or her to use neat handwriting as a courtesy to the reader. Feel free to help your child at any point as he or she makes final revisions.

9.   Once finished, encourage the members of your family or household to listen to the final story. This practice will instill confidence in your child as he or she shares his or her writing at school.

10.   We cordially invite you to come to school with your child, if possible, to share the writing you have done together. Your child will appreciate the support, and we would like to talk with you.

Thank you for your help. We appreciate your involvement. If you have an interesting or special experience and are unable to come to school with your child, we would appreciate hearing about these. Please call us or send a note with your child. We will be glad to call back or visit with you. Thanks again for your support. We hope you enjoyed your experiences!

From "Traveling Tales: Connecting Parents and Children in Writing," by D. R. Reutzel and P. C. Fawson, 1990, *The Reading Teacher, 44,* pp. 222–227. Copyright 1990 by the International Reading Association. Reprinted by permission of D. Ray Reutzel and the International Reading Association.

When children struggle in learning to read, it is important to know where one can go to get help. The programs shared in the following pages are excellent places to begin.

many thousands of dollars trying to help struggling readers close the gap between them and their peers and get back on track with their education. Unfortunately, many students are never able to close the gap between their performance and their potential. In this section, we summarize an effective approach for assisting early readers who struggle.

Reading Recovery: A Program for Assisting Struggling First Graders

In recent years, many reading researchers and practitioners have recognized the need for direct and focused attention on beginning literacy problems in our schools. The idea is to recover early those children who are having problems in beginning reading. This can spare children a lifetime of emotional and economic damage related to literacy problems, and schools can preserve valuable resources otherwise spent on remedial education (Fielding, Kerr, & Rosier, 1998).

Reading Recovery is one of several successful early intervention programs for rescuing young struggling readers. Developed by Marie Clay (1993a&b), an educator from New Zealand, Reading Recovery identifies struggling readers during their first year of formal reading instruction and provides them with individualized tutoring for 30 minutes each day. The program has experienced success in both New Zealand and in the United States (Pinnell, Fried, & Estice, 1990). Pinnell, Lyons, DeFord, Bryk, and Seltzer (1994) showed that compared with three other treatment groups and a control group, Chapter 1 students assigned to Reading Recovery produced the only statistically significant gains on all reading measures used in the study. Other researchers have called into question the effectiveness of Reading Recovery, but up to this point have offered no well-documented alternatives (Shanahan & Barr, 1995).

A typical tutoring session (Clay, 1993b) includes the following activities:

- Rereading two or more familiar books
- Rereading yesterday's new book and taking a running record
- Letter identification (plastic letters on a magnetic board)
- Writing a story (including hearing sounds in words)
- Cut-up story to be rearranged
- New book introduced
- New book attempted

Reading Recovery is founded upon the ground breaking work of and authored by the New Zealand psychologist and educator, Marie Clay.

Reading Recovery is effective with struggling readers for several very obvious reasons. First, it provides young children with a great deal of individual attention and focused instruction, which can be very beneficial for struggling readers who feel insecure in a classroom setting. It also immerses children in pleasurable and teacher-guided oral reading and writing opportunities with teacher feedback. Such guided instruction promotes risk taking, attachment to favorite literature, self-selection of books, and creative writing production. Finally, teachers are better able to adjust the learning program and respond to student needs because of the one-on-one tutorial setup. In essence, Reading Recovery offers struggling readers a daily, individualized, balanced literacy teaching program with heavy emphasis on writing and reading in appropriately challenging and interesting children's fiction and nonfiction books.

Adapting Instruction to Meet the Needs of Limited English Proficient Learners

Several researchers (Koskinen, Wilson, & Jensema, 1985; Neuman & Koskinen, 1992) have found that closed caption television is a particularly effective way of adapting reading instruction for limited English proficient (LEP) children. **Closed caption television,** which uses written subtitles, provides LEP students with meaningful and motivating reading material set in the evolving context of a TV program. Materials necessary for using closed caption TV to teach LEP students to read include: (1) a video recorder, (2) a video monitor, (3) close captioning reader, and (4) videotapes.

Begin by carefully selecting high-interest television programs, recording and previewing programs before making final selections. Next, introduce the TV program(s) selected to students. Pay particular attention to teaching new vocabulary and connecting the program content to children's prior knowledge (Koskinen et al., 1985). Three elements are integral to a successful closed caption TV lesson.

Turn off the sound and read the TV! Closed captioning provides just such an opportunity for the struggling reader.

1. Children watch a part of the captioned TV program together (5 to 10 minutes). The teacher stops the tape and asks students to predict what will happen next in the program. Then, the teacher continues showing the program so that students can check their predictions.
2. Students watch a segment of the program that has examples of certain kinds of phonic patterns, word uses, or punctuation. For example, students can be alerted to the use of quotation marks and the fact that these marks signal dialogue. After alerting students to particular print or conceptual content, they might watch the remainder of the tape to identify dialogue using their newly acquired awareness and knowledge of quotation marks.
3. After watching a closed caption TV program, students practice reading aloud along with the captions. If necessary, both the auditory portion and the

closed captioning can be played simultaneously to provide LEP students with support through their initial attempts to read. At some later point, students can be allowed to practice reading the captioning without the auditory portion of the program. Koskinen et al. (1985) add that they "do not recommend that the sound be turned off if this, in effect, turns off the children. The major advantage of captioned television is the multi-sensory stimulation of viewing the drama, hearing the sound, and seeing the captions." (p. 6)

Summary

Remember to refer to Chapter 8 for descriptions of other effective reading programs for working with struggling readers.

This chapter was designed to help you, the novice or experienced teacher, provide effective, scientifically based literacy instruction in K–3 classrooms. It began with a discussion of characteristics of exemplary K–3 teachers and teaching. Next, it talked about how to design an annual curriculum plan for providing standards-based and scientifically based reading instruction. Following up on the curriculum, it discussed how to develop an annual assessment plan and how to use data to inform instruction based on student performance and literacy learning expectation by grade level.

After addressing assessment, it discussed how to use the Primary Grades Reading-Writing Workshop to plan and deliver effective, scientifically based literacy instruction in K–3 classrooms. It covered interactive reading aloud, shared reading, shared writing, morning message, interactive writing, guided reading, literacy centers, and working with words and strategies. It provided sample center rotation plans and weeklong planning guides for using the Primary Grades Reading-Writing Workshop.

Next, the importance of developing, nurturing, and evaluating parent, family, and community involvement programs in reading and writing in the early grades was addressed. Then, in-depth descriptions of one reading and one writing project that effectively increased parent, family, and community involvement were provided.

Check your understanding of chapter concepts by using the self assessment for Chapter 11 on our Companion Website at www.prenhall.com/ reutzel.

The chapter concluded with a discussion of how instruction can be adapted to meet the needs of struggling readers and LEP learners. It focused on Reading Recovery, a program that has shown promise in accelerating the reading and writing progress of early struggling readers. It also described the use of captioned TV to motivate and increase reading and writing language and skill acquisition among limited English proficient learners in the early years.

Concept Applications

In the Classroom

1. Obtain a copy of a local school district's reading and writing curriculum. Evaluate the contents of this curriculum against the seven major components of early reading instruction: phonemic awareness, letter knowledge and alphabetics, phonics, vocabulary, guided oral reading, fluency, and comprehension. Describe weaknesses and strengths in your analysis.
2. Obtain a copy of your state's curriculum standards. How do the outcomes specified in these state standards compare to the grade-level expectations described in the book *Starting Out Right?* Determine where the state standards agree and disagree with these nationally published reading and writing expectations.
3. Ask your professor to obtain copies of three norm-referenced (standardized) reading tests. Carefully analyze what these tests measure and

how they measure each reading skill, concept, or process in small groups. Write a critical essay on these tests. Describe the one you feel is a better measure of young children's reading abilities and support your assertions with experience, research, or examples. When each group is finished, present your findings to the class.

4. Go to the Internet in small collaborative study groups. Research several reading programs such as Reading Recovery, Open Court, Accelerated Reader, and Success for All. Present your findings using a PowerPoint® multimedia presentation to the class.

5. Develop a first-year plan to increase parental, family, and community involvement in your anticipated classroom. Go to the library and Internet to obtain copies of letters, training curricula, and communications ideas. Present your plan in the form of a trifold brochure to your classmates. Schedule a day when you can exchange and discuss each other's brochures and ideas.

In the Field

1. Make an appointment to visit a primary grade teacher. Interview him about how he plans, tracks, uses, and interprets informal assessment tools to guide his instructional decision making. Ask if you can have copies of several of his informal assessment tools. Following the visit, make an annual assessment plan using the one in Chapter 11 as a model.

2. Ask a local publisher's sales representative to send you a copy of the promotion materials for its most recently published reading/writing/literacy program for K–3. Carefully study the materials, noting where the publisher's claim to be basing its product in the findings of scientifically based reading research. Compare the program elements to the recommendations of the National Reading Panel.

3. Visit an primary grade elementary classroom to observe a teacher doing one of the following: a) read aloud, b) shared reading, c) interactive or shared writing, or d) guided reading lesson. Describe what you saw in detail in a brief report. Also, discuss weaknesses or strengths you observed in the teacher's instruction as compared to that which you have learned from reading this text and discussion in your college classes.

4. Prepare and teach a guided reading lesson in a local primary grade classroom. Copy and share your lesson plan with others.

5. With a small group of students in your class, prepare a family literacy night program. Seek permission and donations to fund the evening so that families receive a meal, free books, and have access to child care and transportation to the location. Write a brief evaluation of the evening. Share your plan and evaluation of the activity with your peers.

Recommended Readings

Armbruster, B. B., Lehr, F., & Osborn, J. (2001). *Putting reading first: The research building blocks for teaching children to read, K–3.* Washington, DC: U.S. Department of Education.

Burns, M. S., Griffin, P., & Snow, C. E. (1999). *Starting out right: A guide to promoting children's reading success.* Washington, DC: National Research Council.

Fountas, I. C., & Pinnell, G. S. (1996). *Guided reading: Good first teaching for all children.* Portsmouth, NH: Heinemann.

McCarrier, A., Pinnell, G. S., & Fountas, I. C. (1999). *Interactive writing: How language and literacy come together, K–2.* Portsmouth, NH: Heinemann.

Pressley, M., Allington, R. L., Wharton-McDonald, R., Collins-Block, C., & Morrow, L. M. (2001). *Learning to read: Lessons from exemplary first-grade classrooms.* New York: Guildford Press.

Reutzel, D. R., & Fawson, P. C. (2002). *Your classroom library: New ways to give it more teaching power.* New York: Scholastic Professional Books.

Roller, C. M. (2002). *Comprehensive reading instruction across the grade levels.* Newark, DE: International Reading Association.

Taylor, B. M., Pearson, P. D., Clark, K. F., & Walpole, S. (1999). *Beating the odds in teaching all children to read* (Report #2-006). Ann Arbor, MI: Center for the Improvement of Early Reading Achievement.

Vopat, J. (1998). *More than bake sales: The resource guide for family involvement in education.* York, ME: Stenhouse.

12

The Transition Years: Grades 4–6

Focus Questions

When you are finished studying this chapter, you should be able to answer these questions:

1. What are the unique challenges facing intermediate level teachers in reading instruction?

2. Why are the intermediate years critical for struggling readers?

3. What are the performance standards in reading for grades 4–6?

4. How should the first days of the school year be organized?

5. Compare and contrast the following ways of organizing reading instruction: Reading Workshop, core book units, and themed literature units.

6. What are the stages of the writing process?

7. How can reading teachers accommodate the needs of English Language Learners (ELL)?

8. Describe three strategies for involving parents with reading and writing development.

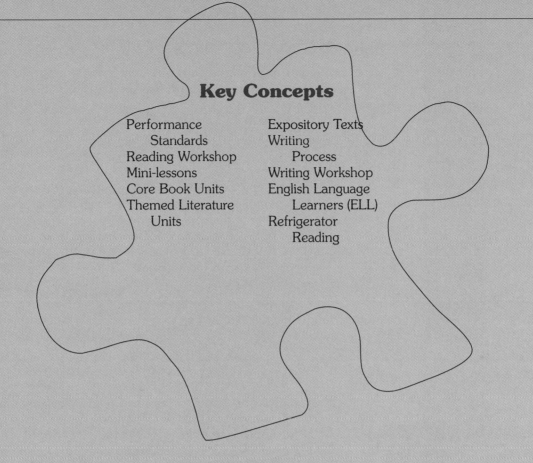

Key Concepts

Performance Standards	Expository Texts
Reading Workshop	Writing Process
Mini-lessons	Writing Workshop
Core Book Units	English Language Learners (ELL)
Themed Literature Units	Refrigerator Reading

Have you ever seen a rerun of the old television series *Leave It to Beaver?* The Beave, as his family often called him, was caught somewhere between the worlds of little kids and big kids. This is where children in grades 4 through 6 are as readers: making the transition from *learning to read* to *reading to learn*.

In *reading to learn* students must acquire new ways of applying reading skills and strategies to understand the world. Our task as reading teachers is to model these strategies, coach students as they navigate the treacherous swamps of informational texts, and help them become as competent in these genres as they are in narrative texts. For reading teachers, that means acquiring new knowledge and skills to help children in their journey.

Visit Chapter 12 of our Companion Website at www.prenhall.com/reutzel to look into the chapter objectives, standards and principles, and pertinent web links associated with The Transitions Years: Grades 4–6.

MS. TRAHAN GETS THINGS POPPING!

It was a spring morning and the green line had made it into town two weeks earlier. Bluebonnets, Indian paintbrush, and honeysuckle adorned the perimeter of Bowie Elementary, and a warm breeze caused the curtains in Ms. Lynn Trahan's classroom to riffle. As the children came into the room, they noticed a brightly colored balloon was tied to the backs of each chair. The students had become accustomed to the unexpected in Ms. Trahan's room and were excited to discover what she had up her sleeve . . . this time.

"As you all know," she began, "we have been using the writing workshop for some time now and, frankly, I think you are getting the hang of it. The question is—how can we go from being good writers to great writers? One of the 'tricks of the trade,' you might say, is to develop an opening line for your story that draws readers in—makes them want to know what happens. These catchy opening lines are known as 'leads.' Let me show you what I mean."

Ms. Trahan, knowing the importance of modeling for students, had come prepared to share some examples of her own. "I've been writing a true story about one of the most scary moments of my life." She could see she already had their rapt attention; kids are always curious about the lives of their teachers. Without further delay, Ms. Trahan pulled out two sheets of paper on which she had begun a draft of her story and began to read.

"What happened was this. My children and I were traveling to school one wintry morning, and there was ice on the road. We lived out in the country then, so the roads were treated for the ice as they are in the city. As we road along in our mini-van we approached a small, narrow bridge—the kind of bridge that has no rails on the sides, just a cement ridge about four inches high along each edge. We were going pretty slow but by the time I saw that the bridge was covered with ice it was too late.

"All of a sudden the van swerved to the right toward the side of the bridge and the angry, swollen river below. I tried to gently—gently as I could in an emergency anyway—steer the van back left to the safety of the bridge. We almost made it. Almost.

"Oh, I bet I'm boring you with my little story. Perhaps we should do something else," said Ms. Trahan. At once the class erupted and plead to hear the ending.

"You see what I mean about catching your audience and holding their attention." The students nodded, and Ms. Trahan knew the initial teaching point was made, so she continued with her story.

"The tires found purchase and our van began to move left. However, the right front wheel caught just outside the tiny ridge that served as a guardrail so that only three of our wheels were on the bridge. The van slid forward rapidly. Then, I felt the front of the van dip down on the right side. Before I knew what was happening, our van rolled over the side of the bridge and tumbled upside down into the river!"

Several children gasped, and more than few sets of eyes were as wide as saucers. "What happened?" asked Hilda. "Was anyone killed?" asked Geraldo with a worried look on his face.

"No," said Ms. Trahan. "Fortunately, two things saved us. First, we were all wearing our seatbelts like we should. I remember seeing my

daughter, Whitney, and the other children upside down held in their seats by the safety belt. Without those seat belts we could have all had broken necks and died right there! The other thing that saved us was that the van landed in shallow water, so I had time to get free and get the children out before anyone drowned. How's that for a scary story?" The class showed their approval with smiles all around.

At once, Ms. Trahan switched on the overhead projector and onto the top glass a transparency she had prepared earlier. On it was written the opening lines of her draft composition. It read:

What happened was this. My children and I were traveling to school one wintry morning, and there was ice on the road. We lived out in the country then, so the roads were not treated for the ice as they are in the city.

"Professional writers," she began, "realize that the very first sentence or two is what causes a reader to want to keep reading . . . or not. For instance, when I was your age I read a lot of comic books as well as chapter books. Money was hard to come by for me, so when I went into a drug store to buy a comic book, I would always read the first few lines of the story to see if it interested me. If I wasn't hooked on the comic book immediately, then I put it back and kept looking for one that did grab my interest.

"Frankly, when I look at my opening sentence in this story I don't believe I would want to read it if I were a reader. The words, 'What happened was this,' just don't get me interested! Let's see if I can come up with something a little better."

With that, Ms. Trahan removed the transparency from the overhead projector and replaced it with a blank one. "Let me see if I can come up with something a little more interesting." She wrote three different opening lines, leads, for the students to consider.

I'll never forget the time my children and I nearly lost our lives on an icy road.
It has been said that when you are about to die your life flashes before your eyes. My children and I once had an opportunity to find out if that is true.
Seat belts save lives. I know this from first-hand experience.

"Which of these leads do you think would entice someone most to want to read my story?" asked Ms. Trahan. After some discussion, a majority of the class agreed that the second alternative lead was best, and that all were better than the first one she had written.

Ms. Trahan continued, "Now I'd like for all of you to go to your writing folders, take out one of your favorite compositions, and create an alternative lead of one to two sentences that you think might be a little better at drawing in readers than what you had originally written. When you think you have something really interesting, you may pop your balloon, and we'll all stop and listen to your new lead." About five minutes later, one by one, great ideas for opening leads were created, and the balloons began to burst.

CHANGING REALITIES: READING INSTRUCTION IN THE TRANSITION YEARS

The years of learning at this level have rightly been referred to as the "transitional grades." Children in grades 4–6 can range widely in their reading development and have to cope with ever-increasing demands in nonfiction materials. At one end of the continuum are students still struggling to conquer basic reading and writing skills, and at the other end are fluent readers champing at the bit for new challenges. Jeanne S. Chall, the Harvard University reading researcher, once wrote:

> The public has become more conscious about the importance of literacy, for students and for adults. The reading achievement of too many children, young people, and adults is not up to what it should be. . . . The students of low-income families and students of all social levels who are predisposed to having reading difficulty—are not doing as well as they can. . . . They need excellent teachers. (1998, pp. 20, 22)

Master teachers in grades 4–6 have a deep understanding of reading and writing standards from the earliest stages through fluency. They also have a significant arsenal of strategies for teaching a wide range of literacy skills. Finally, they are able to establish effective and flexible classroom routines involving small- and large-group instruction, learning centers, and independent learning activities.

From our own experiences as upper-elementary teachers, we can assure you that teaching at this level is as exciting as it is rewarding.

Keeping Our "Balance"

There can be a great deal of pressure at the intermediate level to show significant literacy gains on state-mandated and norm-referenced tests. Grade 4 has especially become a pressure point. President Clinton's national goal established in 1997 called for all students to be reading on grade level by the end of third grade. President Bush extended this goal in his No Child Left Behind Act. In various forms it has been reinforced with high-stakes testing in most states as of this writing.

Other academic pressures commonly occur during grades 4–6. We all remember as children being introduced to cursive writing, long division, and more in-depth studies of science, social studies, and the arts during intermediate years. If we are not careful, we can lose our balance and forget to continue developing reading and writing skills in our students. As one teacher recently remarked,

> "I have come to understand that, in a very real way, children do not truly begin learning to read until the upper elementary years. Before that time, they are mostly learning to decode. Now, they learn how to use those skills to understand their world."
> *(Earlene Mills-House)*

Teachers should continue to consider reading and writing instruction the core of each learning day. Because these skills can easily be developed within the context of other subject areas, continuing to maintain a comprehensive reading program is not as problematic as it may seem. Indeed, it is a necessity!

A Turning Point for Struggling Readers

Problems for struggling readers can become acute during the upper elementary years and, if not addressed, can set the stage for severe discouragement. Students not reading on or near grade level by the end of grade 3 typically do not close the performance gap. Indeed, the gap can widen and contribute to the drop-out crisis in grades 9 and 10. Thus, it is critical that struggling readers benefit from expert teaching in grades 4–6 and supplemental support from Title I or special education classes, if needed.

Good Decoding Is Not Sufficient for Comprehension Development

A common pitfall facing reading teachers at this level, and their students, is the assumption that students who are good decoders will spontaneously develop higher order comprehension skills. Not so. Inferential and evaluative comprehension skills, commonly referred to as "higher order thinking," require extensive and direct instruction in a variety of text genres.

During the upper elementary years, students must develop higher order thinking skills.

Each student has her own zone of proximal development for the myriad higher order thinking skills they must develop; thus, careful assessment, needs-based grouping, and instruction using modeling and guided practice are required. We address this and other critical issues for these youngsters in this chapter.

SKILLS TO BE LEARNED: READING STANDARDS FOR GRADES 4–6

Teachers in grades 4–6 must have a clear understanding of the **performance standards** expected of normally developing readers, as well as early reading skills for those still struggling with basic skills. In this section we provide you with our adaptation of the *reading standards*—grade level goals and accompanying performance objectives—developed by the state of California. Since they are founded on evidence-based reading research, the California standards essentially mirror those developed by the other states. Reading standards should make up the backbone of assessment and teaching preparations. For more information, see the box on pages 426–429.

THE FIRST DAYS AND WEEKS OF SCHOOL

Effective intermediate level teachers begin to establish procedures and routines from the first day of school (Wong & Wong, 1998; Fountas & Pinnell, 2001). Children enjoy feeling successful and generally want to please their teacher. As one colleague remarked, "No child gets up in the morning and says, 'I'm think I'm going to *fail* in school today and make everyone angry!' " An efficient classroom, like an efficient machine, is productive and enjoyable to work with; but when a teacher is constantly dealing with an unruly group of students, everyone loses. Your goal is to maximize time-on-task behavior so that children can learn. The key is to begin the year on the right foot.

The First Day

Be Professional

At the risk of sounding a little old fashioned, we want to offer some advice on this point (because it may well be that we're the only ones who will tell you). Dress professionally. Children, parents, fellow teachers, and principals are all affected by the way you present yourself. Business attire should be worn at all times when you are in the teacher role. NEVER wear jeans, running shoes, exercise clothes, or other casual wear (unless you are a physical education instructor). If you want to be treated as a professional in our world, you must look the part.

Professional dress and posted credentials will gain you the respect of students and their parents.

STANDARD 1: WORD ANALYSIS, FLUENCY, AND VOCABULARY DEVELOPMENT*

*Coding System
First numeral = Grade level expectation
Second numeral = Standard
Third numeral = Skill number
Example: **5.2.2** = Fifth grade expectation, Standard #2 (Reading Comprehension),
Skill #2 (Analyze text that is organized in sequential or chronological order.)

Standards: Grades 4–6

Grade 4: Students understand the basic features of reading. They select letter patterns
and know how to translate them into spoken language by using phonics, syllabication,
and word parts. They apply this knowledge to achieve fluent oral and silent reading.

Grades 5 & 6: Students use their knowledge of word origins and word relationships,
as well as historical and literary context clues, to determine the meaning of specialized
vocabulary and to understand the precise meaning of grade-level-appropriate words.

Performance Objectives: Grades 4–6

Word Recognition
- 4.1.1 Read narrative and expository text aloud with grade-appropriate fluency and
  accuracy and with appropriate pacing, intonation, and expression. *(Authors' note:
  A rate of 90 words per minute [wpm] minimum is required in the Texas standards,
  and 162 wpm is NAEP standard for fluent reading.)*
- 5.1.1 Read aloud narrative and expository text fluently and accurately and with appropriate pacing, intonation, and expression. *(Authors' note: A rate of 100 words
  per minute [wpm] minimum is required in the Texas standards, and 180 wpm is
  NAEP standard for fluent reading.)*
- 6.1.1 Read aloud narrative and expository text fluently and accurately and with appropriate pacing, intonation, and expression.

Vocabulary and Concept Development
- 4.1.2 Apply knowledge of word origins, derivations, synonyms, antonyms, and idioms to determine the meaning of words and phrases.
- 4.1.3 Use knowledge of root words to determine the meaning of unknown words
  within a passage.
- 4.1.4 Know common roots and affixes derived from Greek and Latin and use this
  knowledge to analyze the meaning of complex words (e.g., *international*).
- 4.1.5 Use a thesaurus to determine related words and concepts.
- 4.1.6 Distinguish and interpret words with multiple meanings.
- 5.1.2 Use word origins to determine the meaning of unknown words.
- 5.1.3 Understand and explain frequently used synonyms, antonyms, and homographs.
- 5.1.4 Know abstract, derived roots and affixes from Greek and Latin and use this
  knowledge to analyze the meaning of complex words (e.g., *controversial*).
- 5.1.5 Understand and explain the figurative and metaphorical use of words in context.
- 6.1.2 Identify and interpret figurative language and words with multiple meanings.
- 6.1.3 Recognize the origins and meanings of frequently used foreign words in
  English and use these words accurately in speaking and writing.
- 6.1.4 Monitor expository text for unknown words or words with novel meanings by
  using word, sentence, and paragraph clues to determine meaning.
- 6.1.5 Understand and explain "shades of meaning" in related words (e.g., *softly*
  and *quietly*).

Source: *Adapted from the California Department of Education English language arts content standards.
http://www.cde.ca.gov/standards/

STANDARD 2: READING COMPREHENSION
Standards: Grades 4–6

Grade 4: Reading Comprehension

Students read and understand grade-level-appropriate material. They draw upon a variety of comprehension strategies as needed (e.g., generating and responding to essential questions, making predictions, comparing information from several sources). The selections in *Recommended Readings in Literature, Kindergarten Through Grade Eight* illustrate the quality and complexity of the materials to be read by students. In addition to their regular school reading, students read one-half million words annually, including a good representation of grade-level-appropriate narrative and expository text (e.g., classic and contemporary literature, magazines, newspapers, online information).

Grade 5: Reading Comprehension (Focus on Informational Materials)

Students read and understand grade-level-appropriate material. They describe and connect the essential ideas, arguments, and perspectives of the text by using their knowledge of text structure, organization, and purpose. The selections in *Recommended Readings in Literature, Kindergarten Through Grade Eight* illustrate the quality and complexity of the materials to be read by students. In addition, by grade eight, students read one million words annually on their own, including a good representation of grade-level-appropriate narrative and expository text (e.g., classic and contemporary literature, magazines, newspapers, online information). In grade five, students make progress toward this goal.

Grade 6: Reading Comprehension (Focus on Informational Materials)

Students read and understand grade-level-appropriate material. They describe and connect the essential ideas, arguments, and perspectives of the text by using their knowledge of text structure, organization, and purpose. The selections in *Recommended Readings in Literature, Kindergarten Through Grade Eight* illustrate the quality and complexity of the materials to be read by students. In addition, by grade eight, students read one million words annually on their own, including a good representation of grade-level-appropriate narrative and expository text (e.g., classic and contemporary literature, magazines, newspapers, online information). In grade six, students continue to make progress toward this goal.

Performance Objectives: Grades 4–6

Structural Features of Informational Materials

- 4.2.1 Identify structural patterns found in informational text (e.g., compare and contrast, cause and effect, sequential or chronological order, proposition and support) to strengthen comprehension.
- 5.2.1 Understand how text features (e.g., format, graphics, sequence, diagrams, illustrations, charts, maps) make information accessible and usable.
- 5.2.2 Analyze text that is organized in sequential or chronological order.
- 6.2.1 Identify the structural features of popular media (e.g., newspapers, magazines, online information) and use the features to obtain information.
- 6.2.2 Analyze text that uses the compare-and-contrast organizational pattern.

Comprehension and Analysis of Grade-Level-Appropriate Text

- 4.2.2 Use appropriate strategies when reading for different purposes (e.g., full comprehension, location of information, personal enjoyment).
- 4.2.3 Make and confirm predictions about text by using prior knowledge and ideas presented in the text itself, including illustrations, titles, topic sentences, important words, and foreshadowing clues.
- 4.2.4 Evaluate new information and hypotheses by testing them against known information and ideas.

(continued)

- 4.2.5 Compare and contrast information on the same topic after reading several passages or articles.
- 4.2.6 Distinguish between cause and effect and between fact and opinion in expository text.
- 4.2.7 Follow multiple-step instructions in a basic technical manual (e.g., how to use computer commands or video games).
- 5.2.3 Discern main ideas and concepts presented in texts, identifying and assessing evidence that supports those ideas.
- 5.2.4 Draw inferences, conclusions, or generalizations about text and support them with textual evidence and prior knowledge.
- 6.2.3 Connect and clarify main ideas by identifying their relationships to other sources and related topics.
- 6.2.4 Clarify an understanding of texts by creating outlines, logical notes, summaries, or reports.
- 6.2.5 Follow multiple-step instructions for preparing applications (e.g., for a public library card, bank savings account, sports club, league membership).

Expository Critique (Grades 5–6)
- 5.2.5 Distinguish facts, supported inferences, and opinions in text.
- 6.2.6 Determine the adequacy and appropriateness of the evidence for an author's conclusions.
- 6.2.7 Make reasonable assertions about a text through accurate, supporting citations.
- 6.2.8 Note instances of unsupported inferences, fallacious reasoning, persuasion, and propaganda in text.

STANDARD 3: LITERARY RESPONSE AND ANALYSIS
Goals: Grades 4–6

Grade 4: Students read and respond to a wide variety of significant works of children's literature. They distinguish between the structural features of the text and the literary terms or elements (e.g., theme, plot, setting, characters). The selections in *Recommended Readings in Literature, Kindergarten Through Grade Eight* illustrate the quality and complexity of the materials to be read by students.

Grade 5: Students read and respond to historically or culturally significant works of literature. They begin to find ways to clarify the ideas and make connections between literary works. The selections in *Recommended Readings in Literature, Kindergarten Through Grade Eight* illustrate the quality and complexity of the materials to be read by students.

Grade 6: Students read and respond to historically or culturally significant works of literature that reflect and enhance their studies of history and social science. They clarify the ideas and connect them to other literary works. The selections in *Recommended Readings in Literature, Kindergarten Through Grade Eight* illustrate the quality and complexity of the materials to be read by students.

Performance Objectives: Grades 4–6
Structural Features of Literature
- 4.3.1 Describe the structural differences of various imaginative forms of literature, including fantasies, fables, myths, legends, and fairy tales.
- 5.3.1 Identify and analyze the characteristics of poetry, drama, fiction, and nonfiction and explain the appropriateness of the literary forms chosen by an author for a specific purpose.

- 6.3.1 Identify the forms of fiction and describe the major characteristics of each form.

Narrative Analysis of Grade-Level-Appropriate Text
- 4.3.2 Identify the main events of the plot, their causes, and the influence of each event on future actions.
- 4.3.3 Use knowledge of the situation and setting and of a character's traits and motivations to determine the causes for that character's actions.
- 4.3.4 Compare and contrast tales from different cultures by tracing the exploits of one character type and develop theories to account for similar tales in diverse cultures (e.g., trickster tales).
- 4.3.5 Define figurative language (e.g., simile, metaphor, hyperbole, personification) and identify its use in literary works.
- 5.3.2 Identify the main problem or conflict of the plot and explain how it is resolved.
- 5.3.3 Contrast the actions, motives (e.g., loyalty, selfishness, conscientiousness), and appearances of characters in a work of fiction and discuss the importance of the contrasts to the plot or theme.
- 5.3.4 Understand that *theme* refers to the meaning or moral of a selection and recognize themes (whether implied or stated directly) in sample works.
- 5.3.5 Describe the function and effect of common literary devices (e.g., imagery, metaphor, symbolism).
- 6.3.2 Analyze the effect of the qualities of the character (e.g., courage or cowardice, ambition or laziness) on the plot and the resolution of the conflict.
- 6.3.3 Analyze the influence of setting on the problem and its resolution.
- 6.3.4 Define how tone or meaning is conveyed in poetry through word choice, figurative language, sentence structure, line length, punctuation, rhythm, repetition, and rhyme.
- 6.3.5 Identify the speaker and recognize the difference between first- and third-person narration (e.g., autobiography compared with biography).
- 6.3.6 Identify and analyze features of themes conveyed through characters, actions, and images.
- 6.3.7 Explain the effects of common literary devices (e.g., symbolism, imagery, metaphor) in a variety of fictional and nonfictional texts.

Literary Criticism (Grades 5–6)
- 5.3.6 Evaluate the meaning of archetypal patterns and symbols that are found in myth and tradition by using literature from different eras and cultures.
- 5.3.7 Evaluate the author's use of various techniques (e.g., appeal of characters in a picture book, logic and credibility of plots and settings, use of figurative language) to influence readers' perspectives.
- 6.3.8 Critique the credibility of characterization and the degree to which a plot is contrived or realistic (e.g., compare use of fact and fantasy in historical fiction).

Post Your Credentials. When you go to a doctor's or attorney's office, you always see their professional credentials prominently displayed. Your credentials, your diploma(s) and your state teaching certificate, should be posted in your classroom. Draw your students' attention to them and explain what they mean. This is one of many indications that the students are in good hands and will have their best year ever!

Be Welcoming

Greet your students with a warm smile when they first arrive at your door. Introduce yourself and welcome them with a smile and a handshake. This makes a personal connection with the students and says they are welcome. Have a stick-on name tag for each student with their name already printed on it and help them put it on first thing.

If parents come with a child on the first day, be sure and introduce yourself and let them know when the first open house will be held. It is a sign of professionalism to offer parents a prepared one-page flier that says a little about yourself, your education and certifications, philosophy, contact information, days and times when parents can visit the classroom, and the procedure for setting up conferences.

Assign Seating

Students should have assigned seats on the first day of school. This comforts them because they know their "place." It also helps you learn their names and avoids having students who do not need to be together setting up camp. Explain that the seating arrangement is not permanent. But, it will help you get to know them and help them learn what they need to know in your classroom quickly. The desks can be arranged in any pattern (clusters, circles, rows) for the first days of school.

Remember to create a seating chart showing where each child is assigned. This will help you learn each student's name and simplify roll-taking duties. In fact, a quick glance will tell you right away who is absent.

It is best to have an assignment for students to work on when they first sit down at their seats. Make it something easy and informative. It will give everyone something in common to talk about in a whole-group session. The assignment should be written on the chalkboard or dry erase board for everyone to see as they come in. Some teachers ask students to complete a brief interest inventory with questions like:

- What is your favorite food?
- What is the name of a movie you liked seeing? What was the best part?
- Who is your favorite person in the whole world?
- If you were given $1 million, what would you do with it?

Develop Critical Skills

Take Time to Learn Each Child's Name. A good way to do this is to begin with the first child, say his/her name, and ask him/her to respond to one of the assigned questions. It's a great icebreaker and gets students talking. As you call on the next child, always go back and repeat the names of those who came before to help you remember their names and help the other children get to know their new classmates. So, for example, when you call on the fifth child in this process, you will say something like this: "All right, our next student is named Todd. Let me see if I can remember everyone's name up to Todd. Please listen everyone. I may need help! We have Maria . . . LaMont . . . Callista . . . Keion . . . and now, Todd."

Create and Practice an Attention-getting Strategy. One of the marks of a great teacher is the ability to quickly gain the attention of her class. Doing so quietly is also a plus. Decide on a signal for your students that means "Students, I need your attention," and expect them to comply. Mrs. Roberts, a gifted teacher from Nashville, Tennessee, simply says in a soft voice, "Children, please get into *position*." *Getting into position* means that each student should stop what they are doing, quietly fold their hands on top of their desk, silently look directly at the teacher, and await for further instructions. Her students, upon hearing Mrs. Robert's directive, say softly to everyone around them "Get into position. Pass it on." Within seconds every student is sitting quietly and waiting. Other teachers simply start counting "One, two, three, four, five" and by *five* everyone is to be sitting quietly waiting for instructions. Whatever signal you prefer, pick one and practice it a number of times during your first day (and week) of school.

Set Up Procedures and Routines and Practice Them. Procedures and routines should become so automatic for students that they could literally run the class themselves if you were absent. *Procedures* are the daily living tasks that must be attended to in your classroom. These include such things as:

- What students should do when they have a question
- What to do when the bell rings
- How to go about sharpening pencils
- How to turn in homework assignments
- How to sign up for a task (teacher's helper, line leader, writing editor)
- How to respond to a fire drill
- What students should do when they have been absent
- What students should do when they finish their work before others
- How to take restroom breaks using a hall pass
- Procedures for going to the library, lunch, etc.

Routines are daily activities engaged in by all class members. This category includes such things as:

- Establishing the daily schedule (Post on a chart.)
- Explaining the reading and writing group rotation schedule
- Explaining expectations for behavior when students are in learning centers
- Showing students how to conduct peer editing conferences in writing workshops
- Instructing students how they are to start the day (We recommend that you always have an assignment posted for students to begin as soon as they arrive.)
- Explaining the routine for making transitions from one activity to another and how students will know where they are to be next

Begin creating a positive atmosphere for learning. Above all else, on the first day of school you should make it clear that each and every student is about to begin their best year ever. Explain that you know this because you are a well-trained professional who knows how to find out what each student needs to be successful and that you intend to help them achieve.

Practice, practice, practice. All of the previous suggestions will help you begin the year successfully, but only if you practice them every day for the first two weeks. For instance, stage students in the learning centers and throughout the room and pretend to be working. After a minute or so, perform your attention-getting strategy and see how long it takes them to come to order. Repeat the exercise several times so that they begin to feel your style of operations. This gives everyone a sense of success. It also helps you demonstrate that you will "*inspect* what you *expect*" throughout the year and hold students accountable.

Procedures and routines are essential for a smooth-running classroom.

The First Weeks: Reading and Writing Instruction

From the first day of school you must show students that you consider them to be competent readers and writers (albeit, at their own stage of development). As we progress through this chapter, we will explain in some detail what should be happening in reading and writing instruction. You will plug in those particular pieces as appropriate to the templates we will provide. In this section, we want to begin this process by offering some general guidelines for structuring reading and writing instruction before we move into the more specific elements. The three areas presented in this section for each week of instruction are *language development, reading instruction,* and *writing instruction.*

Week 1

Language Development. The goal in the first week is to acquaint students with your classroom layout, procedures, and routines and begin to increase students' vocabularies (listening, speaking, reading, writing). Here are some particulars for language development in week 1:

- Use whole-group instruction for these first language development sessions.
- Read aloud books several times a day, favoring nonfiction sources.
- Invite verbal responses to your read aloud sessions.
- Use spelling tests to begin to assess what students know about words.
- Introduce any centers that will be used for reading, writing, and language development, including content area centers such as science and mathematics.

Reading Instruction. We want to begin immersing students in a variety of texts in the first week and introduce them to the routines you will use for reading instruction. A spirit of success and confidence should be instilled, particularly with struggling readers. Here are some key considerations for week one:

- Introduce reading mini-lessons in a whole-group setting using such topics as self-selecting books for DEAR time (Drop Everything and Read), locating books in the media center/library, and responding to what has been read.
- Provide direct and explicit instructions about how students will rotate from small-group instruction to learning centers to independent practice sessions.
- Do daily book talks to increase student interest in nonfiction books and other genres.
- Begin daily independent reading (DEAR or SSR [sustained silent reading]) making sure that struggling readers are supported by working in pairs with a more advanced peer.
- Listen to each child read passages aloud on a variety of levels for early assessments, using an informal reading inventory (IRI) (see Chapter 9 for information on IRIs).

Write Net is a valuable resource for teachers interested in teaching imaginative writing. Link to their site from Chapter 12 on our Companion Website at www. prenhall.com/reutzel.

Writing Instruction. Writing and reading are reciprocal processes and should be started at once. In order to get a sense of momentum established right away, do the following:

- Introduce writing mini-lessons working with the whole group. Mini-lesson could focus on selecting appropriate topics, using a graphic organizer, opening sentences (leads), conventions.

- Make in-class writing assignments to help you begin the assessment process.
- Introduce students to the writing center, the variety of tools included, and their purposes/correct uses.
- Introduce students to the writer's notebook concept and have them begin making entries.

Weeks 2–3

In weeks two and three we want routines and procedures to gel and become standard operating practices. Teachers should also finish their initial assessments and begin introducing small-group instruction based on student needs.

Language Development
- Introduce the permanent daily schedule for reading, writing, and language study.
- Provide mini-lessons using a combination of whole-group language development and small-group instruction based on data obtained from your week 1 activities (spelling quizzes, writing assignments).
- Have students, working in pairs, practice new skills learned in mini-lessons.
- Continue read aloud activities in a variety of genre several times a day (e.g., nonfiction texts related to the content curriculum, historic fiction, poetry).
- Continue book talks to spark student interest in a variety of literary genres.

Reading Instruction
- Conclude your preliminary assessments listening to each student read in both narrative and expository texts using an informal reading inventory. (Note: An IRI in Spanish may be needed in bilingual classrooms for some English Language Learners [ELL].)
- Begin literature response discussions using read aloud experiences and book talks.
- Have students begin using reading response journals and sharing entries with a reading buddy.
- Continue using the SSR/DEAR as an independent reading activity (20 minutes daily).
- Conduct whole-group and small-group mini-lessons based on needs assessed thus far, as well as discussions about the variety of literary genre available to them as intermediate students, and different ways/styles of responding to reading selections (letters, newspaper articles, picture books, etc.).
- Introduce the reading workshop format and begin "rehearsals" to help students learn the routine (week 3).
- Begin listening to two to three students read each day from a self-selected book to determine fluency and vocabulary development needs and to fine tune small-group instruction.

Writing Instruction
- Conduct mini-lessons in small- and large-group settings focusing primarily on prewriting and drafting activities.
- Begin small-group sessions (mini-lessons) on aspects of the writing workshop.
- Teach group etiquette rules for peer editing conferences.
- Begin "author's chair" as students complete compositions.
- Explain how student writing folders are to be used to store work.

- Introduce the rudiments of letter writing and have students use that format to write a letter to a friend or family member.

Weeks 4–6

By the end of the first six weeks, routines and procedures should be crystallized and automatic in classroom operations. More general activities are established.

Language Development
- Introduce content-area (i.e., science, social studies) word walls and making words activities to broaden students' vocabulary knowledge.
- Enhance word study through mini-lessons in small groups.
- Use dyads or buddy study to help students review new vocabulary.

Reading Instruction
- Introduce "State of the Class" charts for reading and writing to help students stay on task and complete assignments in a timely manner.
- Continue listening to one to two students read orally each day from self-selected books and/or content selections from their textbooks to monitor student progress and needs.
- Begin guided reading groups, themed literature units, or core book units according to student needs and/or curriculum requirements.
- Conduct mini-lessons in small-group sessions focusing on higher order comprehension strategies, fluency, word learning, and word identification skills according to student needs.
- If adult volunteers are available, begin to assign them to struggling readers to assist in specific areas of need. You must first train the volunteers on reading activities they can deliver, then match them to students having that particular need.

Writing Instruction
- Conduct mini-lessons in small- and large-group settings, focusing primarily on revising and editing fundamentals.
- Share and post numerous model writing samples for each stage of the writing process that meet curriculum or state assessment requirements for best quality work. Students need to see examples of competent work to understand the expectations.
- Conference with two to three students per day about the progress of their work according to work samples in their writing folders.
- Conduct small- and whole-group guided writing sessions.
- Introduce writing backpacks as a homework assignment that involves parents.
- If adult volunteers are available, begin to assign them to struggling writers to assist in specific areas of need. You must first train the volunteers on writing activities they can deliver, then match them to students having that particular need.

Beyond the First Six Weeks of School

After the first six weeks of school, all routines and procedures should be automatic in your classroom. Schedules and behavior expectations are understood and respected. In the remainder of the chapter, we dig deeper into the specifics of reading and writing instruction during the intermediate years.

Vocabulary University provides fun, interactive vocabulary puzzles to increase mastery. Link to their site from Chapter 12 on our Companion Website at www.prenhall.com/reutzel.

Standards Note
Standard 2.12: The reading professional will know classic and contemporary children's and young adult's literature, and easy-reading fiction and nonfiction. To teach "beyond the basal" you'll need an excellent handle on a wide array of titles, old and new. As you read, list titles that you see as suitable for infusion into your own Reading Workshop.

ORGANIZING FOR READING INSTRUCTION

Developing Integrated Curriculums

In Chapter 11, we saw how emerging reading and writing abilities are facilitated by literacy-learning events in the classroom. As children move into the intermediate years, their teachers seek ways of facilitating and advancing their literacy development to inspire lifelong reading and writing activities. Because of the complementary benefits of reading and writing instruction (K. S. Goodman & Goodman, 1983; Squire, 1983; Shanahan, 1984), teachers frequently seek ways of involving the two simultaneously. An integrated curriculum is a powerful vehicle for merging reading and writing instruction, problem-solving skills, cooperative learning, and other desirable curriculum elements in authentic learning situations.

Integrated curriculums are usually accomplished in two *transition* stages. At the first level of integration, the language arts curriculum (reading, writing, listening, speaking) makes the transition from a fragmented schedule to a more unified model; this is often accomplished using a reading workshop format. At the second level of curriculum integration, the language arts are integrated across the curriculum; this is often accomplished through *interdisciplinary thematic units*.

In the remainder of this chapter, we focus on the first level of curriculum integration: how reading workshops are constructed, and how the writing process can be used effectively in the intermediate grades.

> An **integrated curriculum** merges reading and writing instruction with other curriculum elements in authentic learning situations.

The Role of Literature and Expository Texts

Several years ago, while visiting a publishers' exhibit at the annual conference of the International Reading Association (IRA), we found that the hot topic that year was the rediscovery of children's literature and expository texts (nonfiction) as primary tools for teaching reading. As this mammoth exhibit opened, thousands of teachers bought virtually every trade book in sight. They seemed motivated to update their classrooms with the latest materials and to feel a part of the literature-based reading movement. Teachers clearly understood the inherent instructional and motivational potential of high-quality books.

In a survey of reading experts in the United States, Commeyras and DeGroff (1998) determined that most (82 percent) feel that the best instruction includes both literature-based and explicit skills instruction. Thus, teachers who want to use literature for reading instruction must also understand how to teach important literacy skills explicitly if they are to deliver truly comprehensive instruction (Freppon & Dahl, 1998).

There are a number of viable literature-based strategies that include explicit skill instruction (Cooter & Griffith, 1989; Hiebert & Colt, 1989; Zarillo, 1989; Reutzel & Cooter, 1990; Cox & Zarillo, 1993). We have found three program designs to be particularly effective: (1) the Reading Workshop, (2) core book units, and (3) themed literature units. With each approach teachers may also choose to include the guided reading approach (Fountas & Pinnell, 1996, 2001) and/or commercial reading programs as supplemental components. Each includes essentially the same components, thus enabling the teacher to mix organizational schemes and keep classroom life interesting!

Since choosing the right books for instruction is key, we begin with a brief review of student reading interests and resources for selecting quality books. Next, we review the essential elements of the Reading Workshop, core book units, and themed literature units.

How to Choose the Best Books for Instruction

First, think about the kinds of books that can hold student interest (Huck & Kuhn, 1968; Harkrader & Moore, 1997). Matching students with books of high interest causes them to read for longer periods and thus strengthen their reading abilities. Second, knowing student interests can help the teacher build on students' concept and vocabulary knowledge by leading them into new genres.

Mary Ann Harkrader and Richard Moore (1997) conducted a recent study of reading interests for students in the middle years. Several insights were gained from their work.

- There are *some* gender differences in the reading preferences of boys and girls, though they both prefer fiction to nonfiction (Harry Potter, anyone?).
- Favored fiction topics for girls include mystery, friendship, adventure, fairy tales, and animal stories. Their favored nonfiction categories include art and hobbies.
- Favored fiction topics for boys include science fiction, mystery, and adventure. Nonfiction categories include earth science, how-to science experiments, and sometimes the arts and hobbies.
- Fiction topics favored by both boys and girls include mystery, adventure, and perhaps science fiction. Nonfiction interests that overlap some include earth science and how-to science experiments, and (sometimes) arts and hobbies.
- Girls tend to prefer fiction books having female main characters, and boys usually prefer male main characters in fiction texts. However, there are some books with a main character of the opposite gender that will interest them.

Using Basal Readers

In Chapter 8 we discussed how basal readers are particularly useful for teachers in their first years of teaching and can be quite helpful to experienced teachers. We encourage you to use basal readers as a part of your instructional program whenever they serve student needs effectively. Some master teachers use basal readers for about one week out of every four or five weeks of their program. Some use basals extensively with struggling readers who may require a great deal of direct instruction.

What role specifically should basal readers play in intermediate classrooms? This is a choice to be made by each teacher based on the needs of his or her children, but we invite you to think about using basal selections for the following purposes:

- Guided reading activities (Fountas & Pinnell, 1996)
- Mini-lessons to teach the previously listed reading skills to small groups
- Construction of assessment activities (running records, cloze passages, fluency checks, comprehension assessments)
- Small-group reading instruction

*The **Reading Work-shop** is another organizational framework for literature-based reading instruction.*

The Reading Workshop

The **Reading Workshop** (Reutzel & Cooter, 1991) is an organizational scheme providing explicit skill instruction and full integration of children's literature and/or basal stories into the reading program. It is intended to provide flexible scaffolding

Figure 12.1   The reading workshop

Reading Workshop (70 minutes)		
Sharing Time (Teacher) (5–10 min) **Mini-Lesson** (10–15 min) **State of the Class** (5 min)		
Self-Selected Reading (SSR), Small Group Work (SGW), & Independent Reading Conferences (35–45 minutes)		
SSR	*Small Group Work (SGW)*	*Individual Reading Conferences (IRC)*
1. Read a self-selected book (alone or with a "buddy") 2. Responding to text readings	1. Guided oral reading 2. Buddy Reading for Fluency 3. Learning Center Activities 4. Group reading response activities	Conduct 2–3 per day involving oral reading, comprehension checks, running records, reading nonfiction texts, vocabulary quiz, etc.
(10–30 min)	(20–30 min)	(10–15 min)
Sharing Time (Students) (5–10 minutes)		

From "Organizing for Effective Instruction: The Reading Workshop" by D. R. Reutzel and R. B. Cooter, Jr., 1991, *The Reading Teacher, 44* (8), pp. 548–555. Copyright 1991 by International Reading Association. Reprinted by permission.

for reading instruction. The five main components are sharing time, mini-lesson, state of the class, Reading Workshop, and sharing time. Each of these components is outlined in Figure 12.1.

Phase 1: Teacher Sharing Time (5 to 10 Minutes)

During *sharing time,* teachers read aloud myriad selections to spark interest in literature forms (e.g., nonfiction in the sciences and social studies, folktales, short stories, poetry). Sometimes, the sharing time activity can serve as a catalyst for Writing Workshop projects (explained later in this chapter) or as an introduction for the Reading Workshop mini-lesson.

Phase 2: Mini-lesson (10 to 15 Minutes)

As teachers work with students in reading and writing instruction, they often note that some students are experiencing difficulties with a similar concept, skill, or procedure. When the teacher notes such shared difficulties, he or she may decide to form a temporary group to provide additional instruction related to a skill, strategy, concept, or procedure. This type of temporary grouping strategy is called *needs grouping.* **Mini-lessons** are typically whole-class or small-group lessons that last approximately 5 to 10 minutes. Mini-lessons are used to teach reading and writing skills, literary response, or a necessary procedure (Hagerty, 1992; Strickland, 1998). Mini-lessons help teachers get to the point with their skill instruction and end the lesson before student attention fades. Thus if a teacher wishes to teach a word identification or comprehension strategy, such as inferring character traits, for example, then a mini-lesson can be offered once each day until students learn the strategy.

Mini-lessons should be developed based on the demonstrated needs of the students and the nonnegotiable skills that must be learned.

Table 12.1   Possible mini-lesson topics

Procedural Mini-lessons	Literary Mini-lessons	Strategy/Skills Mini-lessons
Where to sit during reading time	Differences between fiction and	How to choose a book
Giving a book talk	nonfiction books	Selecting literature log topics
How to be a good listener in a	Learning from dedications	Connecting reading material to
share session	Books that show emotion	your own life
What is an appropriate noise level	Books written in the first, second,	Tips for reading aloud
during reading time	or third person	Figuring out unknown words
What to do when you finish a	Author studies	Using context
book	How authors use quotations	Substituting
What kinds of questions to ask	How the story setting fits the story	Using picture clues
during a share session	Characteristics of different genres	Using the sounds of blends,
Running a small-group discussion	Development of characters, plot,	vowels, contractions, etc.
Self-evaluation	theme, mood	Using Post-its to mark interesting
Getting ready for a conference	How leads hook us	parts
How to have a peer conference	How authors use the problem/	Monitoring comprehension (Does
Where to sit during mini-lessons	event/solution pattern	this make sense and sound
Taking care of books	Differences between a picture	right?)
Keeping track of books read	book and a novel	Asking questions while reading
Rules of the workshop	Titles and their meanings	Making predictions
	Characters' points of view	Emergent strategies
	Examples of similes and	Concept of story
	metaphors	Concept that print carries
	Examples of foreshadowing	meaning
	How authors use dialogue	Making sense
	Predictable and surprise endings	Mapping a story
	Use of descriptive words and	How to retell a story orally
	phrases	Looking for relationships
	How illustrations enhance the	Looking for important ideas
	story	Making inferences
	Secrets in books	Drawing conclusions
		Summarizing a story
		Distinguishing fact from opinion
		Emergent reader skills:
		directionality, concept of "word,"
		sound/symbol relationships

From *Readers' Workshop: Real Reading* (pp. 113–115), by P. Hagerty, 1992, Ontario, Canada: Scholastic Canada, Ltd. Copyright 1992 by Patricia Hagerty. Reprinted by permission.

Types of Mini-lessons. Hagerty (1992) describes three types of mini-lessons: procedural, literary, and strategy/skill. A listing of possible mini-lesson topics is found in Table 12.1. A *procedural mini-lesson,* for example, might involve the teacher and students in learning how to handle new books received for the classroom library and how to repair worn books. The teacher may demonstrate how to break in a new book's binding by standing the book on its spine, opening a few pages on either side of the center of the book, and carefully pressing them down. Cellophane tape and staplers can be used to demonstrate how to repair tears in a book's pages or covers.

Mini-lessons are a major teaching tool for explicit demonstrations of skilled reading and writing behaviors, necessary procedural knowledge, and a greater understanding of literary and stylistic devices. A *literary mini-lesson* for readers, for example, might involve a student presenting the teacher with a small booklet written at home in the shape of an ax blade that retells favorite parts from the book *Hatchet* (Paulsen, 1987). The teacher could share the book as a demonstration of how a class-mate shared his or her ideas using the writing process in the form of a shape book. (Watch out—after such sharing, a rash of shape books is likely to result.) As a liter-ary mini-lesson for the upper elementary level, a student may assemble a poster re-sembling the front page of a newspaper to show major events from a just-read novel, such as Betsy Byars's (1970) *The Summer of the Swans.*

A strategy/skill mini-lesson for early readers might occur during the reading of the big book *Cats and Mice* (Gelman, 1985), where the teacher notes that many of the words in the book end with -*ing* and draws children's attention to the function of -*ing*. While rereading the big book the next day, the teacher may cover each -*ing* end-ing with a small self-adhesive note. During the group rereading of the book, the teacher reveals the -*ing* ending at the end of the words covered. On subsequent read-ings, the teacher invites students to join in the reading while emphasizing the -*ing* sound at the end of words. Other words that children know are written at the board, and an -*ing* ending is added.

A skill mini-lesson for more advanced readers might cover patterns used by non-fiction writers to make abstract information better understood (e.g., cause–effect, de-scription, problem–solution, and comparisons). This mini-lesson could involve (a) describing the patterns used; (b) searching for examples in science, mathematics, and social studies materials; then (c) students' writing/creating their examples of these patterns pertaining to a topic of choice.

Length of Time for Daily Mini-lessons. We recommend that mini-lessons be short in duration (10–15 minutes) so that student attention can be held. It is important to know that you cannot teach a new skill in 10 to 15 minutes. Rather, your teaching is segmented into 10 to 15 minute units so that attention remains high. Thus, you will have a series of mini-lessons spread over a number of days usually in small group set-tings.

Teaching Skills Using Mini-lessons. Mini-lessons begin with engaging stories or other texts and work down to the essential strategy or skill to be developed. This process allows students to see the new strategy related to real reading tasks. There are three steps or phases to presenting a comprehensive mini-lesson:

- *Skill Introduction*
- *Guided Practice*
- *Student Performance*

Following is a sample mini-lesson and accompanying explanation describing the three components of mini-lessons.

MINI-LESSON SCHEDULE (WHOLE-TO-PARTS-TO-WHOLE)

Skill from the curriculum (6th grade level):* (6.3.2) Analyze the effect of the qualities of the character (e.g., courage or cowardice, ambition or laziness) on the plot and the resolution of the conflict.

Subskill to learn: Inferring character traits from accounts in the story.

Materials needed: Multiple copies of *Harry Potter and the Sorcerer's Stone* (Rowling, 1997).

*Adapted from the California Department of Education English-Language Arts Content Standards.

Step 1: Skill Introduction (within the context of a reading passage)

1. *Begin with a reading selection.* After having students in your reading group read *Harry Potter and the Sorcerer's Stone,* discuss key points of the story with the group and list their favorite parts on chart paper (post in sequence using tape for each sheet of paper with individual points on each). This step provides a "whole text" context from which the new skill can be introduced.

2. *Teacher Modeling.* The point of teacher modeling is to show the students what the new skill to be learned "looks like" when a competent reader (the teacher) uses it. First, the teacher introduces the skill or "part" of reading to be learned. (In this case we will emphasize a subskill of #6.3.2—"Inferring character traits from accounts in the story.") Modeling of the skill is essentially a "think aloud" activity where the teacher talks through the thinking process used to apply the skill. In this instance, she may begin by explaining, "Sometimes we are able to learn a lot about a character by noting how he reacts to difficult situations in the story. I sometimes list things I remember the character did in the story to help me decide what kind of person he or she is." The teacher might then direct the class to reread key passages with a specific character in mind and list key events on chart paper. If Harry Potter were chosen by the teacher for modeling this thinking strategy, the resulting notes made on chart paper with the group may look something like this:

CHARACTER: HARRY POTTER

Examples of Things That Happened:

Harry was patient and kind even though he was mistreated by the Dursleys (Chapter 1) Harry wanted to stay in the same house with his new friends at Hogwarts (Chapter 7)

Harry used the invisibility cloak to go into dangerous places (Chapter 12)

Character Traits We Can INFER:

Kind, patient with others, loyal to friends, brave

Finally, the teacher discusses (thinks aloud) about how all of the pieces of information, when taken together, paint a vivid picture of the character, so much so that it is not difficult to list his character traits. *This process of (a) explaining the skill to be used, (b) thinking aloud while drawing relevant information clues from the text, and (c) demonstrating how the skill can be used in real reading situations are the key elements of the Skill Introduction phase of mini-lessons.*

Step 2: Guided Practice

In the guided practice phase of mini-lessons students develop a growing understanding of the new strategy to be learned; it begins to crystallize. To make this strategy their own they must practice it themselves repeatedly, but with assistance available when needed. Here's how:

1. *First, choose an identical situation from the same text selection used during the Skill Introduction phase (with a different part of the story or character).* In this example, the teacher might begin shifting responsibility for using the skill to the learners (see gradual release of responsibility in Chapter 5 for a refresher on this concept) by selecting another character from *Harry Potter and the Sorcerer's Stone* for a character trait analysis. Children could be asked to complete their analysis by first listing key events, then inferring character traits based on those events or facts. The students' predictions, as with those modeled by the teacher earlier, should be based on what is known about the character from earlier accounts in the

book. In other words, during guided practice students try using the skill with support from the teacher or in collaboration with other more advanced readers. Again, notice that students typically use the same reading selection as that used by the teacher during the introduction phase. The difference is that a different character from another episode is used. This saves time and keeps students on familiar turf (reading-wise). For example, during guided practice you might spend some time outlining some of the character traits learned from *Harry Potter and the Sorcerer's Stone* about other characters and list them on chart paper, perhaps Draco Malfoy (Harry's not-so-nice rival), Ron (his red-headed friend), and Hermione (Harry's smart female friend). For Malfoy, a student may end up listing something like the following:

CHARACTER: DRACO MALFOY

Examples of Things That Happened:

Malfoy's family were part of the evil group led by Voldemort (Chapter 6)

Malfoy was part of the rival house, Slytherin, at Hogarts (Chapter 7)

Malfoy and his friends made fun of Harry during potions class (Chapter 8)

Malfoy picked on weaker students at the lunch table, and took away Longbottom's gift from home saying, "It's that stupid thing Longbottom's gran sent him." (Chapter 9)

Character Traits We Can INFER:

Selfish, mean, possibly evil

Support students as they work through numerous examples to gain skill and confidence. This is essential during guided practice. Sometimes students are assumed to have competence prematurely. If in doubt, *over-practice* the new skill until students are marinated in the new experience, and be there to lend assistance as needed. It is comparable to a child first learning to ride a bike (and YOU are the training wheels!). *Be sure students can demonstrate their ability verbally, graphically, or in writing.*

When you feel reasonably certain the new skill is "owned" by the student, move on to the last phase of the mini-lesson.

Step 3: Student Performance

The final mini-lesson stage involves students demonstrating their newly acquired skill in another text or reading situation. Unlike the guided practice phase where students have help available when they try out the new skill, in student performance students use the new skill independently. The length of the passage is not very important. Your goal is to make sure that the new skill has been learned permanently and that students can apply it in other reading situations. To demonstrate their competence using the skill of inferring character traits from events presented in the reading selection, you might use such fiction texts as *The Lion, the Witch, and the Wardrobe* (Lewis, 1961), *Julie of the Wolves* (George, 1972), or nonfiction accounts of such figures as Christa MacAuliffe, Martin Luther King, Anne Frank, Barbara Jordan, or Winston Churchill.

In Figure 12.2 we present a simple mini-lesson planning guide, developed by R. Cooter (2003), you might use to help structure your teaching.

Phase 3: State of the Class (3 to 5 Minutes)

One of the management concerns for teachers using a Reading Workshop format is monitoring what youngsters do during independent work periods. *State of the class is a wonderful classroom management tool that informs teachers of student activities*

Once a mini-lesson skill is "owned" by the student, the last mini-lesson stage is to have the student demonstrate that skill in another text or reading situation.

State of the class *helps teachers monitor student learning and helps students stay on task.*

Figure 12.2 Mini-lesson planning guide[*]

Mini-Lesson Planning Guide

PRE-PLANNING

Objective of the mini-lesson series (Based on student need or curriculum requirements.):

_____
_____

Materials Needed[†] for teacher modeling, guided practice, and student performance/assessment:

_____
_____
_____

[†] Reading selections for upper elementary instruction may include narratives (stories), informational texts (expository), and/or bridging books (i.e., part story/part information).

STEP 1: SKILL INTRODUCTION

A. Reading & Discussion to Create a Context for Learning (Specify the task to be used.):

_____
_____

B. Skill Introduction and Teacher Modeling

- **Skill Introduction** (Write out the language you will use to introduce and explain the new skill to be learned using words students can understand.):

_____
_____

- **Teacher Modeling** (Activities you will use to model the new skill for your reading novices. Remember the "think-aloud" aspect of modeling, and have multiple modeling experiences ready to help students fully understand what you expect them to do.):

Modeling Activity #1:

_____
_____

Modeling Activity #2:

_____
_____

Modeling Activity #3:

_____
_____

STEP 2: GUIDED PRACTICE (*with* coaching/support)

Practice activities that will be used to help students learn the skill *thoroughly* (Note: Remember that the guided practice experiences should mirror those used by the teacher in modeling—same format, same text sources, if possible):

Guided Practice Activity #1:

_____
_____
_____

Coaching Resource (teacher, another student, or an adult volunteer):

Guided Practice Activity #2:

_____
_____

Figure 12.2   *continued**

Coaching Resource (teacher, another student, or an adult volunteer): _____

Guided Practice Activity #3:

_____
_____
_____

Coaching Resource (teacher, another student, or an adult volunteer): _____

STEP 3: STUDENT PERFORMANCE
Explain how learning will be assessed. (Specific [quantifiable] criteria should be
listed to objectively determine whether the student has mastered the new skill or
strategy.)

_____
_____
_____

---

*Derived in part from the *TEXAS TWO-STEP Model: Emphasis on Schema-Building,* developed for
Bowie Elementary School in Grand Prairie. TX by R. Cooter (2003).

each day and reminds students of their responsibilities during the workshop period.
Each day, students fill in a state of the class chart like the one shown in Figure 12.3,
explaining their major activities for the next day. Just before the SSR and response
period begins (see next section), the teacher reviews the chart with the students to
help them remember what they are supposed to be doing and assign deadlines. Some
teachers, like Nancy Atwell (1987), prefer to complete the chart themselves with the
whole class. Atwell describes state of the class as a brief (3 to 5 minutes) and effective way of "eavesdropping" on students' plans and activities during independent activity periods.

When problems are observed, such as a student's spending several days on one
task with no apparent progress, then a "house call" or teacher-student conference is
scheduled (see individual reading conferences in Figure 12.1). This simple process
ensures that students having difficulty do not fall through the cracks and provides
teachers with a daily audit trail of each student's work that can be referred to during
conferences with parents and when planning mini-lessons.

Phase 4: Self-Selected Reading and Response (40 Minutes)

Self-selected reading and response (SSR&R) is the beginning of the reading period.
It involves three student activities: SSR, literature response (LR), and individual reading conferences (IRC).

Self-Selected Reading. During SSR, also known as Sustained Silent Reading (SSR)
or Drop Everything and Read (DEAR), students may become involved in one or more
activities. To begin the workshop period, students and teachers engage in free reading of a book they have chosen for 10 to 20 minutes of SSR. Another option is for
students to read goal pages established by their LRG. *Goal pages* are daily reading
goals established by students themselves in order to read the book within a given time.

*Struggling readers
should always read
with a more able part-
ner (buddy or "dyad"
reading) during SSR pe-
riods. Choral reading
and Neurological Im-
press are two proven
activities for struggling
readers.*

Figure 12.3   State of the class chart

State of the Class Chart					
Student Name	M	T	W	TH	F
John	LR-GM	LR-GM			
Maria	LR-NM	IRC			
Jalissa	LR-NM	LR-GM			
Sue	IRC	LR-NM			
Miguel	SSR-LRG	SSR-LRG			
Yumiko	IRC	SSR-LRG			
Jamie Lee	LR-NM	LR-GM			
Seth	SSR-SSB	SSR-SSB			
Andrea	SSR-SSB	SSR-RL			
Martin	IRC	SSR-SSB			
Heather	SSR-SSB	SSR-SSB			
April	LR-NM	LR-GM			
Jason	ABSENT	SSR-SSB			
Malik	LR-GM	IRC			
Juanita	SSR-LRG	SSR-LRG			
J.T.	SSR-LRG	SSR-LRG			
Francesca	ABSENT	IRC			
Shelley	LR-NM	LR-GP			
Melanie	SSR-SSB	SSR-LRG			

Key

SSR:	Self-selected reading	RK:	Record keeping
SSB:	Self-selected book	LR:	Literature-response group
LRG:	Literature-response group goal pages	GM:	Group meeting for response
		NM:	New meeting
RL:	Responding to literature	RM:	Determining new response
		IRC:	Individual reading conference

From "Organizing for Effective Instruction: The Reading Workshop" by D. R. Reutzel and R. B. Cooter, Jr., 1991, *The Reading Teacher, 44*(8), pp. 548–555. Copyright 1991 by the International Reading Association. Reprinted by permission.

Students who continue SSR while others rotate through the SGM activities may engage in four activities. First, they must complete their SSR goal pages. Next, they may work on literature response projects. Third, they update their reading records—filling in book time and title logs, updating their activities on the state of the class chart, or signing up for an IRC with the teacher.

Small Group Work (SGW). After the initial 10 minutes of SSR, most students will be rotating through small group work (SGW) activities and spend about 20 minutes in each group. They will participate in guided oral reading for about 20 to 30 minutes, then rotate to one of the other activities. Here's how is works.

Student Assignments During SGW

• *Guided Oral Reading*   As mentioned, most students will work with the teacher each day in a guided oral reading group to build reading fluency, vocabulary, and learn new skills and strategies (see Chapter 6).

• *Buddy Reading*   Another group of children may be working in pairs on reading activities assigned them by the teacher.

• *Learning Center Work*   About one-third of your students should spend about 20 minutes in one of the learning centers. They will work in a different center each day according to your rotation schedule.

• *Group Literature Response*   Finally, some students may be working on a group literature response activity as part of a themed literature unit or core book activity.

Burgess Summary. A kind of cloze passage, Burgess summaries (T. D. Johnson & Louis, 1987) are teacher constructed, using a summary of a selected story. Instead of blanks representing selected missing words from the story, nonsense words replace the missing words. The ratio suggested for replacement words to regular text is about 1:12. Burgess summaries may need to be simplified greatly when used with younger children in the early stages of reading development. Figure 12.4 is a brief example of a passage developed from E. B. White's (1970) *The Trumpet of the Swan*.

*A **Burgess summary** is essentially a modified cloze activity.*

Character and Author Report Cards. Although children often have a great deal of anxiety concerning their own report cards, they enjoy giving grades to others. In this activity, students have the opportunity to grade the author or character(s) in the book they have been reading. Character and author report cards (T. D. Johnson & Louis, 1987) are developed by the teacher with appropriate categories for grading included. Students grade each aspect called for, then write a justification for the grade based on evidence from the book. Both explicit (factual) and implicit (inferred) justifications should be identified. Figure 12.5 offers a simple example of a character report card.

Clue Cards. Clue cards (T. D. Johnson & Louis, 1987) are a relatively simple idea useful in developing vocabulary knowledge. The child draws cards from a deck specially prepared for a particular book. On the front of the card is a sentence summarizing or defining the target word using context from the story. The word being emphasized is

Figure 12.4   Burgess summary for *The Trumpet of the Swan* (E. B. White, 1970)

Lewis was a trumpeter swan born without a <u>blurber</u>. Lewis' father, the cob, decided that something must be done. If Lewis <u>ciz</u> ever to have a chance for a normal life he <u>wrost</u> need a trumpet, the kind humans play in a band. The cob flew into the nearest town, Billings, in <u>dweeb</u> of the needed trumpet. Then he saw it, a <u>renzee</u> store with a shiny, new trumpet with a dangling red cord hanging in <u>sas</u> window. Now was his chance to risk everything on one bold move.

Figure 12.5 Character report card

| Clemmons School |
| Ms. Robert's Third Grade |
| Character Report Card |

Name: _____

Date: _____

Character: Lewis's Father

Book: *The Trumpet of the Swan*

Subject	Grade	Comments
Honesty		
Commitment		
Courage		
Love of family		

Figure 12.6 Clue cards for *The Red Pony* (Steinbeck, 1937)

Front of the card   *Back of the card*

Sometimes I had to talk to Jody as though I was his father.	**Billy Buck**

Sounded the triangle in the morning and said irritably, "Don't you go out until you get a good breakfast in you."	**Jody's mother**

printed on the back so that children can self-monitor their prediction. Figure 12.6 offers several examples drawn from *The Red Pony* by John Steinbeck (1937).

The Unknown Character. The Unknown Character is an activity patterned after 20 Questions. The teacher assumes the role of one of the characters from a book or story. Students ask questions that can be answered with a simple *yes* or *no*. Teachers find this activity a natural vehicle for teaching children about characterization and inferential comprehension. (Teaching hint: A greater sense of drama can be created if the teacher puts on some sort of "Unknown Character" mask while in this role.)

Yakity-Yak. Yakity-Yak is a reciprocal retelling procedure involving groups of two students. After the initial reading of the whole story, each pair of students sits together with copies of the story. Students then take turns rereading sections, usually

Yakity-Yak involves both oral reading and retelling activities.

paragraphs, then stop to retell their partner what they have just read. Then the process is repeated by the other student using the next section of text. Yakity-Yak can be combined with Manzo's (1969) ReQuest procedure in upper elementary grades for comprehensive student analysis of the passage.

ReQuest. ReQuest (Manzo, 1969) is very similar to Yakity-Yak in that it is also a reciprocal response procedure that follows an initial reading of the whole text. Typically, students working together in a one-to-one setting take turns silently rereading a portion of text. Next, one team member asks the other as many questions as possible about the portion of text just read. After the questioning is complete, the students continue reading the next unit of text and the second partner assumes the role of questioner. In Manzo's (1969) scheme, the story is reread sentence by sentence, but larger units of text are often preferred. Manzo also presents ReQuest as a procedure to be practiced between the teacher and one student, usually in a tutorial setting. However, questioning could easily be addressed in a whole-class mini-lesson, thus allowing students to work together.

Yakity-Yak and ReQuest could easily be combined in the following format:

1. Students read the entire selection or chapter independently.
2. Student groups of two each are created.
3. The children begin by rereading portions of the text. Then, one partner (called the "listener") says "Yakity-Yak!" indicating that the teller should retell the passage just read. After the retelling is complete, the "listener" asks his or her partner (the "teller") as many questions as possible related to story elements not mentioned.
4. The process is repeated over and over with the children switching roles each time.

Newspaper Reports. Using various newspaper reporting styles offers motivating ways to help students develop many important comprehension abilities. Some of the formats that newspaper reports can follow are:

- *Ads*
    Wanted—Time Traveler! Have mutant VCR capable of zapping people back in time. Need partner to help stop robbery and shooting of relative. No pay, just thrills. Phone Kelly at 293-4321. (Pfeffer, 1989)
- *Headlines*
    CHILDREN DISCOVER WORLD THROUGH OLD WARDROBE
    TRACK COACH RESNICK SAYS "TAKE A LONG JUMP"!
    JOHN HENRY BEATS STEAM HAMMER, WINS RACE!
- *Crossword:* Can be developed for *Henry and Beezus* (Cleary, 1952) using a Minnesota Educational Computing Consortium (MECC) computer program.
- *Other:* Stimulating literature-response projects using the newspaper motif also include Letters to the Editor, Dear Gabby, editorials, sports, and cooking.

Literature-Response Logs. Literature-response logs are regular records, usually daily, that children keep as running diaries of their readings. Many authorities in the field recommend that children avoid simply summarizing their daily readings, but rather react to what they have read (Parsons, 1990).

Newspaper reports have students summarize main ideas using brief and precise language.

Develop some literature-response log entries using popular children's books to use as modeling activities during mini-lessons.

Individual Reading Conferences. During the last 10 to 15 minutes of each Reading Workshop, or whenever it is most appropriate, the teacher usually meets with two children for individual reading conferences (IRCs). Students make appointments on a sign-up board at least one day in advance, usually at the teacher's request, during the state of the class period; the advance notice gives the teacher enough lead time to review the student's reading profile (see Chapter 9) and decide what to assess. We recommend as a goal three individual conferences per quarter (9 weeks) with each student. If students forget or avoid conferences, the teacher should inform them of their next appointment. During IRC time, students not involved return to the previously described activities. Assessment activities described later in this chapter for themed literature units work just as well for IRC time in the Reading Workshop. In Chapter 9, we also discussed in some detail additional assessment activities that might be selected for IRC time.

Phase 5: Student Sharing Time (5 to 10 Minutes)

As a daily closing activity in the Reading Workshop, we recommend a sharing time for teachers and children to come together for a few minutes to share with the group their written activities, books, poetry, and projects. Student groups might share progress reports on their literature-response projects, such as play practices, murals, or readers' theatre scripts. Some children may wish to share books they have been reading during SSR in the form of book talks. Others can share their responses to books discussed in their SGW. Teachers may sometimes discuss the accomplishments of individual children, though this is really intended to be a time for student presentations. The only problem associated with this second block of sharing time is sticking to the 10-minute time limit because children sincerely enjoy sharing their ideas, work, and discoveries.

Core Book Units

Core book units can be enjoyable literacy experiences for students when used in conjunction with small group skill instruction and writing activities.

Core book units are four- to five-weeklong reading plans organized around a single book read by a small group of students or the entire class. With core book units, enough copies must be acquired so that each student has one. When used in conjunction with small-group skill instruction and writing activities, core book units can be powerful and enjoyable literacy experiences.

Teachers typically follow a pattern when planning a core book unit (Zarillo, 1989; Cox & Zarillo, 1993). First, they allow students to preselect books from an extensive list of popular literature. Be sure to consult such lists as "Children's Choices" and "Teachers' Choices" for the best new books being released, which are published annually by the International Reading Association in its journal *The Reading Teacher.* Teachers begin the unit by presenting the book selected to the class with enthusiasm and drama. Sometimes selected students are involved in introducing the book using a readers' theatre (play production) format. Teacher book talks and shared book experiences are also effective. Most important, successful teachers use the core book as a springboard for independent reading and writing activities.

Cautions About Using Core Book Units

Perhaps the greatest concern about using core books is the idea of requiring all children to read the same book. Although there are many books that educators hope children will not miss, there are probably none that should be required of every child (Huck, Helper, & Hickman, 1987; Zarillo, 1989). Whenever the element of choice is removed from students, teachers run the risk of alienating them from books. Further, the use of core books as the only method of instruction in a literature-based program ignores the importance of allowing children to match books to their individual interests.

Another concern relates to allowing children to read the core book independently. Students should be allowed to read the book at their own pace. Sometimes children become so absorbed by a book that they want to read it quickly. Let them! There are plenty of other related books of high quality they can read while their classmates are still reading. On the other hand, some children may not get very far into the book without some direction. To solve this problem, many teachers assign goal pages each night to keep the class moving and to let readers know which part of the book will be discussed next in class.

Core book units usually have several fundamental parts and follow a common sequence. Figure 12.7 is a template we have used in planning core book units. As with all teaching suggestions, these should be tried out in the classroom and adapted to suit the teacher's needs.

Figure 12.7 A template for planning core book units

Background Preparations

- Confer with authoritative sources (other teachers, media specialists/librarians, lists of popular children's and adolescent books) concerning possible core books, then make your selection.
- Read the selected core book.
- Obtain background information about the book, author, and general theme of the book.
- Order multiple copies of the core book so that each student will have a copy. For bilingual classrooms and students early in their learning of English, obtain, if available, translated editions of the core book.
- Obtain a book jacket, pictures, and other props to use in "selling" the book.
- Obtain extension materials related to the general theme of the book (these will be part of a temporary classroom library and/or reference center).
- Make a list of literature-response projects that may be suggested to students (numerous examples are suggested later in this chapter).

Part 1: Book and Author Introduction

The primary purpose is to introduce the core book and other books by the same author and/or suggest related books that might be enticing to students. Teachers should also describe in a general way choices that will be available to students pertaining to literature response, written responses, and group collaborations. Following are typical activities that transpire in Phase 1:

- **Book introduction** using book jacket and other displays or props.
- **Sharing information** about the author and why he or she wrote the book (Note: for a great example, see Jerry Spinelli's 1991 article "Catching Maniac Magee" in which he explains his motives in writing this Newbery Award winning book.)
- **Book talk** — the teacher dramatically reads an interesting portion of the book leading up to a thrilling point, then leaves the class hanging.
- **Distribution of the book**
- **Sustained Silent Reading (SSR)** to permit students to begin reading the core book and, hopefully, get hooked.
- **Description of initial choices for literature response,** which usually are of an individual nature (i.e., reading response journals, reading logs, story mapping, etc.).
- **Introduction of the library and resource centers,** which house additional free-reading materials for self-selected reading and research into related topics.
- **Assignment of goal pages** so that students are aware of minimal reading expectations for coming days.

(continued)

Figure 12.7 *continued*

Part 2: Reading and Response

In this phase, students read and discuss events in the book with the teacher and peers. Literature-response activities, including written response, commence. Phase 2 activities may include

- **Discussion of responses** noted in reading journals pertaining to the goal pages.
- **Read alouds/choral rereadings** by the teacher or students who have rehearsed with a partner(s). Choral readings are intended to assist students in developing fluency.
- **Group response sessions** wherein students develop a project to demonstrate their comprehension of the book (e.g., discussion webs, "Novels in the News," dramatic portrayals).
- **Student-teacher conferences,** which permit one-on-one interaction for the purpose of ongoing assessment
- **SSR time** to allow students time to read portions of the core book during school hours and subtly remind students that "reading is a priority" in our education.
- **Literacy skill/strategy activities** in which teacher-led mini-lessons are presented to help students continue their development in such areas as vocabulary knowledge, comprehension strategies, study skills, decoding abilities, writing/composition, and fluency.

Part 3: Conclusion and Presentations

In the final phase, students complete the reading and analysis of the core book. Group and individual response projects are presented to the class. Phase 3 often involves

- **Class discussions** about the book and other related books read by class members.
- **Presentations of literature-response activities,** such as murals, posters, mobiles, dramatizations, and panel discussions.
- **Closure activities** led by the teacher to help bring about a sense of completion and inspire a continuing desire to read other books by the same author or by other authors in the same genre.

Themed Literature Units

Themed literature units are organized around a central theme or concept.

Themed literature units (Cooter & Griffith, 1989) organize reading and writing activities around a central concept or theme. They differ significantly from the *themed studies* approach discussed in Chapter 13 in that themed studies integrate content areas (e.g., science, mathematics, literature, and social studies) and integrate reading and writing into the prescribed content curriculum. *Themed literature* units, on the other hand are intended for building reading abilities and mainly involve reading fiction and nonfiction texts not necessarily connected to the school district's required curriculum in subjects like math and science.

With themed literature units, students are permitted to choose a book from a short list of book options selected by the teacher. After reading the book, *reader response groups,* also called literature-response groups, are formed to develop a project that demonstrates their comprehension of the book.

The professional literature concerning themed literature units suggests certain common elements.

- Themes are linked to high-quality literature and expository texts. Themes help teachers select from the vast numbers of quality children's literature and nonfiction books.
- A good theme is broad enough to allow the selection of books that accommodate a wide range of student interests and abilities, yet narrow enough to be manageable.

Figure 12.8 Journeys theme web

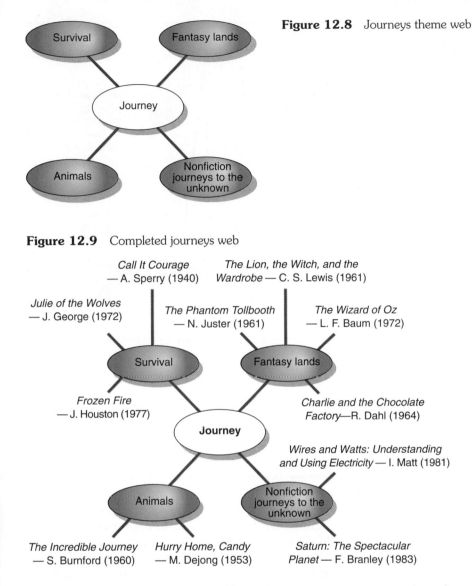

Figure 12.9 Completed journeys web

- Themes are not limited to fictional stories or narrative text but often involve content themes in science, social studies, health, etc.

One of the more successful themed literature units developed for intermediate grades is called "journeys." In planning a unit using the journeys theme, teachers first brainstorm as many interpretations as possible for the theme and diagram them on paper in the form of a web (see the example in Figure 12.8). After subtopics have been identified, teachers search for popular children's books that might go along with each subtheme.

For instance, in children's literature, characters are often seen going on long journeys to fantasy lands full of mystery and danger. *The Lion, the Witch, and the Wardrobe* (Lewis, 1961), *The Phantom Tollbooth* (Juster, 1961), *Charlie and the Chocolate Factory* (Dahl, 1964), or the old favorite by Frank Baum (1900/1972), *The Wizard of Oz,* all fit nicely into this interpretation of journeys. Figure 12.9 shows a completed web for the journeys theme with subtopics and possible book titles.

"Journeys" and "courage" are two popular themes often selected by teachers.

Figure 12.10
Completed courage
theme web

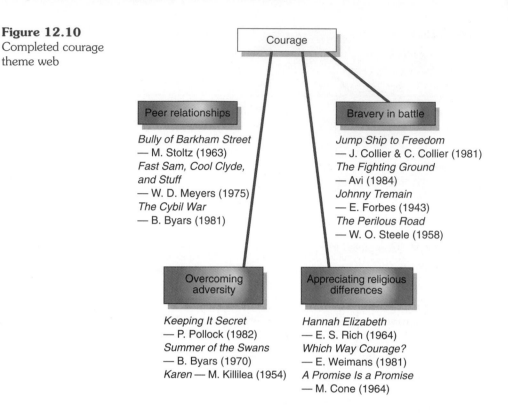

Another popular theme is "courage." It is a superb theme because it can be interpreted in many ways, yet allows teachers to choose books from a manageable body of literature. Again, teachers wishing to develop a themed literature unit using courage as the theme should begin by "webbing out" several interpretations or subtopics. For instance, there is the kind of courage demonstrated on a battlefield that might be called "bravery in battle." Another interpretation involves the kind of courage exhibited by people having to cope with problems of the human condition; this subtopic might be called "overcoming adversity." Many times, young people have to develop courage when dealing with "peer relationships." These are only a few interpretations that could be used in a themed literature unit titled "Courage." Figure 12.10 shows a fully developed web with book possibilities for a "courage" theme for upper elementary students.

To review, a good theme is broadly interpretable and can be linked to quality children's books. When these criteria are met, planning a successful themed literature unit is possible. A number of viable themes collected from several school systems using themed literature units are included in the list in Figure 12.11. In-service teachers have classified them into specific grade levels. Students have the freedom to choose which books they wish to read. When possible, students should be permitted to select themes so as to enhance interest (Jacobs & Borland, 1986). Each theme should include a variety of choices that reflect the diversity of interests and ability levels in the classroom. This view of reading instruction is in sharp contrast to the over-structured "teacher as dictator" forms of teaching. After previewing each of the book choices through teacher book talks, students are then able to make their selection.

Literature response allows students to demonstrate what they have learned. In addition to answering teacher-generated comprehension questions, students com-

Figure 12.11 Selected themes by grade level: Prekindergarten through sixth grade

Prekindergarten and Kindergarten	Giants	Tales–Tails
	Grandparents*	Wheels*
ABC	Native Americans*	
Color	Sea*	***Fifth Grade***
Community Helpers*	Space*	Cultures*
Dinosaurs*	Tall Tales	Fantasy–Fairy tales
Fairy tales	Weather*	Friends
Families*		Journeys
Friends	***Third Grade***	Little People–Giants
Holidays*	Adventure	Monsters
Monsters	Beasts/Creatures	Occupations*
Pets*	Biographies*	Prejudices*
School*	Culture*	Seasons of Life*
Seasons*	Folktales	Survival
	Legends	The Future*
First Grade	Magic	Transportation*
Animals*	Mystery	
Famous People*	Pioneers*	***Sixth Grade***
Feelings	Sports*	Adventure
Food*	War*	Animals*
Growing Up*	Western Stories	Cars and Motorcycles*
Insects*	Witches	Conflict*
Numbers		Family*
Poems	***Fourth Grade***	Ghosts
Travel*	Changes in Life*	Heroes*
	Explorers*	Humor
Second Grade	Geographical Regions*	Music*
Author (specific)*	Heroes*	Overcoming Adversity
Birthdays	Mysteries	Seasonal
Deserts*	Myths*	Sports*
Fable	Night Frights	Survival
Fairy Tales	Space*	

Note: Many of the themes could be used at different grade levels
*Nonfiction and/or expository text.

plete special projects pertaining to the book's content. These projects may take the form of student dramas, creative writing projects, or other creative responses.

Team planning and collaboration help teachers efficiently develop themed literature units. In themed literature units, the teacher guides students toward new and exciting discoveries in a seemingly effortless fashion. The secret to a good themed literature unit, however, is adequate planning. Themed literature units are usually developed through team planning involving reading and language arts teachers at each grade level. Team planning allows teachers to develop units quicker and with greater depth. The old adage "two heads are better than one" definitely holds true here. Sometimes teachers from various academic disciplines join in to help plan interdisciplinary units.

An important consideration for the success of themed literature units is school system support. Developing effective themed literature units is a major undertaking requiring a great deal of teacher planning time, financial resources (primarily for the purchase of paperback books), and administrative approval. This means that school

A good theme can be interpreted in many ways and linked to quality reading selections.

Notice that teachers creating themed literature units prefer to work on them collaboratively.

Standards Note
Standard 2.13: The reading professional will recognize the importance of giving learners opportunities in all aspects of literacy (e.g., as readers, writers, thinkers, reactors, or responders). This chapter is filled with many "activities" that meet the needs of all learners. Pick four (e.g., Radio Plays) and analyze how you'd organize them to meet specific literacy needs at both ends of the skills continuum.

systems should provide teachers with some form of compensated planning time after school hours or release time during the school day. It may be most desirable for school districts to address this need during the summer season when schools are usually not in session. Additionally, school districts should carefully select in-service leaders to assist teachers planning themed literature units for the first time. Leaders should be up to date on the professional literature concerning themed literature units and should have classroom experience using these procedures.

Teaching Themed Literature Units: The Nuts and Bolts

Gathering Learning Resources

After the teacher has selected a theme, resources must be assembled. Although large amounts of capital are not required, a substantial commitment of time and other assets is needed for full implementation. One school system using our approach began piloting themed literature units for about $1,500 per school, most of which was spent on multiple copies of paperback books.

Here is a short shopping list of items needed for themed literature units:

- Multiple copies of books selected ("perma-bound" books are preferred)
- Classroom library related to theme (textbooks, trade books from the school library, filmstrips, recordings)
- Art supplies for literature-response projects (e.g., markers, scissors, tag board, rulers)
- Classroom computers
- Reference books (e.g., dictionaries, encyclopedia, thesaurus)

Documenting Learning with Literacy-Learning Milestones

As mentioned in previous chapters, most school systems have mandated performance objectives for students that tend to be based on or correlate highly with, basal reader scope and sequence charts and state curriculum requirements. In Chapter 9, we outlined our own literacy-learning milestones for learning to read that are quite similar. A common concern among administrators about themed literature units or other literature-based reading programs is documentation of student performance objectives. This is one of the political realities to which teachers must give some attention.

These student performance objectives can easily be addressed in the early planning stages of a themed literature unit. Observing the following considerations will help teachers account for performance objectives, or literacy-learning milestones, and avoid difficulties in justifying the themed literature program.

1. Secure a copy of the state and local curriculum guides and identify all required objectives for the grade level(s) involved.
2. Study the objectives thoroughly, and identify possible learning experiences that could satisfy the requirements. Be sure to consider alternative grouping patterns and materials for each learning experience.
3. As plans for the themed literature unit are drawn up, all objectives should be clearly stated and plans for assessing each objective described.

Figure 12.12   Themed literature unit timeline for fifth or sixth grade students

WEEK 1:	Class introduction to the theme.
	Book talks and book selection.
	Self-selected reading (SSR).
WEEK 2:	Reading response groups are formed.
	Response projects approved by the teacher.
	Groups begin work on projects.
WEEKS 3 to 4:	Response project work continues.
	Teacher conducts mini-lessons (student performance objectives).
WEEK 5:	Students present response projects to class.
	Closure activities by the teacher and class.

It is not unusual for teachers to discover that some objectives cannot be easily accommodated in themed literature units. These objectives can be addressed through short-term, whole-group mini-lessons.

Themed Literature Unit Time Line: An Example

Themed literature units could be relatively short (one to two weeks), but usually last from four to six weeks. Factors such as grade or developmental level of the students, the nature of the theme itself, and school district curriculum requirements usually help teachers decide which time frame is best. For illustrative purposes, a five-week timeline for upper elementary students has been selected (see Figure 12.12).

Week 1: Introducing the Theme

Many teachers like to begin themed literature units with introductory activities of some sort. The purposes are to activate students' prior knowledge and generate motivational feelings about the theme to be studied. Introductory activities might include a collage bulletin board depicting many interpretations of the new theme, role-playing, a guest speaker, or group participation activities.

One classroom about to begin work using the courage theme reviewed a teacher-made collage bulletin board. The teacher had clipped pictures from magazines depicting several interpretations of the word *courage*—two police officers on patrol in their squad car, a young woman in a wheelchair, a young student making a speech, and a soldier on a battlefield. The teacher and class had a most productive discussion, and the stage was set for the introduction of the books. A similar bulletin board could be constructed using jackets from the books to be introduced. Lines could spiral out from the theme word in a web format and connect to each book jacket, introducing the theme and book choices at once.

Many other theme introductions are possible. A guest speaker might come. For the theme "animals," a local veterinarian could visit the class and speak about specific animals portrayed in the books selected. In one instance we observed, the presenter brought along some of the instruments used for administering medicine to animals, talked about some of the myths and facts about the animals under study, and answered questions from the class. This experience created strong interest in the

Get together with a colleague and brainstorm ways students could be introduced to a theme of your choice.

theme and resulted in a great deal of recreational reading in the library and student writing (in the form of language experience stories).

Other introductory activities may involve drama. Role-playing, readers' theatre, and even an occasional video production can be used for theme introduction. Once a mind-set has been created, the teacher is ready to introduce the books.

Book talks call on teachers to use their drama skills to entice students into choosing a book of interest.

Book Talks. One of the most enjoyable parts of a themed literature unit, for both teacher and students, is book talks (Fader, 1976). The object is to draw the children into the books and interest them deeply, so they will want to read. When the book talk is well executed, all children want to read several of the books mentioned. In fact, a little frustration may result as each student tries to choose the one book he or she most wants to read.

The book talk activity is very easy to do. First, the teacher finds an enticing section in each of the books to be used (about six titles for a class of 25, with five copies of each title available). We recommend that the section of the book take about 5 to 10 minutes to read and come from the first third of the book. Second, the teacher enthusiastically tells the class about each book, perhaps adding some background information about the author, then reads a juicy part of the book to the class. Naturally, the more drama and excitement a teacher puts into the book talk, the easier it will be to get the class hooked on each book. Third, the teacher should conclude the reading without giving away the plot. In other words, the book talk should be a cliffhanger. In fact, the suspense of not knowing what will happen to the characters in the story should create an almost overpowering urge to read the book. After each book has been introduced, the children are ready to make their selection.

Student Self-Selection. An important element for the success of any holistic reading program is for students to feel that they have choices. In themed literature units, students are allowed to choose which of the books they will read. As mentioned, about six titles (five copies of each title) usually are selected for a class of 25 children.

In helping children choose which book to read, a good way to avoid peer pressure is to have them select their books by secret ballot. Ask the children to write their names on a blank piece of paper, then list in order their first, second, and third choices. Inform them that they will be given one of their choices and, if at all possible, their first choice.

During the teacher's planning period, he or she simply lists on a sheet of paper the title for each book and writes the numbers from one to five under each title (this corresponds to the multiple copies acquired for each title). Next, the teacher opens the ballots and gives each child his or her first choice. Should the teacher run out of a given title, he or she simply gives the child the second choice. Even if the teacher has to give children their second choice, the children still feel they were given a book of their own choosing instead of one chosen by the teacher. Figure 12.13 illustrates a typical class assignment chart. Sometimes only one child chooses a given title. In this event, the student simply works through the project alone. In fact, during the course of a school year, all children should have an opportunity to work alone at least once.

Self-Selected Reading (SSR). Once the book assignments have been announced, the children are ready to begin reading. It is recommended that the unit begin in earnest by allowing students uninterrupted time to read their books. We call this read-

Figure 12.13   Themed literature unit assignment chart example

Themed Unit Title: "Courage"

Book: *Fast Sam, Cool Clyde, and Stuff*
1.   Jason B.
2.   Jina M.
3.   Melanie C.
4.   Bill J.
5.   Mark S.

Book: *Summer of the Swans*
1.   Austin K.
2.   Sutton E.
3.   Jill E.
4.   Emilio C.
5.   Bruce W.

Book: *Johnny Tremain*
1.   Shelley P.
2.   Jackson B.
3.   Deb F.
4.
5.

Book: *The Perilous Road*
1.   Christen M.
2.   Ramesh B.
3.   Michelle L.
4.   Jason L.
5.

Book: *Which Way Courage?*
1.   Skip C.
2.   Margarette S.
3.   Julian G.
4.   Jason U.
5.

Book: *The Cybil War*
1.   Toni G.
2.   Marion H.
3.   Luis J.
4.   Jillian Y.
5.   Charesse D.

ing period *self-selected reading* (SSR), rather than the usual label *sustained silent reading,* simply because readers may want to share an exciting reading discovery with a friend during the period. These positive encounters with books should be encouraged as long as class disruption does not become a factor.

The purpose of SSR in this situation is threefold. First, children are given time to read, an activity that improves reading ability over time. Second, the children are allowed to get involved with their books, which creates a strong motivation to continue reading. A third purpose is to allow children who may have selected a book that is too difficult time to change their minds and trade their book in for one of the remaining titles. Usually, a 24-hour grace period is allowed for exchanging books. The equivalent of two reading class periods on consecutive days is a good start for SSR.

Teachers frequently ask how long students should take to complete their books. Some teachers feel that when students are given a great deal of time to finish reading their books, say three to four weeks, students simply procrastinate until one or two days before the deadline. The result is a not-so-pleasurable reading experience, opposite of our intended purpose. To counteract this, some teachers prefer a shortened timetable, say five to seven days for a 120-page book. With this timetable comes a mild sense of urgency, a feeling on the part of the student that "I better get busy reading or I won't be finished in time."

Some books naturally require more time than others because of length or complexity. Usually, the teacher can work out a formula to determine how many days should be allowed for each book. For instance, if the teacher feels that the average child can read 20 pages of a given book per night, then a 300-page book will require at least 15 days to read. Teachers should also consider such factors as print size, number of words per page, and the author's writing style when developing these formulas. Whatever the formula used, teachers should try to come up with reasonable limits that help students stay on task and enjoy the book.

Children spend at least two reading periods reading their new book selections.

Time limits are usually set for students to finish reading their books.

Week 2: Beginning Literature-Response Projects

Literature-response groups begin work during the second week.

As teachers well know, sometimes students can be very reluctant readers. Literature-response activities are a wonderful vehicle for spurring interest in books and can create writing opportunities. During the second week, students begin work with their literature-response groups (LRGs). They are grouped by mutual interest, namely, which book they chose. For example, all students (up to four or five) who choose to read *Henry and Beezus* (Cleary, 1952) as part of a friendship theme become the Henry and Beezus Group. All children reading *The Lion, the Witch, and the Wardrobe* (Lewis, 1961) as part of the journeys theme become The Lion, the Witch, and the Wardrobe Group. This type of grouping capitalizes on students' intrinsic interests, needs, and motivations.

Think about some of the advantages of LRG projects over traditional reading follow-up activities.

Students working in LRGs are required to conceive of a project that demonstrates their comprehension of their book. All project ideas are subject to approval by the teacher because refinement of some ideas will be required. We observed one group who read Lewis's *The Lion, the Witch, and the Wardrobe* create a "Narnia game" that was constructed in the image of popular trivia games. Contestants landing on certain spaces on the game board were required to answer questions related to the book. Because students in the LRG were required to write all questions and answers for the game (on a variety of cognitive levels), comprehension of the book seemed to be deeper than one might typically expect from, for example, workbook exercises.

There are several LRG project ideas that have been successful with themed literature units. Some are rather extensive and take considerable preparation, whereas others may be accomplished in just one or two sessions.

Student Dramas. Reenactment of major events in a book is a particularly popular LRG activity for students in elementary through upper elementary grades. These student dramas foster deeper understanding of story structures and narrative competence (Martinez, 1993), facilitate content mastery, and provide a marvelous forum in which to display oral fluency skills. Only minimal props and costumes are needed to help students participate.

Students begin by choosing a favorite part of the book to retell through drama. Next, they develop a script based on a combination of actual dialogue in the book and narration. Usually the narration is delivered by a reader or narrator, who explains such story elements as setting, problem, and other pertinent information. Typically, the drama is presented as a one-act play and concludes in the same way as a book talk—it leaves the audience in suspense. This often makes the audience (other students in the class) want to select the book themselves for recreational reading.

Martinez (1993) points out that modeling can be especially helpful in encouraging students to choose this option for literature response. Inviting a professional or amateur actor to explain to students some of the rudiments of performance is a good way to stimulate interest. Figure 12.14 shows a script developed by students for the novel *Fast Sam, Cool Clyde, and Stuff* (Myers, 1975). This script includes dialogue excerpts from the book along with narration developed by the students.

Dialogue Retellings. Cudd and Roberts (1993) suggest another drama form using fables to help students better understand the importance of dialogue. First, the teacher selects a short fable having two characters and reads it to the class; Cudd and Roberts suggest Arnold Lobel's (1983) *Fables.* Second, the teacher chooses two students to

Figure 12.14 Script for *Fast Sam, Cool Clyde, and Stuff*

Stuff:	Sam and Clyde were going to enter the contest. Only, one of them was going to get decked out like a girl.
Sam:	You can be the woman, and I'll be the man, and we can win this contest. Ain't nobody around going to beat us. And that's a f-a-c-t fact.
Clyde:	How come I have to be the woman? You can be the woman, and I can be the guy.
Sam:	I got to be the guy. Because I can't be no woman.
Clyde:	Why not?
Sam:	Because it messes with my image.
Clyde:	And it messes with my image, too.
Sam:	Anyway, I'm so manly that anybody looking at me could tell I was a man.
Stuff:	We told Angel and Maria and it was decided that me, Angel, and Maria would decide who would be the girl and who would be the guy. Me and Angel figured the guy who was the more manly would be the guy and the other person would be the girl. Maria, Angel's sister, said the guy who was the most manly would be the girl "cause it wouldn't bother him as much being the girl." Which made sense in a funny kind of way. Anyway, we had a manly contest to see who was the most manly between Clyde and Sam.

The contest was simple. Whoever did the manliest thing was going to be the woman, and the other guy would be the man. We figured we had three votes, and it couldn't be a tie. But that was before we considered Maria.

Sam and Clyde, me, Angel, and Maria all met at Clyde's house. Sam was supposed to do his manly thing first. |
Sam:	I am going to do 50 push-ups. Every time I go down I'll go all the way down until my *mustache* touches the floor.
Stuff:	When he said "mustache" he gave Clyde a look because Sam was the only one in the whole bunch who had even a little bit of a mustache.
Clyde:	He got his mustache by having a transplant from under his arms.
Sam:	Yeah, baby, but match these 50.
Stuff:	Sam then did 50 push-ups. I think he could have done more if he wanted to, too. Then it was Clyde's turn. Clyde announced that he was going to take any *torture* that Sam could dish out. Torture!!!
Angel:	You're going to let him torture you?
Clyde:	Right, and I'm going to take it without giving up.
Sam:	You got to be jiving, man. I'll put you through so many changes that you won't even remember your name. I'll put bamboo splinters under your eyelids and tap dance over your forehead. You might as well give it up, turkey, because you're going to be crying for mercy in the worse kind of way.
Stuff:	Clyde laid down on the floor and crossed his arms over his chest.
Clyde:	Sock it to me, and see what a real man can take.
Stuff:	Now, man. If you dudes want to know what came down next, you gotta read the book. You know man, if you wanna see the show you gotta pay the toll!

Adapted from the text by R. Cooter, 1990.

retell the fable orally, each assuming the part of one character. The other students listen for story sequence and help supply any missing parts. The whole class has a discussion about how dialogue is important to story and character development. Third, the teacher provides each student with a copy of the fable for rereading and analysis of the dialogue mechanics in writing. Fourth, students working in pairs write a retelling of the fable from memory with each student assuming one of the character roles. As they write/retell the dialogue and their character speaks, the paper used to create the draft should be physically handed to the appropriate person so that they are constantly reminded, for example, to indent. In the final stages of this activity, students can share their dialogues with the class, then create their own original fables individually, in pairs, or in groups.

Radio plays involve both reading and writing activities.

Radio Play. Developing a radio play involves virtually the same process as any other student drama, except that it involves a purely oral–aural (i.e., speaking–listening) delivery. Students first write a one-act play based on their book as described in the preceding section. Next, materials are gathered for the purpose of creating needed sound effects (police whistles, recorded train sound effects, door opening/closing, etc.), and different human sounds are practiced (such as a girl's or boy's scream, tongue clicking noise, and throat clearing). After thorough rehearsal of the script with sound effects, the radio play is taped on a cassette recorder and played over the school's public address system into the classroom.

Teachers may want to obtain recordings of old radio shows, such as *The Shadow,* to help students better understand the concept. Another source is Garrison Keillor's radio program, *A Prairie Home Companion,* which airs every Saturday night on National Public Radio stations and usually has several radio dramas each week.

Think of ways parent volunteers could assist students with LRG projects.

Evening Newscast. Students enjoy acting out book summaries in the form of a nightly newscast, often titled something like the "10 O'clock Eyewitness Action News." Each student prepares a news story script (using the Writing Workshop method described later in this chapter) that retells an important event or piece of information in the book. After LRG members have helped each other refine their scripts, they dress up and rehearse as news reporters until the performance is ready for presentation to the class. The evening newscast can either be acted out before the class or recorded using a video camera, then replayed to the class on television.

Novels in the News. Rice (1991) describes an activity called *novels in the news,* which has students learn to combine the journalistic style found in newspaper headlines with the story structure of novels. The idea is to reduce major events in the novel or nonfiction book to simplest terms, then display these mock headlines on a bulletin board. Thus, one might see such headlines as LOCAL SCARECROW SEEKS BRAIN IMPLANT for *The Wizard of Oz* (Baum, 1900/1972), COB STEALS TRUMPET FROM LOCAL MUSIC STORE for *The Trumpet of the Swan* (White, 1970), or LOCAL BOY BECOMES FOOTBALL HERO for *Forrest Gump* (Groom, 1986).

In a more advanced version, a mock newspaper front page is created. News stories are created with each LRG member acting as a writer/reporter in much the same way as in the evening newscast activity. Stories are typed at the computer, printed out, then pasted onto a large piece of poster board using a newspaper front-page style. The front page is then displayed in a prominent place and presented to the class. (Hint: Show the class a copy of the book *The True Story of the 3 Little Pigs: By A. Wolf* (Scieszka, 1989) which has an excellent example on the front cover).

Formula Retelling. Many popular authors are *formula* writers; they have discovered a successful basic story line, which is altered in each book in terms of setting, characters, and problem. In *formula retelling* (Cooter, 1994), students in LRGs read two or three stories or books by the same author, chart the basic story line, then respond through group writing to create their own short story using the author's formula. For example, Donald Sobol, author of the popular *Encyclopedia Brown* series, appears to have used a formula in creating these detective stories. These titles are also excellent choices for a themed literature unit with young readers because of their high-interest content, easy readability, and avoidance of profanity and adult situations that might cause some parents to object. Group members (usually a group of five) begin by reading at least one story in an *Encyclopedia Brown* book, with all the chapters read by someone in the group. As the stories are read and the plots unfold, students begin a comparison grid detailing major points in the story. Eventually the stories are completed, as is the comparison grid. After carefully examining the comparison grid and discussing similarities, the final step is for students to create their own short story using common elements from the author's formula.

Many popular, best-selling writers are formula writers.

In Figure 12.15, a completed formula retelling comparison grid is shown depicting Sobol's formula for three stories in *Encyclopedia Brown Solves Them All*. The students' short story can be presented to the class using a dramatic reading format, printed copies of the short story, a radio play, or a dramatic production. Teachers in middle elementary grades may want to consider some of the works of such authors as E. B. White, C. S. Lewis, Beverly Cleary, and Betsy Byars for formula-retelling activities.

A Meeting of Minds. In the early days of television, Steve Allen hosted a program called *A Meeting of Minds.* Famous people of the past were played by actors who held high-level discussions about issues of their time and problems they were trying to solve. Peggy Lathlaen (1993) has adapted *A Meeting of Minds* in her classroom and found it especially useful with biographies.

List some popular TV shows of the past and present that could serve as a template for this kind of project.

Students begin by thoroughly researching their famous person from the past so that they can later "become" this person before the class. This work involves careful reading of one or more books, construction of a timeline for this person's life (which is then compared to a general timeline recording significant inventions and world events at the time), research into costumes of the era, developing Venn diagrams comparing their person to others being researched in the LRGs, and searching Bartlett's *Familiar Quotations* for memorable quotes made by the individual. Reenactments of famous events and question–answer sessions are typical presentations made by students. Famous figures portrayed in Lathlaen's classroom include Thomas Jefferson, Queen Elizabeth I, Barbara Jordan, and George Bush.

Dioramas. A diorama is an important scene from the chosen book that is re-created for presentation. Students, usually working in pairs, often re-create the scene on a small scale using art materials. The diorama is presented to the class along with a prepared explanation of why this scene was deemed important to the book. Multiple dioramas can be presented to portray a visual sequence retelling key scenes in the book.

Big Book or Predictable Book with Captions. A great response activity that can be constructed by individuals or groups is a big book or predictable book version of the novel or nonfiction book. The idea is for students to create a simplified version

Figure 12.15   Formula retelling comparison grid (plot similarities noted in bold)

	The Case of the Missing Clues	*The Case of Sir Biscuit-Shooter*	*The Case of the Muscle Maker*	*Our Story*
The hero	**Encyclopedia Brown**	**Encyclopedia Brown**	**Encyclopedia Brown**	
Problem to solve	Is Bugs threatening Abner?	Who robbed Princess Marta?	Is the Hercules's Strength Tonic fake?	
How Encyclopedia gets involved	Abner **hires** him	Sally **asks him to help**	Cadmus **hires** him	
Villain	Bugs Meany	Kitty, the bareback rider	Wilford Wiggins	
What Encyclopedia does	**Listens** to Abner, examines clubhouse, **finds inconsistencies**	**Listens** to accusations against Barney, **finds inconsistencies**	**Listens** to Wilford's claims, **finds inconsistencies**	
Clues	Cherries	Noise of pots and pans	Suit coat	
In the end	**Encyclopedia proves Bugs lied**	**Encyclopedia proves Kitty lied**	**Encyclopedia proves Wilford lied**	
Results	Bugs repaid Abner	Kitty confessed	Wilford repaid Cadmus	

Stories from *Encyclopedia Brown Solves Them All* by Donald Sobol

of the book, which can be shared with kindergarten or first grade audiences. One upper elementary student adopting our themed literature units model decided to construct a multiple-page predictable book retelling the story line of *Huckleberry Finn* (Figure 12.16). After completion of his project, he shared his predictable book with first grade classes at the neighboring elementary school—a treat for the young children and the author alike!

Discussion Webs. Discussion webs are a kind of graphic aid for teaching students to look at both sides of an issue before making final judgments (Alvermann, 1991). They may be useful with novels and other narrative selections, but we feel they are particularly useful with nonfiction. Adapted from the work of social studies teacher James

Figure 12.16 Student holding book he made in class

Duthie (1986), there are five steps in using discussion webs. The first step is much like traditional reading activities in that a discussion is held to activate background knowledge, discuss new or challenging vocabulary, and provide a purpose for reading. Students then read, or begin reading, the selection. The second step is to state the central question to be considered and introduce the discussion web. Students complete both the *yes* and *no* columns individually, usually recording key thoughts as opposed to complete sentences. The third step is for students to be paired for comparing responses and beginning to work toward consensus. Later, two pairs work together for the purpose of further consensus building. In the fourth step, a group spokesperson reports to the whole class which of the reasons best reflects the consensus of the group; usually, a 3-minute period is allotted for reporting. The final step suggested is that students individually write a follow-up position paper about their judgment on the matter. In Figure 12.17, we present a discussion web completed by students researching whether television cameras should be permitted in courtrooms.

Homemade Filmstrip. Homemade filmstrips are an interesting way for students to retell the sequence of a story. Pictures are made with captions that retell important parts of the book. The pictures are then taped together in sequence and viewed with the aid of an opaque projector (if available). It is similar in purpose to the creation of big books or predictable books described earlier.

Figure 12.17   Students' discussion web: TV cameras in courtrooms?

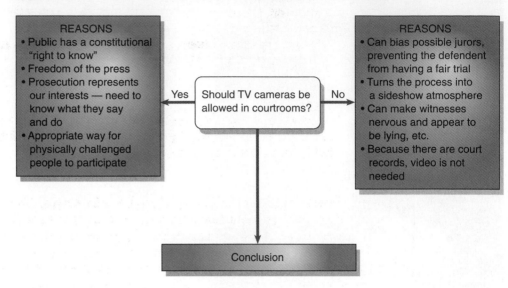

David Letterman or Oprah Talk Show. In a combination of drama, action news, and *A Meeting of Minds,* students write a script for a TV talk show. One of the students is cast as a TV host or interviewer ("Dave" or "Oprah"), and the other team members represent characters from their chosen book being interviewed. The talk show can be acted out in front of the class, followed by questions and answers, or videotaped and shown over television to the class using VCR/TV equipment.

For schools not having video equipment, teachers can check with the high school football coach; coaches have such equipment and may be willing to make it available at convenient times.

Giant Comic Strips. Similar to a mural in size, giant comic strips are made by students to re-create and retell the main story line of a book they've read. First, the group sketches out a comic strip having, typically, six to eight panels that retell an important part of a narrative story or facts explained in a nonfiction book. Next, the comic strip sketch is reviewed by the teacher for accuracy and approved for final stages. The group then reproduces the comic strip on a large sheet of butcher paper and displays it on a wall in the classroom. Giant comic strips are helpful in assessing understanding of sequence. Figure 12.18 shows a giant comic strip created by an intermediate-level group.

Students must be helped to learn appropriate group behavior; it doesn't occur naturally.

Group Etiquette for Successful Literature-Response Groups. Finally, note that students do not work in groups harmoniously by accident; some careful training must occur. Through role-playing experiences, children can be helped to understand appropriate kinds of behavior expected while working in LRGs. One group of teachers in Kenton, Ohio, came up with a wonderful idea for teaching group etiquette. One day after school, teachers at each grade level met to dramatize both positive and negative group behavior. They dressed in the clothing styles of young adolescents and role-played negative group behavior, then positive group behavior. These performances were recorded on videocassette tape and shown to their classes during the introduction to themed literature units. Students enjoyed the production and were able to identify "do's and don'ts" for their LRGs. Figure 12.19 shows some typical rules that might emerge from a discussion of group etiquette.

Figure 12.18 Student-made giant comic strip

Figure 12.19 Group etiquette rules (student generated)

1. Remember that we are taking part in a discussion to learn and help others to learn.
2. We need to bring a paper and pencil to each meeting.
3. Listen to people without interrupting when they talk. Let everyone have their say.
4. Don't show off in a discussion.
5. Everyone has to take part in the discussion.
6. It's OK to change your mind when you have been proven wrong.
7. If someone is having trouble saying what they mean and you understand, help them say it in another way.
8. Always have one member of the group write down important ideas.

Weeks 3 and 4: LRG Projects and Skill Mini-lessons

Work continues on LRG projects in weeks 3 and 4, but the teacher claims part of the time for mini-lessons. Mini-lessons, as applied to themed literature units, allow teachers to (a) help students develop reading and study strategies within the context of the theme and (b) satisfy local or state mandates regarding student performance objectives. For example, if the class is reading books related to the theme "animal stories," then the teacher may prepare a related mini-lesson about using the card catalog in the library to locate other books on animals.

In weeks 3 and 4 of the unit, students should be allowed approximately one-half to two-thirds of the time for working on LRG projects and SSR. Students who feel they require more time to work on their LRG projects should do so out of class as homework.

Week 5: Project Presentations and Closure Activities

The final week of themed literature units is for students to present their projects to the class. These presentations serve two important functions. First, they are a sharing time that provides LRGs with an opportunity to make public their efforts. Second, students in the class are reintroduced to the books they did not read, a process that often stimulates further recreational reading.

Themes should be concluded with some sort of closure activity that brings about a positive sense that the work is now complete and the class is ready to move on to something new. Closure activities might include a guest speaker, a field trip, or perhaps a film presentation related to the theme.

Evaluating Themed Literature Units

Themed literature units provide many assessment opportunities.

Teachers can accumulate evidence of student growth in themed literature units in many ways. Generally, a typical themed literature unit presents 5 to 10 assessment opportunities. The following list includes some of the potential sources for student assessments:

- *Book Tests*   Teachers often give a brief paper-and-pencil test for the middle and end of each book.
- *Literature-Response Projects* Teachers quickly realize that a few students will sometimes attempt to let their fellow group members do all of the work, then claim their share of the credit. This attitude is rarely successful for very long, mainly as a result of peer pressure. Using the following evaluation scheme tends to produce fair and defensible grades:

1. *Class Evaluations*   Each student in the class viewing the project presentations completes an evaluation form (teacher designed) for each group. Criteria for evaluating each group should be negotiated with the LRG at the beginning of week 2, then used by the class members as evaluation criteria during the class presentation.

2. *Intragroup Evaluation*   Each member in the LRG should rate the productivity and contribution of each of the other group members.

3. *Teacher's Evaluation*   Based on the preceding criteria, the teacher awards each individual group member an LRG grade.

- *Mini-lesson Grades*   Summative grades and evaluations accumulated during mini-lessons become part of the overall assessment.
- *Student-Teacher Conferences*   These generally take the form described in the section on the Reading Workshop.

In Chapter 9, we discussed many other assessment methods that can be applied to themed literature units.

COMPREHENSION: FOCUS ON EXPOSITORY TEXTS

The ability to decode words in print is an important early skill that is practiced a good deal in narrative texts in early elementary years. In the more adult-like reading world of grades 4–6, however, students are expected to apply those skills in informational or **expository texts.** In Chapter 13, we take a closer look at the specific demands of subject area texts. This knowledge will provide you with valuable insights for helping students better comprehend these materials.

THE WRITING PROCESS: MAKING AUTHORS OF READERS

Understanding the Writing Process

Writing process instruction teaches students the kinds of thinking processes skilled writers use in producing different forms of text and how to become authors themselves. As authors, children are better able to read books in order to learn how skillful writers paint pictures with words in the reader's mind, discover words that convey just the right meaning for a given thought, and phrases that grab the attention of readers. Through writing process instruction, children become wordsmiths and begin to enjoy the works of other authors on new and higher levels.

Teaching the writing process helps students appreciate the power of words and ideas.

Writing instruction has changed significantly in recent years. Teachers once assigned students such tasks as preparing research papers or reports as the primary mode of instruction. In this "one-draft mentality" (Calkins, 1986) students handed in their report, the reports were graded by the teacher, returned, and most likely forgotten. In recent years, researcher-practitioners like Donald Graves (1983) and his protégé Lucy Calkins (1994) have helped teachers (and students) understand that writing is a process instead of a one-time "quick and dirty" project. Children are taught to understand and use the phases of authorship.

Skills to Be Learned: Writing Standards for Grades 4–6

As with reading, there are certain writing standards (skills) students are expected to achieve by the end of each grade. Knowing the specific scope and sequence of these skills will help you conduct research-based writing assessments, plan for instruction that is sequenced properly, and assist you in plugging the holes in learning that struggling writers often have. See a listing of these skill expectations for grades 4–6 based on the California standards on pages 468–471.

Writers do not move rigidly from one stage of development to another; they sometimes move back and forth from one phase to another, or even quit in the middle of a writing project to start another. It is very instructive to examine the various stages writers go through in producing text: *prewriting, drafting, revising and editing,* and *publishing.* As teachers, we are in a position to help students learn these stages through our modeling, mini-lessons, and practice sessions.

Prewriting Stage

Prewriting is the getting-ready-to-write stage (Tompkins, 1994). Writing begins with an idea or message the writer wants to express. Many teachers help students begin the writing process by asking them to brainstorm a list of topics they might be interested in writing about at some point in the future. They should be topics that generate a certain amount of emotion for the student.

Prewriting is the getting-ready stage.

Donald Graves, in his classic *Writing: Teachers and Children at Work* (1983), suggests that teachers model each of the stages in the writing process to help children see adult examples. For this first step of brainstorming, the teacher might list at

STANDARD 1: WRITING STRATEGIES*

*Coding System
First numeral = Grade level expectation
Second numeral = Standard
Third numeral = Skill number
Example: 5.2.3 = Fifth grade expectation, Standard 2 (Writing Applications), Skill #3
(Write research reports about important ideas, issues, or events. . .)

Standards 1: Grades 4–6

Grade 4: Students write clear, coherent sentences and paragraphs that develop a central idea. Their writing shows they consider the audience and purpose. Students progress through the stages of the writing process (e.g., prewriting, drafting, revising, editing successive versions).

Grade 5: Students write clear, coherent, and focused essays. The writing exhibits the students' awareness of the audience and purpose. Essays contain formal introductions, supporting evidence, and conclusions. Students progress through the stages of the writing process as needed.

Grade 6: Students write clear, coherent, and focused essays. The writing exhibits students' awareness of the audience and purpose. Essays contain formal introductions, supporting evidence, and conclusions. Students progress through the stages of the writing process as needed.

Performance Objectives: Grades 4–6

Organization and Focus
- 4.1.1 Select a focus, an organizational structure, and a point of view based upon purpose, audience, length, and format requirements.
- 4.1.2 Create multiple-paragraph compositions:
  a. Provide an introductory paragraph.
  b. Establish and support a central idea with a topic sentence at or near the beginning of the first paragraph.
  c. Include supporting paragraphs with simple facts, details, and explanations.
  d. Conclude with a paragraph that summarizes the points.
  e. Use correct indention.
- 4.1.3 Use traditional structures for conveying information (e.g., chronological order, cause and effect, similarity and difference, and posing and answering a question).
- 5.1.1 Create multiple-paragraph narrative compositions:
  a. Establish and develop a situation or plot.
  b. Describe the setting.
  c. Present an ending.
- 5.1.2 Create multiple-paragraph expository compositions:
  a. Establish a topic, important ideas, or events in sequence or chronological order.
  b. Provide details and transitional expressions that link one paragraph to another in a clear line of thought.
  c. Offer a concluding paragraph that summarizes important ideas and details.
- 6.1.1 Choose the form of writing (e.g., personal letter, letter to the editor, review, poem, report, narrative) that best suits the intended purpose.
- 6.1.2 Create multiple-paragraph expository compositions:
  a. Engage the interest of the reader and state a clear purpose.
  b. Develop the topic with supporting details and precise verbs, nouns, and adjectives to paint a visual image in the mind of the reader.
  c. Conclude with a detailed summary linked to the purpose of the composition.

- 6.1.3 Use a variety of effective and coherent organizational patterns, including comparison and contrast; organization by categories; and arrangement by spatial order, order of importance, or climactic order.

Penmanship
- 4.1.4 Write fluidly and legibly in cursive or joined italic.

Research and Technology
- 4.1.5 Quote or paraphrase information sources, citing them appropriately.
- 4.1.6 Locate information in reference texts by using organizational features (e.g., prefaces, appendixes).
- 4.1.7 Use various reference materials (e.g., dictionary, thesaurus, card catalog, encyclopedia, online information) as an aid to writing.
- 4.1.8 Understand the organization of almanacs, newspapers, and periodicals and how to use those print materials.
- 4.1.9 Demonstrate basic keyboarding skills and familiarity with computer terminology (e.g., cursor, software, memory, disk drive, hard drive).
- 5.1.3 Use organizational features of printed text (e.g., citations, end notes, bibliographic references) to locate relevant information.
- 5.1.4 Create simple documents by using electronic media and employing organizational features (e.g., passwords, entry and pull-down menus, word searches, the thesaurus, spell checks).
- 5.1.5 Use a thesaurus to identify alternative word choices and meanings.
- 6.1.4 Use organizational features of electronic text (e.g., bulletin boards, databases, keyword searches, e-mail addresses) to locate information.
- 6.1.5 Compose documents with appropriate formatting by using word-processing skills and principles of design (e.g., margins, tabs, spacing, columns, page orientation).

Evaluation and Revision
- 4.1.10 Edit and revise selected drafts to improve coherence and progression by adding, deleting, consolidating, and rearranging text.
- 5.1.6 Edit and revise manuscripts to improve the meaning and focus of writing by adding, deleting, consolidating, clarifying, and rearranging words and sentences.
- 6.1.6 Revise writing to improve the organization and consistency of ideas within and between paragraphs.

STANDARD 2: WRITING APPLICATIONS: GENRES AND THEIR CHARACTERISTICS
Standard 2: Grades 4–6

Grade 4: Students write compositions that describe and explain familiar objects, events, and experiences. Student writing demonstrates a command of standard American English and the drafting, research, and organizational strategies outlined in Writing Standard 1.0.

Grade 5: Students write narrative, expository, persuasive, and descriptive texts of at least 500 to 700 words in each genre. Student writing demonstrates a command of standard American English and the research, organizational, and drafting strategies outlined in Writing Standard 1.0.

Grade 6: Students write narrative, expository, persuasive, and descriptive texts of at least 500 to 700 words in each genre. Student writing demonstrates a command of standard American English and the research, organizational, and drafting strategies outlined in Writing Standard 1.0.

Using the outlined in Writing Standard 1.0, students:
Write Narratives
- 4.2.1 *Write narratives:*
    a. Relate ideas, observations, or recollections of an event or experience.
    b. Provide a context to enable the reader to imagine the world of the event or experience.

(continued)

c. Use concrete sensory details.

d. Provide insight into why the selected event or experience is memorable.

- 5.2.1 Write narratives:
  a. Establish a plot, point of view, setting, and conflict.
  b. Show, rather than tell, the events of the story.
- 6.2.1 Write narratives:
  a. Establish and develop a plot and setting and present a point of view that is appropriate to the stories.
  b. Include sensory details and concrete language to develop plot and character.
  c. Use a range of narrative devices (e.g., dialogue, suspense).

Write Responses to Literature

- 4.2.2 Write responses to literature:
  a. Demonstrate an understanding of the literary work.
  b. Support judgments through references to both the text and prior knowledge.
- 5.2.2 Write responses to literature:
  a. Demonstrate an understanding of a literary work.
  b. Support judgments through references to the text and to prior knowledge.
  c. Develop interpretations that exhibit careful reading and understanding.
- 6.2.4 Write responses to literature:
  a. Develop an interpretation exhibiting careful reading, understanding, and insight.
  b. Organize the interpretation around several clear ideas, premises, or images.
  c. Develop and justify the interpretation through sustained use of examples and textual evidence.

Write Information/Research Reports

- 4.2.3 Write information reports:
  a. Frame a central question about an issue or situation.
  b. Include facts and details for focus.
  c. Draw from more than one source of information (e.g., speakers, books, newspapers, other media sources).
- 4.2.4 Write summaries that contain the main ideas of the reading selection and the most significant details.
- 5.2.3 Write research reports about important ideas, issues, or events by using the following guidelines:
  a. Frame questions that direct the investigation.
  b. Establish a controlling idea or topic.
  c. Develop the topic with simple facts, details, examples, and explanations.
- 6.2.3 Write research reports:
  a. Pose relevant questions with a scope narrow enough to be thoroughly covered.
  b. Support the main idea or ideas with facts, details, examples, and explanations from multiple authoritative sources (e.g., speakers, periodicals, online information searches).
  c. Include a bibliography.

Write Persuasive Letters or Compositions

- 5.2.4 Write persuasive letters or compositions:
  a. State a clear position in support of a proposal.
  b. Support a position with relevant evidence.
  c. Follow a simple organizational pattern.
  d. Address reader concerns.
- 6.2.2 Write expository compositions (e.g., description, explanation, comparison and contrast, problem and solution):
  a. State the thesis or purpose.
  b. Explain the situation.
  c. Follow an organizational pattern appropriate to the type of composition.
  d. Offer persuasive evidence to validate arguments and conclusions as needed.

- 6.2.5 Write persuasive compositions:
  a. State a clear position on a proposition or proposal.
  b. Support the position with organized and relevant evidence.
  c. Anticipate and address reader concerns and counterarguments.

STANDARD 3: WRITTEN AND ORAL ENGLISH LANGUAGE CONVENTIONS
Standard 3: Grades 4–6

Grade 4–6: Students write and speak with a command of standard English conventions appropriate to this grade level.

Performance Objectives: Grades 4–6

Sentence Structure
- 4.3.1 Use simple and compound sentences in writing and speaking.
- 4.3.2 Combine short, related sentences with appositives, participial phrases, adjectives, adverbs, and prepositional phrases.
- 5.3.1 Identify and correctly use prepositional phrases, appositives, and independent and dependent clauses; use transitions and conjunctions to connect ideas.
- 6.3.1 Use simple, compound, and compound-complex sentences; use effective coordination and subordination of ideas to express complete thoughts.

Grammar
- 4.3.3 Identify and use regular and irregular verbs, adverbs, prepositions, and coordinating conjunctions in writing and speaking.
- 5.3.2 Identify and correctly use verbs that are often misused (e.g., *lie/lay*, *sit/set*, *rise/raise*), modifiers, and pronouns.
- 6.3.2 Identify and properly use indefinite pronouns and present perfect, past perfect, and future perfect verb tenses; ensure that verbs agree with compound subjects.

Punctuation
- 4.3.4 Use parentheses, commas in direct quotations, and apostrophes in the possessive case of nouns and in contractions.
- 4.3.5 Use underlining, quotation marks, or italics to identify titles of documents.
- 5.3.3 Use a colon to separate hours and minutes and to introduce a list; use quotation marks around the exact words of a speaker and titles of poems, songs, short stories, and so forth.
- 6.3.3 Use colons after the salutation in business letters, semicolons to connect independent clauses, and commas when linking two clauses with a conjunction in compound sentences.

Capitalization
- 4.3.6 Capitalize names of magazines, newspapers, works of art, musical compositions, organizations, and the first word in quotations when appropriate.
- 5.3.4 Use correct capitalization.
- 6.3.4 Use correct capitalization.

Spelling
- 4.3.7 Spell correctly roots, inflections, suffixes and prefixes, and syllable constructions.
  5.3.5 Spell roots, suffixes, prefixes, contractions, and syllable constructions correctly.
  6.3.5 Spell frequently misspelled words correctly.

Source: http://www.cde.ca.gov/standards/
*Adapted from the California Department of Education English Language Arts Content Standards

Figure 12.20   Sample outline format

Reading Workshop (70 min)		
Sharing Time (5–10 min) Mini-lesson (5–10 min) State of the Class (5 min)		
Self-Selected Reading (SSR) and Response (35–45 min)		

SSR
1. Self-selected book
2. Reading their goal pages for literature-response group
3. Responding to literature
4. Record keeping
  a. Book time and title logs
  b. Updating state of class
  c. Signing up for individual reading conference
 	
10 min
	Literature response
	1. Group meeting for response
	2. New meeting
	3. Determine new response mode
	
	15–20 min
		Individual reading conferences
		1. Two a day
		2. Running record
		  a. Taped
		  b. Retellings
		
		10–15 min

Sharing time (children) (5–10 min)		

the overhead projector or chalkboard several topics that he or she is interested in writing about—sailing, collecting antiques, attending wrestling matches, or traveling to South Pacific islands. It is important that teachers explain to the class *why* each topic is appealing to them. A brainstorming session sometimes helps children who are having difficulty discovering topics of interest. The key to success is helping students find topics that generate emotion, which helps drive the entire writing process through to completion.

After students have selected an interesting topic, they gather information—conduct their research. Depending on the topic, students may need to go to the library to gather background information, surf the Internet for the latest news on their subject, interview people in their family or community, or write to local, state, or federal agencies.

Once the student-writer has settled on a topic and collected useful support information, he or she is ready to begin organizing ideas for presentation; in short, to develop an outline of some kind. The outline's form is not really important, but the writer should have some kind of organizational scheme for the composition. This step helps make the piece clear, concise, and thorough. Several outline formats depicting the story theme "My Birthday Trip to Universal Studios" written by an intermediate student named Jina are presented as examples in Figures 12.20, 12.21, and 12.22.

Once the outline of ideas has been completed, the writer creates several opening sentences or *alternative leads* for the story. Having an interesting beginning, one that grabs the reader, helps create a successful composition. For example, in the story entitled "My Birthday Trip to Universal Studios," Jina may have begun her story thus:

On my birthday my family and I went to Universal Studios. It was a very fun day that I will never forget.

On the other hand, if Jina wrote several alternative leads, then picked the most exciting one to begin her story, perhaps she would come up with a beginning more like this:

Figure 12.21 Semantic web

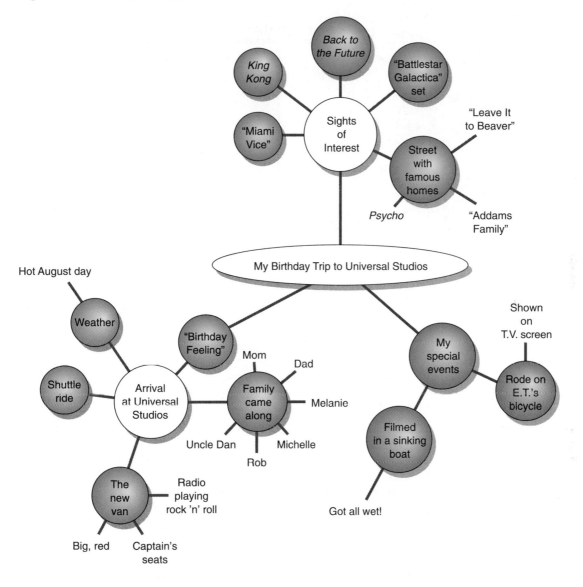

Imagine a birthday party with King Kong, E.T., and the stars from Miami Vice *as your guests! That's exactly what happened to me on my 13th birthday. If you think that's something, hold on to your seat while I tell you the rest of my story.*

Sometimes children have a difficult time getting started with their composition, or even coming up with an idea compelling enough to commit to paper. In this situation, it is usually helpful to engage in free writing. *Free writing,* simply means that students sit down for a sustained period of time and write down anything at all that comes to mind. What often emerges is a rather rambling narrative with many idea fragments. Lucy Calkins (1986, 1994) suggests that children begin by simply listing things in their immediate environment until they come to an idea they wish to write

Free writing is a simple strategy for helping students come up with ideas for their compositions.

Figure 12.22 Structured overview

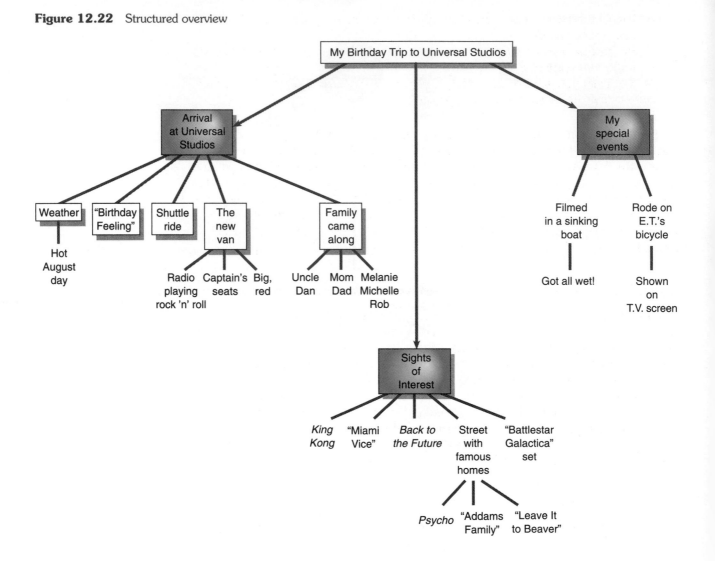

about. After students have an organized set of ideas about which to write and have constructed alternative leads, they are ready for the drafting stage.

Drafting Stage

The *drafting stage* represents an author's first attempt to get ideas down on paper. Teachers should emphasize that the most important part of drafting is simply getting thoughts down on paper, not mechanical correctness. The first draft is often referred to as sloppy copy. Such fine points as verb-tense agreement or spelling correctness are *not* important at this stage; *ideas* are the most important consideration. The following are useful tips for students as they are drafting:

- Write as though you were telling a story to an interested friend.
- Use your own "voice" instead of trying to sound like your favorite author.

- Use words that create a picture in the reader's mind. Your words should be descriptive and clear.
- Be sure to describe sights, sounds, smells, and other sensory images that are important parts of the story you want to tell.
- Say what you want to say directly (*more* is not necessarily *better,* sometimes *less* is *more* if words are chosen well).

Struggling students may have difficulty getting ideas down on paper the first time they attempt drafting. Frequently their handwriting ability is slower than the flow of their ideas. One solution is to have students dictate their story into a tape recorder and then transcribe the story onto paper later. This solution helps keep struggling students from becoming frustrated and improves their ability to transcribe a composition to paper. Another option is to allow students to dictate their story to an older student or a peer tutor. The advantage here is that the storyteller can get valuable and immediate feedback from the peer tutor, aiding in the clarity of the composition.

Revising and Editing

Once the draft has been completed, the author is ready to begin the stages of revising and editing. *Revising,* or "re-visioning" (taking a second look), is changing the manuscript to include new ideas for improving the manuscript. *Editing* is rereading the manuscript to find errors and omissions. It is often a joint effort between the author and "peer editors" who offer constructive criticism.

Editing often involves checking the correctness of spelling, punctuation, grammar, subject-verb agreement, and so on.

The revision process can begin in many ways. Perhaps the most traditional method is the student-teacher writing conference, in which students meet with the teacher after she has read the composition. The teacher asks questions and offers suggestions for revisions. Some teachers like to use a form for recording their comments (see Figure 12.23).

Figure 12.23 Writing evaluation form

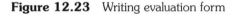

Writing Evaluation Form

Student Name _____   Date _____
Title of Composition _____

Overall Evaluation of the Composition:

_____→

Underdeveloped   Partially Ready   Advanced   Excellent

Areas Needing Further Development

_____ Character development   _____ Spelling
_____ Setting   _____ Grammar
_____ Conflict description   _____ Punctuation
_____ Conflict resolution   _____ Capitalization
_____ Story closure

Another option for helping students improve their compositions is *peer editing.* Many students prefer to get suggestions from their peers before the final publishing stage. Peer editing allows students to help in a collaborative and risk-free environment. Though some students are able to work one-on-one with their peers successfully, peer editing is often more effective in small groups known as *teacherless writing teams or peer editing conferences.* Three to four students work together to develop the best compositions possible. At each stage of the writing process, students share their work with the team, and team members question the author and offer suggestions for improvement.

Editing is checking the composition for incorrect spellings, usage errors, poor sentence constructions, missing topic sentences, awkward language, and whether the composition makes sense. Many teachers encourage children to use word banks (key word lists on the subject), thesaurus, and dictionaries or spelling and grammar checking features on word processing programs. Although some advocate the use of reference tools during the drafting stage, Calkins (1986, 1994) recommends reserving them for these final stages of the writing process.

During the editing stage writers use *proofreaders' marks.* These are notations that an author uses to add, delete, or rearrange information on manuscripts. Figure 12.24 depicts a few examples teachers might consider demonstrating to young writers.

Many schools now provide students with personal computers (PCs) for writing projects. These make the editing process both quick and relatively painless for young writers, but students must first learn keyboarding skills. Selected computer applications for assisting writing development are discussed in greater detail later in this chapter.

Publishing

A natural desire for most authors, young or seasoned, is to share their composition with an audience. For children, publishing can take many exciting forms. One publishing experience common in elementary classrooms is called the *author's chair.* Each day at a designated time, young authors who have completed a composition can sign up to share their most recent compositions in the author's chair. When the appointed time arrives, children take turns reading their creations to the class, answering questions about their story, and reaping generous applause. Other forms of publishing include letter writing to pen pals, school, officials, favorite authors, and media stars or making stories into classroom books, newspapers, and yearbooks. The key to success in publishing is that students feel their writing projects have an audience.

Figure 12.24   Proofreaders' marks

Text with Proofreader Markings	Explanation
injured Jamie carried the͜puppy home.	∧ is for inserting missing words
Let's go⌐to Mark's house⌐over.	∩ for moving text
Let's go to Mark's house ~~over.~~	ℓ for marking out text

Figure 12.25   The Writing Workshop

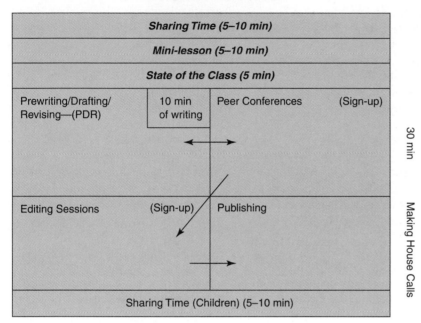

The Writing Workshop

Writing Workshop (60 min)			
Sharing Time (5–10 min)			
Mini-lesson (5–10 min)			
State of the Class (5 min)			
Prewriting/Drafting/Revising—(PDR)	10 min of writing	Peer Conferences	(Sign-up)
Editing Sessions	(Sign-up)	Publishing	
Sharing Time (Children) (5–10 min)			

(right side labels: 30 min / Making House Calls)

The Writing Workshop

The **Writing Workshop** is an organizational structure for teaching composition skills that can be modified as needed. Instruction can be organized into five phases: teacher sharing time, mini-lesson, state of the class, workshop activities, and student sharing time. Figure 12.25 depicts the organizational scheme for the Writing Workshop.

> The **Writing Workshop** is an organizational scheme for planning instruction.

Phase 1: Teacher Sharing Time (5 to 10 Minutes)

The purpose of *teacher sharing time* is to present children with language and experiences through writing that stimulate the natural energies of thinking (Holdaway, 1984). The substance of these teacher-led presentations is usually an assortment of brain-enticing poems, songs, stories, and exposition written by the teacher. The goal is to inspire students to strike out on new adventures in writing. This phase should be brief, perhaps 5 to 10 minutes, and serve as a stimulating introduction to the rest of the writing period.

Phase 2: Mini-lesson (5 to 10 Minutes)

The mini-lesson (Calkins, 1986, 1994), as in the Reading Workshop, is a brief time for teaching the skills outlined in the standards. Class discussions about such topics as selecting good ideas to write about, gathering reference materials, conducting

> *Mini-lessons focus on all aspects of the writing process, such as webbing, creating lists of needed words, and proofreaders' marks.*

interviews, organizing information, and publishing are all viable. Some examples of common mini-lesson topics suggested by Atwell (1987) are:

Illustrations	Narrative leads
Essay writing	Spelling
Form	Writing good fiction
Mythology	The dictionary
Resume writing	Genre
Writing conferences with yourself	Job applications
Correspondence	Punctuation
Focus	Style
Greek mythology	Writing short stories

Teachers usually share examples from their own writing or those volunteered by students during mini-lessons. The main focus of the mini-lesson at all grade levels is helping students write with quality at their stage of development.

Phase 3: State of the Class (5 Minutes)

The *state of the class* phase for the Writing Workshop takes the same form as in the Reading Workshop: The teacher simply lists each student's name on the left of the chart, and students fill in the blanks for each day, indicating what they will be doing (e.g., drafting, peer conferences, editing session, or publishing). Sometimes writing instructors, like Atwell (1987), prefer to complete the state of the class chart in a whole-class setting.

> I think the [state of the class] conference is worth three minutes of the whole class's time. I can't begin to know all the ways my students find ideas for writing, but I do know that eavesdropping is right up there. When they make their plans publicly, writers naturally teach each other about new options for topic and genre. (Atwell, 1987, p. 90)

By recording students' plans for writing and saving them over the weeks of the school year, teachers can see almost at a glance which students are failing to progress (Atwell, 1987). State of the class helps teachers set deadlines for key stages of the writing process with individual students, hold students accountable, and determine when "house calls" may be needed.

Phase 4: Workshop Activities (30 Minutes)

Four activities operate concurrently during the workshop activities phase: (1) prewriting, drafting, and revising; (2) peer editing conferences; (3) editing sessions (with the teacher or peers); and (4) preparing for publishing. Students sign up for one of these activities each day and work accordingly during the workshop period. For descriptive purposes, it may be useful to distinguish between activities the teacher is engaged in versus those of the students.

For the teacher, several activities take place during this time. In the first 10 minutes or so of the Writing Workshop, teachers themselves engage in sustained silent writing (SSW). While working on a written product of his or her choice, the teacher provides children with (a) a model of positive writing behavior and (b) examples for teacher sharing time. After the teacher's SSW period, he or she is ready to move on to making individual "house calls" and working with students in private editing sessions.

Children largely move at their own pace during writing workshop activities and select from the four alternatives. In the *prewriting, drafting, and revising* option, children may choose topics for narratives, gather resources and references, conduct interviews, or create an outline for organizing their stories, and eventually produce a draft.

Once children finish their first drafts, they are ready to sign up for a *peer conference*. Peer conferences are small groups of children, usually three or four, who sign up to read each other's first drafts and make recommendations for revisions. Peer conferences are sometimes known as *teacherless writing groups* because the teacher is not involved during this analysis phase unless invited by the group for consulting purposes.

Teachers have told us that some students learning the Writing Workshop system want peer conference almost all the time. This can be problematic because a goal of comprehensive instruction is to promote peer collaboration and cooperation. One solution is to establish guidelines differentiating peer conferences from what might be termed "one-minute conferences." When children need a quick opinion on their composition, they can usually arrange a one-minute conference with a peer. Students should not require more than three one-minute conferences during a workshop activity period.

Group etiquette rules for student interactions should be established early in the school year to ensure maximum productivity and to minimize conflicts. Role-playing is one way to form group-developed rules. (Remember the teachers who made a videotape acting out positive and negative group behavior in the Reading Workshop section.) Students themselves also have no problem coming up with a list of their own group etiquette rules, which function well in all group experiences.

A word regarding classroom noise levels seems warranted. Whenever teachers begin to experiment with modes of learning that allow children to work on their own or in small groups, the noise level will invariably go up. This may be distressing at first for some teachers, but this issue can be addressed. If the class becomes unruly, then appropriate steps must be taken to maintain class control. More often than not, however, the increase in classroom noise should be viewed as the sound of learning and creative interaction. Silvia Ashton-Warner (1963) refers to this kind of classroom hubbub as "peaceful noise."

Once the peer conference group meets and considers each child's manuscript, suggestions are made for improving the writing project. Of course, authors are free to accept or reject their suggestions. Thus, manuscript revisions follow the peer conference in preparation for the editing session with the teacher.

Editing sessions are special times for students to meet with the teacher to discuss their writing project and receive independent skill instruction or coaching. To take part in the editing session, children sign up the day before the conference and submit a copy of their writing project. This allows teachers time to read the composition and prepare notes for the student the evening before (there goes your social life!). Avoid writing directly on the composition. Instead, remarks should be made on a separate sheet of paper or a stick-on note to prevent defacing the project. When examining some narrative compositions, it may be a good idea to refer to a story grammar outline to make sure all-important elements have been included. Semantic and syntactic considerations should also be discussed.

After the editing session, students frequently need to edit or revise further before publishing. It may be desirable for the student and teacher to have an additional editing session to go over modifications before publishing. A visit to the *publishing center* to put the writing project into final form is the last stop.

Peer conferences are a means for helping students learn to help each other instead of having total dependence on the teacher.

Role-playing is a great way to help students write group etiquette rules.

One final point—*publishing* does not necessarily happen with every writing project. Sometimes a student will say to the teacher, "I'm running out of interest for this story. May I work on another one?" Most writers occasionally run out of gas during a project and start a new one. Some may have several projects in process. It is not the number of publications a child produces during a given period that is important, but the process itself. Although it is desirable for the child to reach closure on a regular basis with writing projects, it does not have to happen every time.

Phase 5: Sharing Time (5 to 10 Minutes)

The Writing Workshop concludes with student *sharing time* or publishing. This period is for sharing and publishing completed writing projects. Children proceed to sharing time only with the approval of the teacher after an editing session.

Even students who may be publishing their writing project outside of class (e.g., putting their book in the school library or submitting their story to a children's magazine) should take part in sharing time. This allows other children to see their finished product and enjoy the story. The most common format for sharing time for students is the *author's chair* experience, where students sit before the group and share their newest composition.

Classroom Computers and Writing Development

When teachers think of computers, word processing often comes to mind. *Word processing* is a general term for software programs that permit someone to write, edit, store, and print text (Strickland, Feeley, & Wepner, 1987, p. 13). In addition to standard word processing packages for elementary and upper elementary-age students, other related computer software programs are available that help students develop as writers.

Because computer software programs come and go so rapidly, it is very difficult to make specific recommendations. Professional publications in the literacy field, such as *The Reading Teacher, Reading Research and Instruction* and *Language Arts* and product journals like *MacWorld* frequently have product reviews that can help guide your decisions. We offer only a brief sampling of writing programs that help students develop and extend their authoring abilities. *Bank Street Writer* is a pioneering effort that is both easy to use and affordable. It is suggested for grades 3 and up. *MacWrite* is the oldest text-processing program for the Macintosh computer and remains one that all Macs can open. Version 4.6 (or even 5), bundled with Mac computers to model SE, remains a very useful format, even with its size limit (*MacWrite 4.6* files can't exceed 64 KB).

IBM's Writing to Read 2000

Writing to Read 2000 is the next generation of IBM's landmark product—*Writing to Read.* It is a beginning reading–writing program based on a modified alphabet idea (one symbol for each of 42 language sounds) for kindergarten and first grade. It was developed by John Henry Martin, a retired teacher and school administrator. The typical routine, usually 30 to 40 minutes per day, takes children through a five-station rotation in a special computer lab. Students begin with the computer station, where they are taught to type 42 phonemes (representing the English language sounds) using color images and synthesized speech. These lessons are repeated in a work jour-

Writing to Read 2000 is a beginning reading-writing program.

nal, then students listen to a tape-recorded story while following along in a book in the listening library. These activities are followed by a typing–writing center, in which students can write compositions of their own choosing. The final center is called "make words," where other reinforcement activities are practiced.

Writing to Read 2000 includes a component called the Computer Center, where "cycle words" teach young children sound/letter relationships. Four other centers support and encourage children to practice these associations using a variety of activities, including work journals, manipulatives, books, and writing. Other components in the new program follow:

- a writing/typing center program called *Write Along*
- graphical menus, audio support, and mouse, enabling easy and independent navigation for young students
- context rhymes that introduce "cycle words"
- teacher options, which include bookmaking, partner support, student management, and reporting information
- a *Writing to Read 2000 Game Board* and assortment of games, puzzles, and manipulatives
- a collection of 23 age-appropriate children's literature books, 16 accompanied by natural, expressive voice cassette recordings
- a teacher's guide that provides cross-curricular connections, curriculum integration, and thematic unit suggestions

LEARNERS WITH SPECIAL NEEDS

Focus on English Language Learners

More and more students in U.S. and Canadian schools speak English as a second language (Reutzel & Cooter, 1999). Helping these **English language learners** (ELL) learn to read and write proficiently in English is critical. Until recently, few books on teaching and learning have attended to the English as a second language (ESL) risk factor (Gunderson, 1991; Fitzgerald, 1995). Many teachers find themselves seeking guidance to promote literacy success for ELL students (Boyle & Peregoy, 1990; Fitzgerald, 1993, 1994, 1995).

In an ideal world, students would become fluent speakers, readers, writers, and listeners in their first language, *then* acquire those same skills in English. Although there have been attempts to do just that in many places, the reality is that there are simply not enough certified bilingual teachers to go around. For instance, the Dallas (Texas) Independent School District estimated that some 600 additional bilingual teachers are needed to adequately staff all classrooms with significant ELL populations (Cooter, 1999). The situation is similar in major urban districts in the West and Southwest regions of the United States. Thus, we must find ways to help ELL students succeed with the tools at our disposal.

It is important to remember that ELL students acquire receptive (listening, reading) and expressive (writing, speaking) skills in the same basic ways as monolingual students. These methods of learning include

- developing classification systems from the most basic to the very complex.
- increasing the length of utterances in both spoken and written forms, beginning with short and simple and gradually growing to the more complex.

There is a major shortage of qualified bilingual teachers to work with ELL populations.

- learning "language labels" for concrete objects and experiences they have had.
- the inclusion of immersion (i.e., modeling) and learning-by-doing (i.e., guided and independent practice) activities as the primary methods of language development.

Strategies for helping ELL students can also help monolingual students develop listening and speaking vocabularies.

Following are some suggestions for helping ELL students succeed. These ideas are also quite useful for assisting monolingual students who have underdeveloped language skills. These suggestions are adapted from a chapter in our activities book for teachers, *Strategies for Reading Assessment and Instruction: Helping Every Child Succeed,* 2nd Edition (Reutzel & Cooter, 2003).

Environmental Print

Using printed matter from the world outside the school enables second language learners to view their own lives, circumstances, and cultural contexts as places for learning and applying their evolving knowledge of English as a second language. Signs, billboards, storefronts, bus schedules, and displays in the everyday lives of ELL students can provide personally relevant bridges from learning English in the school classroom to learning and using English beyond the classroom. The use of environmental print has proven worthwhile for developing both first and second language oral and written skills among younger learners (Hiebert & Ham, 1981).

Students can make collections of environmental print they can read by storing these items in scrapbooks, files, or envelopes. Students can use these easily recognizable print items to compose books, sentences, or other written texts. Bulletin boards can be filled with environmental print items. Some teachers organize environmental print items into alphabetical categories to practice alphabet knowledge. Environmental print items are inexpensive and provide wide access to print beyond the boundaries of school classrooms.

Sentence Strips

Notice how sentence strips can be used to increase awareness of common English sentence patterns.

Dictated sentences recorded on sentence strips can be used to further develop awareness of English sentence patterns (Gunderson, 1991). Sentence strips are especially useful for teaching second language learners because the length of the text is limited, and they provide basic examples of the most rudimentary meaningful units in language. You will need colored marking pens, masking tape for hanging the strips on the wall, and pre-cut sentence strips (which can be purchased in a variety of colors from a teacher-supply store). Another useful tool is a wall sentence strip hanger, shown in Figure 12.26. Storing and displaying sentence strips can present some opportunities for classroom teachers to encourage incidental language learning. For example, constructing a wall hanger for sentence strips provides just such an opportunity. When composing sentence strips, teachers initially dictate the sentences, but students should be invited to dictate their own as soon as they seem willing. Using words drawn from student word banks (discussed in Chapter 7) can serve as a rich resource for building sentences from known and familiar language. In addition, using words from a word bank allows students to manipulate words and sentences and provides a record of language development.

Sentence strips can be copied and stored by punching a hole in the upper right-hand corner of each strip and hanging them on a cup hook, hanger, or peg on the wall. Later, sentence strips can be copied from stories and literature the children are

Figure 12.26 Sentence strip wall hanger

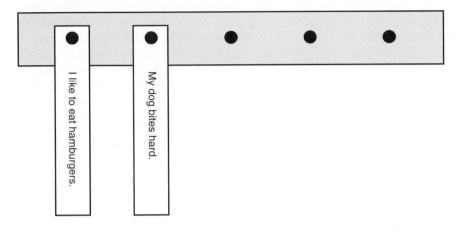

reading. Students can be invited to trace over these sentence strips or copy the sentences onto a space on the strips directly beneath the original sentence.

One way of using sentence strips with ELL students is to have the teacher tell students that they will practice reading in English today. The teacher then writes the sentence onto a sentence strip as students watch: "I like to eat hamburgers!" Then the teacher says, while pointing to the sentence, "This says I like to eat hamburgers!" Next, the teacher points to the sentence strip and asks, "What does this say?" The student responds with the text written on the sentence strip. Students are then encouraged to share their sentence strips with others by reading them or inviting others to read their sentence strips.

Active Listening

Reading researchers (Walters & Gunderson, 1985; Blum, 1995) have discovered reading achievement benefits for ELL students listening to stories read aloud in their first and second languages. In some studies, the stories were simply read aloud by volunteers, whereas in others they were prerecorded on cassette tapes. One of the many benefits cited was that students with Limited English Proficiency (LEP) and an ability to read in the first language learned how terms from the first and second languages translate. Stories, poems, jokes, riddles, or other enticing texts to be read aloud, as always, are the starting point. Adult language models for the read-aloud experiences can be accomplished either through a volunteer program and/or by using prerecorded audiotapes.

For some beginning students, wordless picture books are a good place to begin, as long as the content is not too young for the students. Read the story or share the book in small, preplanned sections. Students can be asked later to dictate a story to match the pictures. The dictation can be typed on the computer by the teacher or a volunteer and printed in a font that resembles common book type (we recommend the fonts *Times, New Roman,* or *Helvetica*). The words can be tape recorded so that students can return to the book later and hear their own dictated language retelling the story based on the pictures.

When using books selected for read aloud, stop reading aloud at strategic points and ask students, "What do you think might happen next?" As a follow-up question, ask students to explain why they think a particular event will take place next in the story.

Audiotaped books can aid ELL students at home in becoming active listeners.

A slightly different version of Active Listening was employed in a study by Blum (1995), where ELL students were provided audiotaped books to extend their classroom literacy instruction into the home context. Books were recorded onto audiotapes by English-speaking adults at a pace that would allow beginning readers to follow along. For turning pages, three seconds were allowed after hearing a sound signaling the need to turn the page. Tape recorders and an electric cord were furnished by the school. Each night, ELL students were allowed to check out a backpack with the tape recorder, cord, book(s) and accompanying audiotape(s). Active listening procedures were followed in listening to the audiotaped books at home. Blum (1995) found that all ESL learners received substantial benefit from active listening at home.

Personal Dictionaries

Personal dictionaries are helpful for increasing the reading and writing vocabularies of both ELL and monolingual students.

For more proficient second language users and for older students, a personal dictionary can be developed to record spellings of words and/or word meanings in English. When younger students demonstrate limited fluency and proficiency in the second language, or when younger or older students begin to ask questions about how English words are spelled or about specific word meanings, they are ready to construct a personal dictionary (Gunderson, 1991). Personal dictionaries can be simple or elaborate in construction. They can be fixed in terms of numbers of pages, or flexible, allowing for more pages to be added with increased language acquisition. But one thing is certain: Personal dictionaries are well worth the effort.

To construct personal dictionaries, students will need a spiral or loose-leaf bound notebook, various drawing media such as crayons, markers, and colored pencils, tabs for marking alphabetic divisions, and (possibly) laminating material for flimsy covers. In the beginning, students will need help setting up their dictionaries and learning how to make entries. Later, when students approach the teacher about how to spell a word or to find out what it means, the teacher can help students become more independent learners by encouraging the use of their personal dictionary.

Standards Note
Standard 5.3: The reading professional will be able to model and discuss reading and writing as valuable, lifelong activities. As you prepare to read about involving families, you are, of course, aware of the powerful influence you have—in some cases, you are the most reliable, stable adult role model in your students' lives. Think further about how you can capitalize upon your position as a "literacy advocate."

Hints about how words begin and listening to the order of the sounds in words can help students figure out the potential spelling of words as well as where to record words in their personal dictionaries. When a student learns a new word he wants to remember from reading or everyday life, he can be invited to write the new word in the dictionary, with a picture and a sentence explaining its meaning. Then, when a student asks how to spell a word or what a word means, teachers can often say, "It's in your personal dictionary!" Making and using a personal dictionary helps students assume more control over their own learning and develop a real spirit of independence in accessing language for their use in reading and writing.

INVOLVING FAMILIES

If we are to maximize the learning potential of every child, we must enlist the aid of family members (Cooter, 2003). We cannot afford to overlook the needs, strengths, contributions, and perspectives that family members can bring to school programs (Handel, 1999, p. 127). Recognition of adult family members as a valuable resource is evident nowadays in such federal legislation as the 1998 Reading Excellence Act, the Workforce Investment Act, and President Bush's No Child Left Behind Act.

Refrigerator Reading

Communication with families is critical. Many times adults will say to teachers, "I would love to help my child become a better reader. . . . I just don't know what to do. Can you help me?" Cooter and others (1999) found that monthly newsletters for families are a great vehicle for communicating easy-to-do activities to primary caregivers. Theirs is called **Refrigerator Reading,** a reference to the age-old practice of putting important school papers on the refrigerator for everyone to see.

Refrigerator Reading newsletters are typically put together on a computer, then photocopied for each child to take home. Thus, you will need access to a computer, printer, and photocopier. The idea is to send home tips for parents on ways they can help their child develop in reading and writing. If you have many English Language Learners (ELL), your newsletter may need to be written on one side in English, and in the native tongue of your learners on the opposite side.

You can include such areas as helping your child self-select high-interest books using the rule of thumb method, how parents can do read aloud activities at home, how to encourage recreational writing, ways to be a good listener when children read, conducting retellings, questioning after reading, study tips, ways to become involved in your child's classroom as a volunteer, and humorous tales about school life (like one principal's "No whining" rule).

Reports from Cooter and his colleagues (1999) are that some parents collect *Refrigerator Reading* newsletters and mail copies to grandmas and new moms, confirming the usefulness of this easy-to-do medium.

Family Projects

Andrea Burkhart (2000), a teacher at a school on the south side of Chicago, asked parents to help her come up with ideas for family–school projects. They responded with many great ideas that she incorporated into her curriculum as *family projects* that get adults at home actively involved.

First of all, you should plan on constructing a monthly newsletter with a full description of the family project assignment and "deliverables" (products you would like for the students to bring to school when the project is done). Sometimes parents are willing to come in with their child to present their product! Figure 12.27 is an outline of the topics Burkhart (2000) developed for her class. You will want to adapt and expand the descriptions to suit your needs and fit grade-level expectations.

Voice Mail

Many teachers have access to their school district's voice mail system and usually have their own account/number. Willman (2000), a remedial reading teacher, uses voice mail during the summer break to keep contact with her students. They report back to her verbally about books they have chosen to read, and parents are often involved. We feel this strategy could be used throughout the school year, as well as during summers for developing readers.

Begin by creating a letter to the parents explaining how the assignment will work, how to access the voice mail system, and your expectations. If you will be using this activity during the school year (as opposed to summer only), plan on conducting this briefing in-person at the first open house of the school year.

Figure 12.27   Family projects curriculum (Burkhart, 2000)

September: Family Tree
Parents and students work together to trace their family roots. They should create a visual display and present an object that reflects their family history, such as an antique picture, clothing, food, music, or literature.

October: Weather
Parents and students predict weather patterns for the next month. They will watch weather reports to compare their predictions and keep track of their work in a journal.

November: Family Reading Month
Parents and students read to or with each other daily. The books read and the amount of time spent reading will be recorded in a daily log and turned in at the end of November.

December: Biographies
Students learn about biographies and how they are constructed in class. They then create interview questions and interview a parent or primary caregiver. Students write a biography of that person and share it with their family.

January: Measurement
Parents and students predict the measurement (length, width, area, etc.) of an object or distance two or three times each week. After actually measuring each object, a journal entry is completed showing the predicted measurement and the actual measurement.

February: Poetry Month
A book of family poetry is created. Students are responsible for educating their families about poetry, collecting the poems, and compiling them into a book.

March: Plants
Each student will take home two plants in milk cartons. The student will care for one, and an adult family member the other. One plant will be given light and the other plant will not. The child and adult together will track the progress of each plant and recorded their progress in a journal entry regularly.

April: Decisions
Two or three times per week students will take home a proposed (hypothetical) question that requires a decision. Topics might include issues related to drugs, gangs, honesty, or others proposed by parents. The parent and child will discuss options together and create a written response.

May: Simple Machines
After learning about simple machines in class, students will construct a simple machine with the guidance of a parent.

Willman (2000) asked students to call in to the voice mail and read aloud for three minutes or summarize a chapter from the book they were reading. You should have specific questions for each book for student response. They can answer these questions when they call in to read. Another adaptation is for students to call in to the school's homework hotline to hear the teacher read aloud portions of the book. This provides a fluent reading model for students. However, a better idea is for parents to read aloud a portion of the book regularly for their child.

Willman (2000) reported that the summer voice mail program succeeded in its inaugural year in preventing all remedial readers from losing ground (26), and one student actually increased his reading level by a half year.

Buddy Journals

Buddy journals (Klobukowski, 2000) are a version of reading logs. Students and parents read the same book together, silently or orally (whatever works best), then respond to each other in a journal. Parents often make superb models of fluent reading and respond well to this activity.

The procedure is simple. The adult family member and child each read the selected book, or portions of the book, then respond in their journals. The adult and child swap journals, read the entry and respond to the entry. Here are some further suggestions from Klobukowski (2000):

- Encourage parents to reread portions of the text orally, if they aren't already reading the book aloud, so that the child can have a reading role model.
- When parents are making entries in their buddy journal, ask them to relate what happened to book characters to themselves and their family and help their child understand these connections.
- Encourage both parents and students to identify the feelings of the characters and share in their journals what they think the characters should do.
- Ask parents to help their child find information in the text and clarify for them any misunderstandings they detect in the buddy journal entries.
- Urge parents to give their child lots of positive reinforcement and praise for what they can do and to avoid negative criticism.
- Parents should try to include humor in their responses.

Let parents know that this activity will work best if there is an appointed time to complete the task at home. This avoids last minute rushes to complete a "homework" assignment.

Buddy journals are an excellent way to involve parents in their children's reading education.

Summary

Reading and writing are closely related processes that have a reciprocal developmental influence. Comprehensive reading programs depend heavily on these processes for overall language development. Several organizational schemes for reading instruction were suggested: the Reading Workshop, core books, and themed literature units. The Reading Workshop is a comprehensive scheme that can be used with either basal readers or trade books. Core book units use a single book as the focal point of the reading curriculum and as a springboard for other reading and writing experiences. Themed literature units are similar to core book units, but students have the added advantage of choice between several books to be read.

The writing process approach helps students learn composition skills similar to those of professional writers. Children learn and progress through a series of writing process stages with each composition: prewriting, drafting, revising, editing, and publishing.

Concept Applications

In the Classroom

1. Develop a themed literature unit using one of the following themes: *courage, relationships, discovering new worlds, changes,* or *animals.* Your plans should include a web of the unit, a list of books chosen from

Check your understanding of chapter concepts by using the self assessment for Chapter 12 on our Companion Website at www.prenhall.com/ reutzel.

popular children's literature, possible reading strategies to be taught in teacher-directed sessions, and suggested ideas for literature-response activities.

2. Develop plans for your own Writing Workshop. Sketch out how you will manage the program within the constraints of a typical classroom environment. What physical facilities (furniture, space) will you need? Draw up a series of lesson plans for demonstrating or modeling to your class how the Writing Workshop will work.

3. Using the section in this chapter on Reading Workshops, map out plans and materials needed to get started. Identify children's literature to be used, sources of ideas for prereading activities and literature-response projects, and materials to be used in literature-response groups.

4. Prepare an annotated bibliography of software available for either Macintosh or PC computers that could be helpful in reading and writing instruction. You should first develop a list of criteria by which each program can be judged, then evaluate the programs accordingly. Use the Internet to locate the latest product information.

In the Field

1. Develop a writing and publishing center for your classroom. It should have a variety of writing instruments, different kinds of paper, an assortment of envelopes, and materials useful for binding stories into books. Solicit parent volunteers to help staff the station on selected days to assist students.

Recommended Readings

Atwell, N. (1987). *In the middle: Writing, reading, and learning with adolescents.* Portsmouth, NH: Heinemann.

Calkins, L. M. (1994). *The art of teaching writing,* (new Ed.) Portsmouth, NH: Heinemann.

Calkins, L. M., & Harwayne, S. (1987). *The writing workshop: A world of difference* (Video). Portsmouth, NH: Heinemann.

Cooter, R. B. (2003). The Texas two-step model: Emphasis on schema-building. Unpublished manuscript, Fort Worth, TX.

Cooter, R. B., Mills-House, E., Marrin, P., Mathews, B., & Campbell, S. (1999). Family and community involvement: The bedrock of reading success. *The Reading Teacher, 52*(8), 891–896.

Fader, D. N. (1976). *The new hooked on books.* New York: Berkley.

Tompkins, G. E. (1994). *Teaching writing: Balancing process and product,* 2nd ed. Upper Saddle River, NJ: Merrill/Prentice Hall.

13 Reading in the Middle School

Focus Questions

When you are finished studying this chapter, you should be able to answer these questions:

1. How do narrative texts and expository texts differ in purpose?

2. What effect does concept load have on the readability of content reading assignments?

3. What are the different expository text patterns used in textbook chapters or units of study?

4. How does one analyze a unit of study in terms of essential information to be conveyed to students?

5. What is an anticipation guide? Why might you choose to use one in a content class?

6. What are some specific efficient reading and study strategies that can be taught within the context of content instruction?

7. What accommodations can be made for struggling readers to help them succeed in content area classrooms?

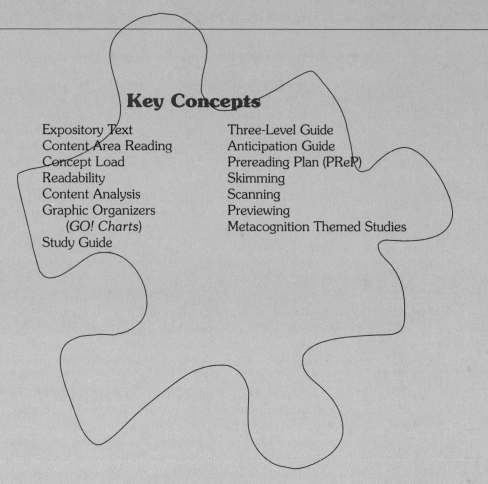

Key Concepts

Expository Text
Content Area Reading
Concept Load
Readability
Content Analysis
Graphic Organizers
    (*GO! Charts*)
Study Guide

Three-Level Guide
Anticipation Guide
Prereading Plan (PReP)
Skimming
Scanning
Previewing
Metacognition Themed Studies

As students make the move from elementary to middle school, they enter a very challenging phase of literacy learning. In the best case scenario, students have become reasonably fluent in reading and are ready to explore in greater detail the myriad subjects offered in their content classes (i.e., the sciences, social studies, mathematics, the arts). As is often said of typical middle schoolers, they have *learned to read* and now *read to learn*.

Visit Chapter 13 of our Companion Website at www.prenhall.com/ reutzel to look into the chapter objectives, standards and principles, and pertinent web links associated with Reading in the Middle School.

CAN YOU ALWAYS BELIEVE WHAT YOU READ?

Willie Barton has taught ninth-grade social studies at Overton High School for eight years and loves his profession. This past summer Mr. Barton signed up for a course on content area reading at the local university and came back to work with new ideas for his students. A favorite unit of study that underwent some redesign pertained to higher-order thinking about social studies in news accounts—discerning author bias and propaganda, to be specific.

The news unit he has designed for this fall uses stories about the same subject as reported by four sources: National Public Radio (NPR), National Geographic magazine, the Washington Times newspaper, and Woodn't You Know (a publication for the lumber industry). The story covered by all four sources was the same—a discussion about the future of rainforests in South America.

Mr. Barton began, "Many people are interested in the future of rain forests in South America, sometimes for quite divergent reasons. This is a splendid topic for us to consider as we look at propaganda in news reports. Theoretically, news accounts are supposed to be unbiased—just report the facts of a situation. Sometimes, however, the reporter is seemingly unable, or unwilling, to keep his or her own biases out of the account. In fact, some people feel that news reporters deliberately report the news in such a way as to sway readers and listeners to their point of view. I believe that is sometimes the case. I also think that you can anticipate bias from certain sources because of their pattern of bias over time. For instance, National Public Radio (NPR) and the New York Times are generally considered to be more liberal in their leanings than some news sources. Likewise, the Washington Times and the New Republic are considered more conservative in their writing. In general, liberal reporters on an issue like rain forests tend to favor conservation and protection of natural resources. Conservatives, on the other hand, tend to favor more pragmatic and economic interests. Both certainly have some valid points.

"One way reporters use their forum to persuade is through the use of meaning-laden words. Another tactic reporters use to sway opinion is through their focus. They attend to only one part of the story so that the consumer feels that it is the most important element. With these two tools—use of vocabulary and topic focus—reporters can provide us with quite different points of view for the very same event."

Mr. Barton then pointed to four enlarged quotes from news accounts on rain forests printed on poster board and displayed on the right-hand sidewall of the classroom for convenient viewing. Each was quite short— just a few sentences. Certain words were underlined in the first example for emphasis. Here is what the first two excerpts said:

SOURCE 1

Hope for the Masses in South American Rain Forests

. . . As one farmer said, "Now that the rain forests are being harvested, there is hope for my grandchildren, they will have land to farm!"

SOURCE 2

Destruction of South American Rain Forests: Another Harbinger of Environmental Collapse

"Many fear that unrestrained disforestation aids in global warming and a reduction in the supply of fresh oxygen worldwide."

Mr. Barton continued, "Let's first take a look at the vocabulary and focus of the first example. The vocabulary that gives us some ideas as to what the bias or 'slant' might be are underlined: hope, masses, harvested, and farm. Notice first that the word 'hope' appears twice; a very positive tone, don't you think? Then the words 'harvested' and 'farm' appear giving a sense of good American values and jobs. When coupled with the word 'masses' in the title, suggesting economic prosperity for a large group of South Americans, then it is not too difficult to figure out from where this writer is coming. I think it is from one of our more conservative publications." The students nodded in assent.

"Now I'd like for you to get into your 'Paper Chase Groups' and read over the quote from Source 2, and be ready to share the vocabulary and focus you feel bring bias to the quote. Please be ready to report your thoughts in about five minutes with the rest of us."

HELPING STUDENTS SUCCEED WITH CONTENT READING MATERIALS

For students still acquiring basic reading abilities, content classes can be a formidable hurdle. One writer points out that reading problems in the middle school become *viral,* attacking student confidence and severely limiting their academic progress (K. S. Cooter, 1999). The job of teaching reading at this level also becomes more rigorous because the stakes are higher. Jeanne S. Chall of Harvard University wrote:

> The public has become more conscious about the importance of literacy, for students and for adults. . . . The reading achievement of too many children, young people, and adults, is not up to what it should be. . . . The students of low-income families and students of all social levels who are predisposed to having reading difficulty—are not doing as well as they can. . . . They need excellent teachers. (1998, pp. 20, 22)

In this chapter, we take a look at ways teachers can help students succeed with the subject area materials commonly found in the middle school. We'll learn about the unique ways subject area texts are written and the reading demands placed on this group of youngsters. Before closing this final chapter of our book, we also consider ways of helping struggling readers.

WHY CONTENT READING IS SO CHALLENGING FOR SOME STUDENTS: THE NATURE OF EXPOSITORY TEXTS

There are at least four different kinds of informational text commonly found in the middle school: *argumentation, description, exposition,* and *narration.* The majority of these readings are informational or **expository texts.** For the middle school

Standard Note
Standard 7.5: The reading professional will be able to ensure that students can use various aspects of text to gain comprehension, including conventions of written English, *text structures* ... As you read the chapter, list the features of expository text that are "considerate" to the reader. List strategies that teachers can employ to ensure that readers do take advantage of these text structures.

Content area reading is the field of study that deals with applying reading skills in expository texts (Cooter & Flynt, 1996).

Middle school students benefit from learning a variety of skills to help them comprehend the diversity of content they will encounter in expository texts.

teacher, formal reading instruction focuses on successful strategies for reading and comprehending expository texts, study skills, and efficient, or "speed," reading strategies. The field that deals with applying reading skills in expository texts is known as **content area reading** (Cooter & Flynt, 1996).

Unlike the stories, or *narrative texts,* commonly used in beginning reading instruction, expository texts have unique organizational patterns. Explaining new ideas to others is a different form of language than storytelling, so different styles must be used to get important points across to the learner. Hence, different writing and reading techniques are employed in content area reading materials.

In this section, we begin with a discussion of the text demands that tend to make reading subject area materials challenging for adolescent readers, such as increased concept load and readability considerations. We then examine the writing patterns or structures commonly used in expository texts.

Specialized Vocabulary and Concepts

A formidable task for every middle school teacher is helping students learn previously unknown concepts and vocabulary. Vocabulary knowledge is developmental and based on background experiences (Heilman, Blair, & Rupley, 2001). Teachers need to lead their students through four levels of vocabulary knowledge—*listening, speaking, reading,* and *writing*—if new content or "specialized" vocabulary is to become part of their permanent memory.

Listening vocabulary, the largest of the four vocabularies, is made up of all words people can hear and understand, which includes not only the words we use in our everyday speech but also those words we can understand only when used in context. For instance, while listening to an evening news report, a child in sixth grade may hear about the latest breakthrough in cancer research. Although the youngster may be able to hear and understand the news report, he or she probably would not

There are four levels of vocabulary knowledge: listening, speaking, reading, and writing.

be able to reproduce the specialized medical terms used (e.g., *carcinomas, metastasis, chemotherapy*). Some have speculated that students entering first grade may have a listening vocabulary of around 20,000 words.

The second level of vocabulary knowledge is called the *speaking vocabulary,* consisting of words we can hear and understand and also use in our everyday speech. The third level of vocabulary knowledge is called *reading vocabulary.* These are words we can hear and understand, use as part of our speech communications, and recognize in print. The final level, *writing vocabulary,* is made up of words we can understand on all levels—listening, speaking, reading, and written communications. In teaching new technical vocabulary like that found in typical content readings, a primary goal is to bring students through each of these levels of vocabulary knowledge.

Students Need "Hands-On" Learning Experiences

The best way to teach students about new ideas is through concrete, or hands-on, experience. For example, if one wanted to teach students from rural Wyoming about life in New York City, the most effective way would be to take them there for a visit. Similarly, the very best way one could teach students about the space shuttle would be to put them through astronaut training and then send them into space on a future mission. Obviously, neither of these experiences is feasible in today's schools, so we must seek the best concrete experiences within our reach as teachers.

The best way to teach new ideas and vocabulary is through "hands-on" experience.

Some educators (Dale, 1969; Estes & Vaughan, 1978) have suggested hierarchies for typical classroom activities, ranging from concrete to abstract experiences. Such hierarchies help prospective teachers select concept and vocabulary development activities of a more concrete nature, and they help practicing teachers review their past practices for evaluative and curriculum redesign purposes. We have developed a composite version of these hierarchies, which is presented in Figure 13.1. Notice that as one ascends toward the top of the *classroom experiences pyramid,* activities become more concrete and thus easier for students to assimilate.

Studies indicate that effective vocabulary development in content classes seems to have three important properties in common (Nagy, 1988): (1) integration of new words with known experiences and concepts, (2) sufficient repetition so that students will recognize words as they read, and (3) meaningful use of new words brought about through stimulating practice experiences. In light of these requirements, we offer several examples of vocabulary development activities for whole-group and individual teaching situations later in this chapter.

Think of ways you could integrate Nagy's (1988) vocabulary development suggestions into a lesson on a science topic of your choice.

Increased Concept Load

Concept load (also called *concept density*) has to do with the number of new ideas and amount of technical vocabulary introduced by an author (Singer & Donlan, 1989); sentences of equal length may, in fact, require very different comprehension skills from a reader. Expository reading materials found in content classrooms are often much more difficult to understand than narrative/story readings because of greater concept load (Harris & Sipay, 1990), because story writers usually present information gradually and build to a conclusion or climax. Elements such as setting, plot, and characterization are laced with information quite familiar to most readers. Expository writers, however, usually present new and abstract information unfamiliar to the reader, which requires the building of new schemas or memory structures in the brain. Authors who introduce several new concepts in a single sentence (high concept load) create a situation that is extremely difficult for all but the best readers.

Concept load *is the number of new ideas introduced by an author.*

Figure 13.1   Pyramid of classroom experiences

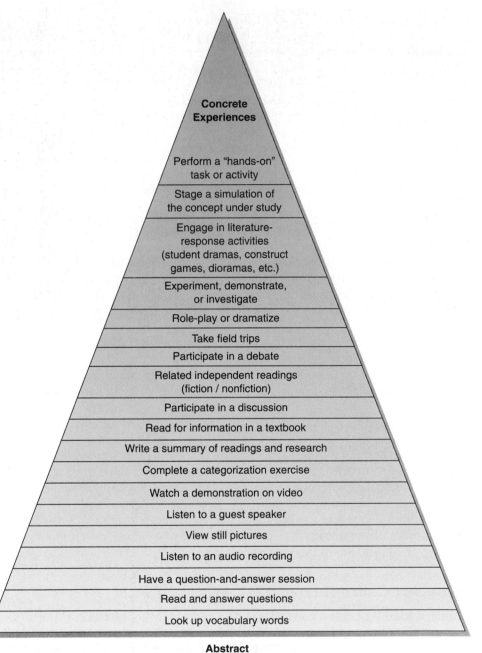

Teachers should consider concept load when they think about ordering new learning materials. High concept load reading materials can create a major obstacle for readers lacking in fluency. One alternative to selecting conceptually dense textbooks is to select several smaller books that concentrate on just a few topics and cover them in some depth. If this option is not possible, the teacher can have students read through materials in dyads (groups of two) and write summaries of key points using good paragraph structure to flesh things out: a topic sentence, which tells the key idea; supporting sentences, which explain the key idea in greater detail; several examples; and a closing summarizing sentence.

Readability Considerations

Another concern of teachers preparing content material for instruction is text difficulty or **readability.** Text difficulty is most often measured using a *readability formula.* The purpose of a readability formula is to assign a grade-level equivalent, or approximate difficulty level, to narrative or expository reading material used to teach children. Sentence length and complexity of vocabulary are two elements often measured in readability formulas.

Readability formulas help teachers judge the difficulty of reading materials.

A number of readability formulas are available for classroom use. The Fry (1977) readability formula (Figure 13.2) is one of the more popular formulas available and bases its estimates on sentence and word length. Another formula, which is significantly quicker and easier to use (Baldwin & Kaufman, 1979), is the Raygor (1977) readability graph (Figure 13.3); instead of having to count the number of syllables contained in a 100-word passage, teachers merely count the number of words having six or more letters.

The problem with readability formulas in general is that they are simplistic and too narrow in scope; many factors determine whether or not students can read a given passage effectively. Klare (1963) concluded that some 289 factors influence readability, 20 of which were found to be significant. Typical readability formulas, such as the Fry (1977) and Raygor (1977), account for only two factors. An important factor affecting both readability and comprehension is interest (Cooter, 1994). If a student is highly interested in a subject, say cooking, then words such as *cuisine, parfait, pastry, pasta,* and *guacamole* likely will be immediately recognizable, even if the text is found to be several years above the student's so-called reading level. Another student at the same point of reading development who is not interested in cooking may find the same words incomprehensible. This is so because interest in a subject usually corresponds directly to a student's background and vocabulary knowledge in that subject area. In summary, readability formulas may be helpful in determining a very general difficulty level, but they should not be considered anything more than a gross estimate.

Unique Writing Patterns

Narrative texts are organized using a story grammar scheme using such common elements as *setting, theme, characterization, plot,* and *resolution.* Expository text, however, is quite different: Its structure tends to be much more compact, detailed, and explanatory (Heilman et al., 2001). Five common expository text structures have been described by Meyer and Freedle (1984): *description, collection, causation, problem/solution,* and *comparison.* When preparing to teach units in the content areas, teachers need to establish which expository text structures are used and organize for instruction accordingly. Meyer and Freedle's (1984) five expository text patterns are described, along with examples taken from content textbooks:

Just as narrative (story) passages use distinct writing patterns, expository texts have five distinct patterns that are commonly used.

Description: Explains something about a topic or presents a characteristic or setting for a topic.

Decimals are another way to write fractions when the denominators are 10, 100, and so on.
(From Merrill Mathematics *[Grade 5], 1985, p. 247)*

Figure 13.2 The Fry readability formula

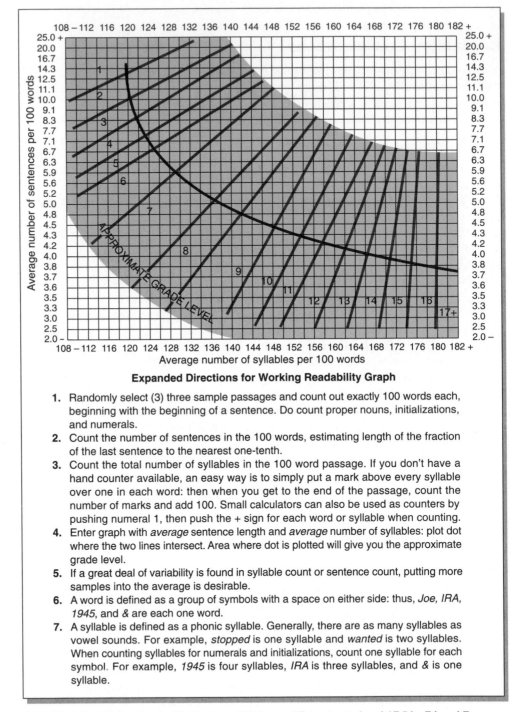

Expanded Directions for Working Readability Graph

1. Randomly select (3) three sample passages and count out exactly 100 words each, beginning with the beginning of a sentence. Do count proper nouns, initializations, and numerals.
2. Count the number of sentences in the 100 words, estimating length of the fraction of the last sentence to the nearest one-tenth.
3. Count the total number of syllables in the 100 word passage. If you don't have a hand counter available, an easy way is to simply put a mark above every syllable over one in each word: then when you get to the end of the passage, count the number of marks and add 100. Small calculators can also be used as counters by pushing numeral 1, then push the + sign for each word or syllable when counting.
4. Enter graph with *average* sentence length and *average* number of syllables: plot dot where the two lines intersect. Area where dot is plotted will give you the approximate grade level.
5. If a great deal of variability is found in syllable count or sentence count, putting more samples into the average is desirable.
6. A word is defined as a group of symbols with a space on either side: thus, *Joe, IRA, 1945*, and *&* are each one word.
7. A syllable is defined as a phonic syllable. Generally, there are as many syllables as vowel sounds. For example, *stopped* is one syllable and *wanted* is two syllables. When counting syllables for numerals and initializations, count one syllable for each symbol. For example, *1945* is four syllables, *IRA* is three syllables, and *&* is one syllable.

From "Fry's Readability Graph: Clarifications, Validity, and Extension to Level 17," by Edward Fry, 1977, *Journal of Reading, 21,* pp. 242–252.

Figure 13.3 The Raygor readability formula

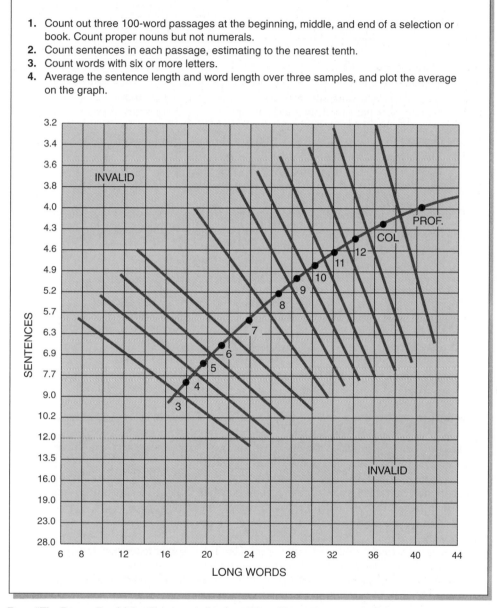

1. Count out three 100-word passages at the beginning, middle, and end of a selection or book. Count proper nouns but not numerals.
2. Count sentences in each passage, estimating to the nearest tenth.
3. Count words with six or more letters.
4. Average the sentence length and word length over three samples, and plot the average on the graph.

From "The Raygor Readability Estimate: A Quick and Easy Way to Determine Difficulty," by A. L. Raygor, in *Reading: Theory, Research and Practice. Twenty-Sixth Yearbook of the National Reading Conference* (pp. 259–263), edited by P. D. Pearson, 1977. Clemson, SC: National Reading Conference.

Collection: A number of descriptions (specifics, characteristics, or settings) presented together.

Water Habitats

Freshwater habitats are found in ponds, bogs, swamps, lakes, and rivers. Each freshwater habitat has special kinds of plants and animals that live there. Some plants and animals live in waters that are very cold. Others live in waters that are warm. Some plants and animals adapt to waters that flow fast. Others adapt to still water.

(From Merrill Science [Grade 3], 1989, p. 226)

Causation includes a time sequence.

Causation: Elements grouped according to time sequence with a cause–effect relationship specified.

America Enters the War

On Sunday, December 7, 1941, World War II came to the United States. At 7:55 A.M. Japanese warplanes swooped through the clouds above *Pearl Harbor.* Pearl Harbor was the American naval base in the Hawaiian Islands. A deadly load of bombs was dropped on the American ships and airfield. It was a day, Roosevelt said, that would "live in infamy." *Infamy* (IN·fuh·mee) means remembered for being evil.

The United States had been attacked. That meant war.

(From The United States: Its History and Neighbors [Grade 5], Harcourt Brace Jovanovich, 1985, p. 493)

Problem/Solution: Includes a relationship (between a problem and its possible causes[s]) and a set of solution possibilities, one of which can break the link between the problem and its cause.

Agreement by Compromise (Events That Led to the Civil War)

For a while there was an equal number of Southern and Northern states. That meant that there were just as many Senators in Congress from slave states as from free states. Neither had more votes in the Senate, so they usually reached agreement on new laws by compromise.

(From The United States and the Other Americas [Grade 5], Macmillan, 1980, p. 190)

Comparison deals with areas of similarity and difference.

Comparison: Organizes factors on the basis of differences and similarities. Comparison does not contain elements of sequence or causality.

Segregation

Segregation laws said that blacks had to live separate, or apart, from whites. Like whites, during segregation blacks had their own parks, hospitals, and swimming pools. Theaters, buses, and trains were segregated.

Many people said that the segregation laws were unfair. But in 1896, the Supreme Court ruled segregation legal if the separate facilities for blacks were equal to those for whites. "Separate but equal" became the law in many parts of the country.

But separate was not equal. . . . One of the most serious problems was education. Black parents felt that their students were not receiving an equal education in segregated schools. Sometimes the segregated schools had teachers who were not as well educated as teachers in the white schools. Textbooks were often very old and out-of-date, if they had any books at all. But in many of the white schools the books were the newest ones. Without a good education, the blacks argued, their students would not be able to get good jobs as adults.

Finally in 1954, the Supreme Court changed the law.

(Adapted from The American People [Grade 6], American Book Company, 1982, p. 364)

Students often have difficulty with comparisons. Why do you think this is so?

PREPARING TO TEACH: ANALYZING READINGS AND CREATING STUDY AIDS

Performing a Content Analysis

A *content analysis* helps teachers determine important facts, concepts, generalizations, and vocabulary that must be taught.

One of the best ways to plan for content area instruction is to perform a content analysis. The purpose of a **content analysis** is to help teachers identify the important *facts, concepts,* and *generalizations* presented in a given unit of study; an essential process for establishing curriculum objectives and learning activities for students (Martorella, 2000). By carefully analyzing new information to be presented, the teacher is able to locate important information, discard useless trivia, and determine which areas of the unit require deeper development for students. As a result of this process, teachers are able to develop a cohesive unit of study that communicates new knowledge to students and helps build new knowledge. In explaining the significance of analyzing informational text prior to teaching, Martorella (1985) remarked:

> What we regard as an individual's knowledge consists of a complex network of the elements of reflection. The fact of our date of birth, for example, is linked in some way to our concept of *birthday*. As further reflection occurs, we incorporate the new information into our network and it becomes related with the old knowledge. (pp. 69–70) [*Authors' note:* This is the stage at which a new generalization is created.]

Facts are individual bits of information, or details, presented in a unit under study. In a science unit dealing with our solar system, some of the facts might be on the atmosphere, satellites, and Saturn. For a history unit pertaining to events surrounding the life of Dr. Martin Luther King, Jr., possible facts found in the readings might relate to the March on Washington, sit-ins, and Civil Rights legislation.

Concepts are categories into which we group all facts or phenomena known through our experiences (Martorella, 2000). In the previous example of a unit about the *solar* system, satellites and Saturn could be grouped into a single concept called *objects orbiting the sun*. Concepts are usually stated in a simple word, phrase, or sentence that captures the main idea.

Concepts *are clusters of related facts.*

A *generalization* is a principle or conclusion that applies to the entire class or sample being examined (T. L. Harris & Hodges, 1995). A generalization is teacher generated, written in the language of the students, and usually expressed in complete sentences. Generalizations organize and summarize a large amount of information, sometimes an entire unit. Two examples are:

Generalizations *are principles or conclusions that relate to an entire unit of study.*

> *There are many reasons why Harry Truman, perhaps an unlikely president, chose public life.*
> *Our solar system is made up of many satellites.*

Once facts, concepts, and generalizations have been identified, the teacher should organize them into some form of graphic representation: a traditional outline, semantic web, structured overview, or other preferred form. Arranging information structurally allows the teacher to analyze the unit and begin making decisions about organizing for instruction. One typical query follows:

> **Question:** *What should a teacher do if the adopted textbook contains information that is not relevant to any of the major concepts?*
> **Answer:** *If the information helps build background understanding for the students that are important to the facts, concepts, and generalizations taught, then the teacher should keep and use that information. If the information serves no real purpose, however, it should not be included in unit activities or discussion.*

Figure 13.4 Partial content analysis of *matter*

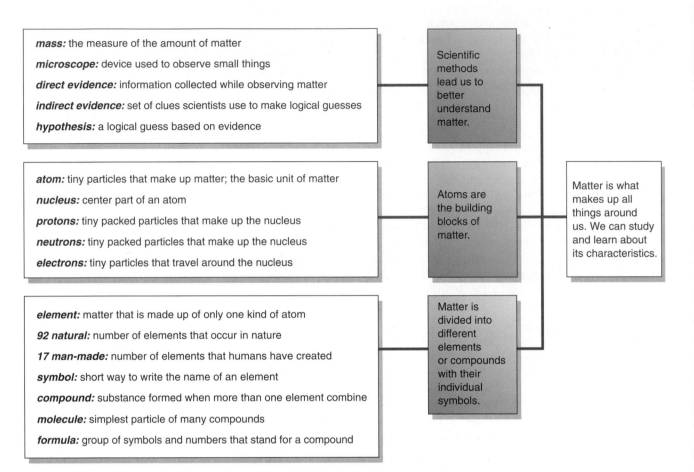

mass: the measure of the amount of matter

microscope: device used to observe small things

direct evidence: information collected while observing matter

indirect evidence: set of clues scientists use to make logical guesses

hypothesis: a logical guess based on evidence

Scientific methods lead us to better understand matter.

atom: tiny particles that make up matter; the basic unit of matter

nucleus: center part of an atom

protons: tiny packed particles that make up the nucleus

neutrons: tiny packed particles that make up the nucleus

electrons: tiny particles that travel around the nucleus

Atoms are the building blocks of matter.

Matter is what makes up all things around us. We can study and learn about its characteristics.

element: matter that is made up of only one kind of atom

92 natural: number of elements that occur in nature

17 man-made: number of elements that humans have created

symbol: short way to write the name of an element

compound: substance formed when more than one element combine

molecule: simplest particle of many compounds

formula: group of symbols and numbers that stand for a compound

Matter is divided into different elements or compounds with their individual symbols.

Courtesy of David Harlan, Fifth Grade Teacher, Sage Creek Elementary School, Springville, UT.

Figures 13.4 and 13.5 are examples of partially finished content analysis graphic representations by two middle school teachers. Notice that they are essentially schema maps.

CONSTRUCTING LEARNING TOOLS

Interesting and informative content area units do not come together by accident; they require deliberate planning and certain key ingredients, which can be drawn from the content analysis you have constructed. Tools you can develop directly from the content analysis are *graphic organizers, vocabulary-* and *concept-learning activities, study guides,* and *expository text response activities.*

Using Graphic Organizers or *GO! Charts*

How are graphic organizers and schema maps alike?

Graphic organizers (sometimes referred to as *GO! Charts*) are maps or graphs that summarize information to be learned and the relationships between ideas (Barron, 1969; Alvermann & Phelps, 2001). It provides a means for presenting new vocab-

Figure 13.5   Partial content analysis of events leading to the Civil War

Generalization

    Differences between states in the North and South led to the Civil War.

Concept

    The northern economy was based on industry; the southern economy was based on agriculture.

Facts

    Samuel Slater built many factories in the North.

    In these factories, Slater discovered that machines could be used instead of people to make things more quickly and cheaply.

    Soon, things made in northern factories were being sold to people living in southern states.

    Farmers discovered that cotton could be processed more quickly and easily with the cotton gin than by hand.

    Many southern farmers grew cotton and sold it to people living in northern states.

    Many immigrants became factory workers; many slaves were forced to work in cotton fields.

Concept

    Both the North and the South fought for control of the government.

Facts

    The North wanted laws favoring business and industry; the South wanted laws favoring farming and slavery.

    Northerners wanted any new states entering the Union to be free states.

    Southerners wanted any new states entering the Union to be slave states.

    In 1820, when Missouri asked to become a state, there were 11 free and 11 slave states in the Union.

    Northerners wanted Missouri to be a free state; Southerners wanted Missouri to be a slave state.

Courtesy of Laurie McNeal, Fifth Grade Unit, Brigham Young University.

ulary and its relationship to larger concepts and generalizations (Tierney, Readence, & Dishner, 1990). Graphic organizers are generally used as an introductory instrument to begin a unit of study, are referred to regularly during the course of the unit, and are used as a review instrument near the end of a unit of study.

    Constructing a graphic organizer is a simple matter once a content analysis has been completed: Simplify or condense the facts, concepts, and generalizations in the unit by reducing each to a single word or phrase, then arrange them graphically in the same hierarchical pattern as the content analysis. If a thorough content analysis is not possible, however, the following steps can be used to develop a graphic organizer (adapted from Barron, 1969):

    1. Identify all facts and vocabulary that are essential to understanding the unit under study, thus forming the bottom layer of information, or subordinate concepts (Thelen, 1984). For the sake of consistency with the content analysis idea discussed earlier in the chapter, we refer to these subordinate concepts as *facts*.

2. Next, group related facts into clusters. These clusters form a second layer of understanding in the unit we refer to as *concepts*.

3. Finally, concepts that relate to each other should be grouped under the major heading for the unit we refer to as a *generalization*. Most often, the unit will have only a single generalization, but occasionally, two or more generalizations may be needed, especially for large or complex units.

Only Use Two or Three *GO! Charts* Formats Each Year

Teachers may wish to use a variety of graphic formats to depict the different units covered each year. However, try to stick to using only two or three each year and use them daily. Most teachers throw too many *formats* at students, never really becoming expert at any. No one style is better than another, but using a different style for each unit may help hold students' attention. Several popular formats for graphic organizers are shown in Figures 13.6 through 13.9 for a unit on the structure of American government.

Figure 13.6 Traditional outline

Structure of American Government

1.   Constitution provides for three branches
    A.   Executive Branch
        1.   President
    B.   Legislative Branch
        1.   House of Representatives
        2.   Senate
    C.   Judicial Branch
        1.   Supreme Court

Figure 13.7 Structured overview

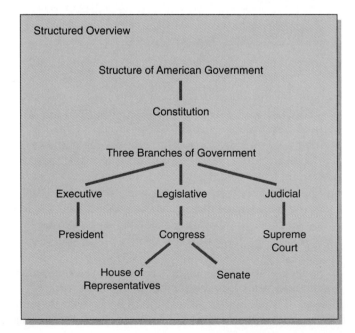

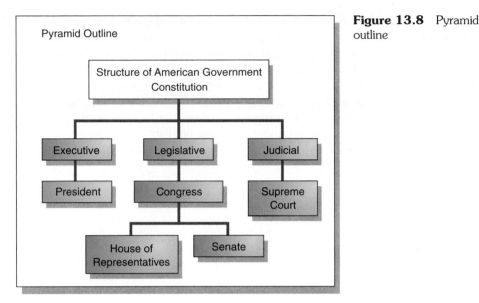

Figure 13.8 Pyramid outline

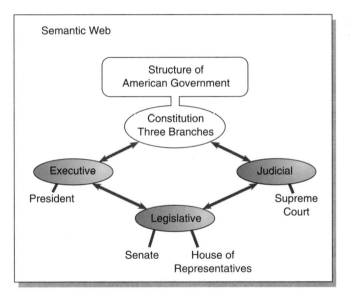

Figure 13.9 Semantic web

Study Guides

Study guides, also known as *reading guides* (A. Manzo, U. Manzo, & Estes, 2000; R. T. Vacca & Vacca, 2001), are teacher-made activities intended to help students move successfully through a unit of study. They can be used before, during, and/or after reading the unit materials (A. Manzo, U. Manzo, & Estes, 2000). Frequently, study guides consist of a series of key questions or problems for students to work through, followed by page references to text materials used in the unit. Students use the references to seek answers and become familiar with the content. Tutolo (1977) described two types of study guides: interlocking and noninterlocking. An *interlocking* study guide groups questions according to three comprehension levels:

Study guides are teacher-made activities that help students progress successfully through a unit of study.

literal, interpretative, and applied. A *noninterlocking* study guide does not use a hierarchical relationship for questions. Tutolo (1977) feels that with some text selections, the reader may need to move from the literal level to the application level and back to the literal level. Thus, grouping of study questions in this situation might be inappropriate.

Many useful study guide formats are appropriate for middle school classrooms. We recommend that teachers use a combination of (a) interlocking or noninterlocking guides for students to use independently along with (b) whole-group activities such as the anticipation guide or prereading plan (PReP). Descriptions of a few examples follow.

Three-Level Guide

A **three-level guide** (Herber, 1978) is a classic interlocking guide in that it leads students from basic levels of comprehension to more advanced levels (A. Manzo, U. Manzo & Estes, 2000). The first level (literal comprehension) helps students understand what the author said, the second level (interpretative comprehension) helps students understand what the author means, and the third level (applied comprehension) helps students understand how text information can be applied (A. Manzo, U. Manzo & Estes, 2000). Although three-level guides have traditionally been constructed using declarative statements, we feel that it is just as appropriate to use a question or problem-solving format.

In constructing a three-level guide, we suggest the following guidelines adapted from R. T. Vacca and Vacca (2001):

1. Begin by constructing the study guide at the interpretative comprehension level by determining what the author means. Write inferences that make sense and that fit the content objectives. Revise your statements so that they are simple and clear. Part 2 of the guide is now completed.

2. Next, search the text for explicit pieces of information (details, facts, and propositions) that support inferences chosen for the second part of the guide. Put these into statement, question, or problem form. Part 1 of the guide is now completed.

3. Next, develop statements, questions, or problems for the applied comprehension level of the guide (Part 3); they should represent additional insights or principles that may be drawn when analyzing parts 1 and 2 of the guide. Part 3 should help students connect what they already know with what they have learned from the study of the unit.

Be flexible when using a three-level guide. The format should be varied from unit to unit to help hold students' attention. It may also be a good idea to occasionally put in *distracter* or "foil" items (i.e., false items); distracters sometimes prevent students from indiscriminately focusing on *every* item and cause them to focus on the information search more carefully (R. T. Vacca & Vacca, 1989).

Finally, include page numbers in parentheses following each question, problem, or statement where answers can be found in the reading assignment. This alerts students to key ideas found on each page and enables them to screen out irrelevant information.

*A **three-level guide** helps students move through basic to advanced comprehension levels.*

Anticipation Guides

Anticipation guides are prereading activities used to survey students' prior knowledge and attitudes about a given subject or topic. They usually consist of three to five teacher-prepared declarative statements that students read and react to before reading the text selection. Statements can be either true or false. The important factor is for students to respond to the statements based on their own experiences (Wiesendanger, 1986). Figure 13.10 shows a sample anticipation guide for "Our Picture of the Universe" (Hawking, 1988).

Prereading Plan

The **prereading plan (PReP)** was developed by Judith Langer (1981) and provides both instructional and assessment benefits. In this three-step process, the teacher first identifies key concepts in the reading selection for the students. Next, the teacher asks students to discuss their associations with each of these terms or concepts. Their associations might be displayed on the chalkboard using a web or structured overview format. Once the group has discussed the different student associations, the teacher "reforms" the associations by asking students if they have any new interpretations to suggest about the major concepts and terms before reading the selection.

> PReP helps teachers assess what students already know about the topic before reading and helps students who may have inadequate knowledge about the topic under study to acquire more background knowledge from their peers and teacher before reading.

Vocabulary Development Activities

Thelen (1984) cited an idea in her book *Improving Reading in Science* that helps "students relate newly learned verbal associations to familiar and emphasized relationships." (p. 36) The format for this categorizing activity is shown in Figure 13.11.

Figure 13.10 Anticipation guide based on "Our Picture of the Universe" from Stephen W. Hawking's *A Brief History of Time* (1988)

Our Picture of the Universe

Directions: Read each statement below and decide whether you agree or disagree with the statement. If you agree with a statement, put an "X" in the ***Before I Read*** blank before that statement. If you disagree, put an "O" in the blank. After you have finished reading "Our Picture of the Universe," complete the blanks labeled ***Hawking's Views,*** indicating how you think the author would answer those same questions.

Before I Read		Hawking's Views
_____	Many of the early scientists, like Aristotle (340 B.C.), believed the Earth was round instead of flat.	_____
_____	The universe was created at some point in time in the past more or less as we observe it today.	_____
_____	An expanding universe theory (big bang) does not preclude a creator.	_____
_____	Knowing how the universe came about millions of years ago can help mankind to survive in the future.	_____

Figure 13.11   Vocabulary reinforcement: Functions of cells

Functions of Cells: Vocabulary Review*

Name _____

1. _____   3. _____

     neutrons   diffusion osmosis

     protons   active transport

     electrons   pinocytosis

2. _____   4. _____

     light reaction   metabolism

     chlorophyll   respiration

     nutrients from soil   homeostasis

*Answers: 1. atoms, 2. photosynthesis, 3. transport, 4. cell functions

Whole-Group Vocabulary Instruction

Whole-group instruction can be an effective mode of teaching vocabulary if not overused.

When teaching in large- or small-group situations, the teacher's primary vehicle for integrating new vocabulary with known experiences, which was discussed earlier in this chapter, is the graphic organizer. Various graphic organizers can be used to introduce and review new words throughout the unit. Because of their schema-like nature, they are ideal for this type of learning situation.

Another way to approach vocabulary instruction is through whole-group vocabulary mini-lessons that involve the entire class in activities demonstrating the meaning of new vocabulary. Whole-group vocabulary mini-lessons will not work with all new vocabulary but may be helpful on an occasional basis. The idea is to provide concrete understanding for abstract ideas. Following is an example for fifth graders learning about the basic components of an atom.

ATOMIC KID POWER!

Step 1: The teacher introduces key information about atomic structure (e.g., nucleus made up of protons and neutrons, electrons orbiting the nucleus).

Step 2: The teacher takes the class out to the play area and assigns students to a role-playing situation wherein they take turns being subatomic particles (e.g., protons, neutrons, electrons). Protons could wear a special hat, colored purple; neutrons wear a white hat; and electrons wear a bright orange hat.

Step 3: A circle large enough for approximately six students to stand within is drawn with chalk on the playground surface. Several students are assigned to play the part of the nucleus, and the appropriate number of children will be the electrons.

Step 4: Finally, the nucleus students stand together in the circle, hopping up and down simulating a live atomic nucleus. The electron children run around the nucleus, keeping about a 20-foot distance at all times. For extra instructional benefit, a parent helper could stand on a ladder (or perhaps the roof of the building), film the simulation using a video camcorder, and replay the film to the class at a later time for review purposes.

Individualized Vocabulary Instruction

Nist and Simpson (1993) argue convincingly that we must help students get to know words and concepts on four distinct levels. The first level is the word's basic definition. Level two concerns understanding of synonyms, antonyms, examples, and nonexamples. Level three involves an understanding of connotations and characteristics of the word. The fourth level of understanding involves applying the word to personal and new situations apart from the original encounter in the content area classroom. Nist and Simpson liken these levels of understanding to an iceberg: The top level that we see first is the dictionary definition, but the bigger picture by far is composed of the three other levels of conceptual word knowledge lying beneath the surface. In this section, we offer two teacher-tested ideas that help achieve these goals.

Thinking Matrix. The *thinking matrix* is designed to help students generate their own questions as an end-of-unit review or to help student groups lead class discussions (McTighe & Lyman, 1988; Alvermann & Phelps, 2001). A concept thinking matrix is easily adapted to vocabulary learning by simply listing key concepts and words to be learned down one axis and the four levels of understanding across the top columns. In Figure 13.12, we illustrate a concept thinking matrix using terms from a lesson on African-American art. Completion of the matrix necessitates higher order analysis of each concept or term and is a perfect opportunity for student collaboration.

Some feel the thinking matrix activity helps students anticipate new information and construct schemas. Consider reasons why.

Figure 13.12 Concept thinking matrix: Lesson on African-American art

Concepts/ Vocabulary	Dictionary Definition	Synonyms, Antonyms, Examples, Nonexamples	Connotations, Characteristics	Other Uses of the Word(s)
race consciousness		Syn.: Ant.: Ex./nonex.:	Connot.: Char.:	
African-American "art idiom"		Syn.: Ant.: Ex./nonex.:	Connot.: Char.:	
images		Syn.: Ant.: Ex./nonex.:	Connot.: Char.:	
flattened space		Syn.: Ant.: Ex./nonex.:	Connot.: Char.:	
compressed gestures		Syn.: Ant.: Ex./nonex.:	Connot.: Char.:	
controlled palette		Syn.: Ant.: Ex./nonex.:	Connot.: Char.:	

Figure 13.13   Content-specific vocabulary card

Content-Specific Vocabulary Cards. Another idea suggested by Nist and Simpson (1993) is *content-specific vocabulary cards.* The cards are like personal dictionaries developed by students and are kept on 3 × 5 index cards in plastic recipe boxes or bound together using steel rings. Nist and Simpson say students typically keep two types of vocabulary cards: general and content specific. General vocabulary cards are for common everyday language, whereas content-specific vocabulary cards, as the name implies, are to assist with learning specialized content area terms (scientific terms, mathematical concepts). The procedure is simple: On one side, the student writes the term or concept to be learned. On the back side, the student writes pertinent information about its meaning, such as a definition, synonyms, antonyms, and examples. Figure 13.13 presents an example of a content-specific vocabulary card for the word *contaminant* from a unit on air pollution.

> *Students essentially create their own dictionaries with* **content-specific vocabulary cards.**

Choosing High-Interest Reading Materials

It is well established through research that middle school students are much more inclined to read when they are offered interesting reading materials (Dewey, 1913; Alexander & Filler, 1976; Krashen, 1992; Worthy, Moorman, & Turner, 1999). With the absolute wealth of materials available on most every subject, there is no reason to limit content information to the district-adopted textbook. Here, for example, is a short list of resources available in most schools to supplement content studies:

> *As interest in a topic increases, so does student learning.*

- trade books (fiction and nonfiction books found in the library)
- journal-magazines (e.g., *National Geographic, The Smithsonian*)
- magazines and other popular press publications
- Internet resources such as World Wide Web tours, search engines, bookmark files in the classroom, and educational Web sites (Cafolla, Kauffman, & Knee, 1997).

What Do Middle School Students Enjoy Reading?

There have been many studies of student reading habits over the years. A recent study of middle school reading preferences (Worthy, Moorman, & Turner, 1999) had some interesting conclusions. First, this team of researchers identified specific reading interests, which are shown in Table 13.1.

Table 13.1 Reading preferences* of sixth grade students

Rank	Type of Material	Percentage of who would read often
1	Scary books or story collections	66%
2	Cartoons and comics	65%
3	*Popular magazines*	*38%*
4	*Sports*	*33%*
5	*Drawing books*	*29%*
6	Cars and trucks	22%
7	Animals	21%
8	Series	21%
9	Funny novels	20%
10	Books written mostly for adults	17%
11	Novels about people	17%
12	Science fiction or fantasy	17%
13	Picture books	16%
14	Almanacs or record books	14%
15	Poetry	12%
16	Biography	10%
17	Adventure novels	9%
18	Information books about history	6%
19	Encyclopedias	6%
20	Information books about science or math	2%

*Note that after #1 and #2 on the list, there is a sharp drop for #3–5, and an even sharper drop after that for the other preferences.

Worthy and her colleagues also posed the following question to the students: "If you could read anything at all, what would it be?" The students' responses were analyzed and are summarized in Table 13.2.

The second conclusion of the researchers was somewhat frustrating. Namely, in the schools studied by the researchers, not many of the preferred materials could be found. Obviously, appropriate reading preferences should be considered and relevant materials obtained when preparing content units.

Students indicate a profound lack of interest in information books about math and science (Worthy, Moorman, & Turner, 1999). What could you do to reverse this trend?

Using Trade Books as Supplements to Textbooks

Trade books (library books) can breathe life into content investigations while also providing needed background information for best comprehension and schema building (Wepner & Feeley, 1993). The key to success in weaving good literature into the content curriculum is remembering that books can be read aesthetically for enjoyment or to learn new information (Cox & Zarillo, 1993). Both purposes are important to encourage the synergy that is possible between good books and content learning.

Table 13.2 Summary of responses to the question: *If you could read anything at all, what would it be?*

Materials or topics named 10 or more times*	Number of responses
Scary	*124*
Sports magazines/books	**41**
Comics and cartoons	28
Teen magazines	26
Mystery	16
Car magazines	14
Science fiction/fantasy	13
Romance	12
Novels written for adults	11
Other fiction	47
Other magazines (e.g., music, ethnic, video games)	24
Other information books	20

*Note the great preference for scary books, followed by a steep drop to practical interest in sports materials, then another steep drop to the other categories.

A good beginning is for the teacher to read a relevant trade book daily to students for about 15 to 20 minutes (Brozo & Simpson, 1995). For example, if a unit on Japan is under way and the teacher decides that some knowledge of feudal times is important, he or she may choose to read aloud *The Coming of the Bear* by Lensey Namioka (1992). In a science class focusing on robotics and mechanization, the teacher could select such traditional favorites as *Jed's Junior Space Patrol* (Marzollo & Marzollo, 1982), *The White Mountain* (Christopher, 1967), or Simon Watson's (1976) *No Man's Land*. Reading aloud great books such as these sparks interest in the subject matter and makes complex ideas more accessible to students.

It is equally important that students be encouraged to read trade books pertaining to the subject under study themselves. Literature-based reading methods described in Chapter 12—reading workshops, core books, themed literature units—have been recommended for adaptation in content classes (Cox & Zarillo, 1993; Brozo & Simpson, 1995). Regardless of the format used to incorporate trade books in content classes, we favor the second-sweep (i.e., second reading) method so that students can enjoy books as literature before seeking needed information.

Use several resources to locate appropriate trade books for content classes. Here are just a few that we have found helpful.

*The **Journal of Adolescent & Adult Literacy** is the premier publication for content area reading.*

- *Journal of Adolescent & Adult Literacy.* International Reading Association. A periodical for middle school and secondary teachers that features a "Books for Adolescents" column and reviews of classroom materials. Substantial summaries presented in these issues are most helpful in planning units.
- Lima, C. & Lima, J. (1993). *A to Zoo: Subject Access to Children's Picture Books.* New York: Bowker. A reference tool useful in locating books for specific topics and themes.
- Norton, D. E. (1998). *Through the Eyes of a Child: An Introduction to Children's Literature* (5th ed.). Upper Saddle River, NJ: Merrill/Prentice Hall. An up-to-

date textbook that offers brief descriptions of trade books and their uses for read alouds, themed studies, and so on.

- *The Newbery and Caldecott Awards: A Guide to Medal and Honor Books.* American Library Association. Provides helpful information regarding some of the most celebrated trade books available.

- *The Reading Teacher.* International Reading Association. A periodical for elementary and upper elementary/middle school teachers that publishes lists of popular books each year called "Children's Choices" (October issue) and "Teachers' Choices" (November issue). Summaries presented in these issues are helpful in planning units.

PROVEN STUDY STRATEGIES: HELPING STUDENTS HELP THEMSELVES

Efficient (Speed Reading) Study Strategies

One of the characteristics of successful mature readers is that they read *selectively* instead of word by word. This means that efficient reading strategies are a conscious or unconscious search for meaning in the text, not a word-by-word, laborious process. Even though much of efficient reading is an unconscious process carried out automatically by the brain (LaBerge & Samuels, 1974), it is desirable for teachers to show students several efficient reading strategies that, when practiced, become internalized in the student over time, resulting in improved reading fluency and comprehension.

Skimming and Scanning

Skimming is an easy strategy to learn and can be useful with a variety of reading materials. It is very helpful with periodicals, popular press materials, and most science and social studies textbooks. Skimming can be used to preview materials or for review purposes.

The object of skimming is quite simple: Students practice forcing their eyes to move quickly across each line of print. As they do so, they try to attend to a few key words from each line. Sometimes it is helpful for students to move their finger rapidly under each line of text, following the text with their eyes (this is called *pacing*). At first, comprehension will drop off dramatically, because students are concentrating more on the physical movement of their eyes than on the meaning of the text. But over time and with practice, students are able to perform the skimming operation with as much or more comprehension than usual.

You should first lead the class through some practice exercises. Emphasis should be on the fact that the key words on each line will tend to be nouns, verbs, and adjectives—in other words, the meaning-carrying words. Articles, conjunctions, and other function words in the sentence add little to the comprehension process and can essentially be ignored.

Scanning is a much simpler strategy to teach and learn. The idea is to have students visually *sweep* or scan a page of text to locate information, such as an important date, key words, or answers to a specific question. Instead of attempting to comprehend all information on the page, the reader is simply trying to locate information "bits." You should be able to demonstrate this strategy for your students through simple modeling.

Standard Note
Standard 8.4: The reading professional will be able to teach students strategies to organize and remember information. When you read about "systems" such as SQ3R and SQRQCQ, list the underlying features of both that make them theoretically sound.

Efficient reading strategies help students make economical use of their study time and generally improve self-esteem and comprehension.

Think of times when you find yourself skimming materials. How is your purpose for reading different from times when you read for pleasure?

Scanning *is a rapid search for a particular type of information, such as a date or a name.*

Previewing

Previewing is especially useful for getting a general idea of heavy reading, such as nonfiction books. Previewing allows readers to cover nonfiction material in a fraction of the usual time with up to 50 percent comprehension. The procedure is simple to teach and learn but may take quite a bit of practice to achieve useful and practical comprehension levels.

The first step is to read the first two paragraphs of the chapter or selection. Most authors provide the reader with an overview of the chapter in the first couple of paragraphs, so reading every word of the first two paragraphs is important. The second step is for students to read only the first sentence of each paragraph thereafter; most professional writers of textbooks and nonfiction texts begin paragraphs with a topic sentence, which summarizes the main idea of each paragraph. Thus, reading the first sentence in each paragraph will provide crucial information to the reader, but remember that some of the important details that follow will be missed. Finally, the student reads the last two paragraphs of the selection, which provides the reader with a summary of major points covered. If the final section is labeled *Summary, Conclusions,* or something similar, then the student should read the entire section.

Fluency: Adjusting Reading Rate to Match the Text Type

Another important efficient reading lesson is varying reading rate. Reading rate is the speed at which readers attempt to process text. Different types of content usually require different reading speeds for best comprehension. For example, some students may be able to read a Hardy Boys mystery at a very fast reading rate. After all, not every word is crucial to understanding the author's message in a book of this kind and a previewing or skimming strategy may be sufficient for good comprehension. On the other hand, when students read a story problem in mathematics, it is important to read each word carefully at a much slower reading rate. Thus, students must become aware of the need to consciously vary their reading rate to match the style and purpose of the text they are reading.

Our Recommended Efficient Reading Strategy

This efficient reading strategy combined elements of previewing and skimming strategies.

After working with scores of students in the middle school, we have arrived at an efficient reading strategy that works with most expository and narrative materials. (The one exception is mathematics, which requires more specialized strategies.) The procedure is a combination of previewing and skimming, as previously described. Here are the steps to follow:

- Read the first two paragraphs of the selection to get an overview of the piece.
- Next, read the first sentence of each successive paragraph. Then skim the remainder of the paragraph to get important supporting details for each topic sentence.
- Read the final two paragraphs of the selection to review main ideas. This procedure has yielded comprehension rates of up to 80 percent with fluent readers but requires only about one-third the time of normal reading.

In addition to the efficient reading strategies, evidence-based research supports the use of many other tactics. It seems that when students understand *what* to study, *how* to study quickly and efficiently, and *why* the information is pertinent to their world, classroom performance is improved.

SQ3R

Perhaps the most classic and widely used study system is *SQ3R* (Robinson, 1946), which is an acronym for *survey, question, read, recite, review.* Especially effective with expository texts, SQ3R provides students with a step-by-step study method that ensures multiple exposures to the new material to be learned. Many students also find that they can trim their study time using SQ3R and still earn better grades.

SQ3R is best taught through teacher modeling followed by a whole-class walk-through. Each step of SQ3R is explained in the following list:

- *Survey:* To survey a chapter in a textbook, students read and think about the title, headings and subheadings, captions under any pictures, vocabulary in bold print, side entries on each page (if there are any), and the summary.

- *Question:* Next, students use the survey information, particularly headings and subheadings, to write prediction questions about what they are about to read. The first few times they use SQ3R students frequently need teacher assistance in developing questions that will alert them to important concepts in the unit.

- *Read:* The third step is for students to read actively (Manzo & Manzo, 1990), looking for answers to their questions. They should also attend to boldface type, graphs, charts, and any other comprehension aid provided.

- *Recite:* Once the material has been read and the questions answered fully, the students should test themselves on the material. Anything difficult to remember should be rehearsed aloud or recited. This multisensory experience helps the difficult material to move into short-term, and with practice, long-term, memory.

- *Review:* The final step is to review the information learned periodically. This can be done orally with a peer, through rewriting notes from memory and comparing to the students' master set of notes, or with mock quizzes developed by a peer or the teacher.

SQ3R is a widely taught study strategy that has met with some success.

SQRQCQ

Although the SQ3R method can be very effective with most expository texts, it is difficult to apply to mathematics. A similar plan developed especially for mathematics story problems (Fay, 1965) is known as *SQRQCQ: survey, question, read, question, compute, question.* As with SQ3R, the teacher should model SQRQCQ with the class and conduct whole-class practice before expecting students to attempt the procedure on their own (P. C. Burns, Roe, & Ross, 1988). The steps of this procedure are:

- *Survey:* Students read through the story problem quickly to get a general feel for what the problem is about.

- *Question:* Next, students should ask themselves general questions related to problem solving, such as, "What is the problem to be solved?" "What do I need to find out?" and "What important information is provided in the story problem?"

What adaptations does the SQRQCQ strategy employ to suit the special needs of mathematics texts?

• *Read:*   Students read the problem again carefully, giving close attention to details and relationships that will assist in the problem-solving process.

• *Question:*   Students answer the question, "What mathematical operation is needed to solve this problem?"

• *Compute:*   Students do the computation associated with the operation decided on in the previous step.

• *Question:*   Students answer the question, "Does this answer make sense?" If it does not, then the students may need to repeat some or all of the process.

Comprehension Monitoring (Metacognition)

Metacognition, or comprehension monitoring, has to do with helping students recognize what they know or need to know about what they are learning. Research suggests that good readers can describe their methods for reading and getting meaning, but poor readers seem virtually unaware of strategies that can be employed (A. Brown, 1982). F. Smith (1965) found that poor readers fail to adjust their reading behavior when reading for different purposes, such as reading for specific details or general impressions. A crucial role for the content area reading teacher is to help students (a) become aware of their own reading comprehension abilities and needs (called *metacognitive awareness*), and (b) learn specific strategies that can be used to fit their own comprehension needs at any given time.

A. Brown (1982) explains why we need to include metacognitive instruction as a fundamental part of study skill instruction:

> I emphasize the need for "cognitive training with awareness" because the whole history of attempts to instill study strategies in ineffectual learners attests to the futility of having students execute some strategy in the absence of a concomitant understanding of why or how that activity works. [For example] . . . we see that outlining itself is not a desired end product, and merely telling students it would be a good idea to outline, underline, or take notes is not going to help them become more effective studiers (A. Brown & Smiley, 1978). Detailed, *informed* instruction of the purposes of outlining and methods of using the strategy intelligently are needed before sizable benefits accrue. (pp. 46–47)

A. Brown (1982) developed a four-step model for teaching students metacognitive processes:

• *Determine the nature of the material to be learned:*   Students should review the text—for example, using the previewing method described earlier in this chapter (see SQ3R)— to learn what kind of material it is (narrative, expository, etc.). Most content area texts and materials in each subject area follow a fairly well-defined pattern. Understanding the pattern involved at the outset helps the reader to anticipate reading demands and expectations.

• *Consider the essential task involved:*   Students need to understand what they are looking for in the text. What is the critical information that will likely appear on tests and other assessment activities? T. H. Anderson and Armbruster (1980) indicate that when students modify their study plans accordingly, they tend to learn more than if the criterion task remains vague.

• *Consider your own strengths and weaknesses:*   As A. Brown (1982) points out, some students are good at numbers or have a good rote memory, whereas others

Standard Note
Standard 8.2: The reading professional will be able to teach students to vary reading rates according to the purpose(s) and difficulty of the material. Think of a comparison/analogy that you'd use to explain this standard: for example, "like the gears of a truck, when you have a heavy load to carry you down shift to the appropriate gear." Then list several specific ways that you'd teach skimming and scanning.

Metacognition has to do with self-monitoring of thinking and learning processes.

may have trouble remembering details or learning new languages (foreign, computer, scientific). In general, the task is to make new, abstract ideas familiar and memorable. Learners need to assess their own strengths and weaknesses in each of the content fields they study in preparation for the final phase of the four-step sequence.

• *Employ appropriate strategies to overcome learning weaknesses:* Once students understand where they have specific learning difficulties, remedial action to overcome these weaknesses is essential. Strategies such as look-backs (going back over text to find key information via scanning), rereading, reading ahead, highlighting, note taking, summary writing, webbing, and outlining suddenly become of great interest to students when they are taught in connection with their new metacognitive self-awareness.

WRITING TO DEEPEN LEARNING: HAVING STUDENTS CREATE THEIR OWN EXPOSITORY TEXTS

Of the many ways to help readers succeed with content materials, teaching them to become authors of expository texts may be the most powerful. There is something about creating our own texts that clarifies and permanently embeds the new concepts, facts, and vocabulary in our minds. It also appears that our interest in content information frequently increases as we gain mastery over it in writing. In this section, we suggest a few ways students create expository texts and, by doing so, become more competent and fluent readers.

Writing helps clarify what we have learned.

Paraphrase Writing

Shelley M. Gahn (1989), an eighth grade language arts teacher in Ohio, recommends paraphrase writing as one way students can re-create content information found in textbooks. The basic idea is that students restate information in their own words, which tends to keep the vocabulary simple and the resulting material brief. This strategy helps students to clarify their personal understanding of what has been studied.

Gahn suggests three types of paraphrase writing: *rephrasing, summarizing,* and *elaborating.* Rephrasing involves rewording relatively short paragraphs from content textbook chapters. Summarizing calls on students to identify the text's major points. Elaborating requires students to compare information in the new text to previous knowledge, sometimes using graphs, charts, or comparison grids. Paraphrase writing is often most effective when students write in small groups or pairs. It is also crucial that teachers model each type of writing for students, showing examples of acceptable paraphrases and those that are flawed.

Using Text Structures

Earlier in this chapter, we discussed expository text patterns (Meyer & Freedle, 1984) frequently found in textbooks. Because these patterns can be difficult for many readers to comprehend, teaching students to write using expository text patterns can often lead to a wonderful breakthrough in understanding. We advocate a four-step process for teaching students how to become authors of these forms of expository writing.

Step 1: The teacher describes the five expository text patterns and explains the differences between description, collection, causation, problem/solution, and

Responding to expository text content can be accomplished through writing activities that ask students to compare information they read.

comparison. The teacher presents examples of each using the overhead projector or chalkboard.

Step 2: The teacher identifies these patterns in content textbooks. Using previously researched materials, the teacher asks students to help locate examples of each expository text pattern on photocopies supplied to them for this purpose.

Step 3: The teacher models the writing of one of the expository text patterns. Beginning with description, the teacher creates an example of a description passage at the overhead projector or chalkboard based on text materials that the class has been reading. The teacher encourages students to coach him or her through premeditated mistakes in the example. The teacher should be sure to think aloud while creating the example, because this is the key element of modeling.

Step 4: The teacher asks students to create their own example. Step 3 is repeated, but this time, the teacher asks students to do the work. As with many writing and reading tasks, it may be profitable for students to work in pairs. Volunteers should be asked to share their examples with the class.

As students become comfortable creating simple expository text structures, they should be encouraged to combine structures in creating more lengthy compositions and projects. Using multiple structures in lengthy pieces is an essential tool for writers. This fact can easily be examined in the adopted textbook.

Cubes

Cubes is an activity that helps students review ideas from six perspectives.

Gail Tompkins (2000) recommends *cubes* as an expository writing activity. She explains that a cube has six sides, and in this activity, students review what they are learning about a topic from six sides, or perspectives, using the following tasks:

- Describe it.
- Compare it to other things you know about.
- Associate it to things it makes you think of.
- Analyze it as to what it is composed of.
- Apply it by explaining what you can do with it.
- Argue for or against it using reasons you have discovered through your investigation.

READING *ACROSS* THE CURRICULUM: THEMED STUDIES

The teaching of reading and writing using a comprehensive reading perspective has been the focus of this book. Although reading and writing have sometimes been presented as separate entities for the sake of clarity, teachers establishing comprehensive reading classrooms typically do not use these literacy skills separately. Rather, they are integrated *across* the curriculum (Savage, 1994) so that these boundaries virtually cease to exist. In full curriculum integration, reading and writing become integral parts of subject area investigations and vice versa via interdisciplinary **themed studies.** A theme such as "changes" or "friends" can become an exciting classroom experience involving social studies, the sciences, mathematics, literature, art history, and other important areas of the curriculum. This themed studies approach is what comprehensive reading teaching is all about in its purest form.

Themed studies are a popular vehicle for applying literacy skills across the curriculum.

The advantages of curriculum integration are numerous. Reading and writing abilities are acquired and refined within a rich context of real world significance, which in turn inspires students to want to know more. Skills are no longer taught in isolation as rote drill but are learned as welcomed tools for communicating ideas. Integration of the curriculum results in a blend of instruction in literacy communication skills and content as well as the planting of seeds for future searches for new knowledge.

In one description of themed studies in Canada, Gamberg, Kwak, Hutchings, and Altheim (1988) identified a number of important characteristics. First, themed studies are in-depth investigations of a topic, concept, or theme. Second, they are high-interest topics that are broad enough to be divided into smaller subtopics. Third, themed studies are not geographically or historically limiting, and they help in breaking down artificial curriculum barriers. For middle school students, "The History of Buildings" and "Around the World in 60 Days" are examples of themes that facilitate themed investigations.

Guidelines for Conducting Themed Studies

Themed studies are very similar to the themed literature units discussed in Chapter 12, differing mainly at the level of curricular integration (language arts integration versus total curriculum integration); thus, a discussion of all the key elements is not necessary. A brief summary of essential components of theme studies—as identified from the work of Paradis (1984) and Gamberg et al. (1988)— follows:

- *Theme selection:* Themes that meet the criteria previously described should be chosen.

- *Identifying resources:* Teaching and learning materials should be identified and collected by the teacher before beginning the unit. Examples include nonfiction

Figure 13.14   Teacher brainstorming web for theme studies

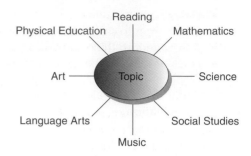

books; other pertinent print media (e.g., documents, travel brochures, and government publications); hands-on materials from the real world that pertain to the topic; community experts; nonprint media (videotapes, films, radio recordings); parent volunteers; relevant basal stories; and identification of possible field trips.

• *Brainstorming:*   Themed studies involve brainstorming for both the teacher and students. Teachers brainstorm as part of the planning process to anticipate ways that curriculums can be integrated into the unit and to assist in the selection of materials. Paradis (1984) offers a brainstorming web (Figure 13.14) to assist teachers in this process. Students are also encouraged to brainstorm as a way of becoming involved initially with the topic. Brainstorming helps students focus their thinking and value each of their peers' ideas, encourages collaboration, and reveals student interests and background knowledge.

• *Learning demonstrations:*   Students complete projects and tasks that demonstrate their newly acquired knowledge. Projects like those cited for themed literature units generally apply here. In addition, students may complete other products such as displays, speeches, demonstration fairs, and guided tours.

Teachers building themed studies search for ways to incorporate reading and other basic literacy skills into content subjects because they know that these processes help students deepen their knowledge of the real world. The dynamic created in these cross-curricular units is quite powerful and spawns many positive outcomes in the classroom, including heightened interest in the subject matter and a sense of empowerment (Cox & Zarillo, 1993; Wepner & Feeley, 1993).

After many years of helping school districts around the nation build thematic units, we have made a few important discoveries that tend to speed the process of curricular integration. The most efficient way to begin is by first constructing a themed literature unit using the process described in Chapter 12; this achieves full integration of the language arts within the context of great literature. Themed literature units also contain all the essential elements for a comprehensive reading program, such as daily reading and writing, the teaching of nonnegotiable skills, literature response, cooperative groups, opportunities to practice fluency, and student self-evaluation. Once teachers build themed literature units as the curriculum core it becomes a relatively simple matter to interlace the content areas. Finally, we have learned that once teachers go through the process we will describe in building thematic units, they better understand all the essential elements and can re-create the process in the future in their own way—keeping some elements, deleting others, to create a balanced learning system that meets the needs of their students.

Planning thematic units involves five major phases, which can be applied equally well in grades 5–8. These phases are *theme selection, setting goals and objectives, webbing, choosing major activities and materials,* and *unit scaffolding.*

Theme Selection

In many ways, the success of thematic units depends on the concept chosen to be the theme. It must be broad enough to accomplish linkage between the various content subjects, address local and state requirements listed in curriculum guides (Pappas, Kiefer, & Levstik, 1990), include quality nonfiction and fictional literature, and still be interesting to youngsters. Topics like "state history" or "nutrition" can be far too confining for the kinds of engaging learning experiences we hope to craft. In Chapter 12, we suggest a large number of possible topics by grade level, which might give the reader a good starting point; these include "legends," "survival," "heroes," "changes," "seasons," and "journeys." If the theme selected is broad enough, teachers will discover creative and enticing ways to weave the various content subjects into the unit. To demonstrate more clearly ways thematic units can be constructed, we build on the themed literature unit called "journeys."

Setting Goals and Objectives

Once the theme has been selected, teachers should consult the district curriculum guide and other available resources to determine possible goals and objectives. Some teachers prefer to do this step first because themes occasionally grow logically out of the required curriculum. Whether done as a first or second step, establishing goals and objectives must come early so that appropriate learning activities and materials can be chosen.

Notice that the skills to be taught are selected after the theme is chosen.

Webbing

The next step in planning thematic units is *webbing,* which is essentially the process of creating a schematic or schema map of the linkage between each aspect of the unit. By creating a web of the major aspects of the proposed unit, the teacher can gain a global view—the big picture. Webs can also be revised and adapted later to use as an advance organizer for students at the beginning of the thematic unit. In Figure 13.15, we see an initial (not fully developed) thematic unit web for the journeys theme. The journeys theme now spans three additional content areas: social studies, science, and mathematics. Major activities have also been suggested, which is the next topic we explore.

Choosing Major Activities and Materials

One of the joys of thematic units is that they infuse the curriculum with great ideas, activities, and materials that energize learners. What a great alternative this is for teachers ready for modest yet powerful change. Activities chosen for thematic units provide students with opportunities to apply literacy skills within a real-world context. Sometimes students complete these activities independently, other times as part of a problem-solving team. Occasions for personal exploration and reflection are also seen as valuable aspects of thematic unit activities.

Figure 13.15   Initial thematic unit web: Journeys

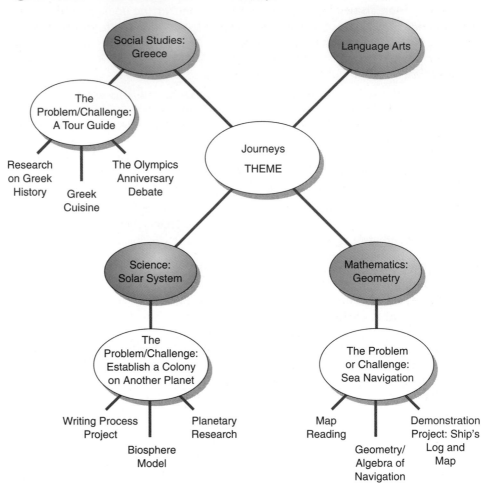

In Figure 13.15, we include several interesting activities that fit the journeys theme nicely and allow the teacher great flexibility. Although it may not be obvious at first glance, various state and district curriculum requirements can be built into the journeys theme. These include studies of Greece, investigations into the solar system, and rudiments of geometry and algebra. A "problem/challenge" scheme has been selected as the means for discovering each curriculum objective within a real world context.

Brainstorm a list of possible problems/ challenges for social studies.

Social Studies. In the social studies component, the problem/challenge activity is for students working in groups of four to assume the role of travel agents charged with the responsibility of developing a "tour guide" for clients traveling to Greece. Required parts of the tour guide involve information about ancient Greece, Greek cuisine, and the founding of the Olympics in ancient Greece. Students in each group present what they have learned to the class, or other classes, in the form of an enlarged travel brochure.

Science. The problem/challenge activity for science has student groups assume the role of astronauts aboard a space shuttle. Their mission is to travel to a planet of their choosing and establish a colony. This activity involves scientific research into such things as what humans need to sustain life, surface conditions on the selected planet, as well as useful natural resources (if any), and information about the building of life-supporting human environments (biospheres). To present their findings, students in each group will draft a report in the form of a book using the writing process, and construct a model of the biosphere they propose to build on the planet surface.

Mathematics. The problem/challenge activity for mathematics is for students to assume the role of sea voyagers who must navigate their ship to Greece from the United States. This is an individual project, or it can be conducted in pairs. Skills involved include basics in map reading, geometry as related to navigation, translation of miles per hour to knots, and journal writing. The product is a ship's log, which details daily destinations, map coordinates, travel times, and (if desired) some brief information about what students see at each port.

Thematic Unit Materials

The preceding examples clearly alert us that many and diverse materials are needed. Both fiction and nonfiction materials are needed to plan rich and interesting activities. The core materials are books, lots of books of every kind. Pappas et al. (1990; Kiefer, Z., Levstik, L. S., & Pappas, C. C., 1998) got it just right when they said, "as with chocolate, you never have enough books!" Essential are reference materials, fictional books to read aloud that awaken imaginations, and nonfiction books to read aloud. Teachers will also need to locate what are known by historians as "primary source materials"—factual, original sources of information. Later in this chapter, we mention a number of time-saving resources for locating specialty books and other media.

Unit Scaffolding

The final stage of planning is *unit scaffolding.* At this point, the teacher determines just how long the unit should run and makes final decisions about which activities to include. Typically, thematic units last one to two weeks in the lower grades (Wiseman, 1992) and up to four or five weeks in the upper grades. The teacher should resist the temptation to run units for months at a time, because this usually becomes too much of a good thing and turns high student interest into boredom.

Assembling the basic daily plans of thematic units is the process known as ***scaffolding.***

One of the decisions to make is whether the unit is to be fully integrated and presented as a seamless curriculum. Some teachers choose to operate in a nondepartmentalized fashion. In this case, our journeys unit may operate for a few days or a week, strictly focusing on the social studies problem/challenge. When the social studies portion is concluded, the class may move on to the science problem/challenge, focusing on that aspect for whole days at a time. The mathematics problem/challenge may come next. The value of seamless integration is that students pursue problems in much the same way as adults in the professional world, incorporating literacy skills throughout the day. Another benefit is that students can move from one problem/challenge to another every few days, thus maintaining a higher level of interest. Unfortunately, seamless integration cannot be achieved very easily in departmentalized schools—self-contained classrooms are generally necessary.

Seamless integration *depends heavily on schedule flexibility.*

Another option for organizing thematic units that can be used either in self-contained or departmentalized situations is segmented integration. In segmented

Figure 13.16   Segmented integration for journeys theme

8:30–9:30	**Language Arts:** Themed Literature Unit on Journeys
9:30–10:45	**Social Studies:** Greece/Tour Guide
10:55–11:30	Computer Lab
11:30–12:30	**Science:** Solar System/Biosphere Model
12:30–1:00	Lunch
1:00–2:15	**Specials:** Library, P.E.
2:30–3:25	**Mathematics:** Sea Navigation

Segmented integration of the curriculum works best in departmentalized and "pod system" schools.

integration, each content area portion is developed concurrently by either the self-contained teacher or content specialists. A sample daily schedule depicting how this integration might occur in a departmentalized middle school setting is shown in Figure 13.16. Segmented integration permits teachers in fully departmentalized schools to develop thematic units collaboratively as faculty teams. Sometimes all teachers in a departmentalized team will choose to take part in the thematic unit; on other occasions, one or two teachers may feel a need to do something different to satisfy district or state mandates. Participation should be a matter of choice. Further, one teacher may decide to run a thematic unit in his or her classroom for three weeks, whereas other teachers may have the unit run for four or five weeks. Whenever possible, however, it is usually a good thing to begin and end the unit at the same time to achieve proper closure.

We have found that planning daily activities is greatly facilitated by webbing each content component separately. Teachers should include in the web such information as key reference books, computer software, important questions to be answered, special activities, and demonstrations that teachers may wish to perform. In Figure 13.17, we share a web used in the science portion of the journeys theme.

PROGRAMS FOR STRUGGLING READERS

The first barrier to overcome for students having learning problems is a negative self-image.

Struggling readers often face feelings of discouragement and bewilderment in content area classes. Reflecting on our own experiences as classroom teachers, we have observed many similarities among readers having learning problems that sometimes compound their learning difficulties. First, and probably most troubling, is a student attitude that says "I'm dumb and can't do the work. . . . " This feeling has usually developed over a period of years and is usually due to unsuccessful experiences in the classroom. For these students, the "classroom safety net" may not have been established or maintained by previous teachers and risk taking on the students' part (trying new learning tasks) is not as likely to occur. Second, middle school students who struggle with content area subjects are usually poorly organized. When students are helped to become systematic in their reading and thinking strategies, positive results follow. Third, readers with learning problems tend to have weak overall reading ability, often characterized by one or more of the following: poor reading comprehension, a slow reading rate, underdeveloped study skills, and limited reading vocabulary.

Figure 13.17 Science web for journeys theme

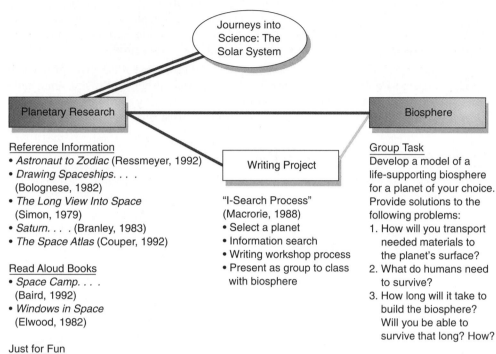

Reference Information
- *Astronaut to Zodiac* (Ressmeyer, 1992)
- *Drawing Spaceships. . . .*
  (Bolognese, 1982)
- *The Long View Into Space*
  (Simon, 1979)
- *Saturn. . . .* (Branley, 1983)
- *The Space Atlas* (Couper, 1992)

Read Aloud Books
- *Space Camp. . . .*
  (Baird, 1992)
- *Windows in Space*
  (Elwood, 1982)

Just for Fun
- *Space Songs* (Livingston, 1988)
- *The Magic School Bus* (Cole, 1990)
- *Look! Look! Look!* (Hoban, 1988)

"I-Search Process"
(Macrorie, 1988)
- Select a planet
- Information search
- Writing workshop process
- Present as group to class
  with biosphere

Group Task
Develop a model of a
life-supporting biosphere
for a planet of your choice.
Provide solutions to the
following problems:
1. How will you transport
   needed materials to
   the planet's surface?
2. What do humans need
   to survive?
3. How long will it take to
   build the biosphere?
   Will you be able to
   survive that long? How?

Fortunately, these problems can be repaired, sometimes easily, within the middle school classroom.

Commercial Programs for Low-Performing Readers

There are new reading programs springing up regularly to assist struggling middle school readers. Their relative financial success is not surprising, especially when considering the growing numbers of students who are struggling in middle school and eventually dropping out as soon as they are old enough to do so. In some large urban centers, for example, drop-out rates have reached 40 percent or more, with a majority of students in these locales reading well below expected levels.

We believe the long-term solution to reading problems lies in improving teacher expertise and providing sufficient learning materials, appropriate and safe classroom environments, and proper support from family and community members. In the end, it really does take a village to properly raise a child.

Nevertheless, some research-proven commercial reading programs can be helpful as supplemental tools in comprehensive reading classrooms. Here are some examples of programs that are useful with certain populations of students. (Be sure to study the research on each program to determine the kinds of students with whom they seem to be most effective—avoid the one-size-fits-all mentality.)

- *Boys Town Reading Program* (Omaha, NE: Boys Town) A four-course reading program developed at the world famous Father Flanagan's Boys Town in Omaha for problem readers. It features a diagnostic component for student placement into one of the four reading courses. The courses progress in difficulty from the first level, which is appropriate for students still learning basic reading skills, to a rather sophisticated level for advanced readers. The intent is for all middle schoolers to have an appropriate reading development course in which they can enroll.

• *Read 180* (New York: Scholastic) A computer-supported program developed at George Peabody College for Teachers of Vanderbilt University, then field tested in Orlando (Florida) and other school districts nationally. It appears to be quite motivating and effective with struggling readers in grades 5–8.

Comprehension "Strategy Families"

You will find two Safety Net Lessons for struggling readers on reading comprehension in Chapter 13 on our Companion Website at www.prenhall.com/ reutzel.

Dana (1989) has grouped several effective reading comprehension strategies for readers with learning problems into what she refers to as *strategy families.* They can be used with relative ease, in minimal time, and they have similar or complementary functions in aiding comprehension. The first strategy family mentioned here, *SIP (summarize, imaging, predict)* helps students focus on content, and the second strategy, called *EEEZ (take it easy, explain, explore, expand),* is a set of elaborative strategies that can be used as a postreading experience to "help anchor the content in memory." (Dana, 1989, p. 32) In each of these strategy families, the acronym reminds students of important steps they are to follow.

• *SIP:* The SIP set of strategies is reportedly consistent with R. C. Anderson's (1970) findings indicating that students benefit from learning task activities that require attention to content and active engagement in processing.

S reminds students to *summarize* the content of each page or naturally divided section of the text. This summarization of text invites students to reflect on and interact with the content in producing a summarized version.

I represents the notion of *imaging.* This is a reminder that students should form an internal visual display of the content while reading, which provides a second imprint of the text's content.

P reminds students to *predict* while reading. As each page or naturally divided section is read, students should pause to predict what they may learn next. While reading the section predicted, students verify, revise, or modify predictions according to what they learned. This process of predicting and verifying can carry students through entire selections and help hold their interest.

• *EEEZ:* The second strategy gets students to elaborate mentally on new content information to facilitate long-term retention. In her introduction to this strategy, Dana (1989) explains,

After reading, it is recommended that students review what they have read in light of the purpose that was set for the reading assignment. Students are told that after reading they should "take it easy" (EEEZ) and make an attempt to *explain* (E) the content in a manner commensurate with the purpose set for reading. They might have to answer questions, generate questions, define a concept, or provide a summary. (p. 33)

The other ideas represented by the EEEZ acronym are

E: *Explore* the same content material as it has been described by other authors of different texts. These comparisons often help students to clarify important ideas.

E: *Expand* the subject matter by reading other texts that go beyond the content covered by the original text.

After expanding, students should respond to the original purpose for reading the assignment given by the teacher and should embellish their responses with additional content discovered during the EEEZ process.

Improving Fluency

All students, and especially struggling readers, should spend significant amounts of time—20 to 30 minutes per day—in the act of reading if they are to grow and progress. Krashen's (1992) research demonstrates that 20 minutes of daily sustained reading in materials of high interest and appropriate difficulty can help students grow by as much as six months per year in overall reading fluency. Daily sustained reading builds vocabulary knowledge and sharpens students' reading skills. Group-assisted reading is one idea that can help you build reading fluency with middle schoolers.

All students should read books they enjoy at least 20 to 30 minutes each day to build fluency (Krashen, 1992).

Group-Assisted Reading

Group-assisted reading (Eldredge, 1990) refers to teachers helping a group of students read text material in unison—emphasizing correct phrasing, intonation, and pitch. In group-assisted reading, teachers read each book many times with students until students can read it fluently with expression. In a variation of group-assisted reading called *dyad* reading groups, the teacher's role is filled with a peer "lead reader." Both group-assisted and dyad reading groups have been shown to be more effective in classroom settings with at-risk readers than more traditional methods (Eldredge & Quinn, 1988; Eldredge, 1990).

Dyad reading is one of the most powerful reading improvement tools.

It is also crucial that a Writing Workshop program be established as part of the comprehensive reading program. Although not empirically tested, we believe a writing-dyad system should be used with students having learning problems. Because of the reciprocal nature of reading and writing, the natural development of word-spelling knowledge and phonic awareness fostered in students through the writing process, as well as the accompanying interest in books and authors that springs from writing experiences, make writing a mainstay in any literacy program for students having reading problems.

HELPING ENGLISH LANGUAGE LEARNERS WITH CONTENT AREA TEXTS

English language learners (ELL students) can be particularly challenged by nonfiction texts. This section describes research-proven ways to help ELL students meet the challenge informational texts can pose.

Modifying Linguistic Variables

Limited knowledge of a second language can prevent learners from making full use of semantic, syntactic, and other clues in content reading materials. Kang (1994) suggests the following tactics to help ELL students with content demands:

- Reduce the vocabulary load.
- Preteach key vocabulary concepts before students read an assigned passage.
- Use prereading questions, highlighting text, notes, or questions in the margins, and graphic organizers to help students attend to important information.
- Use postreading discussion groups to expose ELL learners to more complex language input.

Modifying Knowledge Variables

A second variable affecting an ELL student's ability to learn from reading content area texts is background knowledge. In some cases, a text may presuppose culture-specific background knowledge that is not part of an ELL student's experiences. Likewise, some ELL readers may focus their reading too heavily on the print (decoding), thus failing to activate their prior knowledge to assist in understanding content area text. In either of these scenarios, Kang (1994) suggests strategies for *before, during,* and *after reading* that may help ELL learners succeed in reading content area texts. (Note: Many of these ideas are discussed more fully in other chapters.)

Before Reading
- Semantic mapping
- Structured overviews
- Discussion that draws attention to:
  contradictions
  opposing examples
  exceptions
  categorization
  comparisons relating to concepts in the native language

During Reading
- Pattern guides
- Marginal glosses

After Reading
- Semantic feature analysis
- Small-group discussion

Literacy Variables

In some cases, ELL students may have limited first language literacy skills. Other ELL students may have insufficient second language proficiency to use well-developed first language literacy skills. In either case, specific *prereading, during reading,* and *postreading* strategies can optimize ELL students' opportunities to read content texts effectively.

Before Reading

- Preview the text by showing students how to use headings, subheadings, bold text, marginal glosses or notes, illustrations, or end-of-chapter questions.
- Help students set a purpose for reading by teaching self-questioning strategies.

During Reading

- Provide directions, signals, and questions to focus students' reading on an interaction with the text and their own knowledge.
- Suggest a study strategy and model its use with the text.
- Help students adjust their reading rate to the text difficulty.
- Help students develop skimming and scanning skills.
- Help students predict outcomes, make and confirm inferences, and solve problems.
- Help students use metacognitive monitoring skills.
- Remind students of when and how to use fix-up or repair strategies when comprehension breaks down.

After Reading

- Writing text summaries or completing text pattern guides will help students get more experience with the organization of various text patterns in content area reading.

Summary

In this final chapter, we have discussed how middle school students can be helped to use *reading to learn* strategies in their content area classes. Expository or informative texts in various forms now make up the daily reading diet of these students. The reading challenges they face include complicated vocabulary, increased concept load, and less readable texts. If not addressed, reading problems in the middle school can become *viral.*

Teachers are able to help students attack these new challenges successfully in many ways. A content analysis helps teachers identify important facts, concepts, and generalizations students must learn. Armed with this knowledge, teachers can construct an array of student-support learning aids, including graphic organizers, study guides, and vocabulary development activities. Students can also be taught various efficient study strategies, such as skimming and scanning techniques. Another important skill middle school students acquire is the ability to monitor and adjust their own reading comprehension, or metacognition.

Students who are struggling with basic reading tasks in the middle school can be helped in a number of ways. Improving reading fluency through sustained reading periods, vocabulary development, and research-proven commercial programs can be instrumental in helping these students succeed.

Finally, it is our responsibility as teachers to make sure that all of our students become as literate as their innate talents and abilities permit them. Literacy is the key that opens the door to opportunity. We accomplish that, at least in part, by continuing to learn about the science and art form of teaching and learning.

Check your understanding of chapter concepts by using the self assessment for Chapter 13 on our Companion Website at www.prenhall.com/reutzel.

Concept Applications

In the Classroom

1. Select a chapter from a middle school social studies book on a level of your choice. Using the descriptors for expository text patterns discussed in this chapter, identify as many patterns (e.g., description, comparison) as possible in the unit and answer the following questions: Which patterns do you find? How often do they occur in the unit? Are any patterns missing? If so, what could you do as the classroom teacher to compensate for these omissions? Is it possible that omission of some patterns could lead to learning difficulties for some children? If so, why?

2. Developing a thorough content analysis is the foundation for the successful teaching of content area subjects. To practice and refine this ability, try the following: Form a group with two or three of your colleagues. Select several lengthy magazine articles having to do with various topics relevant to middle school subjects. You may want to consider such magazines as *Air & Space* or *National Geographic* for the articles. After reading their article, each person should develop a content analysis to present to the rest of the group. By comparing analyses, it will be possible to detect whether important bits of information (or for that matter, superfluous information) have been included.

In the Field

Computer applications in education account for one of the fastest growing industries in the world. Perform a library search, and compile a list of the latest software and Internet Web sites available for the teaching of content area vocabulary and concepts for two topics (Mount Everest, the field of Quantum Physics, research on automobile safety). Perhaps a media specialist at a local middle school will assist you in this effort. After your list has been compiled, write to the various sources requesting more detailed information. This process will help you to determine which programs are most beneficial, and it may be possible to order new software and other resources for your school's library/media center in the future.

Recommended Readings

Cafolla, R., Kauffman, D., & Knee, R. (1997). *World Wide Web for teachers: An interactive guide.* Boston: Allyn & Bacon.
Cooter, R. B., Jr., & Flynt, E. S. (1996). *Teaching reading in the content areas: Developing content literacy for all students.* Upper Saddle River, NJ: Merrill/Prentice Hall.

Comprehensive Literacy Resources for Teachers

A message to our literacy education colleagues ... The purpose of Appendix A is to offer our readers a selection of resources useful in constructing Reading Resource Rooms and/or classroom libraries that facilitate Comprehensive Literacy Instruction. These materials and ideas are meant as only a starting point, and we hope that readers will consider helping us to continue building this "database" by contacting us individually or through our publisher.

HOW TO CREATE A READING RESOURCE ROOM

What Is a Reading Resource Room?

Many schools are finding that they can make their dollars go farther by setting up a room in which to place all of the books that are suitable for Guided Reading. Many of these books have been purchased with Title I money and other district resources (in other words, books NOT purchased with the teacher's own personal funds), then distributed to various classrooms. As a result, no one teacher has a large enough range of books (i.e., multiple copies of single titles, topics, etc.) for the students in her/his room. When all of the books in the school have been gathered, sorted by level using Reading Recovery or other similar formulae, and cataloged in one place, teachers can then check out the books they need by choosing the appropriate level and the number of books.

What If I Don't Have a Room?

Some schools have been able to find space in the media center; others have used an office once used by a teaching assistant, and so on. A central location works best.

What Grade Levels Would Find a Reading Resource Room Useful, and When?

Kindergarten teachers begin to use the books sometime after the winter holidays, grades 1–3 use the room anytime during the school year, and grades 4–6 use the room if they have students struggling in reading. As the room grows in content, most schools add chapter books for the upper grades.

How Much Does a Reading Resource Room Cost?

If you had to start from scratch, the cost would be close to $25,000, however most schools have many books that have been purchased previously by district or federal funds.

How Do I Begin?

1. Locate a space.
2. Locate all of the suitable books already in the school.
3. Involve *all* teachers in the planning, especially in grades K–3.

What's the Bottom Line for What I Need?

- When you have located the **books** you now have you will need to order some books to fill in the gaps so that you have enough titles for each level. You will need:
  - 20–25 titles (per Reading Recovery or Guided Reading levels)
  - 12–15 copies of each title

  Again, remember to start with what you have and gradually build from there.

- After the space has been determined, you'll need to locate some **shelving.** The shelving does not have to be fancy. Home Depot, Lowes, and other warehouse stores have plastic shelves for about $40, but you may be able to find some cheaper. (You can get 70 magazine boxes on the shelves if you use both sides.)
- You will need some **magazine boxes** to contain the books. These can be ordered locally. The number needed will be determined by how many books you have or plan to order. Plastic boxes are also available, but are more expensive.
- **Labels** can be purchased at any office supply. We suggest Avery #5165. This is a single sheet of self-stick labels—100 sheets per box.
- **Clothespins** to use in checking out books can be purchased at Wal-Mart or Target. Each teacher using the room will need 20–30 clothespins, which can be stored in a resealable plastic bag. The teacher places a clothespin with his/her name on it to the front of the box of the books being borrowed.
- You will need some **rubber stamps with the school name** to stamp each book.
- If you include Big Books for Shared Reading in your room, you will need six big **plastic tubs.** These can be found at Target, Wal-Mart, and so on for about $5 each.

Can the Room Be Used for Anything Else Other Than Guided Reading Books?

Some schools have added Big Books, read-alouds, and so on to the room.

GUIDED READING LEVELING COMPARISONS

- Following is a handy guide for helping you to translate books that are listed from publishers using Guided Reading ratings to leveling systems— http://www.rigby.com/corrlevel/level/charts/readlevel.asp

General Explanation of Criteria for determining Guided Reading Levels of texts can be found in Chapter 11. We also recommend the following websites for information about leveled books and how to level books in differing ways.

Websites Offering Lists and Downloadable Leveled Books:

- http://registration.beaverton.k12.or.us/lbdb
- http://faculty.tamu.commerce.edu/espinoza/s/ellis-b-rdlevl.htm
- http://www.k12.or.us/instruction/literacy/leveled_books
- http://www.coe.ufl.edu/Special/Pages/LaneEEX6936/booksources.htm
- http://www.leveledbooks.com
- http://readinga-z.com
- http://www.geocities.com/teachingwithheart/levelbooks.html

Websites Describing Differing Leveling Processes and Comparison Charts

- http://www.readometer.com
- http://www.renlearn.com/ar/atossummary.htm
- http://www.rigby.com/corrlevel/level/charts/readlevel.asp
- http://www.lexile.com

SELECTED GUIDED READING BOOKS—LEVELS A–Z (ENGLISH)

Title	Levels: GR	RR	Publisher	Author/Series
Adventures of Huck Finn & Tom Sawyer	Z	-	Scholastic	Twain, Mark
After the Flood	G	12	Rigby	PM Green/Exten Add-to
Airplane, The	B	2	Wright Group	Sunshine
All Fall Down	C	3	Oxford	Wildsmith, Brian
All Over Me	B	2	Steck-Vaughn	Pair-It Books
Amanda's Bear	G	12	Dominie Press	Reading Corners
Amazing Popple Seed, The	F	11	Rigby	Read-Alongs/Stg. 1
Amber Brown Sees Red	N	-	Scholastic	Danziger, Paula
Amelia Bedelia	L	-	Harper Trophy	Parrish, Peggy
Animal Farm	Z	-	Harcourt Brace	Orwell, George
Animal Habitats	C	3	Sundance	Little Red Readers
Animal Homes	B	2	Sundance	Little Red Readers
Anne Frank: Life in Hiding	W	-	Avon	Hurwitz, Johanna
Anne of Green Gables	V	-	Bantam Doubleday Dell	Montgomery, L.M.
Applebird	A	1	Oxford	Wildsmith, Brian
Are You a Ladybug?	E	7	Wright Group	Sunshine
Arguments	J–K	18	Wright Group	Sunshine
Ask Nicely	F	10	Rigby	Literacy 2000
At School	B	2	Wright Group	Sunshine
At the Farm	B	2	Sundance	Little Red Readers
At the Library	C	3	Rigby	PM Starters 2
At the Zoo	A	1–2	Kaeden Books	Kloes, Carol
Baby Elephant's New Bike	F	10	Wright Group	Foundations
Baby Monkey	I	16	Scott-Foresman	Reading Unlimited
Baby Sitters Club Mystery	O	-	Scholastic	Martin, Ann M.
Babysitter, The	G	13	Rigby	PM Green/Exten Add-to
Banana Shake	D	4	Wright Group	Book Bank
Barbeque	A	1–2	Wright Group	Sunshine
Bare Feet	B	2	Wright Group	Visions
Barrel of Gold, A	J–K	18	Wright Group	Storybox

Title	Levels: GR	RR	Publisher	Author/Series
Basketball	A	1	Wright Group	Wonder World
Bath for a Beagle, A	D	5	Troll	First Start
Bears in the Night	D	4	Random House	Berenstain
Bee, The	C	3	Wright Group	Storybox
Ben's Tooth	G	13	Rigby	PM/Green Level
Bicycle, The	C	3	Wright Group	Storybox
Big Chase, The	A	1–2	Wright Group	Foundations
Big Kick, The	D	4	Rigby	PM/Red Level
Big Toe, The	E	7	Wright Group	Storybox Read-Togethers
Biggest Cake in the World, The	E	9	Richard Owen	Ready to Read
Birthday Cake	D	5	Rigby	Guided Reading/Stg. 1
Blackbird's Nest	G	12	Richard Owen	Ready to Read
Blue Jay, The	H	14	D. C. Heath	Little Readers
Boggywooga	I	16	Wright Group	Sunshine
Bone Dance	X	-	Random House	Brooks, Martha
Boston Tea Party, The	S	-	Children's Press	Cornerstones of Freedom
Boxcar Children	O	-	Albert Whitman & Co.	Warner, Gertrude C.
Boy Who Cried Wolf, The	I	16	Wright Group	Aesop
Brave Triceratops	G	12	Rigby	PM/Green Level
Bronze Bow	U	-	Houghton Mifflin	Speare, Elizabeth G.
Brown Bear, Brown Bear	D	4	Holt	Martin, Bill
Bull Run	Y	-	Harper Collins	Fleischman, Paul
Bunnicula	Q	-	Avon	Howe, James
Bus Ride, The	D	4	Scott-Foresman	Reading Unlimited
Caddie Woodlawn	R	-	Bantam Doubleday Dell	Brink, Carol R.
Call It Courage	X	-	Alladin	Armstrong, Sperry
Call of the Wild	Y	-	Signet Classics	London, Jack
Cam Jansen and the Chocolate Fudge Mystery	L	-	Puffin Books	Adler, David A.
Camping	E	7	Wright Group	Sunshine Ext.
Carrot Seed, The	G	12	Harper & Collins	Kraus, Ruth
Carrots	B	2	Grolier, Capstone	Pebble Books
Cat and Mouse	B	2	Rigby	PM Starters 2
Cat on the Mat	B	2	Oxford	Wildsmith, Brian
Caterpillars	P	-	Steck-Vaughn	Mini Pets
Charlie and the Chocolate Factory	R	-	Bantam Doubleday Dell	Dahl, Roald
Chew Chew Chew	D	5	Rigby	Guided Reading/Stg. 2
Chicken Pox	H	14	D. C. Heath	Little Readers
Choosing a Puppy	E	7	Rigby	PM Yellow/Exten Add-to
Christmas Tree, The	F	10	Rigby	PM/Blue Level
Circus Train, The	A	1–2	Sundance	Little Red Readers
Clifford, the Big Red Dog	J–K	18	Scholastic	Bridwell, Norman
Clothes	C	3	Rigby	Interaction
Count and See	A	1–2	MacMillan	Hoban, Tana
Coyote Plants a Peach Tree	I	16	Richard Owen	Young Learners
Creepy Caterpillar	E	7	D. C. Heath	Little Readers
Dad	A	1–2	PM Starters	Rigby
Dad's Headache	F	10	Wright Group	Sunshine
Dad's New Path	F	10	Wright Group	Foundations
Danger	D	4	Wright Group	Storybox
Daughter of the Mountains	V	-	Penguin Group	Rankin, Louis
Day No Pigs Would Die	Z	-	Random House	Peck, Sylvia

SELECTED GUIDED READING BOOKS—LEVELS A–Z (ENGLISH)—CONT'D

Title	Levels: GR	RR	Publisher	Author/Series
Dear Santa	B	2	Rigby	Guided Reading/Stg. 2
Dig	C	3–4	KinderReaders	Rigby
Dizzy Lizzy	E	8	Rigby	Guided Reading/Stg. 2
Don't Forget the Bacon	J–K	20	Greenwillow	Hutchins, Pat
Don't Wake the Baby	B	2	Rigby	Guided Reading/Stg. 1
Dr. Green	G	12	D. C. Heath	Little Readers
Dreaming	B	2	Rigby	Smart Starts
Dressing Up	A	1	Rigby	PM Starters 1
Earthquake	J–K	20	Wright Group	Wonder World
Eggshell Garden, The	A	1–2	Wright Group	Sunshine
Elephants Good For?	G	13	Dominie Press	Reading Corners
Encyclopedia Brown	P	-	Bantam Doubleday Dell	Sobal, Donald & Rose
Exploding Frog	I	16	Modern Curriculum	Language Works
Fall	B	2	Newbridge	Discovery Links
Families	B	2	Rigby	Interaction
Farm Concert, The	D	5	Wright Group	Storybox Read-Togethers
Farm, The	A	1	Rigby	Guided Reading/Stg. 1
Father Bear Goes Fishing	D	5	Rigby	PM/Red Level
Feet	D	5	Wright Group	Storybox
First Day at School	D	5	Dominie Press	Carousel Readers
Five Little Monkeys Jumping on the Bed	E	8	Clarion	Christelow, Eileen
Flat Stanley	M	-	Harper Trophy	Brown, Jeff
Fledgling, The	U	-	Scholastic	Langton, Jane
Flying Fish, The	H	14	Rigby	PM Green/Exten Add-to
Four Ice Creams	D	4	Rigby	PM Starters 2
Fox and the Little Red Hen, The	J–K	19	Rigby	Traditional Tales 1
Freckle Juice	M	-	Bantam Doubleday Dell	Blume, Judy
Friends are Forever	J–K	18	Rigby	Literacy 2000 Satellites
Frog and Toad Are Friends	J–K	19	Harper & Collins	Lobel, Arnold
Frogs	A	1–2	Wright Group	Twig
George Washington Carver	N	-	Biography	Benchmark Education
Getting Dressed	A	1	Wright Group	Sunshine
Gingerbread Boy, The (story)	F	10	Stech-Vaughn	New Way (red)
Gingerbread Man, The	E	9	D. C. Heath	Little Readers
Going to School	A	1–2	Rigby	Smart Starts
Going Up and Down	B	2	Pioneer Valley	Early Emergent
Goldilocks and the Three Bears	G	13	Rigby	Traditional Tales 1
Goodnight Moon	H	14	Harper & Row	Brown
Got the Sun	I	17	D. C. Heath	Little Readers
Grandpa Snored	E	9	Rigby	Guided Reading/Stg. 2
Grasshopper on the Road	L	-	Harper Trophy	Lobel, Arnold
Great African Americans. . .	T	-	Crabtree	Rediger, Pat
Great Big Enormous Turnip	G	13	Scott-Foresman	Reading Unlimited
Great Gilly Hopkins, The	S	-	Hearst	Patterson, Katherine
Growing Up	P	-	It's Science	Children's Press
Hair	A	1–2	Dominie	Carousel Earlybirds
Hand-Me-Downs, The	G	12	D. C. Heath	Little Readers
Happy Birthday!	D	4	Rigby	Guided Reading/Stg. 1
Harriet the Spy	T	-	Harper Collins	Fitzhugh, Louise

Title	Levels: GR	RR	Publisher	Author/Series
Harry Potter. . .	V	-	Scholastic	Rowling, J.K.
Haunted House, The	E	7	Wright Group	Storybox
Have You Seen the Crocodile?	E	9	Harper & Row	West, Colin
Helen Keller: From Tragedy To Triumph	O	-	Alladin	
Help I'm Trapped	Q	-	Scholastic	Strasser, Todd
Henny Penny	I	16	Clarion	Galdone
Henry's Choice	J–K	20	Scott-Foresman	Reading Unlimited
Hobbit, The	Z	-	Ballantine Books	Tolkien, J.R.R.
Hole in Harry's Pocket, The	H	15	D. C. Heath	Little Readers
Honk!	B	2	Mondo Publishing	Book Shop
Horrible Thing with Hairy Feet	H	14	Rigby	Read-Alongs/Stg. 2
How Do I Put It On	H	14	Penguin	Watanabe, Shigeo
How to Ride a Giraffe	I	16	D. C. Heath	Little Readers
Hungry Giant, The	F	10	Wright Group	Storybox Read-Togethers
I Am a Dentist	C	3	Dominie Press	Read More Books
I Am a Fireman	E	6	Dominie Press	Read More Books
I Am a Photographer	E	7	Dominie Press	Read More Books
I Can Make Music	A	1	Sundance	Little Red Readers
I Can Read	B	2	Richard Owen	Ready to Read
I Like to Eat	A	1	Dominie Press	Reading Corners
I Like to Paint	A	1	Dominie Press	Reading Corners
I Live in a House	E	6	Dominie Press	Read More Books
I Live in an Apartment	E	6	Dominie Press	Read More Books
I Want Ice Cream	C	3	Wright Group	Storybox
I'm the King of the Mountain	G	12	Richard Owen	Ready to Read
In a Dark, Dark Wood	E	7	Wright Group	Storybox Read-Togethers
In Spring	B	2	Newbridge	Discovery Links
In the Teacup	A	1–2	Rigby	Kindereaders
Invisible	I	16	Rigby	Read-Alongs/Stg. 2
Island of the Blue Dolphins	V	-	Bantam Doubleday Dell	O'Dell, Scott
It Looked Like Spilt Milk	E	7	Harper & Row	Shaw, Charles
Jack and the Beanstalk	H	15	Rigby	Traditional Tales 2
Jack-O-Lantern	A	1	Wright Group	Twig Books
Jackson's Monster	I	16	D. C. Heath	Little Readers
James Is Hiding	A	1–2	Rigby	Windmill
Joe and the Mouse	F	10	Oxford Univ. Press	Reading Tree
Joe's Father	E	7	Wright Group	Book Bank
Jungle Book, The	U	-	Scholastic	Kipling, Rudyard
Jungle Parade: A Singing Game	D	5	Scott-Foresman	Little Celebrations
Jungle Spots	B	2	Celebration Press	Little Celebration
Just Like Daddy	E	9	Simon & Schuster	Asch, Frank
Just Like Grandpa	E	8	Rigby	Guided Reading/Stg. 3
Just Like Me	E	7	Children's Press	Rookie Readers
Kangaroo	D	4	Dominie Press	Reading Corners
Keep Out	A	1–2	Modern Curriculum	Ready Readers
Kites	B	2	Scott-Foresman	Special Practice Books
Late for Football	F	11	Rigby	PM/Blue Level
Lion and the Mouse, The	G	12	Rigby	Traditional Tales 1
Little Gorilla	I	17	Clarion	Bornstein, Ruth
Little House	Q	-	Harper Trophy	Wilder, Laura E.
Little Red Hen, The	J–K	18	Viking	Galdone, Paul

SELECTED GUIDED READING BOOKS—LEVELS A–Z (ENGLISH)—CONT'D

Title	Levels: GR	RR	Publisher	Author/Series
Little Women	M	-	Random House	Bullseye
Lizard Loses His Tail	D	5	Rigby	PM/Red Level
Lizards and Salamanders	J–K	20	Scott-Foresman	Reading Unlimited
Log Cabin in the Woods	R	-	Scholastic	Henry, Joanne L.
Look at Me	B	2	Rigby	PM Starters 1
Looking for Halloween	D	4	Kaeden Corp.	Urmston, K.
Lots of Cats	E	6	Scott-Foresman	Special Practice Books
Lots of Things	A	1	Dominie	Reading Corners
Lunch Time	D	5	Dominie Press	Carousel Readers
Lunchbox Mystery, The	N	-	Scholastic	Lohans, Alison
Magic School Bus	P	-	Scholastic	Cole, J. & Degen, B.
Making Oatmeal	E	7	Rigby	Interaction
Mark Twain	W	-	Scholastic	Cox, Clinton
Matthew Likes to Read	I	17	Richard Owen	Ready to Read
Me	C	3	Dominie Press	Reading Corners
Michael in the Hospital	E	8	Oxford Univ. Press	Reading Tree
Mike's New Bike	E	9	Troll	First Start Easy
Miss Nelson is Missing	L	-	Houghton Mifflin	Allard, Harry
Miss Nelson Is Missing	J–K	20	Houghton Mifflin	Allard, Harry
Mom	A	1	Rigby	PM Starters 1
Moms and Dads	A	1	Rigby	PM Starters 1
Monkeys	G	12	Scott-Foresman	Special Practice Books
Monster Party, The	D	4	Wright Group	Storybox Read-Togethers
Monster	H	15	Rigby	Read-Alongs/Stg. 3
More Spaghetti I Say	F	11	Scholastic	Gilman, Rita
Mosquito Buzzed, A	E	8	D. C. Heath	Little Readers
Mother and Me	B	2	Kaeden Books	Spinelli, Nancy L.
Mouse and the Elephant, The	I	17	D. C. Heath	Little Readers
Moving	B	2	Sundance	Little Red Readers
Mrs. Wishy Washy	E	8	Wright Group	Storybox Read-Togethers
Mud Pie	D	4	Rigby	Guided Reading/Stg. 1
Mumps	E	6	Rigby	PM/Yellow Level
My Bike	E	8	Richard Owen	Ready to Read
My Birthday Party	A	1	D. C. Heath	Little Readers
My Book	A	1	Penguin	Maris, Ron
My Brother Sam Is Dead	Y	-	Scholastic	Collier, J. & C.
My Computer	F	11	Wright Group	Wonder World
My Hiroshima	T	-	Penguin Group	Morimoto, Junko
My Holiday Diary	F	10	Around the World	Hall, N., & Robinson, A.
My Shadow	C	3	Wright Group	Sunshine
New Baby, The	E	7	Rigby	PM/Yellow Level
New House, The	A	1	Wright Group	Sunshine
Nicole Helps Grandma	B	2	Univ. of Maine	Univ. of Maine
Night the Lights Went Out, The	H	14	D. C. Heath	Little Readers
Noisy Nora	I	16	Dial	Wells, Rosemary
On a Cold, Cold Day	C	3	Rigby	Tadpoles
On Top of Spaghetti	F	11	Scott-Foresman	Little Celebrations
One Sock, Two Socks	G	12	Dominie Press	Reading Corners
One-Eyed Jake	M	-	Morrow	Hutchins, Pat
Orphan of Ellis Island, The	S	-	Scholastic	Woodruff, Elvira

Title	Levels: GR	RR	Publisher	Author/Series
Orphan Train Adventures. . .	W	-	Dell	Nixon, Joan L.
Ouch!	A	1	Rigby	Smart Starts
Our Rocket	B	2	Celebration Press	Learning Media Literacy
Our Teacher, Miss Pool	E	6	Richard Owen	Ready to Read
Paint the Sky	A	1	Wright Group	Sunshine
Pancakes	F	11	Wright Group	Foundations
Pet Hamster	E	6	Scott-Foresman	Special Practice Books
Pip and the Little Monkey	F	10	Oxford University Press	Reading Tree
Pip at the Zoo	E	9	Oxford University Press	Reading Tree
Popcorn Book, The	J–K	18	Scott-Foresman	Reading Unlimited
Rabbits	F	11	Scott-Foresman	Special Practice Books
Rain	B	2	Dominie Press	Reading Corners
Rain, Rain	D	5	Richard Owen	Ready to Read
Ramona	O	-	Avon	Cleary, Beverly
Reading Is Everywhere	D	5	Wright Group	Sunshine-Social Studies
Recess	B	2	Dominie	Teachers' Choice Series
Red and Blue Mittens	J–K	20	Scott-Foresman	Reading Unlimited
Rescue, The	J–K	19	Richard Owen	Ready to Read
Ribbit!	A	1	Celebration Press	Little Celebrations
Ride, Ride, Ride	E	8	Macmillan	Series R
Roll of Thunder, Hear My Cry	W	-	Penguin Group	Taylor, Mildred D.
Roll Over: A Counting People Song	D	4	Clarion	Peek, Merle
Rosa Parks: My Story	U	-	Scholastic	Parks, Rosa
Rosie's Walk	E	9	Macmillan	Hutchins, Pat
Rumpelstiltskin	J–K	20	Wright Group	Once Upon a Time
Sadie and the Snowman	L	-	Scholastic	Morgan, Allen
Safe Place, The	H	14	Richard Owen	Ready to Read
Sam's Ball	E	6	Morrow	Lindgren, Barbro
Sausages	D	4	Rigby	PM/Red Level
Say Hello!	A	1–2	Hampton-Brown	Rise & Shine
Secret Garden	U	-	Scholastic	Burnett, Frances H.
Shadow of the Wolf	N	-	Random House	Gloria, Whelan
Shoe Grabber, The	I	16	Rigby	Read-Alongs/Stg. 2
Shopping at the Mall	G	12	Kaeden Corp.	Urmston, K., & Evans, K.
Shopping	C	3	Sundance	Little Red Readers
Smarty Pants	E	8	Wright Group	Storybox Read-Togethers
Snake Slithers, A	H	14	Scott-Foresman	Special Practice Books
Snow Walk	D	5	Dominie Press	Reading Corners
Snow	B	2	Newbridge	Discovery Links
Soccer at the Park	E	8	Rigby	PM Yellow/Exten Add-to
Soldier Boy	T	-	Language for Learning	Burks, Brian
Sounder	T	-	Scholastic	Armstrong, William
Space Journey	A	1	Wright Group	Sunshine
Space Race	I	17	Wright Group	Sunshine
Splish Splash	E	6	Scott-Foresman	Little Celebrations
Star Fisher, The	S	-	Scholastic	Yep, Lawrence
Sticky Stanley	F	10	Troll	First Start Easy
Strawberry Hill	Y	-	Simon & Shuster	LaFaye, A.
Sun/Wind/Rain	H	15	Scott-Foresman	Special Practice Books
Superfudge	Q	-	Bantam Doubleday Dell	Blume, Judy
Surprise for Mom, A	E	9	Kaeden Corp.	Urmston, K., & Evans, K.
Susie Goes Shopping	F	10	Troll	First Start Easy

SELECTED GUIDED READING BOOKS—LEVELS A–Z (ENGLISH)—CONT'D

Title	Levels: GR	RR	Publisher	Author/Series
Taste of Blackberries	P	-	Scholastic	Buchanan Smith, Doris
Team Sports	B	2	Wright Group	Twig
Tecumseh	R	-	Learning Media Ltd.	Morris, Rod
Tee-Ball	C	3	Scott-Foresman	Little Celebrations
Teeny, Tiny Woman, The	I	16	Scholastic	Seuling, Barbara
Ten Little Bears	F	11	Scott-Foresman	Reading Unlimited
Tents	H	15	Scott-Foresman	Reading Unlimited
Thank You	I	17	Richard Owen	Ready to Read
There's a Nightmare in My Closet	I	16	Dial	Mayer, Mercer
Things I Like	D	5	Knopf	Browne, Anthony
Things to Read	A	1–2	University of Maine	Univ. of Maine
Three Billy Goats Gruff	G	12	D. C. Heath	Little Readers
Three Little Pigs	G	13	Scott-Foresman	Reading Unlimited
Three Little Pigs, The	G	13	Dominie Press	Reading Corners
Tidy Titch	I	16	Greenwillow	Hutchins, Pat
To the Beach	E	6	Kaeden Corporation	Urmston, K., & Evans, K.
Too Fast	A	1	Dominie Press	Reading Corners
Toot, Toot	C	3	Oxford	Wildsmith, Brian
Tracks	E	7	Scott-Foresman	Special Practice Books
Tree House, The	B	2	Wright Group	Storybox
Trojan Horse, The	N	-	Rigby	Literacy 2000
Try It	D	5	Dominie Press	Reading Corners
T-Shirts	E	9	Richard Owen	Ready to Read
Tuck Everlasting	U	-	Farrar, Straus, & Giroux	Babbitt, Natalie
Ugly Duckling, The	J–K	18	Rigby	Traditional Tales 2
Under the Bed	A	1–2	Rigby	Smart Starts
Underwater	F	11	Wright Group	Twig Books
Vacations	B	2	Rigby	Smart Starts
Vampires Don't Wear Polka Dots	M	-	Scholastic	Dadey, D. & Jones, M. T.
Velveteen Rabbit	Q	-	Hearst	Williams, Margery
Very Hungry Caterpillar, The	J–K	18	Putnam	Carle, Eric
Wagon, The	G	13	Scott-Foresman	Special Practice Books
Wait Skates	F	11	Children's Press	Rookie Readers
Walk, The	G	12	Scott-Foresman	Special Practice Books
Watcher, The	Z	-	Simon & Shuster	Howe, James
Watching TV	B	2	Wright Group	Sunshine Extensions
We Ski	B	2	Shortland Publications	Story-Teller First Snow
What a Dog	E	9	Troll	First Start Easy
What Am I?	G	12	Wright Group	Sunshine
What Animals Do You See?	D	4	Dominie Press	Read More Books
What Can I Do?	D	4	Dominie Press	Read More Books
What Comes Out at Night?	B	2	Sundance	Little Red Readers
What Do You Like to Wear?	D	5	Dominie Press	Read More Books
What Goes in the Bathtub?	C	3	Rigby	Guided Reading/Stg. 1
What Is It Called?	D	5	Scott-Foresman	Special Practice Books
What Is Scary?	B	2	Rigby	Windmill
What's for Dinner?	E	7	Seedling	Salem, L., & Stewart, J.
What's Round?	A	1–2	Newbridge	Discovery Links
Wheels on the Bus	E	9	Random House	Ziefert
When Dad Came Home	E	9	Rigby	Guided Reading/Stg. 2

Title	Levels: GR	RR	Publisher	Author/Series
When the Circus Comes to Town	A	1	Sundance	Little Red Readers
Where Are My Socks?	E	6	Richard Owen	Ready to Read
Where Is Miss Pool?	E	6	Richard Owen	Ready to Read
Where Is the Cat?	D	4	Dominie Press	Read More Books
Where the Red Fern Grows	X	-	Bantam Doubleday Dell	Rawls, Wilson
White Fang	Y	-	Scholastic	London, Jack
Who Ate the Broccoli	E	7	D. C. Heath	Little Readers
Who Likes Ice Cream	A	1	Rigby	Guided Reading/Stg. 1
Who Took the Farmer's Hat?	H	15	Scholastic	Nodset, Joan
Wiggly, Jiggly, Joggly, Tooth, A	E	7	Scott-Foresman	Little Celebrations
Willy the Helper	E	6	D. C. Heath	Little Readers
Wind, The	E	8	Richard Owen	Ready to Read
Winter Sleeps	E	9	Dominie Press	Reading Corners
Witch of Blackbird Pond	W	-	Bantam Doubleday Dell	Speare, Elizabeth G.
Witch's Haircut, The	G	12	Wright Group	Windmill
World of Adventure. . .	R	-	Bantam Doubleday Dell	Paulsen, Gary
Worms for Breakfast	I	16	D. C. Heath	Little Readers
Wrinkle in Time	V	-	Bantam Doubleday Dell	L'Engle, Madeleine
Yearling	X	-	Simon & Shuster	Rawlings, Marjorie K.
Young Merlin Trilogy	S	-	Scholastic	Yolen, Jane
Zebras	O	-	Capstone Press	Holmes, Kevin
Zoo Food	D	4	Dominie Press	Reading Corners
Zoo, A	A	1	Rigby	Literacy 2000

SELECTED GUIDED READING BOOKS (SPANISH)

Title	Level: GR	RR	Publisher	Author/Series
El caldo	A	1	Celebration Press	Más Piñata–Stage 1
La charreada	A	1	Celebration Press	Más Piñata–Stage 1
Mi muñeco de nieve	C	3	Celebration Press	Más Piñata–Stage 1
Un pajarito	E	5	Celebration Press	Más Piñata–Stage 1
¡Yo bailo!	B	2	Celebration Press	Más Piñata– Stage 1
¡A tocar?	E	6	Celebration Press	Más Piñata–Stage 2
Insectos, insectos	D	4	Celebration Press	Más Piñata–Stage 2
¿Qué puedo comprar?	E	8	Celebration Press	Más Piñata–Stage 2
Compartiendo a un papá	E	9	Celebration Press	Pequeñitas Cel
Las gallinas de Señora Sato	E	6	Celebration Press	Pequeñitas Cel
Los cinco dinosaurios	E	7	Celebration Press	Pequeñitas Cel
El renacuajo	F	10	Celebration Press	Piñata Series 2
¿Qué dia es hoy?	F	10	Celebration Press	Piñata Series 2
¿Qué viene en grupos de tres?	E	5/6	Creative Teaching	Marlene Beierle/Anne SylvanPress
A través de la semana con Gato Perro	E	8	Creative Teaching	Rozanne, L.
Cuidemos a la Tierra	E	6	Creative Teaching	Science Series
¿Qué hay en mi bolsillo?	D	5	Creative Teaching	Science Series
¿Quién vive aqui?	E	6	Creative Teaching	Science Series Press
Primer dia de escuela	G	12	Dominie Press	Carrusel A
Algo para compartir	F	11	Dominie Press	Carrusel D
Una amiga especial	F	11	Dominie Press	Carrusel E
Los Payasos	C	3	Dominie Press	Col. Cándida

SELECTED GUIDED READING BOOKS (SPANISH)—CONT'D

Title	Level: GR	RR	Publisher	Author/Series
A mi Tambien	C	3	Dominie Press	Series 1/Col. para el maestro
Felices fiestas	B	2	Dominie Press	Series 1/Col. para el maestro
Pasatiempo invernal	C	3	Dominie Press	Series 1/Col. para el maestro
Acerca de los dino saurios	C	3	Dominie Press	Series 2/Col. para el maestro
La amistad	E	9	Dominie Press	Fiesta de los Libros
De compras	E	7	Dominie Press	Leamos Más
Mi casa	E	7	Dominie Press	Leamos Más
Un dia en mi apartamento	E	6	Dominie Press	Leamos Más
Cinco de mayo	H	14	Dominie Press	Librios Dias Festivos
El cuatro de Julio	I	16	Dominie Press	Librios Dias Festivos
El Dia de las Madres	H	15	Dominie Press	Librios Dias Festivos
La Navidad	G	12	Dominie Press	Librios Dias Festivos
¿Dónde estará el Chango Feliz?	C	3	Dominie Press	Librios Alegria A
La luna	E	6	Dominie Press	Librios Alegria C
Cuenta con la familia	A	1	Hampton-Brown	Pan y Canela–A
El chivo comilón	B	2	Hampton-Brown	Pan y Canela–A
La feria	B	2	Hampton-Brown	Pan y Canela–A
Mi caballito	D	4	Hampton-Brown	Pan y Canela–A
Chiles	E	8	Hampton-Brown	Pan y Canela–B
Papi y yo	C	3	Hampton-Brown	Pan y Canela–B
Uno, dos, tres, y cuatro	E	6	Hampton-Brown	Pan y Canela–B
¿Cuál es el mío	E	8	Hampton-Brown	Pan y Canela–B
Pedrito el exagerado	G	13	Hampton-Brown	
El jardin de Gregorio	F	11	Oxford Press	William Stobbs
El perro de Gregorio	E	6	Oxford Press	
Tomás y su tractor	E	8	Oxford Press	
Tuu tuu	C	3	Oxford Press	
¡Pum! ¡Pum! ¡Pum!	D	5	Oxford Press	
Los edificios de Nueva York	F	9/10	Richard C. Owen	Ann Mace
El Zorro	C	3	Richard C. Owen	Janice Boland
Pájaro, pajaro (AIS*)	D	5	Richard C. Owen	Margaret Mahy
¡Los cerdos espían!	D	5	Richard C. Owen	Rhonda Cox
Colas		RATK	Rigby	Arbol de Lit/Animal Antics
El pirata y el perico	E	8	Rigby	Arbol de Lit/Animal Antics
Mi abuelito roncaba	E	8	Rigby	Arbol de Lit/Animal Antics
Soy un gato	E	8	Rigby	Arbol de Lit/Animal Antics
¿Qué viste?	E	7	Rigby	Arbol de Lit/Animal Antics
El sombrero mágico	B	2	Rigby	Arbol de Lit/Food & Fun
La fiesta sorpresa	C	3	Rigby	Arbol de Lit/Food & Fun
Los koalas	D	4	Rigby	Arbol de Lit/Food & Fun
Manos, manos, manos	C	3	Rigby	Arbol de Lit/Food & Fun
Me gusta pintar	B	2	Rigby	Arbol de Lit/Food & Fun
Picos	E	5	Rigby	Arbol de Lit/Food & Fun
¿Quién se comió la lechuga?	C	3	Rigby	Arbol de Lit/Food & Fun
Ana va a la escuela	F	9	Rigby	Arbol de Lit/Let's Get Togt.
Camiones	E	7	Rigby	Arbol de Lit/Let's Get Togt.

Title	Level: GR	RR	Publisher	Author/Series
En la noche	E	6	Rigby	Arbol de Lit/Let's Get Togt.
La semilla de Sara	G	12	Rigby	Arbol de Lit/Let's Get Togt.
¿Y Cuco?	E	8	Rigby	Arbol de Lit/Let's Get Togt.
Gregoria el gigante gruñón	H	14	Rigby	Arbol de Lit/Out & About
La piel	F	11	Rigby	Arbol de Lit/Safe & Sound
Pizza Par Cenar	F	10	Rigby	Arbol de Lit/Out & About
¡Qué Barbaridad!	H	14	Rigby	Arbol de Lit/Out & About
Las fotos de la familia	G	12	Rigby	Arbol de Lit/Safe & Sound
Si te gustan las fresas, no leas este libro	G	12	Rigby	Arbol de Lit/Safe & Sound
Feliz cumpleaños patito	F	10	Rigby	Arbol de Lit/Times & Seasons
Un Amigo	F	10	Rigby	Arbol de Lit/Times & Seasons
Amarillo	B	2	Rigby	Arbol de Lit/Work & Play
Nuestra casa nueva	D	5	Rigby	Arbol de Lit/Work & Play
El Rancho	A	1	Rigby	Lit. 2000–Nivel 1
Un Zoológico	A	1	Rigby	Lit. 2000–Nivel 1
El fantasma	E	8	Rigby	Lit. 2000–Nivel 2
El árbol de Diego	E	9	Rigby	Lit. 2000–Nivel 3
Cuando Laura estuvo ausente	F	11	Rigby	Mary Cappelini
El enorme escarabajo negro	E	9	Rigby	Mary Cappelini
El goloso pulpo gris	G	13	Rigby	Mary Cappelini
El almuerzo de ranita	F	11	Scholastic	Beginning Literacy
En el Barrio	H	14	Scholastic	Beginning Literacy
Tortillas	F	10	Scholastic	Beginning Literacy
Una noche	F	10	Scholastic	Beginning Literacy
La cucaracha correlona	E	9	Scholastic	Cecilia Avalos-Iguana
Las Palomitas	A	1	Scholastic	Cecilia Avalos-Iguana
Día de Futbol	F	11	Seedling Publications	Mariana Robles
Recados de Mamá	H	14	Seedling Publications	Mariana Robles
Un dibujo	D	5	Shortland Publications	Augie Hunter
¿Qué es?	C	3	Shortland Publications	Dorothy Avery
El monstruo de la playa	F	10	Shortland Publications	Dot Meharry
Pintura Fresca	E	7	Shortland Publications	Edwin Johns
Los tres cabritos	F	9	Shortland Publications	Ian Douglas
Las Cuerdas	D	4	Shortland Publications	Jennifer Waters
Mi bebé	D	5	Shortland Publications	May Nelson
El coyote y mi Tata	B	2	SpanPress, Inc.	Arroz con Leche
Las Paredes de mi barrio	B	2	SpanPress, Inc.	Arroz con Leche
Sonrisas	B	2	SpanPress, Inc.	Arroz con Leche
Papa Noel y su sorpresa	E	9	Troll	Janet Craig
Federiquito el sapo	F	10	Troll	R. Greydanus
Gota a gota	E	9	Troll	Sharon Gordon
Un dinosauro en peligro	F	11	Troll	Sharon Gordon
Abuelito, abuelito	G	12	Wright Group	La Caja de Cuentos
El cerdito	D	5	Wright Group	La Caja de Cuentos
El concierto de los animal	E	6	Wright Group	La Caja de Cuentos
El gigante hambriento	F	11	Wright Group	La Caja de Cuentos
El pastel de chocolate	B	2	Wright Group	La Caja de Cuentos
La rosa roja	E	9	Wright Group	La Caja de Cuentos
¿Quién pude ser mi mamá?	E	9	Wright Group	La Caja de Cuentos
La mamá gallina	D	4	Wright Group	Para leer juntos

SELECTED GUIDED READING BOOKS (SPANISH)—CONT'D

Title	Level: GR	RR	Publisher	Author/Series
Huggles hace un viaje	A	1	Wright Group	Sunshine–Set A
Nos Vestimos Como	A	1	Wright Group	Sunshine–Set AA
Mi perrito	B	2	Wright Group	Sunshine–Set B
Sopa Fuchi	B	2	Wright Group	Sunshine–Set B
Mi hogar	C	3	Wright Group	Sunshine–Set C
La granja	A	1	Wright Group	Sunshine–Set CC
Sopa	I	17	Wright Group	Sunshine Fiction
La confusa Señora Clara Cort	I	16	Wright Group	Sunshine Read Together
La Fiesta del Gato	G	12	Wright Group	Sunshine Read Together
Paco el raton gloton	H	14	Wright Group	Sunshine Read Together
Silencio en la biblioteca	E	9	Wright Group	Sunshine Read Together

B Selected Resources for Teachers

Great Books to Read Aloud or to Recommend to Students

Long-Lasting Literature

Aardema, V. (1975). *Why mosquitoes buzz in people's ears.* New York: Scholastic.

Ahlberg, J., & Ahlberg, A. (1986). *The jolly postman or other people's letters.* Boston: Little, Brown.

Andersen, H. C. (1965). *The ugly duckling* (R. P. Keigwin, Translator, & A. Adams, Illustrator). New York: Scribner.

Asbjornsen, P. C. (1973). *The three billy goats gruff* (P. Galdone, Illustrator). New York: Seaburry Press.

Avi, W. (1984). *The fighting ground.* Philadelphia: J. B. Lippincott.

Aylesworth, J. (1992). *Old black fly* (S. Gammell, Illustrator). New York: Holt.

Barrett, J. (1978). *Cloudy with a chance of meatballs* (R. Barrett, Illustrator). Hartford, CT: Atheneum.

Barrett, N. S. (1984). *Trucks* (T. Bryan, Illustrator). London, NY: F. Watts.

Barrett, N. S. (1989). *Spiders.* London, NY: F. Watts.

Base, G. (1986). *Animalia.* New York: Harry Abrams.

Battle-Lavert, G. (1994). *The barber's cutting edge.* Emeryville, CA: Children's Book Press.

Baum, L. F. (1972). *The Wizard of Oz.* Chicago: World.

Bonne, R. (1985). *I know an old lady.* New York: Scholastic.

Bourgeois, P., & Clark, B. (1986). *Franklin in the dark.* New York: Scholastic.

Boyd, C. D., & Cooper, F. (1995). *Daddy, Daddy, be there.* New York: Philomel Books.

Branley, F. (1983). *Saturn: The spectacular planet.* New York: HarperCollins.

Brown, M. (1947). *Stone soup.* New York: Scribner.

Bunting, E. (1990). *The wall.* New York: Clarion.

Burnford, S. (1960). *The incredible journey.* Boston: Little, Brown.

Byars, B. (1970). *The summer of the swans.* New York: Viking.

Byars, B. (1981). *The Cybil war.* New York: Viking.

Carle, E. (1986). *The grouchy ladybug.* New York: HarperCollins.

Carle, E. (1993). *Today is Monday.* New York: Philomel.

Chase, R. (1948). *Grandfather tales.* Boston: Houghton Mifflin.

Cherry, L. (1992). *A river ran wild: An environmental history.* San Diego: Gulliver/Harcourt Brace.

Christelow, E. (1992). *Don't wake up Mama! Another five little monkeys story.* New York: Clarion.

Cleary, B. (1952). *Henry and Beezus.* New York: William Morrow.

Clements, A., & Savadier, E. (1992). *Billy and the bad teacher.* New York: Simon & Schuster Books for Young Readers.

Cohn, A. L. (1994). *From sea to shining sea: A treasury of American folklore and folk songs.* New York: Scholastic.

Cole, J. (1992). *The magic school bus on the ocean floor* (B. Degen, Illustrator). New York: Scholastic.

Collier, J., & Collier, C. (1981). *Jump ship to freedom.* New York: Delacorte.

Collins, D. (1992). *Malcolm X: Black rage.* Minneapolis, MN: Dillon Press.

Cone, M. (1964). *A promise is a promise.* Boston: Houghton Mifflin.

Conroy, P. (1990). *The water is wide.* Atlanta, GA: Old New York Book Shop Press.

Cowley, J. (1980). *Hairy bear.* San Diego, CA: The Wright Group.

Cowley, J. (1982). *What a mess!* San Diego, CA: The Wright Group.

Dahl, R. (1961). *James and the giant peach: A children's story* (N. E. Burkert, Illustrator). New York: Alfred A. Knopf.

Dahl, R. (1964). *Charlie and the chocolate factory.* New York: Alfred A. Knopf.

Dakos, K. (1992). *Don't read this book, whatever you do! More poems about school* (G. B. Karas, Illustrator). New York: Four Winds.

Davis, D. (1990). *Listening for the crack of dawn.* Little Rock, AR: August House.

DeJong, M. (1953). *Hurry home, Candy.* New York: Harper.

Drew, D. (1989). *The life of the butterfly.* Crystal Lake, IL: Rigby.

Duke, K. (1992). *Aunt Isabel tells a good one.* New York: Dutton.

Fisher-Nagel, H. (1987). *The life of a butterfly.* Minneapolis, MN: Carolrhoda Books.

Fleischman, S. (1986). *The whipping boy.* Mahwah, NJ: Troll Associates.

Forbes, E. (1943). *Johnny Tremain.* Boston: Houghton Mifflin.

Fox, P. (1973). *The slave dancer.* New York: Bradbury.

Fox, P. (1986). *The moonlight man.* New York: Bradbury.

Garner, J. F. (1994). *Politically correct bedtime stories.* New York: Macmillan.

Gelman, R. G. (1976). *Why can't I fly?* (J. Kent, Illustrator). New York: Scholastic.

Gelman, R. G. (1977). *More spaghetti, I say!* New York: Scholastic.

Gelman, R. G. (1985). *Cats and mice.* New York: Scholastic.

George, J. (1972). *Julie of the wolves.* New York: HarperCollins.

The Gingerbread Man. (1985). (K. Schmidt, Illustrator). New York: Scholastic.

Goble, P. (1993). *The lost children.* New York: Bradbury.

Gonzalez, L. M. (1997). *Senor Cat's romance.* New York: Scholastic Press.

Gwynne, F. (1970). *A chocolate moose for dinner.* New York: Windmill Books.

Gwynne, F. (1976). *The king who rained.* New York: Windmill Books.

Harlow, R., & Morgan, G. (1992). *Amazing nature experiments* (Kuo Kan Chen, Illustrator). New York: Random House.

Haskins, J. (1992). *I have a dream: The life and words of Martin Luther King, Jr.* Brookfield, CT: Millbrook.

Henwood, C. (1988). *Frogs* (B. Watts, Photographer). London, NY: Franklin Watts.

Herron, C. (1997). *Nappy hair.* New York: Alfred A. Knopf. (Author's note: Due to the rather sensitive nature of this topic, it is recommended for use by our African American teacher-colleagues only.)

Houston, J. (1977). *Frozen fire.* New York: Atheneum.

Hudson, W. (1998). *Anthony's big surprise.* East Orange, NJ: Just Us Books.

Hurwitz, J. (1985). *The adventures of Ali Babba Bernstein.* New York: Scholastic.

Jackson, G. N. (1993). *Garrett Morgan: Inventor.* Cleveland, OH: Modern Curriculum.

Johnson, D. W. (1976). *Jack and the beanstalk* (D. W. Johnson, Illustrator). Boston: Little, Brown.

Juster, N. (1961). *The phantom tollbooth.* New York: Random House.

Killilea, M. (1954). *Karen.* New York: Dodd, Mead.

Kinsey-Warnock, N., & Kinsey, H. (1993). *The bear that heard crying.* New York: Cobblehill.

Krauss, R. (1945). *The carrot seed* (C. Johnson, Illustrator). New York: Scholastic.

Krumgold, J. (1953). *. . . and now Miguel.* New York: Harper Trophy.

L'Engle, M. (1962). *A wrinkle in time.* New York: Dell.

Lewis, C. S. (1961). *The lion, the witch, and the wardrobe.* New York: Macmillan.

Lisle, J. T. (1989). *Afternoon of the elves.* New York: Franklin Watts.

The Little Red Hen. (1985). (L. McQueen, Illustrator). New York: Scholastic.

Littlejohn, C. (1988). *The lion and the mouse.* New York: Dial Books for Young Readers.

Lobel, A. (1981). *On Market Street* (Anita Lobel, Illustrator). New York: Scholastic.

Lock, S. (1980). *Hubert hunts his hum* (J. Newnham, Illustrator). Sydney, Australia: Ashton Scholastic.

Lowry, L. (1993). *The giver.* Boston: Houghton Mifflin.

Martin, B. (1983). *Brown Bear, Brown Bear, what do you see?* (E. Carle, Illustrator). New York: Henry Holt.

Martin, J. R., & Marx, P. (1993). *Now everybody really hates me* (R. Chast, Illustrator). New York: HarperCollins.

Math, I. (1981). *Wires and watts: Understanding and using electricity.* New York: Charles Scribner's Sons.

Mayer, M. (1976). *Ah-Choo*. New York: Dial Books for Young Readers.

Mayer, M. (1976). *Hiccup*. New York: Dial Books for Young Readers.

McKissack, P. C. (1986). *Flossie & the fox*. New York: Dial Books for Young Readers.

Monjo, F. N. (1970). *The drinking gourd*. New York: Harper & Row.

Myers, W. D. (1975). *Fast Sam, Cool Clyde, and Stuff*. New York: Puffin Books.

Numeroff, L. J. (1985). *If you give a mouse a cookie*. New York: Scholastic.

Palatini, M. (1995). *Piggie pie!* New York: Clarion.

Parish, P. (1980). *Good work, Amelia Bedelia* (L. Sweat, Illustrator). New York: Avon Books.

Paulsen, G. (1991). *The river*. New York: Delacourt.

Perlman, J. (1993). *Cinderella Penguin* (J. Perlman, Illustrator). New York: Viking.

Pfeffer, S. B. (1989). *Claire at sixteen*. New York: Bantam Books.

Polacco, P. (1992). *Chicken Sunday*. New York: Scholastic.

Potter, B. (1953). *The tale of Peter Rabbit* (R. Ruth, Illustrator). Racine, WI: Golden Press.

Provensen, A., & Provensen, M. (1983). *The glorious flight: Across the channel with Louis Bleriot*. New York: Viking Penguin.

Reuter, E. (1993). *Best friends* (A. Becker, Illustrator). Pitspopany Press.

Rice, J. (1992). *Texas night before Christmas*. Gretna, LA: Pelican.

Rich, E. S. (1964). *Hannah Elizabeth*. New York: HarperCollins.

Ross, T. (1986). *I want my potty*. Brooklyn, NY: Kane/Miller.

Schwartz, D. M. (1985). *How much is a million?* Richard Hill, Ontario: Scholastic-TAB.

Scieszka, J. (1989). *The true story of the 3 little pigs! By A. Wolf*. New York: Viking Kestrel.

Scieszka, J. (1992). *The stinky cheese man and other fairly stupid tales* (L. Smith, Illustrator). New York: Viking.

Sendak, M. (1962). *Chicken soup with rice*. New York: Scholastic.

Sendak, M. (1963). *Where the wild things are*. New York: HarperCollins.

Seuss, D. (1954). *Horton hears a Who!* New York: Random House.

Seuss, D. (1998). *Hooray for Diffendoofer Day!* New York: Alfred A. Knopf.

Sharmat, M. W. (1980). *Gila monsters meet you at the airport*. New York: Aladdin.

Skaar, G. (1972). *What do the animals say?* New York: Scholastic.

Smith, K. A. (1989). *A checkup with the doctor*. New York: McDougal, Littell.

Smith, R. K. (1981). *Jelly belly*. New York: Dell.

Speare, E. G. (1958). *The witch of Blackbird Pond*. New York: Dell.

Sperry, A. (1940). *Call it courage*. New York: Macmillan.

Spier, P. (1977). *Noah's ark*. Garden City, NY: Doubleday.

Steele, W. O. (1958). *The perilous road*. Orlando, FL: Harcourt, Brace.

Steinbeck, J. (1937). *The red pony*. New York: Bantam Books.

Stolz, M. (1963). *Bully on Barkham Street*. New York: Harper.

Thaler, M. (1989). *The teacher from the black lagoon*. New York: Scholastic.

Thompson, C. (1992). *The paper bag prince*. New York: Knopf.

Van Allsburg, C. (1985). *The polar express*. Boston: Houghton Mifflin.

Van Allsburg, C. (1987). *The Z was zapped*. Boston: Houghton Mifflin.

Viorst, J. (1972). *Alexander and the terrible horrible no good very bad day* (R. Cruz, Illustrator). New York: Atheneum.

Vozar, D. (1993). *Yo, hungry wolf!* (B. Lewin, Illustrator). Garden City, NY: Doubleday/Bantam Doubleday Dell.

Wells, R. (1973). *Noisy Nora*. New York: Scholastic.

White, E. B. (1952). *Charlotte's web*. New York: HarperCollins.

White, E. B. (1970). *The trumpet of the swan*. New York: HarperCollins.

Wood, A. (1984). *The napping house*. (D. Wood, Illustrator). San Diego: Harcourt Brace.

Wood, A. (1990). *Weird parents*. New York: Dial Books for Young Readers.

Young, E. (1992). *Seven blind mice*. New York: Philomel.

Alphabet Books

Anno, M. (1975). *Anno's alphabet: An adventure in imagination*. New York: Crowell.

Baldwin, R. M. (1972). *One hundred nineteenth-century rhyming alphabets in English.* Carbondale, IL: Southern Illinois University.

Brent, I. (1993). *An alphabet of animals.* Boston: Little, Brown.

Chwast, S. (1991). *Alphabet parade.* Fort Worth, TX: Harcourt Brace.

Crowther, R. (1978). *The most amazing hide-and-seek alphabet book.* New York: Viking.

Ehlert, L. (1989). *Eating the alphabet: Fruits and vegetables from A to Z.* Fort Worth, TX: Harcourt Brace.

Emberley, E. (1978). *Ed Emberley's ABC.* Boston: Little, Brown.

Feelings, M. (1974). *Jambo means Hello: Swahili alphabet book.* New York: Dial.

Hoban, T. (1987). *26 letters and 99 cents.* New York: Greenwillow.

Hughes, S, (1998). *Alfie's ABC.* New York: Lothrop, Lee & Shepard Books.

Hunt, J. (1989). *Illuminations.* New York: Bradbury.

Jonas, A. (1990). *Disembark.* New York: Greenwillow.

Kitchen, B. (1984). *Animal alphabet.* New York: Dial.

Lobel, A. (1990). *Alison's zinnia.* New York: Greenwillow.

McCurdy, M. (1998). *The sailor's alphabet.* Boston: Houghton Mifflin.

Merriam, E. (1987). *Halloween ABC.* New York: Macmillan.

Musgrove, M. (1976). *Ashanti to Zulu: African traditions.* New York: Dial.

Press, J. (1998). *Alphabet art: with A–Z animal art and fingerplays* (S. Dennen, Illustrator). Charlotte, VT: Williamson Publishing.

Provensen, A., & Provensen, M. (1978). *A peaceable kingdom: The Shaker abecedarius.* New York: Viking.

Ressmeyer, R. (1992). *Astronaut to zodiac.* New York: Crown.

Rosen, M. (1998). *Avalanche* (D. Butler, Illustrator). Cambridge, MA: Candlewick.

Thornhill, J. (1990). *The wildlife ABC: A nature alphabet book.* New York: Simon & Schuster.

Fantastic Fun and Facts

Burns, M. (1987). *The I hate mathematics book* (M. Hairston, Illustrator). Cambridge, MA: Cambridge University Press.

Cullinan, B. E. (1987). *Children's literature in the reading program.* Newark, DE: International Reading Association.

Kelley, L. (1998). *The scrambled states of America.* New York: Henry Holt.

Kobrin, B. (1988). *Eyeopeners!* New York: Penguin Books.

Lipson, E. R. (1988). *Parent's guide to the best books for children.* New York: Times Books.

McKenna, V. (1998). *Back to the blue* (I. Andrew, Illustrator). Brookfield, CT: Milbrook Press.

Norton, D. (1999). *Through the eyes of a child: An introduction to children's literature* (5th ed.). Upper Saddle River, NJ: Merrill/Prentice Hall.

Ohanian, S. (1984). Hot new item or same old stew? *Classroom Computer Learning, 5,* 30–31.

Reed, A. (1988). *Comics to classics.* Newark, DE: International Reading Association.

Trelease, J. (1989). *The new read-aloud handbook.* New York: Penguin Books.

Wankelman, W., Wigg, P., & Wigg, M. (1968). *A handbook of arts and crafts.* Dubuque, IA: Wm. C. Brown.

Wacky and Weighty Words

Hall, R. (1984). *Sniglets.* New York: Macmillan.

Levitt, P. M., Burger, D. A., & Guralnick, E. S. (1985). *The weighty word book.* Longmont, CO: Bookmakers Guild.

Mahy, M. (1997) *Boom, baby, boom, boom!* (P. MacCarthy, Illustrator). New York: Penguin books USA.

Nash, B., & Nash, G. (1980). *Pundles.* New York: Stone Song Press.

Poetry, Rhythm, and Rhyme

Adoff, A. (1991). *In for winter, out for spring.* Fort Worth, TX: Harcourt Brace.

Baracca, D., & Baracca, S. (1990). *Taxi dog.* New York: Dial.

Carle, E. (1989). *Eric Carle's animals, animals.* New York: Philomel.

Cassidy, S. (1987). *Roomrimes.* New York: Crowell.

Coe, W. (1979). *Dinosaurs and beasts of yore.* New York: Philomel Books.

Demi. (Ed.). (1992). *In the eyes of the cat. Japanese poetry for all seasons.* New York: Holt.

Fleishman, P. (1988). *Joyful noise: Poems for two voices.* New York: HarperCollins.

Florian, D. (1998). *Insectlopedia: Poems and Paintings*. San Diego, CA: Harcourt Brace.

Hoberman, M. (1998). *Miss Mary Mack: A handclapping rhyme*. Boston: Little Brown.

Hollyer, B. (1999). *Dreamtime: A book of lullabies* (R. Corfield, Illustrator). New York: Viking.

Hudson, W. (1993). *Pass it on: African-American poetry for children*. New York: Scholastic.

Kennedy, X. J., & Kennedy, D. (Eds.). (1982). *Knock at a star: A child's introduction to poetry*. Boston: Little, Brown.

Loveday, J. (Ed.). (1981). *Over the bridge: An anthology of new poems*. New York: Kestrel, Penguin.

Mahy, M. (1989). *Nonstop nonsense*. New York: Macmillan.

McCurdy, M. (1998). *The sailor's alphabet*. Boston: Houghton Mifflin.

O'Neill, M. (1961). *Hailstones and halibut bones*. Garden City, NY: Doubleday.

Poems teachers ask for. (1979). New York: Granger Book.

Prelutsky, J. (1976). *Nightmares: Poems to trouble your sleep*. New York: Greenwillow Books.

Prelutsky, J. (Ed.). (1983). *The Random House book of poetry for children*. New York: Random House.

Prelutsky, J. (1984). *The new kid on the block*. New York: Greenwillow Books.

Prelutsky, J. (1986). *Ride a purple pelican*. New York: Greenwillow Books.

Prelutsky, J. (1988). *Tyrannosaurus was a beast: Dinosaur poems*. New York: Greenwillow Books.

Prelutsky, J. (1990). *Something big has been here*. New York: Greenwillow Books.

Prelutsky, J. (1991). *For laughing out loud: Poems to tickle your funnybone*. New York: Alfred A. Knopf.

Schwartz, A. (1992). *And the green grass grew all around: Folk poetry from everyone*. New York: HarperCollins.

Silverstein, S. (1974). *Where the sidewalk ends*. New York: HarperCollins.

Silverstein, S. (1981). *A light in the attic*. New York: HarperCollins.

Sky-Peck, K. (Ed.). (1991). *Who has seen the wind? An illustrated collection of poetry for young people*. Boston: Museum of Fine Arts, Boston, & Rizzoli.

Yolen, J. (1998). *Here Be The Ghosts* (D. Wilgus, Illustrator). San Diego, CA: Harcourt Brace.

Yolen, J. (1998). *Snow, Snow: Winter Poems for Children*. Honesdale, PA: Wordsong/Boyds Miller Press.

Wordless Books

Anno, M. (1980). *Anno's Italy*. New York: Collins.

Anno, M. (1982). *Anno's Britain*. New York: Philomel.

Collington, P. (1987). *The angel and the soldier boy*. New York: Alfred A. Knopf.

dePaola, T. (1978). *Pancakes for breakfast*. Fort Worth, TX: Harcourt Brace.

Drescher, H. (1987). *The yellow umbrella*. New York: Bradbury.

Goodall, J. (1987). *The story of a main street*. New York: Macmillan.

Hoban, T. (1996). *Just look*. New York: Greenwillow Books.

McCully, E. A. (1987). *School*. New York: HarperCollins.

McCully, E. A. (1988). *New baby*. New York: HarperCollins.

Spier, P. (1977). *Noah's ark*. Garden City, NY: Doubleday.

Wiesner, D. (1988). *Free fall*. New York: Lothrop, Lee & Shepard.

Wiesner, D. (1991). *Tuesday*. New York: Clarion.

Almost Wordless Books

Dubanevich, A. (1983). *Pigs in hiding*. New York: Four Winds.

Martin, R. (1989). *Will's mammoth*. New York: Putnam.

Munro, R. (1987). *The inside-out book of Washington, D.C*. New York: E. P. Dutton.

Tafuri, N. (1983). *Early morning in the barn*. New York: Greenwillow.

Sing and Read Books

Bierhorst. J. (1979). *A cry from the earth: Music of the North American Indians*. New York: Four Winds.

Carroll, L. (1979). *Songs from* Alice. New York: Holiday House.

Cohn, A. L. (Ed.). (1993). *From sea to shining sea: A treasury of American folklore and folk songs*. New York: Scholastic.

Dallin, L., & Dallin, L. (1980). *Heritage songster.* Dubuque, IA: Wm. C. Brown.

Delacre, L. (1989). *Arroz con leche: Popular songs and rhymes from Latin America.* New York: Scholastic.

Fox, D. (Ed.). (1987). *Go in and out the window: An illustrated songbook for young people.* New York: Metropolitan Museum of Art & Holt, Rinehart & Winston.

Glazer, T. (1988). *Treasury of songs for children.* Garden City, NY: Doubleday.

Hollyer, B.; selections. (1999). *Dreamtime: A book of lullabyes* (Robin Bell Corfield, Illustrator). New York: Viking.

Johnson, J. W. (1993). *Lift every voice and sing.* New York: Walker.

Keller, C. (1976). *The silly song book.* Englewood Cliffs, NJ: Prentice Hall.

Knight, H. (1981). *Hillary Knight's the twelve days of Christmas.* New York: Macmillan.

Nye, V. (1983). *Music for young children.* Dubuque, IA: Wm. C. Brown.

Pankake, M., & Pankake, J. (1988). *A Prairie Home Companion folk song book.* New York: Viking.

Peek, M. (1987). *The balancing act: A counting song.* New York: Clarion.

Rubin, R. (1980). *The all-year-long song book.* New York: Scholastic.

Seeger, R. C. (1948). *American folksongs for children—In home, school, and nursery school.* New York: Doubleday.

Spier, P. (1970). *The Erie canal.* New York: Doubleday.

Spier, P. (1970). *The fox went out on a chilly night.* New York: Doubleday.

Surplus, R. W. (1963). *The alphabet of music.* Minneapolis: Lerner.

Zinar, R. (1983). *Music in your classroom.* New York: Parker.

Chanting with Children

Cole, J., & Calmenson, S. (1990). *Mary Mack and other children's street rhymes.* New York: Morrow Junior Books.

Colgin, M. L. (Compiler). (1982). *Chants for children.* Manlius, NY: Colgin.

Dunn, S. (1987). *Butterscotch dreams.* Markham, Ontario: Pembroke.

Dunn, S. (1990). *Crackers and crumbs: Chants for whole language.* Portsmouth, NH: Heinemann.

Hoberman, M. (1998). *Miss Mary Mack: A hand-clapping rhyme.* Boston: Little Brown.

Blank Miscue Grid

	MIS-PRONUN.	SUB-STITUTION	OMISSION	INSERTION	TCHR. ASSIST.	SELF-CORRECT.	MEANING DISRUPTION
TOTALS							

Notes:

	MIS-PRONUN.	SUB-STITUTION	OMISSION	INSERTION	TCHR. ASSIST.	SELF-CORRECT.	MEANING DISRUPTION
TOTALS							

Notes:

	MIS-PRONUN.	SUB-STITUTION	OMISSION	INSERTION	TCHR. ASSIST.	SELF-CORRECT.	MEANING DISRUPTION
TOTALS							

Notes:

References

Aardema, V. (1975). *Why mosquitoes buzz in people's ears.* New York: Scholastic.

Aaron, R. L., & Gillespie, C. (1990). Gates-MacGinitie Reading Tests, 3rd Ed. [Test review]. In R. B. Cooter, Jr. (Ed.), *The teacher's guide to reading tests.* Scottsdale, AZ: Gorsuch Scarisbrick.

Adams, M. J. (1990a). *Beginning to read: Thinking and learning about print.* Cambridge, MA: MIT Press.

Adams, M. J. (1990b). *Beginning to read: Thinking and learning about print (Summary).* Urbana-Champaign, IL: Center for the Study of Reading.

Adams, M. J. (1994). *Beginning to read: Thinking and learning about print.* Cambridge, MA: MIT Press.

Adams, M. J. (2001). Alphabetic anxiety and explicit, systematic phonics instruction: A cognitive science perspective. In S. B. Neuman & D. K. Dickinson (Eds.), *Handbook of early literacy research.* New York: Guildford Press.

Adams, M. J., Allington, R. L., Chaney, J. H., Goodman, Y. M., Kapinus, B. A., McGee, L. M., et al. (1991). Beginning to read: A critique by literacy professionals and a response by Marilyn Jager Adams. *The Reading Teacher, 44(6),* 370–395.

Ahlberg, J., & Ahlberg, A. (1986). *The jolly postman or other people's letters.* Boston: Little, Brown.

Aldridge, J. T., & Rust, D. (1987). A beginning reading strategy. *Academic Therapy, 22(3),* 323–326.

Alexander, J. E. (Ed.). (1983). *Teaching reading,* 2nd Ed. Boston: Little, Brown.

Alexander, J. E., & Filler, R. C. (1976). *Attitudes and reading.*
Newark, DE: International Reading Association.

Alexander, J. E., & Heathington, B. S. (1988). *Assessing and correcting classroom reading problems.* Glenview, IL: Scott, Foresman.

Alexander, P. A., & Jetton, T. L. (2000). Learning from text: A multidimensional perspective. In M. L. Kamil, P. B. Mosenthal, P. D. Pearson, and R. Barr (Eds.), *Handbook of reading research* (Vol. 3, pp. 285–310). Mahwah, NJ: Erlbaum.

Allan, K. K. (1982). The development of young children's metalinguistic understanding of the word. *Journal of Educational Research, 76,* 89–93.

Allington, R. (1997, August/September). Commentary: Overselling phonics. *Reading Today,* 15–16.

Allington, R. L. (1977). If they don't read much, how they ever gonna get good? *Journal of Reading, 21,* 57–61.

Allington, R. L. (1980). Teacher interruption behaviors during primary grade oral reading. *Journal of Educational Psychology, 72,* 371–377.

Allington, R. L. (1983a). Fluency: The neglected reading goal. *The Reading Teacher, 36(6),* 556–561.

Allington, R. L. (1983b). The reading instruction provided readers of differing reading ability. *Elementary School Journal, 83,* 255–265.

Allington, R. L. (1984). Oral reading. In R. Barr, M. L. Kamil, & P. Mosenthal (Eds), *Handbook of Reading Research.* New York: Longman.

Allington, R. L. (1992). How to get information on several proven programs for accelerating the progress of low-achieving children. *The Reading Teacher, 46(3),* 246–248.
Allington, R. L. (1997, August–September). Overselling phonics. *Reading Today, 14,* 15.

Allington, R. L. (2001). *What really matters for struggling readers: Designing research-based programs.* New York: Addison Wesley Longman.

Allington, R. L. (2002). *Big brother and the national reading curriculum: How ideology trumped evidence.* Portsmouth, NH: Heinemann.

Allington, R. L., & Cunningham, P. M. (1996). *Schools that work: Where all children read and write.* New York: HarperCollins.

Allington, R. L., & Woodside-Jiron, H. (1998). Thirty years of research in reading: When is a research summary not a research summary? In K. S. Goodman (Ed.), *In defense of good teaching: What teachers need to know about the "reading wars"* (pp. 143–158). York: ME: Stenhouse.

Altwerger, B., Edelsky, C., & Flores, B. M. (1987). Whole language: What's new? *The Reading Teacher, 41(2),* 144–154.

Altwerger, B., & Flores, B. (1989). Abandoning the basal: Some aspects of the change process. *Theory Into Practice, 28(4),* 288–294.

Alvermann, D. E. (1991). The discussion web: A graphic aid for learning across the curriculum. *The Reading Teacher, 45(2),* 92–99.

Alvermann, D. E., & Boothby, P. R. (1982). Text differences: Children's perceptions at the transition stage in reading. *The Reading Teacher, 36(3),* 298–302.

Alvermann, D. E., Dillon, D. R., & O'Brien, D. G. (1987). *Using discussion to promote reading comprehension.* Newark; DE: International Reading Association.

Alvermann, D. E., & Phelps, S. F. (1994). *Content reading and literacy.* Boston: Allyn & Bacon.

Alvermann, D. E., & Phelps, P. (2001). *Content reading and literacy: Succeeding in today's diverse classrooms*, 3rd Ed. New York: Allyn & Bacon.

Alvermann, D. E., Smith, L. C., & Readence, J. E. (1985). Prior knowledge activation and the comprehension of compatible and incompatible text. *Reading Research Quarterly, 20*(4), 420–436.

Amarel, M., Bussis, A., & Chittenden, E. A. (1977). An approach to the study of beginning reading: Longitudinal case studies. Paper presented at the National Reading Conference, New Orleans, LA.

American Federation of Teachers. (1999). *Teaching reading is rocket science. What expert teachers of reading should know and be able to do.* Washington, DC: Author.

American people, The (Grade 6). (1982). New York: American.

Ancona, G. (1994). *The piñata maker: Piñatero.* San Diego, CA: Harcourt Brace.

Andersen, H. C. (1965). *The ugly duckling* (R. P. Keigwin, Trans., & A. Adams, Illustrator). New York: Scribner.

Anderson, L., Evertson, C., & Brophy, J. (1979). An experimental study of effective teaching in first-grade reading groups. *The Elementary School Journal, 79,* 193–222.

Anderson, R. C. (1970). Control of student mediating processes during verbal learning and instruction. *Review of Educational Research, 40,* 349–369.

Anderson, R. C., & Freebody, P. (1981). Vocabulary knowledge. In J. T. Guthrie (Ed.), *Comprehension and teaching: Research reviews* (pp. 80–82). Newark, DE: International Reading Association.

Anderson, R. C., Hiebert, E. F., Scott, J. A., & Wilkinson, I. A. G. (1985). *Becoming a nation of readers: The report of the commission on reading.* Washington, DC: The National Institute of Education.

Anderson, R. C., Mason, J., & Shirey, L. (1984). The reading group: An experimental investigation of a labyrinth. *Reading Research Quarterly, 20*(1), 6–38.

Anderson, R. C., Osborn, J., & Tierney, R. J. (1984). *Learning to read in American schools.* Hillsdale, NJ: Erlbaum.

Anderson, R. C., & Pearson, P. D. (1984). A schema-theoretic view of basic processes in reading. In D. P. Pearson (Ed.), *Handbook of reading research* (pp. 255–291). New York: Longman.

Anderson, R. C., Reynolds, R. E., Schallert, D. L., & Goetz, E. T. (1977). Frameworks for comprehending discourse. *American Educational Research Journal, 14,* 367–382.

Anderson, R. C., Wilson, P. T., & Fielding, L. G. (1988). Growth in reading and how children spend their time outside of school. *Reading Research Quarterly, 23*(3), 285–303.

Anderson, T. H., & Armbruster, B. B. (1980). Studying. In P. D. Pearson (Ed.), *Handbook of reading research* (pp. 657–680). New York: Longman.

Anderson, V. (1991). *A teacher development project in transactional strategy instruction for teacher of severely reading disabled adolescents.* Paper presented at the National Reading Conference annual meeting. Palm Springs, CA.

Anton, W. (1999). *Corn: From farm to table.* New York: Newbridge.

Apple Computer. (1984). *Macwrite* [Computer program]. Cupertino, CA: Author.

Applebee, A. N. (1979). *The child's concept of story: Ages two to seventeen.* Chicago, IL: The University of Chicago Press.

Applebee, A. N., Langer, J. A., & Mullis, I. V. S. (1988). *Who reads best.* Princeton, NJ: Educational Testing Service.

Appleby, E. (2001). *The three billy goats gruff: A Norwegian tale.* New York: Scholastic.

Armbruster, B., & Anderson, T. (1981). *Content area textbooks* (Reading Education Report No. 23). Urbana-Champaign: University of Illinois at Urbana-Champaign, Center for the Study of Reading.

Armbruster, B. B. (1984). The problem of "inconsiderate text." In G. G. Duffy, L. R. Roehler, & J. Mason (Eds.), *Comprehension instruction: Perspective and suggestions.* New York: Longman.

Armbruster, B. B., Lehr, F., & Osborn, J. (2001). *Put reading first: The research building blocks of teaching children to read.* Jessup, MD: National Institute for Literacy/ED.

Asbjornsen, P. C. (1973). *The three billy goats gruff* (Paul Galdone, Illustrator). New York: Seaburry Press.

Asch, F. (1993). *Moondance.* New York: Scholastic.

Asheim, L., Baker, D. P., & Mathews, V. H. (1983). *Reading and successful living: The family school partnership.* Hamden, CT: Library Professional.

Asher, S. R. (1977). *Sex differences in reading achievement.* (Reading Education Report No. 2). Urbana-Champaign: University of Illinois at Urbana-Champaign, Center for the Study of Reading.

Asher, S. R. (1980). Topic interest and children's reading comprehension. In R. J. Spiro, B. C. Bruce, & W. F. Brewer (Eds.), *Theoretical issues in reading comprehension* (pp. 525–534). Hillsdale, NJ: Erlbaum.

Ashton-Warner, S. (1963). *Teacher.* New York: Touchstone Press.

Atwell, N. (1987). *In the middle: Writing, reading, and learning with adolescents.* Portsmouth, NH: Heinemann.

Au, K. H. (1993). *Literacy instruction in multicultural settings.* Fort Worth, TX: Harcourt Brace.

Au, K. H. (1997). *Literacy instruction in multicultural settings.* Belmont, CA: Wadsworth.

Au, T. K., Depretto, M., & Song, Y. K. (1994). Input vs. constraints: Early word acquisition in Korean and English. *Journal of Memory and Language, 33,* 567–582.

Aukerman, R. (1981). *The basal reader approach to reading.* New York: Wiley.

Ausubel, D. P. (1959). Viewpoints from related disciplines: Human growth and development. *Teachers College Record, 60,* 245–254.

Avi. W. (1984). *The fighting ground.* Philadelphia: Lippincott.

Bacharach, N., & Alexander, P. (1986). Basal reader manuals: What do teachers think of them? *Reading Psychology, 3,* 163–172.

Bader, L. A. (1984). Instructional adjustments to vision problems. *The Reading Teacher, 37*(7), 566–569.

Baker, L., & Brown, A. L. (1984). Cognitive monitoring in reading. In J. Flood (Ed.), *Understanding reading comprehension* (pp. 21–44). Newark, DE: International Reading Association.

Baker, L., Dreher, M. J., & Guthrie, J. T. (2000). *Engaging young readers: Promoting achievement and motivation.* New York: Guilford Press.

Baldwin, R. S., & Kaufman, R. K. (1979). A concurrent validity study of the Raygor readability estimate. *Journal of Reading, 23,* 148–153.

Bank Street writer [Computer program]. (1990). Jefferson City, MO: Scholastic Software.

Bantam. (1985). *Choose your own adventure.* New York: Bantam.

Barker, R. (1978). Stream of individual behavior. In R. Barker & Associates (Eds.), *Habitats, environments, and human behavior* (pp. 3–16). San Francisco: Jossey-Bass.

Barracca, D., & Barracca, S. (1990). *Taxi dog.* New York: Dial Books.

Barrentine, S. B. (1996). Engaging with reading through interactive read-alouds. *The Reading Teacher, 50*(1), 36–43.

Barrentine, S. J. (1999). *Reading assessment: Principles and practices for elementary teachers.* Newark, DE: International Reading Association.

Barrett, F. L. (1982). *A teacher's guide to shared reading.* Richmond Hill, Ontario, Canada: Scholastic-TAB.

Barrett, J. (1978). *Cloudy with a chance of meatballs* (R. Barrett, Illustrator). Hartford, CT: Atheneum.

Barrett, N. S. (1984). *Trucks* (Tony Bryan, Illustrator). London, NY: F. Watts.

Barrett, N. S. (1989). *Spiders.* London, NY: F. Watts.

Barrett, T. (1972). Taxonomy of reading comprehension. *Reading 360 monograph.* Boston: Ginn.

Barron, R. F. (1969). The use of vocabulary as an advance organizer. In H. L. Herber & P. L. Sanders (Eds.), *Research in reading in the content areas: First year report.* Syracuse, NY: Reading and Language Arts Center, Syracuse University.

Bartlett, B. J. (1978). *Top-level structure as an organizational strategy for recall of classroom text.* Unpublished doctoral dissertation, Arizona State University.

Barton, D., Miller, R., & Macken, M. A. (1980). Do children treat clusters as one unit or two? *Papers and Reports on Child Language Development, 18,* 137.

Basal reading texts. What's in them to comprehend? (1984). *The Reading Teacher,* 194–195.

Base, G. (1986). *Animalia.* New York: Harry N. Abrams.

Baum, L. F. (1972). *The Wizard of Oz.* World.

Baumann, J. F. (1992). Basal reading programs and the deskilling of teachers: A critical examination of the argument. *Reading Research Quarterly, 27*(4), 390–398.

Baumann, J. F. (1993). Letters to the editor: Is it "You just don't understand," or am I simply confused? A response to Shannon. *Reading Research Quarterly, 28*(2), 86–87.

Baumann, J. F. (1996). Do basal readers deskill teachers: A national survey of educators' use and opinions of basals. *Elementary School Journal, 96*(5), 511–526.

Baumann, J. F., & Bergeron, B. S. (1993). Story map instruction using children's literature: Effects on first graders' comprehension of central narrative elements. *Journal of Reading Behavior, 25,* 407–437.

Baumann, J. F., Jones, L. A., & Siefert-Kessell, N. (1993). Using think alouds to enhance children's comprehension monitoring abilities. *The Reading Teacher, 47*(3), 184–193.

Baumann, J. F., & Stevenson, J. A. (1986). Teaching students to comprehend anaphoric relations. In J. W. Irwin (Ed.), *Understanding and teaching cohesion comprehension* (pp. 3–8). Newark, DE: International Reading Association.

Baylor, B. (1976). *Hawk, I'm your brother.* New York: Macmillan.

Bear, D. R., Inverizzi, M., Templeton, S., & Johnston, F. (2000). *Words their way: Word study for phonics, vocabulary, and spelling instruction.* Upper Saddle River, NJ: Merrill/Prentice Hall.

Bear, D. R., Templeton, S., Invernizzi, M., & Johnston, F. (1996). *Words their way: Word study for phonics, vocabulary, and spelling instruction.* Upper Saddle River, NJ: Merrill/Prentice Hall.

Beaver, J. (2001). *Developmental reading assessment.* Parsippany, NJ: Celebration Press.

Beck, I. L. (1986). Using research on reading. *Educational Leadership, 43*(7), 13–15.

Beck, I. L. (1997). Response to "Overselling phonics" [Letter to the editor]. *Reading Today*, p. 17.

Beck, I. L., Armbruster, B., Raphael, T., McKeown, M. G., Ringler, L., & Ogle, D. (1989). *Reading today and tomorrow: Treasures. Level 3.* New York: Holt, Rinehart and Winston.

Beck, I. L., & McKeown, M. G. (1981). Developing questions that promote comprehension: The story map. *Language Arts, 58,* 913–918.

Beck, I. L., & McKeown, M. G. (2001). Text talk: Capturing the benefits of read-aloud experiences for young children. *Reading Teacher, 55*(1), 10–20.

Beck, I. L., McKeown, M. G., Omanson, R. C., & Pople, M. T. (1984). Improving the comprehensibility of stories: The effects of revisions that improve coherence. *Reading Research Quarterly, 19,* 263–277.

Beck, I. L., Omanson, R. C., & McKeown, M. G. (1982). An instructional redesign of reading lessons: Effects on comprehension. *Reading Research Quarterly, 17,* 462–481.

Bennett, W. J. (2001, April 24). A cure for the illiteracy epidemic. *Wall Street Journal*, p. A24.

Benson & Cummins (2000). *The Power of retelling.* Wright Group/McGraw Hill, NY.

Berger, M. (1996). *Amazing water.* New York: Newbridge.

Berlak, H. (1992). The need for a new science of assessment. In H. Berlak et al., *Toward a new science of educational testing and assessment.* New York: State University of New York Press.

Betts, E. A. (1946). *Foundation of reading instruction.* New York: American Book.

Bilingual writing center, The. (1992). Fremont, CA: The Learning Company. (Aidenwood Tech Park, 493 Kaiser Drive, Fremont, CA 94555, (800) 852-2255.)

Bintz, W. P. (1991). Staying connected—Exploring new functions for assessment. *Contemporary Education, 62*(4), 307–312.

Birdshaw, D., Burns, S., Carlisle, J. F., Duke, N. K., Garcia, G. E., Hoffman, J. V. et al. (2001). *Teaching every child to read: Frequently asked questions.* Ann Arbor, MI: Center for the Improvement of Early Reading Achievement.

Bissex, G. L. (1980). *Gnys at wrk: A child learns to write and read.* Cambridge, MA: Harvard University Press.

Blachman, B. A. (1984). Relationship of rapid naming ability and language analysis skills to kindergarten and first-grade reading achievement. *Journal of Educational Psychology, 76,* 610–622.

Blachowicz, C. L. Z. (1977). Cloze activities for primary readers. *The Reading Teacher, 31*(3), 300–302.

Blachowicz, C. L. Z. (1986). Making connections: Alternatives to the vocabulary notebook. *Journal of Reading, 29*(7), 643–649.

Blackburn, L. (1997). *Whole music: A whole language approach to teaching music.* Westport, CT: Heinemann.

Blair, S. M., and Williams, K. A. (1999). *Balanced reading instruction: Achieving success with every child.* Newark, DE: International Reading Association.

Blanchard, J., & Rottenberg, C. J. (1990). Hypertext and hypermedia: Discovering and creating meaningful learning environments. *The Reading Teacher, 43*(9), 656–661.

Blanchard, J. S., Mason, G. E., & Daniel, D. (1987). *Computer applications in reading.* Newark, DE: International Reading Association.

Blanton, W. E., & Moorman, G. B. (1985). *Presentation of reading lessons. Technical Report No. 1.* Boone, NC: Center for Excellence on Teacher Education, Appalachian State University.

Blanton, W. E., Moorman, G. B., & Wood, K. D. (1986). A model of direct instruction applied to the basal skills lesson. *The Reading Teacher, 40,* 299–305.

Blecher, S., & Jaffee, K. (1998). *Weaving in the arts: Widening the learning circle.* Westport, CT: Heinemann.

Bleich, D. (1978). *Subjective criticism.* Baltimore, MD: Johns Hopkins University Press.

Blevins, W. (1997). *Phonemic awareness activities for early reading success.* New York: Scholastic.

Blevins, W. (1998). *Phonics from A to Z.* New York: Scholastic.

Block, C. C. (1993). Strategy instruction in a literature-based program. *Elementary School Journal, 94,* 103–120.

Block, C. C., Gambrell, L. B., Hamilton, V., Hartman, D. K., Hasselbring, T. S., Klein, A., et al. (2000). *Scholastic literacy place.* New York: Scholastic.

Block, C. C., & Mangieri, J. (1996). *Reasons to read: Thinking strategies for life through literature* (Vols. 1–3), Menlo Park, CA: Addison.

Block, C. C., Oakar, M., & Hurt, N. (2002). The expertise of literacy teachers: A continuum from preschool to Grade 5. *Reading Research Quarterly, 37*(2), 178–206.

Block, J. H. (1989). *Building effective mastery learning schools.* New York: Longman.

Blok, H., Oostdam, R., Otter, M. E., & Overmaat, M. (2002). Computer-assisted instruction in support of beginning reading instruction: A review. *Review of Educational Research, 72*(1), 101–130.

Bloom, A. (1987). *The closing of the American mind: How higher education has failed democracy and impoverished the souls of today's students.* New York: Simon & Schuster.

Bloom, B. (1956). *Taxonomy of educational objectives.* New York: David McKay.

Blum, I. (1995). Using audiotaped books to extend classroom literacy instruction into the homes of second-language learners. *Journal of Reading Behavior, 27*(4), 535–563.

Blume, J. (1972). *Tales of a fourth grade nothing.* New York: Dell.

Bohning, G. (1986). The McGuffey eclectic readers: 1836–1986. *The Reading Teacher, 40,* 263–269.

Bond, G. L., & Dykstra, R. (1967). The cooperative research program in first-grade reading instruction. *Reading Research Quarterly, 2,* 5–142.

Bonne, R. (1985). *I know an old lady.* New York: Scholastic.

Bonners, S. (1989). *Just in passing.* New York: Lothrop, Lee & Shepard.

Booth, J. (1985). *Impressions.* Toronto: Holt, Rinehart and Winston.

Bourgeois, P., & Clark, B. (1986). *Franklin in the dark.* New York: Scholastic.

Boyle, O. F., & Peregoy, S. F. (1990). Literacy scaffolds: Strategies for first- and second-language readers and writers. *The Reading Teacher, 44*(3), 194–200.

Brackett, G. (1989). *Super story tree.* Jefferson City, MO: Scholastic.

Branley, F. (1983). *Saturn: The spectacular planet.* New York: HarperCollins.

Bransford, J. C., & Johnson, M. K. (1972). Contextual prerequisites for understanding: Some investigations of comprehension and recall. *Journal of Verbal Learning and Verbal Behavior, 11,* 717–726.

Bransford, J. D., & Franks, J. J. (1971). The abstraction of linguistic ideas. *Cognitive Psychology, 2,* 331–350.

Braun, C. (1969). Interest-loading and modality effects on textual response acquisition. *Reading Research Quarterly, 4,* 428–444.

Brennan, J. (1994, September 3). Been there done that: Three John Grisham stories, one John Grisham plot. *Fort Worth Star Telegram,* p. 1E.

Bridge, C. (1978). Predictable materials for beginning readers. *Language Arts, 55,* 593–597.

Bridge, C. A., Winograd, P. N., & Haley, D. (1983). Using predictable materials vs. preprimers to teach beginning sight words. *The Reading Teacher, 36,* 84–91.

Brigance, A. H. (1999). *Brigance® comprehensive inventory of basic skills–revised.* North Billerica, MA: Curriculum Associates.

Brimner, L. D. (1992). *A migrant family.* Minneapolis, MN: Lerner.

Bromley, K. D. (1991). *Webbing with literature: Creating story maps with children's books.* Boston: Allyn & Bacon.

Bronfenbrenner, U. (1977). Toward an experimental ecology of human development. *American Psychologist, 32,* 513–531.

Bronfenbrenner, U., McClelland, P., Wethington, E., Moen, P., & Ceci, S. J. (1996). *The state of Americans.* New York: Free Press.

Brown, A. (1982). Learning how to learn from reading. In J. A. Langer & M. T. Smith-Burke (Eds.), *Reader meets author: Bridging the gap* (pp. 26–54). Newark, DE: International Reading Association.

Brown, A., & Smiley, S. S. (1978). The development of strategies for studying texts. *Child Development, 49,* 1076–1088.

Brown, D. J., Engin, A. W., & Wallbrown, F. J. (1979). Developmental changes in reading attitudes during the intermediate grades. *Journal of Experimental Education, 47,* 262–279.

Brown, K. J. (2000). What kind of text—For whom and when? Textual scaffolding for beginning readers. *The Reading Teacher, 53*(4), 292–307.

Brown, M. (1947). *Stone soup.* New York: Scribner.

Brown, R., Pressley, M., Van Meter, P., & Schuder, T. (1996). A quasi-experimental validation of transactional strategies instruction with low-achieving second grade readers. *Journal of Educational Psychology, 88,* 18–37.

Brown, T. (1986). *Hello, amigos.* New York: Holt, Rinehart and Winston.

Brozo, W. G., & Simpson, M. L. (1995). *Readers, teachers, learners: Expanding literacy in secondary schools.* Upper Saddle River, NJ: Merrill/Prentice Hall.

Bruner, J. (1986). *Actual minds, Possible worlds.* Cambridge, MA: Harvard University Press.

Burke, C. (1987). Burke reading interview. In Goodman, Y., Watson, D., & Burke, C. (Eds.), *Reading miscue inventory: Alternative procedures.* New York: Owen.

Burkhart, A. L. (2000). Breaking the parental barrier. In T. V. Rasinski, N. D. Padak et al. (Eds.), *Motivating recreational reading and promoting home–school connections* (pp. 110–113). Newark, DE: International Reading Association.

Burnford, S. (1960). *The incredible journey.* Boston: Little, Brown.

Burns, M. (1987). *The I hate mathematics book* (Martha Hairston, Illustrator). Cambridge, MA: Cambridge University Press.

Burns, M. S., Griffin, P., & Snow, C. E. (1999). *Starting out right: A guide to promoting children's reading success.* Washington, DC: National Academy Press.

Burns, P. C., Roe, B. D., & Ross, E. P. (1992). *Teaching reading in today's elementary schools,* 5th Ed. Dallas: Houghton Mifflin.

Byars, B. (1970). *The summer of the swans.* New York: Viking.

Byars, B. (1981). *The Cybil war.* New York: Viking.

Byrne, B., & Fielding-Barnsley, R. (1989). Phonemic awareness and letter knowledge in the child's acquisition of the alphabetic principle. *Journal of Educational Psychology, 81,* 313–321.

Byrne, B., & Fielding-Barnsley, R. (1990). Acquiring the alphabetic principle: A case for teaching recognition of phoneme identity. *Journal of Educational Psychology, 82*(4), 805–812.

Byrne, B., Freebody, P., & Gates, A. (1992). Longitudinal data on the relations of word-reading strategies to comprehension, reading time, and phonemic awareness. *Reading Research Quarterly, 27*(2), 140–151.

Cafolla, R., Kauffman, D., & Knee, R. (1997). *World Wide Web for teachers: An interactive guide.* Boston: Allyn & Bacon.

California Department of Education. (1980). *Report on the special studies of selected ECE schools with increasing and decreasing reading scores.* (Available from Publication Sales, California State Department of Education, P.O. Box 271, Sacramento, CA 95802.)

California Reading Task Force. (1995). *Every child a reader: The report of the California Reading Task Force.* Sacramento, CA: California Department of Education.

Calkins, L. (1986). *The art of teaching writing.* Portsmouth, NH: Heinemann.

Calkins, L. (1994). *The art of teaching writing,* New Ed. Portsmouth, CT: Heinemann.

Calkins, L. (2001). *The art of teaching reading.* New York: Addison Wesley.

Calkins, L. M. (1980). When children want to punctuate: Basic skills belong in context. *Language Arts, 57,* 567–573.

Calkins, L. M., & Harwayne, S. (1987). *The writing workshop: A world of difference* (Video). Portsmouth, NH: Heinemann.

Cambourne, B. (1988). *The whole story: Natural learning and the acquisition of literacy in the classroom.* New York: Ashton-Scholastic.

Cambourne, B., & Turbill, J. (1990). Assessment in whole-language classrooms: Theory into practice. *Elementary School Journal, 90*(3), 337–349.

Campbell, R. (1992). *Reading real books.* Philadelphia: Open University Press.

Canney, G., & Winograd, P. (1979). *Schemata for reading and reading comprehension performance* (Technical Report No. 120). Urbana-Champaign: University of Illinois at Urbana-Champaign, Center for the Study of Reading. (ERIC Document Reproduction Service)

Cantrell, S. C. (1999). Effective teaching and literacy learning: A look inside primary classrooms. *The Reading Teacher, 52*(4), 370–378.

Carbo, M. (1988). The evidence supporting reading styles: A response to Stahl. *Phi Delta Kappan, 70,* 323–327.

Carle, E. (1981). *The very hungry caterpillar.* New York: HarperCollins.

Carle, E. (1986). *The grouchy ladybug.* New York: HarperCollins.

Carr, E. (1985). The vocabulary overview guide: A metacognitive strategy to improve vocabulary comprehension and retention. *Journal of Reading, 28*(8), 684–689.

Carr, E., Dewitz, P., & Patberg, J. (1989). Using cloze for inference training with expository text. *The Reading Teacher, 43*(6), 380–385.

Carr, E., & Wixson, K. K. (1986). Guidelines for evaluating vocabulary instruction. *Journal of Reading, 29*(7), 588–589.

Carr, H. K. (1986). *Developing metacognitive skills: The key to success in reading and learning.* For the MERIT, Chapter 2 project, The School District of Philadelphia, H. K. Carr, MERIT supervisor. Philadelphia: School District of Philadelphia.

Carroll, J. B., Davies, P., & Richman, B. (1971). *Word frequency book.* Boston: Houghton Mifflin.

Carroll, L. (1872). *Through the looking glass.* New York: Macmillan.

Cassidy, J. (1981). Grey power in the reading program—a direction for the eighties. *The Reading Teacher, 35,* 287–291.

Cattell, J. M. (1885). Ueber die Zeit der Erkennung und Bennenung von Schriftzeichen, Bildern und Farben. *Philosophische Studien, 2,* 635–650.

Caverly, D. C., & Buswell, J. (1988). Computer assisted instruction that supports whole language instruction. *Colorado Communicator, 11*(3), 6–7.

Chall, J. S. (1967). *Learning to read: The great debate.* New York: McGraw-Hill.

Chall, J. S. (1979). The great debate: Ten years later, with a modest proposal for reading stages. In Resnick, L. B., & Weaver, P. Λ. (Eds.), *Theory and practice of early reading* (pp. 29–55). Hillsdale, NJ: Erlbaum.

Chall, J. S. (1983). *Stages of reading development.* New York: McGraw-Hill.

Chall, J. S. (1998). My life in reading. In E. Sturtevant,

J. Dugan, P. Linder, & W. Linek (Eds.), *Literacy and community, the twentieth yearbook of the College Reading Association, USA,* 12–24.

Chapman, L. J., & Hoffman, M. (1977). *Developing fluent reading.* Milton Keynes, England: Open University Press.

Chard, S. C. (1998). *The project approach: Making curriculum come alive,* Book 1. New York: Scholastic Professional Books.

Chase, R. (1948). *Grandfather tales.* Boston: Houghton Mifflin.

Cheney, L. V. (1990). *Tyrannical machines.* Washington, DC: National Endowment for the Humanities.

Chisom, F. P. (1989). *Jump start: The federal role in adult literacy.* Southport, CT: Southport Institute for Policy Analysis.

Choi, S. N. (1991). *Year of impossible goodbyes.* Boston: Houghton Mifflin.

Chomsky, C. (1971). Write first, read later. *Childhood Education, 47,* 230–237.

Chomsky, N. (1974). *Aspects of the theory of syntax.* Cambridge, MA: MIT Press.

Chomsky, N. (1975). *The logical structure of linguistic theory.* Chicago: The University of Chicago Press.

Chomsky, N. (1979). Human language and other semiotic systems. *Semiotica, 25,* 31–44.

Christopher, J. (1967). *The white mountains.* New York: Macmillan.

Clark, E. (1993). *The lexicon in acquisition.* Cambridge, UK: Cambridge University Press.

Clark, H. H., & Clark, E. V. (1977). *Psychology and language: An introduction to psycholinguistics.* New York: Harcourt Brace Jovanovich.

Clarke, M. A. (1989). Negotiating agendas: Preliminary considerations. *Language Arts, 66*(4), 370–380.

Clay, M. M. (1967). The reading behaviour of five year old

children: A research report. *New Zealand Journal of Educational Studies, 2*(1), 11–31.

Clay, M. M. (1972). *Reading: The patterning of complex behaviour.* Exeter, NH: Heinemann.

Clay, M. M. (1975). *What did I write? Beginning writing behaviour.* Portsmouth, NH: Heinemann.

Clay, M. M. (1985). *The early detection of reading difficulties,* 3rd Ed. Portsmouth, NH: Heinemann.

Clay, M. M. (1987). *Writing begins at home: Preparing children for writing before they go to school.* Portsmouth, NH: Heinemann.

Clay, M. M. (1990a). The Reading Recovery Programme, 1984–88: Coverage, outcomes and Education Board district figures. *New Zealand Journal of Educational Studies, 25,* 61–70.

Clay, M. M. (1990b). What is and what might be in evaluation (Research currents). *Language Arts, 67*(3), 288–298.

Clay, M. M. (1993a). *An observation survey for early literacy achievement.* Portsmouth, NH: Heinemann.

Clay, M. M. (1993b). *Reading recovery: A guidebook for teachers in training.* Portsmouth, NH: Heinemann.

Clay, M. M. (1997). *Running Records for classroom teachers.* Portsmouth, NH: Heinemann.

Clay, M. M. (1998). *By different paths to common outcomes.* York, ME: Stenhouse.

Cleary, B. (1952). *Henry and Beezus.* New York: William Morrow.

Clifford, J. (1991). *The experience of reading: Louise Rosenblatt and reader-response theory.* Portsmouth, NH: Heinemann.

Cochrane, O., Cochrane, D., Scalena, D., & Buchanan, E. (1984). *Reading, writing and caring.* New York: Owen.

Cohen, M. (1980). *First grade takes a test.* New York: Dell Books.

Cole, B. (1983). *The trouble with mom.* New York: Coward-McCann.

Cole, J. (1986). *This is the place for me.* New York: Scholastic.

Cole, J. (1990). *The magic school bus lost in the solar system.* New York: Scholastic.

Cole, J., & Calmenson, S. (1990). *Miss Mary Mack.* New York: Morrow Junior Books.

Cole, R. (1997). *The world of matter.* New York: Newbridge Educational.

Collier, J., & Collier, C. (1981). *Jump ship to freedom.* New York: Delacorte.

Collins, A., & Smith, E. (1980). *Teaching the process of reading comprehension* (Tech. Rep. No. 182). Urbana-Champaign: University of Illinois at Urbana-Champaign, Center for the Study of Reading.

Collins, A. M., & Quillian, M. R. (1969). Retrieval time from semantic memory. *Journal of Verbal Learning and Verbal Behavior, 8,* 240–247.

Collins, C. (1988). Research windows. *The Computing Teacher, 15,* 15–16, 61.

Collins C. (1991). Reading instruction that increases thinking abilities. *Journal of Reading, 34,* 510–515.

Collins-Block, C., Gambrell, L. B., & Pressley, M. (2003). *Improving comprehension instruction: Advances in research, theory, and classroom practice.* San Francisco, CA: Jossey-Bass.

Collins-Block, C., & Mangeri, J. (1996). *Reason to read: Thinking strategies for life through literature,* Palo Alto, CA: Addison-Wesley.

Collins-Block, C., Oaker, M., & Hurt, N. (2002). The expertise of literacy teachers: A continuum from preschool to grade 3. *Reading Research Quarterly, 37*(2), 178–206.

Collins-Block, C., & Pressley, M. (2002). *Comprehension instruction: Research-based best practices.* New York: Guilford Press.

Commeyras, M., & DeGroff, L. (1998). Literacy professionals' perspectives on professional development and pedagogy: A United States survey. *Reading Research Quarterly, 33*(4), 434–472.

Cone, M. (1964). *A promise is a promise.* Boston: Houghton Mifflin.

Cooter, R. B., Jr. (1988). Effects of Ritalin on reading. *Academic Therapy, 23,* 461–468.

Cooter, R. B., Jr. (Ed.). (1990). *The teacher's guide to reading tests.* Scottsdale, AZ: Gorsuch Scarisbrick.

Cooter, R. B., Jr. (1993). *Improving oral reading fluency through repeated readings using simultaneous recordings.* Unpublished manuscript, PDS Urban Schools Project, Texas Christian University.

Cooter, R. B., Jr. (1994). Assessing affective and conative factors in reading. *Reading Psychology, 15*(2), 77–90.

Cooter, R. B., Jr. (1998). *Balanced literacy instructional strands.* Reading Research Report #91, Dallas, TX.

Cooter, R. B., Jr. (1999). *Realizing the dream: Meeting the literacy needs of Dallas children.* Dallas, TX: Unpublished manuscript.

Cooter, R. B. (Ed.). (2003). *Perspectives on rescuing urban literacy education: Spies, saboteurs & saints.* Mahwah, NJ: Erlbaum.

Cooter, R. B., Jr., & Cooter, K. S. (1999). *BLAST!: Balanced Literacy Assessment System and Training.* Ft. Worth, TX: Unpublished manuscript, Ft. Worth TX.

Cooter, R. B., & Cooter, K. S. (2002). The Fluency Formula: A comprehensive model of instruction. *Creating Comprehensive Reading Programs.* Symposium series for Title I teachers and administrators, Wichita, KS.

Cooter, R. B., Jr., Diffily, D., Gist-Evans, D., & Sacken, M. A. (1994). *Literacy development milestones research project* (Report No. 94–100). Unpublished manuscript, Texas Christian University, Fort Worth, TX.

Cooter, R. B., Jr., & Flynt, E. S. (1989). Blending basal reader and whole language instruction. *Reading Horizons, 29*(4), 275–282.

Cooter, R. B., Jr., & Flynt, E. S. (1996). *Teaching reading in the content areas: Developing content literacy for all students.* Upper Saddle River, NJ: Merrill/Prentice Hall.

Cooter, R. B., Jr., & Griffith, R. (1989). Thematic units for middle school: An honorable seduction. *Journal of Reading, 32*(8), 676–681.

Cooter, R. B., Jr., Jacobson, J. J., & Cooter, K. S. (1998). *Technically simple and socially complex: Three school-based attempts to improve literacy achievement.* Paper presented at The National Reading Conference Annual Convention, Austin, TX, December 5, 1998.

Cooter, R. B., Jr., Joseph, D. G., & Flynt, E. S. (1987). Eliminating the literal pursuit in reading comprehension. *Journal of Clinical Reading, 2*(1), 9–11.

Cooter, R. B., Jr., Mills-House, E., Marrin, P., Mathews, B., & Campbell, S. (1999). Family and community involvement: The bedrock of reading success. *The Reading Teacher, 52*(8), 891–896.

Cooter, R. B., Mills-House, E., Marrin, P., Mathews, B. A., Campbell, S., and Baker, T. (1999) Family and community involvement: The bedrock of reading. *The Reading Teacher, 52*(8), 891–896.

Cooter, R. B., Jr., & Reutzel, D. R. (1987). Teaching reading skills for mastery. *Academic Therapy, 23*(2), 127–134.

Cooter, R. B., Jr., & Reutzel, D. R. (1990). *Yakity-yak: A reciprocal response procedure for improving reading comprehension.* Unpublished manuscript, Brigham Young University, Department of Elementary Education, Provo, UT.

Cooter, R. B., Jr., Reutzel, D. R., & Cooter, K. S. (1998). *Sequence of development and instruction for phonemic awareness.* Unpublished paper.

Cornejo, R. (1972). *Spanish high frequency word list.* Austin, TX: Southwestern Educational Laboratory.

Corno, L., & Randi, J. (1997). Motivation, volition, and collaborative innovation in classroom literacy. In J. T. Guthrie & A. Wigfield (Eds.), *Reading engagement: Motivating readers through integrated instruction.* Newark, DE: International Reading Association.

Cousin, P. T., Weekly, T., & Gerard, J. (1993). The functional uses of language and literacy by students with severe language and learning problems. *Language Arts, 70*(7), 548–556.

Cowley, J. (1980). *Hairy bear.* San Diego, CA: The Wright Group.

Cowley, J. (1982). *What a mess!* San Diego, CA: The Wright Group.

Cox, C., & Zarillo, J. (1993). *Teaching reading with children's literature.* Upper Saddle River, NJ: Merrill/Prentice Hall.

Craft, H., & Krout, J. (1970). *The adventure of the American people.* Chicago, IL: Rand McNally.

Crist, B. I. (1975). One capsule a week—A painless remedy for vocabulary ills. *Journal of Reading, 19*(2), 147–149.

Cronin, V., Farrell, D., & Delaney, M. (1999). Environmental print and word reading. *Journal of Research in Reading, 22*(3), 271–282.

CTB McGraw-Hill. (2000). *Fox in a box*. Monterey, CA: CTB McGraw-Hill.

Cudd, E. T., & Roberts, L. L. (1987). Using story frames to develop reading comprehension in a 1st grade classroom. *The Reading Teacher, 41*(1), 74–81.

Cudd, E. T., & Roberts, L. L. (1993). A scaffolding technique to develop sentence sense and vocabulary. *The Reading Teacher, 47*(4), 346–349.

Cunningham, A. E., & Stanovich, K. E. (1998). What reading does for the mind. *American Educator, 22,* 8–15.

Cunningham, P. (1980). Teaching were, with, what, and other "four-letter" words. *The Reading Teacher 34,* 160–163.

Cunningham, P. A., Hall, D. P., & Defee, M. (1998). Nonability-grouped, multi-level instruction: Eight years later. *The Reading Teacher, 51*(8), 652–664.

Cunningham, P. M. (1995). *Phonics they use: Words for reading and writing,* 2nd Ed. New York: HarperCollins.

Cunningham, P. M. (2000). *Phonics they use: Words for reading and writing.* New York: Longman.

Cunningham, P. M., Hall, D. P., & Sigmon, C. M. (2001). *The teacher's guide to the four-blocks: A multimethod, multilevel framework for grades 1–3.* Greensboro, NC: Carson Dellosa.

Dahl, R. (1961). *James and the giant peach: A children's story* (Nancy Ekholm Burkert, Illustrator). New York: Alfred A. Knopf.

Dahl, R. (1964). *Charlie and the chocolate factory.* New York: Alfred A. Knopf.

Dale, E. (1969), *Audiovisual methods in teaching,* 3rd Ed. New York: Holt, Rinehart and Winston.

Dallin, L., & Dallin, L. (1980). *Heritage songster.* Dubuque, IA: William C. Brown.

Dana, C. (1989). Strategy families for disabled readers. *Journal of Reading, 33*(1), 30–35.

Daniels, H. (2002). *Literature circles: Voice and choice in book clubs and reading groups,* 2nd Ed. York, ME: Stenhouse.

Davis, D. (1990). *Listening for the crack of dawn.* Little Rock, AR: August House.

Day, K. C., & Day, H. D. (1979). Development of kindergarten children's understanding of concepts about print and oral language. In M. L. Damil & A. H. Moe (Eds.), *Twenty-eighth yearbook of the National Reading Conference* (pp. 19–22). Clemson, SC: National Reading Conference.

DeBruin-Parecki, A., & Krol-Sinclair, B. (2003). *Family literacy: From theory to practice.* Newark, DE: International Reading Association.

Dechant, E. V. (1970). *Improving the teaching of reading,* 2nd Ed. Upper Saddle River, NJ: Prentice Hall.

DeFord, D., & Harste, J. C. (1982). Child language research and curriculum. *Language Arts, 59*(6), 590–601.

DeFord, D. E. (1985). Validating the construct of theoretical orientation in reading instruction. *Reading Research Quarterly, 20*(3), 351–367.

DeFord, D. E., Lyons, C. A., & Pinnell, G. S. (1991). *Bridges to literacy: Learning from Reading Recovery.* Portsmouth, NH: Heinemann.

DeGroff, L. (1990). Is there a place for computers in whole language classrooms? *The Reading Teacher, 43*(8), 568–572.

DeJong, M. (1953). *Hurry home, Candy.* New York: Harper.

Delacre, L. (1996). *Golden tales: Myths, legends and folktales from Latin America.* New York: Scholastic.

Delpit, L. D. (1988). The silenced dialogue: Power and pedagogy in educating other people's children.

Harvard Educational Review, 58(3), 280–298.

dePaola, T. (1978). *The popcorn book.* New York: Holiday House.

Department of Education. (1985). *Reading in junior classes. Wellington, New Zealand.* New York: Owen.

De Ridder, I. (2002). Visible or invisible links: Does the highlighting of hyperlinks affect incidental vocabulary learning, text comprehension, and the reading process? *Language Learning & Technology, 6*(1), 123–146.

D.E.S. (1975). *A language for life (The Bulloch Report).* London: H.M.S.O.

Developmental Learning Materials. (1985). *The writing adventure.* Allen, TX: Developmental Learning Materials.

Devillar, R. A., Faltis, C. J., & Cummins, J. P. (1994). *Cultural diversity in schools: From rhetoric to practice.* Albany, NY: SUNY Press.

Dewey, J. (1913). *Interest and effort in education.* New York: Houghton Mifflin.

Dewey, J., & Bentley, A. F. (1949). *Knowing and the known.* Boston: Beacon Press.

Dewitz, P., & Carr, E. M. (1987). Teaching comprehension as a student directed process. In P. Dewitz (Chair), *Teaching reading comprehension, summarizing and writing in content area.* Symposium conducted at the National Reading Conference, Orlando, Florida.

Dewitz, P., Stammer, J., & Jensen, J. (1980). *The development of linguistic awareness in young children from label reading to word recognition.* Paper presented at the annual meeting of the National Reading Conference, San Diego, CA.

Dickinson, D. K., & Tabors, P. O. (2001). *Beginning literacy with language.* Baltimore, MD: Paul H. Brookes.

Dickson, S. V., Simmons, D. C., & Kameenui, E. J. (1998a). Text organization: Instructional and curricular basics and implications. In D. C. Simmons & E. J. Kameenui (Eds.), *What reading research tells us about children with diverse learning needs*. Mahwah, NJ: Erlbaum (p. 279–302).

Dickson, S. V., Simmons, D. C., & Kameenui, E. J. (1998b). Text organization: Research bases. In D. C. Simmons and E. J. Kameenui (Eds.), *What reading research tells us about children with diverse learning needs* (pp. 239–278). Mahwah, NJ: Erlbaum.

Dickson, S. V., Simmons, D. C., & Kameenui, E. J. (1998b). Text organization: Instructional and curricular basics and implications (279–294). In D. C. Simmons & E. J. Kameenui (Eds.), *What reading research tells us about children with diverse learning needs: Bases and basics*. Mahwah, NJ: Lawrence Erlbaum Associates.

Diffily, D. (1994, April). *Portfolio assessment in early literacy settings*. Paper presented at a professional development schools workshop at Texas Christian University, Fort Worth, TX.

Dillner, M. (1993–1994). Using hypermedia to enhance content area instruction. *Journal of Reading, 37*(4), 260–270.

Dixon-Krauss, L. (1996). *Vygotsky in the classroom: Mediated literacy instruction and assessment*. New York: Longman.

Doctorow, M., Wittrock, M. C., & Marks, C. (1978). Generative processes in reading comprehension. *Journal of Educational Psychology, 70*(2), 109–118.

D'Odorico, L. (1984). Nonsegmental features in prelinguistic communications: An analysis of some types of infant cry and noncry vocalizations. *Journal of Child Language, 11,* 17–27.

Dole, J. A., Brown, K. J., & Trathen, W. (1996). The effects of strategy instruction on the comprehension performance of at-risk students. *Reading Research Quarterly, 31,* 62–88.

Dole, J. A., Osborn, J., & Lehr, F. (1990). *A guide to selecting basal reader programs*. Champaign, IL: Center for the Study of Reading.

Dole, J. A., Rogers, T., & Osborn, J. (1987). Improving the selection of basal reading programs: A report of the textbook adoption guidelines project. *Elementary School Journal, 87,* 282–298.

Donelson, K. L., & Nilsen, A. P. (1985). *Literature for today's young adults*. Boston: Scott, Foresman.

Dowd, C. A., & Sinatra, R. (1990). Computer programs and the learning of text structure. *Journal of Reading, 34*(2), 104–112.

Dowhower, S. (1987). Effects of repeated readings on second-grade transitional readers' fluency and comprehension. *Reading Research Quarterly, 22,* 389–406.

Dowhower, S. (1991). Speaking of prosody: Fluency's unattended bedfellow. *Theory Into Practice, 30*(3), 158–164.

Downing, J. (1977). How society creates reading disability. *The Elementary School Journal, 77,* 274–279.

Downing, J., & Oliver, P. (1973). The child's concept of a word. *Reading Research Quarterly, 9,* 568–582.

Downing, J., & Thomson, D. (1977). Sex role stereotypes in learning to read. *Research in the Teaching of English, 11,* 149–155.

Downing, J. G. (1990). *A study of the relationship between literacy levels and institutional behaviors of incarcerated male felons*. Unpublished doctoral dissertation, Ball State University, Muncie, IN.

Doyle, C. (1988). Creative applications of computer assisted reading and writing instruction. *Journal of Reading, 32*(3), 236–239.

Dreher, M. J., & Gambrell, L. B. (1985). Teaching children to use a self-questioning strategy for studying expository prose. *Reading Improvement, 22,* 2–7.

Drew, D. (1989). *The life of the butterfly*. Crystal Lake, IL: Rigby.

Driscoll, M. P. (1994). *Psychology of learning for instruction*. Boston: Allyn & Bacon.

Drucker, P. F. (1998, August 24). The next information revolution. *Forbes ASAP.* 47–58.

Duffy, G. G., Roehler, L. R., & Putnam, J. (1987). Putting the teacher in control: Basal reading textbooks and instructional decision making. *The Elementary School Journal, 87*(3), 357–366.

Duke, N. K. (2000a). For the rich it's richer: print experiences and environments offered to children in very low- and very high-socioeconomic status first-grade classrooms. *American Educational Research Journal, 37,* 441–478.

Duke, N. K. (2000b). 3.6 minutes per day: The scarcity of informational texts in first grade. *Reading Research Quarterly, 35*(2), 202–24.

Duke, N. K., Bennett-Armistead, S., Roberts, E. M. (2002). Incorporating informational text in the primary grades 40–54. In C. M. Roller (Ed.), *Comprehensive reading instruction across the grade levels: A collection of papers from the 2001 reading research conference*. Newark, DE: International Reading Association.

Duke, N. K., & Purcell-Gates, V. (In press). Genres at home and at school: Bridging the new to the known. *The Reading Teacher.*

Dunn, L., & Dunn, L. M. (1997). *Peabody picture vocabulary test—third edition* (PPVT-III). Circle Pines, MN: American Guidance Service.

Dunn, L., Lugo, D. E., Padilla, E. R., & Dunn, L. M. (1986). *Test de Vocabulario en Imágenes*

Peabody (TVIP). Circle Pines, MN: American Guidance Service.

Dunn, L. M., & Markwardt, F. C. (1970). *Peabody individual achievement test.* Circle Pines, MN: American Guidance Service.

Dunn, R. (1988). Teaching students through their perceptual strengths or preferences. *Journal of Reading, 31,* 304–309.

Dunn, S. (1987). *Butterscotch dreams.* Markham, Ontario: Pembroke.

Durkin, D. (1966). *Children who read early: Two longitudinal studies.* New York: Teachers College Press.

Durkin, D. (1974). A six year study of children who learned to read in school at the age of four. *Reading Research Quarterly, 10,* 9–61.

Durkin, D. (1978). What classroom observations reveal about reading comprehension instruction. *Reading Research Quarterly, 14*(4), 482–533.

Durkin, D. (1981a). Reading comprehension in five basal reader series. *Reading Research Quarterly, 16*(4), 515–543.

Durkin, D. (1981b). What is the value of the new interest in reading comprehension? *Language Arts, 58,* 23–43.

Durkin, D. (1983). *Reading comprehension instruction: What the research says.* Presentation at the first Tarleton State University Reading Conference, Stephenville, TX.

Durkin, D. (1984). Is there a match between what elementary teachers do and what basal reader manuals recommend? *The Reading Teacher, 37,* 734–745.

Durkin, D. (1987). *Teaching young children to read,* (4th Ed. New York: Allyn & Bacon.

Durkin, D. (1989). *Teaching them to read,* 5th Ed. New York: Allyn & Bacon.

Durrell, D. D. (1940). *Improvement of basic reading abilities.* New York: World Book.

Duthie, J. (1986). The web: A powerful tool for the teaching and evaluation of the expository essay. *The History and Social Science Teacher, 21,* 232–236.

Dyer, P. C. (1992). Reading Recovery: A cost-effectiveness and educational-outcomes analysis. *ERS Spectrum, 10,* 10–19.

Eastlund, J. (1980). Working with the language deficient child. *Music Educators Journal, 67*(3), 60–65.

Eckhoff, B. (1983). How reading affects children's writing. *Language Arts, 60*(5), 607–616.

Edelsky, C. (1988). Living in the author's world: Analyzing the author's craft. *The California Reader, 21,* 14–17.

Edelsky, C., Altwerger, B., & Flores, B. (1991). *Whole language: What's the difference?* Portsmouth, NH: Heinemann.

Eder, D. (1983). Ability grouping and student's academic self-concepts: A case study. *The Elementary School Journal, 84,* 149–161.

Educational Testing Service. (1988). *Who reads best?* Princeton, NJ: Educational Testing Service.

Edwards, P. (1999). *A path to follow: Learning to listen to parents.* Portsmouth, NH: Heinemann.

Ehri, L. C. (1984). How orthography alters spoken language competencies in children. In J. Downing & R. Valtin (Eds.), *Language awareness and learning to read* (pp. 118–147). New York: Springer-Verlag.

Ehri, L. C. & Sweet, J. (1991). Fingerpoint-reading of memorized text: What enables beginners to process the print? *Reading Research Quarterly, 26,* 442–462.

Ehri, L. C., & Wilce, L. C. (1980). The influence of orthography on readers' conceptualization of the phonemic structure of words. *Applied Psycholinguistics, 1,* 371–385.

Ehri, L. C., & Wilce, L. C. (1985). Movement into reading: Is the first stage of printed word learning visual or phonetic? *Reading Research Quarterly, 20,* 163–179.

Ekwall, E. E., & Shanker, J. L. (1989). *Teaching reading in the elementary school,* 2nd Ed. Upper Saddle River, NJ: Merrill/Prentice Hall.

Elbow, P. (1994). Will the virtues of portfolios blind us to their potential dangers? In L. Black, D. Daiker, J. Sommers, & G. Stygall (Eds.), *New directions in portfolio assessment* (pp. 40–55). Portsmouth, NH: Boynton/Cook.

Eldredge, J. L. (1990). Increasing the performance of poor readers in the third grade with a group assisted strategy. *Journal of Educational Research, 84*(2), 69–77.

Eldredge, J. L., & Quinn, D. W. (1988). Increasing reading performance of low-achieving second graders with dyad reading groups. *Journal of Educational Research, 82,* 40–46.

Eldredge, J. L., Reutzel, D. R., & Hollingsworth, P. M. (1996). Comparing the effectiveness of two oral reading practices: Round-robin reading and the shared book experience. *Journal of Literacy Research, 28*(2), 201–225.

Ellis, A. K., & Fouts, J. T. (1993). *Research on educational innovations.* Princeton Junction, NJ: Eye on Education.

Ellison, C. (1989, January). PCs in the schools: An American tragedy. *PC/Computing,* 96–104.

Engelmann, S., & Bruner, E. C. (1995). *Reading mastery I: Presentation book C,* Rainbow Edition. Columbus, OH: Science Research Associates/Macmillan/McGraw-Hill.

Engelmann, S., & Bruner, E. C. (2002). *SRA reading mastery plus.* Columbus, OH: SRA-McGraw Hill.

Englert, C. S., & Tarrant, K. L. (1995). Creating collaborative cultures for educational change.

Remedial and Special Education, 16(6), 325–336.

Ericson, L., & Juliebo, M. F. (1998). *The phonological awareness handbook for kindergarten and primary teachers.* Newark, DE: International Reading Association.

Ervin, J. (1982). *How to have a successful parents and reading program: A practical guide.* New York: Allyn & Bacon.

Esch, M. (1991, February 17). Whole language teaches reading. *The Daily Herald* (Provo, UT), p. D1.

Estes, T. H., & Vaughn, J. L. (1978). *Reading and learning in the content classroom.* Boston: Allyn & Bacon.

Fader, D. N. (1976). *The new hooked on books.* New York: Berkley.

Farr, R. (1991). *Portfolios: Assessment in the language arts.* ED334603.

Farr, R., & Tone, B. (1994). *Portfolio and performance assessment.* Fort Worth, TX: Harcourt Brace.

Farr, R., & Tulley, M. (1989). State level adoption of basal readers: Goals, processes, and recommendations. *Theory Into Practice, 28*(4), 248–253.

Farr, R., Tulley, M. A., & Powell, D. (1987). The evaluation and selection of basal readers. *The Elementary School Journal, 87,* 267–281.

Farrar, M. T. (1984). Asking better questions. *The Reading Teacher, 38,* 10–17.

Fawson, P. C., & Reutzel, D. R. (2000). But I only have a basal: Implementing guided reading in the early grades. *The Reading Teacher, 54*(1), 84–97.

Fay, L. (1965). Reading study skills: Math and science. In J. A. Figurel (Ed.), *Reading and inquiry.* Newark, DE: International Reading Association.

Felmlee, D., & Eder, D. (1983). Contextual effects in the classroom: The impact of ability groups on student attention. *Sociology of Education, 56,* 77–87.

Ferreiro, E., & Teberosky, A. (1982). *Literacy before schooling.* Portsmouth, NH: Heinemann.

Fielding, L., Kerr, N., & Rosier, P. (1998). *The 90% reading goal.* Kennewick, WA: National Reading Foundation.

Fields, M. V., & Spangler, K. L. (2000). *Let's begin reading right: A developmental approach to emergent literacy.* Upper Saddle River, NJ: Merrill.

Fillmore, D. (1968). The case for case. *Universals of linguistic theory.* New York: Holt, Rinehart, & Winston.

Finchler, J. (2001). *Testing Miss Malarkey.* New York: Walker & Company.

Fisher-Nagel, H. (1987). *The life of a butterfly.* Minneapolis: Carolrhoda Books.

Fitzgerald, J. (1993). Literacy and students who are learning English as a second language. *The Reading Teacher, 46*(8), 638–647.

Fitzgerald, J. (1994). Crossing boundaries: What do second-language-learning theories say to reading and writing teachers of English-as-a-second-language learners? *Reading Horizons, 34*(4), 339–355.

Fitzgerald, J. (1995). English-as-a-second-language reading instruction in the United States: A research review. *Journal of Reading Behavior, 27*(2), 115–152.

Fitzgerald, J. (1999). What is this thing called "balance"? *The Reading Teacher, 53*(2), 100–115.

Fleischman, S. (1986). *The whipping boy.* Mahwah, NJ: Troll Associates.

Flesch, R. (1955). *Why Johnny can't read.* New York: HarperCollins.

Flesch, R. (1979, November 1). Why Johnny still can't read. *Family Circle, 26,* 43–46.

Flesch, R. (1981). *Why Johnny still can't read.* New York: HarperCollins.

Flippo, R. F. (2001). *Reading researchers in search of common ground.* Newark, DE: International Reading Association.

Flood, J., & Lapp, D. (1986). Types of texts: The match between what students read in basals and what they encounter in tests. *Reading Research Quarterly, 21,* 284–297.

Flynt, E. S., & Cooter, R. B. (2001). *The Flynt/Cooter Reading Inventory for the Classroom,* 4th Ed. Upper Saddle River, NJ: Merrill/Prentice Hall.

Flynt, E. S., & Cooter, R. B, Jr. (1999). *The Flynt/Cooter English * Español reading inventory.* Upper Saddle River, NJ: Merrill/Prentice Hall.

Flynt, E. S., & Cooter, R. B., Jr. (2004). *The Flynt/Cooter Reading Inventory for the Classroom,* 5th Ed. Upper Saddle River, NJ: Merrill/Prentice Hall.

Follett, R. (1985). The school textbook adoption process. *Book Research Quarterly, 1,* 19–23.

Foorman, B. R., et al. (1997). Early intervention for children with reading problems: Study designs and preliminary findings. *Learning Disabilities: A Multidisciplinary Journal, 8*(1), 63–71.

Foorman, B. R., Francis, D. J., Fletcher, J. M., Schatschneider, C., & Mehta, P. (1998). The role of instruction in learning to read: Preventing reading failure in at-risk children. *Journal of Educational Psychology, 90,* 37–55.

Forbes, E. (1943). *Johnny Tremain.* Boston: Houghton Mifflin.

Fosnot, C. T. (1996). *Constructivism: Theory, perspectives, and practice.* New York: Teachers College Press.

Fountas, I. C., & Pinnell, G. S. (1996). *Guided reading instruction: Good first teaching for all children.* Portsmouth, NH: Heinemann Educational Books.

Fountas, I. C., & Pinnell, G. S. (1999). *Matching books to readers: Using leveled books in reading, K–3.* Portsmouth, NH: Heinemann Educational Books.

Fountas, I. C., & Pinnell, G. S. (2001). *Guiding readers and writers: Grades 3–6. Teaching comprehension genre, and content literacy.* Portsmouth, NH: Heinemann.

Fowler, G. L. (1982). Developing comprehension skills in primary students through the use of story frames. *The Reading Teacher, 36*(2), 176–179.

Fox, B. J. (1996). *Strategies for word identification: Phonics from a new perspective.* Upper Saddle River, NJ: Merrill/Prentice Hall.

Fox, B. J., & Hull, M. A. (2002). *Phonics for the teacher of reading,* 8th Ed. Upper Saddle River, NJ: Prentice Hall.

Fox, P. (1973). *The slave dancer.* New York: Bradbury.

Fox, P. (1986). *The moonlight man.* New York: Bradbury.

Fractor, J. S., Woodruff, M. C., Martinez, M. G., & Teale, W. H. (1993). Let's not miss opportunities to promote voluntary reading: Classroom libraries in the elementary school. *The Reading Teacher, 46,* 476–484.

Fredericks, A. D., & Rasinski, T. V. (1990). Working with parents: Involving the uninvolved: How to. *The Reading Teacher, 43*(6), 424–425.

Freeman, D. E., & Freeman, Y. S. (1994). *Between worlds: Access to second language acquisition.* Portsmouth, NH: Heinemann.

Freeman, D. E., & Freeman, Y S. (2000). *Teaching reading in multilingual classrooms.* Portsmouth, NH: Heinemann.

Freeman, Y. S., & Freeman, D. E. (1992). *Whole language for second language learners.* Portsmouth, NH: Heinemann.

Freppon, P. A., & Dahl, K. L. (1998). Balanced instruction: Insights and considerations. *Reading Research Quarterly, 33*(2), 240–251.

Fry, E. (1977). Fry's readability graph: Clarifications, validity, and extension to level 17. *Journal of Reading, 21,* 242–252.

Fry, E. (1980). The new instant word list. *The Reading Teacher, 34,* 284–289.

Fry, E. B., Kress, J. E., & Fountoukidis, D. (2000). *The reading teacher's book of lists.* New York: Jossey-Bass.

Fry, E. B., Polk, J. K., & Fountoukidis, D. (1984). *The reading teacher's book of lists.* Upper Saddle River, NJ: Prentice Hall.

Gahn, S. M. (1989). A practical guide for teaching writing in the content areas. *Journal of Reading, 33,* 525–531.

Galindo, R., & Escamilla, K. (1995). A biographical perspective on Chicano educational success. *Urban Review, 27*(1), 1–25.

Galdone, Paul. *The little red hen.* L. McQueen, Illustrator. New York: Scholastic.

Gall, M. D., Ward, B. A., Berliner, D. C., Cahen, L. S., Crown, K. A., Elashoff, J. D., et al. (1975). *The effects of teacher use of questioning techniques on student achievement and attitude.* San Francisco: Far West Laboratory for Educational Research and Development.

Gallant, M. G. (1986). *More fun with Dick and Jane.* New York: Penquin Books.

Gallup, G. (1969). *The Gallup poll.* New York: American Institute of Public Opinion.

Gamberg, R., Kwak, W., Hutchings, M., & Altheim, J. (1988). *Learning and loving it: Theme studies in the classroom.* Portsmouth, NH: Heinemann.

Gambrell, L. B. (1985). Dialogue journals: Reading-writing instruction. *The Reading Teacher, 38*(6), 512–515.

Gambrell, L. B., & Almasi, J. F. (1996). *Lively discussions: Fostering engaged reading.* Newark, DE: International Reading Association.

Gambrell, L. B., & Bales, R. J. (1986). Mental imagery and the comprehension-monitoring performance of fourth- and fifth-grade poor readers. *Reading Research Quarterly, 21*(4), 454–464.

Gambrell, L. B., & Marnak, B. A. (1997). Incentives and intrinsic motivation to read. In J. T. Guthrie & A. Wigfield (Eds.), *Reading engagement: Motivating readers through integrated instruction* (pp. 205–217). Newark, DE: International Reading Association.

Gambrell, L. B., Morrow, L. M., Neuman, S. B., & Pressley, M. (1999). *Best practices in literacy instruction.* New York: Guilford Press.

Gambrell, L. B., Pfeiffer, W., & Wilson, R. (1985). The effects of retelling upon reading comprehension and recall of text information. *Journal of Educational Research, 78,* 216–220.

Gambrell, L. B., Wilson, R. M., & Gnatt, W. N. (1981). Classroom observations of task-attending behaviors of good and poor readers. *Journal of Educational Research, 74,* 400–404.

Garcia, S. B., & Malkin, D. H. (1993). Toward defining programs and services for culturally and linguistically diverse learners in special education. *Teaching Exceptional Children,* Fall, 52–58.

Gardener, H. (1993). *Frames of mind: The theory of multiple intelligences.* New York: Basic Books.

Garza, C. L. (1990). *Cuadros de familia: Family pictures.* San Francisco: Children's Book Press.

Gates, A. I. (1921). An experimental and statistical study of reading and reading tests (in three parts). *Journal of Educational Psychology, 12,* 303–314, 378–391, 445–465.

Gates, A. I. (1937). The necessary mental age for beginning reading. *Elementary School Journal, 37,* 497–508.

Gates, A. I. (1961). Sex differences in reading ability. *Elementary School Journal, 61,* 431–434.

Gelman, R. G. (1976). *Why can't I fly?* New York: Scholastic.

Gelman, R. G. (1977). *More spaghetti, I say!* New York: Scholastic.

Gelman, R. G. (1985). *Cats and mice.* New York: Scholastic.

Gentry, R. (1987). *Spel. . . is a four-letter word.* Portsmouth, NH: Heinemann.

George, J. (1972). *Julie of the wolves.* New York: HarperCollins.

Gertson, R., Fuchs, L. S., Williams, J. P., & Baker, S. (2001). Teaching reading comprehension strategies to students with learning disabilities: A review of research. *Review of Educational Research, 71*(2), 279–320.

Gibson, E. J., & Levin, H. (1975). *The psychology of reading.* Cambridge, MA: MIT Press.

Gillet, J. W., & Temple, C. (1986). *Understanding reading problems: Assessment and instruction.* Boston: Little, Brown.

Gingerbread man, The. (1985). K. Schmidt, Illustrator. New York: Scholastic.

Giordano, G. (2001). *Twentieth-century reading education: Understanding practices of today in terms of patterns of the past.* New York: JAI Press.

Gipe, J. P. (1980). Use of a relevant context helps kids learn new word meanings. *The Reading Teacher, 33,* 398–402.

Gipe, J. P. (1987). *Corrective reading techniques for the classroom teacher.* Scottsdale, AZ: Gorsuch Scarisbrick.

Glatthorn, A. A. (1993). Outcome-based education: Reform and the curriculum process. *Journal of Curriculum and Supervision, 8*(4), 354–363.

Glazer, S. M. (1989). Oral language and literacy development. In D. S. Strickland & L. M. Morrow (Eds.), *Emerging literacy: Young children learn to read and write* (pp. 16–26). Newark, DE: International Reading Association.

Glazer, S. M., & Brown, C. S. (1993). *Portfolios and beyond: Collaborative assessment in reading and writing.* Norwood, MA: Christopher-Gordon.

Gleason, J. B. (1989). *The development of language,* 2nd Ed. Upper Saddle River. NJ: Merrill/Prentice Hall.

Glowacki, D., Lanucha, C., & Pietrus, D. (2001). *Improving vocabulary acquisition through direct and indirect teaching.* Syracuse, NY: Educational Resources Information Center (ERIC) Document Reproduction Service.

Goetz, E. T., Reynolds, R. E., Schallert, D. L., & Radin, D. I. (1983). Reading in perspective: What real cops and pretend burglars look for in a story. *Journal of Educational Psychology, 75*(4), 500–510.

Golden, J. M. (1992). The growth of story meaning. *Language Arts, 69*(1), 22–27.

Good, T. (1979). Teacher effectiveness in the elementary school. *The Journal of Teacher Education, 30,* 52–64.

Goodman, K., Shannon, P., Freeman, Y., & Murphy, S. (1988). *Report card on basal readers.* Katona, NY: Owen.

Goodman, K., Smith, E. B., Meredith, R., & Goodman, Y. M. (1987). *Language and thinking in school: A whole-language curriculum.* Katona, NY: Owen.

Goodman, K. S. (1967). Reading: A psycholinguistic guessing game. *Journal of the Reading Specialist, 6,* 126–135.

Goodman, K. S. (1968). *Study of children's behavior while reading orally* (Final Report, Project No. S 425). Washington, DC: U.S. Department of Health, Education, and Welfare.

Goodman, K. S. (1976). Behind the eye: What happens in reading. In H. Singer & R. B. Ruddell (Eds.), *Theoretical models and processes of reading,* 2nd Ed. (pp. 470–496). Newark, DE: International Reading Association.

Goodman, K. S. (1985). Unity in reading. In H. Singer & R. B. Ruddell (Eds.), *Theoretical models and processes of reading,* 3rd Ed. Newark, DE: International Reading Association.

Goodman, K. S. (1986). *What's whole in whole language?* Ontario, Canada: Scholastic.

Goodman, K. S. (1987). Look what they've done to Judy Blume!: The "basalization" of children's literature. *The New Advocate, 1*(1), 29–41.

Goodman, K. S., & Goodman, Y. M. (1983). Reading and writing relationships: Pragmatic functions. *Language Arts, 60*(5), 590–599.

Goodman, Y. M. (1986). Children coming to know literacy. In W. H. Teale & E. Sulzby (Eds.), *Emergent literacy: Writing and reading* (pp. 1–14). Norwood, NJ: Ablex.

Goodman, Y. M., & Altwerger, B. (1981). *Print awareness in preschool children: A study of the development of literacy in preschool children.* Occasional paper, Program in Language and Literacy. Tucson, AZ: University of Arizona.

Gordon, C. J., & Braun, C. (1983). Using story schema as an aid to reading and writing. *The Reading Teacher, 37*(2), 116–121.

Gordon, N. (Ed.). (1984). *Classroom experiences: The writing process in action.* Exeter, NH: Heinemann.

Goswami, U., & Bryant, P. (1990). *Phonological skills and learning to read.* East Sussex, UK: Erlbaum.

Goswami, U., & Mead, F. (1992). Onset and rime awareness and analogies in reading. *Reading*

Research Quarterly, 27(2), 152–163.

Gough, P. B. (1972). One second of reading. In J. F. Kavanagh & I. G. Mattingly (Eds.), *Language by ear and by eye.* Cambridge, MA: MIT Press.

Gove, M. K. (1983). Clarifying teacher's beliefs about reading. *The Reading Teacher, 37*(3), 261–268.

Graesser, A., Golding, J. M., & Long, D. L. (1991). Narrative representation and comprehension. In R. Barr, M. L. Kamil, P. Mosenthal, & P. D. Pearson (Eds.), *Handbook of reading research:* Vol. 2. (pp. 171–205). New York: Longman.

Graves, D. H. (1983). *Writing: Teachers and children at work.* Portsmouth, NH: Heinemann.

Graves, M. F., & Slater, W. H. (1987). Development of reading vocabularies in rural disadvantaged students, intercity disadvantaged students and middle class suburban students. Paper presented at AERA conference, Washington, DC.

Greaney, V. (1994). World illiteracy. In F. Lehr & J. Osborn (Eds.), *Reading, language, and literacy: Instruction for the twenty-first century.* Hillsdale, NJ: Erlbaum.

Greene, F. P. (1970). *Paired reading.* Unpublished manuscript, Syracuse University, New York.

Greene, F. P. (1973). *OPIN.* Unpublished paper, McGill University, Montreal, Quebec, Canada.

Griffith, P. L., & Olson, M. W. (1992). Phonemic awareness helps beginning readers break the code. *The Reading Teacher, 45,* 516–523.

Groff, P. J. (1984). Resolving the letter name controversy. *The Reading Teacher, 37*(4), 384–389.

Groom, W. (1986). *Forrest Gump.* New York: Pocket Books.

Gross, A. D. (1978). The relationship between sex differences and reading ability in an Israeli kibbutz system. In D. Feitelson (Ed.), *Cross-cultural perspectives on reading and reading research* (pp. 72–88). Newark, DE: International Reading Association.

Grossen, B. (1997). *30 years of research: What we know about how children learn to read.* Santa Cruz, CA: The Center for the Future of Teaching and Learning.

Guilfoile, E. (1957). *Nobody listens to Andrew.* Cleveland, OH: Modern Curriculum Press.

Gunderson, L. (1991). *ESL literacy instruction: A guidebook to theory and practice.* Upper Saddle River, NJ: Prentice Hall.

Guszak, F. J. (1967). Teacher questioning and reading. *The Reading Teacher, 21*(1), 227–234.

Guthrie, J. T. (1982). Effective teaching practices. *The Reading Teacher, 35*(7), 766–768.

Guthrie, J. T., & McCann, A. D. (1997). Characteristics of classrooms that promote motivations and strategies for learning. In J. T. Guthrie & A. Wigfield (Eds.), *Reading engagement: Motivating readers through integrated instruction.* Newark, DE: International Reading Association.

Guthrie, J. T., Seifert, M., Burnham, N. A., & Caplan, R. J. (1974). The maze technique to assess and monitor reading comprehension. *The Reading Teacher, 28*(2), 161–168.

Gwynne, F. (1970). *A chocolate moose for dinner.* New York: Windmill Books.

Gwynne, F. (1976). *The king who rained.* New York: Windmill Books.

Gwynne, F. (1999). *A chocolate moose for dinner.* New York: Bt Bound.

Hagerty, P. (1992). *Reader's workshop: Real reading.* New York: Scholastic.

Haggard, M. R. (1986). The vocabulary self-collection strategy: Using student interest and world knowledge to enhance vocabulary growth. *Journal of Reading, 29*(7), 634–642.

Hagood, B. F. (1997). Reading and writing with help from story grammar. *Teaching Exceptional Children, 29*(4), 10–14.

Hall, M. A. (1978). *The language experience approach for teaching reading: A research perspective.* Newark, DE: International Reading Association.

Hall, M. A. (1981). *Teaching reading as a language experience,* 3rd Ed. Upper Saddle River, NJ: Merrill/Prentice Hall.

Hall, N. (1987). *The emergence of literacy.* Portsmouth, NH: Heinemann.

Hall, R. (1984). *Sniglets.* Upper Saddle River, NJ: Merrill/Prentice Hall.

Haller, E. J., & Waterman, M. (1985). The criteria of reading group assignments. *The Reading Teacher, 38,* 772–781.

Halliday, M. A. K. (1975). *Learning how to mean: Explorations in the development of language.* London: Edward Arnold.

Hallinan, M. T., & Sorensen, A. B. (1985). Ability grouping and student friendships. *American Educational Research Journal, 22,* 485–499.

Hammill, D., & Larsen, S. C. (1974). The relationship of selected auditory perceptual skills and reading ability. *Journal of Learning Disabilities, 7,* 429–435.

Handel, R. D. (1999). The multiple meanings of family literacy. *Education of Urban Society, 32*(1), 127–144.

Hansen, J. (1981). The effects of inference training and practice on young children's reading comprehension. *Reading Research Quarterly, 16*(3), 391–417.

Hansen, J. (1987). *When writers read.* Portsmouth, NH: Heinemann.

Harkrader, M. A., & Moore, R. (1997). Literature preferences of fourth graders. *Reading Research and Instruction, 36*(4), 325–339.

Harp, B. (1988). When the principal asks: "Why are your kids singing during reading time?" *The Reading Teacher, 41*(4), 454–457.

Harp, B. (1989a). What do we do in the place of ability grouping? *The Reading Teacher, 42,* 534–535.

Harp, B. (1989b). When the principal asks: "Why don't you ask comprehension questions?" *The Reading Teacher, 42*(8), 638–639.

Harris, A. J., & Hodges, R. E. (Eds.). (1981). *A dictionary of reading and related terms.* Newark, DE: International Reading Association.

Harris, A. J., & Sipay, E. R. (1990). *How to increase reading ability,* 9th Ed. New York: Longman.

Harris, T., Matteoni, L., Anderson, L., & Creekmore, M. (1975). *Keys to reading.* Oklahoma City: Economy.

Harris, T. L., & Hodges, R. E. (Eds.). (1995). *The literacy dictionary: The vocabulary of reading and writing.* Newark, DE: International Reading Association.

Harste, J. C., & Burke, C. L. (1977). A new hypothesis for reading teacher research: Both the teaching and learning of reading are theoretically based. In Pearson, D. P. (Ed.). *Reading: Theory, research, and practice* (pp. 32–40). Clemson, SC: National Reading Conference.

Harste, J. C., Short, K. G., & Burke, C. (1988). *Creating classrooms for authors: The reading writing connection.* Portsmouth, NH: Heinemann.

Harste, J. C., Woodward, V. A., & Burke, C. L. (1984). *Language stories and literacy lessons.* Portsmouth, NH: Heinemann.

Harwayne, S. (1992). *Lasting impressions.* Portsmouth, NH: Heinemann.

Hasbrouck, J. E., & Tindal, G. (1992). Curriculum-based oral reading fluency for students in grades 2 through 5. *Teaching Exceptional Children, 24*(3), 41–44.

Hawking, S. W. (1988). *A brief history of time: From the big bang to black holes.* Toronto: Bantam.

Heald-Taylor, G. (1989). *The administrator's guide to whole language.* Katona, NY: Owen.

Heald-Taylor, G. (1991). *Whole language strategies for ESL students.* San Diego, CA: Dominie Press.

Heald-Taylor, G. (2001). *The beginning reading handbook: Strategies for success.* Portsmouth, NH: Heinemann.

Healy, J. M. (1990). *Endangered minds: Why children don't think and what can be done about it.* New York: Touchstone.

Heath. (no date). *Quill* [computer program]. Lexington, MA: Heath.

Heathington, B. S. (1990). Test review: Concepts about print test. In R. B. Cooter, Jr. (Ed.). *The teacher's guide to reading tests* (pp. 110–114). Scottsdale, AZ: Gorsuch Scarisbrick.

Heckleman, R. G. (1966). Using the neurological impress remedial reading technique. *Academic Therapy, 1,* 235–239, 250.

Heckleman, R. G. (1969). A neurological impress method of remedial reading instruction. *Academic Therapy, 4,* 277–282.

Heide, F. P., & Gilliland, J. H. (1990). *Day of Ahmed's secret.* New York: Lothrop, Lee & Shepard Books.

Heilman, A. W., Blair, T. R., & Rupley, W. H. (2001). *Principles and practices of teaching reading,* 10th Ed. Upper Saddle River, NJ: Merrill/Prentice Hall.

Henderson, J. (2001). *Incidental vocabulary acquisition: Learning new vocabulary from reading silently and listening to stories read aloud.* Syracuse, NY: Educational Resources Information Center (ERIC) Document Reproduction Service.

Henk, W. A. (1983). Adapting the NIM to improve comprehension. *Academic Therapy, 19,* 97–101.

Henk, W. A., & Holmes, B. C. (1988). Effects of content-related attitude on the comprehension and retention of expository text. *Reading Psychology, 9*(3), 203–225.

Hennings, K. (1974). Drama reading, an on-going classroom activity at the elementary school level. *Elementary English, 51,* 48–51.

Henwood, C. (1988). *Frogs* (Barrie Watts, Photographer). London, NY: Franklin Watts.

Herber, H. L. (1978). *Teaching reading in the content areas,* 2nd Ed. Upper Saddle River, NJ: Prentice Hall.

Heymsfeld, C. R. (1989, March). Filling the hole in whole language. *Educational Leadership,* pp. 65–68.

Hiebert, E. (1978). Preschool children's understanding of written language. *Child Development, 49,* 1231–1241.

Hiebert, E. (1981). Developmental patterns and interrelationships of preschool children's print awareness. *Reading Research Quarterly, 16,* 236–260.

Hiebert E., & Ham, D. (1981). *Young children and environmental print.* Paper presented at the annual meeting of the National Reading Conference, Dallas, TX.

Hiebert, E. H. (1983). An examination of ability grouping for reading instruction. *Reading Research Quarterly, 18,* 231–255.

Hiebert, E. H. (1999). Text matters in learning to read. *The Reading Teacher, 52*(6), 552–566.

Hiebert, E. H., & Colt, J. (1989). Patterns of literature-based reading. *The Reading Teacher, 43*(1), 14–20.

Hiebert, E. H., & Martin, L. A. (2001). The texts of beginning reading instruction. In S. B. Neuman & D. K. Dickinson (Eds.), *Handbook of Early Literacy*. New York: Guildford Press.

Hill, B., & Ruptic, C. (1994). *Practical aspects of authentic assessment: Putting the pieces together*. Norwood, MA: Christopher-Gordon.

Hill, S. (1990a). *Raps and rhymes*. Armadale, Victoria, Australia: Eleanor Curtain.

Hill, S. (1990b). *Readers theatre: Performing the text*. Armadale, Victoria, Australia: Eleanor Curtain.

Hirsch, E. D. (1987). *Cultural literacy: What every American needs to know*. Boston: Houghton Mifflin.

Hirschfelder, A. B., & Singer, B. R. (1992). *Rising voices: Writing of young Native Americans*. New York: Scribner's.

Hoffman, J. V. (1987). Rethinking the role of oral reading in basal instruction. *The Elementary School Journal, 87*(3), 367–374.

Hoffman, J. V. (2001). *WORDS (on words in leveled texts for beginning readers)*. Ann Arbor, MI: Center for the Improvement of Early Reading Achievement. Available at *http://www.ciera.org/library/presos/2001/*.

Hoffman, J. V. (2001). *WORDS (on Words in Leveled Texts for Beginning Readers)*. Paper presented at 2001 National Reading Conference, San Antonio, Texas.

Hoffman, J. V., McCarthey, S. J., Abbott, J., Christian, C., Corman, L., Curry, et al. (1994). So what's new in the new basals? A focus on first grade. *Journal of Reading Behavior, 26*(1), 47–73.

Hoffman, J. V., Roser, N., & Battle, J. (1993). Reading aloud in classrooms: From the modal to a "model." *The Reading Teacher, 46*(6), 496–503.

Hoffman, J. V., & Segel, K. W. (1982). *Oral reading instruction: A century of controversy*. (ERIC Document Reproduction Service).

Hoffman, M. (1991). *Amazing grace*. New York: Dial Books.

Holdaway, D. (1979). *The foundations of literacy*. Exeter, NH: Heinemann.

Holdaway, D. (1981). Shared book experience: Teaching reading using favorite books. *Theory Into Practice, 21,* 293–300.

Holdaway, D. (1984). *Stability and change in literacy learning*. Portsmouth, NH: Heinemann.

Hollingsworth, P. H. (1978). An experimental approach to the impress method of teaching reading. *The Reading Teacher, 31,* 624–626.

Hollingsworth, P. M., & Reutzel, D. R. (1988). Get a grip on comprehension. *Reading Horizons, 29*(1), 71–78.

Hollingsworth, P. M., & Reutzel, D. R. (1990). Prior knowledge, content-related attitude, reading comprehension: Testing Mathewson's affective model of reading. *The Journal of Educational Research, 83*(4), 194–200.

Holmes, J. A. (1953). *The substrata-factor theory of reading*. Berkeley, CA: California Books.

Homan, S. P., Klesius, J. P., & Hite, C. (1993). Effects of repeated readings and non-repetitive strategies on students' fluency and comprehension. *Journal of Educational Research, 87*(2), 94–99.

Hook, P. E., and Jones, S. (2002). The importance of automaticity and fluency for efficient reading comprehension. *Perspectives, 28*(1), 9–14.

Hopkins, C. (1979). Using every-pupil response techniques in reading instruction. *The Reading Teacher, 33,* 173–175.

Hoskisson, K., & Tompkins, G. E. (1987). *Language arts: Content and teaching strategies*. Upper Saddle River, NJ: Merrill/Prentice Hall.

Houston, J. (1977). *Frozen fire*. New York: Atheneum.

Hoyt, L. (1999). *Revisit, reflect; retell: Strategies for improving reading comprehension*. Portsmouth, NH: Heinemann.

Huck, C. S., Helper, S., & Hickman, J. (1987). *Children's literature in the elementary school*. New York: Holt, Rinehart and Winston.

Huck, C. S., & Kuhn, D. Y. (1968). *Children's literature in the elementary school*. New York: Holt, Rinehart and Winston.

Hughes, T. O. (1975). *Sentence-combining: A means of increasing reading comprehension*. Kalamazoo: Western Michigan University, Department of English.

Hull, M. A. (1989). *Phonics for the teacher of reading*. Upper Saddle River, NJ: Merrill/Prentice Hall.

Hunt, L. C. (1970). Effect of self-selection, interest, and motivation upon independent, instructional, and frustrational levels. *Reading Teacher, 24,* 146–151.

Hunter, M. (1984). Knowing, teaching and supervising. In P. L. Hosford (Ed.), *Using what we know about teaching*. Alexandria, VA: Association for Supervision and Curriculum Development.

Hymes, D. (Ed.). (1964). *Language in culture and society*. New York: HarperCollins.

Invernizzi, M., Juel, C., & Rosemary, C. (1997). A community volunteer tutorial that works. *Reading Teacher, 50*(4), 304–311.

Irvin, J. L. (2001). Assisting struggling readers in building vocabulary and background knowledge. *Voices from the Middle, 8*(4), 37–43.

Irwin, J. W. (1996). *Teaching reading comprehension processes,* 2nd Ed. Englewood Cliffs, NJ: Prentice Hall.

Jachym, N. K., Allington, R. L., & Broikou, K. A. (1989). Estimating the cost of seatwork. *The Reading Teacher, 43,* 30–37.

Jacobs, H. H., & Borland, J. H. (1986). The interdisciplinary concept model: Theory and practice. *Gifted Child Quarterly, 30*(4), 159–163.

Jaffe, N. (1993). *The uninvited guest and other Jewish holiday tales.* New York: Scholastic.

Jenkins, R. (1990). *Whole language in Australia.* Scholastic Co. workshop at Brigham Young University, Provo, UT.

Jobe, F. W. (1976). *Screening vision in schools.* Newark, DE: International Reading Association.

Johns, J. L. (1980). First graders' concepts about print. *Reading Research Quarterly, 15,* 529–549.

Johns, J. L. (1986). Students: Perceptions of reading: Thirty years of inquiry. In D. B. Yaden, Jr. & S. Templeton (Eds.), *Awareness and beginning literacy: Conceptualizing what it means to read and write* (pp. 31–40). Portsmouth, NH: Heinemann.

Johns, J. L., & Ellis, D. W. (1976). Reading: Children tell it like it is. *Reading World, 16,* 115–128.

Johns, J. L., & Johns, A. L. (1971). How do children in the elementary school view the reading process? *The Michigan Reading Journal, 5,* 44–53.

Johns, J. L., & Lunn, M. K. (1983). The informal reading inventory: 1910–1980. *Reading World, 23*(1), 8–18.

Johnson, D. (1989). *Pressing problems in world literacy: The plight of the homeless.* Paper presented at the 23rd annual meeting of the Utah Council of the International Reading Association, Salt Lake City, UT.

Johnson, D., & Pearson, P. D. (1984). *Teaching reading vocabulary.* New York: Holt, Rinehart and Winston.

Johnson, D. D. (1973). Sex differences in reading across cultures. *Reading Research Quarterly, 9*(1), 67–86.

Johnson, D. D. (2001). *Vocabulary in the elementary and middle school.* Needham Heights, MA: Allyn & Bacon.

Johnson, D. D., & Baumann, J. F. (1984). Word identification. In P. D. Pearson (Ed.), *Handbook of reading research* (pp. 583–608). New York: Longman.

Johnson, D. D., & Pearson. P. D. (1975). Skills management systems: A critique. *The Reading Teacher, 28,* 757–764.

Johnson, D. D., & Pearson, P. D. (1984). *Teaching reading vocabulary.* New York: Holt, Rinehart and Winston.

Johnson, D. W. (1976). *Jack and the beanstalk* (D. William Johnson, Illustrator). Boston: Little, Brown.

Johnson, D. W., & Johnson, R. T. (1999). *Learning together and alone: Cooperative, competitive, and individualistic learning,* 5th Ed. Boston: Allyn & Bacon.

Johnson, D. W., Maruyama, G., Johnson, R. T., Nelson, D., & Skon, L. (1981). Effects of cooperative, competitive and individualistic goal structures on achievement: A meta-analysis. *Psychological Bulletin, 89,* 47–62.

Johnson, T. D., & Louis, D. R. (1987). *Literacy through literature.* Portsmouth, NH: Heinemann.

Johnston, F. R. (1998). The reader, the text, and the task: Learning words in first grade. *The Reading Teacher, 51,* 666–676.

Jones, M. B., & Nessel, D. D. (1985). Enhancing the curriculum with experience stories. *The Reading Teacher, 39,* 18–23.

Jongsma, K. S. (1989). Questions & answers: Portfolio assessment. *The Reading Teacher, 43*(3), 264–265.

Jongsma, K. S. (1990). Questions & Answers: Collaborative Learning, *The Reading Teacher, 43*(4), 346–347.

Joseph, D. G., Flynt, E. S., & Cooter, R. B., Jr. (1987, March). *Diagnosis and correction of reading difficulties: A new model.* Paper presented at the National Association of School Psychologists annual convention, New Orleans, LA.

Juel, C. (1988). Learning to read and write: A longitudinal study of the fifty-four children from first through fourth grade. *Journal of Educational Psychology, 80*(4), 437–47.

Juel, C. (1991). Cross-age tutoring between student athletes and at-risk children. *Reading Teacher, 45*(3), 178–186.

Juster, N. (1961). *The phantom tollbooth.* New York: Random House.

Kagan, J. (1966). Reflection-impulsivity: The generality and dynamics of conceptual tempo. *Journal of Abnormal Psychology, 71,* 17–24.

Kang, H. W. (1994). Helping second language readers learn from content area text through collaboration and support. *The Journal of Reading, 37*(8), 646–652.

Karlsen, B., & Gardner, E. F. (1984). *Stanford diagnostic reading test,* 3rd Ed. New York: Harcourt Brace.

Kaufman, A. S., & Kaufman, N. L. (1997). *Kaufman Test of Educational Achievement-Normative Update (K-TEA/NU).* Circle Pines, MN: AGS.

Kearsley, R. (1973). The newborn's response to auditory stimulation: A demonstration of orienting and defensive behavior. *Child Development, 44,* 582–590.

Keegan, M. (1991). *Pueblo boy: Growing up in two worlds.* New York: Cobblehill Books.

Keene, E. O., & Zimmerman, S. (1997). *Mosaic of thought.* Portsmouth, NH: Heinemann.

Keith, S. (1981). *Politics of textbook selection* (Research report No. 81-AT). Stanford, CA: Stanford University School of Education, Institute for Research on School Finance and Governance.

Kemp, M. (1987). *Watching children read and write.* Portsmouth, NH: Heinemann.

Kessen, W., Levine, J., & Wendrich, K. (1979). The imitation of pitch in infants. *Infant Behavior and Development, 2,* 93–100.

Kiefer, Z., Levstik, L. S., & Pappas, C. C. (1998). *An integrated language perspective in the elementary school: An action approach*, 3rd Ed. Boston: Addison-Wesley.

Killilea, M. (1954). *Karen.* New York: Dodd, Mead.

Kintsch, W. (1974). *The representation of meaning in memory.* Hillsdale, NJ: Erlbaum.

Kirsch, I. S., Jungeblut, A., Jenkins, L., & Kolstad, A. (1993). *Adult literacy in America: A first look at the results of the national adult literacy survey.* Washington, DC: National Center for Educational Statistics.

Kirshner, D., & Whitson, J. A. (1997). *Situated cognition: Social, semiotic, and psychological perspectives.* Mahwah, NJ: Lawrence Erlbaum Associates.

Klare, G. R. (1963). Assessing readability. *Reading Research Quarterly, 10,* 62–102.

Klenk, L., & Kibby, M. W. (2000). Re-mediating reading difficulties: Appraising the past, reconciling the present, constructing the future. In M. L. Kamil, P. B. Mosenthal, P. D., Pearson, and R. Barr (Eds.), *Handbook of Reading Research,* Vol. 3. Mahwah, NJ: Erlbaum.

Klobukowski, P. (2000). Parents, buddy journals, and teacher response. In T. V. Rasinski, N. D. Padak, et al. (Eds.), *Motivating recreational reading and promoting home-school connections* (pp. 51–52). Newark, DE: International Reading Association.

Knapp, M. S. (1991). *What is taught, and how, to the children of poverty: Interim report from a two-year investigation.* Menlo Park, CA: SRI.

Koskinen, P., Wilson, R., & Jensema, C. (1985). Closed-captioned television: A new tool for reading instruction. *Reading World, 24,* 1–7.

Koskinen, P. S., Blum, I. H., Bisson, S. A., Phillips, S. M., Creamer, T. S., & Baker, T. K. (1999). Shared reading, books, and audiotapes: Supporting diverse students in school and at home. *The Reading Teacher, 52*(5), 430–444.

Kownslar, A. O. (1977). *People and our world: A study of world history.* New York: Holt, Rinehart and Winston.

Kozol, J. (1985). *Illiterate America.* New York: New American Library.

Krashen, S. (1982). *Principles and practices in second language acquisition.* New York: Pergamon Press.

Krashen, S. (1992). *The power of reading.* Englewood, CO: Libraries Unlimited.

Krashen, S. (1993). *The power of reading: Insights from the research.* Englewood. CO: Libraries Unlimited.

Krashen, S., & Biber, D. (1988). *On course.* Sacramento, CA: CABE.

Krauss, R. (1945). *The carrot seed* (Crockett Johnson, Illustrator). New York: Scholastic.

Krulik, N. E. (1991). *My picture book of the planets.* New York: Scholastic.

Kuby, P., & Aldridge, J. (1997). Direct vs. indirect environmental print instruction and early reading ability in kindergarten children. *Reading Psychology 15*(1), 1–9.

Kuby, P., Aldridge, J., & Snyder, S. (1994). Developmental progression of environmental print recognition in kindergarten children. *Reading Psychology 18*(2), 91–104.

Kuby, P., Kirkland, L., & Aldridge, J. (1996). Learning about environmental print through picture books. *Early Childhood Education Journal, 24*(1), 33–36.

Kuchinskas, G., & Radencich, M. C. (1986). *The semantic mapper.* Gainesville, FL: Teacher Support Software.

Kulik, C. C., & Kulik, J. A. (1982). Effects of ability grouping on secondary students: A meta-analysis of evaluation findings. *American Educational Research Journal, 19,* 415–428.

Labbo, L. D. (2001). Supporting children's comprehension of informational text through interactive read alouds. *Literacy and Nonfiction Series, 1*(2), 1–4.

LaBerge, D., & Samuels, S. J. (1974). Toward a theory of automatic information processing in reading. *Cognitive Psychology, 6,* 293–323.

LaBerge, D., & Samuels, S. J. (1985). Toward a theory of automatic information processing in reading. In H. Singer & R. B. Ruddell (Eds.), *Theoretical models and processes of reading* (pp. 689–718). Newark, DE: International Reading Association.

Lamme, L. L., & Hysmith, C. (1991). One school's adventure into portfolio assessment. *Language Arts, 68,* 629–640.

Lamoreaux, L., & Lee, D. M. (1943). *Learning to read through experience.* New York: Appleton-Century-Crofts.

Langer, J. (1981). From theory to practice: A prereading plan. *Journal of Reading, 25,* 152–156.

Langer, J. A. (1984). Examining background knowledge and text comprehension. *Reading Research Quarterly, 19,* 468–481.

Langer, J. A. (1985). Levels of questioning: An alternative view.

Reading Research Quarterly, 20(5), 586–602.

Langer, P., Kalk, J. M., & Searls, D. T. (1984). Age of admission and trends in achievement: A comparison of blacks and Caucasians. *American Educational Research Journal, 21,* 61–78.

Larsen, N. (1994). *The publisher's chopping block: What happens to children's trade books when they are published in a basal reading series?* Unpublished master's projects, Brigham Young University.

Lass, B., & Davis, B. (1985). *The remedial reading handbook.* Upper Saddle River, NJ: Prentice Hall.

Lathlaen, P. (1993). A meeting of minds: Teaching using biographies. *The Reading Teacher, 46*(6), 529–531.

Law, B., & Eckes, M. (1990). *The more than just surviving handbook: ESL for every classroom teacher.* Winnipeg, Canada: Peguis.

Leinhardt, G., Zigmond, N., & Cooley, W. (1981). Reading instruction and its effects. *American Educational Research Journal, 18,* 343–361.

Lemann, N. (1997, November). The reading wars. *The Atlantic Monthly, 280*(5), 128–134.

L'Engle, M. (1962). *A wrinkle in time.* New York: Dell.

Lenneberg, E. H. (1964). *New directions in the study of language.* Cambridge, MA: MIT Press.

Levin, J.-R., Johnson, D. D., Pittelman, S. D., Levin, K., Shriberg, L. K., Toms-Bronowski, S., & Hayes, B. (1984). A comparison of semantic- and mnemonic-based vocabulary-learning strategies. *Reading Psychology, 5,* 1–15.

Levin, J. R., Levin, M. E., Glasman, L. D., & Nordwall, M. B. (1992). Mnemonic vocabulary instruction: Additional effectiveness

evidence. *Contemporary Educational Psychology, 17,* 156–174.

Levine, S. S. (1976). *The effect of transformational sentence-combining exercises on the reading comprehension and written composition of third-grade children.* Unpublished doctoral dissertation, Hofstra University, NY.

Lewis, C. S. (1961). *The lion, the witch, and the wardrobe.* New York: Macmillan.

Liberman, I. Y., Shankweiler, D., Liberman, A., Fowler, C., & Fischer, F. (1977). Phonetic segmentation and decoding in the beginning reader. In A. S. Reber & D. L. Scarborough (Eds.), *Toward a psychology of reading* (pp. 207–225). Hillsdale, NJ: Erlbaum.

Lima, C., & Lima, J. (1993). *A to zoo: A subject access to children's picture books.* New York: Bowker.

Lindsay, P. H., & Norman, D. A. (1977). *Human information processing: An introduction to psychology.* New York: Academic Press.

Lipson, M. Y. (1983). The influence of religious affiliation on children's memory for text information. *Reading Research Quarterly, 18*(4), 448–457.

Lipson, M. Y. (1984). Some unexpected issues in prior knowledge and comprehension. *The Reading Teacher, 37*(8), 760–764.

Lisle, J. T. (1989). *Afternoon of the elves.* New York: Franklin Watts.

Littlejohn, C. (1988). *The lion and the mouse.* New York: Dial Books for Young Readers.

Livingston, N., & Birrell, J. R. (1994). Learning about cultural diversity through literature. *BYU Children's Book Review, 54*(5), 1–6.

Lobel, A. (1981). *On Market Street* (Pictures by Anita Lobel). New York: Scholastic.

Lobel, A. (1983). *Fables.* New York: Harper & Row.

Lock, S. (1980). *Hubert hunts his hum* (J. Newnham, Illustrator). Sydney, Australia: Ashton Scholastic.

Lomax, R. G., & McGee, L. M. (1987). Young children's concepts about print and reading: Toward a model of word reading acquisition. *Reading Research Quarterly, 22*(2), 237–256.

Loranger, A. L. (1997). Comprehension strategies instruction: Does it make a difference? *Reading Psychology, 18*(1), 31–68.

Loughlin, C. E., & Martin, M. D. (1987). *Supporting literacy: Developing effective learning environments.* New York: Columbia Teachers College Press.

Lowery, L. F., & Grafft, W. (1967). Paperback books and reading attitudes. *The Reading Teacher, 21*(7), 618–623.

Luria, A. R., & Yudovich, F. I. (1971). *Speech and the development of mental processes in the child.* London: Staples press.

Lyman, F. (1988). Think-Pair-Share, Wait time two, and on . . . *Mid-Atlantic Association for Cooperation in Education Cooperative News, 2,* 1.

Lyon, G. R. (1997). Statement of G. Reid Lyon to The Committee on Education and the Workforce, U.S. House of Representatives (July 19, 1997). Washington, DC.

Lyon, G. R. (1998). Why reading is not a natural process. *Educational Leadership, 55*(6), 14–18.

Lyon, R. (1977). Auditory-perceptual training: The state of the art. *Journal of Learning Disabilities, 10,* 564–572.

Lyons, C. A., & Beaver, J. (1995). Reducing retention and learning disability placement through reading recovery: An educationally sound, cost-effective choice. In R. L. Allington & S. A. Walmsley (Eds.), *No quick* fix: Rethinking literacy programs in America's elementary schools. New York: Teachers College Press.

MacGinitie, W. H. (1969). Evaluating readiness for learning to read: A critical review and evaluation of research. *Reading Research Quarterly, 4,* 396–410.

MacGinitie, W. H., & MacGinitie, R. K. (1989). *Gates-MacGinitie reading tests,* 3rd Ed. Chicago: Riverside.

Macmillan/McGraw-Hill. (1993). *Macmillan/McGraw-Hill reading/language: A new view.* New York: Author.

Manarino-Leggett, P., & Salomon, P. A. (1989, April–May). *Cooperation vs. competition: Techniques for keeping your classroom alive but not endangered.* Paper presented at the thirty-fourth annual convention of the International Reading Association, New Orleans, LA.

Mandler, J. M., & Johnson, N. S. (1977). Remembrance of things parsed: Story structure and recall. *Cognitive Psychology, 9,* 111–151.

Manzo, A. V. (1969). The request procedure. *The Journal of Reading, 13,* 123–126.

Manzo, A. V., & Manzo, U. C. (1990). *Content area reading: A heuristic approach.* Upper Saddle River, NJ: Merrill/Prentice Hall.

Manzo, A. V., Manzo, U. C., & Estes, T. (2000). *Content area literacy: Interactive teaching for active learning,* 3rd Ed. San Francisco, CA: John Wiles & Sons.

Marchionini, G. (1988). Hypermedia and learning: Freedom and chaos. *Educational Technology, 28,* 8–12.

Martin, B. (1990). *Brown Bear, Brown Bear, What do you see?* New York: Henry Holt.

Martin, B. (1991). *Polar Bear, Polar Bear, What do you hear?* New York: Henry Holt.

Martin, B., & Archaumbalt, J. (1987). *Knots on a counting rope.* New York: Holt, Rinehart and Winston.

Martin, J. H. (1987). *Writing to read* [Computer program]. Boca Raton, FL: IBM.

Martinez, M. (1993). Motivating dramatic story reenactments. *The Reading Teacher, 46*(8), 682–688.

Martinez, M., & Nash, M. F. (1990). Bookalogues: Talking about children's literature. *Language Arts, 67,* 576–580.

Martorella, P. H. (1985). *Elementary social studies.* Boston: Little, Brown.

Martorella, P. H. (2000). *Teaching social studies in middle and secondary schools.* Upper Saddle River, NJ: Prentice Hall.

Marzano, R. J. (1993–1994). When two world views collide. *Educational Leadership, 51*(4), 6–11.

Marzollo, J., & Marzollo, C. (1982). *Jed's junior space patrol: A science fiction easy to read.* New York: Dial.

Mason, J. (1983). An examination of reading instruction in third and fourth grades. *The Reading Teacher, 36*(9), 906–913.

Mason, J. M. (1980). When do children begin to read: An exploration of four-year-old children's letter and word reading competencies. *Reading Research Quarterly, 15,* 203–227.

Masonheimer, P. E., Drum, P. A., & Ehri, L. C. (1984). Does environmental print identification lead children into word reading? *Journal of Reading Behavior, 16,* 257–271.

Math, I. (1981). *Wires and watts: Understanding and using electricity.* New York: Scribner's.

Mathes, P. G. (1997). Cooperative story mapping. *Remedial and Special Education, 18*(1), 20–27.

Mathes, P. G., Simmons, D. C., & Davis, B. I. (1992). Assisted reading techniques for developing reading fluency. *Reading Research and Instruction, 31*(4), 70–77.

Mathewson, G. C. (1985). Toward a comprehensive model of affect in the reading process. In H. Singer & R. B. Ruddell (Eds.), *Theoretical models and processes of reading,* 3rd Ed. (pp. 841–856). Newark, DE: International Reading Association.

Mathewson, G. C. (1994). Model of attitude influence upon reading and learning to read. In H. Singer & R. B. Ruddell (Eds.), *Theoretical models and processes of reading,* 4th Ed. (pp. 1131–1161). Newark, DE: International Reading Association.

Maxim, G. (1989). *The very young: Guiding children from infancy through the early years,* 3rd Ed. Upper Saddle River, NJ: Merrill/Prentice Hall.

May, F. B., & Elliot, S. B. (1978). *To help children read: Mastery performance modules for teachers in training,* 2nd Ed. Upper Saddle River, NJ: Merrill/Prentice Hall.

May, F. B., & Rizzardi, L. (2002). *Reading as communication,* 6th Ed. Upper Saddle River, NJ: Merrill/Prentice Hall.

Mayer, M. (1976a). *Ah-choo.* New York: Dial Books.

Mayer, M. (1976b). *Hiccup.* New York: Dial Books.

McCallum, R. D. (1988). Don't throw the basals out with the bath water. *The Reading Teacher, 42,* 204–209.

McCarrier, A., Pinnell, G. S., & Fountas, I. C. (1999). *Interactive writing: How language & literacy come together, K–2.* Portsmouth, NH: Heinemann.

McCarthey, S. J., Hoffman, J. V., Christian, C., Corman, L., Elliott, B., Matherne, D., & Stahle, D. (1994). Engaging the new basal readers. *Reading*

Research and Instruction, 33(3), 233–256.

McCormick, C. E., & Mason, J. (1986). Intervention procedures for increasing preschool children's interest in and knowledge about reading. In W. H. Teale & E. Sulzby (Eds.), *Emergent literacy: Writing and reading* (pp. 90–115). Norwood, NJ: Ablex Publishing.

McCormick, S. (1995). *Instructing students who have literacy problems.* Upper Saddle River, NJ: Merrill/Prentice Hall.

McCracken, R. A., & McCracken, M. J. (1978). Modeling is the key to sustained reading. *The Reading Teacher, 31,* 406–408.

McDermott, G. (1993). *Raven: Trickster tale from the Pacific Northwest.* San Diego, CA: Harcourt Brace.

McGee, L. M., Lomax, R. G., & Head, M. H. (1988). Young children's written language knowledge: What environmental and functional print reading reveals. *Journal of Reading Behavior, 20*(2), 99–118.

McGee, L. M., Ratliff, J. L., Sinex, A., Head, M., & LaCroix, K. (1984). Influence of story schema and concept of story on children's story compositions. In J. A. Niles & L. A. Harris (Eds.), *Thirty-third yearbook of the National Reading Conference* (pp. 270–277). Rochester, NY: National Reading Conference.

McGee, L. M., & Richgels, D. J. (2000). *Literacy's beginnings: Supporting young readers and writers,* 3rd Ed. Needham, MA: Allyn & Bacon.

McGuire, F. N. (1984). How arts instruction affects reading and language: Theory and research. *The Reading Teacher, 37*(9), 835–839.

McInnes, J. (1983). *Networks.* Toronto: Nelson of Canada.

McKee, D. (1990). *Elmer.* London: Red Fox.

McKeown, M. G., & Beck, I. L. (1988). Learning vocabulary: Different ways for different goals. *Remedial and Special Education, 9*(1), 42–52.

McKeown, M. G., Beck, I. L., & Worthy, M. J. (1993). Grappling with text ideas: Questioning the author. *The Reading Teacher, 46*(7), 560–565.

McKissack, P. C. (1986). *Flossie & the fox.* New York: Dial Books for Young Readers.

McKuen, R. (1990). Ten books on CD ROM. *MacWorld, 7*(12), 217–218.

McMahon, S. I., & Raphael, T. E. (1997). *The book club connection: Literacy learning and classroom talk.* New York: Teachers College Press.

McNeil, J. D. (1987). *Reading comprehension,* 2nd Ed. Glenview, IL: Scott, Foresman.

McTighe, J., & Lyman, F. T. (1988). Cueing thinking in the classroom: The promise of theory-embedded tools. *Educational Leadership, 45*(7), 18–24.

Meade, E. L. (1973). The first R-A point of view. *Reading World, 12,* 169–180.

MECC. (1984). *Writing a narrative* (computer program). St. Paul, MN: Minnesota Educational Computing Consortium.

Medina, M., & Escamilla, K. (1994). Language acquisition and gender for limited-language-proficient Mexican Americans in a maintenance bilingual program. *Hispanic Journal of Behavioral Sciences, 16*(4), 422–437.

Menke, D. J., & Pressley, M. (1994). Elaborative interrogation: Using "why" questions to enhance learning from text. *Journal of Reading, 37*(8), 642–645.

Menyuk, P. (1988). *Language development knowledge and use.* Glenview, IL: Scott, Foresman/Little, Brown.

Merrill Mathematics (Grade 5). (1985). Upper Saddle River, NJ: Merrill/Prentice Hall.

Merrill Science (Grade 3). (1989). Upper Saddle River, NJ: Merrill/Prentice Hall.

Meyer, B., Brandt, D., & Bluth, G. (1980). Use of top-level structure in text for reading comprehension of ninth-grade students. *Reading Research Quarterly, 16,* 72–103.

Meyer, B. J. (1979). Organizational patterns in prose and their use in reading. In M. L. Kamil & A. J. Moe (Eds.), *Reading research: Studies and applications* (pp. 109–117). Twenty-eighth Yearbook of the National Reading Conference.

Meyer, B. J. F., & Freedle, R. O. (1984). Effects of discourse type on recall. *American Educational Research Journal, 21*(1), 121–143.

Mezynski, K. (1983). Issues concerning the acquisition of knowledge: Effects of vocabulary training on reading comprehension. *Review of Educational Research, 53*(2), 253–279.

Michaels, J. R. (2001). *Dancing with words: Helping students love language through authentic vocabulary instruction.* Urbana, IL: National Council of Teachers of English.

Miller, B. F., Rosenberg, E. B., & Stackowski, B. L. (1971). *Investigating your health.* Boston: Houghton Mifflin.

Mindplay. (1990). *Author! Author!* Danvers, MA: Methods and Solutions.

Moe, A. J., & Irwin, J. W. (1986). Cohesion, coherence, and comprehension. In J. W. Irwin (Ed.), *Understanding and teaching cohesion comprehension* (pp. 3–8). Newark, DE: International Reading Association.

Moffett, J. (1983). *Teaching the universe of discourse.* Boston: Houghton Mifflin.

Moffett, J., & Wagner, B. J. (1976). *Student-centered language arts and reading K–13. A handbook* for teachers, 2nd Ed. Boston: Houghton Mifflin.

Monjo, F. N. (1970). *The drinking gourd.* New York: HarperCollins.

Mooney, M. E. (1990). *Reading to, with, and by children.* Katonah, NY: Owen.

Moore, M. A. (1991). Electronic dialoguing: An avenue to literacy. *The Reading Teacher, 45*(4), 280–286.

Morphett, M. V., & Washburne, C. (1931). When should children begin to read? *Elementary School Journal, 31,* 496–503.

Morris, D., Shaw, B., & Perney, J. (1990). Helping low readers in grades 2 & 3: An after-school volunteer tutoring program. *Elementary School Journal, 91,* 133–150.

Morrow, L. M. (1984). Reading stories to young children: Effects of story structure and traditional questioning strategies on comprehension. *Journal of Reading Behavior, 16,* 273–288.

Morrow, L. M. (1985). Retelling stories: A strategy for improving children's comprehension, concept of story structure and oral language complexity. *Elementary School Journal, 85,* 647–661.

Morrow, L. M. (1988a). Retelling as a diagnostic tool. In S. M. Glazer, L. W. Searfoss, & L. Gentile (Eds.), *Re-examining reading diagnosis: New trends and procedures in classrooms and clinics* (pp. 128–149). Newark, DE: International Reading Association.

Morrow, L. M. (1988b). Young children's responses to one-to-one story reading in school settings. *The Reading Teacher, 23*(1), 89–107.

Morrow, L. M. (1990). Preparing the classroom environment to promote literacy during play. *Early Childhood Education Research Quarterly, 5,* 537–554.

Morrow, L. M. (1993). *Literacy development in the early years: Helping children read and write,* 2nd Ed. Boston: Allyn & Bacon.

Morrow, L. M. (1995). *Family literacy: Connections in schools and communities.* Newark, DE: International Reading Association.

Morrow, L. M. (2001). *Literacy development in the early years: Helping children read and write,* 4th Ed. Needham Heights, MA: Allyn & Bacon.

Morrow, L. M. (2002). *The literacy center: Contexts for reading and writing,* 2nd Ed. Portland, ME: Stenhouse.

Morrow, L. M., & Rand, M. K. (1991). Promoting literacy during play by designing early childhood classroom environments. *The Reading Teacher, 44*(6), 396–402.

Morrow, L. M., Tracey, D. H., Woo, D. G., & Pressley, M. (1999). Characteristics of exemplary first-grade literacy instruction. *The Reading Teacher, 52*(5), 462–476.

Mosenthal, P. B. (1989a). From random events to predictive reading models. *The Reading Teacher, 42*(7), 524–525.

Mosenthal, P. B. (1989b). The whole language approach: Teachers between a rock and a hard place. *The Reading Teacher, 42*(8), 628–629.

Moss, B., & Newton, E. (2001). An examination of the information text genre in basal readers. *Reading Psychology, 23*(1), 1–13.

Moustafa, M. (1997). *Beyond traditional phonics: Research discoveries and reading instruction.* Portsmouth, NH: Heinemann.

Moustafa, M., & Maldonado-Colon, E. (1999). Whole-to-parts phonics instruction: Building on what children know to help them know more. *The Reading Teacher, 52*(5), 448–458.

Mullis, I. V. S., Campbell, J. R., & Farstrup, A. E. (Eds.). (1993). *NAEP 1992 reading report card for the nation and the states* (Report No. 23-ST06). Washington, DC: National Center for Education Statistics, USDOE.

Munsch, R. (1980). *The paper bag princess.* Toronto: Annick Press.

Muth, K. D. (1989). *Children's comprehension of text: Research into practice.* Newark, DE: International Reading Association.

Myers, W. D. (1975). *Fast Sam, Cool Clyde, and Stuff.* New York: Puffin Books.

Nagy, W. (1988). *Teaching vocabulary to improve reading comprehension.* Unpublished manuscript, Champaign, IL: Center for the Study of Reading.

Nagy, W. E., & Anderson, R. C. (1984). How many words are there in printed school English? *Reading Research Quarterly, 19*(3), 304–330.

Nagy, W. E., Anderson, R., & Herman, P. (1987). Learning word meanings from context during normal reading. *American Educational Research Journal, 24,* 237–270.

Nagy, W. E., Herman, P. A., & Anderson, R. C. (1985). Learning words from context. *Reading Research Quarterly, 20,* 233–253.

Naiden, N. (1976). Ratio of boys to girls among disabled readers. *The Reading Teacher, 29*(6), 439–442.

Namioka, L. (1992). *Yang the youngest and his terrible ear.* Boston: Little, Brown.

Nash, B., & Nash, G. (1980). *Pundles.* New York: Stone Song Press.

Naslund, J. C., & Samuel, J. S. (1992). Automatic access to word sounds and meaning in decoding written text. *Reading and Writing Quarterly, 8*(2), 135–156.

National Assessment of Educational Progress. (1990). *Learning to read in our nation's schools: Instruction and achievement in*

1988 at grades 4, 8, and 12. Princeton, NJ: Author.

National Assessment of Educational Progress NAEP. (1996). *Results from the NAEP 1994 reading assessment—at a glance.* Washington, DC: National Center for Educational Statistics.

National Assessment of Educational Progress. (2000). Washington, DC: Department of Education.

National Association for the Education of Young Children. (1986). Position statement on developmentally appropriate practice in programs for 4- and 5-year-olds. *Young Children, 41*(6), 20–29.

National Center for Education Statistics. (1999). *NAEP 1998 Reading Report Card: National & state highlights.* Washington, DC: National Center for Education Statistics.

National Commission on Teaching and America's Future. (1996). *What matters most: Teachers for America's future.* Woodbridge, VA: Author.

National Education Association (NEA). (2000). *Report of the National Education Association's Task Force on Reading 2000.* Washington, DC: Author.

National Institute of Child Health and Human Development. (2000). *Why children succeed or fail at reading. Research from NICHD's program in learning disabilities.* Retrieved from http://www.nichd.nih.gov/publica tions/pubs/readbro.htm

National Institute of Child Health and Human Development. (2000). *Report of the National Reading Panel: Teaching children to read.* Washington, DC.

National Reading Panel (NRP). (2000). *Report of the National Reading Panel: Teaching children to read* (NIH pub 00-4769). Washington, DC: National Institute of Child Health and Human Development.

National Research Council. (1998). Preventing reading difficulties in young children. Washington, DC: U.S. Department of Education. (available at *http://www.nap.edu/ readingroom/enter2.cgi?030906 418X.html*)

Nelson, T. (1988, January). Managing immense storage. *Byte,* 225–238.

Neuman, S., & Koskinen, P. (1992). Captioned television as comprehensible input: Effects of incidental word learning from context for language minority students. *Reading Research Quarterly, 27*(3), 94–106.

Neuman, S., & Roskos, K. (1992). Literacy objects as cultural tools: Effects on children's literacy behaviors in play. *Reading Research Quarterly, 27*(3), 203–225.

Neuman, S. B. (1981). Effect of teaching auditory perceptual skill on reading achievement in first grade. *The Reading Teacher, 34,* 422–426.

Neuman, S. B. (1999). Books make a difference: a study of access to literacy. *Reading Research Quarterly, 34*(3), 2–31.

Neuman, S. B. (2001). The role of knowledge in early literacy. *Reading Research Quarterly, 36*(4), 468–475.

Neuman, S. B., & Celano, D. (2001). Access to print in low-income and middle-income communities: An ecological study of four neighborhoods. *Reading Research Quarterly, 36*(1), 8–27.

Neuman, S. B., & Roskos, K. (1990). Play, print, and purpose: Enriching play environments for literacy development. *The Reading Teacher, 44*(3), 214–221.

Neuman, S. B., & Roskos, K. (1993). *Language and literacy learning in the early years: An integrated approach.* New York: Harcourt Brace.

Neuman, S. B., & Roskos, K. (1997). Literacy knowledge in practice: Contexts of participation

for young writers and readers. *Reading Research Quarterly, 32*(1), 10–33.

Newman, J. M. (1985a). Yes, that's an interesting idea, but. . . . In J. M. Newman (Ed.), *Whole language: Theory in use* (pp. 181–186). Portsmouth, NH: Heinemann.

Newman, J. M. (Ed.). (1985b). *Whole language: Theory in use.* Portsmouth, NH: Heinemann.

Newman, M. L. (1996). *The association of academic achievement, types of offenses, family, and other characteristics of males who have been adjudicated as juvenile delinquents.* Unpublished masters thesis, California State University, Long Beach, CA.

Nilsen, A. P., & Nilsen, D. L. F. (2002). Lessons in the teaching of vocabulary from September 11 and Harry Potter. *Journal of Adolescent & Adult Literacy, 46*(3), 254–260.

Nist, S. L., & Simpson, M. L. (1993). *Developing vocabulary concepts for college thinking.* Lexington, MA: Heath.

Nolan, E. A., & Berry, M. (1993). Learning to listen. *The Reading Teacher, 46*(7), 606–608.

Nordquist, V. M., & Twardosz, S. (1990). Preventing behavior problems in early childhood special education classrooms through environmental organization. *Education and Treatment of Children, 13*(4), 274–287.

Norton, D. E. (1998). *Through the eyes of a child: An introduction to children's literature,* 5th Ed. Upper Saddle River, NJ: Merrill/Prentice Hall.

Norton, D. E., & Norton, S. (2003). *Through the eyes of a child: An introduction to children's literature,* 6th Ed. Upper Saddle River, NJ: Merrill/Prentice Hall.

Novick, R. (2002). Learning to read the heart: Nurturing emotional literacy. *Young Children, 57*(3), 84–89.

Numeroff, L. J. (1985). *If you give a mouse a cookie.* New York: Scholastic.

Nurss, J. R., Hough, R. A., & Goodson, M. S. (1981). Prereading/language development in two day care centers. *Journal of Reading Behavior, 13,* 23–31.

Oakes, J. (1992). Can tracking research inform practice? *Educational Researcher, 21*(4), 12–21.

O'Bruba, W. S. (1987). Reading through the creative arts. *Reading Horizons, 27*(3), 170–177.

Ogle, D. M. (1986). K-W-L: A teaching model that develops active reading of expository text. *The Reading Teacher, 39*(6), 564–570.

Ohanian, S. (1984). Hot new item or same old stew? *Classroom Computer Learning, 5,* 30–31.

O'Huigin, S. (1988). *Scary poems for rotten kids.* New York: Firefly Books.

Olson, M. W., & Gee, T. C. (1988). Understanding narratives: A review of story grammar research. *Childhood Education, 64*(4), 302–306.

Olson, M. W., & Longnion, B. (1982). Pattern guides: A workable alternative for content teachers. *Journal of Reading, 25,* 736–741.

Opitz, M. F. (1992). The cooperative reading activity: An alternative to ability grouping. *The Reading Teacher, 45*(9), 736–738.

Opitz, M. F. (1998). *Flexible grouping in reading: Practical ways to help all students become better readers.* New York: Scholastic.

Opitz, M. F., & Ford, M. P. (2001). *Reaching readers: Flexible and innovative strategies for guided reading.* Portsmouth, NH: Heinemann.

Opitz, M. F., & Rasinski, T. V. (1998). *Good-bye round robin: 25 effective oral reading strategies.* Portsmouth, NH: Heinemann.

Orellana, M. F., & Hernandez, A. (1999). Talking the walk: Children reading urban environmental print. *The Reading Teacher, 52*(6), 612–619.

Osborn, J. (1984). The purposes, uses, and contents of workbooks and some guidelines for publishers. In R. C. Anderson, J. Osborn, & R. J. Tierney (Eds.), *Learning to read in American schools* (pp. 45–112). Hillsdale, NJ: Erlbaum.

Osborn, J. (1985). Workbooks: Counting, matching, and judging. In J. Osborn, P. T. Wilson, & R. C. Anderson (Eds.), *Reading education: Foundations for a literate America* (pp. 11–28). Lexington, MA: Lexington Books.

Otto, J. (1982). The new debate in reading. *The Reading Teacher, 36*(1), 14–18.

Palincsar, A. S., & Brown, A. L. (1984). Reciprocal teaching of comprehension-fostering and monitoring activities. *Cognition and Instruction, 1,* 117–175.

Palincsar, A. S., & Brown, A. L. (1985). Reciprocal teaching: A means to a meaningful end. In J. Osborn, P. T. Wilson, & R. C. Anderson (Eds.), *Reading education: Foundations for a Literate America* (pp. 299–310). Lexington, MA: Heath.

Pankake, M., & Pankake, J. (1988). *A Prairie Home Companion folk song book.* New York: Viking.

Pappas, C. C., Kiefer, B. Z., & Levstik, L. S. (1990). *An integrated language perspective in the elementary school.* New York: Longman.

Paradis, E., & Peterson, J. (1975). Readiness training implications from research. *The Reading Teacher, 28*(5), 445–448.

Paradis, E. E. (1974). The appropriateness of visual discrimination exercises in reading readiness materials. *Journal of Educational Research, 67,* 276–278.

Paradis, E. E. (1984). *Comprehension: Thematic units* (videotape). Laramie: University of Wyoming.

Paris, S. G., Lipson, M. Y., & Wixson, K. K. (1983). Issues concerning the acquisition of knowledge: Effects of vocabulary training on reading comprehension. *Review of Educational Research, 53,* 293–316.

Parish, P. (1963). *Amelia Bedelia.* New York: HarperCollins.

Park, L. S. (2001). *A single shard.* New York: Clarion.

Parker, A., & Paradis, E. (1986). Attitude development toward reading in grades one through six. *Journal of Educational Research, 79*(5), 313–315.

Parkes, B. (1986a). *The enormous watermelon.* Crystal Lake, IL: Rigby.

Parkes, B. (1986b). *Who's in the shed?* Crystal Lake, IL: Rigby.

Parsons, L. (1990). *Response journals.* Portsmouth, NH: Heinemann.

Partnership for Reading (2001). *Put reading first: The research building blocks for teaching children to read.* Washington. DC: The Partnership for Reading. Report available online at *www.nifl.gov/ partnershipforreading.*

Paterson, K. (1977). *Bridge to Terabithia.* New York: Thomas Y. Crowell.

Paulsen, G. (1987). *Hatchet.* New York: Simon & Schuster.

Payne, C. D., & Schulman, M. B. (1998). *Getting the most out of morning message and other shared writing lessons.* New York: Scholastic.

Payne, R. (1998). *A framework for understanding poverty.* Highlands, TX: RFT.

Pearson, P. D. (1974). The effects of grammatical complexity on children's comprehension, recall, and conception of certain semantic relations. *Reading Research Quarterly, 10*(2), 155–192.

Pearson, P. D. (1985). Changing the face of reading comprehension instruction. *The Reading Teacher, 38*(8), 724–738.

Pearson, P. D. (1989a). *Improving national reading assessment: The key to improved reading instruction*. Paper presented at the 1989 annual reading conference of the Utah Council of the International Reading Association, Salt Lake City, UT.

Pearson, P. D. (1989b). Reading the whole language movement. *Elementary School Journal, 90*(2), 231–242.

Pearson, P. D. (2000). *What sorts of programs and practices are supported by research? A reading from the radical middle*. Ann Arbor, MI: Center for the Improvement of Early Reading Instruction.

Pearson, P. D., & Duke, N. (2002). Comprehension instruction in the primary grades. In C. Collins-Block & M. Pressley (Eds.), *Comprehension instruction: Research-based best practices* (pp. 247–258). New York: Guildford Press.

Pearson, P. D., & Fielding, L. (1982). Listening comprehension. *Language Arts, 59*(6), 617–629.

Pearson, P. D., & Gallagher, M. C. (1983). The instruction of reading comprehension. *Contemporary Educational Psychology, 8*(3), 317–344.

Pearson, P. D., Hansen, J., & Gordon, C. (1979). The effect of background knowledge on children's comprehension of implicit and explicit information. *Journal of Reading Behavior, 11*(3), 201–209.

Pearson, P. D., & Johnson, D. D. (1978). *Teaching reading comprehension*. New York: Holt, Rinehart and Winston.

Peregoy, S. F., & Boyle, O. F. (1993). *Reading, writing, and learning in ESL*. New York: Longman.

Perez, S. A. (1983). Teaching writing from the inside: Teachers as writers. *Language Arts, 60*(7), 847–850.

Perfetti, C. A., & Lesgold, A. M. (1977). Discourse comprehension and sources of individual differences. In M. A. Just & P. A. Carpenter (Eds.), *Cognitive processes in comprehension* (pp. 141–184). Hillsdale, NJ: Erlbaum.

Perkins, J. H. (2001). Listen to their teachers' voices: Effective reading instruction for fourth grade African American students. *Reading Horizons, 41*(4), 239–255.

Perspectives on basal readers (Special issue). (1989). *Theory Into Practice, 28*(4).

Peterson, B. (1991). Selecting books for beginning readers. In D. E. DeFord, C. A. Lyons, & G. S. Pinnell (Eds.), *Bridges to literacy: Learning from reading recovery* (pp. 119–147). Portsmouth, NH: Heinemann.

Peterson, R., & Eeds, M. (1990). *Grand conversations: Literature groups in action*. New York: Scholastic.

Pfeffer, S. B. (1989). *Future forward*. New York: Holt.

Piaget, J. (1955). *The language and thought of the child*. New York: World.

Pikulski, J. J. (1985). Questions and answers. *The Reading Teacher, 39*(1), 127–128.

Pikulski, J. J., & Templeton, S. (1997). The role of phonemic awareness in learning to read. *Invitations to Literacy*. Boston: Houghton Mifflin.

Pinkney, A. D. (1993). *Alvin Ailey*. New York: Hyperion Books for Children.

Pinnell, G. S., Deford, D. E., & Lyons, C. A. (1994). Comparing instructional models for the literacy education of high-risk first graders. *Reading Research Quarterly, 29*(1), 8–39.

Pinnell, G. S., & Fountas, I. C. (1997a). *A handbook for volunteers: Help America read*. Portsmouth, NH: Heinemann.

Pinnell, G. S., & Fountas, I. C. (1997b). *Help America read: Coordinator's guide*. Portsmouth, NH: Heinemann.

Pinnell, G. S., & Fountas, I. C. (1998). *Word matters*. Portsmouth, NH: Heinemann.

Pinnell, G. S., & Fountas, I. C. (2002). *Leveled books for readers grades 3–6: A companion volume to guiding readers and writers*. Portsmouth, NH: Heineman.

Pinnell, G. S., Fried, M. D., & Estice, R. M. (1990). Reading recovery: Learning how to make a difference. *The Reading Teacher, 43*, 282–295.

Pinnell, G. S., Lyons, C. A., DeFord, D. E., Bryk, A. S., & Seltzer, M. (1994). Comparing instructional models for the literacy education of high-risk first graders. *Reading Research Quarterly, 29*(1), 8–39.

Pino, E. (1978). *Schools are out of proportion to man*. Seminar on discipline, Utah State University, Logan, UT.

Pintrich, P. R., & DeGroot, E. V. (1990). Motivational and self-regulated learning components of classroom academic performance. *Journal of Educational Psychology, 82*, 33–40.

Piper, T. (1993). *Language for all our children*. New York: Merrill/Macmillan.

Point/counterpoint. The value of basal readers. (1989, August–September). *Reading Today, 7*, 18.

Polacco, P. (2002). *When lightning comes in a jar*. New York: Philomel.

Pollack, P. (1982). *Keeping it secret*. New York: Putnam.

Potter, B. (1903). *The tale of Peter Rabbit*. New York: F. Warne.

Powell, D. A. (1986). *Retrospective case studies of individual and group decision making in district-level elementary reading textbook selection*. Unpublished doctoral dissertation, Indiana University, Bloomington, IN.

Pray, R. T. (1983). *A comparison of good and poor readers in an adult, incarcerated population*. Unpublished doctoral dissertation, Harvard University, Cambridge, MA.

Prelutsky, J. (1976). *Nightmares: Poems to trouble your sleep*. New York: Greenwillow Books.

Prelutsky, J. (1984). *A new kid on the block*. New York: Greenwillow Books.

Prelutsky, J. (1990). *Something big has been here*. New York: Greenwillow Books.

Prelutsky, J. (1991). *Poems for laughing out loud*. New York: Alfred A. Knopf.

Prelutsky, J. (1996). *A pizza the size of the sun*. New York: Greenwillow Books.

Pressley, M. (2000). What should comprehension instruction be the instruction of? In M. L. Kamil, P. B. Mosenthal, P. D. Pearson, & R. Barr (Eds.), *Handbook of Reading Research,* Vol. 3 Mahwah, NJ: Erlbaum.

Pressley, M. (2002a). Comprehension strategies instruction: A turn-of-the-century status report. In C. Collins-Block, & M. Pressley (Eds.) *Improving comprehension instruction: Advances in research, theory, and classroom practice* (pp. 11–27). New York: Guilford Press.

Pressley, M. (2002). *Reading instruction that works: The case for balanced teaching,* 2nd Ed. New York: Guilford Press.

Pressley, M., Allington, R. L., Wharton-McDonald, R., Collins-Block, C., and Morrow, L. M. (2001). *Learning to read: Lessons from exemplary first-grade classrooms*. New York: Guildford Press.

Prince, A. T., & Mancus, D. S. (1987). Enriching comprehension: A schema altered basal reading lesson. *Reading Research and Instruction, 27,* 45–53.

Proudfoot, G. (1992). Pssst! There is literacy at the laundromat. *English Quarterly, 24*(1), 10–11.

Provensen, A., & Provensen, M. (1983). *The glorious flight: Across the channel with Louis Bleriot*. New York: Viking Penguin.

Puckett, M. B., & Black, J. K. (1994). *Authentic assessment of the young child*. Upper Saddle River, NJ: Merrill/Prentice Hall.

Pulver, C. J. (1986). Teaching students to understand explicit and implicit connectives. In J. W. Irwin (Ed.), *Understanding and teaching cohesion comprehension* (pp. 3–8). Newark, DE: International Reading Association.

Radencich, M., Beers, P., & Schumm, J. S. (1995). *Handbook for the K–12 reading specialist*. Boston, MA: Allyn and Bacon.

Ramirez, G., & Ramirez, J. L. (1994). *Multiethnic literature*. Albany, NY: Delmar.

RAND Reading Study Group. (2001). *Reading for understanding: Towards an R & D program in reading comprehension*. Washington, DC: Author/OERI/ Department of Education.

Raphael, T. E. (1982). Question-answering strategies for children. *The Reading Teacher, 36,* 186–191.

Raphael, T. E. (1986). Teaching question-answer relationships, revisited. *The Reading Teacher, 39*(6), 516–523.

Raphael, T. E., Pardo, L., Highfield, K., & McMahon, S. I. (1997). *Book club: A literature-based curriculum*. Littleton, MA: Small Planet Communications.

Raphael, T. E., & Pearson, P. D. (1982). *The effect of metacognitive awareness training on children's question answering behavior* (Tech. Rep. No. 238). Urbana-Champaign: University of Illinois at Urbana-Champaign, Center for the Study of Reading.

Rasinski, T. (1989). Fluency for everyone: Incorporating fluency instruction in the classroom. *The Reading Teacher, 42*(9), 690–693.

Rasinski, T. (1990b). Investigating measure of reading fluency. *Educational Research Quarterly, 14*(3), 37–44.

Rasinski, T. (1998, September). *Reading to learn: Vocabulary development strategies*. Paper presented at the Fall Session of the Dallas Reading Plan Grades 4–6 Professional Development Series, Dallas, TX.

Rasinski, T. (2000). Speed does matter. *The Reading Teacher, 54*(2), 146–151.

Rasinski, T., & Opitz, M. F. (1998). *Good-bye round robin: 25 effective oral reading strategies*. Portsmouth, NH: Heinemann.

Rasinski, T., & Padak, N. D. (1990). Multicultural learning through children's literature. *Language Arts, 69,* 14–20.

Rasinski, T. V. (1984). *Developing Models of Reading Fluency*. ERIC Document Reproduction Service No. ED269721.

Rasinski, T. V. (1990). Effects of repeated reading and listening-while-reading on reading fluency. *Journal of Educational Research, 83*(2), 147–150.

Rasinski, T. V. (1995). *Parents and teachers: Helping children learn* to read and write. New York: Harcourt Brace.

Rasinski, T. V. & Fredericks, A. D. (1988). Sharing literacy: Guiding principles and practices for parent involvement. *The Reading Teacher, 41,* 508–512.

Rasinski, T. V., & Fredericks, A. D. (1989). Working with parents: What do parents think about reading in the schools? *The Reading Teacher, 43*(3), 262–263.

Rasinski, T. V., and Padak, N. (1996). Five lessons to increase reading fluency. In L. R. Putnam (Ed.), *How to become a better reading teacher: Strategies for assessment and intervention.* Columbus, OH: Merrill/Prentice Hall.

Raven, J. (1992). A model of competence, motivation, and behavior, and a paradigm for assessment. In H. Berlak, *Toward a new science of educational testing and assessment.* New York: State University of New York Press.

Ravitch, D., & Finn, C. E., Jr. (1987). *What do our 17-year-olds know?* New York: HarperCollins.

Rawls, W. (1961). *Where the red fern grows.* New York: Doubleday.

Raygor, A. L. (1977). The Raygor readability estimate: A quick and easy way to determine difficulty. In P. D. Pearson (Ed.), *Reading: Theory, research and practice* (pp. 259–263). Clemson, SC: National Reading Conference.

Rayner, K., Foorman, B. R., Perfetti, C. A., Pesetsky, D., and Seidenberg, M. S. (2001). How psychological science informs the teaching of reading. *Psychological Science in the Public Interest 2*(2), 31–74.

Rayner, K., Foorman, B. R., Perfetti, C. A., Pesetsky, D., and Seidenberg, M. S. (2002, March). How should reading be taught? *Scientific American,* 85–91.

Read, C. (1971). Preschool children's knowledge of English phonology. *Harvard Educational Review, 41,* 1–34.

Read, S. J., & Rosson, M. B. (1982). Rewriting history: The biasing effects of attitudes on memory. *Social Cognition, 1,* 240–255.

Reid, J. F. (1966). Learning to think about reading. *Educational Research, 9,* 56–62.

Reimer, B. L. (1983). Recipes for language experience stories. *The Reading Teacher, 36*(4), 396–401.

Reinking, D. (Ed.) (1987). *Computers and reading: Issues for theory and practice.* New York: Teachers College Press.

Reinking, D., & Rickman, S. S. (1990). The effects of computer-mediated texts on the vocabulary learning and comprehension of intermediate-grade readers. *Journal of Reading Behavior, 22*(4), 395–409.

Reutzel, D. R. (1985a). Reconciling schema theory and the basal reading lesson. *The Reading Teacher, 39,* 194–197.

Reutzel, D. R. (1985b). Story maps improve comprehension. *The Reading Teacher, 38*(4), 400–405.

Reutzel, D. R. (1991). Understanding and using basal readers effectively. In Bernard L. Hayes (Ed.), *Reading instruction and the effective teacher* (pp. 254–280). New York: Allyn & Bacon.

Reutzel, D. R. (1992). Breaking the letter a week tradition: Conveying the alphabetic principle to young children. *Childhood Education, 69*(1), 20–23.

Reutzel, D. R. (1995). Fingerpoint-reading and beyond: Learning about print strategies (LAPS). *Reading Horizons, 35*(4), 310–328.

Reutzel, D. R. (1996a). A balanced reading approach. In J. Baltas & S. Shafer (Eds.), *Scholastic guide to balanced reading: Grade 3–6,* 7–11. New York: Scholastic.

Reutzel, D. R. (1996b). A balanced reading approach. In J. Baltas & S. Shafer (Eds.), *Scholastic guide to balanced reading: K-2.* New York: Scholastic.

Reutzel, D. R. (1999a). On balanced reading. *The Reading Teacher, 52*(4), 2–4.

Reutzel, D. R. (1999b). Organizing literacy instruction: Effective grouping strategies and organizational plans. In L. M Morrow, L. B. Gambrell, S. Neuman, & M. Pressley (Eds.), *Best practices for literacy instruction.* New York: Guilford Press.

Reutzel, D. R., Camperell, K., & Smith, J. A. (2002). Helping struggling readers make sense of reading. In C. Collins-Block, L. B. Gambrell, & M. Pressley (Eds.), *Improving comprehension instruction: Advances in research, theory, and classroom practice.* San Francisco, CA: Jossey-Bass.

Reutzel, D. R., & Cooter, R. B., Jr. (1990). Whole language: Comparative effects on first-grade reading achievement. *Journal of Educational Research, 83,* 252–257.

Reutzel, D. R., & Cooter, R. B., Jr. (1991). Organizing for effective instruction: The reading workshop. *The Reading Teacher, 44*(8), 548–555.

Reutzel, D. R., & Cooter, R. B., Jr. (1999). *Balanced reading strategies and practices: Assessing and assisting readers with special needs.* Upper Saddle River, NJ: Merrill/Prentice Hall.

Reutzel, D. R., & Cooter, R. B. (2003). *Strategies for reading assessment and instruction: Helping every child succeed,* 2nd Ed. Upper Saddle River, NJ: Merrill/Prentice Hall.

Reutzel, D. R., & Cooter, R. B. (2003). *Strategies for assessment & intervention.* Upper Saddle River, NJ: Merrill/Prentice Hall.

Reutzel, D. R., & Daines, D. (1987a). The instructional cohesion of reading lessons in seven basal reading series. *Reading Psychology, 8,* 33–44.

Reutzel, D. R., & Daines, D. (1987b). The text-relatedness of seven basal reading series. *Reading Research and Instruction, 27,* 26–35.

Reutzel, D. R., & Fawson, P. C. (1989). Using a literature webbing strategy lesson with predictable books. *The Reading Teacher, 43*(3), 208–215.

Reutzel, D. R., & Fawson, P. C. (1990). Traveling tales: Connecting parents and children in writing. *The Reading Teacher, 44,* 222–227.

Reutzel, D. R., & Fawson, P. C. (1991). Literature webbing predictable books: A prediction strategy that helps below-average, first-grade readers. *Reading Research and Instruction, 30*(4), 20–30.

Reutzel, D. R., & Fawson, P. C. (1998). Global literacy connections: Stepping into the future. *Think, 8*(2), 32–34.

Reutzel, D. R., & Fawson, P. C. (2002). *Your classroom library—giving it more teaching power: Research-based strategies for developing better readers and writers.* New York: Scholastic Professional Books.

Reutzel, D. R., Fawson, P. C., Young, J. R., Morrison, T. G., & Wilcox, B. (in press). Reading environmental print: What is the role of concepts about print in discriminating young readers' responses. *Reading Psychology.*

Reutzel, D. R., & Gali, K. (1998). The art of children's book selection: A labyrinth unexplored. *Reading Psychology, 19*(1), 3–50.

Reutzel, D. R., & Hollingsworth, P. M. (1988a). Highlighting key vocabulary: A generative-reciprocal procedure for teaching selected inference types. *Reading Research Quarterly, 23*(3), 358–378.

Reutzel, D. R., & Hollingsworth, P. M. (1988b). Whole language and the

practitioner. *Academic Therapy, 23*(4), 405–416.

Reutzel, D. R., & Hollingsworth, P. M. (1991a). Investigating the development of topic-related attitude: Effect on children's reading and remembering text. *Journal of Educational Research, 84*(5), 334–344.

Reutzel, D. R., & Hollingsworth, P. M. (1991b). Reading comprehension skills: Testing the skills distinctiveness hypothesis. *Reading Research and Instruction, 30*(2), 32–46.

Reutzel, D. R., & Hollingsworth, P. M. (1991c). Reading time in school: Effect on fourth graders' performance on a criterion-referenced comprehension test. *Journal of Educational Research, 84*(3), 170–176.

Reutzel, D. R., & Hollingsworth, P. M. (1991d). Using literature webbing for books with predictable narrative: Improving young readers' predictions, comprehension, & story structure knowledge. *Reading Psychology, 12*(4), 319–333.

Reutzel, D. R., & Hollingsworth, P. M. (1993). Effects of fluency training on second grader's reading comprehension. *Journal of Educational Research, 86*(6), 325–331.

Reutzel, D. R., Hollingsworth, P. M., & Eldredge, J. L. (1994). Oral reading instruction: The impact on student reading development. *Reading Research Quarterly, 23*(1), 40–62.

Reutzel, D. R., & Larsen, N. S. (1995). Look what they've done to real children's books in the new basal readers. *Language Arts, 72*(7), 495–507.

Reutzel, D. R., & Morgan, B. C. (1990). Effects of prior knowledge, explicitness, and clause order on children's comprehension of causal relationships. *Reading Psychology: An International Quarterly, 11,* 93–114.

Reutzel, D. R., Oda, L. K., & Moore, B. H. (1989). Developing print awareness: The effect of three instructional approaches on kindergartners: Print awareness, reading readiness, and word reading. *Journal of Reading Behavior, 21*(3), 197–217.

Reutzel, D. R., & Sabey, B. (1995). Teacher beliefs about reading and children's conceptions: Are there connections? *Reading Research and Instruction, 35*(4), 323–342.

Reutzel, D. R., & Wolfersberger, M. (1996). An environmental impact statement: Designing supportive literacy classrooms for young children. *Reading Horizons, 36*(3), 266–282.

Reznitskaya, A., & Anderson, R. C. (2002). The argument schema and learning to reason. In C. Collins-Block, L. B. Gambrell, & M. Pressley (Eds.) *Improving comprehension instruction: Advances in research, theory, and classroom practice* (pp. 319–334). San Francisco, CA: Jossey-Bass.

Rhodes, L. K., & Dudley-Marling, C. (1988). *Readers and writers with a difference.* Portsmouth, NH: Heinemann.

Rhodes, L. K., & Shanklin, N. (1993). *Windows into literacy: Assessing learners K–8.* Portsmouth, NH: Heinemann.

Ribowsky, H. (1985). *The effects of a code emphasis approach and a whole language approach upon emergent literacy of kindergarten children* (Report No. CS-008-397). (ERIC Document Reproduction Service)

Rice, P. E. (1991). Novels in the news. *The Reading Teacher, 45*(2), 159–160.

Rich, E. S. (1964). *Hannah Elizabeth.* New York: HarperCollins.

Richards, M. (2000). Be a good detective: Solve the case of oral reading fluency. *The Reading Teacher, 53*(7), 534–539.

Richek, M. A. (1978). Readiness skills that predict initial word learning using 2 different methods of instruction. *Reading Research Quarterly, 13,* 200–222.

Richgels, D. J. (2001). Invented spelling, phonemic awareness, and reading and writing instruction, pp. 142–155. In Neuman, S. B., & Dickinson, D. K. (Eds.), *Handbook of early literacy research.* New York: Guilford Press.

Richgels, D. J., & Wold, L. S. (1998). Literacy on the road: Backpacking partnerships between school and home. *The Reading Teacher, 52*(1), 18–29.

Riley, R. E. (1993). *Adult literacy in America.* Washington, DC: United States Department of Education.

Roberts, B. (1992). The evolution of the young child's concept of word as a unit of spoken and written language. *Reading Research Quarterly, 27*(2), 124–139.

Roberts, T. (1975). Skills of analysis and synthesis in the early stages of reading. *British Journal of Educational Psychology, 45,* 3–9.

Robinson, A. (In press). *American Reading Instruction.* Newark, DE: International Reading Association.

Robinson, B. (1972). *The best Christmas pageant ever.* New York: HarperCollins.

Robinson, F. (1946). *Effective study.* New York: Harper Brothers.

Robinson, H. M. (1972). Perceptual training—does it result in reading improvement? In R. C. Aukerman (Ed.), *Some persistent questions on beginning reading* (pp. 135–150). Newark, DE: International Reading Association.

Rogg, L. J. (2001). *Early literacy instruction in kindergarten.* Newark, DE: International Reading Association.

Roller, C. M. (2002). *Comprehensive reading instruction across the grade levels: A collection of papers from the Reading Research 2001 Conference.* Newark, DE: International Reading Association.

Romero, G. G. (1983). *Print awareness of the preschool bilingual Spanish English speaking child.* Unpublished doctoral dissertation, University of Arizona Tucson.

Rosenbaum, J. (1980). *Making inequality: The hidden curriculum of high school tracking.* New York: Wiley.

Rosenblatt, L. M. (1978). *The reader, the text, and the poem.* Carbondale, IL: Southern Illinois University Press.

Rosenblatt, L. M. (1989). Writing and reading: The transactional theory. In J. M. Mason (Ed.), *Reading and writing connections.* Boston: Allyn & Bacon.

Rosenhouse, J., Feitelson, D., & Kita, B. (1997). Interactive reading aloud to Israeli first graders: its contribution to literacy development. *Reading Research Quarterly, 32,* 168–183.

Rosenshine, B., & Meister, C. (1994). Reciprocal teaching: A review of nineteen experimental studies. *Review of Educational Research, 64,* 479–530.

Rosenshine, B. V. (1980). Skill hierarchies in reading comprehension. In R. J. Spiro, B. C. Bruce, & W. F. Brewer (Eds.), *Theoretical issues in reading comprehension* (pp. 535–554). Hillsdale, NJ: Erlbaum.

Roser, N. L., Hoffman, J. V., & Farest, C. (1990). Language, literature, and at-risk children. *The Reading Teacher, 43*(8), 554–561.

Roskos, K., & Neuman, S. B. (2001). Environment and its influences for early literacy teaching and learning. In S. B. Neuman & D. K. Dickinson (Eds.), *Handbook of Early Literacy Research* (pp. 281–294). New York: Guildford Press.

Routman, R. (1988). *Transitions: From literature to literacy.* Portsmouth, NH: Heinemann.

Routman, R. (1996). *Literacy at the crossroads: Crucial talk about reading, writing, and other teaching dilemmas.* Portsmouth, NH: Heinemann.

Routman, R. (2003). *Reading Essentials: The specifics you need to know to teach reading well.* Portsmouth, NH: Heinemann.

Rowe, M. B. (1974). Wait-time and rewards as instructional variables, their influence on language, logic, and fate control: Part one—wait time. *Journal of Research in Science Teaching, 11,* 81–94.

Rowling, J. K. (1998). *Harry Potter and the Sorcerer's Stone.* New York: Scholastic.

Ruddell, R. (1974). *Reading-language instruction: Innovative practices.* Upper Saddle River, NJ: Prentice Hall.

Ruddell, R. B., & Ruddell, M. R. (1995). *Teaching children to read and write: Becoming an influential teacher.* Boston: Allyn & Bacon.

Ruddell, R. B., & Unrau, N. J. (1997). The role of responsive teaching in focusing reader intention and developing reader motivation. In J. T. Guthrie & A. Wigfield (Eds.), *Reading engagement: Motivating readers through integrated instruction.* Newark, DE: International Reading Association.

Rule, A. C. (2001). Alphabetizing with environmental print. *The Reading Teacher, 54*(6), 558–562.

Rumelhart, D. E. (1975). Notes on a schema for stories. In D. G. Bobrow & A. Collins (Eds.), *Representation and understanding: Studies in cognitive science* (pp. 211–236). New York: Academic Press.

Rumelhart, D. E. (1980). Schemata: The building blocks of cognition.

In R. J. Spiro (Ed.), *Theoretical issues in reading comprehension* (pp. 33–58). Hillsdale, NJ: Erlbaum.

Rumelhart, D. E. (1981). Schemata: The building blocks of cognition. In Guthrie, J. T. (Ed.), *Comprehension and teaching: Research reviews* (pp. 3–26). Newark, DE: International Reading Association.

Rumelhart, D. E. (1984). Understanding understanding. In J. Flood (Ed.), *Understanding reading comprehension* (pp. 1–20). Newark, DE: International Reading Association.

Rupley, W., & Blair, T. (1987). Assignment and supervision of reading seatwork: Looking in on 12 primary teachers. *The Reading Teacher, 40*(4), 391–393.

Rupley, W. H., & Blair, T. R. (1978). Teacher effectiveness in reading instruction. *The Reading Teacher, 31*, 970–973.

Ryder, R. J., & Graves, M. F. (1994). Vocabulary instruction presented prior to reading in two basal readers. *Elementary School Journal, 95*, 139–153.

Rye, J. (1982). *Cloze procedure and the teaching of reading.* Portsmouth, NH: Heinemann.

Sadoski, M., & Quast, Z. (1990). Reader response and long-term recall for journalistic text: The roles of imagery, affect, and importance. *Reading Research Quarterly, 24*(4), 256–272.

Sadow, M. W. (1982). The use of story grammar in the design of questions. *The Reading Teacher, 35*, 518–523.

Samuels, S. J. (1967). Attentional process in reading: The effect of pictures on the acquisition of reading responses. *Journal of Educational Psychology, 58*, 337–342.

Samuels, S. J. (1970). Effects of pictures on learning to read, comprehension, and attitudes.

Review of Educational Research, 40, 397–408.

Samuels, S. J. (1979). The method of repeated readings. *The Reading Teacher, 32*(4), 403–408.

Sandora, C., Beck, I. L., & McKeown, M. G. (1999). A comparison of two discussion strategies on students' comprehension and interpretation of complex literature. *Reading Psychology, 20*(3), 177–212.

Sanford, A. J., & Garrod, S. C. (1981). *Understanding written language.* New York: Wiley.

Santa, C. (1990). *Reporting on the Montana Teacher Change Project: Kallispell reading/language initiative.* Utah Council of the International Reading Association, Salt Lake City, UT.

Santa, C. M. (1997). School change and literacy engagement: Preparing teaching and learning environments. In J. T. Guthrie & A. Wigfield (Eds.), *Reading engagement: Motivating readers through integrated instruction.* Newark, DE: International Reading Association.

Santa, C. M., & Heien, T. (1998). An assessment of Early Steps: A program for early interventions of reading problems. *Reading Research Quarterly, 34*(1), 54–79.

Savage, J. F. (1994). *Teaching reading using literature.* Madison, WI: Brown & Benchmark.

Schneider, W., & Shiffrin, R. M. (1977). Controlled and automatic human information processing: 1. Detection, search, and attention, *Psychological Review, 84*(1), 1–66.

Scholastic. (1986). *Talking text* (computer program). Jefferson City, MO: Scholastic.

Scholastic. (1990). *Bank Street writer III* (computer program). Jefferson City, MO: Scholastic Software.

Scholastic. (1995). *Literary place program.* New York: Author.

Schreiber, A., & Tuchman, G. (1997). *Scholastic Phonics*

Readers The Big Hit: Book 14. New York: Scholastic.

Schunk, D. H., & Zimmerman, B. J. (1997). Developing self-efficacious readers and writers: The role of social and self-regulatory processes. In J. T. Guthrie and A. Wigfield (Eds.), *Reading engagement: Motivating readers through integrated instruction* (pp. 34–50). Newark, DE: International Reading Association.

Schwartz, D. M. (1985). *How much is a million?* Richard Hill, Ontario: Scholastic-TAB.

Schwartz, R. M., & Raphael, T. E. (1985). Concept of definition: A key to improving students' vocabulary. *The Reading Teacher, 39*(2), 198–205.

Scieszka, J. (1989). *The true story of the 3 little pigs: By A. Wolf.* New York: Viking Kestrel.

Searfoss, L. W. (1975). Radio reading. *The Reading Teacher, 29*, 295–296.

Searfoss, L. W., & Readence, J. E. (1989). *Helping children learn to read,* 2nd Ed. Upper Saddle River, NJ: Prentice Hall.

Seefeldt, C., & Barbour, N. (1986). *Early childhood education: An introduction.* Upper Saddle River, NJ: Merrill/Prentice Hall.

Sendak, M. (1962). *Chicken soup with rice.* New York: Scholastic.

Sendak, M. (1963). *Where the wild things are.* New York: HarperCollins.

Senechal, M., & Cornell, E. H. (1993). Vocabulary acquisition through shared reading experiences. *Reading Research Quarterly, 28*(4), 361–373.

Seuss, D. (1954). *Horton hears a Who!* New York: Random House.

Shake, M. (1986). Teacher interruptions during oral reading instruction: Self-monitoring as an impetus for change in corrective feedback. *Remedial and Special Education, 7*(5), 18–24.

Shake, M. C., & Allington, R. L. (1985). Where do teacher's

questions come from? *The Reading Teacher, 38,* 432–439.

Shanahan, T. (1984). Nature of the reading-writing relation: An exploratory multi-variate analysis. *Journal of Educational Psychology, 76,* 466–477.

Shanahan, T., & Barr, R. (1995). Reading Recovery: An independent evaluation of the effects of an early intervention for at-risk learners. *Reading Research Quarterly, 30*(40), 958–996.

Shanahan, T., & Lomax, R. G. (1986). An analysis and comparison of theoretical models of the reading-writing relationship. *Journal of Educational Psychology, 78,* 116–123.

Shanklin, N. L., & Rhodes, L. K. (1989). Comprehension instruction as sharing and extending. *The Reading Teacher, 43*(7), 496–500.

Shannon, P. (1983). The use of commercial reading materials in American elementary schools. *Reading Research Quarterly, 19,* 68–85.

Shannon, P. (1989a). Basal readers: Three perspectives. *Theory Into Practice, 28*(4), 235–239.

Shannon, P. (1989b). *Broken promises.* Granby, MA: Bergin & Garvey.

Shannon, P. (1992). *Becoming political: Readings and writings in the politics of literacy education.* Portsmouth, NH: Heinemann.

Shannon, P. (1993). Letters to the editor: Comments on Baumann. *Reading Research Quarterly, 28*(2), 86.

Shannon, P., & Goodman, K. (1994). *Basal readers: A second look.* New York: Owen.

Sharmat, M. W. (1980). *Gila monsters meet you at the airport.* New York: Aladdin.

Shockley, B., Michalove, B., & Allen, J. (1995). *Engaging Families.* Portsmouth, NH: Heinemann.

Short, K. G., Harste, J. C., & Burke, C. (1996). *Creating classrooms for authors and inquirers.* Portsmouth, NH: Heinemann.

Siegel, M. (1983). *Reading as signification.* Unpublished doctoral dissertation, Indiana University.

Silvaroli, N. J. (1986). *Classroom reading inventory,* 5th Ed. Dubuque, IA: William C. Brown.

Silverstein, S. (1974). *Where the sidewalk ends.* New York: HarperCollins.

Silverstein, S. (1996). *Falling Up.* New York: HarperCollins.

Simmons, D. C., & Kameenui, E. J. (1998). *What reading research tells us about children with diverse learning needs: Bases and basics.* Mahwah, NJ: Erlbaum.

Sinatra, R. C., Stahl-Gemake, J., & Berg, W. (1984). Improving reading comprehension of disabled readers through semantic mapping. *Reading Teacher, 38*(1), 22–29.

Singer, H. (1960). *Conceptual ability in the substrata-factor theory of reading.* Unpublished doctoral dissertation, University of California at Berkeley.

Singer, H. (1978a). Active comprehension: From answering to asking questions. *The Reading Teacher, 31,* 901–908.

Singer, H. (1978b). Research in reading that should make a difference in classroom instruction. In *What research has to say about reading instruction* (pp. 57–71). Newark, DE: International Reading Association.

Singer, H., & Donlan, D. (1989). *Reading and learning from text,* 2nd Ed. Hillsdale, NJ: Erlbaum.

Sippola, A. E. (1994). Holistic analysis of basal readers: An assessment tool. *Reading Horizons, 34*(3), 234–246.

Skaar, G. (1972). *What do the animals say?* New York: Scholastic.

Slaughter, H. B. (1988). Indirect and direct teaching in a whole language program. *The Reading Teacher, 42*(1), 30–35.

Slavin, R. E. (1987). Ability grouping and student achievement in elementary schools: A best-evidence synthesis. *Review of Educational Research, 57*(3), 293–336.

Slavin, R. E. (1988). Cooperative learning and student achievement. *Educational Leadership, 45,* 31–33.

Slavin, R. E. (1991). Are cooperative learning and "untracking" harmful to the gifted? *Education Leadership, 48*(6), 68–71.

Slavin, R. E. (1995). *Cooperative learning: Theory, research, and practice.* Needham Heights, MA: Allyn & Bacon.

Slavin, R. E., & Madden, N. (1995). Effects of success for all on the achievement of English language learners. Paper presented at the annual meeting of the American Educational Research Association, San Francisco, CA, April, 1995.

Slavin, R. E., Madden, N. A., Karweit, N. L., Livermon, B. J., & Dolan, L. (1990). Success for all: First-year outcomes of a comprehensive plan for reforming urban education. *American Educational Research Journal, 27,* 255–278.

Slavin, R. E., Madden, N. L., Dolan, L., & Wasik, B. A. (1996). *Every child, every school: Success for All.* Thousand Oaks, CA: Corwin.

Slavin, R. E., Madden, N. L., Karweit, N. L., Dolan, L., & Wasik, B. A. (1992). *Success for All: A relentless approach to prevention and early intervention in elementary schools.* Arlington, VA: Educational Research Services.

Slosson, R. L. (1971). *Slosson intelligence test.* East Aurora, NY: Slosson Educational Publications.

Sloyer, S. (1982). *Reader's theater: Story dramatization in the* classroom. Urbana, IL: National Council of Teachers of English.

Smith, D. E. P. (1967). *Learning to learn.* New York: Harcourt Brace.

Smith, E. B., Goodman, K. S., & Meredith, R. (1976). *Language and thinking in school,* 2nd Ed. New York: Holt, Rinehart and Winston.

Smith, F. (1977). The uses of language. *Language Arts, 54*(6), 638–644.

Smith, F. (1983). *Essays into literacy.* Exeter, NH: Heinemann.

Smith, F. (1985). *Reading without nonsense,* 2nd Ed. New York: Teachers College Press.

Smith, F. (1987). *Insult to intelligence.* New York: Arbor House.

Smith, F. (1988). *Understanding reading,* 4th Ed. Hillsdale, NJ: Erlbaum.

Smith, K. A. (1989). *A checkup with the doctor.* New York: McDougal, Littell.

Smith, M. W. & Dickinson, D. K. (2002). *Early language and literacy classroom observation (ELLCO).* Baltimore, MD: Paul H. Brookes.

Smith, N. B. (1965). *American reading instruction.* Newark, DE: International Reading Association.

Smith, N. B. (1986). *American Reading Instruction.* Newark, DE: International Reading Association.

Smith, R. K. (1981). *Jelly belly.* New York: Dell.

Smolkin, L. B., & Donovan, C. A. (2000). *The contexts of comprehension: Information book read alouds and comprehension acquisition.* (CIERA Report #2-009). Ann Arbor, MI: Center for the Improvement of Early Reading Achievement.

Smoot, R. C., & Price, J. (1975). *Chemistry, a modern course.* Upper Saddle River, NJ: Merrill/Prentice Hall.

Snow, C. (1999). *Preventing reading difficulties.* Keynote address at the Second Annual Commissioner's Reading Day, Austin, TX.

Snow, C. E., Burns, M. S., & Griffin, P. (1998). *Preventing reading difficulties in young children.* Washington, DC: National Academy Press.

Snow, C. E., Burns, M. S., & Griffin, P. (1998). *Preventing reading failure in young children.* Washington, DC: National Academy Press.

Snowball, D., & Bolton, F. (1999). *Spelling K–8: Planning and teaching.* York, ME: Stenhouse.

Soto, G. (1993). *Local news.* San Diego, CA: Harcourt Brace.

Spache, G., & Spache, E. (1977). *Reading in the elementary school,* 4th Ed. Boston: Allyn & Bacon.

Spady, W., & Marshall, K. J. (1991). Beyond traditional outcome-based education. *Educational Leadership, 48,* 67–72.

Spangler, K. L. (1983). Reading interests vs. reading preferences: Using the research. *The Reading Teacher, 36*(9), 876–878.

Speare, E. G. (1958). *The witch of Blackbird Pond.* New York: Dell.

Sperry, A. (1940). *Call it courage.* New York: Macmillan.

Spiegel, D. L. (1981). Six alternatives to the directed reading activity. *The Reading Teacher, 34,* 914–922.

Spiegel, D. L. (1999). The perspective of the balanced approach. In S. M. Blair-Larsen & K. A. Williams (Eds.), *The balanced reading program: Helping all students achieve success,* pp. 8–23. Newark, DE: International Reading Association.

Spier, P. (1977). *Noah's ark.* Garden City, NY: Doubleday.

Spinelli, J. (1991). Catching Maniac Magee. *The Reading Teacher, 45*(3), 174–176.

Spivak, M. (1973). Archetypal place. *Architectural Forum, 140,* 44–49.

Squire, J. R. (1983). Composing and comprehending: Two sides of the same basic process. *Language Arts, 60*(5), 581–589.

Squire, J. R. (1989). A reading program for all seasons. *Theory into Practice, 28*(4), 254–257.

Stahl, S. A. (1986). Three principles of effective vocabulary instruction. *Journal of Reading, 29*(7), 662–668.

Stahl, S. A., & Fairbanks, M. M. (1986). The effects of vocabulary instruction: A model-based meta-analysis. *Review of Educational Research, 56*(1), 72–110.

Stahl, S. A., Hare, V. C., Sinatra, R., & Gregory, J. F. (1991). Defining the role of prior knowledge and vocabulary in reading comprehension: The retiring of number 41. *Journal of Reading Behavior, 23*(4), 487–507.

Stahl, S. A., & Jacobson, M. G. (1986). Vocabulary difficulty, prior knowledge, and text comprehension. *Journal of Reading Behavior, 18*(4), 309–319.

Stahl, S. A., & Kapinus, B. (2001). *Word power: What every educator needs to know about teaching vocabulary.* Washington, DC: National Education Association.

Stahl, S. A., & Miller, P. D. (1989). Whole language and language experience approaches for beginning reading: A quantitative research synthesis. *Review of Educational Research, 59,* 87–116.

Stahl, S. A., & Murray, B. A. (1993). Environmental print, phonemic awareness, letter recognition, and word recognition. In D. J. Leu & C. I. Kinzer (Eds.), *Examining central issues in literacy research, theory, and practice* (pp. 227–233). Chicago: National Reading Conference.

Standard for the English Language Arts. (1996). A project of The International Reading Association and National Council of Teachers of English. Newark, DE: International Reading Association.

Stanovich, K. (1980). Toward an interactive-compensatory model of individual differences in the development of reading fluency. *Reading Research Quarterly, 16*(1), 37–71.

Stauffer, R. G. (1969). *Directing reading maturity as a cognitive process.* New York: HarperCollins.

Stauffer, R. G. (1975). *Directing the reading-thinking process.* New York: HarperCollins.

Stayter, F. Z., & Allington, R. L. (1991). Fluency and the understanding of texts. *Theory Into Practice, 30*(3), 143–148.

Stedman, L. C., & Kaestle, C. E. (1987). Literacy and reading performance in the United States from 1880 to the present. *Reading Research Quarterly, 22,* 8–46.

Steele, W. O. (1958). *The perilous road.* Orlando, FL: Harcourt Brace.

Stein, M. (1993). *The beginning reading instruction study.* Syracuse, NY: Educational Resources Information Center (ERIC) Document Reproduction Service.

Stein, N. L., & Glenn, C. G. (1979). An analysis of story comprehension in elementary school children. In R. O. Freedle (Ed.), *New directions in discourse processing* (pp. 53–120). Hillsdale, NJ: Erlbaum.

Steinbeck, J. (1937). *The red pony.* New York: Bantam Books.

Stenner, A. J. (1996). *Measuring reading comprehension with the Lexile framework.* Washington, DC: Paper presented at the 4th North American Conference on Adolescent/Adult Literacy.

Stenner, A. J., & Burdick, D. S. (1997). *The objective measurement of reading comprehension.* Durham, NC: MetaMetrics.

Steptoe, J. (1987). *Mufaro's beautiful daughters: An African tale.* New York: Lothrop, Lee, & Shepard Books.

Stern, D. N., & Wasserman, G. A. (1979). *Maternal language to infants.* Paper presented at a meeting of the Society for Research in Child Development. Ann Arbor, Michigan.

Stevens, R., & Rosenshine, B. (1981). Advances in research on teaching. *Exceptional Education Quarterly, 2,* 1–9.

Stevens, R. J., Madden, N. A., Slavin, R. E., & Farnish, A. (1987a). *Cooperative integrated reading and composition: A brief overview of the CIRC program.* Baltimore, MD: Johns Hopkins University, Center for Research on Elementary and Middle Schools.

Stevens, R. J., Madden, N. A., Slavin, R. E., & Farnish, A. M. (1987b). Cooperative integrated reading and composition: Two field experiments. *Reading Research Quarterly, 22*(4), 433–454.

Stevens, R. J., & Slavin, R. E. (1995). Effects of a cooperative learning approach in reading and writing on academically handicapped and nonhandicapped students. *Elementary School Journal, 95*(3), 241–262.

Stolz, M. (1963). *Bully on Barkham Street.* New York: HarperCollins.

Stoodt, B. D. (1989). *Reading instruction.* New York: HarperCollins.

Strickland, D. S. (1998). *Teaching phonics today: A primer for educators.* Newark, DE: International Reading Association.

Strickland, D. S., Feeley, J. T., & Wepner, S. B. (1987). *Using computers in the teaching of reading.* New York: Teachers College Press.

Strickland, D., Snow, C., Griffin, P., Burns, M. S., & McNamara, P. (2002). *Preparing our teachers: Opportunities for better reading instruction.* Washington, D.C.: Joseph Henry Press.

Sucher, F., & Allred, R. A. (1986). *Sucher-Allred group reading placement test.* Oklahoma City: Economy.

Sukhomlinsky, V. (1981). *To children I give my heart.* Moscow, USSR: Progress.

Sulzby, E. (1985). Children's emergent reading of favorite storybooks: A developmental study. *Reading Research Quarterly, 20*(4), 458–481.

Sulzby, E. (1991). Assessment of emergent literacy: Storybook reading. *The Reading Teacher, 44*(7), 498–500.

Sulzby, E., Hoffman, J., Niles, J., Shanahan, T., & Teale, W. (1989). *McGraw-Hill reading.* New York: McGraw-Hill.

Sunburst. (1987). *The puzzler.* Pleasantville, NY: Sunburst Communications.

Swafford, J. (1995). I wish all my groups were like this one: Facilitating peer interaction during group work. *Journal of Reading, 38*(8), 626–631.

Sweet, A. (1997). Teacher perceptions of student motivation and their relation to literacy learning. In J. T. Guthrie & A. Wigfield (Eds.), *Reading engagement: Motivating readers through integrated instruction.* Newark, DE: International Reading Association.

Szymusiak, K., & Sibberson, F. (2001). *Beyond leveled books: Supporting transitional readers in grades 2–5.* York, ME: Stenhouse.

Taba, H. (1975). *Teacher's handbook for elementary social studies.* Reading, MA: Addison-Wesley.

Tarver, S. G., & Dawson, M. M. (1978). Modality preference and the teaching of reading: A review. *Journal of Learning Disabilities, 11*(1), 5–17.

Taxel, J. (1993). The politics of children's literature: Reflections on multiculturalism and Christopher Columbus. In V. J. Harris (Ed.), *Teaching multicultural literature in grades K–8* (pp. 1–36). Norwood, MA: Christopher Gordon.

Taylor, B., Harris, L. A., & Pearson, P. D. (1988). *Reading* difficulties: Instruction and assessment. New York: Random House.

Taylor, B. M., Frye, B. J., & Gaetz, T. M. (1990). Reducing the number of reading skill activities in the elementary classroom. *Journal of Reading Behavior, 22*(2), 167–180.

Taylor, B. M., Graves, M. F., & Van den Broek, P. (2000). *Reading for meaning: Fostering comprehension in the middle grades.* New York: Teachers College Press.

Taylor, B. M., Pearson, P. D., Clark, K. F., & Walpole, S. (1999). *Beating the odds in teaching all children to read* (Report #2-006). Ann Arbor, MI: Center for the Improvement of Early Reading Achievement.

Taylor, B. M, Pearson, P. D., Clark, K. F., & Walpole, S. (2000). Effective schools and accomplished teachers: Lessons about primary grade reading instruction in low-income schools. *Elementary School Journal, 101*, 121–165.

Taylor, D. (1983). *Family literacy: Young children learning to read and write.* Portsmouth, NH: Heinemann.

Taylor, D., & Strickland, D. S. (1986). *Family storybook reading.* Portsmouth, NH: Heinemann.

Taylor, G. C. (1981). ERIC/RCS report: Music in language arts instruction. *Language Arts, 58,* 363–368.

Taylor, M. D. (1990). *Road to Memphis.* New York: Dial Books.

Taylor, N. E. (1986). Developing beginning literacy concepts: Content and context. In D. B. Yaden, Jr., & S. Templeton (Eds.), *Metalinguistic awareness and beginning literacy* (pp. 173–184). Portsmouth, NH: Heinemann.

Taylor, N. E., Blum, I. H., & Logsdon, M. (1986). The development of written language awareness: Environmental aspects and program characteristics. *Reading Research Quarterly, 21*(2), 132–149.

Taylor, W. L. (1953). Cloze procedure: A new tool for measuring readability. *Journalism Quarterly, 30,* 415–433.

Teale, W. H. (1987). Emergent literacy: Reading and writing development in early childhood. In J. E. Readence, R. S. Baldwin, J. P. Konopak, & H. Newton (Eds.), *Research in literacy: Merging perspectives* (pp. 45–74). Rochester, NY: National Reading Conference.

Teale, W. H., & Martinez, M. (1986a). Reading in a kindergarten classroom library. *The Reading Teacher, 41*(6), 568–73.

Teale, W. H., & Martinez, M. (1986b). *Teachers reading to their students: Differing styles, different effects?* ERIC Document Reproduction Service.

Teale, W. H., & Sulzby, E. (1986). *Emergent literacy: Writing and reading.* Norwood, NJ: Ablex.

Temple, C., & Gillet, J. (1996). *Language and literacy: A lively approach.* New York: HarperCollins.

Temple, C., Nathan, R., Burris, N., & Temple, F. (1993). *The beginnings of writing,* 3rd Ed. Newton, MA: Allyn & Bacon.

Templeton, S. (1995). *Children's literacy: Contexts for meaningful learning.* Princeton, NJ: Houghton Mifflin.

Texas Education Agency. (2003–2004). *Texas primary reading inventory* (TPRI). Austin, TX: Author. Available online, in both English and Spanish, at Reading Initiative at *http:// www.tea.state.tx.us/reading/.*

Thaler, M. (1989). *The teacher from the Black Lagoon.* New York: Scholastic.

Tharp, R. (1982). The effective instruction of comprehension: Results and description of the Kamehameha Early Education Program. *Reading Research Quarterly, 17*(4), 503–527.

Tharpe, R. G., & Gallimore, R. (1988). *Rousing minds to life.* Cambridge, MA: Cambridge University Press.

Thelen, J. N. (1984). *Improving reading in science.* Newark, DE: International Reading Association.

Thomas, D. G., & Readence, J. E. (1988). Effects of differential vocabulary instruction and lesson frameworks on the reading comprehension of primary children. *Reading Research and Instruction, 28,* 1–13.

Thompson, R. (1997). The philosophy of balanced reading instruction. *The Journal of Balanced Reading Instruction, 4*(D1), 28–29.

Thorndike, R. L. (1973). *Reading comprehension education in fifteen countries: An empirical study.* New York: Wiley.

Thorndyke, P. N. (1977). Cognitive structure in comprehension and memory of narrative discourse. *Cognitive Psychology, 9*(1), 77–110.

Tierney, R. J. (1992). Setting a new agenda for assessment. *Learning, 21*(2), 61–64.

Tierney, R. J., Carter, M. A., & Desai, L. E. (1991). *Portfolio assessment in the reading-writing classroom.* Norwood, MA: Christopher-Gordon.

Tierney, R. J., & Cunningham, J. W. (1984). Research on teaching reading comprehension. In P. D. Pearson (Ed.), *Reading research handbook* (pp. 609–656). New York: Longman.

Tierney, R. J., & Pearson, P. D. (1983). Toward a composing model of reading. *Language Arts, 60*(5), 568–580.

Tierney, R. J., Readence, J. E., & Dishner, E. K. (1985). *Reading strategies and practices: A compendium,* 2nd Ed. Boston: Allyn & Bacon.

Tomasello, M. (1996). Piagetian and Vygotskian approaches to language acquisition. *Human Development, 39,* 269–276.

Tompkins, G. E. (2000). *Teaching writing: Balancing process and product*, 3rd Ed. Upper Saddle River, NJ: Merrill/Prentice Hall.

Tompkins, G. E. (2003). *Literacy for the 21st Century*, 3rd Ed. Upper Saddle River, NJ: Merrill/Prentice Hall.

Tompkins, G. E., & Hoskisson, K. (1995). *Language arts: Content and teaching strategies,* 3rd Ed. Upper Saddle River, NJ: Merrill/Prentice Hall.

Topping, K. (1989). Peer tutoring and paired reading: Combining two powerful techniques. *The Reading Teacher, 42,* 488–494.

Torgesen, Wagner, Rashotte, Alexander, & Conroy, 1997. Prevention and remediation of severe reading disabilities: Keeping the end in mind. *Scientific Studies of Reading, 1*(3), 217–234.

Torrey, J. W. (1979). Reading that comes naturally. In G. Waller & G. E. MacKinnon (Eds.), *Reading research: Advance in theory and practice,* Vol. 1, (pp. 115–144). New York: Academic Press.

Tovey, D. R., & Kerber, J. E. (Eds.) (1986). *Roles in literacy learning.* Newark, DE: International Reading Association.

Towers, J. M. (1992). Outcome-based education: Another educational bandwagon. *Educational Forum, 56*(3), 291–305.

Towle, (1993). *The real McCoy: The life of an African American inventor.* New York: Scholastic.

Town, S., & Holbrook, N. M. (1857). *Progressive Primer.* Boston: Carter, Bazin & Company.

Trabasso, T. (1980). *On the making of inferences during reading and their assessment.* (Tech. Rep. No. 157). Urbana-Champaign: University of Illinois, Center for the Study of Reading.

Treiman, R. (1985). Onsets and rimes as units of spoken syllables: Evidence from children. *Journal of Experimental Child Psychology, 39,* 161–181.

Trelease, J. (1995). *The new read-aloud handbook.* 4th Ed. New York: Penguin.

Tunnell, M. O., & Jacobs, J. S. (1989). Using "real" books: Research findings on literature based reading instruction. *The Reading Teacher, 42,* 470–477.

Tutolo, D. (1977). The study guide: Types, purpose and value. *Journal of Reading, 20,* 503–507.

U.S. Bureau of Labor. (1995). *Final report: Governor's Council on School-to-Work Transition.* Washington, DC: U.S. Department of Education.

U.S. Department of Education. (1997). *President Clinton's America's Reading Challenge.* Washington, DC: U.S. Department of Education.

U.S. Department of Education. *National Assessment of Educational Progress: The Nation's Report Card Reading 2000.* Washington, DC: U.S. Department of Education, Office of Educational Research and Improvement.

United States and the other Americas, The (Grade 5). (1980). Upper Saddle River, NJ: Merrill/Prentice Hall.

United States: Its history and neighbors, The (Grade 5). (1985). San Diego. CA: Harcourt Brace.

Unsworth, L. (1984). Meeting individual needs through flexible within-class grouping of pupils. *The Reading Teacher, 38*(3), 298–304.

Vacca, J. L., Vacca, R. T., & Gove, M. K. (1995). *Reading and learning to read,* 3rd Ed. Boston: Little, Brown.

Vacca, R. T., & Vacca, J. L. (2001). *Content area reading: Literacy and learning across the curriculum*, 7th Ed. New York: Allyn & Bacon.

Vacca, R. T., Vacca, J. L., Gove, M. K., Burkey, L. C., Lenhart, L. A., & McKeon, C. A. (2003). *Reading and learning to read,* 5th Ed. Needham Heights, MA: Allyn & Bacon.

Valencia, S. (1990). A portfolio approach to classroom reading assessment: The whys, whats, and hows. *The Reading Teacher, 43*(4), 338–340.

Valencia, S. (1998). *Portfolios in action.* New York: HarperCollins.

Valencia, S., McGinley, W., & Pearson, P. D. (1990). *Assessing reading and writing: Building a more complete picture for middle school assessment* (Tech. Rep. No. 500). Urbana, IL: Center for the Study of Reading. (ERIC Document Reproduction Service).

Valencia, S., & Pearson, P. D. (1987). Reading assessment: Time for a change. *The Reading Teacher, 40*(8), 726–733.

Vallecorsa, A. L., & deBettencourt, L. U. (1997). Using a mapping procedure to teach reading and writing skills to middle grade students with learning disabilities. *Education and the Treatment of Children, 20*(2), 173–188.

Van Allsburg, C. (1985). *The polar express.* Boston: Houghton Mifflin.

Van Allsburg, C. (1987). *The Z was zapped.* Boston: Houghton Mifflin.

Van Manen, M. (1986). *The tone of teaching.* Ontario: Scholastic.

Varble, M. E. (1990). Analysis of writing samples of students taught by teachers using whole language and traditional approaches. *Journal of Educational Research, 83*(5), 245–251.

Veatch, J. (1968). *How to teach reading with children's books.* New York: Owen.

Veatch, J. (1978). *Reading in the elementary school,* 2nd Ed. New York: Owen.

Veatch, J., & Cooter, R. B., Jr. (1986). The effect of teacher selection on reading achievement. *Language Arts, 63*(4), 364–368.

Viorst, J. (1972). *Alexander and the terrible, horrible, no good, very bad day* (R. Cruz, Illustrator). New York: Atheneum.

Viorst, J. (1987). *Alexander and the terrible, horrible, no good, very bad day*. New York: Aladdin.

Voltz, D. L., & Demiano-Lantz, M. (1993, Summer). Developing ownership in learning. *Teaching Exceptional Children,* pp. 18–22.

Vopat, J. (1994). *The parent project: A workshop approach to parent involvement.* York, ME: Stenhouse.

Vopat, J. (1998). *More than bake sales: The resource guide for family involvement in education.* York: ME: Stenhouse.

Vukelich, C. (1994). Effects of play interventions on young children's reading of environmental print. *Early Childhood Research Quarterly, 9*(2), 153–170.

Vygotsky, L. S. (1939). Thought and speech. *Psychiatry, 2,* 29–54.

Vygotsky, L. S. (1962). *Thought and language.* Cambridge, MA: MIT Press.

Vygotsky, L. S. (1978). *Mind in society.* Cambridge, MA: Harvard University Press.

Wade, S. E., & Moje, E. B. (2000). The role of text in classroom learning. In M. L. Kamil, P. B. Mosenthal, P. D. Pearson, & R. Barr (Eds.), *Handbook of Reading Research,* Vol. 3. Mahwah, NJ: Erlbaum.

Wagner, R., Torgesen, J., & Rashotte, C. (1999). *Comprehensive Test of Phonological Processing (CTOPP).* Circle Pines, MN: AGS.

Walker, B. J. (2004). *Diagnostic teaching of reading: Techniques for instruction and assessment.* Upper Saddle River, NJ: Merrill/Prentice-Hall..

Walker, J. E. (1991, May). *Affect in naturalistic assessment: Implementation and implications.* Paper presented at the 36th annual convention of the International Reading Association, Las Vegas, NV.

Wallach, L., Wallach, M. A., Dozier, M. G., & Kaplan, N. E. (1977). Poor children learning to read do not have trouble with auditory discrimination but do have trouble with phoneme recognition. *Journal of Educational Psychology, 69,* 36–39.

Walley, C. (1993). An invitation to reading fluency. *The Reading Teacher, 46*(6), 526–527.

Walters, K., & Gunderson, L. (1985). Effects of parent volunteers reading first language (L1) books to ESL students. *The Reading Teacher, 39*(1), 66–69.

Wang, M., Haertel, G., and Walberg, H. (1994, December). What helps students learn? *Educational Leadership,* 74–79.

Wasik, B. A. (1998). Using volunteers as reading tutors: Guidelines for successful practices. *The Reading Teacher, 51*(7), 562–573.

Watson, D., & Crowley, P. (1988). How can we implement a whole-language approach? In C. Weaver (Ed.), *Reading process and practice* (pp. 232–279). Portsmouth, NH: Heinemann.

Watson, R. (2001). Literacy and oral language: Implications for early literacy acquisition. In S. B. Neuman & D. K. Dickinson (Eds), *Handbook of Early Literacy Research,* (pp. 43–53). New York: Guilford Press.

Watson, S. (1976). *No man's land.* New York: Greenwillow.

Weaver, C. (1994). *Reading process and practice: From socio-psycholinguistics to whole language, 2nd Ed.* Portsmouth, NH: Heinemann.

Weaver, C. (1998). *Reconsidering a balanced approach to reading.* Urbana, IL: National Council of Teachers of English.

Weaver, C., Chaston, J., & Peterson, S. (1993). *Theme exploration: A voyage of discovery.* Portsmouth, NH: Heinemann.

Webb, K., & Willoughby, N. (1993). An analytic rubric for scoring graphs. *The Texas School Teacher, 22*(3), 14–15.

Webb, M., & Schwartz, W. (1988, October). Children teaching children: A good way to learn. *PTA Today,* pp. 16–17.

Weimans, E. (1981). *Which way courage?* New York: Atheneum.

Weinstein, R. S. (1976). Reading group membership in first grade: Teacher behaviors and pupil experience over time. *Journal of Educational Psychology, 68,* 103–116.

Weintraub, S., & Denny, T. P. (1965). What do beginning first graders say about reading? *Childhood Education, 41,* 326–327.

Wells, R. (1973). *Noisy Nora.* New York: Scholastic.

Wepner, S. B. (1985). Linking logos with print for beginning reading success. *The Reading Teacher, 38*(7), 633–39.

Wepner, S. B. (1990). Holistic computer applications in literature-based classrooms. *The Reading Teacher, 44*(1), 12–19.

Wepner, S. B. (1992). Technology and text sets. *The Reading Teacher, 46*(1), 68–71.

Wepner, S. B. (1993). Technology and thematic units: An elementary example on Japan. *The Reading Teacher, 46*(5), 442–445.

Wepner, S. B., & Feeley, J. T. (1993). *Moving forward with literature: Basals, books, and beyond.* Upper Saddle River, NJ: Merrill/Prentice Hall.

Wepner, S. B., Feeley, J. T., & Strickland, D. S. (1995). *The administration and supervision of reading programs, 2nd Ed.* New York: Teacher's College Columbia Press.

Wessells, M. G. (1990). *Computer, self, and society.* Upper Saddle River, NJ: Prentice Hall.

Whaley, J. F. (1981). Readers' expectations for story structures. *Reading Research Quarterly, 17,* 90–114.

Wharton-McDonald, R., Pressley, M., Rankin, J., Mistretta, J., Yokoi, L., & Ettenberger, S. (1997). Effective primary-grades literacy instruction = balanced literacy instruction. *The Reading Teacher, 50*(6), 518–521.

Wheatley, E. A., Muller, D. H., & Miller, R. B. (1993). Computer-assisted vocabulary instruction. *Journal of Reading, 37*(2), 92–102.

Whitaker, B. T., Schwartz, E., & Vockell, E. (1989). *The computer in the reading curriculum.* New York: McGraw-Hill.

White, C. S. (1983). Learning style and reading instruction. *The Reading Teacher, 36,* 842–845.

White, E. B. (1952). *Charlotte's web.* New York: HarperCollins.

White, E. B. (1970). *The trumpet of the swan.* New York: HarperCollins.

Wiener, R. B., & Cohen, J. H. (1997). *Literacy portfolios: Using assessment to guide instruction.* Upper Saddle River, NJ: Merrill/Prentice Hall.

Wiesendanger, W. D. (1986). Durkin revisited. *Reading Horizons, 26,* 89–97.

Wigfield, A. (1997). Motivations, beliefs, and self-efficacy in literacy development. In J. T. Guthrie & A. Wigfield (Eds.), *Reading engagement: Motivating readers through integrated instruction.* Newark, DE: International Reading Association.

Wigfield, A. (1997b). Children's motivations for reading and reading engagement. In J. T. Guthrie and A. Wigfield (Eds.), *Reading engagement: Motivating reading through integrated instruction* (pp. 14–33). Newark, DE: International Reading Association.

Wigfield, A. (2000). Facilitating children's reading motivation. In L. Baker, M. J. Dreher, and J. T. Guthrie (Eds.), *Engaging young readers: Promoting achievement and motivation*

(pp. 140–158). New York: Guilford Press.

Wigfield, A., & Guthrie, J. T. (1997). Relations of children's motivation for reading to the amount and breadth of their reading. *Journal of Educational Psychology, 89,* 420–432.

Wiggins, R. A. (1994). Large group lesson/small group follow-up: Flexible grouping in a basal reading program. *The Reading Teacher, 47*(6), 450–460.

Wilde, S. (1997). *What's a schwa sound anyway?* Portsmouth, NH: Heinemann.

Williams, J. P., Brown, L. G., Silverstein, A. K., & deCari, J. S. (1994). An instructional program in comprehension of narrative themes for adolescents with learning disabilities. *Learning Disability Quarterly, 17,* 205–221.

Willman, A. T. (2000). "Hello, Mrs. Willman, it's me!: Keep kids reading over the summer by using voice mail." In T. V. Rasinski, N. D. Padak, et al. (Eds.), *Motivating recreational reading and promoting home-school connections* (pp. 51–52). Newark, DE: International Reading Association.

Wilson, R. M., & Gambrell, L. B. (1988). *Reading comprehension in the elementary school.* Boston: Allyn & Bacon.

Wilson, R. M., Hall, M. A., Leu, D. J., & Kinzer, C. K. (2001). *Phonics, phonemic awareness, and word analysis for teachers: An interactive tutorial,* 7th Ed. Upper Saddle River, NJ: Prentice Hall.

Winograd, P. (1989). Improving basal reading instruction: Beyond the carrot and the stick. *Theory Into Practice, 28*(4), 240–247.

Winograd, P. N. (1989). Introduction: Understanding reading instruction. In P. N. Winograd, K. K. Wixson, & M. Y. Lipson (Eds.). *Improving*

basal reader instruction (pp. 1–20). New York: Teachers College Press.

Winograd, P. N., Paris, S., & Bridge, C. (1991). Improving the assessment of literacy. *The Reading Teacher, 45*(2), 108–116.

Winograd, P. N., Wixson, K. K., & Lipson, M. Y. (Eds.). (1989). *Improving basal reader instruction.* New York: Teachers College Press.

Wiseman, D. L. (1992). *Learning to read with literature.* Boston: Allyn & Bacon.

Wittrock, M. C. (1974). Learning as a generative process. *Educational Psychologist, 11,* 87–95.

Wixson, K. K., Peters, C. W., Weber, E. M., & Roeber, E. D. (1987). New directions in statewide reading assessment. *The Reading Teacher, 40*(8), 749–755.

Wong, H., & Wong, R. (1998). *The first days of school: How to be an effective teacher.* Mountain View, CA: Harry K. Wong.

Wong, J. W., & Au, K. H. (1985). The concept-text-application approach: Helping elementary students comprehend expository text. *The Reading Teacher, 38*(7), 612–618.

Wood, A. (1984). *The napping house* (Don Wood, Illustrator). San Diego, CA: Harcourt Brace.

Wood, A. (1990). *Weird parents.* New York: Dial Books for Young Readers.

Wood, A., & Wood, D. (1988). *Elbert's bad word.* New York: Harcourt, Brace, & Jovanovich.

Wood, E., Pressley, M., & Winne, P. H. (1990). Elaborative interrogation effects on children's learning of factual content. *Journal of Educational Psychology, 82,* 741–48.

Wood, K. D. (1983). A variation on an old theme: 4-way oral reading. *The Reading Teacher, 37*(1), 38–41.

Wood, K. D. (1987). Fostering cooperative learning in middle and secondary level classrooms. *Journal of Reading, 31,* 10–18.

Woodcock, R., Mather, N., & Barnes, E. K. (1987). *Woodcock reading mastery tests–revised.* Circle Pines, MN: American Guidance Service.

Woodcock, R. W. (1997). *Woodcock Reading Mastery Tests–Revised (WRMT–R).* Circle Pines, MN: AGS.

Woodcock, R. W., & Muñoz-Sandoval, A. F. (1993). *Woodcock-Muñoz language survey* (WMLS), English and Spanish forms. Chicago: Riverside.

Worby, D. Z. (1980). *An honorable seduction: Thematic studies in literature.* Arlington, VA: ERIC Document Reproduction Service. (ERIC Document Reproduction Service).

Worthy, J., Moorman, M., & Turner, M. (1999). What Johnny likes to read is hard to find in school. *Reading Research Quarterly, 34*(1), 12–27.

Yaden, D. B., Jr. (1982). A multivariate analysis of first graders' print awareness as related to reading achievement, intelligence, and gender. *Dissertation Abstracts International, 43,* 1912A. (University Microfilms No. 82–25, 520)

Yashima, T. (1983). *Crow boy.* New York: Viking.

Yellin, D., & Blake, M. E. (1994). *Integrating language arts: A holistic approach.* New York: HarperCollins.

Yep, L. (1989). *The rainbow people.* New York: HarperCollins.

Ylisto, I. P. (1967). An empirical investigation of early reading responses of young children (doctoral dissertation, The University of Michigan, 1967). *Dissertation Abstracts International, 28,* 2153A. (University Microfilms No. 67–15, 728).

Yolen, J. (1976). *An invitation to a butterfly ball: A counting rhyme.* New York: Philomel.

Yolen, J. (1988). *The devil's arithmetic.* New York: Viking Kestrel.

Yopp, H. K. (1988). The validity and reliability of phonemic awareness tests. *Reading Research Quarterly, 23,* 159–177.

Yopp, H. K. (1992). Developing phonemic awareness in young children. *The Reading Teacher, 45*(9), 696–703.

Yopp, H. K., & Troyer, S. (1992). *Training phonemic awareness in young children.* Unpublished manuscript.

Yopp, R. H., & Yopp, H. K. (2000). *Literature-based reading activities* (3rd Ed.). New York: Allyn & Bacon.

Young, E. (1989). *Lon Po Po.* New York: Philomel Books.

Young, T. A., & Vardell, S. (1993). Weaving readers theatre and nonfiction into the curriculum. *The Reading Teacher, 46,* 396–406.

Zahar, R., Cobb, T., & Sapda, N. (2001). Acquiring vocabulary through reading: Effects of frequency and contextual richness. *Canadian Modern Language Review, 57*(4), 541–572.

Zarillo, J. (1989). Teachers' interpretations of literature-based reading. *The Reading Teacher, 43*(1), 22–29.

Zemelman, S., Daniels, H., & Hyde, A. (1993). *Best practice: New standards for teaching and learning in America's schools.* Portsmouth, NH: Heinemann.

Zentall, S. S. (1993). Research on the educational implications of attention deficit hyperactivity disorder. *Exceptional Children, 60*(2), 143–153.

Zintz, M. V., & Maggart, Z. R. (1989). *The reading process: The teacher and the learner.* Dubuque, IA: William C. Brown.

Zlatos, B. (1993). Outcomes-based outrage. *Executive Educator, 15*(9), 12–16.

Zutell, J., & Rasinski, T. (1991). Training teachers to attend to their students' oral reading fluency. *Theory Into Practice, 30*(3), 211–217.

Name Index

Subject Index

ABOUT THE AUTHORS

D. Ray Reutzel

D. Ray Reutzel is the Provost and academic vice president at Southern Utah University. He was formerly a Karl G. Maeser Research Professor and Chair of the Department of Elementary Education at Brigham Young University. He earned his doctorate in Curriculum and Instruction with an emphasis in reading and language arts from the University of Wyoming, Laramie, in 1982. He teaches courses in research design, reading, and language arts for preservice and in-service teachers at BYU. He has taught in kindergarten and grades 1, 3, 5, and 6 as an elementary school teacher.

Dr. Reutzel took a leave from his university faculty position to return to full-time, first-grade classroom teaching in Sage Creek Elementary School in 1987–1988. While in the elementary classroom, he established a model first-grade whole language classroom that has been visited by observers from throughout the country. In 1987, Dr. Reutzel received BYU's College of Education Excellence in Research Award. In the same year, his work was recognized by the American Educational Research Association (AERA) as one of the Distinguished Research Papers at the 1988 Annual Meeting.

Dr. Reutzel is the author of more than 100 articles, books, book chapters, and monographs. He has published in *Reading Research Quarterly, Journal of Reading Behavior, Journal of Educational Research, Reading Psychology, Reading Research and Instruction,* and *The Reading Teacher,* among others. He has served as an editorial review board member or guest reviewer for *The Elementary School Journal, The Reading Teacher, Reading Research Quarterly, The Journal of Reading Behavior, The Reading Teacher, The NRC Yearbook, American Reading Forum Yearbook, Reading Psychology,* and *Reading Research and Instruction.* Dr. Reutzel is an author of the *Literacy Place* program published by Scholastic, Inc. of New York.

Dr. Reutzel lives in Cedar City, Utah, with his wife, daughter, four sons, a dog, and a cat. His hobbies include reading, skiing, fishing, singing, playing the piano, and trying to keep up with his wife and children.

Robert B. Cooter, Jr., Ed.D.

Dr. Robert Cooter is Professor of Reading & Urban Literacy Education and Director of the National Center for Urban Literacy Research at The University of Texas at Arlington. Dr. Cooter teaches undergraduate and graduate courses in reading, literacy assessment, early and emergent literacy, and language arts education. He is particularly interested in ways to offer comprehensive literacy programs to city kids in grades PK–12, and in the assessment and correction of reading difficulties. Cooter has worked with teachers and school districts around the nation seeking to create comprehensive literacy programs. He has taught grades 1, 3, 4, 7, 11, and 12 in the public schools, and also served as a Title I reading specialist.

Professor Cooter recently served as the first "Reading Czar" (or Associate Superintendent for Reading/Language Arts) for the Dallas Independent School District, Texas. Bob engineered the district's highly acclaimed *Dallas Reading Plan,* a collaborative project supported by Dallas area business and community enterprises involving the training of approximately 3,000 teachers in "balanced literacy instruction." In March of 1998, Dr. Cooter was recognized as a "Texas State Champion for Reading" by then-Governor, George W. Bush, and Texas First Lady, Laura Bush, as a result of the many successes of the Dallas Reading Plan initiative.

In addition to his best-selling text *Teaching Children to Read: Putting the Pieces Together,* which is currently used at over 200 universities and colleges to prepare elementary teachers, Cooter has also authored or co-authored six other professional books. These include the *Flynt/Cooter Reading Inventory for the Classroom* (Merrill/Prentice-Hall, 2004), *Strategies for Reading Assessment and Instruction: Helping Every Child Succeed* (Merrill/Prentice-Hall, 2003) and the *Flynt/Cooter English-Español Reading Inventory* (Merrill/Prentice-Hall, 1999). Robert Cooter recently served as contributing editor to a new book titled *Perspectives on Rescuing Urban Literacy Education: Spies, Saboteurs, & Saints* (Lawrence Erlbaum Associates, 2003).

Bob is currently working on several new books dealing with urban literacy education, reading assessment, and the teaching of the language arts. He has had over 50 articles on reading assessment and education published in such journals as *The Reading Teacher, Journal of Reading, Language Arts*, and the *Journal of Educational Research*. Robert Cooter currently contributes a regular Urban Literacy column for *The Reading Teacher* (professional journal of the International Reading Association).

A native of Nashville, Tennessee, Bob now lives in Fort Worth, Texas, with his wife, Kathleen Spencer Cooter, a popular education consultant, Special Education professor, and Director of Laboratory Schools at Texas Christian University. He enjoys vacationing with his wife on their houseboat, "Our Last Child," performing Southern folktales, listening to good Blues, and dining on catfish and cheese grits. Bob Cooter is the proud father of five children and three stepchildren, has eight grandchildren, and is owned by a hound dog of unknown breed and questionable utility.